HIV and AIDS in Africa

HIV AND AIDS IN AFRICA

Christian Reflection, Public Health, Social Transformation

Edited by
Jacquineau Azetsop, S.J.

ORBIS BOOKS
Maryknoll, New York 10545

ORBIS BOOKS
Maryknoll, New York 10545

Fathers and Brothers
MARYKNOLL
TOGETHER IN GOD'S MISSION OF MERCY

Founded in 1970, Orbis Books endeavors to publish works that enlighten the mind, nourish the spirit, and challenge the conscience. The publishing arm of the Maryknoll Fathers and Brothers, Orbis seeks to explore the global dimensions of the Christian faith and mission, to invite dialogue with diverse cultures and religious traditions, and to serve the cause of reconciliation and peace. The books published reflect the views of their authors and do not represent the official position of the Maryknoll Society. To learn more about Maryknoll and Orbis Books, please visit our website at www.maryknollsociety.org.

Library of Congress Cataloging-in-Publication Data

Names: Azetsop, Jacquineau, editor.
Title: HIV & AIDS in Africa : Christian reflection, public health, social
    transformation / edited by Jacquineau Azetsop, S.J.
Other titles: HIV and AIDS in Africa
Description: Maryknoll, NY : Orbis Books, [2016] | Includes bibliographical
    references and index. | Description based on print version record and CIP
    data provided by publisher; resource not viewed.
Identifiers: LCCN 2016020516 (print) | LCCN 2016006986 (ebook) |
    ISBN 9781608336715 (ebook) | ISBN 9781626982000 (pbk.)
Subjects: LCSH: AIDS (Disease)—Africa. | HIV infections—Africa.
Classification: LCC RA643.86.A35 (print) | LCC RA643.86.A35 H55125 2016
    (ebook) | DDC 362.19697/920096—dc23
LC record available at https://lccn.loc.gov/2016020516

To Ted Rogers, SJ, and Michael J. Kelly, SJ,

two men of faith and of great pastoral intelligence,

who taught us to care for God's people

when the divinity is hidden.

CONTENTS

Part One
The Sociohistorical, Cultural, and Political Context of the Pandemic

Part Two
Methodological and Normative Concerns of an Applied Theology on HIV and AIDS

ACKNOWLEDGMENTS

A volume of such magnitude is obviously the product of many formal and informal meetings and discussions, of the tireless efforts of many men and women interested in developing a Christian theological response to the HIV and AIDS crisis in Africa, and of the unflagging desires to add some more theological voices to the many voices that have attempted to bring hope when HIV strikes.

I am grateful to the people who have supported the development and production of this volume. First of all, I would like to thank Wilfrid Okambawa, whose ideas inspired this project, and Paterne Mombe, who endorsed it as a project of the African Jesuit AIDS Network (AJAN). The idea to write this volume came from the programmatic and broad contribution of Wilfrid Okambawa in the last AJAN volume. I was encouraged to take the lead of this book project after discussion with Okambawa and Mombe, the director of AJAN. I then drafted the outline of the project and discussed it in the Hekima College dean's office with Emmanuel Foro, the dean of Hekima College, and Festos Mkenda, the director of the African Jesuit Historical Institute in Nairobi, in July 2014. The following day, Emmanuel and I held a meeting with Joseph Healey, a Maryknoll priest living in Nairobi, who supported this project right away and encouraged us to publish it with Orbis Books. I sincerely thank Foro, Mkenda, and Healey for their unfailing contributions and encouragement.

The advisory committee of this book provided me with a sense of direction from the beginning of the project. Without the support of this very active committee, this book would not have taken the shape it has now. My sincere thanks to Laurenti Magesa, Peter Kanyandago, Lisa S. Cahill, Wilfrid Okambawa, Teresia Hinga, and Paterne Mombé in guiding me to lead this project to its completion.

The review process of the individual contributions was coordinated by an editorial committee made up of Philippe Denis, Anthony Egan, Emmanuel Foro, Dossou Davy, Odomaro Mubangizi, Festo Mkenda, and Ludovic Lado. Without forgetting the anonymous reviewers, I sincerely thank all the members of this committee. I also thank Jim Keane and his hardworking staff and colleagues at Orbis Books. Orbis Books and AJAN have financially supported this book's production.

A special word of thanks and gratitude to Shawn Copeland, Lisa Cahill, and James F. Keenan from Boston College, who willingly encouraged and supported this project. Shawn Copeland wrote the Foreword for the volume,

Lisa S. Cahill wrote the Concluding Remarks, and James F. Keenan wrote the Post Scriptum.

I thank all the contributors, especially Evelyn Manyanja, Edwina Ward, Stuart Bate, Ignace Ndongala, Caroline Mbonu, Bernard Tonde, Fabien Yedo, Susan Rakoczy, and Elias Bongmba for the special dedication to this project.

Last but not least, special thanks to Davy Dossou and Raphael Bazebizonza, whose support and care were quite instrumental in organizing the manuscript.

I dedicate this volume to Michael J. Kelly and Ted Rogers, who have been in the front line in the battle against AIDS and in caring for the victims for many years. Michael Kelly, an Irish Jesuit priest and university professor of literature, worked in Zambia and wrote a number of books on HIV. Ted Rogers, a British Jesuit priest and a social worker in Zimbabwe, pioneered the Catholic response to AIDS for the entire region of southern Africa. These two men dedicated an important part of their lives to writing about and fighting against HIV and AIDS in those initial years when being infected simply meant getting ready to die. Although neither is an academic theologian, both shed the light of God's kingdom in the darkness of human existence and wrote about AIDS from their care for God's wounded people.

Jacquineau Azetsop, S.J.

FOREWORD

You hold in your hands a vital, important, and timely collection of essays about HIV and AIDS on the continent of Africa. Do not put it down. Read it. No matter your age, culture, race, nationality, or religion; no matter your gender, sexual orientation, political affiliation, or physical-ableness: Read it. Please. Yes, this volume is about HIV and AIDS on the continent of Africa, but it is also about us—*all of us*. As former UN secretary-general Kofi Annan put it, "In the ruthless world of AIDS, there is no us and them."

In 2012, roughly 23 million people in sub-Saharan Africa were infected with the HIV virus that causes AIDS. This epidemic figures among the most complex and unsettling religious, cultural, and social experiences for millions of children, women, and men who call the continent of Africa home. Since its eruption, AIDS has never been solely about disease, although it is that precisely—a biomedical and biological disease. Governments, cultures, and religions have invested the disease with a wide range of meanings, definitions, and implications. When the outbreak of the virus was first diagnosed, some African governments disregarded it, while others derided warnings of the disease as a Western invention. Some cultural groups, infuriated by the sexual insinuations of the disease, ignored it; others prescribed homeopathic remedies, while some demanded a return to traditional sexual abstinence. Some religious groups focused their preaching and teaching on the sexual transmission of the disease, linking HIV infection to punishment from God; other groups looked away, abandoning children, women, and men to a painful fate. But other groups, through advocacy and practical care, committed themselves to accompany those suffering with the disease and to do so in faith, hope, and love. These women and men understand that "nothing in death or life . . . can separate us from the love of Christ" (Rom. 8:38–39); through advocacy and practical care, they profess that we—all humanity—as the eschatological and Trinitarian Body of Christ suffer from and live with HIV.

This theological perspective is passionately, lovingly, and vividly upheld in this volume of essays, edited by Jacquineau Azetsop, S.J. As a group, these thirty-one women and men—biblical exegetes, ethicists, historians, pastoral practitioners, philosophers, social scientists, and theologians—through their considerable scholarly and pastoral experience offer in their various essays a comprehensive and nuanced exploration of the multiple factors shaping the HIV and AIDS crisis in Africa. These authors uncover the sociohistorical, cultural, and political context of the pandemic; deploy creative and rigorous interpretive skills to recapture the import of traditional healing; and open pertinent biblical texts in response to the stigma and suffering that HIV infection causes. They revisit foundational theological issues such as theodicy, theological anthropology, or Christology and probe the very meaning of moral agency and norms, given the extreme vulnerability the disease provokes. By reflecting on theological education, spiritual direction, liturgy, and sacraments, these women and men address ways to initiate and cultivate authentic solidarity with and among those who have been socially marginalized by the disease. Finally, the authors demonstrate that providing adequate medical treatment for AIDS cannot be divorced from providing adequate and long-term solutions to social predicaments of poverty, hunger, and malnutrition; of civil conflict, devaluation of rural livelihoods, and migration; of education and medical care; and of colonialism, geopolitical relations, and global economic policies.

Read this book. Why? For all their weightiness, the essays in this collection radiate with creative thinking and energy. The HIV and AIDS crisis may fuel and may be fueled by the social vulnerabilities of Africa's people, but it does not deprive them of hope—a search for alternative strategies to meet crucial human needs, compassionate and practical solidarity in the face of massive suffering, development and implementation of more effective prevention programs, devotedness to community and one another, prayer and dynamic religious life. Second, these essays contest those lingering colonial-cum-Hollywood images as well as media depictions that demean Africans and their cultural practices as fearful, backward, and promiscuous. Our socially constructed conceptions of AIDS contribute to the influence of such representations, and more often than not these conceptions are rife with stereotype, exaggeration, and bias. The persistence in Africa of the HIV and AIDS epidemic and its cruel impacts on human lives and communities primarily stems not from a woman's or a man's character or culture and cultural practices, but rather from lack of access to potentially life-saving antiretroviral drugs and medical care. What may be medically treated in one sector of our global village remains lethal in another. Third, over the past thirty-five years, hundreds of books and articles have been written about the HIV and AIDS epidemic; several of these have taken a theological approach. This volume not only builds on prior theological reflection, it draws on ongoing and new multidisciplinary research in order to enrich and expand on that reflection.

The most radical import of these essays is this: *There is no "us" and "them"; there is only we.* We are the body of Christ, we are infected with and affected by the HIV virus and the disease it causes.

Read this book. Please.

M. Shawn Copeland
Professor of Systematic Theology, Boston College, USA

INTRODUCTION

Theological Creativity, Christian Imagination, and Ecclesial Practices in a Time of AIDS

Jacquineau Azetsop

Many theological papers and books addressing all sorts of issues in relation to the AIDS pandemic have been written in Africa and worldwide. However, so far, none goes as far as putting to the fore a comprehensive reflection on the AIDS pandemic, from an African perspective, that harnesses the resources of the different branches of theology as well as the intention of designing a model of theological reflection for future public health crises. This is precisely the void that this book intends to fill. The idea of embarking upon this project stems from the seminal contribution of Wilfrid Okambawa to *AIDS, 30 Years Down the Line: Faith-Based Reflections about the Epidemic in Africa*, a volume published by the African Jesuit AIDS Network in 2012. Okambawa titled his piece, "African HIV/AIDS Theology: Toward a Holistic Approach to the HIV and AIDS Issue."[1] He endeavored to sketch an African HIV and AIDS' theology—and succeeded quite well in doing so. Even though Okambawa's write-up was deep and dense, the scope of his project goes beyond a mere book chapter. Many of the theological perspectives, concepts, and trends included in his paper need to be unpacked, deepened, and expanded. Among the numerous aspects of a conceivable theology of HIV and AIDS that Okambawa discussed, some stood out. This volume builds on Okambawa's attempts to develop an African-biblical HIV and AIDS hermeneutics and theodicy in addition to a pastoral, moral, spiritual, and systematic theology as well as a theology of healing.

The HIV virus and related consequences have threatened human life for more than three decades—three decades of fight against and reflection on a virus and disease that have deeply challenged African countries and the entire world. With Africa being the epicenter of the epidemic, the entire continent has

---

[1] Wilfrid Okambawa, "African HIV/AIDS Theology: Toward a Holistic Approach to the HIV/AIDS Issue," in *AIDS, 30 Years Down the Line: Faith-Based Reflections about the Epidemic in Africa*, ed. Paterne A. Mombé, Agbonkhianmeghe E. Orobator, and Danielle Vella (Nairobi: Paulines Publications Africa, 2013), 335–48.

fought relentlessly; the continent had to fight both the disease and stigmatization by the whole world. Theologians, pastoral agents, clergy, and faithful from
Christian churches, most often in collaboration with other faith-based and
social constituencies and institutions, have significantly contributed to efforts
aiming at reducing incident cases and managing AIDS. Fighting in hope, Christian churches have certainly learned from the AIDS tragedies and can now
turn them into life-giving realities calling for a radical social transformation
of national communities that still need good leaders who will govern well and
anticipate the future of their respective countries. Since theology is a reflection
on human existence in the light of the divine revelation guided by the tradition of the churches, it cannot ignore AIDS' attacks on life and how it affects
(particularly) socially disadvantaged populations, who face poverty, violence,
international injustice, racism, ethnic conflict, denial of children's rights, and
discrimination on the basis of gender and socioeconomic status.

This volume builds on traditions of Christian churches and reflections
from scholars around the African continent and abroad in providing a distinctive Christian approach to issues in the HIV and AIDS pandemic, bearing
in mind the existing theological resources and interventions that have been
developed to contain the epidemic. Each chapter of this collection specially
highlights the methodology, concepts, and tools that may be helpful for future
theological reflections in times of a pandemic or major epidemics. The theological contributions to the volume are essentially interdisciplinary, shaped by
data borrowed from contextualizing sciences, peace studies, human rights and
legal studies, biomedicine, public health, philosophy, and cultural studies. This
book endeavors to produce a radical, lasting, and highly elaborated approach
to an African theological handling of HIV and AIDS. Each author takes into
consideration the fact that AIDS is an issue of integral human development and
justice that requires a holistic response. Theological responses to the pandemic
are multifaceted, rooted in reality and cognizant of global health policy and
financing. The chapters of the book are written in such a way that the entire book
may be used as a reference for whoever intends to do theological work on future
pandemics or public health crises.

Even though this book aims at being quite ambitious, it does not
attempt to offer the last word on the theological and ecclesial contributions to the fight against the HIV and AIDS pandemic. Instead, the authors
highlight how the churches have thought about, struggled with, and fought
against the pandemic. Most essays attempt to perceive the HIV and AIDS
crisis as a sociopolitical game changer, highlighting the imperative of social
transformation as the best means for HIV prevention and AIDS management at the population level. The book takes to heart the breathtaking and
angry words of Emmanuel Katongole: "The AIDS pandemic uncovers the

ongoing process of malfunctioning . . . which results in an endless disenfranchising by and within the DNA of the social, political, economic systems in Africa."[2] The healing of a social immune system that is deeply compromised calls for a new vision of society grounded in a social justice perspective that integrates all social constituencies and seeks to promote the welfare of all. Policies, interventions, and practices that will maximize efforts to prevent and fight AIDS are not alien to those that will help to heal society from ailments that open the way to public health crises and catastrophes of all sorts. Didier Fassin traces the deep roots of the AIDS crisis in South Africa to apartheid and, before that, to the colonial period.[3] AIDS appears to him as a social condition as opposed to being a human or an individual health condition.[4] Paul Farmer alerted both the political and public health communities to the simple yet shocking connection between public health crises and structural violence in Haiti, while perceiving inequality as the real monster in the room.[5] Social forces that sustain the kingdom of the unjustifiably unequal are the very same forces that structure access to life-saving solutions when inequality becomes pathological.[6] The healing of the so-called hopeless continent by afro-pessimists is the precondition for the promotion of people's well-being and respect by others. AIDS has reinforced afro-pessimism and negative stereotypes of the black continent.[7] Yet if the challenge of AIDS is taken seriously, the continent can take up this opportunity as a chance to emerge into greater light.

The paramount thing that this volume aims to achieve is to depart from a narrow moralistic and individual-based appraisal and view of sexuality to understand the risks for HIV infection and the occurrence of AIDS as involving

---

[2] Emmanuel Katongole, "An Age of Miraculous Medicine," in *AIDS in Africa: Theological Reflections*, ed. Bénézet Bujo and Michael Czerny (Nairobi: Publications Africa, 2007), 114.

[3] Didier Fassin, *When Bodies Remember: Experiences and Politics of AIDS in South Africa* (Berkeley: University of California Press, 2007).

[4] Didier Fassin, "Embodiment of Inequality: AIDS as a Social Condition and the Historical Experience in South Africa," *EMBO Reports*, special issue 4 (2003): S5–S9.

[5] Paul Farmer, *Pathologies of Power: Health, Human Rights, and the New War on the Poor* (Berkeley: University of California Press, 2003).

[6] Ibid.

[7] Brooke G. Schoepf, "AIDS in Africa: Structure, Agency, and Risk," in *HIV and AIDS in Africa: Beyond Epidemiology*, ed. E. Kalepeni, S. Craddock, J. R. Oppong, and J. Ghosi (Malden, MA: Blackwell Publishing, 2004), 15–28; Axelle Kabou, *Et si l'Afrique refusait le développement?* (Paris: L'Harmattan, 1991); Etounga Manguélé, *L'Afrique a-t-elle besoin d'un plan d'ajustement culturel?* (Ivry: Edition Nouvelles du Sud, 1993); René Dumont, *L'Afrique noire est mal partie* (Paris: Le Seuil, 1962); J. Giri, *L'Afrique en panne: vingt-cinq ans de développement* (Paris: Karthala, 1986).

both personal and socioglobal responsibility. Such a narrow-minded behavioral approach can be a challenge for the redemptorist bishop of the Rutenburg Diocese. Talking about the AIDS crisis as it found a favorable ground in the South African social fabric, Bishop Kevin Dowling once said, "I think we're facing an enormously difficult challenge. The brutalization of this society through apartheid and the hopelessness among so many youths who can't get jobs, a deep lack of self-esteem and just a fatalistic spirit, makes people shrug their shoulders and say, 'I'm going to get it [HIV] anyway.'"[8] Hence, a theological reflection on AIDS cannot solely focus on virtues and health education as a preventive intervention that should be passed on to individuals in order to form their character in such a way that they can avoid being infected or passing the virus to someone else. It must also focus on socioglobal values that need to inform institutions so as to promote the well-being of all and to uphold life-promoting practices. Religious approaches to AIDS that are found in this volume shy away from one-sidedness and an unjustifiably narrow-minded moralism that divides more than unites and increases the stigma and discrimination against those who live with HIV or are affected by it.

AIDS has been with us for more than thirty years. We have learned enough to allow ourselves to accept ideological and disempowering solutions. Theology and religious perspectives on AIDS that emerge from this book are critically rooted in African culture and politics as well as in global dynamics. Although we are critical of how we live, we also draw attention to some good practices and values that emerge from local cultures and our positive coping with the challenges of life and with AIDS. Agbonkhianmeghe Emmanuel Orobator rightly noticed that "the AIDS crisis has spawned an intriguing variety of expressions depicting its impact on the church: 'the body of Christ has AIDS'; 'Our church has AIDS'; 'The church living positively with AIDS'; and so on."[9] Instead of falling into despair sustained by a disempowering pessimism, just like Orobator, we envision the HIV crisis as *kairos*. This book issues one cry, which is the combination of many cries that call Christian churches to foster the move from the HIV crisis to the social *kairos*, by becoming healing and servant churches that seek, with the Savior's help, to redeem the continent from the night of AIDS and structural violence to the light of peace and systemic justice. Hence, this volume underscores another important point: theological reflections on HIV and AIDS include, somehow, a theology of society and of culture. Far from focusing their thought exclusively on the virus and sex, contributors to

---

[8] IRIN Africa, "South Africa: Bishop Kevin Dowling: The Best Available Means We Have to Protect Life Is the Condom" (August 2008), www.irinnews.org/.

[9] Agbonkhianmeghe E. Orobator, *From Crisis to Kairos: The Mission of the Church in the Time of HIV/AIDS—Refugees and Poverty* (Nairobi: Pauline Publications Africa, 2005), 121.

this volume have sought to disclose the reasons why the African continent is a fertile ground for HIV.

This book is composed of seven parts. Part 1 sets out the sociohistorical environment within which the AIDS pandemic spread as well as socioanthropological paradigms used to fight the HIV virus. Festo Mkenda outlines the sociohistorical context of AIDS in Africa. Festo's contribution is a sociopastoral analysis of the past that allows one to understand the context, discern opportunities, and commit oneself to working for positive change. Laurenti Magesa argues that a realistic prevention approach needs to reckon with the African spiritual approach to sexuality, which determines the foundation and legitimation of what the majority of people do. True change starts with acknowledging people's worldviews. Lado Tonlieu Ludovic offers a socioanthropological rereading of the strategies used to fight AIDS in Africa by showing, from literature, how they constantly shifted between methodological individualism and methodological holism, depending on whether the focus was on individuals as social actors, on culture as collective heritage, or on social structures.

The four authors of part 2 address the methodological and normative concerns of an applied theology on HIV and AIDS. Albert Ngengi Mundele argues that the Bible, the Word of God, displays the experience of the community of the Israelites as well as individuals with God. As with every human experience, the biblical stories could be read as a memory of the ancestors (Job 8:8–10) to which Africans turn in every circumstance of their life, to see how they should behave in critical situations like AIDS. Using a historical, cultural, and political economy approach to vulnerability that reflects a comprehensive understanding of HIV risks in a marginalized continent, Jacquineau Azetsop argues that a simplistic reliance on individual rational choice to change risky behavior cannot account for social conditions and structures that limit people's options and predispose them to certain behavior, making HIV risks more a socially produced reality than a purely behavioral one. Philippe Denis demonstrates how AIDS has changed the social landscape in South Africa, which includes the churches, affecting religious institutions at the institutional level by prompting them to create a multiplicity of faith-based AIDS organizations, to reinvest in the health-care sector after long years of absence, and to move away from narrow moralism, which sustains stigmatizing and discriminatory behaviors against people living with HIV (PLWH). Small Christian Communities (SCCs) tend to be one of the best places where such abilities to transfer can be passed on to Christians and their neighbors with lasting effects. Joseph Healey demonstrates that the active involvement of SCC members in reaching out to people with HIV as responders, health-care workers, caregivers, and counselors is a pastoral and social priority. SCC members have a special opportunity to minister to families and couples living with HIV in Eastern Africa.

Part 3 of this volume seeks to lay down the biblical foundations of the fight against AIDS, scrutinize the concepts of sin and healing, unveil the meaning of moral responsibility in times of sickness, and raise gender issues. Paul Rene Ondoua surveys the New Testament to grasp Jesus's healing praxis in order to outline its significance for the churches' mission and for individual Christians when confronted with sickness. The miracles of Jesus are not to be considered as sensational illustrations or demonstrations of a therapeutic power from another world, aiming to strike people's imagination. They are bound to his Word, which is strength and joy, truth and life, and that allows one to enter into the divine logic of salvation. Hence, avoidance of fatalism and demonization of AIDS call for a return to the word of God. Conrad Folifack scrutinizes the contours of Psalm 38 to see how its use may enlighten the plight of PLWH. Using semantic connections between verses, he shows how they unfold narrative elements and highlight the change in relationship patterns in situations of sickness. The use of Psalm 38 may foster identification between the sick of the Psalms and PLWH. It can also be used by the sick themselves to seek an intimate connection with God. Wilfrid Okambawa endeavors to sketch an African HIV and AIDS hermeneutics from Isaiah 53:5. As a well of wisdom that influences New Testament Christologies, Isaiah 52:13–53:12 can help PLWH to become a source of wisdom and healing for others. However, PLWH first need to move from the status of victims suffering from an incurable infection to that of people voluntarily taking on their suffering in obedient love in the interest of others. For Caroline Mbonu, the question of Jesus's disciples in John 9:2 can be perceived as a wake-up call for Africans to look inward and to draw up a holistic agenda for a way forward. The healing of the blind man is also a restoration for the parents and the community. Mbonu employs hermeneutics of resonance as well as cultural hermeneutics to elicit the familial and communal character of sin and responsibility as it pertains to the pandemic, and also proposes a response in curbing the spread of HIV. Priscille Djomhoué insists that the gospel calls wife and husband to love in a reciprocal submission. Ephesians 5:21–31 clearly echoes this call. However, this text is one of those most used in the church, by some pastors and Christians especially, to validate inequalities between men and women. Djomhoué challenges the churches to change, since inequality is at the core of the feminization of HIV.

Part 4 focuses on the theological foundations of the churches' fight against AIDS. Dossou Davy opens this section by perceiving AIDS as a theodicy question. AIDS is altogether a physical, moral, and metaphysical evil that has challenged medicine and human society. No matter the destructive nature of AIDS, human society cannot remain at the level of questioning but needs to move on to action by opening up to the transcendent being and seeking the best ways of intervening. Eugène Goussikindey grapples with a key Christological reference as PLWH and people affected by HIV attempt to find meaning and raise questions about the relevance of faith in the face of the AIDS pandemic. What answer can be given to Jesus's question ("Who do you say that I am?) in a continent devastated by AIDS? Goussikindey responds to this burning question with what he calls "a Christology in the time of distress" by sketching out an image of Jesus Christ when things fall apart. As an institution called to enact Jesus's practice, the church's mission in the Catholic Diocese of Kinshasa is deeply challenged by HIV and AIDS, as Ignace Ndongala demonstrates. The church is called to become a brotherhood of God's children: a community of service (*diakonia*), a healer of human beings and a defender of life.

Odomaro Mubangizi comes up with an African theological anthropology grounded in local cosmology that challenges a global political economy that neglects the care of HIV- and AIDS-affected and -infected persons. He suggests a theology of global compassion (Matt. 25:31–46) as both a theoretical and practical solution to the HIV and AIDS pandemic. In fact, only through collaboration among Christian churches and with other constituencies can such a great vision can be implemented. Nyambura Njoroge attempts to capture the kinds of theologies and methodologies African Christians have created in response to the AIDS pandemic. The contributions of the World Council of Churches since 1980, the Circle of Concerned African Women Theologians, and the African founding members of the International Network of Religious Leaders Living with or Personally Affected by HIV and AIDS (INERELA+) stand out.

The five contributors to part 5 of this volume raise important ethical and structural questions about the magnitude of the AIDS pandemic as they relate to the global marginalization of Africa, gender discrimination, global health challenges, public policy in Africa, and stigma issues. Peter Kanyandago suggests that AIDS can only be adequately addressed if it is situated within the general and ethical context that underscores, as a categorical imperative, the necessity of ensuring what is needed to promote and defend the dignity and identity of each human being. The dehumanizing effects of marginalization of Africa and the violent structures of neoliberalism are unethical. Christian churches ought to address AIDS in ways that are context-specific.

According to Teresia Hinga, AIDS is both a pandemic and a syndemic. As a syndemic, AIDS thrives in a symbiotic relationship with other diseases and comorbidities as well as in the context of "metaphorical viruses" such as stigma, denial, sexism, racism, and other situations affected by pathologies of power. With regard to gender issues, transforming power dynamics to enhance mutuality instead of domination is a fundamental strategy that turns the global and gendered syndemic into a locus of social transformation. Anthony Egan addresses the question of the Catholic Church's complex relationship with global health, with particular reference to the AIDS pandemic in Africa on controversial issues of condom usage and global justice. These two issues are among the points of divergence between global health organizations and the Catholic Church. However, cooperation is essential to serve the common good. Operating with the Shona concept of *ukama* (relatedness of all citizens), which is equivalent to the biblical notion that we are each other's keeper (Gen. 4:9–16), Ezra Chitando challenges public policy in the time of HIV to take seriously the need to protect the poor, the marginalized, and the stigmatized in society. By acknowledging the relatedness among all the people of God, public policy can become more attuned to the struggles and needs of the most vulnerable citizens. Elias K. Bongmba discusses stigma, its impact, and responses from faith communities. Even though Christian churches have done a lot in addressing stigma, the fight against stigma is not yet over. As the ecclesial community moves forward in its combat against public health crises, faith communities should bear in mind that they have gone through a rough history of responding to HIV and AIDS and the stigma that has accompanied it.

How do we worship the God of life in times of distress and sickness? Part 6 starts with the dense and well-researched contribution of Elochukwu Uzukwu, a senior scholar and liturgist. Uzukwu addresses the monstrosity of the AIDS pandemic from the indigenous African perception of ominous diseases and indicates some ritual community and individual gestures toward the *disease*, toward the patient, and toward the deities, Jesus-God. Uzukwu further provides indications for liberation clues from liturgical spiritualities that appear to claim that suffering empowers community and individuals: schooled by suffering, the affected Christian community and PLWH make sense of the generosity and fragility of a God who revealed himself in Jesus Christ. Spiritual direction is one of the ways through which Jesus accompanies PLWH and the spiritual director. Susan Rakoczy focuses her contribution on some of the inner dynamics of spiritual direction when HIV and AIDS become part of the direction conversation because of the personal experience of either the director, the seeker, or both. The presence of HIV and AIDS in the spiritual direction relationship through the experience of seeker and director offers the opportunity for growth in both persons' relationship with God.

The fundamental pastoral exercise of prayer care of the sick and dying is the bringing of life to the sick, their families, and the communities they inhabit. Stuart Bate emphasizes that this spiritual journey may lead to being raised up to new life, whether in recovery from the sickness or in passing on to new life in the reign of God. The Christ event gives meaning to this journey, which is why Christian churches need to be agents of healing graces in times of AIDS. The churches' response to sickness and death should reflect Jesus's response to the sickness, death, and raising up of Lazarus. Training to enact and effect Jesus's praxis is definitely important. Edwina Ward argues that the curriculum in theological education must include leadership training for seminarians and students of theology, if they are to become active and informed leaders in their respective communities. In times of AIDS, Christian churches are challenged to once again find their prophetic voices by properly educating and communicating to those infected and affected ways of preventing further spread of the disease.

Violent conflicts and wars have contributed to an increased vulnerability to HIV and its spread. Bernard Tondé argues that the eradication of HIV and AIDS in Africa requires more than medicine, a greater political commitment to peace. A credible fight against the AIDS pandemic should include a conflict prevention component. Through its self-perception as the family of God, the church can be a vector of peace and togetherness, being welcoming to all. Using an interdisciplinary approach to address the AIDS pandemic and the need for a serious political commitment, Evelyn Mayanja argues that unless the leadership deficit and insecurity are viewed as contributing factors to the pandemic and strategies aiming at strengthening stewardship leadership and national security are developed, the AIDS pandemic will continue to escalate. Countries with positive interventions toward AIDS are those with stewardship leadership and the political will for national security.

Part 7 of this volume presents two important pastoral initiatives at the national level as well as the testimony of one HIV interventionist pioneer. Seeking to suggest a pastoral theology methodology to address a changing epidemic, Fabien Yedo Akpa argues that a methodology used as a framework for preventing HIV and managing AIDS cannot be definitive. Program implementation needs to consider the circumstances in which people live and how they cope with the infection. Father Ted Rogers, the HIV interventionist pioneer, worked tirelessly in Zimbabwe and encouraged many young Jesuits to embark on the fight against the AIDS pandemic. Rogers is no less than "a fire that kindles other fires."[10] Open-mindedness, compassion, and courage sustained Ted Rogers's ministry as an early AIDS interventionist pioneer at the moment where being a priest and an AIDS worker sounded awkward. The courage of faith led him to be the inspiration for the conference of Southern African Catholic Bishops' AIDS program in 1988 and of the African Jesuit AIDS Network created in 2002. Drawing on his own personal and pastoral experience and on what goes on in Zambia, Leonard Chiti reflects on the emergence of the home-based care (HBC) system in the late 1980s as a complement to the mainstream health-care delivery system for PLWH. He points to the theology, Zambian cultural background, religious values, and faith dimension of HBC.

---

[10] Society of Jesus, 35th General Congregation (Rome: Curia Generaliza, 2008).

Part One

The Sociohistorical, Cultural, and Political Context of the Pandemic

CHAPTER 1

OF THINGS OLD AND NEW

The African Sociohistorical Context of
an HIV-and-AIDS Theology

Festo Mkenda

In his *Spiritual Exercises*, Ignatius of Loyola proposes that the exercitant attempt to view the world as the three divine persons did before resolving that the second person should become the incarnate savior of humanity. He even suggests what the divine persons probably saw: a world, full of people, "so diverse in dress and behavior: some white and others black, some in peace and others at war, some weeping and others laughing, some healthy and others sick, some being born and others dying."[1] The divine persons saw a varied reality of mixed opportunities on earth, which determined their response. Here, the image one gets is that of a "movable God"—God who, as Pope (now Saint) John Paul II broadly showed, is not the unmovable mover of philosophers but the living God who is moved to specific action by the human condition.[2]

The action of the second person becoming the incarnate savior culminated in the highest expression of his love for humanity and of his determination to see his work accomplished, as was manifested on the cross. St. Ignatius invites the prayerful disciple to face this limitless love and then ask introspectively, "What have I done for Christ? What am I doing for Christ? What ought I to do for Christ?"[3] In the end, one is invited to engage in a theological reflection—an act of seeing the world the way God sees it, of determining what appropriate action, and of committing oneself to bringing desired change. In a way, this is an exercise in sociopastoral analysis that allows one to understand a context, discern opportunities, and commit oneself to working for positive change in a manner similar to that of the divine persons on the eternal eve of the incarnation.

---

[1] George E. Ganss, *The Spiritual Exercises of Saint Ignatius: A Translation and Commentary* (Chicago: Loyola Press, 1992), nos. 102–8.

[2] John Paul II, *Crossing the Threshold of Hope* (London: Jonathan Cape, 1994).

[3] Ganss, *Spiritual Exercises*, no. 53.

For quite some time now, theologians have viewed the context and experience of HIV and AIDS as a *kairos*,[4] an opportune moment for seeing the universe afresh and taking appropriate action. The HIV and AIDS pandemic, especially as has been experienced in its African epicenter, offers the church and humanity that rare opportunity to look back to old ways, draw wisdom from the past, and commit to new approaches that are more life-giving. Sociohistorical facts about HIV and AIDS force us to theologize anew, for the alternative is to preach a sterile gospel that is out of touch with sacred human experience. Well over thirty years since the virus and the disease were definitively identified, we have collected data and gathered information that are sufficient for isolating facts from fabrications and thus see the HIV and AIDS reality nearly as accurately as the divine persons must be seeing it. This is the first step in any theological exercise and, for the purpose of this essay, the main part. The second step is to discern opportunities and determine appropriate action.

The Sociohistorical Context of HIV and AIDS in Africa

If God looked down on earth to assess the devastation wrought by HIV and AIDS, God would first see Africa. The reality in other parts of the world would only be a cut-down representation of the real thing. From the mid-1980s, authors outdid one another in painting the most graphic situation on the continent, substantiating their shocking descriptions with undeniable facts and figures. It was estimated that 12 million Africans would die of AIDS in the 1990s alone, a figure "equivalent to the obliteration of the entire population of a medium-sized African country," suggested Paul Nugent, or "the number of Africans transported to the New World during the trans-Atlantic slave trade over three-and-a-half centuries."[5] The predicted figure was actually exceeded, for 17 million Africans had already succumbed to the disease by the year 2002, and another 29 million probably lived with the virus in that year.[6] By 2004 "Sub-Saharan Africa had an estimated 12 million AIDS orphans," who constituted "about 95 percent of all the world's AIDS orphans."[7] At the same time, 90 percent of children infected with HIV were in Africa. In 2008 Africa had only

---

[4] Cf. Agbonkhianmeghe E. Orobator, *From Crisis to Kairos: The Mission of the Church in the Time of HIV/AIDS, Refugees and Poverty* (Nairobi: Paulines Publications, 2008), 121–22.

[5] Paul Nugent, *Africa since Independence: A Comparative History* (NY: Palgrave Macmillan, 2004), 362.

[6] Robert Guest, *The Shackled Continent: Africa's Past, Present, and Future* (London: Macmillan, 2004), 89.

[7] John Iliffe, *The African AIDS Pandemic: A History* (Oxford: James Currey, 2006), 116.

11 percent of the world's population, but it was reported to have approximately 67 percent of the global number of people living with HIV or suffering from AIDS.[8] This reality imposed itself on every observer. From the year 2000 HIV and AIDS constituted an essential chapter or a substantial part of a chapter in every monograph on Africa worth its salt.

Describing the devastation of AIDS in Africa as "Sisyphean Nightmare" and "Nature's Holocaust," Peter Schwab said that "the figures jump off the page" to "shock and numb."[9] Yet, if it lasted longer than a few moments, numbness would cause inaction. The reality of HIV and AIDS called for action even from the most reluctant quarters, and those who initially dithered eventually had to do something. The calling came in the form of two questions: First, why such devastation in Africa, and second, what could one do about it?

If, like us, God needed literature in order to comprehend the devastation, he would probably have on his reading list John Iliffe's already-cited 2006 book, *The African AIDS Epidemic: A History.* This is the only book-length work by a leading historian of Africa (known to the current author) that traces the entire length of the African epidemic from its earliest days to the time of its publication and carefully maps the spread of HIV to different parts of the continent. Most importantly, Iliffe sets out to "suggest" an answer to the "why" question that many have raised, but most pointedly Thabo Mbeki, the former president of South Africa: "Why has Africa had a uniquely terrible HIV/AIDS epidemic?"[10] Mbeki proposed poverty and exploitation as constituting an adequate response or the main blocks of a comprehensive answer. He attracted fans who hailed his challenge to "the HIV-causes-AIDS theory that the world has become so used to,"[11] as well as critics who counted him among denialists of the causal link between the virus and the disease.[12] Going beyond Mbeki's partial answer, Iliffe shows the necessity of looking at the entire history of the epidemic in order to grasp the nexus of factors that made Africa such a fertile ground for the virus that caused AIDS.

To begin to fathom the African devastation, for example, it is important to contend with questions of origins. For Iliffe, the proven preexistence in some monkeys in Africa's western equatorial region of simian immunodeficiency virus (SIV)—which he describes as "the natural ancestor of HIV"—and the presence

---

[8] "HIV/AIDS Pandemic Affects Development in Africa," *DevelopAfrica*, www.developafrica.org.

[9] Peter Schwab, *Africa: A Continent Self-Destructs* (NY: Palgrave, 2001), 111.

[10] Iliffe, *African AIDS Pandemic*, 1; also see Thabo Mbeki, "South African President Thabo Mbeki's Letter to World Leaders on AIDS in Africa" (April 3, 2000), www.virusmyth.com.

[11] Huw Christie, "The Great AIDS Debate That Will Change the World," *New African* (May 2000): 8.

[12] Guest, *Shackled Continent*, 105–6.

in the same region of the full range of viral subtypes that caused AIDS, "is a compelling reason to believe that the epidemic began there."[13] Retrospective examination of stored blood samples further indicated that a case of HIV was identified in Kinshasa, the capital of today's Democratic Republic of Congo (DRC), in 1959. AIDS' peculiarly lengthy incubation period—that is, the time between infection with HIV and full-blown AIDS, which could be anything from two to over ten years—meant that new infections could occur and the virus could be transported from one place to another long before the disease could be felt and steps taken to check it. In this view, the fact that first known cases of AIDS were identified in Los Angeles need not suggest that the epidemic started there. Rather, as Iliffe concludes, "Africa had the worst epidemic because it had the first epidemic."[14]

To many, Iliffe's conclusion—already held by many before him—is quite helpful in understanding the disproportionate catastrophe in Africa. Yet the suggestion that the virus could have its origin in Africa triggered reactions that were drawn from a distant, largely unrelated, past. "Old colonial myths about the rampant promiscuity of Africans were dusted down and given a pseudo-scientific gloss," says Nugent.[15] Conversely, several Africans manifested a feeling of stigma and assumed the most defensive stance, which unmasked Africa's own insecurity in the global society. For them, Africa was under siege yet again. Emmanuel Katongole dedicated a significant part of a twelve-page essay to the history of past Western prejudices against Africa from Hegel's Africa-has-no-history claim to Hitler's list of most hated races, all in an effort to show that the HIV's Africa-origin argument could as well be the latest.[16] Rather unfortunately, with a reference to "untamed barbaric instinct," he gave the impression of having read into the argument an accusation of bestiality,[17] which is entirely needless since a virus "leap" from animals to humans through blood contact— hardly new in epidemiological history—could take place in many different and probably accidental situations. An alternative explanation quickly came to the fore, suggesting that AIDS was a "Western import or Western fabrication . . . no more than racist propaganda designed to dampen the sexual ardor and reproductive capacity of Africans."[18] This alternative was met with signifi-

---

[13] Iliffe, *African AIDS Pandemic*, 4–5, 158.

[14] Ibid., 158.

[15] Nugent, *Africa since Independence*, 358.

[16] Emmanuel M. Katongole, *A Future for Africa: Critical Essays in Christian Social Imagination* (Scranton, PA: University of Scranton Press, 2005), 32–36.

[17] Katongole, *Future for Africa*, 32.

[18] Martin Meredith, *The State of Africa: A History of Fifty Years of Independence* (London: Free Press, 2005), 366; also see Nugent, *Africa since Independence*, 358; Guest, *Shacked Continent*, 106; Katongole, *Future for Africa*, 37; and Michael J. Kelly, "The Churches and a Stigmatising Disease," in *AIDS, 30 Years Down the Line: Faith-Based Reflec-*

cant enthusiasm. In his letter to world leaders, President Mbeki made a direct connection between the racism practiced under apartheid and world reaction to his position on HIV and AIDS. For Mbeki, to deny a voice to those who opposed the link between HIV and AIDS was "to do precisely the same thing that the racist apartheid tyranny we opposed did, because, it is said, there exists a scientific view that is supported by the majority, against which dissent is prohibited."[19] Such reactions were pulled out of Africa's bitter past; after tempers had been lowered, few judged them to have been appropriate responses to the new AIDS pandemic.

Time wasted responding inappropriately also accounts for the devastation of HIV and AIDS in Africa. Some initial responses betrayed a sense of denial that was informed by Africa's own rampant prejudice, for example, against homosexuality. An official in Botswana declared AIDS to be "not a problem in Botswana" since "AIDS is primarily a disease of homosexuals and there is no homosexual in Botswana," and was joined by the country's health minister who "allayed fear by mentioning that the modes of transmission of the disease means that it could not become a big epidemic." Just about a year later, the same minister was talking of "a scourge that could decimate a large portion of the human race."[20] The Johannesburg *Star* understood AIDS to be a disease for homosexuals as it announced, "Gay Plague Hits South Africa."[21] In Zimbabwe, the minister of health "ordered doctors not to identify AIDS as a cause of death," and in Kenya, as in Zambia, the government was "more concerned to protect its reputation as a thriving tourist destination than to alert its own people about the hazards they faced."[22]

Had they not found allies in religious opinion, the inadequate political responses would not have had the devastating impact they ended up having. Most responses to HIV and AIDS in Africa, especially most of the caring, were inspired by religious belief. The Catholic Church alone held an impeccable record, recognized by UNAIDS, of running up to 26 percent of health institutions that offered AIDS-related services globally; in Africa, the figure rose to 50 percent.[23] Yet this record was largely clouded by initial responses from several religious leaders, which tended to be moralistic, sometimes even

tions about the Epidemic in Africa, ed. Paterne A. Mombé, Agbonkhianmeghe E. Orobator, and Danielle Vella (Nairobi: Paulines Publications, 2012), 248–49.

[19] Mbeki, "Letter to World Leaders."

[20] Iliffe, *African AIDS Pandemic*, 38.

[21] *The Star*, January 1983, as cited in Iliffe, *African AIDS Pandemic*, 43.

[22] Meredith, *State of Africa*, 366; cf. Nugent, *Africa since Independence*, 358.

[23] Michael Czerny, "The Second African Synod and AIDS in Africa," in *Reconciliation, Justice, and Peace: The Second African Synod*, ed. Agbonkhianmeghe E. Orobator (Maryknoll, NY: Orbis Books, 2011), 194–95.

celebratory, as they understood AIDS to be the "wages of sin."²⁴ An independent church leader in Botswana is said to have declared HIV and AIDS to be "a punishment sent by God, as Sodom and Gomorrah."²⁵ Many more felt that rampant homosexuality, bisexuality, and promiscuity among those who would not follow God's demands were finally being punished.²⁶ Such "crude providentialism" (as Iliffe called it) also informed religious action. A Catholic priest in Kenya was reported to have refused to conduct funeral services for AIDS victims, fearing that "the church might be seen to be encouraging the spread of the disease."²⁷ This religious disapproval preyed on traditional African cultures in which "shame"—understood as "an emotional response to falling short of social norm" or to the "disapproval coming from others"²⁸—enforced social order. In the end, it compounded the stigma that came to be associated with AIDS, which condemned victims of the epidemic into silence and made it difficult for them to access treatment and care.²⁹ "I would like to talk to my priest, but he would condemn me," said one Bernard to Gillian Paterson, adding that "AIDS is not a nice thing to mention to a man of God."³⁰ AIDS victims suffered an unnecessarily heavier burden, not because they were "guilty" of sin—for that God would have forgiven them even before they expressed remorse—but because fellow humans made them feel like social failures and outcasts.

The argument that a dithering political response that was fueled by denial, which found an ally in stigmatizing religious positions, actually helped to worsen the AIDS pandemic in Africa is best corroborated by two celebrated cases of appropriate initial responses in Senegal and Uganda. Regarding Senegal, some authors have cautioned against a blanket attribution of its lower rate of HIV infection to its initial response without taking into consideration other factors, especially Islamic strictures on mostly young women who otherwise might have exposed themselves to greater risk by exploring their sexual opportunities earlier in life; such strictures seem to have translated into less HIV prevalence

²⁴ Nugent, *Africa since Independence*, 364.

²⁵ Iliffe, *African AIDS Pandemic*, 94.

²⁶ Laurenti Magesa, "AIDS and Survival in Africa: A Tentative Reflection," in *Moral and Ethical Issues in African Christianity: Exploratory Essays in Moral Theology*, 2nd ed., ed. J. K. N. Mugambi and Anne Nasimiyu-Wasike (Nairobi: Acton Publishers, 1999), 208.

²⁷ Iliffe, *African AIDS Pandemic*, 94.

²⁸ F. B. Welbourn, "Some Problems of African Christianity: Guilt and Shame," in *Christianity in Tropical Africa: Studies Presented and Discussed at the Seventh International African Seminar, University of Ghana, April 1965*, ed. C. G. Baëta (Oxford: Oxford University Press, 1968), 184, 189.

²⁹ Norbert Litoing, "Religion and HIV/AIDS-Related Stigma in Africa: An Interreligious Perspective," in Mombé, Orobator, and Vella, *AIDS, 30 Years*, 157.

³⁰ Gillian Paterson, *Stigma in the Context of Development: A Christian Response to the HIV Pandemic* (London: Progressio, 2009).

in other Muslim countries in Africa.[31] It is generally accepted, however, that Senegal's initial response helped to limit the spread of the virus, keeping its prevalence consistently below 1 percent among its adult population. There is even greater agreement that Uganda's political leadership, especially President Yoweri Museveni, together with religious authorities in the country, wasted no time with futile denials; instead, they created a conducive environment for establishing concerted multisectoral programs that helped reverse the spread of the virus, bringing it down from, for example, 21.1 percent in 1991 to 6.1 percent in 2000 among pregnant women.[32] These facts add to the conclusion that Africa had the worst epidemic because most of its initial responses were inappropriate.

The now enormous literature on HIV and AIDS also manifests a third reason for Africa's disproportionate share of the pandemic's malevolence—what I would like to call the continent's inadequate socioeconomic hardware. A society's capacity to build and sustain structures for the provision of health care, including treatment, depends not only on political will but also on economic muscle. Economically, Africa was at its weakest moment in the mid-1980s, largely following the structural adjustment programs that had been dictated upon African states by the World Bank and the International Monetary Fund. Among the many disastrous consequences of these programs were the weakening of the postindependence state and its near complete exit from provision of health care to masses of poor Africans. That up to 10 percent of new infections in Nigeria between 1995 and 2005 were still being contracted through blood transfusion shows how derelict the health system was in that country, as indeed it was in Chad and in so many other places.[33] States receiving foreign aid had to stop seriously investing in health care, for the logic of the structural adjustment programs was that individual Africans deserved no health care unless they could afford it out-of-pocket. AIDS spread fastest and widest in Africa during this disastrous economic episode in postindependence history. In the process, it disproportionately affected the most impoverished members of the society and then went on to increase their economic misery as breadwinners died and their dependents were left helpless. HIV was indeed a "misery-seeking missile"[34] and, even more importantly, was itself a misery-making machine.

---

[31] Magesa, "AIDS and Survival," 201; Nugent, *Africa since Independence*, 365; Iliffe, *African AIDS Pandemic*, 55–57.

[32] Paterne A. Mombé, Agbonkhianmeghe E. Orobator, and Danielle Vella, "Introduction: AIDS, Thirty Years down the Line?" in Mombé, Orobator, and Vella, *AIDS, 30 Years*, 26–27.

[33] Iliffe, *African AIDS Pandemic*, 57; cf. Jacquineau Azetsop, "Universal Access to Antiretroviral Treatment in Chad and Social Equity: Barriers to Access and Public Health Leadership," in Mombé, Orobator, and Vella, *AIDS, 30 Years*, 296 and passim.

[34] Renée Sabatier, *Blaming Others: Prejudice, Race, and Worldwide AIDS* (London: New Society Publishers, 1988), 147.

AIDS, as the Panos Dossier concluded in 1992, is "a cause as well as a symptom of poverty and disadvantage."[35]

Poverty is a compound concept, which attracts to itself a host of other wicked attendants. To "rampant poverty," Mombé, Orobator, and Vella have associated ignorance, commercial or transactional sex, and nutritional deficits.[36] This list could be almost infinitely prolonged. Several diseases go untreated for lack of resources, for example, and, in turn, expose poor people to a greater risk of contracting HIV. It is also mainly as culturally created, economically margin-alized groups that women and children in Africa suffered the effects of the disease more than senior men. Moreover, to the collapse of health systems as a consequence of poverty, and to ignorance as an associate of that same poverty, we can also append the easiness with which people turned to witchcraft and ineffective traditional healing methods as alternative remedies for HIV and AIDS[37] or believed in dangerous myths like sexual-intercourse-with-a-virgin-wipes-out-the-disease.[38] These factors complicate the poverty equation even before the question of universal access to proven but expensive antiretroviral therapy is introduced to it.

On the matter of access to available therapy, a few successful cases once more help to strengthen the argument that Africa suffered the worst epidemic because it had the largest number of individuals and communities living in absolute poverty. They could not pay for treatment or care, and their govern-ments could not provide them for free. Yet antiretroviral treatment held an almost magical formula for a revolution that turned a deadly disease into a manageable chronic condition and reduced significantly the transmission of the virus from mother to child and more generally from one person to another.[39] As Alison Munro has shown, when the South African government finally put its act in order, and with huge support from faith-based initia-tives, the country used its better economic endowment at home and aid from outside to facilitate access to antiretroviral treatment, ultimately preventing an already bad situation from becoming worse.[40] Indeed it is no mere coin-

---

[35] From the back cover of the Panos Dossier, *The Hidden Cost of AIDS: The Challenge of HIV to Development* (London: Panos Institute, 1992).

[36] Mombé, Orobator, and Vella, "Introduction," 25.

[37] Nugent, *Africa since Independence*, 363; Iliffe, *African AIDS Pandemic*, 92; Richard Dowden, *Africa: Altered States, Ordinary Miracles* (London: Portobello Books, 2008), 325.

[38] Guest, *Shackled Continent*, 99; Dawden, *Africa*, 336.

[39] Paterne A. Mombé, "Responsibility in an Era of Antiretroviral Treatment Revolu-tion," in Mombé, Orobator, and Vella, *AIDS, 30 Years*, 263.

[40] Alison Munro, "Is Universal Access to Antiretroviral Treatment a Myth or Reality? Some Experiences of the Catholic Church in South Africa," in Mombé, Orobator, and Vella, *AIDS, 30 Years*, 320–32.

cidence that AIDS-related deaths began to decline overall in Africa in 2007, the same time as prices of antiretroviral drugs were significantly lowered and made accessible to a large number of those who needed them most. By 2013, there were 33 percent fewer new HIV infections than in 2001 and 32 percent fewer AIDS-related deaths than in 2005.[41]

Discerning Opportunities and Determining Appropriate Action

One of the great lessons we draw from the preincarnation divine observation of the human condition is God's complete trust of the world. The second person would not come into that world with a host of angels to assist him as apostles and disciples, but would make use of opportunities still extant on earth. The observation must have gone beyond understanding the context to identifying opportunities for action. What, we may ask, would the divine persons have identified as opportunities for action in the context of HIV and AIDS in Africa?

In the last thirty years, we saw a concerted effort in the scientific community to find vaccines against HIV and treatment for AIDS. This needs to be continued and even doubled. Much has also been done to alleviate poverty and reduce the economic burden of those oppressed by the disease. Politicians and activists, armed with ethical arguments, shamed pharmaceutical companies that were bent on making capital out of the pandemic, and the net result has been a reduced cost of varieties of antiretroviral therapy per person per year from about $10,000 in the mid-1990s to about $130 in the mid-2000s. Consequently, there were more than 7 million people in Africa accessing treatment in 2013[42]—a small fraction that, nevertheless, points to the fact that more can be done.

Besides the obvious gains that must be consolidated, HIV and AIDS have brought to light Africa's treasure of social mechanisms that are available to her in crises, which may as well be acknowledged and developed. They have also manifested cultural fault lines that might need fixing or changing if the continent is to survive this pandemic or withstand any other crisis—the recent Ebola outbreak in West Africa, for example.

One of the lessons we derive from HIV and AIDS is that, in Africa, as in any other place on earth, we are more socially connected than we often think. Population movements for all sorts of reasons were among major factors in the African AIDS epidemic, explaining both its speed and its breadth.[43] Even more

---

[41] UNAIDS Special Report, May 2013, 10, www.unAIDS.org.

[42] Ibid., 15.

[43] Magesa, "AIDS and Survival," 201.

importantly, this social connectedness negates the false boundaries between rich and poor, both among individuals in a society and among nations. If poor people were exposed to the risk of contracting HIV because of their misery, the rich were at the same risk because of their wealth. "The fact that the most privileged sections of society have been felled is none too surprising," writes Nugent, "because power and sexual access tend to go together."[44] As AIDS gnaws on the poor, it stings the rich with its tail, and the same can be said about women and men. The need to combat AIDS is thus a societal, even global, responsibility. Humanity has probably never had a greater reason for standing together as a family.

More intimately, human beings are more sexually connected than they are prepared to admit publicly. After the demise of traditional structures that safely handled the topic, African adults conspired with Christianity and so-called Western civilization never to mention sex to the young. Today, thanks to the regretted ravages of HIV and AIDS, sex has once more become part of necessary conversation between the young and the old. This, too, is an opportunity, albeit one that must be handled well. Some people might present the subject as that scary, dirty thing that is to be avoided or else it will send you to the grave. As Emmanuel Katongole warns, others might present it casually as a playful thing in need of no serious commitment as long as one "plays safe"—say, by wearing a condom.[45] In Africa, even adults are having another chance to learn new, positive, and nonmoralizing ways of talking about the gift of sex.

The African woman and the African family stand out as two pillars without which society should have collapsed under the AIDS crisis. "Although HIV/AIDS bore especially hard on women," reported Iliffe, "it also provided them with opportunities to regain the active political role that they had often played in nationalist movements but had lost at independence."[46] "Since we began volunteering, other people look at us differently," said a woman in Mozambique, and continued,

> Often, when we pass someone on a walkway in the barrio, that person will give us a special gesture of dignity because of our work. . . . They say that we are people that can help others. . . . When someone is sick, the community leaders come to us for help. Before we were nobodies. So now we feel good; we feel honoured.[47]

A whole community was rediscovering the strength of its women, thanks to the regrettable ravages of HIV and AIDS. "Home care"—that African inven-

---

[44] Nugent, *Africa since Independence*, 363.
[45] Katongole, *Future for Africa*, 43.
[46] Iliffe, *African AIDS Pandemic*, 101.
[47] As presented in Iliffe, *African AIDS Pandemic*, 107.

tion that occupied the empty space of proper health facilities—"was indeed a euphemism for women's work."[48] With AIDS, old myths and societal structures that depended on them have been shaken, and patriarchy can no longer hold. Making a similar observation, Orobator suggests that the active role of women, both lay and religious, in combating HIV and AIDS reveals a higher meaning of being church and beckons to a different ecclesiology.[49] This, too, has to be seen as an opportunity.

Like the woman, the African extended family absorbed the heaviest shocks of AIDS. A study conducted in the worst affected parts of Zambia in 2002 showed that up to 72 percent of households had taken in one or more children orphaned by the disease.[50] UNAIDS estimated that, in 2004, 90 percent of care in Africa was provided by family members.[51] To be sure, there were reports of children being abused in such settings, but, largely, the extended family lived up to its description as "Africa's great heritage [and] its strongest mechanism for human survival."[52] Iliffe acknowledged variations in family responses, but said "predominantly they—and 'they' meant chiefly women—provided care with a selflessness that was one of the most heroic features of the epidemic." In his estimation, "Had Africa's family systems been less resilient, the impact of the first AIDS epidemic could have been terrible beyond imagining." Arguing that "for the family the shame of not caring was worse than the shame of AIDS," he identified what he called the "self-evident obligation of kinship" in Africa.[53] Despite the stress under which families found themselves, Guest still concluded that "[not] even AIDS can break the African extended family."[54] When such self-evident family bonds are placed against the image of a church minister refusing to bury a fellow Christian who died of AIDS for fear of embarrassing the church, one wonders whether Africans do not have a reason to consider kinship blood to be thicker than the waters of baptism; one wonders whether, in the context of AIDS, the church does not have a unique opportunity to learn from Africa what it means to be a family!

Finally, as already indicated, reactions to the possibility of an African origin of HIV clearly manifested a lingering historical woundedness that is still crying for healing. It might be the case that far too often the West absolves itself of responsibility for Africa's past ills, urging Africans simply to accept the reality and get

---

[48] Iliffe, *African AIDS Pandemic*, 109.

[49] Orobator, *From Crisis to Kairos*, 133–38; see also Kelly, "Churches and a Stigmatising Disease," 252–53.

[50] Guest, *Shackled Continent*, 98.

[51] Iliffe, *African AIDS Pandemic*, 109.

[52] Dawden, *Africa*, 327.

[53] Iliffe, *African AIDS Pandemic*, 98, 103–4.

[54] Guest, *Shackled Continent*, 98.

on with life. The problem with accepting blame, though, is that Africans might demand reparation or at least an apology. As Guest observed, "Today's Westerners do not feel particularly guilty about the sins of dead people who happened to come from the same country."[55] The issue is certainly more complex than Guest expresses it here, but a point is being communicated. Africans may also have not come up with ways of addressing their own woundedness. They may even have perpetuated structures that worsen their condition, continually making them aliens in a globalized arena, as Katongole suggests Western "civilization" does.[56] What is sure is that HIV and AIDS have brought to light a preexisting condition that needs healing, and ignoring it might hamper current efforts to combat the disease as well as cripple Africa's preparedness for another crisis.

Conclusion

A suggestion was made at the start of this essay that we imitate the divine persons on the eve of the incarnation as we look at the reality of HIV and AIDS today. The purpose of such an exercise would be to understand the pandemic's devastation, especially in Africa. As has been proposed, the longer prevalence of HIV on the continent before AIDS was identified, the poor initial response from some quarters, and the socioeconomic misery in which the virus thrived all account for Africa's disproportionately larger share of the global tragedy. Furthermore, it was also suggested that, characteristically, the divine persons see opportunities for positive action where humans might see none. Learning from them, we might identify similar opportunities even in the cinders left behind by the regretted virus and disease. We could appreciate our connectedness better; we could understand the gift of sexuality more deeply; we could treat women as equal members of the human family and allow them the credit they deserve for their irreplaceable role in society; we could strengthen the African family rather than watch by as it crushes under the onslaught of so-called modernity; we could even look back, admit our woundedness, and, together as members of the one human family, seek durable healing. It is unthinkable that, in such an enormous task, theology—the queen of all the sciences—would not play a major role.

---

[55] Ibid., 11.

[56] Katongole, *Future for Africa*, 35–36.

CHAPTER 2

CONTEXTUALIZING HIV AND AIDS
IN THE AFRICAN REALITY

Laurenti Magesa

The History and Epidemiology of
HIV and AIDS in Africa

A few cases of acquired immunodeficiency syndrome (AIDS) were first detected among some members of the black gay community and intravenous drug users in New York City, Los Angeles, and San Francisco in the United States in 1981.[1] Scientists soon came to isolate the cause of AIDS to be the human immunodeficiency virus (HIV). Apparently, the virus had earlier been noticed in primates, and John Iliffe notes that suspicions that the virus had already infected humans by 1959 seem to be backed by evidence. In 1982 the syndrome was identified among some fishermen at the Kasensero landing site of the Kyotera village community in Rakai District in Uganda, reportedly the first sure incidence of AIDS on the continent. In the following years, the disease spread rapidly across the sub-Saharan region, killing countless numbers of people.[2] Transmitted through intimate bodily contact with fluids from a person already infected with the virus, it was soon established that, in the case of Africa at least, the virus was spread mainly through heterosexual activity.

No country of sub-Saharan Africa has remained untouched by the epidemic; differences apply only to numbers of people affected in each place.[3] South Africa, Nigeria, and Kenya are reported to be among the countries experiencing the highest occurrence of HIV infection, but they are obviously not the only ones. Swaziland, Botswana, and Lesotho are among the countries that suffer the greatest rate of incidences of HIV infection per capita worldwide. Researcher Linda Morison reports this sad fact: "While only 10 percent of

---

[1] Symptoms of the illness were first published in 1981 by the US Centers for Disease Control (CDC) in Atlanta.

[2] John Iliffe, *The African AIDS Epidemic: A History* (Athens: Ohio University Press, 2000), 23–24.

[3] Ananya Mandal, "History of AIDS," www.news.medical.net.

the world's population lives in sub-Saharan Africa, an estimated 70 percent of all HIV-infected adults and children are found there."[4] Almost 3 percent, or 23.5 million people out of the continent's population of 850 million, are said to carry the virus. Therefore, the devastating and long-lasting consequences of HIV and AIDS on the psychological, social, and economic aspects of life on the continent can easily be imagined.

The prevalence of HIV infection in sub-Saharan Africa cuts across all social groups and geographical divisions. For a number of years after it was identified, AIDS was popularly branded as a "city disease," since it most predominantly occurred in the urban and otherwise comparatively more densely populated areas. But probably because of rapid human mobility and increased social contact, this view changed as AIDS rapidly spread to the rural areas as well. Thus, apart from the issue of statistics, the distinction between urban and rural HIV prevalence today is academic. However, the prevalence of HIV seropositivity in Africa indeed differs among social classes and between the sexes: the poor in general and women in particular suffer more from the infection than the wealthy and the men.

In terms of gender, Linda Morison again records that sub-Saharan Africa "is the only region [of the world] where more women than men are infected."[5] According to her research, this is due to certain sexual practices embedded in the African social reality. "Patterns of sexual behavior whereby young women have sex with older men, in combination with high susceptibility to infection in very young women has resulted in extremely high infection rates in young women in some parts of Africa."[6] This phenomenon is sometimes characterized as the feminization of AIDS in Africa. Though transmission by intravenous drug users also occurs here, particularly in large urban centers, it accounts for only a small percentage of the overall HIV infection cases; by far the majority occur as a result of heterosexual intercourse, as has already been noted.

Perceptions, Attitudes, and HIV and AIDS Prevention Strategies

The modes of HIV transmission have been widely publicized in Africa, thanks to vigorous awareness campaigns by governments and various nongovernmental organizations (NGOs) across the continent. Internationally, the scientific and medical communities have expended great effort to try to under-

---

[4] Linda Morison, "The Global Epidemiology of HIV/AIDS," *British Medical Bulletin* 58, no. 7 (September 2001): 7.

[5] Ibid.

[6] Ibid.

stand and spread knowledge about the nature of the epidemic and how to tame it. As yet, however, researchers have not discovered an effective vaccine against HIV or a cure for AIDS. Certainly, some remarkable advances have taken place in the medical field in the fight against the virus. With the production of anti-retroviral drugs (ARVs) that control the consequences of the HIV infection by slowing down the physical hazards of AIDS, research has produced quite posi-tive results. Whereas previously infection by the virus spelled certain death, in the regions of the world where people can access and afford them, ARVs have helped many to lead relatively long, normal, and productive lives after infec-tion. In many areas of sub-Saharan Africa, however, these medications are still beyond easy reach of the majority poor, especially in the rural areas.

These biomedical approaches leading to some therapeutic successes concern themselves with what may be described as the "symptoms" of the pandemic. From this point of view, they do not address its root causes. The issue is that an equally, if not more serious problem concerning HIV and AIDS is a sociological and economic one. This fact has not been sufficiently recognized, or has even been rejected, in the past. For example, when in July 2000 Thabo Mbeki, then President of South Africa, suggested that poverty, together with sexual activity, should be included as a major reason for the transmission of HIV, and that in Africa drugs alone were not enough to stem its spread, he was severely accused of "denialism" and blamed as a peddler of death to boot.[7] But a decade and a half later, poverty is indeed generally acknowledged as a major contributing factor to the spread of the infection. According to Michel S. Kamanzi, poverty must be included, together with corruption, ignorance, and political instability, as both a cause and a conse-quence of AIDS.[8]

Eileen Stillwaggon argues likewise that HIV and AIDS transmission "is a predictable outcome of an environment of poverty, worsening nutrition, chronic parasitic infection, and limited access to medical care." These are the conditions that condemn people to all sorts of infectious illnesses, "no matter how they are transmitted."[9] Stillwaggon has no doubt that "HIV is a disease of poverty in the African context." Actually, she places more emphasis on poverty than on behavior as the foundational factor in the transmission and spread of HIV and AIDS.[10] Edwin Cameron adds to this the elements of race

---

[7] See Nicoli Nattrass, *Mortal Combat: AIDS Denialism and the Struggle for Antiretro-virals in South Africa* (Scottsville, South Africa: University of KwaZulu-Natal Press, 2007).

[8] Michel S. Kamanzi, "Solidarity, a New Categorical Imperative," in *AIDS in Africa: Theological Reflections*, ed. Bénézet Bujo and Michael Czerny (Nairobi: Paulines Publications Africa, 2007), 22–24.

[9] Eileen Stillwaggon, *AIDS and the Ecology of Poverty* (Oxford: Oxford University Press, 2006), 69.

[10] Ibid., 78.

and homophobic bigotry, since for some time AIDS was seen as a disease of blacks and gays.[11]

When all is said and done, however, the cultural perception in HIV diffusion has received little attention in Africa. The key strategy in the campaigns to prevent HIV transmission has hitherto involved providing awareness against risky sexual behaviors, with emphasis on the importance of sexual abstinence, absolute faithfulness to one's sexual partner, or the use of condoms, also known as "condomization." The approach is dubbed the ABC method (for *A*bstinence, *B*e Faithful, *C*ondom Use). This tactic has had ambiguous results in Africa. Actually, in terms of sustainability, the ABC paradigm does not seem to have accomplished much positive response, if the numbers of confirmed new HIV cases in many of the countries provide any indication. Therefore, the unavoidable question is "Why?" Why do many Africans of all ages continue to engage in what are quite clearly and objectively "risky" sexual behaviors, with some getting infected? Is everyone in question unable to abstain from sexual activity? Why are some individuals unwilling to use condoms?

One cannot suggest blanket answers to these questions. Arguing that it is simply a case of hedonism—where people either cannot control their sexuality, or do not care about their lives or those of their loved ones—is unreasonable. But it makes sense to hypothesize, in the case of sub-Saharan Africa, that people who do not adhere to the ABC method may have cultural reasons for at least part of their behavior. Anders Breidlid takes that position. "The failure of modernist interventions to achieve behavioral change," he says, "makes it urgent to explore the extent to which traditional processes, practices, dynamics, structures, and networks within communities are under-reported and under-utilized as resources to support or facilitate behavioral change." He suggests, "There is a sense that reference to traditional norms and values stand a better chance of being accepted and adhered to than alien modernist interventions that so far have been met with massive, if tacit, resistance on the behavioral level." According to Breidlid, "Interventions devoid of acknowledgment of cultural and contextual specificity may be those that would have detrimental consequences for success in reducing the effects of the pandemic."[12]

Beliefs That Count in the African Worldview

Breidlid could be right. "A people's cosmology, their understanding of their own particular world, shapes the way they act in relation to themselves

---

[11] Edwin Cameron, *Witness to AIDS* (London: I. B. Tauris, 2005), 75–102.

[12] Anders Breidlid, "HIV/AIDS, Cultural Constraints and Educational Intervention Strategies," in *HIV/AIDS in Sub-Saharan Africa: Understanding the Implications of Culture and Context*, ed. Jean Baxen and Anders Breidlid (Cape Town: UCT Press, 2009), 32.

and to each other, [and to the world around them], and how they interpret the consequences of their actions."[13] The construal of sexual relations as moral behavior, therefore, relies very much on the predominant cosmology of a people at any given time, because the latter "forms the context in which ultimate reality is interpreted."[14] Illness and death constitute for Africans dimensions of "ultimate reality" that contradict life. For the issue in question, the question is what role HIV and AIDS play in Africa's perception of the world on the one hand, and the construction of sexual moral attitudes and behavior on the other.[15] In other words, how do sexual attitudes and behavior reflect Africans' value systems toward the meaning of life and death?

The African worldview is spiritual but deeply life-oriented in practice. Seemingly "ordinary" behavior is invariably laden with mystical (spiritual) meaning whose import must be constantly interpreted in as much as it tran-scends conventional appearances. From this perspective, the ultimate meaning of any thought, act, or word must be sought in its relationship to, and effects on, human existence: whether it promotes the good life that is the door to transcendent existence. And the "good life" is understood quite pragmatically as virtuous relationships resulting in personal and communal wealth, health, dignity, and happiness for everyone. Whereas other more mundane dimensions of these realities are not neglected, everything coheres in the ultimate goal of generation of life—essentially, having children. This quality is what is known as *Ubuntu*; perpetuation of life in this way is what gives authenticity to the person as an authentic human being, *umuntu*.[16] Humanity's central requirement involves responsibilities to fulfill in community, in which process an individual gains one's rights.

P. H. Coetzee and A. P. J. Roux explain it this way:

> Living in relation with others directly involves a person in social and moral roles, duties, obligations, and commitments which the individual person must fulfill. The natural relationality of the person thus immediately plunges him/her into a moral universe, making morality an essentially social and trans-individual phenomenon focused in the

---

[13] Laurenti Magesa, "AIDS and Survival in Africa: A Tentative Reflection," in *Moral and Ethical Issues in African Christianity—A Challenge for African Christianity*, ed. J. N. K. Mugambi and A. Nasimiyu-Wasike (Nairobi: Acton Publishers, 1999), 198.

[14] Ibid.

[15] Ibid.

[16] The notion implies the fullness of humanity, "a person's self-realization and manifes-tation as a human being." See Mluleki Munyaka and Mokgethi Motlhabi, "*Ubuntu* and Its Sociomoral Significance," in *African Ethics: An Anthology of Comparative and Applied Ethics*, ed. Munyaradzi Felix Murove (Scottsville, South Africa: University of KwaZulu-Natal Press, 2009), 63, 73.

well-being of others. Our natural sociality then prescribes or mandates a morality that, clearly, should be weighted on the side of duty, i.e. on that which one has to do for others.[17]

But it is in doing "for others," "in losing oneself" for them (see Matt. 10:39; 16:25) that, in the African perception, one gains oneself as a full and fulfilled human being. There is no greater goal for human existence from this point of view than, through mutual life-giving relationships, to grow into full or complete humanity on earth and so achieve the transformed and transcendental ancestral status in the world hereafter. Thus, as Matthew Michael notes, for the African, "The most important thing . . . is to attain or acquire personhood and thus the greatest achievement is to be conferred or recognized as a 'person.'"[18] Quoting Clinton R. Sanders's description of this interpretation of personhood, he says that it points to "an element of social designation that may be acquired or forfeited, given or taken away," depending on the interpersonal performance of the individual in society.[19] In this view, personhood is more than just an ontological given; it is a life goal to be achieved.

It is in this sense that "an individual is never born whole and fully human," as L. Lungile Pato explains. "The family, the clan, the community . . . to which one belongs enables the individual to become a mature human person." It means socialization into a trend of behavior by which one is "given an identity, a place of belonging, human dignity, and personhood" in, by, and through the community.[20] The "life force" of the community is therefore "the most important" element of human development, Klaus Nurnberger explains. "Life is life in community; there is no other possible life."[21] The power of life is not only preserved but enhanced by its transmission through community relationships, especially by way of physical generation of children. This explains the central role of sexuality and sexual relations in the African community structure. "Even if sexuality was not the only value appreciated and treasured by traditional African societies," Method Mwihava argues, "it characterized the life of the community." To a large extent, it defined the purpose of human existence and stood as the criterion for "[all] other values."[22] Mwihava maintains that for

---

[17] In Munyaka and Motlhabi, "*Ubuntu* and Its Sociomoral Significance," 73–74. Also Klaus Nurnberger, *The Living Dead and the Living God: Christ and the Ancestors in a Changing Africa* (Pietermaritzburg: Cluster Publications, 2007), 19–55.

[18] Matthew Michael, *Christian Theology and African Traditions* (Eugene, OR: Resource Publications, 2013), 101.

[19] Ibid., 103.

[20] Ibid., 115.

[21] Nurnberger, *Living Dead and the Living God*, 22–23.

[22] Method Mwihava, "The Role of the Community within the Realm of Sexuality in Africa" (unpublished doctoral dissertation, 2014), n.p.

African peoples, "Sexuality was therefore the thread that connected humans to each other, to God and the community as the governing authority. It was believed that by exercising one's sexuality, the individual was providing a service to the community."[23]

> This inter-connectivity fashioned the progression of each person from birth to the entrance in [the] world of the ancestors. From conception, in fact, the child (or zygote) began a journey of vital progression through experience and time. This time travel . . . was characterized by one's ability to effectively progress from the past to the present and on to the future. These transitions entailed both ethical and moral growth, and depending on the quality and level of that growth, could lead an individual to true excellence.[24]

The fundamental ethos of indigenous cultures of black Africa is one that is geared toward the promotion and perpetuation of life, in both its physical and mystical or transcendental dimensions. In everything that one does, the goal must be that the life of the family, clan, or ethnic group is advanced; the contrary is counted as unethical behavior because it negatively affects the life not only of the living but also that of the unborn and the entire community of goods (creation). Unethical behavior affects communion between and among the existential human community and other forces in the invisible world. Despite various mutations in cultural outlook, it remains strong and continues to influence the economic, political, social, and religious perspectives of the majority of the sub-Saharan African populations.

The sexual practices of many Africans as individuals and communities can best be understood when situated in this "life" context. Current approaches to arresting HIV transmission and the spread of AIDS must, therefore, confront questions such as the following: How deeply is the traditional worldview still adhered to by African communities and individuals? How does it impact the perception and practice of human sexuality in a situation of HIV and AIDS?

The Challenge

What today challenges the traditional approach to sexuality and sexual relations is its practical application in a changed environment of HIV and AIDS prevalence. It seems that in the interests of the central value of life, something must change fundamentally in indigenous thinking and attitudes. The fact that HIV is transmitted in the region mainly through heterosexual intercourse now comes

---

[23] Ibid.
[24] Ibid.

into direct confrontation with the conviction that it is through sexual activity that the most important ethical values in the life of the person—*Ubuntu*—are achieved. The situation has become extremely ambiguous, even paradoxical.

If sexual relations constitute the ideal channel of life's fulfillment on the one hand, but also the probable transmission of physical death on the other, what is the resolution? The paradox distresses many Africans. The dilemma is accentuated by the proffered standard ABC approaches of curbing the pandemic, in that these methods simultaneously seem to curtail the optimum way of attaining the meaning and purpose of life through the begetting of children (an evil) as they help to limit the chances of certain death, the enemy of life (a good). But there is an added dimension to the dilemma: if the African indigenous logic is to be pursued to its ultimate conclusion, to die of AIDS is viewed as a "bad death" that may disqualify one from attaining ancestral status. But the ABC approach may curb this evil and make possible a "good death" in ripe old age. Again, what is the resolution?

Given the available statistics, it is evident in which direction the moral sympathies of probably the majority of African people are leaning. Individuals who contract the virus through rape or other coerced or promiscuous sexual activity—such as, for example, child marriage or prostitution—are generally condemned. These behaviors are recognized as evil and proscribed as antilife. What constitute the paradox are those circumstances where risky sexual activity is engaged in as a result of conscious, free, and consensual decisions of adults for a spiritual goal. Here issues pertaining to fundamental cultural perspectives and beliefs cannot be easily brushed aside. For example, the practice of "wife inheritance" still goes on among some ethnic groups, even after death of a partner by AIDS, for the sake of assuring the continued existence of a relative. Also, some Africans continue to insist upon full adherence to all cultural mortuary customs that may involve sexual contact.

These instances by no means represent isolated cases, nor are they confined to a specific class of people or area. Peter Knox studied South African beliefs in the ancestral cult, closely related to widespread African peoples' attitudes toward sexuality, sexual relations, and death rituals. He found that ancestral control over perceptions of life in terms of physical fecundity is still significant, and reached the conclusion that "the ancestor cult cannot be dismissed as a bygone relic; it is a vital and widespread dimension of the religious landscape [of Africa], and it features in the awareness and practice of ordinary . . . Africans, including practicing Christians."[25] African Christians liberally take part in these rituals, he reports, unconvinced that they are not committed to their Christian

---

[25] Peter Knox, *AIDS, Ancestors, and Salvation: Local Beliefs in Christian Ministry to the Sick* (Nairobi: Pauline Publications Africa, 2008), 94–95.

faith. In the words of Nurnberger, to many African persons and communities, "Ancestors are present in terms of authority; ancestors are present in terms of time, space and power; ancestors are present in terms of familiarity."[26] In a sense, consciousness of their presence in and wishes for the community dictate behavior. The same applies to some sexual customs, despite known risks of acquiring HIV. What must be done?

Cultural Empowerment

Although the HIV and AIDS pandemic has devastated the continent in many ways, Africa's identity must not be equated with it. Emmanuel M. Katongole maintains that this attitude toward Africa has unfortunately turned the continent into a depository of condoms as *the* solution to the epidemic. But Katongole proposes "cultural empowerment" as the more dignified route by which Africa can achieve a holistic redemption from the scourge. The notion "does not simply mean the retrieval and affirmation of African traditional culture (although it includes it)." Above all, it concerns "the provision of alternative cultural symbols and images to displace the present [false] power that AIDS seems to hold over Africa."[27]

What is needed is an approach that can transform Africa's own symbolism, imagery and linguistic frames of reference toward abundant life. What are required are perceptions that take into account what this central value entails in the current context of HIV and AIDS. Upon examination, three major, interrelated components emerge from within African culture itself as sources of transforming action: namely, solidarity, compassion, and responsibility—all of them intrinsic dimensions of African community.

Community calls for solidarity with people infected with HIV or affected by AIDS. Knox describes this kind of cohesion as the basis of "social healing," illustrated by the healing ritual practice among the Zulu people of South Africa. For them, healing is not confined to the "physiological dimension of the patient's life." It is also essentially social, a process of reconciliation and integration. In the case of AIDS, the ritual is called *inhlambuluko yegceke* or family therapy; it involves the whole family "reaffirming the belonging and thus the personhood of the patient" and invites "reconciliation within the family." Referring to Pope John Paul II's exhortation *Ecclesia in Africa* on social healing, Knox asserts, "In the case of AIDS, the [Zulu] ritual helps to remove misunderstandings and accusations regarding the cause of the disease. AIDS is thus fought in

---

[26] Nurnberger, *Living Dead and the Living* God, 51.

[27] Emmanuel M. Katongole, *A Future for Africa: Critical Essays in Christian Social Imagination* (Scranton, PA: University of Scranton Press, 2005), 29–47.

the spirit of the 'African family of God' [inspiring] 'care for others, solidarity, warmth in human relationships, acceptance, dialogue and trust.'"[28]

The African community spirit at the center of this ritual dictates reintegration of all people suffering from HIV and AIDS "without stigmatization in their rights as full members of society."[29] If community is central in Africa—that is to say, if "the 'I' is actualized only in the 'we,'"—then exclusion is a mockery of this foundation. "To become untouchable because of AIDS means ceasing to exist to some extent, or to exist as a public danger."[30] On the contrary, what practical solidarity involves is affection toward people with AIDS, an attitude that brings hope to them, offering them in the expression of Pope John Paul II, "all possible material, moral, and spiritual comfort." This describes true solidarity which is an invitation to wholeness of society.

The notion of peace—the biblical *shalom*—denotes a similar idea. As explained by Tammy R. Williams, the meaning of shalom in the Bible applies directly to the African cultural understanding of the imperative of community, especially in the face of HIV and AIDS, because it "best captures the concept of health. It suggests the idea of completeness, soundness, well-being, and prosperity, and includes every aspect of life: personal, relational, and national." As in the New Testament, "Healing consistently involves not only physical recovery from sickness but the renewal of relationships with God and others."[31]

The principle of African solidarity requires the integration of the community in compassion, love, and care for all, including anyone suffering from AIDS. At the same time, it also places responsibility upon the person with the illness to uphold the health of the community, the most important duty of any member of the community in whatever situation: namely, to make sure that it is maintained in health. This is a dimension of fecundity: one is as productive in this way just as if one had physical offspring. Though not-yet-born, they are actual realities nonetheless. A person infected with HIV is, according to this principle, therefore obligated to avoid transmitting the virus in any manner; to do so is to cause death, the equivalent of "witchcraft," a most heinous crime, something that disqualifies anyone from *Ubuntu*.

From this perspective, the ABC approaches for the purpose of preventing the transmission of HIV must be seen as a gift of life to the community. The decision to do any of these does not imply a denial of the ancestral procreative imperative, even though it may appear as such "from a purely biological point

---

[28]   Knox, *AIDS, Ancestors, and Salvation*, 177.

[29]   Paterne Auxence Mombe, "Compassion of Christ," in Bujo and Czerny, *AIDS in Africa*, 45.

[30]   Kamanzi, "Solidarity," 29.

[31]   Quoted in Emmanuel Katongole, "An Age of Miraculous Medicine," in Bujo and Czerny, *AIDS in Africa*, 111.

of view." The choice to avoid sexual behavior with potential lethal results actually recovers the mandate to procreate through a deeper paternity or maternity that unites one with the ancestral procreative force by safeguarding the life of the other and the yet-to-be-born. The resolution makes sexuality "an even richer reality"[32] by moving "from being a destroyer to a protector of life."[33]

The decision demands discipline. It grows out of and extends the principle of safeguarding and perpetuating life and can, therefore, be embraced by Africans with much more understanding and greater social approbation. Rather than being seen as villain, the person who does so is actually a hero from the point of view of African communitarian ethics on account of protecting the inviolability of the life of the community. Such a person demonstrates conversion into, and reconciliation with, the community, despite previous unethical behavior.

Transforming Language

An indispensable tool in the transformation and empowerment of culture is language. Language constitutes the carrier of culture by the power of the "word" in Africa. The clout of language and its associated symbols is that they do not only describe but also shape attitudes of the community. Yet language can also be ambivalent; it can be used to integrate or exclude, to liberate or oppress. At issue here is language about the body. The question is, How is the female and male body depicted in language?

Often in African languages, women's bodies are portrayed as objects of men's pleasure through various symbols and metaphors. As a consequence, women are deprived of a voice in negotiating sexual experience—precisely, when, how, or where sexual activity can take place. This fosters cultural gender inequalities and renders women vulnerable to sexual manipulation. By stereotyping women, such language does not affirm their humanity; it leads, instead, to women's sexual mistreatment and thus dishonors their role in African culture as the main custodians of life. It violates the deeper unity of the female and male life force on which African spiritual traditions base themselves.

Needing particular transformation are therefore linguistic imageries and metaphors that encourage attitudes that foster behaviors leading to the transmission of HIV. Sayings such as, "Honey sucker which drinks at distant pools," depicting male pride about promiscuity, must be changed through a form of

---

[32] See Mwihava, "Role of Community."

[33] Creispin Ilombe Wilondja, "Rights and Duties of Persons Living with HIV," in *AIDS, 30 Years Down the Line: Faith-Based Reflections about the Epidemic in Africa,* ed. Paterne Mombe, Agbonkhianmeghe E. Orobator and Danielle Vella (Nairobi: Paulines Publications Africa, 2012), 221.

socialization that underlines respect for women. The process must be comprehensive, for whereas metaphors of masculinity embolden men "to be sexually
adventurous, even predatory . . . norms of femininity encourage women to
be 'innocent' and 'compliant' in sexual decisions."[34] Imageries that encourage
sexual promiscuity in both sexes, like "a person cannot eat palm nut soup all
the time,"[35] must likewise be radically challenged because they foster conduct
destructive of life.

Conclusion

To begin to indicate an adequate and realistic approach to the prevention of the HIV and AIDS crisis in Africa, the significance of the African
spiritual understanding of sexuality must be acknowledged. It is essential to
appreciate what "being human" in the African worldview means and requires
in the context of sexuality. African perceptions and attitudes toward kinship
relationships based on the fullness of life continue to shape attitudes toward
sexuality and sexual relations there. If we understand and respect these perceptions and attitudes, it will be possible to reinterpret them to address effectively
the situation of HIV and AIDS in contemporary Africa. Even if it is true that
culture does not totally determine social behavior, it forms the foundation and
legitimation of what the majority of people do. Therefore, "Any effective change
begins with addressing people's worldview. In the case of [HIV and AIDS] in
Africa . . . [this] appears to be the approach that should achieve results, a healing
from the roots."[36]

---

[34] SAT Programme, *Mainstreaming Gender in Response to AIDS in Southern Africa:
A Guide for the Integration of Gender Issues into the Work of AIDS Service Organisations*
(Harare: Southern African AIDS Training Programme, 2001), 5.

[35] See Emevwo Biakole, Joyce Mathangwane, and Dan Odallo, *The Discourse of HIV/
AIDS in Africa* (Gaborone: University of Botswana, 2003).

[36] Laurenti Magesa, "Taking Culture Seriously: Recognizing the Reality of African
Religion in Tanzania," in *Catholic Ethicists on HIV/AIDS Prevention*, ed. James F. Keenan
(New York: Continuum, 2000), 84.

CHAPTER 3

SOCIOANTHROPOLOGICAL DIMENSIONS OF THE FIGHT AGAINST HIV AND AIDS IN AFRICA

Lado Tonlieu Ludovic

It is a truism in social sciences today that disease, just as with health care, is a social and cultural reality along all levels of the chain—from etiology to the understanding of health, from therapeutic routes to the actors involved in the process. Compared to other equally deadly pandemics in Africa such as malaria and more recently Ebola, AIDS is perhaps unique in that it strikes at the heart of social institutions and symbol-dense realities such as sexuality, procreation, the family, and so on, while upheaving centuries-old practices and beliefs.[1]

From this point of view, AIDS has been, for Africa in particular, a social and cultural earthquake with far-reaching political, economic, religious, and legal ramifications. The AIDS pandemic is a complex and dense phenomenon that reminds us of what Marcel Mauss, a pioneer of modern sociology, calls "total social fact."[2] This paper intends to offer a socioanthropological rereading of the strategies used to fight AIDS in Africa by showing, from literature, how the strategies constantly shifted between methodological individualism and methodological holism, depending on whether the focus is on individuals as social actors, on culture as collective heritage, or on social structures.

The Paradigm of Methodological Individualism

In social sciences, the term *methodological individualism* refers to "the explanatory approach that accounts for a collective phenomenon (macroscopic) and its analysis as the result of a set of actions, beliefs, or single attitudes (microscopic)."[3] The literature shows that the fight against AIDS in Africa

---

[1] Annabel Desgrées du Loû, "Santé de la Reproduction et Sida en Afrique Subsaharienne. Enjeux et Défis," *Population*, no. 4 (July–August 1998): 701–30.

[2] Marcel Mauss, *Sociologie et Anthropologie* (Paris: Les Presses universitaires de France, 1968).

[3] Bernard Valade, "Individualisme Méthodologique," www.universalis.fr.

has had its phases of methodological individualism. This perspective focuses on individual responsibility in the spread of HIV and the need to encourage behavioral changes at the individual level in order to reduce AIDS. Indeed, the spread of AIDS being closely linked to sexual habits, the first attempts to fight against the pandemic favored the change of those sexual habits, especially in light of the fact that in sub-Saharan Africa, its transmission is mostly hetero-sexual.[4]

HIV is transmitted mainly through sexual, and therefore social, contact between a man and a woman, often initiated by the man, given the prevailing social conventions. It was therefore quite logical to focus the first-line strategies against HIV on behavioral changes. The ABC approach (Abstain, Be faithful, Use *Condoms*) is part of this approach, because it addresses awareness, even responsibility, in negotiating sexual contact.

A number of empirical studies were conducted to identify most-at-risk groups and conceptualize pathways of infection within such groups.[5] They were mostly found to be sex workers, truck drivers, migrants and homosexuals. Identification of these groups was intended to determine the riskiest sexual partners, and then to be able to generate more responsible behavior,[6] including abstinence, fidelity, and condom use, within these groups. In this approach, men are particularly singled out and called on to change their habits and behaviors. They are considered more likely to have multiple sexual partners and engage in casual sex and other risky behavior, and less likely to use condoms.[7] Messages with a moral overtone, issued by the various religions, follow this same logic of responsible sexual behavior. Their aim is to guide the faithful to greater sexual discipline as a divine requirement, as some religious leaders have interpreted AIDS as divine punishment, striking down sexual libertines.

However, the limits of this individualistic approach soon became evident. The first drawback was the recycling of colonial prejudices of the allegedly unbridled sexuality of Africans, for whom having multiple sexual partners is the norm and the main cause of the spread of HIV. Hence, according to this view, Africans had only to discipline their sexual selves in order to defeat AIDS. Such

---

[4] Mburano Rwenge, "Facteurs Contextuels de la Transmission Sexuelle du Sida en Afrique Subsaharienne: Une synthèse," www.codesria.org/.

[5] Brodie Ramin, "Anthropology Speaks to Medicine: The Case of HIV/AIDS in Africa," *McGill Journal of Medicine* 10, no. 2 (2007): 127–32.

[6] Carolyn Baylies, "HIV/AIDS and Older Women in Zambia: Concern for Self, Worry over Daughters, Towers of Strength," *Third World Quarterly* 23, no. 2 (April 2002): 351–75.

[7] Victor Agadjanian and Cecilia Menjívar, "Talking about the 'Epidemic of the Millennium': Religion, Informal Communication, and HIV/AIDS in Sub-Saharan Africa," *Social Problems* 55, no. 3 (August 2008): 301–21.

prejudice has its roots in colonial anthropology.[8] A second risk was stigmatization, even "scapegoating" of groups considered "at risk," by presenting them as the main vectors of transmission of HIV. The third issue was the assumption of a causal link between the knowledge of the risks for infection and the ability to change one's sexual behavior. Indeed, the actors in the fight against AIDS were soon to find that an awareness of the risk did not necessarily result in a change of sexual habits. It appeared that educating on the risks of infection, although important and in which huge sums were invested, was not enough, and that one had to consider the social and cultural factors of the transmission of AIDS. This is what a culturalist paradigm will initiate, making a step toward methodological holism.

Culturalist Paradigm

Medical anthropology entered the field of social sciences via culturalism, in particular via ethnomedicine, which focuses on endogenous therapeutic systems as cultural structures. Indeed, classical medical anthropology postulates that culture and health are closely related. This applies for the health systems in traditional African societies as it does for modern medicine.[9] From this perspective, some anthropologists have focused on the local representations of AIDS in many African countries. Gausset and Mogensen show, for example, that in the Ntonga community of Zambia, AIDS is considered, because of a convergence of symptoms (weight loss and coughing), like a local disease known as Kahungo, an illness believed to be linked to sexual pollution. This combination allows Ntonga people to integrate this new disease in their cultural system and give it meaning. Even if some believe that these local etiological complexes constitute an obstacle to AIDS prevention because they distort its understanding, Gausset and Mogensen recall in terms that echo the writings of the English anthropologist Evans-Pritchard on witchcraft that "the distinction between the biomedical aspect of AIDS and its association with Kahungo holds in the how and the why. . . . The Ntonga know, as far as they are concerned, how AIDS is transmitted and how one protects from it. There remains the question of why."[10]

The distinction between the how and the why explains well why the reference to witchcraft still occupies a prominent place in the etiological complex associated with AIDS in Africa. In such a scheme, the use of modern medicine does not

---

[8] Cf. Douglas Webb, *HIV and AIDS in Africa* (London: Pluto Press, 1997).

[9] Bonginkosi Maxwell Nkosi, "Understanding and Exploring Illness and Disease in South Africa: A Medical Anthropology Context," *International Journal of Humanities and Social Science* 2, no. 24 (December 2012): 84–93.

[10] Quentin Gausset and Hanne O. Mogensen, "Sida et Pollutions Sexuelles chez les Tonga de Zambie," *Cahiers d'Études Africaines* 36, no. 143 (1996): 473.

necessarily exclude the concomitant use of traditional medicine, which combines medicinal plants and therapeutic rituals to appease the anger of the spirits or ancestors. In some contexts, such as South Africa, where traditional medicine still occupies a prominent place, voices have even been raised to encourage collaboration between doctors and traditional healers on AIDS.[11] This approach has not been hugely successful. However, taking into account the multiple social, economic, and political factors that limit patients' access to modern medicine, traditional medicine in Africa still has a bright future ahead. Fortunately, more and more young Africans are specializing in pharmacology and work, with the support of traditional healers, for a better understanding of the therapeutic properties of plants.

But for many authors, African culture has proven in many cases not to be an ally in the fight against AIDS. Some cultural behaviors are often pinned as factors aggravating risks for HIV transmission. These are mainly the practice of polygamy, levirate marriage, traditional circumcision, payment of dowry, and others. Before AIDS, these practices were harmoniously integrated into cultural systems, often oriented toward the promotion of life and the preservation of family integrity. For example, the levirate marriage allowed a woman to marry the brother of her late husband, giving her the opportunity to stay in the family of the latter and benefit from some sort of protection. Among the Luo community of Kenya, for example, argues Mugambe,[12] a woman who just lost her child cannot leave the house without having had sex with her husband or another man. This practice, which symbolized the promise of another child, and therefore of life, becomes in an AIDS-striking era the risk for a possible promise of death.

Those who argue for the eradication or the evolution of these cultural practices often insist, from the position of gender theory, on the increased vulnerability of women resulting from these practices. *Vulnerability* here refers to the lack of power, opportunity, and ability to make and implement decisions that impact personal life. In 2013, women represented 58 percent of the total number of people living with HIV in sub-Saharan Africa and have always been among the most infected and affected social classes.

The unequal power relations in a marriage, in which the wife has no control over the sexual life of her husband outside the house, and in which she has no ability to force him to get tested or use a condom, make her more vulnerable to sexually transmitted diseases, including AIDS.[13] Hence it is important to add

---

[11] Ellen Giarelli, Linda A. Jacobs, and Sandra Hartnett, "Traditional Healing and HIV-AIDS in KwaZulu-Natal, South Africa," *American Journal of Nursing* 103, no. 10 (October 2003): 36–47.

[12] Lydia Mugambe, "Rethinking Culture in the Face of HIV/AIDS in East Africa," *Empowering Women for Gender Equity*, no. 68 (2006): 73–78.

[13] Mugambe, "Rethinking Culture in the Face of HIV/AIDS in East Africa," 73.

a gender component to all interventions aiming at HIV prevention or AIDS treatment. Indeed, the ABC trilogy of Abstinence, Be faithful, Condom Use makes sense for HIV prevention among women only if they have a marginal control or genuine power over their sexuality and over their sexual partners. The inability of women to escape vulnerability is even more pronounced when it comes to cultural practices that are imposed on them by the group. The culture here is a "social fact" characterized, in the Durkheimian sense of the term, by the constraint that it exercised on the individual, leaving little room for individual freedom.[14]

But the diversity of cultures and contexts in Africa does not readily favor broad generalizations about women's powerlessness. Other studies, without necessarily denying the greater vulnerability of women in negotiating sexual relations in general and marriage in particular, relativize the powerlessness of women. This is to avoid the risk of painting African women as passive victims in the face of all-powerful men. From a survey conducted in Malawi, for example, Schatz shows that when addressing the risk of contracting HIV in marriage, women say they talk to their husbands, use their social network for advice and support, confront their husbands' extramarital partners, and divorce their husbands if they are not willing to adopt responsible practices such as condom use.[15] Desgrées du Loû also relativizes the absolute vulnerability of women in conjugal sexuality, citing surveys among the Yoruba of Nigeria, showing that the woman can refuse sex to her husband, even if it means having to face consequences.[16] However, compared to the pressures to impose cultural change from the outside, often in the name of equality, endogenous solutions are preferred because they are more lasting. The aim is to involve all components of the local communities, both men and women, in a cultural discernment process for rethinking cultural practices that put them at risk.[17]

But is culture really the problem? Some authors do not think so. Laurent Vidal, one of the greatest HIV and AIDS anthropologists in Francophone Africa, warns against the temptation of culturalist reductionism—not to negate the risk of HIV transmission related to cultural practices, but to relativize the scope of culture. According to Vidal, the scale of the pandemic in sub-Saharan Africa prompted the reorientation of medical anthropology, from

---

[14] Vicki Tallis, "Gendering the Response to HIV/AIDS: Challenging Gender Inequality," *Agenda: Empowering Women for Gender Equity*, no. 44 (2000): 58–66.

[15] Enid Schatz, "'Take Your Mat and Go!' Rural Malawian Women's Strategies in the HIV/AIDS Era," *Culture, Health, and Sexuality* 7, no. 5 (September–October 2005): 479–92.

[16] Desgrées du Loû, "Santé de la reproduction et sida en Afrique subsaharienne," 709.

[17] Margaret A. Farley, "Partnership in Hope: Gender, Faith, and Responses to HIV/AIDS in Africa," *Journal of Feminist Studies in Religion* 20, no. 1 (2004): 147.

a focus on local conceptions of the illness and therapeutic-religious practices to the study of health and health-care delivery systems more sensitive to global sociopolitical issues. According to Vidal, within a narrow culturalist approach to explain the spread of HIV in Africa, social factors may be overshadowed by cultural factors. Furthermore, such an approach may sustain the justification of the moral stigmatization of the sick and of African cultures.[18] Whether it is polygamy, levirate marriage, or any other cultural practice, these are not inherently HIV transmission vectors. A polygamous family where the man and his wives have been subjected to a test and where fidelity is practiced cannot be exposed to HIV.

Despite these limitations, it can be acknowledged that the culturalist paradigm initiates the beginning of a break away from the individualistic approach by directing attention to the cultural and social factors that determine sexual behavior. The culturalist paradigm is halfway between methodological individualism and methodological holism, represented by the paradigm of structural inequalities.

AIDS and Structural Inequalities

This approach is rooted in political economy since the structural paradigm is interested in the production and distribution of wealth in a country, and in the influence of political processes on economic activity. It pays close attention to structural relationships that generate, among others, situations of dependence, hegemony, domination, exploitation, and exclusion. The global economy is shaped by the close link that exists between political power and economic power, whereby the poorest are at the same time those who are most excluded from decision-making centers.[19]

Physician-anthropologist Paul Farmer deserves credit for drawing the attention of the international community to the fact that there was a close link between poverty and AIDS at a time when individualistic cultural approaches were thriving. This poverty is caused by structural inequalities that are often rooted in social parameters such as race, class, gender, and political violence. From the poignant life stories collected in the Central Plateau region of Haiti, Farmer shows how social forces symptomatic of the political economy of violence break down on the ground, at national and international levels, in distress and disease in

---

[18] Laurent Vidal, "The Shortcomings of Culturalism and the Relevance of the Social Dimension in the Approach to AIDS in Africa," in *HIV/AIDS Stigma and Discrimination: An Anthropological Approach*, ed. UNESCO, issue no. 20 (Paris: Studies and Reports, 2002), 11–14.

[19] Seiji Yamada, "An Anthropological Examination of the HIV/AIDS Epidemic," *Pacific Health Dialog* 6, no. 2 (1999): 310–16.

individual lives.[20] These forces determine citizens' access to or lack of food, health, water, wood, and housing.

The poorest regions in the world are the epicenters of the pandemic, with the greatest infection rates. This correlation characterizes AIDS as a disease of poverty that affects women more than men, and rural more than urban residents. Deborah Bryceson shows, for example, that when it comes to disparities between rural and urban environments, such as that in Malawi, where the population is 80 percent rural, AIDS-related deaths have significantly weakened the agricultural production force, exposing families to extreme poverty, mainly to food insecurity.[21] Mutangadura and Sandkjaer make the same observation in rural southern Africa, where AIDS weakens family agriculture, because women constituted more than 70 percent of the workforce and 80 percent of the agricultural production force. These socially insecure and vulnerable situations are often at the root of migration of those searching for work, leading to prostitution, trade in goods against sexual favors, and so on, which in turn expose individuals to the risk of sexually transmitted infections, among which is AIDS.[22] When it comes to racial discrimination, in the United States as well as in South Africa, where racism experienced periods of institutionalization, statistics show that AIDS affects the long-marginalized black communities more than any other community.[23] The poorest and most excluded social classes also turn out to be the most vulnerable.

The sociopolitical and economic roots of the disease have become an important dimension of critical medical anthropology. Africa often falls prey to multifaceted crises, which ruin efforts to eradicate poverty. The many civil wars

---

[20] Paul Farmer, "On Suffering and Structural Violence: A View from Below," *Daedalus* 125, no. 1 (Winter 1996): 261–83; see also Paul Farmer, "Global AIDS: New Challenges for Health and Human Rights," *Perspectives in Biology and Medicine* 48, no. 1 (Winter 2005): 10–16.

[21] Deborah Fahy Bryceson, "Ganyu Casual Labour, Famine, and HIV/AIDS in Rural Malawi: Causality and Casualty," *Journal of Modern African Studies*, no. 44 (2006): 173–202; see also Adam B. S. Mwakalobo, "Implications of HIV/AIDS for Rural Livelihoods in Tanzania: The Example of Rungwe District," *African Studies Review* 50, no. 3 (December 2007): 51–73.

[22] Gladys B. Mutangadura and Bjorg Sandkjaer, "Mitigating the Impact of HIV and AIDS on Rural Livelihoods in Southern Africa," *Development in Practice* 19, no. 2 (April 2009): 214–26; Sonja Merten and Tobias Haller, "Culture, Changing Livelihoods, and HIV/AIDS Discourse: Reframing the Institutionalization of Fish-for-Sex Exchange in the Zambian Kafue Flats," *Culture, Health, and Sexuality* 9, no. 1 (January–February 2007): 69–83.

[23] Richard Parker, "The Global HIV/AIDS Pandemic, Structural Inequalities, and the Politics of International Health," *American Journal of Public Health* 92, no. 3 (March 2002): 343–46.

that contribute to the continent's political instability are sources of vulnerability for the most disadvantaged, such as women and children. The rape suffered by women in areas affected by violence, such as the eastern Democratic Republic of Congo, increases their vulnerability to HIV. Such violence is often maintained by the lust for natural resources, including illegal logging; that lust feeds an opaque global market, while extending the wealth of warlords.[24] In many African countries, poor governance, also reflected in the misappropriation of the funds intended for the fight against AIDS, tuberculosis, and malaria, deprives the patient of the means of prevention and access to care. From this perspective, some authors point out the social costs of structural adjustment programs initiated by the World Bank and International Monetary Fund to help African countries improve their economy. The cuts in social spending have weakened the education and health sectors at the expense of the poorest. It must be concluded that the strategies against the HIV and AIDS pandemic should also include initiatives for a more equitable world economic order, the elimination of political violence, better global governance, fight against poverty, racism, and sexual discrimination.[25]

Conclusion

Strategies for fighting AIDS cannot rely on one single monolithic paradigm. The debate about the link between religion and AIDS illustrates this well. In the African context in general, AIDS and religion often meet. As Marc Eric Gruénais wrote, "AIDS as the disease—and not anymore the risk of infection with HIV—is thought of, by the believers, as an event which forms part of a deep religious experience." The outstanding contribution of religious organizations in the fight against AIDS in Africa is recognized today. But from another point of view, religions, in some aspects, have been criticized as an obstacle to the fight against AIDS in Africa. The controversies focus on certain beliefs and norms that could perpetuate the vulnerability of their faithful.[26] Margaret Farley criticizes both their moral conservatism and their slowness to question the beliefs and practices that perpetuate situations that favor the spread of the disease.[27]

---

[24] Zaryab Iqbal and Christopher Zorn, "Violent Conflict and the Spread of HIV/AIDS in Africa," *Journal of Politics* 72, no. 1 (January 2010): 149–62.

[25] Roberto De Vogli and Gretchen L. Birbeck, "Potential Impact of Adjustment Policies on Vulnerability of Women and Children to HIV/AIDS in Sub-Saharan Africa," *Journal of Health, Population, and Nutrition* 23, no. 2 (June 2005): 105–20; see also Parker, "Global HIV/AIDS Pandemic."

[26] Marc-Éric Gruénais, "La religion préserve-t-elle du sida? Des congrégations religieuses congolaises face à la pandémie de l'infection par le VIH," *Cahiers d'Études Africaines* 39, no. 154 (1999): 256.

[27] Eudora Chikwendu, "Faith-Based Organizations in Anti-HIV/AIDS Work among

At the very least, one can conclude that no single strategy against AIDS is ideologically neutral.[28] The current predominant approaches are largely determined by the neoliberal ideology of a sexuality centered on personal freedom and a self-determining power. The transfer of funds and strategies is also sometimes accompanied by pressure to impose the ideology, norms, and sexual values of the countries of origin. The battle against HIV and AIDS will only be won by continuing to fight on three fronts: individual responsibility, which calls for changing behavior and attitudes; the culture that embodies the values and established practices; and structural changes that aim to eradicate social structures that cause poverty and injustice, in favor of a fairer global, political, and economic order.

African Youth and Women," *Dialectical Anthropology* 28, no. 3/4 (2004): 307–27.

[28] Hansjörg Dilger, "'Living Positively in Tanzania': The Global Dynamics of AIDS and the Meaning of Religion for International and Local AIDS Work," *Africa Spectrum* 36, no. 1 (2001): 73–90.

Part Two

Methodological and Normative Concerns of an Applied Theology on HIV and AIDS

CHAPTER 4

AIDS and Biblical Hermeneutics

How to Read the Bible in a
Continent Wounded by Health Crises

Albert Ngengi Mundele

Since its emergence as a dangerous pandemic, AIDS has negatively impacted the most precious value of Africa: Life. It has affected and killed—and continues to affect and kill—countless Africans. Individuals, communities, and nations are wounded in both a worldwide and specific sense. An HIV vaccine has not yet been found. Antiretroviral treatment is far from being an absolute solution. With all this in mind, we might be tempted to raise the following question: Is AIDS the result of divine punishment against the wicked who do not keep the laws of God (Deut. 7:15; 28:20–29)? Is it an application of the ancient tradition of retribution: God blesses the upright and punishes the wicked (Job 4:7–9; 8:3–10, 13–15, 20; 11:13–20; Ezek. 18:21–32)?

This chapter focuses on AIDS and biblical hermeneutics. The Bible in general and the OT in particular do not talk about HIV/AIDS. However, there are concepts that describe illness, sickness, and plague (for example, see Deut. 7:15 and 2 Kgs. 5:1). Their physical and psychological impact on victims and communities can be compared with the impact of AIDS in Africa today: many victims are hopeless and excluded from communities, and orphans are chased away from their families.

How can an African read the Bible in today's situation? Normally, "When an African reads the Bible, he is fully immersed in his historical and cultural background."[1] The Bible, Word of God, displays the experience of a community/people (Israel) as well as individuals with God. As with every human experience, the biblical stories could be read as a memory of the ancestors/elders (Job 8:8–10) to which Africans turn in every circumstance of their life, to see how they should behave in critical situations like AIDS.

---

[1] Albert Ngengi Mundele, *A Handbook on African Approaches to Biblical Interpretation* (Limuru, Kenya: Kolbe Press, 2012), 17.

Issues of suffering and disease/illness/sickness are expressed in many books of the Bible.[2] I have chosen two stories: first, the story of Job, and second, the story of the hemorrhaging woman. The first points out that the human being does not have the ultimate solution for all that happens to him: God the creator is wiser than human beings (Job 38–39). Second, the story of the hemorrhaging woman (Mark 5:25–34) singles out that the solution to her problem is found in approaching God (Jesus) after human beings failed to resolve it. Africans facing the AIDS pandemic could be seen from these perspectives.

This chapter is divided into four parts: a general overview of biblical publications/research on HIV and AIDS in Africa, two biblical characters (Job and the woman with hemorrhages) in their respective socioanthropological contexts, the traditional African view on life, and as a conclusion, a hermeneutical and theological reading of the Bible from the historical perspective in a wounded Africa with HIV and AIDS.

General Overview of Biblical Research on HIV and AIDS in Africa

Since AIDS was revealed to the world in 1981, many authors have reflected on the pandemic from many perspectives with regard to Africa. From a biblical point of view, there are also many writings that pertain to HIV and AIDS, including these selections from African Anglophone countries:

• *Ghislain Tshikendwa Matadi*: His reflections on Job related to HIV and AIDS led Ghislain Tshikendwa Matadi to recommend a theology of hope and life that "can accompany all those who suffer in moving from despair to hope and from lamentation to the new life which arises from a sincere encounter with God."[3] This theology entails several features: accompanying the afflicted and encouraging them to express their fear and anger, hoping against hope (Rom. 4:18) and struggling against current afro-pessimism, defending the

---

[2] For example: Num. 12:10 (Miriam: skin disease / leprosy); Pss. 13; 22; 55; Lam. 73; 86:14–17; 88; 103:3 (diseases/maladies); 1 Sam. 16:14 (Saul afflicted by an evil spirit); 2 Sam. 12:15–18 (death of David's son / Bathsheba); 24:25 (pestilence); 1 Kgs. 8:37–39 (Solomon's prayer: v. 27 = pest/plague; v. 38 = plea and sickness); 2 Kgs. 5:1–27 (Naaman); the book of Job; Mark 5:25–43 (the woman with a hemorrhage); Matt. 15:21–28 (woman with demonical daughter); 27:45–46 (Jesus's crucifixion).

[3] Ghislain Tshikendwa Matadi, *Suffering, Belief, Hope: The Wisdom of Job for an AIDS-Stricken Africa* (Nairobi: Paulines Publications Africa, 2005; original French title: *De l'Absurdité de la Souffrance à l'Espérance. Une Lecture du Livre de Job en Temps du VIH/ SIDA*). Matadi also wrote "How Long, O Lord," in *AIDS in Africa: Theological Reflections*, ed. Bénézet Bujo and Michael Czerny (Nairobi: Paulines Publications, 2007), 31–42.

dignity of all who suffer, putting special emphasis on medicine instead of miracles and witchcraft, considering the reality of death as a passage to life, and promoting the dignity of human sexuality.[4] Ghislain Tshikendwa Matadi underlines one of the most important elements to be considered by people who are infected by HIV or affected by AIDS. He encourages people not to give room to resignation when facing the pandemic.

• *Musa W. Dube: HIV/AIDS and the Curriculum: Methods of Integrating HIV/AIDS in Theological Programmes,*[5] contains four contributions on biblical studies and HIV and AIDS: Musa W. Dube, "Methods of Integrating HIV/AIDS in Biblical Studies"; Johanna Stiebert, "Does the Hebrew Bible Have Anything to Tell Us about HIV/AIDS?"; Madipoane Masenya (ngwana'Mphahlele), "Prophecy as a Method of Speaking about the HIV/AIDS Epidemic in Southern Africa," and Musa W. Dube, "The Prophetic Method in the New Testament." These contributions are part of a search for ways and means in pedagogy "to train theological educators on how and why to implement the HIV/AIDS curriculum in their educational institutions." They bring awareness to students in theological institutions on "how our teaching can become part of the solution by helping the church and society in general to reduce the spread of HIV/AIDS and to provide quality care to those who are infected and affected is urgent."[6] Musa W. Dube also contributed to *Compassionate Circles: African Women Theologians Facing HIV.*[7] This work is about rereading and reinterpreting the scriptures from an African woman's perspective that leads to responsible creativity, healing, and wholeness.

• *Teresa Okure* has written several articles on the Bible and HIV and AIDS.[8] Throughout her work, she insists on the hermeneutic of life. The

---

[4] Matadi, *Suffering*, 114–15.

[5] Musa W. Dube, ed., *HIV/AIDS and the Curriculum: Methods of Integrating HIV/AIDS in Theological Programmes* (Geneva: WCC Publications, 2003). From that volume, see Dube, "Methods of Integrating HIV/AIDS in Biblical Studies," 10–23; Johanna Stiebert, "Does the Hebrew Bible Have Anything to Tell Us about HIV/AIDS?" 24–34; Madipoane Masenya (ngwana' Mphahlele): "Prophecy as a Method of Speaking about the HIV/AIDS Epidemic in Southern Africa," 35–42; Dube, "The Prophetic Method in the New Testament," 43–58.

[6] Dube, *HIV/AIDS and the Curriculum*, xi.

[7] Musa W. Dube, "In the Circle of Life: African Women Theologians' Engagement with HIV and AIDS" in E. Chitando and N. Hadebe, eds., *Compassionate Circles: African Women Theologians Facing HIV* (Geneva: WCC Publications), 233.

[8] Among others, see a commissioned paper for CAFOD titled *HIV and Women: Gender Issues, Culture and Church* (April 14, 1998); "First Was Life, Not the Book" in Okure, ed., *To Cast Fire upon the Earth: Bible and Mission Collaborating in Today's Multicultural Global Context* (Natal, South Africa: Cluster, 2000), 194–214; "HIV/AIDS and Africa: The Real Issues," in *The Church and HIV/AIDS in the West African Context*, ed. Ferdinand Nwaigbo et

Bible is about life and for promoting life; everybody should therefore read the biblical text in order to discover life. As HIV is a threat to life, everybody should commit to eradicating that danger. Life is considered as a high value in Africa; to each endeavor that prevents or stops the destruction of life, thereby promoting life, should be upheld.

Scholars, including Felicitas Becker, Paul Isaak, Ezra Chitando, and Masiivwa Gunda,[9] who have also undertaken biblical studies in relation to HIV and AIDS, highlight the relevance of awareness about the dangers that HIV and AIDS pose in Africa today. Their respective reflections are based on some important passages of the sacred Scriptures that enlighten the ways of facing HIV and AIDS in this continent.

The Suffering of Two Biblical Characters: Job and the Woman with Hemorrhages

Here I analyze from a socioanthropological aspect two biblical characters whose suffering highlights their human and communal environmental framework, their role or status in their respective societies, and especially their view on the past history of their forefathers up to themselves.

Job's Life

The story of Job has always been considered as a paradigm for suffering in general and suffering of an innocent in particular. Nevertheless it is not the only story of its type in the Ancient Near East: "the Sumerian Job" (*ANET* 589–91), the *Ludlul bel nemeqi* ("the Babylonian Job"), and the Suffering Righteous in Mesopotamian Literature all tell about a man who was afflicted but who did not know the reason because he had been faithful in all his duties to the gods (*ANET* 596–601).[10]

Taking into account literary considerations, people generally divide the book of Job into two parts: the prose that contains the prologue and the epilogue of the book (1:1–2:13; 42:7–17) and the so-called poetic part (3:1–42:6).

---

al. (Port Harcourt, Nigeria: CIWA Publications, 2005), 66–94.

[9] Felicitas Becker, "The Virus and the Scriptures," *Journal of Religion in Africa* 37, no. 1 (2007): 16–20; Paul Isaak, "A Biblical and Ethical Response to HIV/AIDS," *Africa Theological Journal* 27, no. 1 (2004): 59–75; Ezra Chitando and Masiiwa Gunda, "HIV and AIDS, Stigma and Liberation in the Old Testament," *Exchange* 36, no. 1 (2007): 184–93.

[10] Cf. H.-P. Müller, *Das Hiobproblem. Seine Stellung und Entstehung im Alten Orient und im Alten Testament* (Darmstadt: Wissenschaftliche Buchgesellschaft, 1995), 49–57, 69–72.

Job in the Prologue (1:1–2:13)

From a socioanthropological view, Job is a preeminent person whose suffering has divided the society surrounding him into two groups. On one side is Job with God his creator: Job is portrayed as a blameless man, upright, a God-fearing person, and rich; the abundance of his possessions and the mention of many workers (servants) shows him as a person of a high status (1:1–5). The relationship with the workers seems to be so good that they immediately inform him of whatever happens to the property: they report to him about the disaster that struck the oxen and the herdsmen (1:15), the sheep and the shepherds (1:16), and the camels and the young guardians (1:17).

Job displays excellent care for his children. He looks after their spiritual life by sanctifying them and offering burnt sacrifices for every one (1:5). He is a good paterfamilias, whose children live a communal life, celebrating feasts together (1:4, 18b). God appreciates him: "there is no one on earth like him, blameless and upright, fearing God and avoiding evil" (1:8; 2:3).

On the other side are Satan, Job's wife, and his friends, who have an idea that his past has caused his current situation of suffering. Job's nameless wife appeared in the narrative only to make a negative remark (2:9: "curse God and die"). She certainly wants to cut off their good past from the bad present. Job's friends come from different places: Eliphaz from Teman, Bildad from Shuh, and Zophar from Naamath. Consolation, comfort, and compassion summarize the reasons the three friends went from their respective home to meet Job. The first sign of this consolation is their gesture of mourning (2:12). Furthermore, silence revealed a wise and powerful message to all, including Job and his friends (2:13). Silence is often the best solution in the face of tragedy.

Such an experience of silence happened to me in March–June 1995. Ebola was killing people in Kikwit in the Democratic Republic of Congo. Two communities of sisters—the Poverelle Sisters and the congregation of St. Joseph of Turin—were put in quarantine, for some of their sisters had died and others were infected. One day we were told that Sr. Eugenie Kabina (thirty-two years old), an infected nursing student from the congregation of St. Joseph of Turin, was developing antibodies; there was hope of survival. The following day, we heard that she had died early in the morning and was immediately buried. We went to visit her community despite the quarantine. When we—four priests of the Theologicum of Kikwit—entered the compound, the sisters were scattered, everyone in her corner, shedding tears in silence. We looked for a chair to sit down, a pillar or wall to lean on; one of us even sat down on the stone floor.

Silence! How long was it before the superior told us about the last moments of Sr. Eugenie? Later those sisters told us that our visit helped them realize that they were still human beings. Since that day I have better understood what happened to Job and his three friends (2:11–13). In some circumstances, presence and silence must be the first ways to console, to show compassion, and to comfort a suffering person.

A Look at the Past

The end of 1:5 underlines something that we normally do not perceive: it summarizes the deeds that have built up Job's life, that is, his past history. The literary triple use of the expression "one day" in 1:6, 13 and 2:1 hints that the narration is referring to repeated past events. Furthermore, the mention of "still holding" in 2:9 indicates something that has been done in the past and that continues in the present. The meeting between God and Satan in the heavenly council (1:7–10; 2:2–6) refers to the past: "Have you not surrounded him and his family and all that he has with your protection?" (1:10).

In the prologue, God, his family, and his livestock are the main parts of his life that Job values. He recognizes that life from its beginning ("from the mother's womb") is a gift from God. That is why, when all his misfortunes happen, Job remains faithful to God and blesses him (1:20–22; 2:10).

Job in the Poem (3:1–42:6)

The poem is characterized by a structured dialogue between Job and his three friends, Eliphaz, Bildad and Zophar (3:1–31:37); the monologue of Elihu (32:1–37:24); God's speech (38:1–41:26); and Job's last speech (42:1–6). I do not analyze all those passages but point out two aspects of this poem: the socio-anthropological aspect of the characters and the recourse to the past (history) as a solution for the future. Silence could be interpreted in a variety of ways, sometimes as the best way to console, comfort, and show compassion, especially when one is present in the suffering. It could also be a time to interiorize such a misfortune, to meditate and reflect on it. However, silence should not last forever. Eventually people need to have discussions with others to find solutions and ways out of suffering.

Their good relationship allows Job's friends to come to him from their homes. It is genuine friendship, not only in good times but also during dreadful periods like Job's misfortune. Job's friends remind him to look back at what the forefathers said or instructed them to do.

Eliphaz appeals to Job to reflect on the traditional doctrine of retribution: "Since when are the upright destroyed? As I see it, those who plow for mischief and sow trouble, reap the same. By the breath of God they perish and by the blast of his wrath they are consumed" (4:7–9).

Bildad speaks in the same way: "Does God pervert judgment, and does the Almighty distort justice? . . . If you inquire of the former generations, and give heed to the experience of the fathers . . . will they not teach you and tell you and utter their words of understanding? . . . Behold, God will not cast away the upright; neither will he take the hand of the wicked" (8:3–4, 8–11, 20).

Zophar invites Job to see the secrets of God's wisdom: "If you remove all iniquity from your conduct, and let not injustice dwell in your tent, surely then you may lift up your face in innocence . . . but the wicked, looking on, shall be consumed with envy" (11:14–15, 20). And he adds: "Do you not know this from olden time, since man was placed upon the earth, that the triumph of the wicked is short and the joy of the impious but for a moment? Though his pride mount up to the heavens and his head reach to the clouds, yet he perishes forever like the fuel of his fire and the onlookers say, 'Where is he?'" (20:4–7).

Job himself knows the traditional theory of retribution, and from his own life he maintains his integrity and innocence in the midst of the attacks of his friends. "Far be it from me to account you right; till I die I will not renounce my innocence. My justice I maintain, and I will not relinquish it; my heart does not reproach me for any of my days" (27:5–6). Job reviews his whole life and assesses his present situation (29–31); he reaffirms his innocence that is rooted in a glorious past. He recalls God's goodness and protection surrounding him, his prominent role within the local judicial assembly at the gate of the city and his active concern for the poor, orphan, stranger, and the unassisted:

> When I went forth to the gate of the city and set up my seat in the square—then the young men saw me and withdrew, while the elders rose up and stood. . . . For me they listened and waited. . . . For I rescued the poor who cried out for help, the orphans, and the unassisted; the blessing of those in extremity came upon me, and the heart of the widow I made joyful. . . . I was eyes to the blind, and feet to the lame was I; I was a father to the needy; the right of the stranger I studied. (29:1–20)

God's speech goes all the way back to the beginning of creation, revealing his initial plan. "Who is this that obscures divine plans with words of ignorance? . . . Where were you when I founded the earth? Tell me if you have understanding" (38:2–4). With a long series of questions, God lets Job know of God's marvelous deeds since creation through nature and human history (38:5–41:6).

Job's final answer (42:1–6) sheds lights on his relationship with God. According to Ghislain Tshikendwa Matadi, verse 5 ("'I had heard of you by word of mouth, but now my eye has seen you'") is "a key verse for the interpretation of the entire Book of Job. It is the climax of the book: what Job gains from his encounter with God. It is no longer a theory about God. This is about experience, the lived, first-person experience of the Lord."[11]

The epilogue (42:17) leads to new insights in the socioanthropological aspect in the story of Job: after God intervened in the debate, he spoke to Job and his friends. Job became, through his prayers for his friends, a mediator in their burnt sacrifices (42:8-9; cf. Eliphaz 22:27). Furthermore, God brought restoration to Job—part of God's mysterious freedom and generosity (42:10), a free divine response to Job's actions and virtues.

*   *   *

We see that all the characters scrutinize the past to find out not only the reason but also the solution to Job's plight. They considered the traditional doctrine of divine retribution, but that teaching does not cover the whole past and explanations about the world and human life (38:1–41:26). This, I think, is why Job's present situation leads us to reconsider the past. Job's friends were seeking the meaning of life in general and of suffering in particular through the theoretical teachings of their forefathers. However, it emerges that sharing reflections and concrete experiences lets Job "know" God as well as the mystery of the world hidden to him. His friends were right to turn back to the past, but they read that history only partially, refusing to face the reality of the concrete facts and deeds in Job's life.

The Woman with Hemorrhages

Another biblical passage that can shed more light on human suffering before we touch upon the current situation of Africa wounded by HIV and AIDS is Mark 5:25–43. The origin of the woman is not revealed, and the reason for her hemorrhages is unknown. Her illness seems to be without cure, for she has met many doctors and spent a lot of money without being healed (v. 26). She has lived as a recluse for twelve years. Is it because of the Jewish purity laws concerning women (Lev. 15:25–27) or because of shame?

Nevertheless she had heard about Jesus, and came incognito in the crowd to touch his garment and was healed (Mark 5:27, 30). One does not know from where she got the news that Jesus has the power to heal. She is convinced of it, though, and goes on to touch his garment (v. 30).

For her, the crowd is a refuge to hide her status and poor condition. A crowd offers anonymity, but sometimes is an obstacle preventing people from meeting God personally. One can see this in the stories of the paralytic in Mark 2:3–4; the blind Bartimaeus in Jericho in Mark 10:46–48, and Zacchaeus in

---

[11] Ibid., 119–20.

Luke 19:3–4. But in the story of the woman with hemorrhages, the crowd "covered" her status (an outcast). She was looking for means of healing without making this known to the public and even to Jesus, the author of healing (v. 29). Another feature of the woman is to confess Jesus the Healer in public (v. 33): she falls prostrate before him and tells him the whole truth. Jesus praises her faith (v. 34). In this story, Jesus brings a solution that is beyond human understanding and capability. Where human beings (doctors) have not succeeded, he brings the solution.

In "Fifty Years of Bleeding: A Storytelling Feminist Reading of Mark 5:24–43," Musa W. Dube views this pericope in combination with a South African resurrection folktale and a contemporary (his)story of Africa. She depicts "how African women have survived during the pre-colonial, colonial, post-independence, globalization, and the HIV/AIDS eras."[12] Teresa Okure also applied this pericope on "Mama Africa," who is still bleeding through the slave trade, through being carved up in the 1885 Berlin Conference, through colonialism, through looting of her mineral resources, through neocolonialism, and through the AIDS pandemic.[13] Other applications may be found in Grant Lemarquand's *An Issue of Relevance*.[14]

Traditional African View on Life

The two biblical stories treated above speak to present African life, especially with reference to HIV and AIDS. With the pandemic, life in Africa is no longer the same as it was thirty years ago. It has affected and infected individuals, families, communities, and nations. In addition to this sad situation, it has also affected some African values.[15] For example, AIDS is impacting the African communitarian spirit that says, as John Mbiti notes, "I am because we are, and since we are, therefore I am."[16] In African traditional philosophy,

---

[12] Musa W. Dube, *Other Ways of Readings: African Women and the Bible* (Atlanta: Society of Biblical Literature, 2001), 5–6.

[13] Teresa Okure, "The Challenge of the Woman with the Hemorrhage (Mark 5:24–34) for African States Fifty Years after Independence," in *L'Eglise en Afrique 50 ans après les indépendances. The Church in Africa 50 Years after States' Independence. A Igreja em África 50 anos depois das independencies*, ed. Nathanaël Yaovi Soede and Ignace Ndongala (Abidjan: Editions ATA, 2013): 401–5.

[14] Grant Lemarquand, *An Issue of Relevance: A Comparative Study of the Story of the Bleeding Woman (Mk 5:25–34; Matt 9:20–22; Lk 8:43–48) in North Atlantic and African Contexts* (New York: Peter Lang, 2004).

[15] Musa W. Dube, ed., *HIV/AIDS and the Curriculum: Methods of Integrating HIV/AIDS in Theological Programs* (Geneva: WCC Publications, 2003), 11.

[16] John Mbiti, *African Religions and Philosophies* (New York: Doubleday and Company, 1970), 141.

when an individual suffers, the whole community suffers along, too. However, AIDS is destroying that communitarian life: its attack on life "affects particularly socially disadvantaged populations, who face poverty, gender inequality, violence, international injustice, racism, ethnicity, denial of children's rights, and discrimination on the basis of sexual orientation and ethnicity."[17] Furthermore, "Its incurability leads to fear, hopelessness, intense search for healing, poverty, death, orphans, widows, and overburdened grandparents who have to take care of orphaned children."[18]

The African conception of life is connected to ancestors who are involved in every aspect of life. The fact that they lived this earthly life makes them best placed to advise, convince, and guide human beings. They are part of the family. If somebody is sick, the whole community is affected, even the ancestors. Moreover, their excellent experiences on earth have made them experts of jurisprudence and reference points in religious, individual, or social communal life. In times when disease strikes, they are consulted and expected to give a solution to the matter. Although the pandemic today has changed African behaviors, especially among families or in hard-hit areas, the African mindset still turns back to the past, to ancestors, to seek solutions in all life-threatening situations.

How to Read the Bible in a Wounded Continent

How can the church preach the gospel of hope while confronting imminent death?[19] In the above analysis, I have pointed out the relevance of human history. The lives of the personalities in the book of Job and the story of the woman suffering from hemorrhage prompted them to learn the lessons from their past experiences and to find out solutions to problems. The Scriptures contain the Word of God, but they also reveal the experiences of human beings as individuals as well as communities. The Scriptures have become a past experience for the African who adheres to and accepts them. Storytelling and rhetoric are part of African history, and they bear significance for the present.

The book of Job is a reflection of the universal reality of human suffering. In the African context, suffering has a strong connection with the past and with one's ancestry. In this way, the African view of suffering resembles the biblical view, especially with regard to God being the most powerful and the greatest healer.

In addition, it has been said that the bleeding woman is a paradigm for all who suffer from a condition that cannot be cured, such as HIV. Consolation,

---

[17]   Dube, *HIV/AIDS and the Curriculum*, 11.

[18]   Ibid.

[19]   Marco Moershbacher, Joseph Kato, and Pius Rutechura, eds., *A Holistic Approach to HIV and AIDS* (Nairobi: Paulines Publications Africa, 2016), 9.

compassion, sharing of experiences, and hope are rooted in the history of the Scriptures. Yahweh, who created this world and human beings, who saved the Sons of Israel from the darkness of Egyptian bondage and the serpent in the wilderness, is ultimately able to do the same in Africa today. Jesus, who extended a solution to the woman with hemorrhages, is shown able to do the same today. Our reading of biblical stories can and should influence our behaviors and our endeavors for life; similarly, the socioanthropological situation of our ancestors (our past memory) when they were facing suffering and disease should be considered in our reading of the Bible today.

CHAPTER 5

HIV RISKS, HUMAN BEHAVIOR, AND SOCIAL CONDITIONS

Jacquineau Azetsop

What I have described here of inequality in the face of death, which is first and foremost inequality in life, and of sexual violence, which is also social violence, exemplifies the inequality and violence that affects bodies and afflicts the weak everywhere in the world.[1]

In the early stages of the AIDS epidemic, a behavioral approach to infection and intervention was most popular. People living with HIV (hereafter PLWH) were seen as morally irresponsible individuals.[2] Interventions were reduced to behavior-change strategies and the provision of sexual education. In all sectors of society, including Christian churches, moralizing leaders spread stigmatizing perceptions of HIV infection as the normal wage of sin. As AIDS spread in the 1990s in most African countries, I went to a faith-based hospital for consultation. Out of nowhere, a general physician asked me, "Isn't it true that God punishes? Don't you think that PLWH deserve what is happening to them? Are they not responsible for their own infection?" I did not know what to say. This physician simply appeared to me as someone who lacked compassion and who could not think beyond the stigmatizing representations that framed the moral underpinning of a disease that may directly or indirectly be connected to sex.

Even today, stigma is the major enemy of HIV prevention. As time has passed, following the failures or limited successes of behavioral interventions, sociologists, anthropologists, and social epidemiologists have brought to light the connections between social conditions and HIV risks. Today, it is common knowledge that, in one way or another, AIDS is about sex; but it is about much more than sex. AIDS is connected to gender inequality, access to resources, cultural practices, political

---

[1] Didier Fassin, *When Bodies Remember: Experiences and Politics of AIDS in South Africa* (Berkeley: University of California Press, 2007), 274.

[2] N. Krieger and S. Zierler, "What Explains the Public's Health? A Call for Epidemiologic Theory," in *New Ethics for the Public's Health*, ed. D. Beauchamp and B. Steinbock (New York: Oxford University Press, 1999), 47.

power, and structural adjustment programs with their neoliberal underpinnings. It is also connected to ideologies—those deeply entrenched in local cultures as well as those imported with colonial power and religions.[3]

The main argument of this chapter is that it is simplistic to appeal to individual rational choice to change risky behavior, when social conditions and structures limit people's options and predispose them to certain behavior, making HIV risks more a socially produced reality than a purely behavioral one. Although human behavior contributes directly or indirectly—or passively or actively—to the infection, special attention needs to be given to social forces that create HIV risk environments and weakened individual and community agency. Given the effects of these social forces, structural interventions ought to be considered as the bedrock on which any intervention may be framed and implemented so as to address both proximal and distal causes of vulnerability, as well as the pathways that link them. To contribute efficiently to prevention efforts, theological ethicists must ask how large-scale social forces come to have their effects on unequally positioned individuals and countries. The quest for understanding features of HIV risk that are obscured by individualist frameworks can sharpen theological reflection on the prevention of future emergent epidemics.

The theological contribution to HIV prevention needs, first, to question the predominance of behavioral and biomedical approaches over a social production approach; second, to provide epidemiologic research with an approach to personhood that accounts for the routes of exposure; third, to determine criteria for judging the morality of human behavior; and fourth, to suggest the option for the poor as a way to promote public health through social transformation. This chapter uses a historical, cultural and political economy approach to vulnerability that reflects a comprehensive understanding of HIV risks in a marginalized continent.

Behavioral and Social Approaches to Infection: Beyond Methodological Individualism

The behavioral approach is premised on the individual's ability to act freely to avert any health-damaging situation. This approach explains determinants of population disease occurrence as behavioral clusters and cultural factors that are shared among individuals. HIV infection is simply understood as an outcome of individual choices among many different options. The ability to choose can

---

[3] Brooke G. Schoepf, "Assessing AIDS Research in Africa: Twenty-Five Years Later," *African Studies Review* 53, no. 1 (2010): 107.

be affected by providing sufficient incentives. To alter AIDS distribution, aggregates of individual choices are measured and individualized interventions are designed.[4] An economic prostitute, a woman living with HIV whose fidelity to an unfaithful husband cannot be doubted, and an infected inner-city poor left with no opportunity are treated as promiscuous and incapable of having control over their behavior. The interconnected explanatory ideas named as lifestyle theory are based on biological, methodological, and moral individualism. Within this perspective, prevention is essentially viewed as a technocratic problem of behavior change involving the ABC trilogy of Abstinence, Be faithful, Condom Use. These solutions, which have been credited for Uganda's decline in HIV incidence, may not have been as successful as has been said.[5]

To be considered successful, behavioral intervention strategies need to address, for example, risk and rate differentials between active females and males.[6] ABC strategies, for example, failed to take into account the context of vulnerability created by structural factors that shape women's lives in most African countries. There is no doubt that "abstinence is meaningless to women who are coerced into sex. Faithfulness offers little protection to wives whose husbands have several partners or were infected before marriage."[7] Women's lack of property rights, differential access to literacy and education, lower wages, and lack of assets shape their HIV risks. Besides ethicoreligious considerations, calls for condom use are meaningless in the context of gender inequality and feminization of poverty. Similarly, calls for abstinence and faithfulness are largely out of touch with the social embeddedness of women's vulnerability. Women's needs and their historical situatedness require gender-focused and multisectoral strategies to shape individual or group behaviors over time. The discovery of the social roots of women's vulnerability leads us to question the underlying assumption that individual decision making rooted in the ideology of rational choice is the key site for risk minimization.[8] As an explanatory framework, individualism ignores or negates the gendered and social contexts in which individuals attempt to enact behavioral changes. The lack of sexual education is not the major obstacle to behavior change. Pressing, more immediate needs often supersede other needs and determine risk taking.[9]

---

[4] Krieger and Zierler, "What Explains the Public's Health?" 48.

[5] Shari L. Dworkin and Anke A. Ehrhardt, "Going beyond ABC to Include 'GEM': Critical Reflections on Progress in the HIV/AIDS Epidemic," *American Journal of Public Health* 1, no. 7 (2007): 13–17.

[6] Ibid., 13.

[7] Ibid., 14.

[8] Ibid., 17.

[9] Joseph R. Oppong and Jayati Ghosh, "Concluding Remarks: Beyond Epidemiology," in *HIV and AIDS in Africa: Beyond Epidemiology*, ed. E. Kalepeni, S. Craddock, J. R. Oppong, and J. Ghosi (Malden, MA: Blackwell Publishing, 2004), 324.

In opposition to the lifestyle theory, "a theory of social production of disease conceptualizes determinants of disease distribution as economic and social relationships forged by a society's political economic structure. Social groups defined by these relationships are differentially helped or harmed by their position relative to each other."[10] These relationships are conveyed in terms of social class, gender and sexism, race/ethnicity, social stratification, and position in society. Each population group's HIV risks and well-being are affected by the inequality that shapes socioeconomic relationships. This theory of disease production explains women's greater vulnerability to HIV, economic prostitution, and marginalized groups' greater exposure to HIV as an outcome of socioeconomic positioning.[11] Hypotheses emerging from this theory propose explanations of HIV transmission in relation to social structures.

The social approach pays attention to contextual factors; we cannot ignore our everyday experience, how we live together as a society, how we prioritize development and design social policies, and how we care for the less fortunate. Individuals cannot be understood solely by looking inside their bodies and brains; one must also look inside their communities, their networks, their workplaces, their families, and even the trajectories of their lives.[12] The focus is shifted from the individual-as-risk-taker to contextual factors. This approach perceives individuals as nested within a system of socioeconomic relationships that potentially influence individuals' choices.

As an economic crisis spread across the African continent in the late 1970s, the HIV virus silently spread as well. Seemingly unrelated, the two phenomena were in fact intimately intertwined. The effects of poverty accelerated the spread of the virus in the 1980s. By the 1990s the ravages of AIDS in turn plunged afflicted regions deeper into economic crisis.[13] HIV infection is mostly confined to worse-off members of the population. HIV remains the exact outcome of poverty, with sexual trade, migration, polygamy, and teenage marriages as the predictors in the sub-Saharan region.[14] Women are often engaged in sexual transactions, sometimes as commercial sexual workers, but more often as part of survival strategies for themselves and their dependents. Early marriage and the passing on of poverty from one generation to another increases vulnerability.

---

[10] Krieger and Zierler, "What Explains the Public's Health?" 48.

[11] Ibid., 49.

[12] Elizabeth Fee and Nancy Krieger, "Understanding AIDS: Historical Interpretation and the Limits of Biomedical Individualism," *American Journal of Public Health* 83, no. 10 (1993): 1481.

[13] Brooke G. Schoepf, "AIDS in Africa: Structure, Agency, and Risk," in *HIV and AIDS in Africa: Beyond Epidemiology*, ed. E. Kalepeni, S. Craddock, J. R. Oppong, and J. Ghosi (Malden, MA: Blackwell Publishing, 2004), 15.

[14] Noel D. Mbirimtengerenji, "Is the HIV/AIDS Epidemic an Outcome of Poverty in Sub-Saharan Africa?" *Croatian Medical Journal* 48 (2007): 605.

Poverty is associated with weak endowments of socioeconomic resources, such as low levels of education, with associated low levels of literacy, lack of marketable skills, poor health status, and low labor productivity as results.[15] Amartya Sen highlights the need for extending understanding of poverty beyond the concept of inadequate income and basic needs to encompass deprivation of substantive freedoms that enable people to lead the kind of life they have reason to value.[16] Sen rejects a reductionist understanding that confines poverty to financial capital, quantified in monetary terms. Poor people do not only lack money, but also they lack skills and assets to transform commodities into actual functionings. Such an approach to "poverty includes deprivation, constrained choices, and unfulfilled capabilities, and refers to interrelated features of wellbeing that impact upon the standard of living and quality of life."[17]

HIV risks are exacerbated by migration flows, often dictated by conflicts or economic deprivation. Most internal and transnational migration patterns began as a result of colonial policies "undermining rural livelihoods and channeling labor into regional industries with high labor demands while fallen economies result from African countries' location in the global economy and underlie continual migratory circuits that heighten vulnerability to HIV, primarily through family dissolution and concomitant shifts in sexual economies toward casual, extramarital, or remunerated relationships."[18] Migratory "movements entail separation from partners and provide opportunities for more sexual interactions, thereby enabling transfer of infection from high seroprevalence areas to lower ones."[19] Although dominant migration patterns involve men acquiring HIV when away from home and then returning to rural female partners, there is evidence that women with absent migrant male partners also become infected outside of their primary relationship.[20]

Disease Causation,
Theological Anthropology, and Ethics

Assigning responsibility for HIV occurrence and intervention should stem from the anthropological vision and the theory of disease etiology that shape epidemiological claims. Both the theory and the anthropological vision ought

---

[15] Ibid., 606.

[16] Amartya Sen, *Development as Freedom* (New York: Alfred A. Knopf, 1999), chapter 4.

[17] Mbirimtengerenji, "Is the HIV/AIDS Epidemic an Outcome of Poverty in Sub-Saharan Africa?" 605.

[18] Susan Craddock, "Beyond Epidemiology: Locating AIDS in Africa," in *HIV and AIDS in Africa: Beyond Epidemiology*, ed. E. Kalepeni, S. Craddock, J. R. Oppong, and J. Ghosi (Malden, MA: Blackwell Publishing, 2004), 7.

[19] Dworkin and Ehrhardt, "Going beyond ABC," 14.

[20] Ibid.

to be broad enough to capture the entire reality about causality and embodiment. The need for a broader vision stems from the fact that social forces that create opportunity for disease often exceed the limits of the physical body and affect the social body as a whole. Moreover, economic globalization and the phenomenon of migration have shown how porous the local space is. The local space is willingly or unwillingly opened to global realities, just as it can itself shed light on global realities. All these facts suggest that it is useful and worthwhile to relate the ethnography of given affected countries to world history.[21]

Personhood and HIV Epidemiology

Theological ethics values the human person but does not acclaim individualism. Our anthropological claim for HIV prevention does not start with an atomistic view of human beings as distinct entities prior to and independent of human existence as communal. The idea of human beings conceived as free and rational entities is alien to most non-Western cultures, in which the moral vision of the human person is essentially relational. Individuals are never totally independent or purely rational, separate, and self-interested. African culture stresses relationality as a distinctive feature of our common humanity, meaning that one's humanity is affirmed by recognizing the humanity of others. This approach to human personhood emphasizes relationships that exist among individuals. These relationships are expressed through institutions of mutual support, regulatory norms, language, and politics. Humans are always caught up in a web of social intercourse that makes them either strong or vulnerable. Understood within such a relational context, sin, grace, redemption, and the option for the poor are properly contextualized.

An epidemic theory informed by such a relational anthropology not only places people's experience at the center of HIV intervention policy but also calls for society's commitment to their well-being as a moral requirement that flows from our common humanity and the call to discipleship. This is not a peripheral enterprise but the very heart of the matter, because the anthropological vision determines epidemiologic theory, ethical judgment about infection, and society's intervention. Early HIV prevention initiatives were sustained by a liberal view of the human subject that matches the features of capitalism. We challenge such a view because it has failed as a framework for HIV prevention. To acknowledge that social sins shape risks for infection, interventions to reduce incident cases should transcend the behavioral paradigm to include the need for social transformation through the option for the poor, which requires structural changes, for the redemptive work of Christ is achieved by grace-filled individuals and institutions that seek to alter the social causes that create opportunities for poor behavior.

---

[21] Fassin, *When Bodies Remember*, 274.

The Fundamental Causes of HIV Infection:
An Epidemic Theory

Just as does our vision of personhood, our epidemic theory needs to provide us with connections between history, social structures, and individual pathologies. The fundamental causes for infection refer to contextual factors that shape HIV risks. Social conditions are linked to a very broad array of diseases.[22] Social factors influence disease processes by creating vulnerability or susceptibility to health risks in general, rather than to any specific disorder. These structural causes are steady, and they include access to basic resources that can be used to reduce exposure to the HIV or avoid the negative outcomes of AIDS. To understand the biosocial etiology of HIV infection, we need to remember that "a syncretic and properly biosocial anthropology of these and other plagues moves us beyond noting, for example, their strong association with poverty and social inequalities to an understanding of how such inequalities are embodied as differential risk for infection."[23] Social conditions are likely to be the fundamental conditions of HIV infection, "because they embody access to important resources, affect[ing] multiple disease outcomes through multiple mechanisms."[24] Poverty and violence are the fundamental causes that determine a myriad of predictors. Consequently, as the last Ebola epidemic in West Africa showed, the fundamental cause maintains an association with disease even when intervening mechanisms change.[25]

As a result of a socially entrenched violence and systemically entertained poverty, AIDS is a pathology of power. This violence is far from being accidental; rather, it is intimately connected to the social conditions that so often determine who will suffer abuse and who will be shielded from harm. The social dimension of HIV infection and of AIDS production demands that the research apprehend how the embodiment of inequality occurs. Cultural-behavioral reductionism that sees local customs and uncontrolled sexual impulse as the only cause of poor behavior does not account for the biosocial history of the epidemic. Thus, tools of classical epidemiology cannot be applied to HIV and AIDS because they determine risk only in terms of individual behavior. Epidemiologic investigation needs the help of contextualizing sciences to point out the social causes of infection.[26]

---

[22] Bruce Link and Jo Phelan, "Social Conditions as Fundamental Causes for Disease," *Journal of Health and Social Behavior* 35 (1995): 80–94.

[23] Paul Farmer, "Anthropology of Structural Violence," *Current Anthropology* 45 (2006): 305.

[24] Link and Phelan, "Social Conditions as Fundamental Causes," 80.

[25] Annie Wilkinson and Melissa Leach, "Briefing: Ebola—Myths, Realities, and Structural Violence," *African Affairs* 114 (2014): 1–13.

[26] Jonathan Mann, "Human Rights and AIDS: The Future of the Pandemic," in

World system theory allows us to capture the transnational nature of vulnerability by revealing the continuous influence of past and present events on individual pathologies.[27] In most African countries, historically deep and geographically broad connections come into view with very little effort. The socialization of human behavior is important to understand how a wounded social context is embodied as a disease caused by an intracellular organism.[28] The epidemic is, in part, an outcome of globalization, defined as imbalances of power privileging industrial nations.[29] The global forces recruit their partners among local politicians and businesspeople. Failure to stop the progress of the pandemic results from the global marginalization of Africa. Reversing the disempowering effects of the exploitation, discrimination, and imperialism that characterize the current world system might yield better results for HIV prevention. Structural adjustment programs (SAP) that were fronted by the International Monetary Fund and the World Bank also contributed in increasing the intensity and extent of poverty within African countries. These neoliberal reforms led to shrinking incomes while the introduction of user fees into the provision of health services meant that the poor were not able to access medical care.[30] SAP exacerbated women's HIV risks. Poor women suffered even greater economic vulnerability under these policies, which depressed income among the lowest socioeconomic sectors of the population, feminizing the epidemic.[31]

HIV Epidemic Theory and Moral Judgment

Most HIV infections happen through direct sexual contact. There is no doubt that behavior and a certain level of moral cooperation are involved. Hence, people should be challenged to uphold high moral standards. However, moral judgments about infection cannot be one-sidedly blamed on people's behavior. The validity of a moral judgment on HIV—and on future epidemics similar to it—requires a clear understanding of agency, causality, responsibility, and routes of exposure. The routes of exposure have already been clearly spelled out in the discussion of disease causation and epidemic theory.

Health and Human Rights: A Reader, ed. J. Mann et al. (New York: Routledge, 1999), 439–52.

[27] Farmer, "Anthropology of Structural Violence," 312.

[28] Ibid., 316.

[29] Craddock, "Beyond Epidemiology," 6.

[30] Solomon Benatar, "The HIV/AIDS Pandemic: A Sign of Instability in a Complex Global System," in *Ethics and AIDS in Africa: The Challenge to Our Thinking*, ed. Anton A. Van Niekerk and Loretta M. Kopelman (Claremont, CA: New African Books, 2005), 53.

[31] Schoepf, "AIDS in Africa," 15.

Agency

Though some hold unjustified and untested assumptions about an individual's ability to prevent AIDS and poor health no matter the location, evidentiary bases of such assumptions have not been proven. No data show that, in locations where social conditions shape HIV risks, cognitive exercise has fundamentally altered these risks. Cognitive-rational assumption entails an exaggeration of human agency that minimizes the role of poverty as the fundamental cause as well as the influence of the social environment on people's health.[32] The notion that the individual is a neoliberal rational subject or agent capable of acting responsibly after being counseled and tested is simply one-sided. Risk for HIV infection does not merely depend on knowledge about the modes of transmission of the virus, but rather on one's freedom to make choices. Decline in HIV incidence cannot be accounted for in terms of interventions such as counseling and testing because decline happened before all these measures were taken. While they only play a small part in HIV prevention, they reinforce the wider community HIV-prevention message.[33] Freedom and responsible behavior can only partly explain the clustering of diseases within poor neighborhoods or marginalized socioeconomic groups, so other factors need to be taken into consideration. Considering the multiplicity of constraints on a human's ability to responsibly control her or his behavior, we need to humbly accept individuals' limitations and propose some venues for structural interventions. People cannot always reduce risk, even in spite of their knowing how infection occurs. If individuals' willpower to control their lifestyle is limited, then, to address issues of HIV risk effectively, moral individualism and behavior change programs are simply and inadequately one-sided.

We need to reckon with the social nature of the human person. Public health science emphasizes the social connectedness that exists between human beings. To alter individual behavior in a sustained and effective manner, we need to address social practices and norms through community mobilization and advocacy. "HIV prevention is a matter of enabling communities, and indirectly their individual members, to develop HIV risk reduction strategies."[34] Here, we do not simply understand human agency in individual terms but also in social ones for "the individual capacities are intimately tied to the enabling (or disabling) character of social norms, practices and institutions, which are, in turn, understood to be modified by community mobilization and social movements."[35]

---

[32] Paul Farmer, *Infections and Inequalities: The Modern Plagues* (Berkeley and Los Angeles: University of California Press, 2001), 257.

[33] Susan Kippax, "Effective HIV Prevention: The Indispensable Role of Social Science," *Journal of the International AIDS Society* 15 (2012): 6.

[34] Ibid.

[35] Ibid.

Causality

Isn't it true that poverty and structural violence are greater contributors to HIV risk than cultural belief and behavior? If we agree that culture is only one axis of HIV causality, why were the other axes absent from early medical literature? Establishing a direct causal link between behavior and HIV infection or between cultural practices and beliefs and HIV risks is simply immodest and misleading, because these claims of causality ignore how inequalities play out in individual pathology.[36] Behavior is the proximate cause, while the whole array of factors—including cultural factors—must be considered in order to identify mediatory causes, which are themselves fueled by poverty and violence. Behaviors are not determined by any single factor, but by an array of elements that, in combination, structure risk behavior. Mediatory causes are merely the particular mechanisms through which more fundamental causes operate, and mediatory causes, as such, will change over time, while the influence of fundamental causes will persist. Addressing these mediatory causes will do little, in the long term, to eliminate disease and to promote health. Instead, it is necessary to confront the fundamental causes themselves, which often have very little to do with AIDS itself. When an epidemic is driven by social conditions, focusing on behavior obscures the process of embodiment, leading to the erasure of biology.[37] A close look at the embodiment process shows that "individual biographies and urban or rural monographs give evidence that being exposed to HIV has directly to do with the configuration of everyday life as structural violence."[38] Hence, unless poverty and violence are addressed more consistently, there will be very little progress in reducing the epidemic and preventing future epidemics. To avoid taking responsibility for the social origin of poor health, a cognitive-cultural explanation can be overemphasized at the expense of a structural one.

Responsibility

Aside from the fact of irrationally concluding that infection is the obvious consequence of misbehavior, the behavioral theory does not provide criteria for understanding how just is the system of blames or rewards relied upon by those who uphold this theory. This theory can be very divisive because it distinguishes between innocent and guilty exactly when society needs to unite against AIDS.[39]

---

[36] Farmer, "Immodest Claims of Causality: Social Scientists and the 'New' Tuberculosis," in *Infections and Inequalities*, 228–61.

[37] Farmer, "Anthropology," 316.

[38] Didier Fassin, "Response to an Anthropology of Structural Violence of Paul Farmer," *Current Anthropology* 45 (2006): 319.

[39] L. M. Kopelman, "If HIV/AIDS Is Punishment, Who Is Bad?" in Van Niekerk and Kopelman, *Ethics and AIDS in Africa*, 208–18.

This theory fails to explain risk and infection rate differentials. Differences in HIV prevalence from one country to another, from one place to another within the same country, and from one continent to another around the globe strongly suggest the need for inquiry into the social environment. Hence, there is no doubt of the risk of infection, as "the epidemic is embedded in so many unjust situations that efforts to roll it back will meet with only limited success if they do not embody practical attention at all levels to the dignity, needs and rights of every person."[40]

Rejecting a sex-focused approach for assigning responsibility for AIDS, Lisa Cahill strongly asserts that "AIDS is a justice issue, not primarily a sex issue. AIDS as a justice issue concerns the social relationships that help spread HIV and fail to alleviate AIDS, relationships of power and vulnerability that are in violation of Catholic norms."[41] She further argues that "an exclusive focus on sexual promiscuity or drug use, condoms or needle exchange programs, obscures the fact that the behaviors that transmit HIV are strongly influenced by social conditions. Likewise, a choice to engage in different behavior patterns—like sexual fidelity in marriage to an uninfected spouse and a healthy lifestyle—is only possible when one's social circumstances offer those different patterns as real possibilities for oneself."[42] With this, Cahill indicates that the focus should be moved from the individual to the social forces and institutions that constrain human agency.

Option for the Poor, Social Justice, and Structural Interventions

Pasteur once famously quipped that "the microbe is nothing, the terrain is everything."[43] The high rates of HIV in Africa are connected to the continent's "terrain" of increasing poverty, widening inequalities, and economic exclusion from a world led by neoliberal greed. It is essential that interventions be attuned to the local "terrain." As a key feature of the African terrain, poverty indicates the need for a pragmatic solidarity with, and for, the worse off.[44] This option is shaped by the transcendence of a God who takes the side of the marginalized and by the liberating praxis of Jesus of Nazareth (Luke 4:17–21). The solidar-

---

[40] Michael J. Kelly, *HIV and AIDS: A Social Justice Perspective* (Nairobi: Paulines Publications Africa, 2010), 7.

[41] Lisa Cahill, "Justice and the Common Good," in *Catholic Ethicists on HIV/AIDS Prevention*, ed. J. F. Keenan (New York: Continuum, 2000), 282.

[42] Ibid.

[43] Kelly, *HIV and AIDS*, 138.

[44] Paul Farmer, *Pathologies of Power: Health, Human Rights, and the New War on the Poor* (Berkeley and Los Angeles: University of California Press, 2003), 145–52.

istic love of God for his people is totally fulfilled through Jesus's life and death, which open a venue for a hermeneutical mediation allowing us to understand the life of destitute sick through Jesus's praxis and life. Hence, the incarnation of the Word of God and Jesus's ministry and earthly existence have an important theological and moral significance for the option for the poor. They play a normative and inspirational function in shaping this option. Theological ethics needs to promote structural change at all levels. Effective solidarity around HIV prevention cannot focus on behavior in isolation from structural issues that create a risk environment. Women, for example, would have more capacity to resist HIV and to counter its effects if they had access to education, income-generating opportunities, and primary health-care services. An epidemic of inequality such as AIDS reveals the dysfunctional nature of most African states and the ever-exclusive civilization of profit seeking that shapes the global economy. The persistence of oppressive structures at the national and international levels reveals the sin of the world that contradicts the kingdom of justice and peace that Jesus of Nazareth inaugurated.

How can theological ethics effectively contribute to prevention efforts? Is it not by advocating for a paradigm shift "away from reliance on informational messages to alter individual behavior and toward social analysis and a search for transformational structural change"?[45] In order to play its transformative and prophetic role, theological ethicists ought to build a strong collaboration with social scientists—as well as with biomedical experts—because they have the theoretical tools for informing ethical reflection with the real-world experience. Social scientists can indeed contribute to understanding prevention in the real world by engaging with HIV prevention in its relationship to the real world. Attempts to radically separate biomedical prevention from behavior change because all prevention effort demands a broad structural transformation without which the fundamental cause of vulnerability and disease will not be addressed.[46]

First, theological ethics needs to disentangle the ideologies that shape the dominant views of prevention by placing human dignity and respect for an entire continent at the center of epidemiologic research. The major policy in the early stage of the pandemic, targeting the behavior risk groups, has proven to be highly risky as a way to reduce HIV incidence because it created a new identity, a new alterity perceived as being dangerous for others.[47] An entire continent was placed in the category of "other," and Africans were then labeled as promiscuous. African women were portrayed as being reservoirs of pathogens. Immodest claims of causality were made, "blaming cultural differences

---

[45] Schoepf, "Assessing AIDS Research," 135.
[46] Kippax, "Effective HIV Prevention," 6.
[47] Schoepf, "AIDS in Africa," 19.

for situations clearly linked to socioeconomic and political inequality."[48] The dominant interpretation of AIDS contributed to the reproduction of problematic colonial representations such as that Africans are promiscuous and African governments are incompetent. The aggregated and cumulative effects of these interpretations strategically elude historical and contemporary Western participation in creating problems such as AIDS in Africa and elsewhere.

To restore the dignity of PLWH and the African continent, theological ethicists need to challenge stigmatizing and race-based epidemiological claims, public attitudes, and social policy rooted in moral and methodological individualism. Questioning the use of individualism as a framework for HIV prevention is nothing other than challenging the dominance of the liberal and neoliberal model in global health and affirming the value of health as a global common and public good. Hence, individualism, in itself, becomes recognized as the source of global structural sins.

Second, theological ethics needs to promote social justice through structural change. After many years of involvement in the fight against HIV, Christian churches can now develop an action theory and a reality-based health-care activism. HIV prevention has heightened social/community mobilization and political commitment to the welfare not only of sick individuals but of the entire population. Increase of social and political capital seems to have a protective effect. The quest for social transformation as a way to improve population health led James Keenan to argue for the expansion of universal access to HIV prevention and AIDS treatment to universal access to care. The social mobilization and coalition with other constituencies created around the fight against HIV supports the need for improving ecumenical, interreligious, and social dialogue on important social issues. Catholic social teaching, with its emphasis on human dignity, common good, and subsidiarity, offers good resources for theorizing and advocating a normative and transformative activism. Relying on church teachings, a multitude of initiatives were launched at all levels—from Small Christian Communities, parishes, and dioceses, and even to the level of the national and regional bishops' conferences—to address the AIDS pandemic. The time has come to theorize and learn from this multidimensional response for the sake of more consistent interventions now and in the future. Most interventions that local churches launch are often carried out by grassroots groups or institutions such as home-based care in southern Africa, Small Christian Communities, local health-care dispensaries, or community-based organizations. These grassroots groups have worked hard to address structures that create risky environments, prevent access to health resources, and ultimately reify the fundamental equality with which human beings have been endowed by the Creator. Structural interventions aim at establishing an environment enabling healthier

---

[48] Ibid.

choices.[49] Structural interventions are consistent with the social justice tradition of the Catholic Church and with the principles of the Ottawa Charter for Health Promotion. Community mobilization, economic and educational interventions, contingent funding, and integration of HIV services are the forms of interventions that grace-filled institutions can use to effect structural change.[50] These interventions have proven to be instrumental to women's empowerment. Empowerment cannot be limited to economic solutions, but must include education and skill training.[51]

Third, theological ethicists need to engage macro-social policy and call for intersectoral interventions as pro-poor initiatives. Engaging health policy or focusing on condom use discussion alone appears to be too narrow a focus for a continent where socioeconomic and cultural pressures create risk environments.[52] For example, the elimination of school fees may reduce HIV incidence among girls, since fewer girls will be forced to drop out of school, which then would reduce the risk of some of them being found on the street. In the same line of thought, the fight against AIDS has taught us that interventions that provide destitute individuals with skill training opportunities that boost their economic status have been shown to improve health outcomes by shifting relationships of power and offering income opportunities outside of the sex industry. To address social policy and justice, the theological discourse of the churches must self-confidently take shape in a larger network of other religions and civil society. The churches need to address the private and public values that shape policy making and challenge the domination of market values over all spheres of social life.

Conclusion

Almost four decades into the AIDS pandemic, we have learned not to accept narrow-minded, one-sided, and untested ideological pronouncements. Theological ethicists cannot rely on ideas and theories that have been shown to be limited or been proven wrong. Throughout this chapter I have endeavored to demonstrate that, to approach the truth about HIV risk and intervention, ethicists need to engage epidemiologic and socioanthropological sources that explain how history, cultural politics, political economy, and socioeconomic

---

[49] K. M. Blankenship, S. R. Friedman, S. Dworkin, and J. E. Mantell, "Structural Interventions: Concepts, Challenges, and Opportunities for Research," *Journal of Urban Health: Bulletin of the New York Academy of Medicine* 83, no. 1(2006): 60.

[50] Ibid., 63–66.

[51] Julia Kim, Paul Pronyk, Tony Barnett, and Charlotte Watts, "Exploring the Role of Economic Empowerment in HIV Prevention," *AIDS* 22, suppl. 4 (2008): S57–S71.

[52] Steven H. Woolf, "Social Policy as Health Policy," *JAMA* 30, no. 11 (2009): 1167.

status determine behavioral options and contribute to AIDS. Dialoguing with such approaches, theological ethics can function as a subversive discipline that challenges ideological theories of disease causation that lead to narrow-minded moralism and misguided intervention. Theology needs to question behavioral and biomedical approaches that easily align with methodological and market individualism by providing a theological anthropology to guide genuine efforts aiming at HIV prevention. With an anthropological perspective that affirms both the individuality and the irreducible sociality of the human person, HIV infection can be recognized as an issue neither only of personal morality nor only of social morality. Without undermining personal responsibility for infection, any moral judgment about infection needs to take into account the social matrix that shapes risk. The ethics of HIV prevention should be primarily a social ethics within which can be anchored personal ethics.

CHAPTER 6

CHANGING RELIGIOUS BELIEFS AND
ATTITUDES AMONG PEOPLE LIVING
WITH HIV IN SOUTH AFRICA

Philippe Denis

Despite some pioneering studies in the last decade of the twentieth century,[1] not until the 2000s did HIV and AIDS and religion become a recognized field of inquiry with a substantial body of works by theologians, anthropologists, and scholars of religion.[2] During the first decades of the epidemic, the key question (in sub-Saharan Africa at least) was whether faith communities and Christianity in particular were an obstacle in the fight against HIV and AIDS through their perceived opposition to public health prevention policies, or an asset by complementing or even replacing failing public health systems on the African continent.[3] The emphasis during this period was on what religious institutions did or did not do to mitigate the effects of the epidemic. If the positive contribution of faith-based medical institutions was widely acknowledged, the response of religious institutions in matters of prevention, stigma, and public representations of the disease remained an object of debate.[4] But, as we move into the fourth decade of the epidemic—with a lower mortality rate among HIV patients, thanks to easier access to antiretroviral treatments— the focus of attention is changing. The focus has turned to the long-term effects

---

[1] Ronald Nicolson, *God in AIDS? A Theological Enquiry* (London: SCM, 1996).

[2] See the Online Bibliographic Database on Religion and HIV compiled by the Collaborative for HIV and AIDS, Religion and Theology (CHART), a project of the School of Religion, Philosophy, and Classics of the University of KwaZulu-Natal (www.chart.ukzn.ac.za). For a review of the literature dealing with HIV and AIDS and religion in sub-Saharan Africa, see Philippe Denis, "HIV/AIDS and Religion in Sub-Saharan Africa: An Emerging Field of Enquiry," *Archives de science sociale des religions* 164 (2013): 43–58.

[3] Jill Olivier and Quentin Wodon, *Strengthening the Evidence for Faith-Inspired Health Engagement in Africa*, 3 vols. (Washington, DC: World Bank, 2012).

[4] I discussed these matters in "HIV, AIDS, and Religion in Sub-Saharan Africa: An Historical Survey," in *Religion and HIV and AIDS: Charting the Terrain*, ed. Beverley Haddad (Pietermaritzburg: University of KwaZulu-Natal Press, 2011), 57–77.

of the epidemic on religious beliefs and attitudes. Has the epidemic changed
the manner of believing? Do people living with HIV and AIDS relate to religious institutions in the same way as before? What effect does the new focus on
health, sexuality, and gender—three categories central in the experience of HIV
and AIDS—have on religious institutions? Has theology changed as a result of
the epidemic?

The changes brought about by HIV and AIDS on the religious scene are
not easy to grasp, because they are incremental and mostly happen at the grassroots level. An important, though by no way unique, source of information I
used for this chapter is the archives of the Sinomlando Centre's Memories of
AIDS Project, a collection of sixty-five oral history interviews and ten group
interviews conducted between 2011 and 2013 in the Pietermaritzburg area in
the South African province of KwaZulu-Natal.[5] The interviewees were nongovernmental organization (NGO) workers, pastoral agents, and support group
members who had dealt with HIV and AIDS in and around Pietermaritzburg since the late 1980s. A third of the informants were people living with
HIV involved in an AIDS support group. Most interviews were conducted in
isiZulu, the local language. The interviewers—postgraduate students or staff
members of the Sinomlando Centre—made use of a topic guide developed by
the research team. The interviewees were asked to elaborate on four themes:
power issues in the AIDS sector, stigma, faith, and sexuality.

Three Decades of Christian Responses to HIV and AIDS in South Africa

One of the very first Christian AIDS activists in South Africa was Archbishop Denis Hurley of Durban, who is mostly known for his contribution to
the Second Vatican Council and his stance against apartheid. In August 1987
he heard the Zimbabwean Jesuit Ted Rogers advocating for a Christian response
to AIDS at the plenary session of the Southern African Bishop's Conference in
Mariannhill. Shortly afterwards, he established a Diocesan AIDS Committee,
later renamed Sinosizo Centre, which pioneered a home-based care program
providing care to AIDS patients and their families throughout the Archdio-

---

[5] The project was conducted by the Sinomlando Centre for Oral History and Memory
Work, a research and community development center of the University of KwaZulu-Natal
in cooperation with Rijk van Dijk (Africa Studies Centre, Leiden) and with the support of
the South African Netherlands Programme on Alternatives in Development (SANPAD).
The audiotapes, transcriptions, and translations are available to researchers at the Alan Paton
Centre, University of KwaZulu-Natal, Pietermaritzburg, subject to the specifications of the
release agreements signed by the interviewees.

cese of Durban.[6] This model was later replicated in other Catholic dioceses of KwaZulu-Natal. Similar programs were developed in Zambia, Uganda, and Zimbabwe during the same period.[7] In 2000 Sinosizo added an orphan-care component to its program to respond to the needs of a growing number of AIDS orphans.

In March 1991 the South African Council of Churches organized a consultation on AIDS in which, apart from AIDS activists and health professionals, a few Methodists and a representative from the Durban-based ecumenical agency Diakonia participated.[8] By 1993, over seven hundred bodies were engaged in AIDS work in South Africa.[9] A significant number of these early projects were of Christian origin. In August 1993, for example, the Salvation Army established Bethesda House, a home for abandoned babies of HIV-infected mothers in Soweto. In 1995 McCord Hospital, a Durban-based Christian hospital, opened an outpatient clinical service that was designed to meet the medical, economic, psychological, and spiritual needs of its patients. In the aftermath of the International AIDS Conference in July 2000, public awareness of the epidemic increased and the number of community-based HIV and AIDS projects rose to an unprecedented level, thanks to a wider availability of donor funding. Some projects were initiated by a local congregation, like the Hillcrest AIDS Centre, a testing and counseling centre established by a pastor of the Methodist church on the outskirts of Durban.[10] Others only had a loose relationship with a church but received funding through it. Many had no links at all to a religious institution but followed a Christian ethos, as witnessed, for example, by the practice of praying before an activity or when visiting a patient. In the Pietermaritzburg area, where the Memories of AIDS Project has been conducted, a remarkably dense network of AIDS-related community organizations—some overtly Christian, others not—covers the urban and peri-urban territory. The result is that anybody affected or infected by HIV has a good chance of encountering, at some point,

---

[6] Paddy Kearney, *Guardian of the Light—Denis Hurley: Renewing the Church, Opposing Apartheid* (New York: Continuum, 2009); Stephen Joshua Muoki, "AIDS Prophets in a Wounded Country: A Memoir of Two Catholic Clerics Involved in Responding to AIDS in South Africa before the Epidemic (1984–1990)," *Oral History Journal of South Africa* 1 (2013): 58–73. On Ted Rogers's AIDS work, see *Ted Rogers, Jesuit, Social Pioneer, and AIDS Activist in Zimbabwe: A Memoir* (Pietermaritzburg: Cluster Publications, 2012), 219–229.

[7] John Illife, *The African AIDS Epidemic. A History* (Oxford: James Currey, 2006), 108.

[8] Witswatersrand University, William Cullen Library, SACC Archives, AC 623, 12.34: Minutes of Church Consultation on AIDS.

[9] Illife, *The African AIDS Epidemic*, 99.

[10] Thomas Ninan, "Toward an HIV-Competent Church: The Hillcrest AIDS Centre, a Pioneering Faith Response to HIV and AIDS in Southern Africa (1990 to 2001)" (unpublished master's thesis, University of KwaZulu-Natal, 2014).

an NGO, a community-based organization (CBO), or a faith-based organization (FBO)—to follow the commonly used categories—be it a home-based-care organization, an orphan-care project, an AIDS hospice, a counseling and testing center, or an AIDS clinic.

Like apartheid a generation before, AIDS has generated a considerable civil response. The biomedical aspects of HIV and AIDS are usually managed, with various degrees of success, by the public health system. By the time of this writing, more than 3 million HIV-positive people survive, thanks to antiretroviral treatment dispensed in state-run clinics or hospitals. But even in this environment, community-based organizations are present in various supportive roles. In this effort Christians and, for a small part, Muslims make a meaningful contribution. To coordinate the church's responses to the epidemic, some of the churches, the Catholic Church in particular,[11] have created an AIDS desk. Their role in advocacy and policy making has been significant. They also channeled international donor funding to grassroots organizations linked directly or indirectly to them.

The interviews document another aspect of this proliferation of faith-based projects. In a society affected by massive unemployment, volunteering in an HIV and AIDS project opens the door to upward social mobility. Well trained and articulate, the volunteers become employable when the occasion arises. All want to increase their chances of employment. They work hard for little money. Their main reward is increased training and social recognition. It is true that, in recent years, the combined effect of the global economic recession, the normalization of AIDS, and the allocation of donor funding to other priorities have resulted in many NGOs and CBOs reducing their programs, retrenching staff, and sometimes closing altogether. But volunteering continues, at least in the most resilient community organizations.

Of all AIDS-related community organizations, HIV and AIDS support groups are the most significant because of their impact on the medical, psychosocial, and spiritual well-being of their members. AIDS support groups create a space for disclosure, mutual support, and assertiveness. But they also constitute a new form of social organization that, like home-based-care organizations or orphan care projects, sometimes has a religious character. By promoting HIV awareness, care, and treatment among their peers and in their communities and producing a well-articulated discourse on AIDS, the support group members contribute to the development of what some authors have described as *therapeutic citizenship*.[12] They develop, thanks to AIDS, new forms of sociability and identity.

---

[11] Alison Munro, "Response of the Catholic Church to AIDS: An SACBC AIDS Office Perspective," in *Catholic Responses to AIDS in Southern Africa*, ed. Stuart Bate and Alison Munro (Pretoria: SACBC, 2013), 21–53.

[12] Vinh-Kim Nguyen, *The Republic of Therapy: Triage and Sovereignty in West Africa's*

Contrasting Responses at the Congregation Level

For most people infected or affected by HIV, what counts is the local congregation. Unless they belong to the leadership structures of their churches, they have never read—and probably never heard of—the statements issued by their church leaders on HIV and AIDS. This does not mean that these statements—and theological work on HIV and AIDS in general—are not important. The messages they propagate can filter down to ordinary people through various channels. Particularly important in this respect is the inclusion of modules on HIV and AIDS in the curriculum of theological institutions. It was to respond to this need that, in 2003, the African theologian Musa Dube published a handbook on AIDS in the theological curriculum under the auspices of the World Council of Churches.[13] Equally significant are the programs aimed at raising AIDS awareness among pastors, such as the Evangelical Seminary of Southern Africa Christian AIDS Program (ECAP), which has been running workshops, mostly for evangelical and Pentecostal pastors, in the Pietermaritzburg area with great success. Some of the pastors who opened the doors of their churches to people living with HIV had been ECAP-trained.

In the early days of the epidemic, blaming the victims of AIDS for their misfortune was not uncommon. Church leaders, including Catholic bishops, were not afraid of saying that AIDS was a punishment of God. Such messages are rarely heard today, at least in the public sphere, but they have not disappeared. The interviews show that in some congregations, stigmatizing statements continue to be made from the pulpit. More pervasive, however, is the attitude consisting in keeping silent on AIDS under the pretext that it is not the business of the church to deal with a sexually transmitted disease. Nonhlanhla, a support group member who had the courage to disclose her HIV status to her congregation, was very shocked when her pastor made her understand that it was out of place:

> What broke my heart is when I heard the pastor saying that the church is a place to talk about the Word of God. He used this phrase to say that the church is not a place to talk about HIV and AIDS. From that time my love lessened, not the love of God, of being saved, but the love of the church. I went less and less to church because of the way they handled the issue of HIV. . . . I went into the pulpit and told them that

Time of AIDS (Durham, NC: Duke University Press, 2010): 108–9; Philippe Denis, "New Patterns of Disclosure: How HIV-Positive Support Group Members from KwaZulu-Natal Speak of Their Status in Oral Narratives," *Medical History* 58, no. 2 (2014): 297.

    [13] Musa Dube, ed., *HIV and AIDS Curriculum for Theological Institutions in Africa* (Geneva: WCC Publications, 2003).

I was HIV-positive and also told them that God has helped me and that I was beautiful, healthy, and fresh, you know, the person who is so thin but fresh. I told them that I was HIV-positive and that God had helped me even though I was not on treatment.

Stigma is the single biggest obstacle to testing, treatment, and care. "We believe," wrote anthropologist Catherine Campbell and her colleagues at a time when antiretroviral medicines were largely out of reach in the South African public health system, "that even after the treatment is available and HIV and AIDS is no longer fatal, the link between HIV and AIDS and 'bad behavior' (i.e., sexual behavior) will still exist in ways that associate the disease with shame and embarrassment."[14] The interviews conducted for the Memories of AIDS Project show that, seven or eight years later, stigma is still prevalent. People living with HIV disclose their status to family members and friends with less hesitation than before, but they rarely go public because of the fear of stigma and discrimination. There are still people, men in particular, who do not go for testing, or if they do, do not take their medicine because they do not want to be seen as HIV-positive. For many South Africans AIDS is not yet a normal disease.

The Churches' Dilemma

One might ask what responsibility religious institutions—and the Christian churches in particular—have in this situation. If all Christians were prepared to accept, as Gideon Byamugisha suggested, an HIV-positive Anglican canon from Uganda, that "the body of Christ may be HIV-positive,"[15] the Christian communities confronted with HIV and AIDS would be free of stigma. Clearly, this is not the case. Why?

The answer lies in the link between AIDS and sexuality. In sub-Saharan Africa the main mode of HIV transmission is sexual. Because of its association with life and fertility, sexuality is seen in positive terms, even though parents in African families find it difficult to speak openly about it to their children. But when it brings disease, the sexual act becomes shameful, and the one who is believed to introduce the sickness in the family—the woman, not the man—is rejected as sinful and impure. Several HIV-positive women referred to the stereotype of the loose woman in the interviews. The first thought that comes

---

[14] Catherine Campbell, Carol Ann Foulis, Sbongile Maimane, and Zweni Sibiya, "'I Have an Evil Child at My House': Stigma and HIV/AIDS Management in a South African Community," *American Journal of Public Health* 95 (2005): 814.

[15] Gideon Byamugisha, John Joshva Raja, and Ezra Chitando, *Is the Body of Christ HIV-Positive? New Ecclesiological Christologies in the Context of HIV-Positive Communities* (Delhi: Indian Society for Promoting Christian Knowledge, 2012).

to mind when a woman tests positive is that she "sleeps around." The fact that faithful women can be infected by husbands or boyfriends having slept with other women is not taken into consideration. The fear of being considered immoral explains why many women are afraid of disclosing their status, especially to men. Their male partners are also afraid, but for other reasons: being affected by a sexually transmitted disease is a sign of weakness. A real man cannot be sick.

All this does not relate, at least directly, to the Christian faith. But there is a relationship. Mainstream Christianity recognizes the value of sexuality but on one condition: that it be strictly practiced in the context of marriage. Outside marriage, sex is necessarily sinful. If a Christian believer is not married—as is the case for numerous South African adults who do not earn enough money to buy a house, perform the traditional rituals, and start a family—and has a sexual partner, that person will see himself or herself as a sinner and fear being so designated by family members and neighbors. Shame is as much a religious phenomenon as a cultural one.

The churches are caught in a dilemma. They are bound to preach the sanctity of marriage, but by doing so, they implicitly declare sinful the vast cohorts of people who, for reasons over which they rarely have control, are unlikely ever to marry.[16] The type of marriage—contracted, customary, civil, or Christian—is not the issue here. What is out of reach for many people is a stable union between a man and a woman under one roof with the intention of raising children. The considerable number of children born to single mothers in South Africa and the ridiculously small number of marriages celebrated in black parishes throughout the country illustrate the seriousness of the problem. The message of the church on the sacrament of marriage is reserved de facto to a minority of church members, middle-class people of various races who can afford to marry. How can one expect young men or young women with little or no income to remain faithful to a sexual partner during their entire life if their chances of living together in a stable environment are almost nonexistent?

This dilemma affects the church's response to HIV and AIDS in two ways. On the first we shall not say much because the subject has been abundantly debated. The choice is between declaring the use of condoms outside the bonds of marriage to always be sinful even when there is risk of HIV infection or accepting and even recommending the use of condoms to people at risk of contracting the virus in order to save lives, knowing that this might bring confu-

---

[16] According to the 2011 census, of South Africans ages twenty or older, 43.7 percent had never been married, 36.7 percent were married at the time of the census, 11.0 percent were living together like married partners, 5.7 percent were widowed, 0.9 percent were separated, and 1.9 percent were divorced.

sion on the Catholic doctrine of marriage.[17] Commenting on the furor caused by the Southern African Catholic Bishops' Conference's 2001 *Message of Hope*, which restricted the use of condoms to discordant couples (where one partner is HIV-infected and the other is not), Alison Munro, the director of the SACBC AIDS Desk, showed that there are ways, even in the Catholic Church, of navigating away from the dilemma of HIV prevention. "The condom issue became something of a non-issue in the AIDS Office," she wrote, "with a policy of informing people of the Church's teaching on sexual practices outside marriage and on the efficacy of condom use, leaving them to make their own decisions."[18]

Less easy to pinpoint because of its relationship to popular culture, the second dilemma facing the Christian churches is perhaps more formidable. The churches have to preach a moral message in sexual matters because sexuality is a human reality that can be handled wrongly and therefore requires moral guidance. But at the same time, the moral message of the churches regarding sexuality can have the unintended effect of reinforcing stigma. This message is not delivered in a vacuum. It is addressed to and received by people who perceive AIDS as shameful because of a cultural environment that declares it as such. Christian pastors do not have to openly discriminate against people living with HIV for being agents of stigma. The very fact of associating sex and sinfulness has this effect. The problem is compounded by the fact that most priests and pastors, even those who are married, do not have the tools to articulate a theology of sexuality. Their theological studies did not equip them for that. In any event, in the African community at least, sexuality is not a subject that one speaks easily about. It is urgent to reexamine the theology of sexuality in the context of AIDS to permit an evangelical perspective on sexuality and marriage devoid of stigmatization, intended or not.

God, the Ancestors, and Biomedicine

Using interviews of AIDS support group members as material, I now examine the manner in which AIDS affects the religious beliefs and attitudes of people living with HIV. As much as religious institutions can be said to have exercised, in various ways, an impact on the course of the epidemic, we should recognize that the epidemic has, in turn, changed the manner of believing and of relating to the church.

The following observations are tentative because they only rely on a small number of oral history interviews in a certain area—Pietermaritzburg—and at

---

[17] On the dilemma of HIV prevention, see the collection of papers edited by James Keenan under the title *Catholic Ethicists on HIV/AIDS Prevention* (New York: Continuum, 2000). See also Denis, "HIV/AIDS and Religion in Sub-Saharan Africa," 53–55.

[18] Munro, "Response of the Catholic Church to AIDS," 45.

a certain time—between 2011 and 2013. They emanate from AIDS support group members who are characterized by a higher degree of awareness and agency in HIV matters than ordinary people, yet these interviews show interesting trends, suggesting that we may be entering a new phase of our collective social and religious history.

The first change, which has been described elsewhere,[19] concerns gender relations. This is of interest to the churches, traditionally interested in relations between men and women in the context of marriage. Historically, the Christian message on gender relations has been understood in contradictory ways, either by promoting mutually respectful relations between men and women or by strengthening patriarchal structures nurturing gender oppression and gender abuse.

The women interviewed for the Memories of AIDS Project displayed a surprising degree of assertiveness in matters of gender relations. They openly criticized their male partners who insisted on having sex without thinking of the consequences, refused to test for HIV, and blamed the women when finding out that they were HIV-positive. If the women referred, in some of the interviews, to the stereotype of the "loose woman" who spreads the virus through her carelessness, it was to distance themselves from it. The interviews make it clear that patriarchal practices persist in the African community, but the women concerned have no hesitation to declare that it is wrong.

In a similar way, the epidemic incites the people directly affected by it to reposition themselves in matters of faith and religion. Some redefine Christianity on their own terms. In contrast to the message often conveyed by religious institutions, especially in the early years of the epidemic, of HIV and AIDS as God's punishment or, in its milder form, as the inevitable consequence of a moral transgression, the support group members refused to take any blame, religious or not, for their HIV condition. Rather they emphasized positive aspects such as love, compassion, reconciliation, and forgiveness.

Here is the manner, for example, in which the founder of an AIDS support group in downtown Pietermaritzburg spoke of her spiritual experience. She described with a great richness of expression the journey that took her from anger to peace of mind. At first she rebelled against God, who had permitted her to be infected despite the fact that she "behaved herself" and avoided "sleeping around":

> My relationship with God has gone through a lot of changes. There was a time where I was very angry with God. I felt angry at a number of levels. Why me? I behaved myself. I was not sleeping around. Why did he allow this to happen to me? You know, that kind of thing. . . . It was

---

[19] Denis, "New Patterns of Disclosure," 289–93.

a journey of finding me and finding God and redefining who God is
to me from the stubborn, rebellious young woman I was to learning to
humble myself at his feet. I appreciate who he is and I surrender to his
will. Once I did that, a lot of things started to flow. He lets me resist,
he lets me fight, he lets me throw tantrums. We had that relationship. I
throw tantrums. I ask questions.

When describing their experience, the AIDS support group members put
more emphasis on the fact of still being alive—thanks to antiretroviral treatment whose power was attributed to God—than on being under the threat of
death. Many interviewees were able to articulate spiritually and, one may say,
theologically their views on God, Jesus, the church, and Christian morality in a
context profoundly transformed by the widespread availability of antiretroviral
treatment.

At the heart of this experience was the lifesaving antiretroviral treatment,
which Nonhlanhla, a forty-five-year-old HIV-positive woman, almost considered as a sacrament:

I just took Christ as my personal Savior. I took him, even in these ARV
tablets, before I put the tablets in my mouth. When I come from the
clinic, I say, "Lord, this is nothing you can do better than these tablets!"

A corollary of the support group members' assertiveness is that they do not hesi-
tate to take on their priests or pastors for incorrectly handing HIV and AIDS
matters—for example, on the issue of condoms. Nontokozo, a Pentecostal
woman, declared that the ministers of religion who refused to promote condoms
during church services were wrong because many born-again Christians were
infected. They did not trust the power of the Holy Spirit:

They say a child of God does not use condoms and then I say, "Please,
can you show me in the Bible where it is written about condoms?" I
used to say at this point that we put the Holy Spirit aside because we all
have the Holy Spirit, the one of speaking in tongues, because we speak
about the reality of life. . . . I feel sorry for my church because a lot of
people have died of AIDS in my church.

One of the most striking developments among people affected and infected
by HIV is the gradual dissipation of the confusion regarding the nature of the
disease. In the first decades of the epidemic, the Western-based biomedical
approach, which defined AIDS as a deficiency of the immune system caused
by a virus called HIV, and the traditional belief systems, which explained the

phenomenon of multiple deaths as the result of a lack of harmony between the living and the dead due, among other reasons, to the transgression of cultural taboos, were in open competition, creating conditions for confusion, silence, and denial.[20] To this we could add that the "healing churches" and, though less frequently, the mainline churches propose a third kind of belief system: for them, God—not Western medicine—heals AIDS when the right prayers are addressed to him.

But things are changing. During the last ten years, millions of South Africans have received information on the virus and its transmission in counseling and testing centers and in HIV clinics. The ideological confusion of the early years is disappearing. The interviews show that, among AIDS support group members and home-based-care volunteers, the respective roles of God, the ancestors, and biomedicine in the experience of the disease are much more clearly distinguished. AIDS is seen as a disease, not a curse. For Nontokozo, for example, the pastors who say that praying makes the virus disappear are "false prophets." They are "gambling with the lives of the people." If God plays a role, it is through the antiretroviral medicines, not directly. There are many reasons to believe that a good number of other people infected or affected by HIV, especially in urban areas, understand the disease in the same way.

Conclusion

AIDS has changed the landscape in South Africa in countless ways, including the church. It has affected religious institutions at the institutional level by prompting them to create or encourage the creation of a multiplicity of faith-based AIDS organizations, small or big, short-lived or of long duration. Slow in the early years, the movement accelerated in the early 2000s thanks to the massive availability of donor funding before slowing down again in recent years due to the combined effect of the global economic recession and the success of antiretroviral therapies. The AIDS epidemic has allowed the churches to reinvest in the domain of health care, largely relinquished when mission hospitals were handed over to the state in the 1960s and 1970s. Throughout South Africa the chances of a person affected or infected by HIV coming across an AIDS project sponsored by a church at some point are quite high.

But the relationship between AIDS and the church is not limited to the institutional level. HIV and AIDS are at the same time biomedical, social, and

---

[20] Peter Delius and Clive Glaser, "Sex, Disease, and Stigma in South Africa: Historical Perspectives," *African Journal of AIDS Research* 4 (2005): 20–36; Deborah Posel, Kathleen Kahn, and Liz Walker, "Living with Death in a Time of AIDS: A Rural South African Case Study," *Scandinavian Journal of Public Health* 35 (2007): 138–46.

cultural phenomena. Religious institutions—and, among them, the Christian churches—shape representations in a powerful way. From that point of view, the role of the churches is ambiguous. The message of compassion they preach to the faithful finds expression in the support their members provide to people living with HIV and their families. But the churches also fuel stigma, most of the time unintentionally, by contributing to the perception than a person having contracted a sexually transmitted disease has committed a shameful act. The only way to avoid this danger is to open the pulpit to people living with HIV who will defeat, by the power of their testimony, any idea of an association between HIV and immorality.

The good news, in this new phase of the epidemic, is that people living with HIV start to become more assertive in matters of gender relation and in matters of faith. They invent a new way of being Christian, based on the idea that HIV, paradoxically, is as much a gift of God as it is a tragedy, thanks to the medicines that give them a new lease on life. They vigorously refuse the idea that they should be blamed for being HIV-positive. Some were heard to say they love their HIV. It is true in the sense that the virus has given them new opportunities and a new sense of purpose.

CHAPTER 7

SMALL CHRISTIAN COMMUNITIES AS AGENTS OF CHANGE IN THE FIGHT AGAINST HIV AND AIDS IN EASTERN AFRICA

Joseph Healey

There are over 180,000 Small Christian Communities (SCCs) in the Catholic Church in the nine AMECEA[1] countries in Eastern Africa today that have some kind of planned practical action; service; and pastoral, social, and mission outreach to local problems and challenges such as people with HIV. How are SCC members important agents of change and transformation in the fight against HIV? The first goal of this chapter is to analyze the reality of people with HIV in Eastern Africa today. The second goal is to demonstrate that the active involvement of SCC members in reaching out to people with HIV as responders, health-care workers, caregivers, counselors, and so on is a pastoral and social priority. SCC members have a special opportunity to minister to families and couples living with HIV in Eastern Africa, such as caring for millions of AIDS orphans and counseling discordant couples (where one partner is HIV-infected and the other is not). Specific stories, case studies, and examples are cited to illustrate these goals in the context of developing an African narrative ecclesiology.

---

[1] AMECEA is an acronym for Association of Member Episcopal Conferences in Eastern Africa. It is a service organization for the National Episcopal Conferences of the nine English-speaking countries of Eastern Africa, namely Eritrea (1993), Ethiopia (1979), Kenya (1961), Malawi (1961), South Sudan (2011), Sudan (1973), Tanzania (1961), Uganda (1961), and Zambia (1961). The Republic of South Sudan became independent on July 9, 2011, but the two Sudans remain part of one Episcopal Conference. Somalia (1995) and Djibouti (2002) are affiliate members. AMECEA is one of the eight Regional Episcopal Conferences of SECAM (Symposium of Episcopal Conferences of Africa and Madagascar).

Listening to the Reality of People
with HIV in Eastern Africa Today

The AMECEA Study Conference in Mukono, Uganda, in 2005 on "Responding to the Challenges of HIV/AIDS within the AMECEA Region" had one pastoral resolution that emphasized "active involvement of SCCs in reaching out to people with HIV/AIDS. SCC members as caregivers, counselors, etc." This can be extended to SCC members reaching out to refugees; internally displaced people (IDP); people traumatized by civil war, violence, and tribalism/ethnicity; street children; and sick, bereaved, and other needy people.[2]

Among the 31 Criteria to Evaluate a Typical Small Christian Community (SCC) in Eastern Africa in the e-book on the *Small Christian Communities Global Collaborative Website* is:

> No. 14: The SCC has some kind of planned practical action/service/ pastoral, social and mission outreach. Ideally this is a communal response where the SCC members carry out the practical action as a group. This service and outreach responds to local challenges and problems such as lax Catholics in the neighborhood, bereavement, sick people, needy and poor people, people with HIV/AIDS, street children, and so on.[3]

Especially in urban areas, Africans of different Christian denominations and religious faiths live side by side. In the traditional African spirit of community, unity, and hospitality, Catholic neighborhood SCCs are inclusive. Christians of other denominations participate in visiting the sick (such as people with HIV), outreach programs such as community health care, and bereavement in the local community.

Pope Francis emphasizes the importance of welcoming, listening to, and accompanying the wounded, marginalized, and people at the peripheries today. No. 20 of The Joy of the Gospel states, "All of us are asked to obey the Lord's call to go forth from our own comfort zone in order to reach all the

---

[2] Nigerian theologian and Jesuit Father Agbonkhianmeghe E. Orobator documents the SCCs' outreach to people with HIV/AIDS and to refugees in Kenya, Tanzania, and Uganda (*From Crisis to Kairos: The Mission of the Church in the Time of HIV/AIDS, Refugees, and Poverty* [Nairobi: Paulines Publications Africa, 2005], 86–179).

[3] Appendix 2 in "Online Resource Materials on the Ongoing Formation and Training of SCC Members," in Joseph G. Healey, *Building the Church as Family of God: Evaluation of Small Christian Communities in Eastern Africa*. The online digital version regularly updated from the 2012 print version is available as a free 741-page ebook as of April 5, 2016, on the Small Christian Communities Global Collaborative Website, www.smallchristiancommunities.org/ebooks/47-ebooks-.html.

'peripheries' in need of the light of the gospel." Part of this new pattern and process is for bishops, priests, brothers, sisters, and lay pastoral agent/workers to become more of a "listening church." Traditionally bishops are officially part of the "teaching church." But regarding the topics of family and marriage, they need to become part of the listening church—to listen to the lived experience of laypeople, husbands and wives, mothers and fathers, even youth and children. In relation to people with HIV, special outreach programs begin with listening, accompanying, and walking with before teaching (the Emmaus model in Luke 24).

Listening to the reality in Eastern Africa today includes tracking the contemporary shifts in HIV and AIDS. An editorial in the August 22, 2014, issue of Kenya's *Daily Nation* titled, "AIDS: What Went Wrong," states,

> The latest global figures provide grim reading, with the revelation that Kenya has the fourth highest number of new infections, meaning a reversal of the gains realized in the past. . . . Antiretrovirals are available to sustain those infected. So are the structures to provide care at home and at the workplace. However, entrenched habits do not seem to have changed, making many vulnerable to infections.[4]

Such entrenched habits include middle-aged men ("sugar daddies") having sex with young women, including young teenagers. These men resist behavior modification or behavioral change in their lifestyle. Recent research covers Mombasa, Kisii, and Kisumu, Kenya; and Mwanza, Tanzania. Among the Luo ethnic group in Kenya and Tanzania, wife inheritance for widows is very strong. In Musoma, Tanzania, there is a high incidence of tuberculosis and an increasing amount of HIV and AIDS due to these strong Luo cultural customs. American Maryknoll missionary Father James Conard emphasizes that unfortunately "African culture triumphs over Tanzania laws."[5]

The Catholic Church in Africa is involved in a two-year (2014–2015) ongoing process of listening, discussion, dialogue, debate, discernment, and proposed pastoral responses on "Family and Marriage" leading up to the Synod of Bishops 14th Ordinary General Assembly took place in Rome, October 4–25, 2015.

---

[4] This is substantiated by numerous recent Kenyan newspaper reports: "Homa Bay Top in New HIV Cases" (*Daily Nation*, August 20, 2014); "Alarm as 7 Infected with HIV Every Day [in Mombasa]" (*Daily Nation*, June 16, 2014); "Young Women Lead in New HIV Infections Study" (*Standard*, August 21, 2014); "Sex Workers Blamed for Soaring HIV Prevalence" (*Standard*, September 9, 2014); "73,000 HIV-Positive in Kisii as Infections Soar" (*Standard*, June 16, 2014).

[5] James Conard, conversation with the author, Kowak, Tanzania, July 8, 2014.

In this process, the AIDS pandemic is a very important challenge for Africa that has a surprising history. Given its very serious effect on marriage, family, and relationships in general, it has received very little attention. It is significant (and disappointing!) that the AIDS threat was not specifically mentioned in the thirty-nine questions of the original questionnaire for the Synod of Bishops' first session in October 2014. Some African countries, including Kenya, did not mention the AIDS crisis in its answer to the last question: "What other challenges or proposals do you consider urgent or useful to treat?" The coordinator of the compilation of answers in Kenya said that this was an oversight due to the pressure of limited time.[6]

Part of the chairman of AMECEA Cardinal Berhaneyesus Souraphiel, archbishop of Addis Ababa, Ethiopia's intervention on "The Pastoral Challenges of the Family, External Pressures on the Family" at the October 2014 session focused on three key pastoral challenges that face Catholic families in Africa:

1. Poverty.
2. Migration.
3. AIDS: a disease which creates division in the family and frequently divorce. Usually, both parents are affected and, sometimes both die, leaving children under the care of grandparents.[7]

We need to understand that these three challenges are interconnected and interrelated, and that they are part of Africa's overall cultural, economic, political, religious, and social context and reality. "71% of the 35 million people living with HIV/AIDS in the world live in sub-Saharan Africa. The call by UNAIDS to close the gap around access to HIV services will not be met unless the delivery of antiretroviral treatment (ARV) is radically reshaped into community-led approaches that adapt to the realities of those living with HIV."[8]

The HIV and AIDS crisis was not mentioned in the Final Report of the 2014 Synod, another indication of the Western influence on the synod discussions and documentation. Cameroonian theologian and Jesuit Father Jacquineau Azetsop says, "HIV was totally absent. The synod was totally dominated by issues from the first world. It is unfortunate that African bishops

---

[6] Kenyan laywoman Theresa Abuya, interview with the author, Nairobi, Kenya, June 25, 2014.

[7] The full text of his presentation is published in AMECEA Online Newsletter no. 70 (November 14, 2014), amecea.blogspot.com/2014/11/ethiopia-extract-of-chairman-of-amecea.html.

[8] "Flexibility in Health Systems and Community Approach That Adapts to the Daily Realities of HIV-Positive People," *Fides News*, November 29, 2014.

forgot about it also."[9] Commentators in North America and Europe are merely saying that the HIV and AIDS problem is being handled by medicine (that is, the "cocktail" of antiretroviral drugs). This is fueled by misleading news reports in the West, such as the following:

> HIV is evolving to become less deadly and less infectious, according to a major scientific study. The team at the University of Oxford shows the virus is being "watered down" as it adapts to our immune systems. It said it was taking longer for HIV infection to cause AIDS and that the changes in the virus may help efforts to contain the pandemic. Some virologists suggest the virus may eventually become "almost harmless" as it continues to evolve.[10]

For this reason, scholars and activists urged the African delegates at the October 2015 synod session to emphasize the challenges of HIV and specific pastoral responses.

Case Study of Volunteer Community Health-Care Workers in the SCCs in Kenya

SCCs in Eastern Africa have developed a new lay health-care ministry, a volunteer community-based health-care apostolate. These voluntary Community Health Care (CHC) workers or ministers focus on reaching out to people with HIV and their families. This important new lay ministry in SCCs is described by American Maryknoll missionary and Kenyatta University Catholic chaplain Father Lance Nadeau:

> In addition to being agents of missionary outreach to the poor, SCCs in Nairobi and elsewhere in East Africa are developing a new, inculturated, and critical form of lay health care ministry: the huduma ya afya (Swahili for "the service of health care"), a volunteer community-based health care apostolate that provides the following services:
>
> 1. Visit the sick in their homes to talk and pray with them.
> 2. Bring nurses and social workers to evaluate the sick.
> 3. Recommend that the sick go to dispensaries and hospitals.

---

[9] Email to the author dated December 1, 2014.
[10] James Gallagher, "HIV Evolving 'into Milder Form,'" BBC News, December 1, 2014, www.bbc.com/news/health-30254697.

4. Accompany the sick to dispensaries and hospitals if necessary.
5. Bring medications to the sick.
6. Train the family members in home care, nutrition, and hygiene.
7. Inform the parish priests if the sick want a visit.[11]

The Twentieth Anniversary Booklet of Eastern Deanery Community-Based Health Care and AIDS Relief Program (EDARP)[12] of the Nairobi Archdiocese explains,

> Our pools of dedicated Community Health Care Workers (CHWs) are members of the Small Christian Communities (SCCs). These are nominated by the SCCs and the parish, though occasionally individual members may nominate themselves. They too must be vetted by the parish. Once potential CHWs are identified, they must undergo training within their respective parishes using the National CHWs Curriculum. . . . CHWs walk in the footsteps of Jesus Christ, making Him more present to the sick person, to the community[13]

---

[11] Lance Nadeau, "The Small Christian Communities' Health-care Ministry: A Model for Future Mission," in African Continent Report for the 1999 International Consultation on Small Christian Communities (Nairobi: Printed Paper, 1999), 33–34. Nairobi's SCCs do not stand alone in developing a new form of health-care ministry. Other communities are making similar contributions to the ministry in the Eastern African church. On the health-care ministry of SCCs in Kampala, Uganda, see Joseph G. Healey, "Inculturation in Africa," New People (May–June 1992), 13–18; Joseph G. Healey, "Twelve Case Studies of Small Christian Communities in Eastern Africa," in *How Local Is the Local Church? Small Christian Communities and Church in Eastern Africa*, ed. Agatha Radoli (Eldoret, Kenya: AMECEA Gaba Publication, 1993) 70–71; Glen Williams and Nassali Tamale, *The Caring Community: Coping with AIDS in Urban Uganda*, Strategies for Hope 6 (London: ActionAid, 1991).

[12] Eastern Deanery AIDS Relief Program (EDARP) is a faith-based program under the Roman Catholic Church founded in 1993 to respond to the numerous incidences of HIV infection that affected the communities on the eastern side of Nairobi, Kenya. EDARP activities have expanded to HIV/TB prevention, counseling, testing, and treatment services. All services offered in EDARP facilities are free. EDARP facilities are located within the following areas within Eastland's Nairobi: Shauri Moyo, Eastleigh, Mathare, Huruma, Baba Dogo, Kariobangi, Dandora, Ruai, Njiru, Komarock, Soweto, Donholm, St. Veronica Eastleigh 1st Avenue, and Dandora Phase 5. See www.edarp.org.

[13] In Pope Benedict XVI's Post-Synodal Apostolic Exhortation Africae Munus, number 133, under "The Church as the Presence of Christ," states,
> The Church is "in Christ, a sacrament—a sign and instrument, that is, of communion with God and of the unity of the entire human race." As the community of Christ's disciples, we are able to make visible and share the love of God. Love "is the light—and in the end, the only light—that can always illuminate a world grown dim and grant us the courage needed to keep living and working." This is clearly seen in the universal Church, in dioceses and parishes, in the SCCs,

and are prophetic against the culture of death in this multi-faceted response.[14]

EDARP has continued to train CHWs as a strategy to implement home-based care to people living with HIV. Kenyan laywoman Alice Njoroge, the managing director of EDARP, reports that as of September 30, 2014, a total of 2,680 CHWs have been trained in the past twenty-one years; 1,051 are presently active. She says, "We use our CHWs as agents of change in our community." They emphasize the sanctity of human life. They are the key people in the information campaign to help people learn about their HIV status, to take the necessary tests, and so forth. Among discordant couples, CHWs encourage the positive partner to take their medicine regularly. As a result, new HIV infections in the Eastland Deanery have dropped from 13 percent to 5.2 percent.[15]

SCC Members Reach Out to People with HIV and AIDS

SCCs in Eastern Africa also have many outreach activities related to HIV prevention and AIDS care. For example, St. Kizito SCC is located in Waruku, an informal settlement area (lower-class housing). It is one of the ten neighborhood, parish-based SCCs in St. Austin's Parish in the Nairobi Archdiocese. The Amani na Wema (Swahili for peace and goodness) Children's Home that has AIDS orphans is part of the SCC. SCC members reach out to the children through joint Bible sharing, praying the rosary, and providing food and gifts. Many SCCs have a lay ecclesial ministry called the Good Neighbor or the Good Samaritan, in which a person is responsible for visiting the sick and reporting news back to the whole small community. This minister visits the AIDS patients to pray with them and to encourage them to persevere. Sometimes the SCC members go as a small group. The members informally counsel patients that the virus is not the end of their lives. They can live with the virus and take helpful and healing medicine. SCC members emphasize the power of God in our lives.

---

in movements and associations, and even in the Christian family itself, which is "called to be a 'domestic church,' a place of faith, of prayer and of loving concern for the true and enduring good of each of its members," a community which lives the sign of peace. Together with the parish, the SCCs and the movements and associations can be helpful places for accepting and living the gift of reconciliation offered by Christ our peace.

[14] *History of Innovative Community Health Care and TB/HIV Prevention, Care, and Treatment* (Nairobi: Eastern Deanery AIDS Relief Program [EDARP], 2013), 14.

[15] Author's interview with Alice Njoroge in Nairobi, Kenya, January 6 and 9, 2015.

From talks with SCC leaders in Kenya,[16] one learns clearly that the HIV stigma continues. People with the virus are embarrassed to talk about it openly; they do not like to be known publicly, so it is much harder for SCC members to reach out to them. SCC members have a special opportunity to minister to families and couples affected by HIV. One concrete example is outreach to the millions of AIDS orphans in Africa. Then there is the challenge of marriage counseling to discordant couples. In an SCC, how does the marriage counselor advise a husband or wife whose spouse has AIDS? How does the uninfected partner avoid getting infected? Should the couple use a condom? How does the SCC marriage counselor advise a faithful Catholic woman who discovers that her husband is sleeping with other women? Should she and her husband first both get the HIV test? Should she deny marital privileges to her husband until he promises to be faithful only to her?

These real questions are complicated, sensitive, and nuanced. At a certain point the SCC marriage counselor may have to refer the questions to a specially trained marriage counselor. Some of the issues to be considered are the primacy of personal conscience informed by the teachings of the church, the use of condoms in special situations, the importance of prayer for deeper discernment, and offering advice on a case-by-case basis.

An Africa Story:
"We Need to Run Out and Meet Lucia"

Regarding SCC members' service and outreach to people with HIV, listen carefully to the story[17] "We Need to Run Out and Meet Lucia":[18]

---

[16] Based on the author's conversations with Josphat Mulinya, chairperson of St. Kizito SCC (Nairobi Archdiocese) in Nairobi on December 31, 2014; Gabriel Mwatela, chairperson of the St. Kizito SCC Peace, Justice, and Reconciliation Committee in Nairobi on January 4, 2015; and Joseph Kamau, chairperson of St. Veronica SCC (Nyahururu Diocese) in Nairobi on January 3, 2015.

[17] Seven other short stories on outreach to people with HIV/AIDS can be found on the section on "AIDS" in Joseph Healey, *African Stories for Preachers and Teachers* (Nairobi: Paulines Publications Africa, 2006; Swahili edition: Hadithi za Kiafrika kwa Wahubiri na Walimu). See also *Far from Powerless: A Selection of Stories Published by AJAN* (Nairobi: AJAN, 2014; free online version; at ajanweb.org).

[18] Story 3 in Appendix 13 on "Stories of Small Christian Communities (SCCs) in Eastern Africa," in Healey, *Building the Church* (which has 127 references to HIV/AIDS), 492. This story is classified as historical fiction. It is based on a true story in Tanzania, but because of our sensitivity to people with HIV/AIDS it is written in a fictionalized way. It is posted as African Story no. 533 in the African Stories Database on the African Proverbs, Sayings, and Stories Website, www.afriprov.org/index.php/resources/storiesdatabase.html?-task=display2&cid[0]=496. The story is also published in different forms in Healey, *Once*

One Thursday afternoon Maryknoll missionary Father Jim Corrigan participated in the Bible Service of the St. Charles Lwanga Small Christian Community (SCC) in the Bomani section of Bunda Town, Tanzania. This SCC has a special concern for the increasing number of people with AIDS in Bunda. Martina Chacha is responsible for the ministry of "Good Neighbor" in her small community. She regularly checks on the sick people in the vicinity of Bomani. During the past week Maria Magesa's daughter Lucia returned after over two months in the TB Ward in Bugando Medical Center in Mwanza. Lucia has AIDS and now is too weak to even get out of bed. The family was too embarrassed to tell anyone, but the word slowly got around. Martina told the SCC leaders about Lucia. They decided to discuss how to help her during the Thursday meeting of the SCC members.

The Gospel of the Fourth Sunday of Lent—the Parable of the Prodigal Son from the 15th chapter of St. Luke—was read and reflected upon. Jim added his thoughts like everyone else. One SCC member pointed out that the father in the story does not wait for his younger son to return. He runs out to meet him. This shows God's great love for us. He is ready to run out to meet us in love, forgiveness and compassionate care.

When the community members discussed a practical action to flow from the Gospel it was immediately clear. As the elderly man James put it: "We need to run out and meet Lucia who is suffering." So after the Bible Service and meeting everyone walked over to Maria Magesa's home to visit Lucia. It was dark inside the small bedroom and Jim had trouble adjusting to the poor light. Lucia has no husband, which is increasingly common these days. Her two young children were sitting quietly in the corner. Lucia herself was lying on her side in bed, too weak to even sit up. Her face was drawn and flushed. Sores on her tongue had bothered her for many days. Her arms were thin and bony. Occasionally Lucia would put her head over the side of the bed and spit into a small can.

Martina Chacha quietly sat down on the bed, held Lucia's hand and told her how much the small community members cared about her. Philipo, the leader of the SCC, explained how suffering can be a special call from God. The SCC's patron saint, Charles Lwanga, had to suffer very much in Uganda before he was burned to death for his Christian faith. There were prayers of intercession and everyone, even the children, laid hands on Lucia to pray for her recovery. Lucia said a

---

upon a Time in Africa: Stories of Wisdom and Joy (Maryknoll, NY: Orbis Books, 2004), 67–68, and in Healey, *African Stories for Preachers and Teachers*, 14–15.

weak "thank you." Philipo gave her mother Maria a small donation of flour and money from the small community.

Then there was a painful moment of silence. Everyone realized how many families in the Bunda area have a loved one who is either sick with AIDS or already had died. Many people like Lucia are coming home to die. The disease is ravishing East Africa especially on the other side of Lake Victoria around Bukoba, Tanzania, and up into Western Uganda. AIDS has no favorites. Rich and poor, old and young, educated and uneducated, city and rural people alike are getting AIDS or are HIV-positive.

Jim was grateful to be part of this SCC outreach to people suffering from AIDS. Recently he had read about one Catholic doctor who said: "As the Christian Churches in Africa at the beginning of the 21st Century, history will judge us by how generously and compassionately we have responded to the AIDS crisis." At first Jim and Michael, the other priest in Bunda Parish, didn't realize how serious the AIDS pandemic really is. But then in walking around the SCCs, Jim began to discover how many people have AIDS. Most families try to hide it. The shame is too great. There is a unique stigma attached to AIDS because it was different from other diseases. Most people in Africa get AIDS from multi-partner heterosexual relationships. People don't want to be confronted and have to examine their personal lifestyles. They don't want to face the challenge of behavior modification. Others pass it off as "just another illness." Still others say that it was "just bad luck" or that they are "bewitched."

But Jim knew differently.

Soon he began to understand the *hali halisi* (Swahili for the "real situation"). Bunda is on a major truck route. Also many people pass through the town on their way to somewhere else. This compounds the problem. There are a lot of multi-partner relationships. It is so very, very hard to convince people to change this sexual behavior. But Jim knew this is the only way. Yet it is going to take a long time. And many people like Lucia are going to suffer and die painful deaths in the meantime.

As he walked out of Lucia's dark room and was temporarily blinded by the bright African sunlight, Jim wondered if and when he would see Lucia again. But the ministry of love and compassion to Lucia and many like her would continue. Jim was proud that the Bunda Parish leaders and the SCCs had responded so generously. He knew that this was what Christianity is all about. He felt deeply that if they really follow Christ it means being compassionate toward suffering people.

The next Sunday Jim Corrigan preached about AIDS in church. He called his homily, "Suffering Faces and Hearts in Bunda Today." He got permission from Lucia to tell her story. Respectfully he told the painful journey of Lucia, "one of our own Small Christian Community members." In using the Gospel story of the prodigal, the priest challenged the people by asking: "Who is the prodigal? The son? The father? In today's world is it the Lucias? Is it the people who accept and love AIDS patients as they are? Let's admit it. We are afraid to talk about AIDS. And meeting a person who is HIV-positive! That is even worse. How much easier to say: 'That is someone else's problem. We have doctors and institutions to take care of these AIDS patients.'

"Each age has its own terrible form of dying. In the First Century it was crucifixion. From pictures and films we know what a painful death Jesus Christ suffered on the cross. In the 14th Century it was the Black Death (bubonic plague) that was an epidemic disease that killed one-third of the people in Europe. Today it is AIDS. If Jesus chose the most ignominious form of death in his time to redeem us, would he choose to die from AIDS today?" That got some gasps from the Christians at the 7:30 a.m. Eucharistic Celebration in the Bunda Town Church.

Jim went on to ask the congregation: "What is the last word that will be spoken in human history?" After giving the people time to think a little bit he quoted from one spiritual writer who said: The last word of history will be "compassion." Jim added two other words: "forgiving love—as in the example of today's Gospel about the 'Prodigal Father.'"

Jim praised the example of St. Charles Lwanga SCC, saying, "Outreach to AIDS patients and their families is a special call and challenge for SCCs in East Africa today. SCCs are a community of believers who care about other people. SCCs are a unique support group in the AIDS ministry. As a communion of extended families the SCCs provide support, encouragement and home care for AIDS patients themselves. We have a responsibility to our brothers and sisters with AIDS. Do not be afraid. Be Christ-like and reach out to others who are suffering. Join local 'caring communities' like SCCs and other special support groups for AIDS and HIV Positive people. Reach out in personal ways too."

Near the end of his homily Jim told the story of Blessed Mother Teresa of Calcutta, whom many had heard about. Her religious community of the Missionaries of Charity works with the poorest of the poor in Dar es Salaam and Tabora, Tanzania. The missionary priest ended his homily by saying: "In talking about people with AIDS

Blessed Mother Teresa tells each of us: 'Today people with AIDS are the most unwanted and unloved brothers and sisters of Jesus. So let us give them our tender love and care and a beautiful smile.'" Then Jim asked: "How about us here in Bunda? Are we ready to give at least a smile and hopefully much more to these people who are in such need?"

Using Various Pastoral Theological Reflection Methods Leading to Change and Transformation

SCCs in Eastern Africa use various pastoral theological reflection methods, such as the three steps of "See, Judge, and Act" that are part of the pastoral spiral (also known as the pastoral circle or pastoral cycle). The term pastoral spiral is preferred because it showed the ongoing-ness of the method or process.

The many examples above, including the story of Lucia and Jim's homily, are moments of pastoral theological reflection as part of African narrative ecclesiology. Real-life storytelling leads to a deeper understanding of the core Christian values of love, compassion, and solidarity. This process helps SCC members to get to a deeper level and insight that can lead to change and trans-formation. This, in turn, leads to a deeper Christian response to people suffering and wounded with HIV, dramatizing the role of SCCs in the neighborhood in a time of suffering and diseases—an ecclesiology that starts with lived experience and opens up to the transformative power of the church in the neighborhood.

The ideal in the "Act" step is that SCC members promote behavioral modi-fication—a change in a person's lifestyle, such as being faithful to one partner. SCC members use a powerful Swahili (East and Central Africa) proverb that says, "It is better to have a still curtain hanging inside the house than a flag blowing to and fro outside the house." The reference is to faithfulness in marriage: it is better to have a single partner, comparable to the curtain in the proverb, than to go back and forth like a flag blowing in the wind. Such exam-ples get people to think more deeply about their behavior.

Various reflection methods are related especially to social justice in the Lumko series, such as the "Amos Program for Small Christian Communities."[19] These programs search for the root causes of common problems, leading to social action. The Amos Program is a form of Bible sharing in five steps where the Bible is read in the context of everyday life realities of the people of our time. The starting point in each case is a concrete social or political problem— poverty, unemployment, corruption, drug use, HIV and AIDS, violence, prostitution, and so on—that is then analyzed in light of the Bible and the Christian tradition. But SCC members do not stop at the steps of analysis and interpretation. Instead, they move on to develop viable solutions that are as

---

[19] No. 9 of the Appendix of Healey, *Building the Church as Family of God.*

realistic and practical as possible. In so doing, they make it possible for life relationships to improve step by step.[20]

RENEW Africa is a dynamic, engaging process for the spiritual renewal of parishes built on the faith experiences of Africans in their daily lives and centered on faith sharing within Small Christian Communities. The overall theme is "Gathered as God's Family." These reflection guides are ideally suited for small faith-sharing communities in parishes and other groups. Each session includes real-life stories of people who experience challenges of global concern, presented in written or video form. Session topics available for download include Global Solidarity, Fair Trade, HIV and AIDS, Hunger, Migration, and Peacebuilding. The series is available for college and university students as The World on Campus.[21]

Conclusion: The Journey Continues

The following question offers a key challenge to Small Christian Communities in Africa: What are the different human problems in Africa that we should reflect on in our SCC meetings in the light of the gospel? (based on no. 89 of St. John Paul II's Apostolic Exhortation "The Church in Africa of the First African Synod"). Rather than being only problem-centered, we need to see the AIDS pandemic as a challenge and even an opportunity to live the gospel in a different and deeper way as we reach out to those people whom Pope Francis calls the wounded and those on the margins and peripheries of society. SCCs can implement the Second African Synod's recommendations for reconciliation and healing services on the local level. SCC members thus become agents of change and transformation.

---

[20] "The Amos Program: Prophetic Action in the World of Today," Catholic Biblical Federation (CBF) Newsletter, 4/2007 edition.

[21] RENEW International, www.renewintl.org/renewafrica.

Part Three

AIDS, Healing, and the Bible

CHAPTER 8

HEALING IN THE NEW TESTAMENT AND HEALING OF AIDS IN AFRICA

Jean Paul René Ondoua Omgba

Africa's wide variety of healing practices is well known. A large segment of the African population exhibits a preference for health-care practices considered traditional, local, and even miraculous. As a result, scientific or so-called objective modern medicine is often neglected, even abandoned. The emergence of faith healers has also contributed to this phenomenon, distinguished by the accelerated establishment of new awakening churches, where miraculous acts of power (healing) seem to happen on a regular basis.[1] These entities damage the credibility of medical science in its fight against AIDS, which requires proper medical tools, and create confusion and mistrust. Such an outcome is particularly harmful when we consider the pain and suffering that overwhelm many African brothers and sisters, especially as the tragedy of the AIDS pandemic keeps decimating African populations in quantity and quality. Faced with the horror of this situation, many people will turn to anything that can help restore their health.

The aim of this chapter is to challenge these attitudes and beliefs, which can be considered dangerous for Africa. The goal, through a holistic appreciation of healing in the New Testament, is to suggest ways that could help the African people escape from the impersonal, systematic nature of the medical care they receive. AIDS is a serious matter that must be treated seriously, and that can only be achieved through the Master, our Lord Jesus Christ, the eternal Word of the Father, who came so that we might have life in abundance (see John 10:10). This approach opens up two main themes for this chapter: a presentation of

---

[1] Cf. M. Hebga et al., *Croyance et guérison* (Yaoundé: Clé, 1973); E. de Rosny, *Ndsimi, Ceux qui soignent dans la nuit* (Yaoundé: Clé, 1974); E. de Rosny, *Les yeux de ma chèvre, Sur les pas des maitres de la nuit en pays douala* (Paris: Plon, Terre humaine, 1981); *L'Afrique des guérisons* (Paris: Karthala, 1992); L. Perrin, *Guérir et sauver: entendre la parole des malades* (Paris: Cerf, 1987); H. Memel-Foté, *La santé, la maladie et les médecines en Afrique, une approche anthropologique* (Abidjan: Cerap, 2008); X. Dijon, *La diversité des pratiques africaines de guérison: repères philosophiques et théologiques* (Yaoundé: Presse de l'UCAC, 2009).

healing miracles in the New Testament and an overview of healing practices in Africa,[2] using the case of AIDS as a backdrop. Finally I suggest ways of better understanding AIDS and its healing.

The Healing Miracles in the New Testament

It is not possible to talk about Jesus's earthly ministry without mentioning healing miracles. The Gospels are full of them, and primitive communities attached great importance to them. This is to recognize and accredit Jesus as Prophet of all times, the one whom God sent to manifest his kingdom among men; and since God was with Jesus, he went about doing good and healing all who were oppressed by the devil (see Gen. 2:21–23; 10:38). In fact, Jesus was teaching not just with his words but also by his actions.[3] The universality of his mission is therefore built into this binary truth; word and action. In this sense, Latourelle can rightly say that the healing stories in the Gospels are linked to the overall meaning of Jesus's life and death.[4] At this point, it is important to take a panoramic tour of the healing stories in the Gospels (focusing on the Gospels of Matthew, Mark, Luke, and John).

Matthew

Matthew 4:23 points out that Jesus went all around Galilee, teaching in synagogues, proclaiming the gospel of the kingdom, and healing every disease and every infirmity among the people. This synopsis clearly indicates that healing is prominent in the earthly mission of Jesus. Matthew reserves a good section (chaps. 8–9) to stories of miracles. This section is preceded by the Sermon on the Mount, a new teaching brought by Jesus (chaps. 5–7). One could argue that miracles are thus another form of teaching. With the same authority, Jesus speaks and acts, heals, forgives, and casts out demons. The first group of miracles in Matthew 8 includes mentions of three specific healings and one multiple healing, ending with a quote of accomplishment: "that it might be fulfilled which was spoken through Isaiah the prophet, saying: He took our infirmities, and bore our diseases" (Matt. 8:17; cf. Isa. 53:4). The

---

[2] M. Hebga présente plusieurs types d'explication du phénomène de guérisons. Il en distingue quatre: l'explication par l'exotérisme et le symbole; l'explication sociologique et psychologique; l'explication para-psychologique; l'explication métaphysique et religieuse. Bien vouloir lire son article "Sorcellerie et maladies en Afrique Noire. Jalon pour une approche catéchétique et pastorale," *Téléma* 4 (1982): 23–30.

[3] W. Kasper, *Jésus le Christ* (Paris: Cerf, 1980), 127.

[4] C. Kolié, "Jésus guérisseur," in *Chemins de la christologie africaine* (Mame-Desclee, 2001), col. "Jésus et Jésus-Christ," 168.

second part of Matthew 9 ends with the look of pity that Jesus throws to the crowds, together with the invitation to pray to the Lord of the Harvest to send out laborers (Matt. 9:36–37). From this, it appears that the healing miracles in Matthew's Gospel are primarily a visible sign of the reign of the kingdom and the fulfillment of the messianic promises announced in the Old Covenant. The purpose of Matthew is to give his readers instructions and catechesis on Jesus, whose actions and words have a meaning for the completion and the coming of the kingdom. In other words, it is not the miracle in itself that matters, but rather the faith in the one who performs: Jesus, Christ and Lord.[5] Thus, from the Matthean perspective, the miracles that Jesus Christ performed were works of mercy, and the Servant of God was thus fulfilling the promises of the Old Testament:[6] "Go and tell John the things which he hears and sees: the blind receive their sight, and the lame walk, the lepers are cleansed, and the deaf hear, and the dead are raised up, and the poor have good tidings preached to them" (11:4–5).

Mark

The miracles in the Gospel of Mark involve four aspects: they simultaneously proclaim the reign of God, they are effective signs of the Messiah, they announce the Passion, and they foreshadow the mission of the church. Indeed, the miracles in Mark's Gospel are intimately linked to Jesus's proclamation of the good news of the kingdom by Jesus. The first chapters of Mark are the illustration of the fundamental message about the reign of God, proclaimed by Jesus Christ (see Mark 1:14–15). But the reign of God is not imposed by force or by signs that alienate human freedom. The kingdom of God is only possible through faith, which explains why Jesus refuses to do miracles where there is no faith. Faith is requested or recognized by Jesus, as shown in most miracles. Examples include the healing of the paralytic (2:5), the healing of the woman afflicted with hemorrhages and the resurrection of Jairus's daughter (5), the healing of the daughter of a Syrophoenician (7:29–30), and the healing of the blind Bartimaeus (10:52).

This faith allows us to see Jesus's miracles, not as *terrata*—that is to say, sensational and magical acts—but rather *dunameis*, acts that demonstrate the power and warmth of God in human misery. Such acts include the founding of a new humanity, acts of salvation and the path from the captive state to the delivered state, acts shattering the evil—in short, acts that establish Jesus as the Divine Savior who destroys the kingdom of Satan and establishes for good the Kingdom of God: "The time is fulfilled, and the kingdom of God is at hand" (Mark 1:15).

---

[5] R. Latourelle, *Miracles de Jésus et théologie du miracle* (Paris: Cerf, 1986), 105.
[6] Ibid., 289.

Luke

Luke's intention in writing the Gospel is expressed in the prologue (1:1–4). He decided to write, for his dear Theophilus, a presentation of the events that were fulfilled among them, according to what was recounted to them by eyewitnesses. Theophilus, who was supportive of Luke's ministry, becomes aware of Jesus's teachings and actions. The Gospel of Luke is therefore a narrative of the events as they occurred. These events relate to Jesus and took place in Jerusalem for the salvation of humanity. Luke clearly wants to present Jesus as the Savior, the one through whom God's salvation is given to us. This salvation already emerges through the signs, miracles, and healing that Jesus performed. In Luke's Gospel (and in Mark's, as already discussed), miracles and healing occur within the teaching of Jesus, showing their intimate connection with the power of his word (4:36). This same connection is apparent with the healings of the demoniac, Simon's mother-in-law (4:31–38), the paralytic (5:17–26), the man with the withered hand (6:6–11), and the servant of the centurion (7:1–10).

Miracles in Luke's Gospel therefore serve to demonstrate and clarify the power of the Word of God. Luke speaks in fact of the *dunamis*, the power of God that acts within human weakness, God's power that lifts up and revives. Before the deployment of this *dunamis*, the crowds exclaims, "A great prophet has come to us! God has come to help his people" (Luke 7:16). The miracle in Luke's Gospel is thus an act of Jesus, who went around doing good (Acts 10:38), an act of Jesus as a Savior who proclaims the victory of good over evil, and an act of God whose Son demonstrates his reign (Luke 11:20). This act of salvation calls for the faith of the one who benefits from it. This is, in reality, the saving faith (Luke 17:19) that allows us to see, through the miracle, the salvation that will reach our whole being, where we see our God as he is (cf. 1 John 3:2; 1 Cor. 13:12).

John

John uses a specific vocabulary to talk about the healing miracles. For him they are *semeia* (signs). In the fourth Gospel, the sign is a gesture that shows the current glory of Jesus and prefigures the glory that will appear when his time comes. From the seven notable signs of the fourth Gospel, three relate to healing: the healing of the son of a royal official (4:46–54), the healing of the paralytic (5:1–9), and the healing of the man born blind (chap. 9). The return to life of Lazarus (11:1–44) can also be added to this list. I consider here the story of the man born blind, paying particular attention to its context, structure, and Christological significance.[7]

---

[7] D. Mollat, "La guérison de l'aveugle-né," *BVC* 23 (1958): 22–31; J. Bligh, "Four Studies in John I: The Man Born Blind," *Heythrop Journal* 7 (1966): 129–44; B. Grigsby,

The main episode of what is called the "Book of Signs" in John's Gospel (chaps. 1–12), the man-born-blind narrative, is developed by two self-revelations of Jesus: "I am the light of the world" (8:12) and "I am the good shepherd" (10:11).

Jesus is the light of the world. We must start from the prologue (1:4–5, 9; cf. 3:19) to understand this revelation. Here, Jesus is the Word-Light who comes into the world to enlighten every man; it is the light that shines in the darkness and one that the darkness cannot stop. And since it is light, it can only walk with those who see—that is to say, those who are in the light because they believe in him. In this broader context, the episode of the healing of the man born blind (chap. 9) is to be placed. Jesus is the light that illuminates the darkness of desolate humanity; he gives man the knowledge of the meaning of life. A parallel must be drawn between this and the account in Genesis 1:3. The first creative act of God was light: "Let there be light, and there was light." God created light first to illuminate the earth that was dim, empty, and covered with darkness (Gen. 1:2). Moreover, the light as the first creation of God supports his creative action and illuminates it from beginning to end. Therefore it is also in light that man is created. And Jesus's mission is to restore this divine creative authority: "While I am in the world, I am the light of the world" (John 9:5).

Jesus is the good shepherd. The image of the shepherd is common in the biblical tradition. Abraham was a nomadic shepherd (Gen. 13:2) and David was also one in Bethlehem (1 Sam. 16:11; 2 Sam. 7:8). The image of the shepherd has a double aspect. On the one hand, it is reminiscent of conduct and governance, and on the other hand it reminds us of care, hospitality, and tenderness. Only God can completely and fully fill the duty of the pastor. The most explicit and most complete text in this regard is Ezekiel 34. In the Gospel of John, Jesus adds a new aspect to the title of pastor. He is the good shepherd, alongside those who behave like mercenaries, with the sole desire to exploit the people and who run away at the slightest trouble, giving up the sheep (John 10:12–13). Jesus is the true shepherd and a pastor of truth who knows his sheep, who sacrifices himself for them, who gives his life for free for them and gives it to them in abundance (10:10; 14). Jesus is the shepherd who kindles and embraces all humanity with the unique sacrifice on the cross. His death and resurrection constitute the height of his offering to humanity as he continues to guide and feed his people through his church and the sacraments (cf. John 21:15–17; Matt. 28:19–20).

As the light of the world and the Good Shepherd, Jesus can only raise the man drowned in darkness and make him walk in the light of life. He heals the

---

"Washing in the Pool of Siloam: A Thematic Anticipation of the Johannine Cross," *Novum Testamentum* 27 (1985): 227–35; F. Manns, "L'évangile de Jean à la lumière du Judaïsme," *Analecta*, Jerusalem 33 (1991): 185–216.

born-blind, he erases the idea of a sin related to this evil, and he is the harbinger of a new world. Blindness (9:1–2, 39–41), sin (9:2–3, 41) and the coming of a new world (9:5, 39) form a triple inclusion at the beginning and at the end of the story, thus ensuring its unity.

The story's unity is also characterized by its dialogical structure:

9:1–7	Jesus's dialogue with the born-blind
9:8–12	Dialogue with citizens
9:13–17	First dialogue of the Pharisees with the one who can finally see
9:18–23	Pharisees' dialogue with parents
9:24–34	Second dialogue with the one who can finally see
9:35–38	Jesus's dialogue with the one who can finally see
9:39–41	Dialogue of Jesus with the Pharisees

A total of seven dialogues include the theme of sin (vv. 2–3, v. 41). The man born blind is not so because he has sinned—his parents even less—but so that the signs of God might be manifested through him. On the other side, the Pharisees are blind because of their sin of refusing to open up to the signs of God. What emerges as important is the openness to the signs of God, being able to read them and embrace them in order to be healed from evil and sin—to stand up again and walk following the one who is the light of the world and the Good Shepherd.

The Christological significance of the story appears clearly with the titles given to Jesus: Rabbi (v. 2), light (v. 5), man (vv. 11, 16), the prophet (v. 17), Christ (v. 22), the Son of Man (v. 35), and the Lord (v. 36). These titles are given to Jesus by himself and by all the characters in the story. Seven signs reveal the divine mission of Jesus, who came to establish a new order and a new humanity in which the one who believes in him sees the achievements of God and then goes from darkness to light, becoming a purified new being, so he finds again the original pride and dignity of the image of God that cannot be damaged or lost into the darkness of oblivion.

What Can Be Learned from Jesus's Miracles?

From all of the above, it is clear that miracles are acts of Christ to awaken humanity's faith and unity in Christ as the ultimate revealer of God's kingdom. Jesus preaches the reign of God. His preaching is nothing more than the proclamation of salvation offered to humankind. In his approach, which is that of God—God who offers free salvation to humankind—Jesus does not linger to link disease to sin nor to condemn the sick. Rather he remains in the dynamic of God's reign, which wants to expunge every form of evil and violence by way of love, forgiveness, and hospitality.

The healing miracles that Jesus performs are at the service of these values. In this sense, miracles are an exceptional grace offered by God in his infinite love and mercy. These founding miracles emphasize the advent of a new world, established by Jesus. His miracles reflect the goodness and love of God for people, and express the salvation that Jesus brought.

Ultimately, the miracles of Jesus are not to be considered as sensational illustrations or demonstrations of a therapeutic power from another world, aiming to strike the imagination of common people. They are bound to his word, which is strength and joy, truth and life, and that allows the entry into the divine logic of the gift of salvation—which is the whole essence of the gospel. The question for the church in Africa, then, is: Will Jesus still do the things he once did on the roads of Galilee and Judea? Does he still do it today and especially in Africa? Can we expect to come out of the darkness of the AIDS disease with him?

The Reality of AIDS in Africa and Its Cure

Only a few years ago, an individual infected with HIV had no option except death.[8] The statistics that have been given are grim: one death every eleven seconds, a contamination every six seconds. However, considerable progress has been made in research since the virus was identified. The number of new cases of HIV infection and deaths associated with this virus have fallen significantly (34.2 million people infected in 2012). Treatment programs have been developed rapidly, accompanied by an unprecedented increase in the number of people receiving antiretroviral drugs and other lifesaving treatments.[9] It is possible today to live with the virus or the disease, because with treatment, AIDS has become a chronic condition that can be managed with proper care.

While these developments also apply to Africa, the real problem many people face on the continent remains shame and stigma associated with the disease. One finds very little or nothing said about it in some villages. The subject is still avoided, and families hush up the truth. In many parts of Africa, HIV has been known by other names, such as "slow poison," "night poison," "fate," "witchcraft," and "diabolical possession." The victims are often encouraged by prophets and dishonest advisers to avoid facing the truth, refuse to check into a hospital, but pathetically throw themselves into the arms of so-called healers who have no moral or religious boundaries and claim they can cure the above-mentioned ills. The obvious consequence is that the "death woman" continues to spread fear and horror in Africa, sometimes decimating

---

[8] OMS (Organisation Mondiale de la Santé), Quatorzième conférence international sur le SIDA, Barcelone du 07 au 12 juillet 2002.

[9] See OMS, *La stratégie mondiale du secteur de la santé sur le VIH/SIDA 2011/2015: intérimaire des progrès: rapport abrégé*, mai 2014.

families. So we repeat it to ourselves in Africa: AIDS is a pernicious and dangerous ill, tedious and disturbing from a mental, social, spiritual, psychological, and physical point of view. It must be taken seriously by trusting medical science, in a context in which many people rightly appreciate the teachings of the New Testament about healing.

One of the major recommendations of the Second Vatican Council was to place the Word of God in the heart of all church activities and all the Christian faithful.[10] This was done in order to establish more concrete involvement in biblical ministry, more interest in existential questions of mankind, so that the Word of God would be at the heart and soul of every ministry dedicated to humanity in each individual's struggle for dignity as a child of God.

The Post-Synodal Apostolic Exhortation *Verbum Domini* does not stray from this dynamic replacement of the Word of God at the center of questions and problems regarding the current and concrete life of humanity. It invites the training of experts in the word of God who could be sensitive to different contexts in which to deploy this Word.[11] One of these contexts is naturally that of human health. We must give back to the Word of God the eternal privilege to be a complete and total healing force. The Word of God feeds and nourishes all human activity. It alone is a source of incomparable and unsurpassable truth propounded for the life of men; it directs and shapes human action; it alone is "listened to and celebrated, especially in the Eucharist, feeds and internally strengthens Christians and makes them capable of authentic testimonial to the gospel in everyday life."[12] The Word of God heals man, saves him, and gives him salvation. It restores salvation in him, his social environment, and his trust in God. The dignity of human life is thus based on the power of the Word of God, and not on that which is offered by traditional and religious healers in Africa. AIDS may indeed be reconsidered under this prism, radiating from the trust in God and his Word that heals and restores to man his pride and dignity, created in the image and likeness of God (Gen. 1:26–27).

The Mission of the Church in Africa

Rooted in the Word of God, the church in Africa today has a difficult mission with regard to HIV and AIDS: to help those made miserable and desperate by the disease to focus on Jesus Christ, to enter in the mystery of the One who sacrificed himself on the cross for their salvation and move forward in the hope of entering with him into the Father's glory. One of the tasks of the

---

[10] Second Vatican Council, *Dei Verbum* (Dogmatic Constitution on Divine Revelation), no. 21.

[11] Benedict XVI, Post-Synodal Apostoloic Exhortation, *Verbum Domini*, no. 75.

[12] Francis, Apostolic Exhortation, *Evangelii Gaudium*, no. 174.

church in Africa is the commitment to hospitality, consideration, and integration of AIDS sufferers by relying on the words of Jesus: "Come to me, all you who are struggling hard and carrying heavy loads, and I will give you rest. Put on my yoke, and learn from me. I'm gentle and humble. And you will find rest for yourselves" (Matt. 11:28–30).

The task of pastors and guides of the church in Africa is to work, tirelessly and without petty ambitions, for those who are weak, suffering, and destitute, to restore the dignity they deserve by making the effort to look at them with the eyes of Jesus—that is, to see with love. The church can accomplish this mission with the assurance of the permanent presence of the risen Lord (Matt. 28:20) and the active, invigorating and fortifying presence of the Holy Spirit (cf. Acts 4:8; 5:32; 8:26; 9:31; 11:24–28; 16:6–7; 20:22–23).[13] Only in this context can the apostolic workers and influential groups act in consideration of the humanity of the weak and the sick. They have the sacrosanct duty, as disciples of Christ, to remain mindful to the breath of the Spirit of the Lord and to guide their actions toward their purpose: the salvation of God, whose words are healing and salvation.[14] Exorcisms and prayers for healing and deliverance will therefore only have meaning in this context (cf. Matt. 10:1–9; Mark 6:7–13; Luke 9:49–50);[15] if they move away or recede, it is reasonable to suspect them of "spiritual embezzlement" and rank them among those whose aim is personal enrichment. We must move away from these chapels of spiritual nuisance, which are said to cure AIDS by the vicious and ritualistic use of the sacraments and sacramental rites.[16]

In this regard, we must reiterate that the Word of God must be at the center of health care, not the gesticulation and magical conjuring of an isolated exorcist, miracle maker, prophet, or healer. The true role of the church and pastors in Africa is to make Jesus Christ present among those suffering with AIDS. The church and pastors must tell the sufferers about Jesus Christ, who has the power to offer healing as a grace and a free gift of salvation. The church and pastors must also give the sufferers Jesus Christ in the Eucharist and the other sacraments (i.e., penance and anointing the sick). In addition, the church and pastors must also demonstrate the healing grace and salvation of Jesus Christ through

---

[13] John Paul II, Encyclical Letter, *Redemptoris Missio* (1990), nos. 21, 24, 28–29; Second Vatican Council, *Ad Gentes* (Decree on the Missionary Activity of the Church, 1965), no. 4.

[14] Patrick Adeso, *Fullness Is Holiness: A Biblical, African Spirituality for the Third Millennium* (Yaoundé: Presses de l'UCAC, 2001), 140.

[15] See Vumukaku Nanga, "Guérison et exorcisme, réflexion théologique dans une perspective pastorale," *Telema* 85 (1996): 48; N. Yaovi Soede, "Prêtres et prière de guérison," in *Année Sacerdotale: Pour maintenir la flamme*, ed. P. Bitjick Likeng (Yaoundé: Presses de l'UCAC, 2012), 73.

[16] Soede, "Prêtres et prière de guérison," 75.

their hospitality, listening, dialogue, assistance, spiritual and educational talks, the fight for rehabilitation, reconciliation and reintegration of patients in their community and family, concrete acts of charity, and more. In this way we will gradually overcome the "fatalization" and "demonization" of AIDS, a disease that should be no more harmful than malaria, tuberculosis, yellow fever, or hepatitis, and even now is less deadly than the Ebola virus and many others.

CHAPTER 9

BIBLICAL NARRATIVES ON SICKNESS AND AIDS PATIENTS' STORIES

The Case of Psalm 38

Conrad A. Folifack D.

In the Hebrew Bible, sickness is rarely described or narrated from the patient's perspective. In many instances, sickness appears in relation to healing, law, conversion, and the need for faithfulness to God. Rarely is the patient given the opportunity to say a word on the predicament of being sick. Only in the book of Job and in the Psalms does one find discourses about sickness and suffering where the patients can personally narrate their suffering. The book of Job in particular has emerged as the central scriptural resource for books and articles on HIV and AIDS in Africa.[1] Therefore scant attention has been given to psalms in biblical research in relation to AIDS in Africa. Sigmund Mowinckel, a leading scholar in the classification of the psalms, has identified a category of Psalms of Lament that echo the experience of suffering in sickness: which include Psalm 6:32 (also a penitential psalm, vv. 3–4); 38 (vv. 3, 5, 7, 17); 39 (v. 3); 41 (v. 3); and also 22 (vv. 6, 14–16); 28 (v. 1); 30 (thanksgiving for healing, v. 2), and 88 (vv. 4–6). This chapter concentrates on Psalm 38 because it seems to present a greater prospect of offering the best insight into the sufferings, feelings, and story of the patient.

---

[1] Madipoane J. Masenya, "Between Unjust Suffering and the 'Silent' God: Job and HIV/AIDS Sufferers in South Africa," *Missionalia* 29, no. 2 (2001): 186–99; Sarojini Nadar, "Re-reading Job in the Midst of Suffering in the HIV/AIDS Era: How Not to Talk of God?" *Old Testament Essays* 16, no. 2 (2003): 343–57; Van Dyk Peet, "The Tale of Two Tragedies: The Book of Job and HIV/AIDS in Africa," *BOSTA*, no. 16 (2004): 7–13; Ghislain Tshikendwa Matadi, *De l'absurdité de la souffrance à l'espérance: Une lecture du livre de Job en temps de VIH/SIDA* (Kinshasa: MediasPaul, 2004); *From Human Suffering to Human Hope: Reading the Book of Job from the African Context of Suffering in Times of HIV/AIDS* (Berkeley: Jesuit School of Theology, 2001).

How does a sick person perceive his or her relationship with God? As Gutierrez puts it, what does he or she say about God in such a situation of suffering?[2] This study analyzes the narrative discourse in the time of sickness in Psalm 38. In general, psalms belong to poetry, and so it may seem quite surprising to refer to them as narratives. Psalms of sickness belong to the Psalms of Lament, which can be personal or national. They echo human distress in various ways: sickness, uncleanliness, sin, and fear of death.[3] The main characteristic of the Psalms of Lament is that one finds always a "shorter or longer description" or narration of distress before God.[4] Therefore, although they belong to poetry, psalms are not, as asserted by Robert Alter, completely "purified of narrative elements."[5] In relation to narrative, Alter distinguishes the following semantic connections between verses in biblical poetic compositions: synonymy with or without verbatim repetition; complementarity; the movement of focusing, heightening, intensification, and specification; and finally consequentiality.[6] Yet one can find in biblical poetry other narrative features, such as time progression or the notion of sequentiality, which may be characterized by a movement from cause to effect,[7] or by verbs marking action.[8]

The study attempts to demonstrate how Psalm 38 can serve to enlighten the plight of a person who is living with HIV (PLWH). The first part of this chapter uses semantic connections between verses to demonstrate how they unfold narrative elements and highlight the change in relationship patterns (with God and neighbor) in situations of sickness. The second part highlights the connection that exists between Psalm 38 and narratives of PLWH to demonstrate how stigmatization can be used to foster a process of identification between the sick persons in the psalms and PLWH. The third part concentrates on the use of this psalm as a source of spiritual nourishment for a person who is living with HIV.

The Sick Person in Psalm 38

Identifying a psalm as relating to sickness is not always easy, because people in ancient times had a much wider notion of sickness than our modern understanding. As Mowinckel puts it, illness "does not cover a medical pathological

---

[2] Gustavo Gutiérrez, *Job: Parler de Dieu à partir de la souffrance de l'innocent* (Paris: Cerf, 1987).

[3] Sigmund Mowinckel, *The Psalms in Israel's Worship*, vol. 2 (Oxford: Basil Blackwell, 1967), 16.

[4] Ibid., 196.

[5] Robert Alter, *The Art of Biblical Poetry* (New York: Basic Books, 1985), 27–28.

[6] Ibid., 29.

[7] Ibid., 38.

[8] Ibid., 44.

notion"; rather, it describes a psychological state of distress, "low spirit, sorrow, shame, in which someone finds himself because he has been hit deep within into what constitutes his 'honor and vitality.'"[9] Therefore, not every psalm has a mere mention of sickness or healing that can be called a psalm of illness. Psalm 38 echoes the petition of a patient suffering from a severe malady, but it is also "a complaint, a confession of sin, a supplication for deliverance from enemies, and a subtle denial of responsibility."[10] Despite this variety of themes, the psalm obviously portrays a person with "ill health" and offers a "compelling illustration" of the way sickness is considered in the psalms, "not as a clinical phenomenon but as a personal experience."[11] Sickness is described physically and psychologically, sociologically and theologically.[12] Therefore, sickness affects the relationship with oneself, one's neighbor, and God.

Physical and Psychological Distress

In a psalm of sickness, the distress is both physical and psychological. The description of sickness moves from a general to a more detailed presentation. The psalm opens (38:4a) with an affirmation about the state of physical health, which is repeated later on (v. 8b). The phrase, "there is no soundness (məṭōm) in my flesh," in v. 4a is paralleled with a similar one (v. 4b), "there is no peace (šälôm) in my bones ('ṣmy)." The pair of words məṭōm and šalôm derive from roots (*tmm* and *šlm*) that express completeness, wholeness, soundness. The soundness concerns the completeness of the physical being, both flesh and bones. The absence of soundness is due to God's anger (v. 4a) and to sin (v. 4b). But the direct cause of the absence of soundness is the evil deeds of one's enemies, in verses 20a and 21b, where one finds the same pair of words as in verse 4b.[13] *There is no peace* (šälôm) *in my bones* ('ṣmy) (v. 4b) forms a ring with *my enemies are strong* (v. 20a: 'ṣm) and *they repay* (v. 21b: šälam) *evil for good*.

Then the sick person goes on explaining in detail the absence of soundness. The sick body is covered with *wounds* (HaBBûrötäy: v. 6a) and he suffers a *plague* (*nega*': v. 12a). The substantive *nega*' is a general term used for *an affliction* of various kinds (1 Kgs. 8:37), but it also means a bodily harm to be judged

---

[9] Mowinckel, *The Psalms in Israel's Worship*, 16.

[10] Samuel Terrien, *The Psalms: Strophic Structure and Theological Commentary*, vol. 1, *Psalms 1–72*, Critical Eerdmans Commentary (Grand Rapids: Eerdmans, 2002), 325.

[11] James Luther Mays, *Psalms: Interpretation*, A Bible Companion for Teaching and Preaching (Louisville, KY: Westminster John Knox Press, 1994), 162.

[12] Ibid.

[13] J. P. Fokkelman, *Major Poems of the Hebrew Bible: At the Interface of Prosody and Structural Analysis*, vol. 2, *85 Psalms and Job 4–14*, Studia Semitica Neerlandica (Assen: Van Gorcum, 2000), 145.

by the Levitical priest (Deut. 21:5). The third meaning is the association of *neḡa'* with leprosy, especially in Leviticus, where the noun *neḡa'* occurs sixty-one times. But the problem is that the expression, *neḡa' ṣārā 'at* is used as a "technical term for various kinds of skin diseases" (Lev. 13:2, 29; 14:3, 32), including leprosy (Lev. 13–14).[14] The symptoms showing that one suffers from *neḡa' ṣārā 'at* are swelling, eruptions, or spots. Also, someone suffering from leprosy and identified as such should be isolated from the community (Lev. 13:3, 45). The sick person in Psalm 38 is suffering from wounds that are rotting and festering, and seems likely to be someone excluded from the community (v. 12).

More than a few scholars have argued that the sick person is suffering from some kind of sickness that is akin to leprosy. But scholars do not agree with a precise identification of the disease in Psalm 38 as leprosy. As P. Craige suggests, the diagnosis of the sickness, despite the existence of some symptoms of leprosy, "draw[s] together the symptoms of a variety of afflictions to portray human condition in sickness. . . . The breadth of the description makes this psalm more appropriate for general usage as a prayer."[15] It is possible that the sick person is afflicted by such a sickness, but "its universal appeal lies in its applicability to the experience of sickness that so many undergo."[16] Yet the language seems "hyperbolic"[17] and not realistic. "The psalmist portrays his suffering, which he believes to be the consequence of his sin. . . . But it must be obvious to any reader that no one in the terrible condition he describes would be fit to recite this psalm as a prayer, let alone to compose it."[18]

Indeed, the sickness is portrayed with realism. The wounds that stink have become odious (v. 6). They putrefy and rot, leaving a strong smell, which might eventually chase away even loved ones, friends, and neighbors (v. 12). The mention of burning loins refers either to fever or to the causes of wounds as an internal infection creating pain (v. 8). Loins and flesh are expressions of the inner and outer man, "seat of procreative power and a symbol of strength and vitality."[19] The heart is also affected. Mentioned twice, it beats (v. 11a) or is in a state of agitation (v. 9b). The result of the festering and rotting wounds and the burning loins is sighing (v. 10b) and groaning (v. 9b).

---

[14] M. Delcor, "*neḡa' to touch*," in *Theological Lexicon of the Old Testament*, vol. 2, ed. Ernst Jenni and Claus Westermann (Peabody, MA: Hendrickson, 1997), 718.

[15] P. C. Craige, *Psalm 1–50*, Word Biblical Commentary (Waco, TX: Word Books, 1983), 304; Allen P. Pross, *A Commentary on the Psalms*, vol. 1, *1–41*, Kregel Exegetical Academy (Grand Rapids: Kregel, 2011), 38; Marc Girard, *Les Psaumes: Analyse structurelle et interpretation* (Montreal: Bellarmin, 1984), 312.

[16] Craige, *Psalm 1–50*, 304.

[17] Pross, *Commentary on the Psalm*, 822.

[18] J. W. Rogerson and J. W. McKay, *Psalms 1–50*, Cambridge Bible Commentary, New English Bible (London: Cambridge University Press, 1977), 38.

[19] Rogerson and McKay, *Psalms 1–50*, 182.

As a result of the strong pain, the sick person cannot stand. He is bowed down (v. 7), feeble, utterly crushed (v. 9a), and devoid of any strength (v. 11b). The fact of *being bent* shows a connection between the patient's psychological state and his physical condition.[20] This impression of being bowed down and crushed by sickness is proof that the sick person is overloaded by a malady that has become a burden. The faithful one is crushed by sickness in the same way that sin and iniquity do (v. 5). Indeed the sick person establishes a relationship between the absence of wholeness and sin (v. 4b). Verses 5, 7, and 9, as Fokkelman puts it, are connected by "the concept of being overwhelmed, where illness, burden, and guilt merge into each other."[21]

So we can conclude that "the psalmist's sickness is never specified, his unfaithful friends and his enemies lack definition, and his illness cannot be diagnosed."[22] With this unspecific description of sickness, the psalm is open to use by any believer in the same situation.

Sickness and Social Relationships

The pain suffered is also sociological. The social network from which the sick suffer ostracism is made up of the "inner cycle" of friends and relatives and of the "outer cycle" that comprises one's enemies. The sick person is socially isolated by loved ones, friends, and intimate neighbors who stand away from him (v. 12). His situation is comparable to that of Job, who is abandoned by brothers, friends, neighbors, relatives, servants, and even his wife (Job 19:13–19).[23]

The outer cycle of relationships is made up of enemies who appear twice in the psalm. In verse 13, their deeds are described with a vocabulary that identifies them as responsible for the sickness. The description uses a set of verbs of action that form a narrative sequence. They *lay* (*nāqaš*) traps, they *seek* (*bāqaš*) his life, and they *seek* (*dāraš*) evil to befall the sick; they *speak* (*dābar*) about destruction, and *plan* (*hāgah*) fraud. So the enemies *plan* or *seek*, *speak*, and *lay*, touching the three areas of human capacity to sin: the mind, words, and actions (v. 13). They would rejoice if the sick should stumble (vv. 17–18a). In verses 20–21, the perpetrators of such evil actions are characterized with more specifications. They are named as enemies (v. 20a: *'ôyēb*) and adversaries (v. 21b: *sāṭan*), meaning those who are hostile toward the sick. The enemies characterized as the strong (*'ṣm*), full of undue hatred, and especially concerned with active evil, repaying evil instead of good, may be identified as the wicked. Despite their wickedness, it is doubtful whether the enemies may be considered

[20] Terrien, *Psalms*, 326.
[21] Fokkelman, *Major Poems of the Hebrew Bible*, 145.
[22] Rogerson and McKay, *Psalms 1–50*, 312.
[23] Terrien, *Psalms*, 327.

as the authors of the sickness. The enemies rather take advantage of the situation of sickness to mock the one who is suffering. It is God who causes the sickness, as one can perceive in verse 2, where the faithful one prays to be spared from God's fury and anger.

The predicament is also characterized by the impossibility of communication, and as such the sick person is isolated and lonely. He is like a dumb and deaf person. The words uttered against him are not only aimed at provoking him but also to drive him to despair. As he remains still, God will respond for him (cf. vv. 15b and 16).[24] This predicament of the sick person in social relations can be labeled as stigmatization.

Sickness and Sin

In the middle of the torment undergone by the sick person, the consciousness of his sinfulness becomes more evident and is expressed in three instances. The first reference to sin is found in verses 2–3, where the sick person prays to be spared from God's anger. If God is angry and fiery, it is because sickness is considered as a consequence of sin, breaking the harmony between the afflicted person and God. The consequence of this anger is described by the image of an arrow and God's hand crushing the sick (v. 3). The images of the hand pressing and the arrow piercing invoke the image of God as an archer, a warrior (cf. Ps. 7:21).[25] After the loss of all of his children and property, and after he is struck by a malign ulcer, Job describes God by using military images (Job 10:17; 19:12).

More specifically, the sick person speaks about his sins in three instances using the same pair of words, sin (vv. 4b, 19: *Hattā't* and iniquities (vv. 5a, 19: *'āwôn*). The two words seem synonymous, but according to their specific meaning, iniquity or guilt (*'āwôn*) is rather a consequence of sin (*Hattā't*). The word *Hattā't*, which belongs mostly to the priestly language,[26] is the theological term in the Old Testament that is most used in relation to sin or error, in terms of violation of God's norms.[27] In v. 4b, *Hattā't* causes lack of soundness in the body, and in v. 19 psychological pain that is anxiety arising from being separated from God. One can say that sin (*Hattā't*) is the cause of total disharmony, both physical and psychological.

The other word for sin is *'āwôn*, which is translated *perversity* or *iniquities* and occurs in verses 5a and 19a. But the correct translation should be *guilt* or *punishment*. The word derives from a verb *'āwah* that means *to curve, to twist,*

---

[24] M. Mannati, *Les psaumes 2* (Paris: Cahiers de la Pierre-qui vire, 1967), 65.

[25] Rogerson and McKay, *Psalms 1–50*, 181.

[26] R. Knierim, " *ajx ḥāṭa' to miss*," in *Theological Lexicon of the Old Testament*, vol. 1, ed. Ernst Jenni and Claus Westermann (Peabody, MA: Hendrickson, 1997), 407.

[27] Ibid., 410.

or *to turn aside*. Then there is the meaning *to bend, to pervert* (Piel), and *to transgress*. The basic meaning of this verb *to bend, to curve*, is used in verse 7a, where using the same root (*ʿāwah*), the sick person expresses the fact that he is "is bent." The link between act and consequence leads sometimes to the translation of *ʿāwôn* by *transgression, perversity*, or *iniquity*.[28] But as a theological term, *ʿāwôn* must be used in a dynamic way to designate a *guilty process* caused by sin from which God must deliver the sinner.[29] Guiltiness (vv. 5a, 19) caused by sin (vv. 4b, 19) leads to the psychological feeling of being bent (v. 7a). The psychological consideration given to the word *ʿāwôn* leads to the metaphor of weight and length used also in verse 5b. Indeed, in his situation, it's not as sin such that causes pain to the sinner, but rather the psychological effect of guiltiness, which has become heavier than what he can actually carry and higher than his normal height. Therefore the fact of being utterly crushed is not physical so much as psychological. In verse 19, the guiltiness, *ʿāwôn*, is a weight so psychologically heavy that the sick is compelled to speak out (*nāgad*). After confession, the person's consciousness is freed from any guilt or culpability. Liberated from the feeling of guiltiness, he can turn to God in confidence as a Savior and a Helper.

Then, in verse 6, sin is also called folly.[30] The word for *folly* (*ʾuwwelet*) belongs to the language of the sages and is an attitude typical of the fool (*ʾewil*) who is the opposite of the wise (Prov. 1:7). This lack of wisdom (v. 6a) not only expresses sinful behavior (vv. 5a, 19a) but is also its cause.

This psalm underlines the connection between sin and sickness, considering sickness as a punishment from God. The description of sin portrays a kind of predicament that is not only physical but also psychological: the fact of being separated from God is added to the social isolation from close ones. This connection between sin and sickness appears in many other psalms: 6:1; 32:3–5; 39:10–11; 41:4; 88:7, 16; 107:17–22; and 103:3.[31]

Sickness and Relation to God

The description of distress in this psalm, whether physical or psychological, alternates with the three references to God. In verses 2 and 3, the prayer of the psalmist expresses a very dark image of God. In the formulaic supplication in the form of parallelism used in verse 2 (also found in Ps. 6:2),[32] God is charac-

---

[28] Knierim, "*ʿāwôn, perversity*," in *Theological Lexicon of the Old Testament*, vol. 2, ed. Ernst Jenni and Claus Westermann (Peabody, MA: Hendrickson, 1997), 864.

[29] Ibid., 865.

[30] Girard, *Les Psaumes*, 308. The fool is not psychopathologically sick but someone whose behavior is, because of the lack of wisdom, morally questionable.

[31] Mays, *Psalms*, 163.

[32] Robert Alter, *The Book of Psalms* (London: W. W. Norton and Company, 2007), 134.

terized as someone angry (*qeṣph*), hot-tempered (*ḥemāh*), and violent, who like a warrior or archer, uses an arrow or his hand to pierce, crush, or mash down. From arrow to hand, God moves from the use of an instrument, the arrow, to the involvement of his physical person, using his hand. This intensification of anger is evident also through the use of words in v. 2; *ḥemāh*, which means *heat* (then the metaphorical use for anger), shows the process of anger that moves to *qeṣeph*, which is actually anger. The sick man is asking to be spared from this angry and violent God because of the intensity of his distress (vv. 4–9).

Verse 10 opens with a move toward God. The sick person expresses his desire and sighing, which has become a continuous prayer for a quick recovery, hiding a clear expression of hope. The description of suffering that follows is more psychological and echoes the stigmatization the person is going through from close ones (v. 12) and from enemies (v. 13), and also loneliness (vv. 14–15). Despite this predicament, in verse 16, there is a clear expression of hope and confidence in God, who is named in the first person: my God. God is no longer the violent warrior (v. 2) but the one who inspires hope (v. 16a: yäHal) that the prayer will be answered (v. 16b). Despite the acknowledgment of his iniquities, a positive self-esteem arises. The sick person recognizes that he is a good man (v. 21), although pursued by enemies who are still active (alive) and in great number (v. 20).

In verses 22–23, the violent and angry God, the archer, is the one who is close at hand (v. 22), the Helper and the Salvation. The sick person, in the final supplication that parallels the initial request to be spared (v. 2), does not ask for healing but for salvation and help. He needs to be saved from the guilt and culpability that oppress him. More than healing, what the psalmist needs is to be restored in a genuine relationship to God (v. 22b). Even though there is no sign of healing as in Psalm 38, trust and hope in God emerge gradually and are able to transform the way in which the burdens of physical and psychological distress are borne. That is the journey PLWH are invited to undertake.

Psalm 38 and Narratives of People Living with HIV

PLWH can easily identify with the patient of this psalm. Indeed, the links between the predicament of the sick one in Psalm 38 and a person living with HIV are many: some bodily symptoms described in the sickness look like those of AIDS, the irresponsible sexual behavior (sin and sickness) that sometimes leads to infection, the stigmatization and discrimination affecting many PLWH. Here we focus on one of the main characteristics of Psalm 38—stigma—and evaluate the possibility for a person living with HIV to pray with this psalm.

Stigmatization appears in terms of isolation, injustice, hatred, and persecution in Psalm 38. The people with stigmatizing behaviors are not only those close to the sick one but also enemies or adversaries. The sick one suffers isolation from kin, loved ones, neighbors, and friends who stay away from him (v. 12). This situation transforms him into a social outcast. But the isolation is also spiritual, involving separation from God (v. 22b). The sick person experiences persecution, injustice, and hatred (v. 20) from outsiders called enemies or adversaries who take advantage of his situation to speak or devise deceitful things and destruction against him (v. 13). The consequence of stigma is silence and the incapacity to argue or counterattack. Indeed, the sick man is like one who is dumb, who cannot open his mouth, and who finds no argument to answer his adversaries (vv. 14b, 15b). Stigma remains one of the main problems for PLWH, although it has received only scant attention in research on HIV and AIDS.[33]

Stigma's Manifestations and Causes

Harriet Deacon argues that the definition of disease stigma among social science researchers "owes much to Goffman (1963), who suggested that people who possess a characteristic defined as socially undesirable (such as HIV infection) acquire a 'spoiled identity,' which then leads to social devaluation and discrimination."[34] She then defines *stigma* as

> a fundamental emotional response to danger that helps people feel safer by projecting controllable risk, and therefore blame, onto out-groups. Stigmatization thus helps to create a sense of control and immunity from danger by an individual and at a group level. HIV-and AIDS-related stigma allows individuals to distance themselves from the other ("promiscuous," "gay," "black," "white," "non-religious," "young," "urban") people who are presumed to be at greater risk of contracting HIV because of their behavior.[35]

But discrimination and structural inequalities resulting from stigmatization can become possible only when particular circumstances enable them.[36] The definition of stigma corresponds to the situation of the sick person in Psalm 38, who suffers continuous blame and devaluation from enemies: "Those who want to harm me speak about destruction, and deceitful things, all the day long, they devise" (v. 13).

---

[33] Harriet Deacon, Leana Uys, and Rakgadi Mohlahlane, "HIV and Stigma in South Africa," in *HIV/AIDS South Africa 25 Years: On Psychosocial Perspectives*, ed. Paul Rohleder, Leslie Swartz, Seth C. Kalichman, and Leickness Chisamu Simbayi (New York: Springer, 2009), 105.

[34] Ibid., 106.

[35] Ibid.

[36] Ibid.

Stigma leveled against PLWH in Africa takes many forms: rejection of infected individuals; compulsory detection of those who have the virus without any guarantee of confidentiality; violence; discrimination of all kinds in recruitment, especially in those companies where workers benefit from medical coverage; rejection or exclusion from families and communities; divorce when a partner is found to be HIV-positive; refusal to register in school those children who are infected or affected; refusal to PLWH to enter some countries or expulsion from others. Everyday life is often populated with the refusal to greet PLWH or to share food, live in the same house, use the same toilets, or eat off the same dishes as PLWH. Abuses in hospitals or attempts against their physical integrity are also part of the daily life of PLWH. In some countries, even pregnant women or young mothers face discrimination in form of devalorization, indexation, and other abuses, especially when mothers decide not to breastfeed their babies.[37]

The causes of stigma vary.[38] Death from AIDS coupled with the fear of being infected and the possible sexually irresponsible behavior resulting in HIV lead people to adopt all kinds of attitudes against PLWH. Furthermore, widespread traditional and religious beliefs hold that HIV is punishment for a moral transgression.

In Psalm 38, not only do those who are close to the sick person reject him (v. 12), but he also faces hatred and injustice from those so-called enemies who stigmatize him. Indeed, they hate him wrongfully, repaying evil instead of good (vv. 20b, 21).

Stigma in the Narrative Discourses of People Living with HIV

In the narrative discourse of people living with HIV, stigma occurs in marital life, educational institutions, and communities. See their own words:

- If you are married, your husband can divorce you.
- Your kin refuse to eat what you have cooked, or refuse to eat in the same dish with you.
- In school, if your HIV-AIDS status is known, your children will also suffer, since they will be isolated.
- In the community you are often indexed and abused in words by some people.[39]

---

[37] Harris Cleaver Tombi, *Prévenir le VIH/Sida en Afrique Subsaharienne* (Paris: Edilivre, 2014), 76–88.

[38] Ibid., 78.

[39] Ibid.

In families, even when accepted, some people suffer constant blame and rejection leading to "isolation and alienation."[40] Busisiwe—a South African mother who together with her child, also HIV-positive, was tolerated in her mother's home—was blamed even in front of others for being "promiscuous":

> So, my mom embarrasses me with that [HIV] even in front of people because I'm HIV-positive. It makes me feel not at home, as if I'm lost. It makes me want to stay outside. Even when I've made a minor mistake like spilling sugar, she would say, 'This is because you are thinking of guys and AIDS and all that'. So you see those things hurt me. They make me realize that I'm alone, there is no one who would tell me not to worry.[41]

Busisiwe's mother is like one of the enemies in Psalm 38, who "speak about destruction, and deceitful things, all the day long, they devise" (v. 13b). Busisiwe is "like a dumb one who cannot open his mouth" (v. 14a) because, in the face of this onslaught of hatred, there is no argument (v. 15b). Besides discrimination, stigma has many other consequences, such as aggressive behaviors, sometimes the desire of PLWH to seek revenge by contaminating others, uneasiness, insecurity, isolation, silence, loss of self-confidence and self-esteem, stress, despair, and the desire to commit suicide.[42]

This stigma can also lead to criminal behavior. In South Africa, for example, PLWH have been murdered, ostensibly as a result of disclosure of their status. The most famous case is the murder of a 35-year-old woman who was killed in 1998, just three weeks after she revealed on a radio station her HIV status.[43]

On a wide scale, the impact of stigma is very damaging, as suggested by a 2009 study on HIV and stigma in South Africa: "Stigma and discrimination reduce the impact of prevention programs, inhibit treatment take-up and adherence, exacerbate the psycho-social effects of HIV infection, and reduce the quality of life of people living with HIV and AIDS."[44]

Praying with Psalm 38

For PLWH who face discrimination and stigma, Psalm 38 can become a way of recovering confidence and strength, through identifying with the

---

[40] Lumka Daniel and Corine Squire, "Experience of People Living with HIV," in Rohleder et al., *HIV/AIDS in South Africa 25 Years*, 259.

[41] Ibid.

[42] Tombi, *Prévenir le VIH/Sida en Afrique Subsaharienne*, 87.

[43] Deacon, Uys, and Mohlahlane, "HIV and Stigma in South Africa," 105.

[44] Ibid.

sick man of the psalm who is in a similar situation. Nevertheless, as James Mays suggests, one should be cautious in reading this as well as other psalms connecting sin to sickness[45] and offer a few insights that can direct the reading of and praying with this psalm.

First, God is the Lord over all aspects of human life, including sickness. Therefore, sickness should be seen as a clinical as well as a religious matter. God's purpose in afflicting a human may not be only punishment or correction but also "instruction, purification, or vicarious suffering."[46]

Second, Psalm 38 does not refer to a particular sin, but to the general condition of human sinfulness. Therefore, a severe sickness that leads a person close to death and the possibility of judgment can bring to light a person's sinfulness and make more urgent the need of grace. Nevertheless, notice that the book of Job, as well as the healing miracles in the Gospels, are an "eloquent protest" against the connection between ill health and sin. Job suffered in spite of his innocence.[47] Jesus affirms explicitly that there is no connection between sickness and the sick one (John 9:2–3). Yet he holds together forgiveness and healing (Mark 2:1–12) as an expression of complete soundness.

In any situation, the reading of Psalm 38, despite the references to punishment (vv. 2–3) and sin (vv. 4, 5, 6), should not bring despair to those people who have serious illnesses like AIDS, but rather reinforce trust and confidence as these people bring their predicament before God. Even though a person living with HIV might be rejected, God does not reject a soul who comes close to him with a contrite heart.

Conclusion

In this chapter I have examined the predicament of the sick person and how sickness affects such a person's relationships either with other human beings or with God. I have also identified stigmatization as one of the consequences of sickness. In the case of poor health caused by HIV, one may find Psalm 38 to be a source of comfort and consolation and learn how one can deal with sickness in faith and in relation to God. Indeed, the sick person is a human being who still deserves God's love, and who is also worthy of others' consideration, whereas stigmatization breaks social relationships and worsens the predicament of the sick. A relationship with God helps one to remain alive and strong, despite the various negative feelings and distress that HIV causes.

---

[45] Mays, *Psalms*, 164–65.

[46] Ibid.,164.

[47] Ibid.

Appendix: Translation of Psalm 38

Psalm of David, for remembrance.

¹ YHWH do not in your anger reproach me,
  nor in your wrath discipline me.

² For your arrow has pierced me,
  and your hand presses me down.

³ There is no soundness in my flesh
  because of your anger,

There is no completeness in my bones
  because of my sins.

⁴ For my iniquities have gone over my head,
  like a heavy burden,
  they are too heavy for me.

⁵ My wounds stink and⁴⁸ fester,
  because of my folly.

⁶ I am bent and greatly bowed down,
  all the day long, mourning,⁴⁹ I walk around.

⁷ For my loins are full with burning,
  and there is no soundness in my flesh.

⁸ I am feeble and utterly crushed,
  I groan because of the agitation of my heart.

⁹ ADONAÏ, before you [are] all my desires,
  and my sighing is not hidden from you.

¹⁰ My heart beat violently,⁵⁰ my strength has left me,
  and the light of my eyes, also, is not with me.

¹¹ My loved ones and my friends stand far off from my plague,
  and my neighbors stand away from me.

---

⁴⁸ LXX and the Samaritan Pentateuch have a copula between the two verbs.

⁴⁹ The verb *qādar* means *grow dark, darken* (Cf. Francis Brown, S. R. Driver, and Charles A. Briggs, *Hebrew and English Lexicon* [Oxford: Clarendon Press, 1972], hereafter BDB). *To mourn* is a figurative meaning.

⁵⁰ BDB consider *sĕḥrḥar* as a Pealal form of *sāḥar to go around, about*. Thus our translation, *to beat violently*.

¹² Those who seek my life set their trap,
   and those who want to harm me speak about destruction,
   and deceitful things all the day long, they devise.

¹³ And I am like a deaf man, I do not hear,
   and like a dumb man who cannot open his mouth.

¹⁴ And I am like a man who does not hear,
   and there is in my mouth no arguments.

¹⁵ For you, YHWH, I wait,
   you will answer, ADONAÏ MY GOD.

¹⁶ For I said, let them not rejoice over me,
   when my foot slips, they magnify themselves against me.

¹⁷ For I am ready to stumble,
   and my pain is continuously before me.

¹⁸ I confess my iniquities,
   I am anxious because of my sin.

¹⁹ My living enemies are strong,
   and they are many those who hate me wrongfully.

²⁰ They repay me evil instead of good,
   they are my adversaries, because of my pursuit of the good.

²¹ Do not abandon me, YHWH, MY GOD,
   do not be far from me.

²² Make haste to my help,
   ADONAÏ, my salvation.

CHAPTER 10

THE HEALING PATIENT

African HIV and AIDS Hermeneutics of Isaiah 52:13–53:12 (with Special Focus on Isaiah 53:5)

Wilfrid F. Okambawa

But he was wounded for our transgressions,
he was bruised for our iniquities;
upon him was the chastisement that made us whole,
and with his stripes we are healed. (Isaiah 53:5) [1]

In this chapter I intend to show how the Suffering Servant of Yahweh (SSY, Isa. 52:13–53:12), the most influential text shaping New Testament Christology and considered as the climax of the OT,[2] is a *healing patient*, by reinterpreting Isa. 53:5 in the light of some therapeutic theories of African Traditional Religions (ATRs), in which the patient is the one in the best position to heal other people and HIV and AIDS hermeneutics. To achieve this, I show first how the SSY is a patient, then how the SSY is a healer. Finally, I lay the foundation for an African Christian theology of HIV and AIDS, showing how victims could become healers and salvific agents for others.

---

[1] Given the limitations of this paper, we do not analyze word for word the whole section of Isa. 52:13–53:12, but we do focus on Isa. 53:5, even though we refer to other parts of the Song when necessary. Regarding the text, although we do not ignore the original Hebrew text, we use the RSV.

[2] Eric Voegelin, *History and Order: Israel and Revelation* (Baton Rouge: Louisiana State University Press, 1956), 299.

The Suffering Servant of Yahweh as a Patient

The Literary Proof: Isaiah 53:5

The Song of the SSY has a concentric structure[3] with noticeable inter-twining of the speakers I, He, We, and They,[4] representing, respectively, God; the SSY; the Israelites, including the narrator;[5] and the nations (*goyim*). The *goyim* never speak in direct speech; their thoughts are only reported by the narrator. However, their presence gives a universal dimension to the Song and to the SSY.

The Song may be divided into four parts:

1. God's prophecy regarding the exaltation of his SSY and his newness (Isa. 52:13–15)
2. The SSY as a patient (man of sorrows) (Isa. 53:1–3)
3. Right and wrong diagnoses / interpretations of the suffering of the SSY (Isa. 53:4–6)
4. Nonviolence and sacrificial death of the SSY (Isa. 53:11–12)

The main argument in favor of this subdivision is that the introduction and conclusion build an *inclusio*.[6] Though Danylak finds the climax of the Song in Isaiah 53:10,[7] I hold that it is rather in Isaiah 53:5, for verse 5 stands clearer at the center of the text than verse 10, which is found almost at the end.

Rhetorical Analysis and Patient Metaphors in Isaiah 53:5

The rhetorical analysis of Isaiah 53:5 proves that its center is the patient, the "mega-metaphor" structuring the whole song. There are synonymous paral-lelisms, on the one hand, between "But he was wounded for our transgressions" and "he was bruised for our iniquities," and on the other hand between "upon

[3] Bernd Janowski, "Isaiah 53 and the Drama of Taking Another's Place," in Bernd Janowski and Peter Stuhlmacher, *The Suffering Servant: Isaiah 53 in Jewish and Christian Sources* (Grand Rapids: Eerdmans, 2004), 61.

[4] David Clines, *I, He, We, and They: A Literary Approach to Is 53* (Sheffield, UK: JSOT, 1976).

[5] John Skinner, *The Book of the Prophet Isaiah: Chapters XL–LXVI* (Cambridge: Cambridge University Press, 1929), 136–37.

[6] David L. Allen, "Substitutionary Atonement and Cultic Terminology in Is 53," in Darrell Bock and Mitch Glaser, eds., *The Gospel according to Isaiah 53: Encountering the Suffering Servant in Jewish and Christian Theology* (Grand Rapids: Kregel Academic, 2012), 185.

[7] Barry Danylak, *Redeeming Singleness: How the Storyline of the Bible Affirms the Single Life* (Wheaton, IL: Crossway, 2010), 99.

him was the chastisement that made us whole" and "and with his stripes we are healed." In fact, "made whole" and "healed" are parallel.[8] In the first set, the words "wounded" and "bruised," and "transgressions" and "iniquities" correspond to one another. In the second set, the words "chastisement" and "stripes," and "made us whole" and "we are healed" belong to the same semantic field. The passive form of the verbs "wound" and "bruise" expresses the divine passive (*passivus divinum*), meaning that God is their real subject. He has wounded the Servant, so that he can have compassion for wounded fellow human beings in a logic of assimilation and *kenosis* (self-emptying). The image of the SSY is a mega-metaphor for all injustices perpetrated against the people of Israel,[9] as well as for all the sicknesses of Israel, in which there are fourteen noticeable micro-metaphors. The most important is that of the wounds (Isa. 53:5) portraying the SSY,[10] for it relates at best to the one of lamb (53:7), sacrifice (53:10), scapegoat (53:12), and sprinkling/priesthood (52:15).

In fact, the image used to describe the SSY as "marred in appearance" connotes a physical disability or disease. This mega-metaphor does not focus on the exact nature of the disability of the SSY but on his social experience, for his disability or disease is framed primarily as a social and political experience and not just as a physical description.[11] There is no doubt that the Song of the SSY bears aspects of prophetic literature, such as oracle, and poetic features like those of lament psalms and thanksgiving psalms, because of its dialectic of suffering and exaltation.[12]

Philological Proof of the Patient's Sickness

The Hebrew word rendered by "sorrows" in Isaiah 53:3 also signifies pain, while the word *holî*, rendered by "grief," also means sickness. In Isaiah 53:10 it

---

[8] Frederick Gaiser, *Healing in the Bible: Theological Insights for Christian Ministry* (Grand Rapids: Baker Academic, 2010), 227.

[9] Michael Giansiracusa, *The Suffering Servant of Camden, NJ: A Journey in 21st-Century Urban Ministry* (Bloomington, IN: Author House, 2014), 31.

[10] According to Shipper, even if the passage uses *hlh* as a metaphor for the condition of others in v. 4 (cf. Isa. 33:24) and speaks metaphorically of their "healing" in v. 5, it does not mean that *hlh* is primarily a metaphor for something other than the servant's disability in v. 3 or 10 (Jeremy Shipper, *Disability and Isaiah's Suffering Servant* [Oxford: Oxford University Press, 2011], 44). In extrabiblical texts, Israel is sometimes portrayed as a person with a disability as a metaphor for its sinfulness; see Judith Abrams, *Judaism and Disability: Portrayals in Ancient Texts from the Tanak through the Bavli* (Washington, DC: Gallaudet University Press, 1998), 76.

[11] Shipper, *Disability and Isaiah's Suffering Servant*, 40–41.

[12] Roger N. Whybray, *Thanksgiving for a Liberated Prophet: An Interpretation of Isaiah Chapter 53* (Sheffield: University of Sheffield, 1978).

means "made him sick." This is also its common and basic meaning; as shown by John Goldingay and David Payne, the parallel of *mak'ōbôt* ["suffering"] is *ḥōlî* ["disease"], which commonly means "illness," and the context speaks more explicitly of harm from other people than of disease. The noun and the verb *ḥālāh* do occasionally mean "wound," but more often the noun denotes "weakness."[13] Maybe the fear of an extreme Pentecostal healing ministry prevents most translations of the fourth song from stressing the sickness and cure of the SSY as forcefully as does the biblical Hebrew (BH). Consequently, Alonso Schökel's translation is exceptional for rendering the verse in the line of the Vulgate and Duhm as follows: "we consider him a leper, wounded and humiliated by God."[14] However, it is difficult to determine whether the SSY had an injury or disability, for the word *ḥlh* has a wide semantic range that includes injury, illness, disease, and disability. Though the Song has forms of the word, many scholars have decided not to associate this repeated use of *ḥlh* with disability or disease.[15]

The SSY is also avoided like a patient with an infectious disease. The act of pouring out the soul in Isaiah 53:12c is a euphemism for death. However, the image suggests the idea of libation of water or blood. Now blood is the symbol of life (the symbol of *nephesh*?). In Isaiah 53:5 the key words are *ḥōlî*, *mūsar*, and *šalom*, while in Jeremiah 10:18–19, trauma is used for "wound" illness.

Historical Proof: Identification of the SSY and His Sickness

Identification of the SSY is one of the major problems that have shaped the interpretation history of the Song. Does he represent an individual or a collective personality? What was the SSY's sickness or disability? Regarding his sickness, the text does not specify its nature. What is sure is that it does not result from his sinfulness; on the contrary it is the consequence of the sinfulness of others. Duhm was the first to reveal the disability imagery of the SSY in 1892,[16] and Budde determined this disability as leprosy.[17] In fact, the image of the SSY presents many remembrances of the one of Job, the collective/corporate personality representing Israel. Job suffered from a skin disease (Job 2:7). Though the original Hebrew text does not mention *sara'at*, medieval physicians

[13] John Goldingay and David Payne, *A Critical and Exegetical Commentary on Isaiah 40–50*, vol. 2 (New York: T&T Clark, 2006), 302.
[14] Thomas D. Hanks, *God So Loved the Third World: The Biblical Vocabulary of Oppression* (Eugene, OR: Wipf and Stock, 2001), 76.
[15] Shipper, *Disability and Isaiah's Suffering Servant*, 44.
[16] Bernhard Duhm, *Das Buch Jesaja* (Göttingen, DE: Vandenhoeck und Ruprecht, 1892).
[17] Karl Budde, "The So-Called 'Ebed-Yahweh Songs' and the Meaning of the Term 'Servant of Yahweh' in Isaiah Chaps. 40–55," *American Journal of Theology* 3 (1899): 503.

identified it as leprosy.[18] Since Job had been healed from this disease, a Muslim tradition considers him as the patron saint of leprosy cures.[19] Going further in the same line, Itkonen identifies the SSY with King Uzziah (2 Chr. 26:19–20),[20] the only leper king in the history of Israel. However, the difference between Uzziah and the SSY is that the leprosy of the former resulted from his sinful action of burning the incense in the house of the Lord and usurping the right of the priests.

According to one tradition, the Hebrews were lepers, cripples, and down-trodden peoples chased away from Egypt (Manetho, Apion): "It was said that when Osarseph, named after Osiris, the god of Heliopolis, joined the lepers, he changed his name and was called Moses."[21] Although Flavius Josephus dismissed this tradition,[22] one should consider it seriously without falling into anti-Semitism.

The Song bears historical elements of a Phoenician background[23] and of the Egyptian Osiris, who had been killed and risen from death, bearing the sins of Seth. The myth of Osiris has the three dimensions of the theological, anthropological, and cosmic worlds. Like the SSY, Osiris is innocent and becomes a source of blessing for his people. As with the SSY, Osiris is nonviolent and was brought back from death to life through the power of Isis's love. However, the myth of Osiris lacks the vicarious aspect of the suffering and death we have in the Song. In the first case, the main agent of bringing back from death to life is Isis, a human being, while in the second case it is God himself.

The Isaianic concept of the SSY has been later developed into that of the son of man found in Daniel, Ezekiel, and apocalyptic literature.[24] Some scholars hold that the SSY refers to Moses—a new Moses performing a new exodus by bringing Israel not only out of the Babylonian captivity but also out of itself like a shepherd.[25] Some other scholars define the SSY as Jeremiah, the prophet

---

[18] Ibid.

[19] Naomi Westbrook Martinez, *God Always Makes Sense: An Illuminating Study of the Book of Job* (Oklahoma City: Tate Publishing, 2011), 16.

[20] Lauri Itkonen, *Deuterojesaja (Jes. 40–55) metrisch untersucht* (Helsinki: Finnischen Literatur-Gesellschaft, 1916), 81–82.

[21] Manetho quoted by Elias J. Bickerman, *The Jews in the Greek Age* (Cambridge, MA: Harvard University Press, 1988), 225.

[22] Flavius Josephus, *Life, Against Apion* (Cambridge, MA: Harvard University Press, 1993).

[23] Mitchell Dahood, "Phoenecian Elements in Is 52:13–53:12," in *Near Eastern Studies in Honor of W. F. Albright*, ed. H. Goedicke (Baltimore: Johns Hopkins Press, 1971).

[24] David Syme Russel, *Daniel, An Active Volcano: Reflections on the Book of Daniel* (Edinburgh, UK: Saint Andrew Press, 1981), 127.

[25] Paul Coxon, *Exploring the New Exodus in John: A Biblical Theological Investigation of John Chapters 5–10* (Eugene, OR: Wipf and Stock, 2015), 288.

of doom, while others see King Joachim behind this image[26] or the writer of Deutero-Isaiah himself: God's salvation will not be achieved through the military endeavors of Cyrus but through the silent ministry of the prophet. Most recent theories state that the SSY represents the returnees from the Babylonian Exile, that is, only a part of Israel.[27]

Another theory holds that the one who suffers is God's enemy,[28] avoiding thereby the kenotic politics of the SSY of the BH.[29] Yet such a reactionary reinterpretation would not have been necessary if, in the original Song, the SSY has been interpreted as a healer.

The Suffering Servant of Yahweh as a Healer

The term rendered as "servant" in Isaiah 52:13 is '*Obed*,' usually understood in the BH as Israel. The same word can also mean "slave." But service can also mean care, a therapy in order to bring deliverance. The verb to "prosper" could also mean to succeed, to overcome. Some scholars translate it as "be intelligent." Its use here supposes that the servant was in a state of complete failure. The verbs "to prosper" and "to be exalted" build a synonymic parallelism. In the medical realm, "to prosper" means "to recover," "to be whole," for disease reduces our strength, energy, wealth, and well-being. The use of "prosper" twice in the poem could invite an interpretation of the word that might be used to support a prosperity gospel reading, though this can hardly be defended.

The Homoeopathic Principle: Healing Suffering through Suffering

The wounds of the SSY are like those made by leprosy (Isa. 53:5). Yet in these very wounds are healing powers. We have here the ancient pharmacological principle of homoeopathy: *similia similibus curantur* (to cure the similar through the similar).[30] A wound is needed to cure human wounds. The principle is not valid only in the field of homeopathy; rather, it is at the core of our whole modern immunology. For example, a vaccine for a virus is made of the virus itself. There is a relationship between suffering, healing, and peace, and

---

[26] Henri Cazelles, "Le roi Yoyakin et le Serviteur du Seigneur," in *Proceedings of the Fifth World Congress of Jewish Studies*, Vol. 1, PELI, 1969, Jerusalem, 121–25.

[27] Frederick Hagglund, *Isaiah 53 in the Light of Homecoming after Exile* (Tübingen, DE: Mohr Siebeck, 2008).

[28] J Stenning, *The Targum of Isaiah* (Oxford: Oxford University Press, 1949), 178–81.

[29] Mark E. Moore, *Kenotic Politics: The Reconfiguration of Power in Jesus's Political Praxis* (London: Bloomsbury Publishing, 2013), 135.

[30] Maurice Selbonne, *Le principe de similitude en thérapeutique 'similia similibus curantur' devient 'contraria contrariis curantur'* (Paris: Hemerlé Petit et Cie, 1935).

so too the Bible will not let us escape the connection between suffering and *shalom*.[31]

God's Plan in Salvation History

The question of grasping God's will in history is raised in verses 53:5 and 53:10, where we come across one of the most difficult theological problems of the Song. First, all of verse 10 aims at explaining why the SSY was bruised in verse 5 with a new element: the will of God. Is this the same as the plan of God? Are we dealing here with predestination? If one of the purposes of the Song was to combat retribution theology, is predestination theology not another face of the same coin? Is the SSY's will identical to God's? If God is good and righteous, how can he will that his SSY might suffer for unrighteous people? If we assume that God's will contains only what is necessary, is suffering necessary then? If God is almighty, could he not handle matters in such a way that his beloved Servant may escape suffering?

In the last line of verse 10 we return to the themes of the will of God and of prosperity. God's success shall be more noticeable through weak people than powerful ones. Though we should be very cautious in addressing the question of suffering, one of the best biblical answers is Joseph's: "You intended to harm me, but God intended it for good to accomplish what is now being done, the saving of your lives" (Gen. 50:20). Consequently, we can say, regarding the Servant, that God intended no suffering: "We might thus infer, what God wills, and so what pleases God, is undying covenant loyalty and suffering for the sake of righteousness and justice. God delights not in the Servant's suffering itself, but in the Servant's willingness to suffer in service to the covenant and to God's covenant people (Isa 53:10b–12)."[32]

Normally, a cleansed leper should perform a sin offering (Lev. 14:12): "The death of the suffering servant compensates for the sins of the people and makes many to be accounted righteous."[33] Because the SSY has freely accepted to die, the will of God will succeed in his life. He is so closely united to God that his prosperity is that of God and vice versa. The mention of the SSY's offspring alludes to a kind of resurrection, whereby the dead Servant survives through his progeny, just as in the African ancestor worship system. The Song presents a special miracle: the success (prosperity) of the SSY, the decisive miracle through which the Servant's work attains its end, to be a blessing and remedy

---

[31] Gaiser, *Healing in the Bible*, 227.

[32] Darrin Snyder Belousek, *Atonement, Justice, and Peace: The Message of the Cross and the Mission of the Church* (Grand Rapids: Eerdmans, 2012), 228.

[33] Gordon Wenham, *Leviticus* (Grand Rapids: Eerdmans, 1979), 110.

for others.[34] This resurrection is like the proof of the innocence of the SSY as well as a call to conversion.

The Suffering Servant of Yahweh in Comparison with Other Figures

The SSY shares five characteristics with Job:

1. Both seem to be corporate personalities representing the whole of Israel.[35]
2. Both are faithful and blameless servants of God.
3. Both suffer from a skin disease to the point of scandalizing the people around them, and both use the language of suffering.[36]
4. Both are promised a bright future as a reward after their suffering.
5. Both stories allude to resurrection and operate in the logic of death and resurrection.

There are also five dissimilarities between the two:

1. Job talks, while the SSY is silent.
2. Job has a name, while the SSY is anonymous.
3. The book of Job is longer and appears as a drama; the latter is shorter and a poem.
4. Job is tempted by Satan with God's permission (Job 1:6–12), while the SSY suffers to bear witness to God.
5. The suffering of the SSY is clearly vicarious, while Job's is displayed as essentially personal, even though both seem to achieve an intercessory ministry.

The SSY is also similar to Jesus in certain ways:

1. Both suffered vicariously in the name of God for the sake of humankind.
2. Both died and were exalted by God.

---

[34] Sigmund Mowinckel, *He That Cometh: The Messiah Concept in the Old Testament and Later Judaism* (Grand Rapids: Eerdmans, 2005), 205.

[35] Contra A. Condamin, "Le Serviteur de Iavé. Un nouvel argument pour le sens individuel messianique," *Revue Biblique* 17 (1908): 162–81.

[36] Jean Charles Bastiaens, "The Language of Suffering in Job 16–19 and in the Suffering Servant Passage in Deutero-Isaiah," in *Studies in the Book of Isaiah, Festschrift Willem A. M. Beuken*, ed. Jacques Reuten and Marc Vervenne (Louvain: Presses Universitaires, 1997), 421–32.

3. Both were innocent and nonviolent, like a lamb.
4. Both heal through their wounds.

However, there are also important differences:

1. The Song of the SSY is far shorter than the stories of Jesus in the Gospels.
2. The SSY appears as a mythical and collective character, while Jesus is portrayed as a historical and individual character.
3. While the Song only hints at further life after death, the stories of Jesus explicitly speak of his resurrection.
4. The divinity of Jesus is more prominent than that of the SSY.

In Matthew 8:17, a quote from Isaiah 53:4 helps create a typology in which Jesus and the Servant become examples of a healer of disabilities rather than a figure with disabilities.[37]

HIV and AIDS in Relation to Isaiah 52:13–53:12

The Stigmatization of the SSY and of People Living with HIV

In Greek, the word *stigma* means a mark, a tattoo, often on the body to distinguish outcasts from "normal" people. It came to be applied to specific diseases like leprosy, some mental illnesses, epilepsy, and nowadays people living with HIV (PLWH). *Disease stigma* is an ideology holding that people with a specific disease are different from normal society, through their infection with a disease agent: "This ideology links the presence of a biological disease agent (or any physical signs of a disease) to negatively defined behaviors or groups in society. Disease stigma is thus negative social 'baggage' associated with a disease."[38] Suffering became salubrious or redemptive only dimly in the Old Testament, by including the power to remove or lessen sickness, and the sinful stigma of sickness.[39] AIDS is the leprosy of our time,[40] and PLWH are simulated to sinners in a process of stigmatization.

---

[37] Shipper, *Disability and Isaiah's Suffering Servant*, 74.

[38] Harriet Deacon, Inez Stephney, and Sandra Prosalendis, *Understanding HIV/AIDS Stigma: A Theoretical and Methodological Analysis* (Cape Town: HRSC, 2005), 19.

[39] Darrel Amundsen, "A 'Christian' Response to Epidemics?: Theological and Historical Considerations," in *Women, HIV, and the Church: In Search of Refuge*, ed. Arthur Ammann and Julie Pons-Ford Holland (Eugene, OR: Cascade Books, 2012), 21.

[40] Willem A. Saayman and Jacques Kriel, *AIDS: The Leprosy of Our Time? Toward a Christian Response to AIDS in Southern and Central Africa* (Johannesburg: Orion Publishers, 1992).

The SSY and the Scapegoat Theory

The scapegoat theory is found in most cultures (Jewish, Greek,[41] Asian, and African).

Cyril was one of the first interpreters to link the SSY and Christ as scapegoats,[42] for both had to be killed outside the camp/Jerusalem. Modern interpretations often reject the scapegoat theory, because it is seen as returning violence for violence: "The power of Jesus in undoing the scapegoat mechanism is that he opens the eyes of people of faith to the truth that the victim rather than the perpetrator of the sacrificial system is God."[43] In African cultures the scapegoat can be seen in numerous rituals and legends, such as the sacrificial *kudio* ritual of the Fon people of Benin. The *kudio*, that is, "change of death,"[44] is a very rare human sacrifice performed when a disease is very serious and hard to heal: the medicine man or woman or another person accepts a vicarious death so that the patient may live. Similar to the *kudio* is the ritual sacrifice of the king so that his people may be spared from a great disease.

The traditional scapegoat shares a number of similarities with the SSY:

- The scapegoat and the SSY share the common destiny of vicarious death.
- Both share the state of being marginalized and are expected to die outside the camp.
- Both are intended to bring peace.
- Both are sacrifices for the sin of others in the expectation of bringing life.

Some differences between the two include the following:

- The scapegoat is chosen even against his will to die for the people, while the SSY suffers *willingly* for the well-being of his people.
- The scapegoat is a sacrifice offered to a spirit, often an evil one; the self-sacrifice of the SSY has nothing to do with any evil spirit.
- The scapegoat dies without any necessary expectation of resurrection, while the SSY has some expectation of survival beyond death.
- The scapegoat is not sick, while the SSY is.
- The scapegoat is only a victim of violence, while the SSY is at the same time the victim and the priest performing the ritual.

---

[41] David Dawson, *Flesh Becomes Word: A Lexicography of the Scapegoat or, The History of an Idea* (East Lansing: Michigan State University Press, 2013).

[42] Cyril, *Letters*, vol. 76 (Washington, DC: Catholic University of America, 1987), 173.

[43] Chris Glaser, *Coming Out as Sacrament* (Louisville, KY: Westminster/John Knox Press, 1998), 104–5.

[44] Wilfrid Okambawa, *Le pardon: une folie libératrice* (Dakar, SN: Lux Africae, 2015), 210.

A Critique of the Scapegoat Theory

Jesus is not simply a scapegoat, but is a model of love and nonviolence. To think of him merely through the scapegoat theory lens might lead to a kind of magic logic that is unacceptable in Jewish-Christian tradition. In his interpretation of the Shoah, Levinas refers to Isaiah 53, emphasizing the godforsakenness of the SSY. If innocents suffer, one cannot help thinking that heaven is empty, for God seems to have covered his face, and the believer is tempted toward atheism. The Jewish meaning of suffering does not lie in any divine plan or mysterious penance for sins, "but in the possibility for the individual of gaining a victory in his conscience, independent of any external . . . "[45] The nonviolence and love of the SSY are expressed through his silence: "yet he opened not his mouth" (Isa. 53:7). Consequently, the power of God's arm is not the power to crush the enemy (sin), but the power, when the enemy has crushed the SSY, to give back love and mercy. The SSY takes on himself the sins of Israel and of the world and, like the scapegoat (Lev. 16:22), bears (*nāśāʾ*; cf. 53:4) those sins away from us.[46] Thus, if suffering can dehumanize a person, true humanity is revealed through the successful test of suffering.

A feminist analysis of the Song can also be fruitful, for the SSY could be seen as a mother in travail during childbirth, dying to give life, emptying herself to give birth to a new child.

The Healing Patient or Wounded Healer in African Traditional Religions

The Ibo of Nigeria believe that a person called by Agwu to be a votary becomes sick (mental illness) if he or she refuses or delays to respond. When the patient becomes a devotee of the deity, he or she is then healed and can become a healer. We find similar practices among many Bantu people, especially the Lemba, the Shona, and the Swazi. The Ngoma, the medicine man or woman, is usually a former patient who undergoes a religious initiation after which the person becomes a healer: "the power of the wounded healer, together with his fellow sufferers, that is transforming sufferer into healer."[47] The paradigm of the wounded healer is also used in disciplines

---

[45] René van Riessen, *Man as a Place of God: Levinas' Hermeneutics of Kenosis* (Dordrecht: Springer, 2007), 119.

[46] John Oswalt, *The Book of Isaiah, Chapters 40–66* (Grand Rapids: Eerdmans, 1998), 376–77.

[47] John M. Janzen, *Nogoma: Discourses of Healing in Central and Southern Africa* (Berkeley: University of California Press, 1997), 87.

like Christology,[48] spirituality,[49] and even psychoanalysis,[50] suggesting that the notion of a wounded healer is an almost universal idea or reality. Jewish, Hindu, and African traditions also have a belief that suffering can be redemptive, and that it is even more purifying when undergone by a pure and righteous person or animal, as a self-sacrifice out of obedient love.

An African Biblical Approach to HIV and AIDS

Among African scholars who have brought biblical hermeneutics to bear on the issue of HIV and AIDS, significant examples are Ghislain Tshikendwa's interpretation of the book of Job,[51] the global interpretation of the Bible by Mchombo and Larko,[52] and womanist hermeneutics of the Bible.[53] In all these studies, the Bible as God's Word can be seen as a medicine for AIDS patients.[54]

If, following Mary Douglas,[55] the pairing of the paradigms of "clean" and "unclean" could be considered the hermeneutical key to the books of the Pentateuch, except for Genesis, is it not the case with the fourth song of the SSY? Here we have a reversal of such a logic by a kind of "transvaluation of all values,"[56] whereby the clean becomes unclean and the unclean clean, the weak is made strong and the strong weak. In fact, in the course of Jewish history, the image of the SSY is one of the most powerful criticisms of classical established Jewish retribution theology, even more than Job.

Willmot Blyden has applied the image of the SSY to African people all over the world, comparing Africa in her service and her suffering to the Hebrews in Egypt:

---

[48] Selwyn Hugues, *Jesus: The Wounded Healer* (Farnham, UK: CWR, 2010).

[49] Henri Nouwen, *The Wounded Healer: Ministry in Contemporary Society* (Garden City, NY: Doubleday, 1972); Linda Grier-Hugues, *The Wounded Healer: Real Stories about Real People Restored to His Glory* (Longwood, FL: XLibris Corporation, 2010).

[50] Eckhard Frick, *Durch Verwundung heilen: zur Psychoanalyse des Heilungsarchetyps* (Göttingen, DE: Vanderhoeck and Ruprecht, 1996).

[51] Ghislain Tshikendwa Matadi, *Suffering, Belief, Hope: The Wisdom of Job for an AIDS-Stricken Africa* (Nairobi: Paulines Publications Africa, 2007).

[52] William Mchombo, Joyce Larko, et al., *Call to Me: How the Bible Speaks in the Age of AIDS* (Oxford: Strategies for Hope Trust, 2010).

[53] M. W. Dube and M. W. D. Shomanah, *Grant Me Justice! HIV/AIDS and Gender Readings of the Bible* (Scranton, PA: University of Scranton, 2008).

[54] Gerald West and Bondi Zengele, "The Medicine of God's Word: What People Living with HIV and AIDS Want (and Get) from the Bible," *Journal of Theology for Southern Africa* 125 (July 2006): 51–63.

[55] Mary Douglas, *Purity and Danger: An Analysis of Concepts of Pollution and Taboo* (London: Routledge, 2013).

[56] Friedrich Nietzsche, *Will to Power: An Attempted Transvaluation of All Values* (LaVergne, TN: Kessinger Publishing, 2010).

The lot of Africa resembles also His who made Himself of no reputation but took upon Himself the form of a servant, and, having been made perfect through suffering, became "the Captain of our salvation." And if the principle laid down by Christ is that by which things are decided above, viz., that he who would be chief must become the servant of all, then we see the position which Africa and the Africans must ultimately occupy. And we must admit that through serving man, Africa [Ethiopia] has been stretching out her hands unto God.[57]

A Contemporary Critique of the SSY Model

In the situation of martyrdom, where the choice is between conversion or death, death can be seen as a form of religious resistance. But what of the case of the Shoah, where death was imposed by law, and defense of life was the only possible way of resistance? Emil Fackenheim and Erving Greenberg hold that since the Holocaust, the paradigm of the SSY is no longer relevant.[58] Perhaps for similar reasons, a fair amount of black preachers in North America have abandoned the theme of suffering of the Negro Spirituals for that of a prosperity gospel theology. Alternatively, some black theologians, including William Jones and Theophus Smith,[59] criticize the theodicy of the SSY, and Anthony Pinn rejects it for discouraging liberation struggles[60]: "classifying black people as God's (collective) contemporary suffering servant is a bad idea. It potentially underwrites suffering in perpetuity."[61]

Similarly, Andrew David takes a humanist, nontheistic position to address the problem of human suffering without focusing on transhistorical and supernatural claims and assumptions. The humanist approach maintains an awareness of the substance of suffering but in ways that also maintain the need for human accountability and responsibility. This approach considers moral evil in relation to the outcome of struggle against injustice: "Rather than the rhetoric of liberation that is drawn from the cross, a nontheistic, humanist interpretation can

---

[57] Edward Wilmot Blyden, *Christianity, Islam, and the Negro Race* (London: Whittingham, 1887), 139.

[58] Jonathan Sacks, *Crisis and Covenant: Jewish Thought after the Holocaust* (Manchester, UK: Manchester University Press, 1992), 17.

[59] William R. Jones, *Is God a White Racist? A Preamble to Black Theology* (Garden City, NY: Anchor Press, 1973); Theophus Smith, *Conjuring Culture: Biblical Formations of Black America* (New York: Oxford University Press, 1994).

[60] Anthony Pinn, *Why Lord? Suffering and Evil in Black Theology* (New York: Continuum, 1995); see also Pinn, *Moral Evil and Redemptive Suffering: A History of Theodicy in African-American Religious Thought* (Gainesville: University Press of Florida, 2002).

[61] William David Hart, *Afro-Eccentricity: Beyond the Standard Narrative of Black Religion* (New York: Palgrave Macmillan, 2011), 196.

recognize the importance of struggle but also the manner in which outcomes are not guaranteed. Instead, this approach suggests that the importance of our struggles to promote the integrity of life is found in the very struggles themselves."[62]

This humanistic approach has the advantage of being concrete and engaging us in the real struggles of our time. However, does it not run the risk of anthropocentrism? Is the human being the center of everything?

Similarities between PLWH and the SSY

People suffering with HIV share some characteristics with the SSY:

- Both suffer in their body as well as in their soul.
- Both are marginalized and stigmatized.

There are many differences between PLWH and the SSY as well:

- No one would willingly contract HIV, while the SSY suffers willingly.
- Some PLWH are responsible for the illness they are suffering from, unlike the SSY, who is completely innocent.
- The vicarious dimension of the SSY is clearer than that of PLWH.
- The "resurrection" of the SSY is clearer than in the case of PLWH.
- The divine aspect of the SSY is clearer than that of the PLWH.

Conclusion

The meaning of a text does not lie only in its past but also in its future, in its capacity to give life, to give birth to new meanings and interpretations. "But where sin increased, grace abounded all the more" (Rom 5:20). An African HIV and AIDS hermeneutics of Isaiah 53:5 helps to make sense of the "non-sense" of suffering in general and HIV and AIDS in particular. The Song can help people living with HIV to become a source of wisdom and healing for others. However, they first need to move from the status of victims suffering from a fatal disease to that of people voluntarily taking on their suffering in obedient love, through a ministry of intercession and conscientization, in the interest of the whole world. By doing so they will become healing, patient, and compassionate medicine men and women.

---

[62] Andrew David, *The Other Journal: Evil* (Eugene, OR: Cascade Books, 2012), 92–93.

CHAPTER 11

SIN AND MORAL RESPONSIBILITY
IN TIMES OF AIDS

"Master, Who Has Sinned?" (John 9:2)

Caroline N. Mbonu

A critical response to the scourge of the HIV and AIDS pandemic transcends the blame game expressed in a phrase like, "Master, who has sinned?" (John 9:2). Any attempt at unearthing the source of suffering in an individual's life remains futile in light of inadequate human knowledge. Similarly, a personal ethical scrutiny may yield little or no result to finding a solution to the spread of the deadly virus. How to stop the spread of the infection remains the vexing question on the African continent and elsewhere.

One might ask: Where have the strict sexual taboos of traditional Africa gone? Perhaps urbanization, with its attendant anonymity, provides a cover for moral decadence. It does appear also that the "I-logic" (rather than the "we-logic") that privileges the individual over the community does a disservice to the fight against the AIDS pandemic in Africa. As a result, the secrecy associated with the blight inadvertently moves it to a moral sphere rather than a public health concern.

In the battle to control the infection's spread, the traditional African response to crisis has been left largely untapped. Here, inculturation theology must look beyond church rituals to embrace well-being at the grass roots. African communalism, a "we-logic" that has sustained life over millennia, remains a significant resource in combating AIDS. This chapter draws insights from John 9:2, to investigate sin and moral responsibility in times of HIV and AIDS. Insights from the teachings of the church on the pandemic as well as the African notion of sin and moral responsibility expand this analysis. In this study, I employ a hermeneutics of resonance as well as cultural hermeneutics to draw out the familial and communal character of sin and responsibility as they pertain to the pandemic. I also propose a response in curbing the spread of the killer virus.

This chapter is a response to the virus from a biblical and African sensibility. The discussion is foregrounded on the question that Jesus's disciples raised: "Master, who has sinned, this man or his parents that he was born blind?" (John 9:2). The first section attempts to locate Africa's position vis-à-vis the pandemic. An exegetical survey of John 9:2 is the subject of the second section. Then I study the African notion of sin, including its individual and communal character. Next I engage HIV and AIDS as a public health concern, with an example from the narrative of Miriam in Numbers 12:10–12. Finally I explore moral responsibility in the present predicament and propose a way forward.

Where We Stand

For a people who have appropriated the biblical faith tradition, the Johannine text (John 9:2) offers an approach to managing the scourge of HIV and AIDS that is at once personal and communal. HIV and AIDS, familiar names since the 1980s, represent perhaps the most dreaded disease until Ebola of recent memory. Africans die by the thousands each day from diseases caused by the virus. The tragedy of AIDS in Africa has not only decimated populations but has impoverished many more. Indeed, the crisis has become one of Homeric proportions. Though a plethora of research findings and pertinent literature, oral and written, from almost every imaginable discipline exist on the subject, proper management of the disease appears to elude experts.

Various governments and agencies around the world, particularly religious bodies such as the Catholic Church, have tried to help in alleviating the suffering caused by the AIDS pandemic and to stop the spread.[1] The Catholic Church's approach to fighting the HIV privileges practices that are consistent with traditional African values—namely, abstinence, fidelity, and chastity. Success in Uganda, where HIV prevalence fell from 21 percent to 6 percent between 1989 and 2003, was credited to abstinence and fidelity. Fidelity or reduction in the number of sex partners, called "zero grazing" in Uganda, was the key to the success.[2] But the larger medical community's insistence on the use of condoms, contraception, and other such measures offers minimum support to the Catholic approach.[3]

---

[1] Following the election of Pope Francis in 2013, UNAIDS wrote that the church "provides support to millions of people living with HIV around the world" and that "Statistics from the Vatican in 2012 indicate that Catholic Church–related organizations provide approximately a quarter of all HIV treatment, care, and support throughout the world and run more than 5,000 hospitals, 18,000 dispensaries, and 9,000 orphanages, many involved in AIDS-related activities."

[2] www.ncbi.nlm.nih.gov/pmc/articles/PMC2602746/.

[3] The Catholic approach to the use of condoms has recently shifted. During his last

Exegetical Survey: John 9:2

His disciples asked him, "Rabbi, who sinned, this man or his parents
that he was born blind?"

Written between AD 90 and 100, John's Gospel is often called the Gospel
of Light. The text under review comes within the pericope (9:1–10) manifesting
Jesus as the Light of the world. As a whole, the Gospel of John also concerns
itself with church and synagogue debates or insider-outsider status. The healing
of the man born blind continues this two-dimensional drama.[4]

The disciples' query into the moral status of the man born blind and that
of his parents betrays some of the cultural drama associated with affliction. The
question reveals a deep-seated Jewish cultural belief that attributes suffering and
disease to sin, an idea that resonates with the African understanding of suffering.[5] Undoubtedly, Jesus's disciples remained connected to the culture and
tradition of their people. The Torah continued to define for them what was
right or wrong, and the Torah makes clear that sin was not necessarily a personal
act; the sin of parents can be visited on their progeny (Exod. 20:5; Num. 14:18),
a determinism that is echoed in the question, "Rabbi, who sinned, this man or
his parents?"[6]

In ancient Israel, family solidarity was fundamental.[7] Children were
conceived as extensions of the personality of the family head—in this case, the
male progenitor. The whole family made up a corporate personality, which was
rewarded or punished as a group.[8] In this milieu, suffering, therefore, was attributed to intergenerational sin (Exod. 20:5). As Rodney A. Whitacre asserts, in

---

visit to Africa before his retirement, Pope Benedict XVI softened Rome's blanket ban on
contraception when he conceded, "In certain cases, where the intention is to reduce the risk
of infection," condoms may be used to save lives in cases of HIV-positive couples and discordant couples. In other words, it would be permissible then for a married couple in which one
partner is HIV-positive to use condoms in order to prevent the other partner from becoming
infected. In this case, then, the use of condoms would be morally justified because it is not
used as a contraceptive. Rather, the intention is to prevent or reduce infection.

[4] Dennis C. Dulings, *The New Testament: History, Literature, and Social Context*, 4th
ed. (Belmont, CA: Wadsworth, 2003), 431–32.

[5] Daniel O. Ihunnia, "Breaking the Evil Yoke: A Challenge for Mission Theology in
Africa," *SEDOS Bulletin* (January 2014): 14.

[6] Matthew's passion narrative ("His blood be on us and on our children!" 27:25)
corroborates the thinking of the era about intergenerational sin expressed by the disciples
in John 9:2.

[7] Frederick L. Moriarty, "Numbers," in *The Jerome Biblical Commentary* (London:
Geoffrey Chapman, 1968), 91.

[8] Ibid.

Jewish thought the man born blind suffers either because of his own sin that caused him to be born blind from the womb or from the sin of his parents who brought him into the world.[9] The Jewish people commonly assumed that disease and disorders on both the personal and national level were due to sin, as summarized in the rabbinic saying from around AD 300 that "there is no death without sin and there is no suffering without iniquity."[10] Many African cultures share similar beliefs around sickness. Daniel O. Ihunnia asserts that many Africans fear curses more than they trust blessings. Consequently, they trace their problems by affiliation to past intergenerational curses.[11] But the prophet Ezekiel (18:20) offers antithesis to such understanding: "The person who sins shall die. A child shall not suffer for the iniquity of a parent, nor a parent suffer for the iniquity of a child." The disciples' question suggests a shift in the understanding of suffering in the deuteronomistic sense. John 9:2, therefore, appears as a request to Jesus to comment on the debate on suffering as a consequence of sin. Jesus corroborates Ezekiel's prophesy in the verses that follow (John 9:3ff.). Jesus refuses to attribute suffering and disease to sin, against the accepted Jewish notion that such a condition was always a punishment implying guilt (Wis. 8:19–20). Indeed, John 5:1–5 supports the idea of suffering as a consequence of personal sin. But can Scripture contradict itself?

The passage on the healing of the man at the Sheep Gate (John 5:1–15) suggests the possibility that suffering in a way can be connected to individual sin. The two incidents (John 5:1–15; 9:2ff.), placed side by side, could create confusion. John 5:1–15 seems to suggest the connection between sin and suffering: "See, you have been made well! Do not sin anymore, so that nothing worse happens to you" (vv. 14). But the latter text suggest otherwise. Regardless of suggestion of divine judgment, both texts awaken the reader to the reality of the human condition. But one should also reject the idea that there is never such a connection between sin and suffering or disease (5:14).[12] Whitacre supports the notion that Jesus's command in John 5 focuses on the man as a sinner, noting the

> striking contrast to the later healing of the man born blind, in which Jesus declines to connect the illness with sin (9:3). These two passages taken together provide important insight into the relation between sin and catastrophes such as illness (cf. Carson 1991:245–46, 361–62). Here a connection is clearly drawn between this man's sin and his

---

[9] Rodney A. Whitacre, *John, The IVP New Testament Commentary Series*, ed. Grant R. Osborne (Downers Grove, IL: InterVarsity Press, 1999), 235.
[10] Ibid.
[11] Ihunnia, "Breaking the Evil Yoke," 15.
[12] Whitacre, *John*, 122.

illness (5:14), whereas the later passage (9:3) seems to suggest that not every illness is directly linked with particular sins.[13]

Although there is a suggestion of personal sin that caused suffering in John 5:1–15, the latter text (John 9:2ff.) presents suffering as an opportunity for God's manifestation. Suffering is thus not an end but rather a means to manifest God's grace either in a person or in a people. That is to say, God does not will evil on a person or a community. Rather, misfortunes, suffering, or disease can have redemptive value. Where sin distorts the image of God in humans, suffering can straighten the relationship. The African notion of sin—its individual and communal character—is not far from the Johannine understanding.

An African Notion of Sin

Close similarities exist between the African and Hebrew worldviews. The Levisons note the "kindred atmosphere" connecting the traditional African culture with the New Testament, and indeed the Hebrew Bible.[14] Thus, a hermeneutics of resonance allows appropriation of John 9:2 for the African context. One can decipher a sense of deuteronomistic determinism in the African perception of suffering. Africans ask questions such as that in John 9:2 when confronted with suffering. Some even attribute HIV and AIDS to a generational or communal curse. Understanding the African approach to sin can illuminate the familial and communal aspects of the pandemic.

Sin can be understood best in the context of African communalism. Sin in its individual and social forms is very much present in the consciousness of the African peoples, as is the need for rites of purification and expiation.[15] I must note that Africa is not a homogeneous entity. Each African group has a unique historical development and economic experience, as well as sociopolitical cultural expressions and religious traditions; as such, there is no single concept or term for sin. This study employs a notion of sin from the Nigerian-Igbo ethnic group.

Although sin is most often an individual act, sin has a communal undertone for the Igbo. Belief in Chukwu (the Supreme Deity) undergirds community actions. The holiness or sinfulness of each reflects on the entire community. Interconnectedness within the group becomes obvious when we consider the

---

[13] Ibid.

[14] John R. Levison and Priscilla Pope-Levison, "Global Perspectives on New Testament Interpretation," in *Hearing the New Testament: Strategies for Interpretation*, ed. Joel B. Green (Grand Rapids: Eerdmans Publishing, 1995), 337.

[15] John Paul II, Apostolic Exhortation *Ecclesia in Africa* (Rome: Libreria Editrice Vaticana, 1995), § 42, 43.

definition of sin in Igbo. Several words translate the term in the language. Three such words are

- *nmehe* (*nme* = do; *ehe* = miss), loosely translates as "miss the target or standard."
- *iheojor* (*ihe* = something, *ojor* = terribly bad), translates as "something terribly bad."
- *aru* (abominable act). *Aru* is an aspect of sin. Every *aru* entails a relational dimension demanding expiation to placate the divinities or ancestors, and to restore communal reconciliation and tranquility.

In the moral order, *nmehe*, missing the standard or doing wrong, suggests a shortfall or a deviation from the standard. Such deviation implies serious consequences for the offender as well as other persons. The consequence of sin transcends the individual who missed the mark. Because the individual is part of the community, whatever affects an individual affects the community as a whole. Hence, the disciples' inquiry in John 9:2 can also become an Igbo dilemma.

The relationship between the individual and the community is an intricate one because the community confers personhood on an individual. The Igbo notion of *ohaka* (the community is supreme) captures this relationship.[16] *Ohaka* corroborates the *Ubuntu* philosophy—"I am because we are, and because we are, therefore I am." Stated differently, a we-logic undergirds African relationality. This we-logic locates the full effect of sin in the life of the community regardless of offender. Elochukwu Uzukwu makes a case for African personhood by insisting that, far from dissolving individuality, African communalism promotes individual gifts for the benefit of the family.[17] We-logic becomes obvious in tending to the cycle of life in which procreation takes a pride of place—hence, the dilemma with battling HIV and AIDS.

To underscore the value placed on sexual practices, Igbo culture includes sex taboos that serve as hedges around sexual practices. Breaking a sex taboo constitutes *nmehe*; such misbehavior attracts the full weight of the law.[18] Against

---

[16] Caroline N. Mbonu, "A Notion of Community in First Corinthians 12:12–26: A Key to Sustain the Igbo Concept of *Ohaka* in the Emerging Global Culture," *Igbo Studies Review*, no. 2 (2014): 112–13.

[17] Elochukwu Uzukwu, *A Listening Church: Autonomy and Communion in African Church* (Maryknoll, NY: Orbis Books, 1996), 78.

[18] In Etche-Igbo tradition, a married man or woman accused of any misconduct would normally swear first by declaring his or her innocence as follows: "I have not gone to bed with another man's wife [woman's husband]." The poignancy of the oath's wording conveys the community sense of sexual sanctity. The belief is that the transgression of marriage vows affects not only the transgressor but the entire community. See Je'adayibe Dogara Gwamna, *Perspectives in African Theology* (Bukuru, Nigeria: African Christian Textbooks, 2008), 172.

this background, the understanding that HIV and AIDS spread through sexual union becomes extremely worrisome. Hence, the attaching of sin to the pandemic emerges from the belief that HIV and AIDS is driven largely by sexual relations outside of marriage.[19] Furthermore, modernity and its attendant urbanization continue to erode traditional values in communities across Africa. Modernity, a process that started in the West with the Enlightenment—to which the African peoples cannot lay direct claim—has not had a wholesome impact on the continent. Cultures influenced by the Enlightenment appear to have lost the sense of the symbolic world, a bastion of the African soul. The African soul is formed and informed by a worldview in which the world of the spirit and the natural world remain connected and intertwined in an endless web of relationship; this worldview appears to be falling apart.[20] Sexual mores appear the hardest hit. Gwamna decries this development in a quote from O'Donovan: "One of the major challenges of modern Africa is how to stop the cancer of sexual degeneration before it destroys the very society.... Sexual sin and degradation is rapidly becoming one of the most deadly realities of modernity in Africa."[21]

An echo of the question, "Rabbi, who has sinned?" resounds in the thought that sexual transgression is *aru*, an abomination that can potentially hurt the entire community. Communities lost their voice in the fight for a collective survival with I-logic that favored secrecy concerning HIV and AIDS patients.[22] *Secrecy* as used here represents what has been sanctified as the "principle of confidentiality," which is grounded in the notion of the "autonomous individual," who first exists before choosing to become a member of the community, a Western anthropological framework. Confidentiality mystifies the disease and creates resentment from other members of the community. Secrecy also deepens the morality of the act and creates room for stigmatization. Individual rights to secrecy concerning a public health issue negate the we-logic that communicates the idea of one's humanity realized only through relationships. The we-logic is based on communalism, a cultured philosophy that supports the idea of a

---

[19]   For a fuller discussion on HIV and AIDS in West Africa, see Benjamin Abotchie Ntreh, "Job," in *Global Bible Commentary*, gen. ed. Danie Patte (Nashville: Abingdon Press, 2004), 141–50.

[20]   The morality deriving from the Enlightenment drives from the "I-logic." The I-logic accentuates individuality to a detriment of solidarity. Solidarity is a principle that undergirds the "we-logic."

[21]   Gwamna, *Perspectives in African Theology*, 155.

[22]   On the Enlightenment, Richard Gula posits, "The communal, relational view of the person is a necessary corrective to the Enlightenment view of the person that has had a far-reaching influence on spirituality and morality. The Enlightenment view of radical individualism thinks of the person as an individual first, not as a social being. As a result, it has focused our moral thinking too much on securing individual rights and liberties." See *The Call to Holiness: Embracing a Fully Christian Life* (New York: Paulist Press, 2003), 103.

person being a being with others, a being for others, and a being through others. In Igbo thought, therefore, a person who contracts HIV and AIDS and conceals the condition from the community negates the personhood of each and every member of the group. Such behavior is consistent with *nmehe* or *iheojor*, or *aru*—a terrible sin, an evil. Group survival remains the raison d'être of community striving.[23] An African concept of sin would include that sin resides not in the individual, as the question in John 9:2 suggests, but could also have a familial or communal dimension. This notion of sin calls for collective moral responsibility. A survival strategy in the face of a disease that could potentially have adverse consequence on the Hebrew people appears to inform the management of Miriam's illness in the book of Numbers.

Managing Public Health Concerns

The Miriam narrative (Num. 12:10–12) offers a paradigm on how to manage communicable disease in the community. There is a trace of a semblance to African attitudes toward persons suffering from HIV and AIDS with Miriam's plight. Reading John 9:2 back into the Miriam story instructs in the relationships between an individual and the community in times of diseases of public health concern.

Scripture is clear on the cause of Miriam's illness; she and Aaron spoke against Moses (Num. 12:1). But Miriam alone is punished, struck with a disease that could potentially harm the entire group. Why Aaron was not punished alongside Miriam remains a puzzle. Gender scholars may intuit a motive, given the patriarchal overtone of the Pentateuch, but there are parallels with the situation of women living with HIV.[24] In Miriam's case, the Israelites' sense of corporate identity was at stake. In a similar way, regarding AIDS, James Alison articulates a viewpoint held in some circles that attributes the illness to divine retribution: "I understood quite clearly at some point in the crisis produced by AIDS, accustomed as I was to hearing talk of AIDS as a punishment from God or a judgment on such and such a behavior, producing the attitude that these

---

[23] Oyeronke Oyewumi: "(Re)Constituting the Cosmology and Sociocultural Institutions," in *African Gender Studies: A Reader*, ed. Oyeronke Oyewumi (New York: Palgrave Macmillan, 2005), 107.

[24] Gender sensibility unearths the parallel between Miriam's punishment and women living with HIV and AIDS. Miriam and Aaron sinned, but only Miriam gets punished. Sophia Chirongoma laments the plight of women in her chapter on women living with HIV in Zimbabwe; see "Women, Poverty, and HIV in Zimbabwe: An Exploration of Inequalities in Health Care," in *African Women, Religion, and Health: Essays in Honor of Mercy Amba Ewudziwa Oduyoye*, ed. Isabel Apawo Phiri and Sarojini Nadar (Maryknoll, NY: Orbis Books, 2006), 173–86.

people deserve what has befallen them, it's not worth the bother of doing something to alleviate the problem."[25]

In the case of Miriam, however, community preservation did not obscure the sense of duty toward the sick and suffering. Restoration of human dignity remains a primary concern for the overall health of any community. The well-being of a community is measured by its attitude toward the weak and infirm. The Miriam narrative offers a response to curbing the killer virus from a cultural viewpoint that resonates with traditional African health management. Moses and the people respond to Miriam in solidarity. Though kept outside the camp for fear of contamination, Miriam was not stigmatized; neither did the community judge her, nor was her humanity degraded. Miriam's ailment would constitute a public health hazard if ill-managed, hence her isolation. Significantly the group did not abandon Miriam in her illness. Indeed, the whole community waited until she recovered and rejoined the group before they continued on their journey (Num. 12:15–16). In this entire episode, the blame game was not an option, and neither was abandonment.

In African ontology, life is not a personal commodity. By implication, when life is in peril, the community is duty bound to come to its rescue. Although community solidarity appears to negate the idea of divine judgment on the sufferer, it does not exonerate one from responsibility for his or her actions.

Moral Responsibility in the Present Predicament: A Way Forward

Just as the disciples in John 9:2 seek to assign moral responsibility to the condition of the man born blind, so too in the present predicament is blame a common reaction. The secrecy, silence, and hushed discussion about issues concerning AIDS tend to intensify the degree to which it is regarded as a moral concern. But one cannot dismiss moral responsibility altogether as an issue attached to the pandemic.

These relativistic times are grossly undermining traditional understandings of morality. Relativism does not dispense one from responsibility, moral or social. Management of the pandemic proves difficult in some parts of Africa because of the moral questions around illicit sexual intercourse that are attached to the mode of the infection's spread. Such thinking supports the false notion that only adults suffer from HIV and AIDS. But like the man born blind in John 9:1–10, many children are born with the disease. Furthermore, some caregivers contract the disease. The various means through which the pandemic spreads

---

[25] James Allison, *Raising Abel: The Recovery of the Eschatological Imagination* (New York: Crossroad, 2002), 158.

compels us to critically find a way out of the quandary. Reading John 9:2ff. from a communal standpoint offers useful insights.

The opening question of the debate, "Rabbi, who has sinned?" (John 9:2), positions Jesus to teach his followers the deeper meaning of sin and suffering. Jesus's response, "Neither this man nor his parents sinned; he was born blind so that God's works might be revealed in him" (John 9:3), locates suffering in the wider range of God's omnipotence. Suffering viewed from this angle moves the scourge out from an individual but into a community. God's self-revelation and creative power reside within a community.[26] God's revelation in Jesus Christ is manifest in giving sight to a man born blind. This healing as well is also a restoration for the parents and the community. Similarly, our theologians can find models of God's self-revelation on African soil. A community dislodged by decades of social and political upheaval and presently being ravaged by AIDS seeks urgently the revelation of God's mighty works—a revelation that would restore dignity and the beauty of the human soul. In the words of Jean Marc Éla, Cameroonian sociologist and theologian, we have to put an end to the reproduction of models that have not been developed within our own African sociocultural context.[27] Such local representation would begin to bring light to the darkness that the pandemic has brought upon the land.

Another way forward in combating the spread of HIV on the continent involves closer attention to the church's teaching on sex and reproductive health. Pope Paul VI's encyclical *Humanae Vitae* is a tool in the fight. *Humanae Vitae* outlined opposition to "artificial birth control" on the basis that it would open a "wide and easy road towards conjugal infidelity and the general lowering of morality,"[28] a problem often associated with urbanization but that also has a religious dimension.

The health of one person is our collective health, and the illness of one person is our collective illness; one person's death becomes a communal death.

---

[26] Caroline N. Mbonu, *Handmaids: The Power of Names in Theology and Society* (Eugene, OR: Wipf and Stock, 2010), 50.

[27] Jean Marc Éla, "Christianity and Liberation in Africa," in *Paths of African Theology*, ed. Rosino Gibellini (Maryknoll, NY: Orbis Books, 1994), 136.

[28] Pope Paul VI, *Humanae Vitae*, www.vatican.va/holy_father/paul_vi/encyclicals/documents/hf_p-vi_enc_25071968_humanae-vitae_en.html. In addition, the Catholic Church's social teaching affirms human life as a mystery, sacred and social (see John Paul II, *Evangelium Vitae* [Rome: Libreria Editrice Vaticana, 1995], § 25, 34, 35, 60, 61). According to John Paul II, human life is social in the sense that it is participated life in kinship and *koinonia*—mutual and reciprocal relationality in which everyone is her or his sister's and brother's keeper (*Evangelium Vitae*, § 19; cf. Gen. 4:9). In other words, believers or persons who profess religious faith are challenged, as responsible and accountable stewards of God's grace, to protect human life, especially when it is most vulnerable, and in this case life threatened by HIV and AIDS.

Therefore, if the HIV and AIDS pandemic is indeed a punishment for sin, then it invites repentance and reconciliation. But Christian faith instructs that God allows suffering to happen usually for reasons beyond human comprehension. Suffering can be a corrective measure against certain tendencies in a person or a people. Perhaps the question asked in John 9:2 is a wakeup call for Africans to look inward and to draw up a holistic agenda for a way forward.

Conclusion

Jesus's disciples' query concerning suffering of the man born blind (John 9:2) draws attention to faith-based responses to the HIV and AIDS pandemic in Africa. Similarities between African cultures and the culture of the land of the Bible facilitate appropriation of the Johannine text in addressing the African AIDS pandemic. A critical study of the biblical texts as they concern suffering would point to God's omnipotence in human situations. Since suffering is often reflected upon as divine judgment, it becomes important to evangelize a belief system that ascribes illness and suffering to God. But one must not also overlook the cultural component of the pandemic. There is a need for a more critical evaluation of the I-logic that emphasizes individual rights, a flaw in the fight against the virulent disease in a we-logic setting. Communities must reclaim their voice in the fight for their collective survival.

By healing the man born blind, Jesus redeems the Jewish idea of personal or intergenerational sin believed to cause suffering. African theologians can show leadership in articulating redemptive aspects of African faith and culture as a new approach to fighting the pandemic of HIV and AIDS. As persons called by God through Jesus Christ, Africans listening and acting on the word of Jesus in the Scriptures would engender a proactive response in eradicating HIV and AIDS from the continent.

CHAPTER 12

GENDER, AIDS, AND THE BIBLE IN AFRICA

A Reading of Ephesians 5:21–31

Priscille Djomhoué

When AIDS first appeared in the 1980s, it was very quickly identified as a disease particular to men, because a large proportion of persons diagnosed in that period were male. But that statistical trend reversed quickly, and the percentage of women among those infected has increased steadily, from 35 percent in 1990 to 41 percent in 1997 and 48 percent in 2004.[1] Indeed, UN secretary-general Kofi Annan made a statement whose profound significance will be evident to every African who knows the foundations of life and the place of women in African culture: "In Africa, AIDS has a woman's face."[2] In 2013, African women represented 58 percent of the total number of people living with HIV.[3] A fact sheet published by UNAIDS in 2014 shows that African women are also more infected than women on other continents.

The fight against inequality between women and men, in the church in particular and in religion and the culture in general, is one avenue that should be explored in order to promote effective measures to eradicate the scourge. My approach leads me to criticize and condemn erroneous readings of the Bible that unfortunately reinforce cultural practices that block African women from making choices that would preserve their health. In this chapter, I seek to highlight the cultural arguments underlying inequalities based on gender, so as to expose their limitations. Moreover, after recognizing that there are several feminist readings of the Bible in relation to HIV and AIDS in Africa, a historical-critical and contextual reading of Ephesians 5:21–31 will allow us to correct

---

[1] UNFPA, "La santé en matière de procréation: une mesure de l'équité," www.unfpa. org/swp/2005/français/ch4/chap4_page1.htm.

[2] Kofi Annan, *New York Times–International Herald Tribune*, December 29, 2002. Comment by Alexandra Suich, www.un.org/french/pubs/chronique/2006/nume-ro2/0206p12.htm.

[3] ONUSIDA, *Fiche d'information, 2014,* http://www.unaids.org/fr/resources/campaigns/2014/2014gapreport/factsheet.

an interpretation frequently propounded in the church to consolidate these inequalities and thereby add to the plight of women in the pandemic—that is, feminization of the pandemic. The gospel calls for a love that is actualized in reciprocal submission of husband and wife, and not in the domination of one by the other. Ephesians 5:21–31 is ideal for my thesis, as this text is one of those most used in the church to validate inequalities between men and women.

Identification and Analysis of Causes

Scholars in numerous disciplines have determined several reasons why women more than men are victims of HIV and AIDS in Africa.[4] While biological factors obviously play a role,[5] the discrepancy in infection rates is better understood in terms of sociocultural and economic factors that validate the marginalization of women, thus creating social conditions that are conducive to increasing the risk of infection.[6]

Sociocultural and Economic Factors

The main causes of women's vulnerability are their inferior status and their sociocultural and economic marginalization. Deprived of all decision-making capacity, they have no means to protect themselves against HIV. Due to the weight of culture and their economic power, men have the leverage to decide on the frequency, timing, and form of sexual relations, as well as the means of prevention. Seeking the economic means to survive may lead poor women to engage in prostitution, a major risk factor. In addition, poverty limits access to information on sexual health and to prevention and treatment technologies. How can women actively fight the pandemic when the culture promotes male dominance, compromises their financial autonomy, and denies them the right to take their own initiative? Many justify the inferiority of women on the basis of cultural and biblical arguments that unfortunately lack substance, which needs most urgently to be established.

---

[4] See Constance R. A. Shisannya, "Violence faites aux femmes: incidences des pratiques sociales et religio-culturelles sur les infections au VIH/SIDA chez les femmes du Kenya," CETA, *Revue de Théologie de Toute l'Afrique* 1, no. 1 (Janvier 2001): 59–71; Robert Igo, *A Window into Hope: An Invitation to Faith in the Context of HIV and AIDS* (Geneva: World Council of Churches, 2009).

[5] OMS, "Genre et VIH/SIDA," www.who.int/gender/hiv_AIDS/fr/.

[6] Priscille Djomhoué, *Les Relations Nouvelles entre hommes et femmes: Préalable au développement de l'Afrique* (Yaoundé: CLE, 2010), 11–12.

Gender and Culture in Africa

The place of women in society is shaped essentially by the ideological constructs that bear on how gender is conceptualized. This thesis is not without its limitations, because a study of some traditional societies reveals that women occupied a prominent place before the Colonial era. For example, in traditional Bamiléké society in Cameroon, we find the prominent position of the Queen Mother called "Mafo" or "Mefeu." She was practically second in rank in the chieftaincy and therefore in that society. Her opinion was very important in the chief's deliberations and decision making. She could even take over when the chief was away. Regarding the Mafo, Maurice Tematio writes,

> This is the title given to the current chief's mother (who is a widow of the late chief) or to her successor (who would thus be a sister of the new leader). This title is always paired with the name of the person in question because one is not born "*Mafo.*" Such a woman possesses special property, and has the right to choose her husband, with whom she does not live. She has her own separate residence where she receives her visitors. Her husband sees her only in private visits to her residence, hence the adage "the mafo is nobody's wife . . . her children belong only to the husband." She enjoys a quasi-masculine status; and, in the absence of the chief, it has happened that an authoritarian *mafo* has exercised effective command of the chieftaincy.[7]

Similarly, in southern Cameroon, there have been women leaders, including Her Majesty Theresa Marie Atangana,[8] chief of the Ewondo and Bene, who reigned in the country's capital. Moreover, numerous women called Kamsi preside over the traditional religious ceremonies in Bamiléké region.[9]

Puzzling, therefore, is why accepting female pastoral ministry in various African countries has been so difficult. Why do women suddenly find themselves excluded from the sphere of decision making? The answer, according to Fatou Sow and Bop Codou,[10] is to be found outside of African culture. The lower status of African women has been imposed upon them for centuries. However, this does not reflect the African cultural background. Women's

---

[7] Maurice Tematio, "Le peuple Bamiléké: origines, traditions, culture, religion et symboles," temation.blogspot.com.

[8] "Obsèques de sa Majesté Marie Thérèse Atangana," corr. Thomas Essomba, www.camer.be.

[9] Every year, Fovu attracts thousands of pilgrims, sometimes from foreign lands, for ceremonies and rites, libations and offerings (Tematio, "Le peuple Bamiléké").

[10] Fatou Sow and Bop Codou, *Notre corps, notre santé: la santé et la sexualité des femmes en Afrique subsaharienne* (Paris: l'Harmattan, 2004), 303.

inferiority comes from foreign influences brought by Islam, Christianity, and colonization. In the case of Christianity, I think this inferior position must be understood as an incorrect reading of the Word of God, because the gospel is by definition good news.

It is also true that certain aspects of African culture can promote a negative conception of woman: notably slavery, the caste system, sorcery and the perception of infertility, and certain rites. In Malawi, for example, ethnic groups such as the Yao, Lomwe, Sena, and Chewa practice initiation rites that mark the passage from puberty to adulthood. After these ceremonies, girls are encouraged to leave the place where the initiation takes place and wash themselves. One of the requirements of this ceremony is to have unprotected sex with an experienced person of the opposite sex. Similar practices are observed among the Bamiléké of Cameroon, in the rite of widowhood. The widow must have sex with a man she has not chosen.

All this cautions us to avoid justifying the low status of women based on fundamentally cultural arguments; these arguments are not unequivocal, so we may be led into error. Conversely, if culture was unequivocal, then all that is cultural would be constructed and therefore open to change. Culture must come under the scrutiny of the gospel, the good news for all. The feminization of the pandemic calls for a reconsideration of antivalues.

The Bible and Male-Female Relationships: A Theology of Equality in Ephesians 5:21–31

There are several African feminist readings of the Bible with respect to HIV and AIDS: M. Dube and M. Kanyoro M., eds., *Grant Me Justice, HIV/ AIDS and Gender Readings of the Bible* (Pietermaritzburg: Cluster Publications and Orbis Books, 2004); Mussa Simon Muneja, *HIV/AIDS and the Bible in Tanzania: A Contextual Rereading of 2 Samuel 13:1–14, 33* (Bamberg: University of Bamberg Press, 2012); M. Masenya, "The Bible, HIV/AIDS, and African–South African Women: A Bosadi (Womanhood) Perspective," http:// uir.unisa.ac.za/; and Musa Dube, "Grant Me Justice: Female and Male Equality in the New Testament," *Journal of Religion and Theology* (Namibia) 3 (2001): 82–115.

The book coedited by Musa Dube and Musimbi Kanyoro highlights biblical readings related to HIV in order to expose social injustices that African women suffer. For them, most biblical readings support the patriarchal system that promotes feminization of the pandemic. Their book offers communities a liberationist approach to Bible reading in the context of HIV, and also shows that the Bible and faith offer models of liberation that can inspire hope. The first part deals with the Old Testament, HIV, and gender. Denise Ackermann, who worked on the text on 2 Samuel 13:1–22, thinks that the subordination of women in this passage is a more virulent virus than HIV. The article by M. Masenya looks at 5 Ephesians and 1 Corinthians 7, but her textual analysis is very cursory.

Following these authors and in the same perspective, I propose a reading of Ephesians 5:21–31 that challenges the erroneous hermeneutical canons that have grounded many interpretations of this text. Such a reexamination aims to provide an exegesis of the text that promotes the fight against the pandemic.[11] The choice of text recalls a marriage blessing ceremony that I concelebrated with a colleague in Cameroon in 2007. My role was to preach while my colleague blessed the couple in question. The liturgy calls for the future spouses to exchange expressions of consent and that we lay our hands on them. My colleague had chosen the liturgical formula that first invites the man and then the woman to pronounce the words of commitment. In fact, the pastor read line by line, and the couple repeated after him.

The man's text was as follows: "I promise to love you, respect you and protect you, to live with you in truth, to remain with you in good times and bad until death do us part." And the woman's response was, "I promise to love you, respect you and assist you, to live with you in the truth, to remain with you in good times and bad, to stay faithful to you until death do us part."

How should we react? The two statements differ. That of the woman differs in two important details: "assist the husband and be faithful to him." My colleague had read the man's text unchanged. But she made a particular point of commenting on the text of the woman, even before the latter spoke. In her commentary she stressed, "To assist the husband should not mean that you oppose him, you do not have the right to take initiatives." By saying this, my colleague assigned to the women the role of a servant rather than a partner. To illustrate her commentary, the pastor intoned this passage of Ephesians 5: "Wives, submit to your husbands."

This text is highly prized in wedding sermons by both pastors and couples. But most of the preaching focuses on the submissive attitude that wives should take in marriage. The reading of the text that defines the couple's relationship as one of male dominance over women and of submission of women to men is linked to a culture of male dominance, which influences the interpretation of Scripture. However, there is a considerable difference between this traditional, biased interpretation and what the text suggests.

Here is my hypothesis: Ephesians 5:21–31 is a revolution in how relations between the partners should develop. It shows that neither member of

---

[11] Priscille Djomhoué, "Des relations nouvelles dans le couple: relecture d'Ephésiens 5,21–31," in *Les Relations Nouvelles entre hommes et femmes: Préalable au développement de l'Afrique*, ed. Priscille Djomhoué (Yaoundé: Clé, 2010), 79–96.

the couple is expected to dominate or be dominated for reasons of gender. The husband and wife owe each other submission and respect. In the interests of deepening our understanding of the text, I proceed in two steps. First is textual exegesis in order to define the meaning of the relationship of husband and wife; second is a suggestion of how Scripture can illuminate our concept of male/ female relationships from the perspective of development and the fight against the AIDS pandemic in Africa.

Understanding the Text

This passage comes right after the exhortation to reject how the world lives and to imitate God instead. In fact, faith in Christ is the starting point of a new life: "Therefore be imitators of God, as beloved children, and live in love, as Christ loved us and gave himself up for us, a fragrant offering and sacrifice to God" (Eph. 5:1–2). This verse is presented to illustrate the example to be followed, that of Christ, seen from the perspective of the relationship that should exist between husband and wife.

A remarkable similarity exists between this first verse of the chapter and the first verse of the passage we are studying. Consider, first, "Therefore be imitators of God, as beloved children" (5:1), and then, "Be subject to one another out of reverence for Christ" (5:21). The two passages are addressed to believers in general, regardless of gender and age. Grammatically, the second-person plural—*imitez* (be imitators) followed by *craignez* (fear) and *soumettez-vous* (be subject)—means that the exhortation is directed toward God's people without distinction. I think verse 21 summarizes everything that will be expounded subsequently. The justification for this assertion is grammatical: the punctuation at the end of verse 21. The modern Greek text (NA[26])[12] uses a comma—a choice of a punctuation, a variation indicating how the rest of the sentence should be read. I support the choice of the *Traduction Oecuménique de la Bible* (TOB) and the *Louis Second* version (revised 2005), which changed the comma in French to a semicolon. Indeed, the semicolon marks an average-strength break, separating two parts of the same sentence, the first clarifying the second. In other words, verse 21 is a kind of summary of what is developed in the rest of the pericope. Thus, the text is an exhortation addressed to the husband and wife, inviting them to submit to one another. Markus Barth notes[13] that

In Eph 5:22 ff., the call for specific subordination of one group to another is indissolubly tied to the mutual order proclaimed in 5:21.

---

[12] Nestlé Aland, *Novum Testamentum Graece*, 26th edition (1984).

[13] The specific call in Ephesians 5:22 for subordination of one group to another is absolutely inseparable from the mutual order declared in 5:21.

> Except in some variant readings . . . the term "subordinate" is not even repeated in vs. 22. The single imperative of vs. 21 ("subordinate Yourselves to one another") anticipates all that Paul is about to say not only to wives, children and slaves, but also to husbands, fathers and masters, about the specific respect they owe because of Christ to those with whom they live together either by choice or by birth, or by historical circumstances.[14]

Thus, the relationship of husband and wife is not situated in the paradigm of power but of love that invites man and woman to mutual submission. Commenting on verses 25 and 26, Michel Boutier says that a single source results in different invitations to the woman and man: submission and love.[15]

Mutual Submission in Marriage

The Greek verb *upotasso*, which means "to submit," does not exist in the twenty-sixth or twenty-seventh editions of the Greek New Testament. The TOB and the versions that place it explicitly in the text have adopted the now-abandoned model of the twenty-fifth edition. Indeed, in the twenty-sixth and twenty-seventh editions, the verb appears in verse 21, in the present participle form, which gives it the connotation of exhortation. The task is to endorse mutual subordination. This verb, therefore, does not appear explicitly in verse 21, which calls upon the woman, but appears clearly in verse 24, which directly addresses the man. Nevertheless, let us try to understand the version of the twenty-fifth edition adopted by the TOB.

The first word at the beginning of verse 22, "wives," is a summons, an apostrophe that unconditionally prepares the reader to listen to a word or message. The same technique is used in verse 25 about the man: "husbands." After employing this apostrophe toward both members of the couple, recommending a mutual submission as evidenced by the use of "vous" (you) and "les uns aux autres" (each other) at the beginning of verse 21, I think Paul addresses each member individually to explain how this submission should be understood.

This text presents an entirely new understanding, a message that will surprise the Jews. It bursts upon them at a very special time in the development of a Christianity that raises challenges to some traditional values. Paul finds himself between the Greco-Roman world and the Jewish world. Jewish society is patriarchal, but Ephesus is a cosmopolitan city with several religions,

---

[14] Markus Barth, *Ephesians 4–6: A New Translation with Introduction and Commentary*, Anchor Bible (New York: Doubleday and Company, 1974), 609.

[15] Michel Boutier, *L'épître de Saint Paul aux Ephésiens* (Geneva: Labor et Fides, 1991), 243.

especially the worship of Artemis and Demeter. In this context, women are in charge of cultural and financial affairs and can flourish without husbands. Thus, not only were they priestesses, they also threatened male authority. Elisabeth Fiorenza says, "As a rule, one finds increasingly frequent recommendations in favor of submission and proper 'feminine' conduct every time there is a rise in the real socio-religious status of women and their power within patriarchy."[16] This text mirrors the problems of the church in Ephesus, which included the desire of Christian women to emulate the priestesses of pagan cults. It is also the aim of the author to redefine the nature of the marital relationship among Christians in an environment where some people, sensing that their authority is waning, try to have women be submissive.

The TOB calls this passage "les relations nouvelles" (new relationships). This title is justified by the fact that the author of Ephesians, in the name of God's love and the light of the gospel, must destroy the very foundations of the prevailing morality. He will do so by employing a subtle teaching method: "Be subject to one another out of reverence for Christ" (5:21).

This verse introduces a new family and social code.[17] The couple's relationships are put under the theme of mutual submission. Paul's exhortation is often focused on Christian humility: Ephesians 2:1–11 says that whoever claims any authority must restrain or abase themselves so as to receive that authority from the hands of God. Similarly, Galatians 5:13 extols this submission in the service of Christians to each other: "through love become slaves to one another." The relationship of husband and wife is not based on a relationship of domination, subordination, or superiority, but of mutual submission.

In the writings of Paul, other lists of duties look different from those of Ephesians; for example, Colossians 3:18–4:1; 1 Timothy 2:11–13; and Titus 2:4–5. Here, the details of the exhortation appear at first glance to be inconsistent with those in Ephesians. Indeed, how can it be said that there is no relationship of inferiority and superiority in the couple when Paul says, "Wives, be subject to your husbands"?

According to Paul, Love Is Submission

Note that in verse 22, the adverb of comparison, "comme" (as)—in the phrase, "as you are to the Lord"—gives the real meaning of the phrase. This adverb appears twice: regarding the wife first and then the husband (v. 25). The

---

[16] Elisabeth Schüssler Fiorenza, *En Mémoire d'Elle* (Paris: Cerf, 1986), 169.

[17] Germans refer to this text as "Haustafeln," following Martin Luther, meaning "household codes." Michel Boutier compares this expression with what is known as *Code Familial* (240). Personally, I think it can be called the *Nouveau Code de la Famille* (*New Family Code*) because it represents a new way to understand the couple's relationships.

meaning of the advice to the couple is compared to the relationship between Jesus and the church. In other words, the woman is submissive to her husband as unto the Lord, and the husband is the head of the wife as Christ is the head of the church. By means of this comparison, Paul gives an entirely different meaning to the word that is translated by "head."

The subtlety of Paul here is at the level of the use of the verb "submit." By using this verb in relation to the attitude of the wife to her husband, he avoids shocking his contemporaries whose traditions imposed inferior status on women. But its meaning changes through Paul's instructive use of a comparison through which he calls on husbands and wives to reconsider the meaning of their relationship. Though we encounter the use of a word to which we are accustomed, that word takes on an unaccustomed meaning.

When Paul says, "Husbands, love your wives," it sounds entirely normal in a society where loving a wife is like loving the food we consume when hungry and put aside when full. We must pay attention, however, to the rest of the sentence. Introducing, "just as Christ loved the church," changes things completely. The meaning of the love that the husband owes to the wife is to be sought in the way that Christ loved the church. The meaning of the husband's duty becomes entirely new, because Christ loved the church until death. In ancient society the husband has the right of life and death over his wife. But according to our text, it is for the husband to sacrifice himself for his wife, as Christ did for the salvation of the world. The relationship in the couple is thereby a parable of the love of God and humanity.

Toward a Theology of Equality

The letter to the Ephesians challenges the patriarchal patterns of a society that wants wives to submit to their husbands' dictates. It invites us to see the husband-wife relationship not as confined within a power structure that constrains each of them, but as expressing love as manifested by Christ. Marital relations, like human relationships in general, are based on love and mutual submission. Here we have a theology of equity. Love does not alienate the other; it amplifies the standing of the person to whom one relates. Our interpretation of Holy Scripture should lead to questioning traditional positions that diminish the other, if not to dismissing them altogether, and adopting positions that elevate the other. Our cultures and practices must be tested against the word of our God who raises our neighbor up and encourages the construction of a new society where men and women live in harmony.

The Church and Gender Integration

Today, no institution, including the church, is blind to the strong link between gender inequality and the feminization of HIV and AIDS. But has this knowledge led to an awareness that materializes in active applications within ecclesial practice? If we look on the level of policy for clear efforts to integrate gender considerations, the church remains the place where resistance is most pronounced. In their practices and structures, the church and religions generally must courageously accept the cultural challenges of the AIDS pandemic and other scourges whose most visible consequence is the delayed development and misery of their members. It is imperative that inequality, the main factor contributing to women's vulnerability, be addressed. The church must engage in a reform centered on the rejection of gender inequality in order to change the unequal social relationships of men and women and stop the spread of HIV infection.

Part Four

Foundations of an African Theology on HIV and AIDS

CHAPTER 13

THE AIDS PANDEMIC AS A
PROBLEM OF THEODICY

Dossou Davy

AIDS is the most lethal pandemic since the Spanish flu of 1918. Patients, doctors, and scientists are not the only ones who are worried by the existential threat of this scourge of society, because AIDS is not only a disease, a human suffering, but also a physical and moral evil. This chapter reflects on the AIDS pandemic as a problem of theodicy. As a subdiscipline of philosophy, theodicy interrogates God in connection with the existence of suffering and evil.

This chapter is organized around three points. First, I show how the pandemic is a challenge to science, medicine, and society. Second, I explain how the AIDS pandemic emerges as a problem of theodicy. Finally, I suggest some philosophical and theological paradigms as ways to relieve or soothe the anxiety of people living with HIV (PLWH).

A Challenge to Science, Medicine, and Society

Scientists have identified the viral origin of AIDS. However, its incredibly fast mutations are a great challenge to biomedical science. In the absence of a cure to the physical pain that AIDS provokes, science has found and proposed palliative treatments to alleviate the patient's pain. Strong cooperation between scientists and clinical researchers, the contribution of the private and public sectors, the intervention of the public health authorities, and finally, the central involvement of PLWH are favorable indicators in the fight against HIV and AIDS.

A Challenge to Society

The recognition of the challenging nature of AIDS and HIV should not be a pretext for inertia and defeatism. Instead, it should be an opportunity to think differently and to act more efficiently. The HIV and AIDS pandemic is a multidimensional problem, because it plunges us into a universe of insecurity where the human being, faced with the pandemic's disastrous consequences, can be powerless and hopeless. AIDS floods us like the waves of a tsunami. It shakes our values, forcing us to question our behaviors. It reveals our selfishness, insofar as many believed that the illness was confined to some well-defined social categories.[1]

The AIDS pandemic challenges the social body to rethink how it cares for people. This entails a thorough scrutiny of social insufficiencies, prejudices, and inequalities that shape daily life and pave the way to infection. From an anthropological standpoint, AIDS challenges both the individual and the community to become responsible agents by performing tasks aiming at improving HIV prevention and AIDS management instead of asking the question, "Where is AIDS from?" These attempts at action can change our perspective from a victim-blaming attitude to that of concrete engagement. On a political level, as a guarantor of the public's health, the state ought to assign an important portion of the national budget to the fight against the pandemic in accordance with strategic planning for effective prevention of the virus. Moreover, the state is the best avenue to design policies and programs aiming at providing the affected and infected individuals with much-needed care.

A Theodicy Issue

Questions about the nature of God are inevitably related to questions around the meaning of human freedom. But these questions become more crucial in the presence—or perhaps more aptly, in the omnipresence—of evil. The AIDS pandemic emerges as a problem of theodicy, because it takes us into the nebulous heart of suffering and evil. It sends people back to themselves in their anguish, existential fragility, and ontological finitude. Raising the phenomenon of AIDS from a theodicy perspective, I attempt here to understand whether the scourge is connected to a deficiency in our human constitution or is the result of the misuse of freedom.

Etymologically, the word "theodicy" is composed of *Théos* and *dikê*. The Greek term *dikê* has several meanings: law, conflict of law, punishment, or trial. The verb *dikaio* means to seek justice, to hold something for fair trial and justification. "Theodicy" does not mean the "trial and justification of God," but a justification of God's goodness and providence in the presence of evil.

Evil is often viewed as a foreign body, an independent entity that can be rejected. It is also seen as a spiritual or material stain, able to affect several links in a chain of forces that have a close relationship with each other. The Congolese theologian Lusala Luka Lu Ne Nkuka affirms that "the African religious

---

[1] Elisabeth Kübler-Ross, *Le Sida, un défi à la société* (Paris: Interéditions, 1988).

conception of evil refers to everything that denies life. It is the earth, the world of human beings with their passions. It is the world of darkness. The obscurity where the will to harm humans beings prevails."[2] As an evil, the AIDS pandemic appears like a dangerous beast that hides in the shadows, destroys personal plans, puts in question the future of humanity, and shakes human relationships unpredictably. It discloses itself as an elusive unknown, a kind of transcendence with a mysterious origin that reveals humanity's impotence to solve the enigma of existence.

Why should we suffer? Why does AIDS exist? God is accused of remaining silent in the face of human suffering. If God loves us, why does he allow us to be affected by AIDS? Is evil included in the workings and nature of human freedom? Can a just God be the cause of evil? How can we hold God responsible for all evil in the world? Taking into consideration the thought of Leibniz, we can give a threefold answer to these questions: physical, metaphysical, and moral.

A Physical Evil

A deep meditation on the book of Job conveys the reality and impacts of physical evil. Just as the silence of God in the face of suffering such as AIDS surprises us to the point of shaking our faith, so, too, Job seeks in vain God's response to his tribulations and questions. But what if, as in Job's case, we hear a call to recognize our created nature and to contemplate the greatness of the one who has mastered the monstrous Leviathan?

Following Leibniz's thesis, God is the physical cause of evil in the world and in human beings, because he is the Creator and the origin of all that exists. Evil caused by AIDS becomes evil suffered by a person who is affected. Titus Njoroge Mbugua affirms that "only God knows AIDS. It is up to us to do our part."[3] Such an assertion seems to hold God responsible for AIDS, since he is the Creator of all existing beings. Remember the famous text from the prophet Isaiah: "I am the Lord, and there is no other. I form the light and create darkness. I make well-being, and I create disaster. I, the Lord, do all these things" (Isa. 45:6–7). The prophet's intention is clear: the affirmation that God is the unique master of good and evil, life and death.[4] Following this logic, would

---

[2] Lusala Luka Lu Ne Nkuka, *Jésus-Christ et la religion africaine: réflexion christologique à partir de l'analyse des mythes d'Osiris, de Gueno, d'Obatala, de Kiranga et NzalaMpanda* (Rome: Gregorian and Biblical Press, 2010), 123.

[3] Réseau Jésuite de Lutte contre le SIDA, *Un peuple qui veut vivre* (Abidjan: Editions du CERAP, 2007), 133.

[4] Charles Journet, *Le mal: Essai théologique* (Suisse: Editions Saint Augustin, 1988), 77.

AIDS have been caused by the working of "God's left hand"[5]—that is, the consequence of his anger?[6] The AIDS pandemic would be something determined in
advance by God, in a way that it is inevitably inscribed in humankind's destiny.
In this regard, humanity is forced to live with an ineradicable and incomprehensible evil.

Regardless of all moral norms, the human tragedy of AIDS awakens in us a
feeling of something unjustifiable: the physical pain, the death. A person living
with HIV has the feeling of facing her- or himself as if facing a stranger, an
unknown that remains an enigma. The person is confronted with the absolutely
opaque character of being unfolding in this human tragedy. Socially, a person
living with HIV is often stigmatized as being dangerous for others. Like Job,
"the suffering innocent," these people are challenged by suffering to the point
of demanding account to God: "Tell me what I did!" Similarly, the scientist
cries out in distress to God, because AIDS puts to the test science's capacity to
discover what can cure such a disease. Faced with AIDS, the patient experiences
human finitude in weakness, loneliness, isolation, and pain. It is an experience
of upheaval for the flesh. As Maurice Merleau-Ponty noted, the flesh holds a
"double meaning of what is felt and what feels."[7]

A Metaphysical Evil

The problem of the existence of evil in the presence of belief in God is
usually parsed on the level of metaphysics and theology, and can be called the
two extreme points of a single intuition of intelligence.[8] In classical philosophical terms, being exists as a positive reality while evil exists as deprivation. We
can truly think of the AIDS pandemic as evil on the philosophical and theological levels if we understand that each human being has a right to one's integrity,
a right to be what the person is—a right to one's *being*.

In a metaphysical sense, evil represents the essential finitude of the creature. As Leibniz notes, "We must consider that there is an original imperfection
in the creature before sin, because the creature is limited in essence, whence it
cannot know everything, and that it can mislead and make other mistakes."[9]

---

[5] This expression comes from Karl Barth, "Dieu et le Néant," in *Dogmatique* (Geneva:
Labor et Fides, 1963).

[6] Paul Ricoeur, "Le mal: un défi à la philosophie et à la théologie," 227.

[7] Extrait de *Le visible et l'invisible* de Maurice Merleau-Ponty cité par Renaud Barbaras,
"De la phénoménologie du corps à l'ontologie de la chair" in *Le Corps* (Paris: Vrin, 1992), 273.

[8] Journet, *Le mal*, 50.

[9] Wilhelm Gottfried Leibniz, *Essai de Théodicée sur la bonté de Dieu, la liberté de
l'homme et l'origine du mal*, ed. Paul Janet (Félix Alcan, 1900), §20.

The source of such evil "must be sought in the ideal nature of the creature."[10] The place of eternal truths is "the ideal cause of evil, so to speak, as well as good."[11] As a result, every creature contains evil within oneself, metaphysically speaking.

AIDS is a metaphysical evil insofar as it becomes a symptom of vulnerability of the being in its ontological finitude. This evil is real and exists as an injury or mutilation of the being. In order to act, AIDS stifles the healthy act, alters the being of the human person, and hampers the creative process. If God is the ruler of the world, is AIDS not the result of a violation of the order of the world? If the life of a person living with AIDS is reduced to a present dominated by suffering and the anguish of death, which no theodicy may reasonably minimize, this is due to the fact that the desire for eternity is now stifled by the disease that impoverishes one's sense of perspective.[12] A person living with HIV views the future with pessimism, reducing the temporality of life to a present dominated by suffering, to which is added the symbolic violence of the looks and the judgment of others.[13]

Ontological humiliation suffered by the human being is an experience whereby one tries to measure the huge distance between what one truly is and what one seems to become in concrete existence. A person is brought to realize that he or she is "less than what he is." This negative experience of situation-limits and limitations reflects "an invincible opposition between a world that would satisfy the spiritual absolute, and the real world where men bend variously under the misfortune that seems to aggravate the contingency with which it has reached out to them."[14] Martin Heidegger illustrates this when he says that the *Dasein* (human being) experiences deprivation, anxiety, and loneliness in a world that does not offer any shelter.

A Moral Evil

AIDS is not only an individual disease; it affects the entire human community. Moral evil—*sin* in religious language—can be seen as an ethical consequence of metaphysical evil. But can God be the cause or bear responsibility for moral evil? According to Leibniz, God is not the cause of moral evil, because God willingly oriented the act of creation toward perfection. It is clear

---

[10] Ibid.

[11] Ibid.

[12] Lucien Ayissi, "Philosophie de la vie et éthique de l'altérité face aux défis du Sida," in *Penser le Sida. Analyses croisées d'une pandémie*, sous la direction de Hubert Mono Ndjana et Lucien Ayissi (Paris: L'Harmattan, "Collection Ethique, Politique et Science," 2010), 11–37.

[13] Claire Marin, *Violence de la maladie, violence de la vie* (Paris: Armand Colin, Collection "L'inspiration philosophique," 2008), cité par Ayissi, 13–14.

[14] Jean Nabert, *Essai sur le mal* (Paris: PUF, 1955), 53.

that when God considers every creature "in itself," God intends the creature to reach perfection. When God considers beings that join with others to form a harmonious whole with a common destiny, God also directs them toward perfection. Therefore, the best possible world is the one that exists in actuality.[15]

If God is not the cause of moral evil, then we can understand evil as being a fault or failure caused by the act of volition of a supernatural being—for example, Satan, the Adversary, in Judeo-Christian anthropology. Satan is the incarnation par excellence of evil, the personification of the original chaos in the order of creation. In this case, Satan could be held responsible for evil in humanity. Another significant fact that deserves mention is the intrinsic link established by some between witchcraft and AIDS. In this case, AIDS would be the logical outward sign or symptom of witchcraft or a curse cast by an evil spirit or force of evil to weaken or destroy the vital force. Or is AIDS the logical consequence of the misuse of freedom by humanity? If HIV occurred by an act of human volition, then perhaps human beings can be held responsible for it.

In African traditional culture, disease is a sign that something is wrong in our interpersonal relationships with God, with other people, or with the rest of creation. Disease is perceived as the consequence of an unhealthy relationship, but also of any improper or indelicate behavior toward God and the cosmos, that disrupts our health. In this light, a person living with AIDS is one who is at odds with both society and the cosmos, either because the person was guilty of a breach of the natural or divine law or a principle that governs the good life.

Lucien Ayissi confirms that the reality of getting sick, of losing one's well-being, "can be interpreted as the result of a cynical and transgressive lifestyle."[16] A person living with HIV is seen as "one whose existence might put society at risk," while "being healthy is proof that the relationship with the cosmos is not yet tainted by fault or sin."[17] The moral damages that patients incur are multiple and multifaceted, ranging from social stigma to professional discrimination, from the threat of the accusing gaze of others to the inclusion within macabre categories where they are condemned to solitude and a lonely death. Even if, objectively and rationally, AIDS is not regarded as a punishment for disordered sexual acts, it is never completely separated from fault or wrongdoing.

If the autonomy of human freedom consists in the determination of one's own will, this autonomy is included from the beginning within the individual soul. Would God therefore be both complicit and the author of evil in a person whose "choice" and "freedom" have already been directed or oriented? On this question, Leibniz's answer is interesting. "The evils sometimes become subsid-

---

[15] Leibniz, *Essai de théodicée*, § 41.
[16] Ayissi, "Philosophie de la vie et éthique de l'altérité face aux défis du Sida," 14.
[17] Ibid.

iary assets, as means for larger goods."[18] Therefore, "Whenever something seems blameworthy to us in the works of God, one should judge that we do not know it enough and believe that a wise man, who would understand it, would judge that we cannot even wish anything better."[19]

From such a perspective, God allows evil for the sake of harmony, and evil is the condition of harmony in the universe. Is God forced to allow evil? If he is compelled to do it, then he is not all-powerful. But can God then freely allow evil? If he can, then he lacks goodness. God "allows" that we do not yet see his reign and that we are still threatened by nothingness.[20] This is the dilemma that HIV and AIDS victims experience. The AIDS pandemic urges us to rethink our autonomy and our human freedom in the cosmos, in relation to the harmony between immanence and transcendence—hence Leibniz's exhortation to prudence, to respecting the sacred order established by nature.

What steps can we take to deal with the challenge of HIV and AIDS? The difficult situation that AIDS places us in compels us to explore two pathways to a healing process and psychological relief for victims.

The Social and Philosophical Pathway

AIDS has ravaged and devastated society; does it not call for social justice—a justice that at the individual level calls for an ethics of otherness, of the loving and welcoming look, and (at the collective level) for an imperative of solidarity? In the words of Paul VI, "If the most extraordinary scientific advances, the most amazing technical prowess, the most prodigious economic growth are not accompanied by a genuine social and moral progress, they turn finally against the human."[21] The dignity of every human being who suffers must be defended vigorously. Instead of casting an accusatory look at people living with HIV, we must demonstrate more in the face of their human suffering. Their suffering is a call to responsibility that "challenges us to do everything we can to restore health to the sick and avert preventable diseases."[22] In addition to ethical commitments, however, the same mandate for social justice requires responsible scientific and medical research. While the benefits of scientific and technological advances "manifest the nobility of man's vocation to participate

---

[18] Leibniz, *Essai de théodicée*, § 35.

[19] Ibid., § 47.

[20] Ricoeur, "Le mal," 227.

[21] Pope Paul VI, Discours à l'occasion du 25ème anniversaire de la FAO (16 novembre 1970), n. 4: AAS 62 (1970): 833, cité par le pape François dans son Encyclique *Laudato Si*, Sur la sauvegarde de la maison commune, donné à Rome, le 24 Mai 2015, 5.

[22] Pierre Meinrad Hebga, "Santé et salut," *Revue Christus* 118 (1983): 166–67.

responsibly in the creative action of God in the world,"[23] it must not, however, give rise to a bacteriological and viral manipulation carried out indiscriminately that ignores the negative effects of these interventions.

The Theological Pathway

In the Old Testament, inexplicable suffering is often attributed to personal and collective sin, known or unknown. The judgment of people today is often not so different from that of people of the Old Testament. For example, some who are themselves living with HIV think that it is a punishment, and ask, What did I do to God?

We all know how quickly we judge as guilty those in our societies who engage in sexual depravity. We hear echoes of this in the New Testament, in the episode of the healing of the blind man: "Rabbi, who sinned, he or his parents, that he was born blind?" In our context, the question thus arises: "Rabbi, who sinned, he or his parents, that he was infected by HIV?" To his disciples as to us today, Jesus replied, "Neither this man nor his parents sinned, but this happened so that the works of God might be displayed in him" (John 9:2–3).

Jesus thus rejects the idea of suffering as punishment from God. He rejects the easy moralization and condemnation. For Jesus, suffering is an opportunity to act, to bear witness to God's liberating action. He offers us an opportunity to abandon searching for the scapegoat in favor of taking personal responsibility. PLWH can be helped to understand that, in the words of Pope Benedict XVI, "It is not escaping the suffering, running away from pain, which heals the man, but the ability to accept the tribulations and mature by them, to find a meaning to life in union with Christ who suffered with infinite love."[24]

Suffering is also an integral part of human existence. The intervention of Jesus does not remove us from the torment of this world, but rather gives us the courage and strength to carry the testimony of faith and hope in the middle of the torment of the AIDS pandemic. Only the acceptance of the grace to enter into the mystery of the cross could make us, the carriers of HIV, victorious in any ordeal. "If, indeed, the goodness of God is shown in how He fought evil since the beginning of Creation," to quote Paul Ricoeur, our fighting against the AIDS pandemic "make us the co-belligerents."[25] If we believe in Christ, and that God conquered evil through Christ, we must also believe that evil cannot destroy us. The AIDS pandemic, far from being regarded as a divine or cosmic punishment, can be a place of learning and exercise of hope.

---

[23] Pope Francis, *Laudato Si*, 102.

[24] Pope Benedict XVI, *Spe Salvi*, 35.

[25] Ricoeur, "Le mal," 228.

CHAPTER 14

CHRISTOLOGY IN A TIME OF DISTRESS

Eugène Didier Goussikindey

The task of deepening our understanding of Christ is a permanent endeavor of the Christian faith for each generation, with its particular context and challenges. The task of exploring the meaning of Christ's person and message in a given circumstance like the HIV and AIDS pandemic is often dominated by the quest for relevancy. In dealing with an issue as fundamental as our understanding of Christ, we must then keep in mind this important reminder of John P. Meier: "Nothing ages faster than relevance."[1] My core concern in this chapter is to explore how the challenges of HIV and AIDS can be illuminated by Christ's own experience as unfolds in Christian tradition.

Our understanding of "who Christ is" has never been a simple and straightforward task. When Jesus himself took the initiative of asking his followers, "Who do men say that the Son of man is?" (Matt. 16:13, 15),[2] he was confronted with different answers to the point of reframing his question: "Who do you say that I am?" Peter's answer—"You are the Christ, the Son of the living God" (Matt. 16:16)—has since set the stage for an unparalleled exploration of the meanings of "Christ" and "Son of God,"[3] which still challenge us today.

Over the past decades, HIV and AIDS have stirred passion and compassion, showing how vulnerable infected people become and how vulnerable affected people are as well. As the cries of so many men and women confronted with HIV and AIDS persist, the unavoidable question arises: "What bearing does Christian response have on the burning problem of the day, and how is all this

---

[1] John P. Meier, *A Marginal Jew: Rethinking the Historical Jesus*, vol. 2 (New York: Doubleday, 1994), 1. As I was concluding this essay, West Africa, where I am living, has been hard hit by Ebola, a deadly virus that gives the immune system hardly any chance to defend itself.

[2] Through this essay, scriptural references are to the Revised Standard Version.

[3] See John P. Meier, *A Marginal Jew: Rethinking the Historical Jesus*, vols. 1–3 (New York: Doubleday, 1991–1999) and 4 (New Haven: Yale University Press, 2009); Raymond E. Brown, *The Birth of the Messiah*, new updated ed. (New York: Doubleday, 1993); Brown, *The Death of the Messiah from Gethsemane to the Grave*, vols. 1–2 (New York: Doubleday, 1993–1994).

related to Christ?"[4] This chapter grapples with the challenges of the pandemic on our understanding of Christ. First, I offer a basic frame of the social context that has determined our reflection; second, I explore some selected elements of biblical tradition that give matters for thought in approaching the issue. Finally, I attempt to recapture a perspective on Christ that could help infected and affected people to continue the life journey with HIV and AIDS.

Framing the Social and Ecclesial Context
of HIV and AIDS

From the outset, we need to reckon with the fact that there are many and diverse stakeholders on matters concerning HIV and AIDS. HIV and AIDS permeate and deeply affect all levels of human society. Governments around the world are concerned with containing the spread of the pandemic. With the help of UNAIDS[5] and in close collaboration with a dozen other UN agencies— especially WHO and UNICEF—the United Nations appears at the forefront of many plans for action. The civil society in a significant number of countries has been advocating the right of people living with HIV and AIDS to live free of discrimination and their right to treatment.

On treatment itself, the scientific community researching HIV and AIDS regularly consider various attempts to tackle the virus and ways to contain it from weakening the immune system. The hope is to win the battle through a vaccine or an appropriate and effective drug with few side effects. Acting in collaboration with and sometimes independently from the scientific medical community are the research and development laboratories of pharmaceutical companies.

Of different concerns are the family and friends affected by their loved ones living with or dead from illness related to HIV and AIDS. Attentive to whatever is said or envisioned on HIV and AIDS, family and friends often have to expend time and resources to care for the sick, the widowed, and the orphaned. Some sufferers are too scared, too weak, or too poor to face the challenges. The greatest burden is carried by people infected by HIV as well as those who have already developed AIDS. With death looming on the horizon, they experience powerlessness and, at times, feeling misunderstood or guilty. They are distressed by what they have to leave behind. Handling one's status is often a burden to carry.

Among the stakeholders, many religious denominations are committed to the cause of fighting HIV and AIDS. The Roman Catholic Church particularly

---

[4] Raimon Panikkar, *Christophany: The Fullness of Man*, trans. Alfred DiLascia (Maryknoll, NY: Orbis Books, 2004), 5.

[5] See www.unAIDS.org, especially "Strategy 2011–2015" and "The Gap Report" (2014).

has a wide range of responses to the pandemic: from medical care in hospitals and health-care centers to pastoral and spiritual care in parishes and Christian communities. The church's commitment is guided by social and moral teachings, and theological principles and guidelines for her members' action. In addition, many theologians have taken up the ministry of deepening the faith within this context. This chapter participates in this effort. To recapture an image of Jesus Christ in this context, I examine three crucial moments in the life journey of Jesus Christ that will be central to our understanding: his incarnation as an expression of God's care, his crucifixion as an expression of God's love, and his resurrection as God's light and continuous presence in the darkness of humanity to the end of time.

Elements of the Biblical Tradition

The Incarnate Lord: A God Who Cares

With Raymond E. Brown, "One may speak of the Gospels as developing backwards," from "the oldest Christian preaching" concerning Jesus's death and resurrection to his birth: "Not only did these events constitute the clearest instance of God's salvific action in Jesus, but also it was through them that the disciples came to a more adequate understanding of who Jesus really was."[6] The infancy narrative can be understood as the culmination or the full maturity of the disciples' experience of Jesus. This experience can be summed up by a catchword from Matthew: "God with us" (1:23).

While Matthew offers a genealogy and Luke a historical context for Jesus's birth, both have brought to the fore the human root of Jesus while preserving in his birth a unique act of God. The bond with God has its deepest expression in the Gospel of John: "In the beginning was the Word and the Word was with God, and the Word was God. ... And the Word became flesh and dwelt among us, full of grace and truth; we have beheld his glory, glory of the Son from the Father" (John 1:1, 14). Ultimately, we owe to Paul the expression of the pivotal stand and unique position of Jesus both in his relation to human beings and to God: "When the time had fully come, God sent forth his Son, born of woman, born under the law, to redeem those who were under the law, so that we might receive adoption as sons" (Gal. 4:4–5).

The basic experience of the early disciples was that of God's nearness in Jesus Christ. They were convinced that, with Jesus Christ, God has made manifest an intimate bond with humankind. In translating this original experience through time and space, new ways of thinking and speaking were carved to fit

---

[6] Brown, *Birth of the Messiah*, 26.

new contexts. Such was the devise of the creed of the Council of Nicaea in 325: "for us humans and for our salvation"[7] he came down and became incarnate, became human, suffered, and rose up on the third day.

Indeed, embedded in the creed is the image of a God who cares by sharing fully in our humanity. This image runs against the common view of God both in the Jewish context and in the Greek worldview. As Paul says, "Jews demand signs and Greeks wisdom, but we preach Christ crucified, a stumbling block to Jews and folly to Gentiles" (1 Cor. 1:22–23). This image of God of the Christian imagination stems from the experience gained in the encounter with Jesus Christ who suffered and rose up.

> Have this mind among yourselves, which was in Christ Jesus, who, though he was in the form of God, did not count equality with God a thing to be grasped, but he emptied himself, taking the form of a servant, being born in the likeness of men. And being found in human form he humbled himself and became obedient unto death, even death on the cross. Therefore God has highly exalted him and bestowed on him the name which is above every name. . . . Jesus Christ is Lord, to the Glory of God the Father. (Phil. 2:6–11)

So, God's manifestation in Christ Jesus is entirely directed toward human beings. The birth of Jesus Christ is by itself an expression of a God who cares for human beings. The coming into the flesh of Jesus Christ is indeed the cornerstone for a fruitful understanding of the challenges brought by the HIV and AIDS epidemic to Christian faith. In Christ, God has taken on our humanity by becoming one of us. So, whatever affects the human condition is no longer stranger to God, because it is no stranger to Jesus Christ: "It was fitting that he, for whom and by whom all things exist, in bringing many sons to glory, should make the pioneer of their salvation perfect through suffering. For he who sanctifies and those who are sanctified have all one origin. That is why he is not ashamed to call them brethren" (Heb. 2:10–11).

Because in Jesus Christ God sets his tents among men, all humanity becomes part of his "household" (Eph. 2:19): brothers and sisters of the same Father, thanks to Jesus Christ. Whatever affects one member of the household affects the entire household. It is, in effect, "for us and for our salvation" that Christ "suffered" and "rose up". Through the incarnation, compassion and care have been manifested as expressions of who God is: "Deus caritas est." In the incarnation, God embraces the human condition for the salvation of all. God is not ashamed of our human condition and its weaknesses. In Jesus Christ, God

---

[7] Norman Tanner, ed., *Decrees of the Ecumenical Councils*, vol. 1 (Washington, DC: Georgetown University Press), 5.

has shown the willingness to shoulder it, to save it. One can say that the incarnation not only reveals how much God, in Christ Jesus, cares for human beings, but it has made manifest that human beings truly matter for God. He is ready to risk himself into the flesh so as to save all by solidarity. The incarnation has made manifest that humanity is not only a concern for God but truly part of God.

The Crucified Lord: A God Who Loves

God's solidarity with human beings in Jesus Christ has been fully manifested in Jesus Christ's compassion for human suffering and by his own suffering and death on the cross. Jesus's compassion for human suffering is epitomized in Luke's story of the widow of Nain:

> Soon afterward, he went to a city called Nain, and his disciples and a great crowd went with him. As he drew near to the gate of the city, behold a man who had died was being carried out, the only son of his mother, and she was a widow. . . . And as the Lord saw her, he had compassion on her and said to her, "Do not weep." (Luke 7:11–14)

At the heart of the drama of the widow of Nain is a life shattered. Jesus's word, "Do not weep," is a grace to "arise." His concern for the sick, the poor, the downtrodden, the marginalized has earned him a famous albeit infamous characterization: "a glutton and a drunkard, a friend of tax collectors and sinners!" (Luke 7:34).

The passion narratives bring to the front Jesus's personal way of coping with suffering. The passion narratives disclose Jesus's attitude when confronted with suffering, betrayal of friendship, desertion of close friends during his trial, sudden distance of a crowd who benefited from his miracles, solitude, silence from his Father, powerless sympathy of some women, and a sense of abandonment, agony, and death. The clear consciousness of his imminent death has been an overwhelming experience whose account challenges, puzzles, and amazes altogether our understanding of God in Jesus Christ. In the Gospels, Jesus was completely aware of the way his words and deeds were received, particularly by the leaders of the time. He announced his passion and death to his disciples. Through his lamentation on Jerusalem we could access his feeling on his mission: "O Jerusalem, Jerusalem, killing the prophets and stoning those who are sent to you! How often would I have gathered your children together as a hen gathers her brood under her wings, and you would not! Behold, your house is forsaken. I tell you, you will not see me until you say, 'Blessed is he who comes in the name of the Lord'" (Luke 13:34–35).

This record of genuine sentiment of things falling apart in the life of Jesus sheds light on the strong experience of the disciples that God, in Jesus Christ, sets to a new stage his bond with human beings. Faced with his imminent death, Jesus seized the opportunity to take charge of his life and offer a proper meaning to the events that soon were to unfold. Few words and simple gestures have forever transformed a dark moment into an empowering symbol. The Passover meal became the expression of a new covenant. So, at the very moment of the tragic end of the Son's mission, a new beginning emerges. The body that will soon be broken under the brutality of fellow human beings is offered as well as the blood shed as an expression of a life given to be life-giving. Despite the disciples' betrayal, Jesus went on to strengthen the bond of friendship with all, including Judas.

The special recommendation found in Luke's Gospel and in Paul's letter to the Corinthians—"Do this in memory of me" (Luke 22:19; 1 Cor. 11:24)— highlights that the new bond entails a commitment to act like Jesus, that is, to lay down one's life as life-giving for others. The passion became an expression of a love that goes to the end: "This is my commandment, that you love one another as I have loved you. Greater love has no man than this, that a man lay down his life for his friends. You are my friends if you do what I command you" (John 15:12–14).

The cross, which historically is a symbol of torture and infamous death, unexpectedly became the revelation of how far God was ready to compromise himself in loving humanity so as to open a new way for mutual love among people. The passion narrative shows the physical, mental, emotional, and spiritual challenges that Jesus Christ had gone through. People infected with as well as affected by HIV and AIDS can turn to Jesus Christ and point out, "We have not a high priest who is unable to sympathize with our weaknesses, but one who in every respect has been tempted as we are, yet without sinning" (Heb. 4:15).

When death is near, the last temptation is to give up, to lose faith in God's continuous presence and love. Jesus Christ has assumed his suffering and death with an unfailing communion with humankind and with his Father. He knows from his own experience what it means to be abandoned by friends; Jesus knows what it means to feel the compassion of the women crying on his way to his execution and the quiet presence of his mother at this tragic moment. He who is in full communion with his Father knows what is it to experience the silence of the Father in Gethsemane and on the cross. Only the resurrection has attested that, in that silence, the bond has never been broken.

The Risen Lord:
A God Who Carries the Wounds of Humanity

The risen Christ announces peace to brokenhearted disciples. The resurrection narratives stand in correlation with the pain, suffering, and despair of the passion. What happened to the crucified has become the cornerstone—

the crucial, decisive, and recurring reference—of the disciples' experience. It is, indeed, the single event that completely changes the course of our understanding of God. As the non-Christian sources about this event are very few, one ultimately has to rely on the New Testament on this matter.

Without engaging in a critical historical and literary study, a close look at the resurrection narratives indicates that they are not just a happy conclusion to a tragic story. Of the different presentations of the resurrection, I explore here: the story of the disciples on the road to Emmaus in the Gospel of Luke (24:13–35), and the experience of the disciples as presented in the Gospel of John (20:1–29). Paul's testimony in the letter to the Corinthians (15:3–7) serves as a conclusion.

The story of the disciples of Emmaus indicates how far the disciples were disappointed: their hope was dashed. The very day when some women went at dawn to the tomb, found it empty, and informed the apostles, two disciples were on the way to Emmaus away from Jerusalem, discussing Jesus of Nazareth and how the "chief priests and rulers delivered him up to be condemned to death, and crucified". They "had hoped that he was the one to redeem Israel."

The resurrection seems to have been an unexpected event; it was not obvious. In fact, it was hard to believe. The women who broke the news were welcomed with men's bias: "an idle tale" (Luke 24:11) not worth believing. The two disciples of Emmaus remained skeptical even when some of their fellows went to the tomb and "found it just as the women had said"; the best they could say is, "They did not see" (Luke 24:24). That the crucified is alive is hard to take. The experience of the arrest and condemnation that ended with execution as a criminal was so strong that the disciples' hope was shattered to the point of no return. The news that Jesus is alive is just unbelievable. They need to "see" by themselves in order to accept the testimony of others. At the heart of the disappointment, there was a belief: he was to "redeem Israel." As the redemption of Israel was expected as an act of God, the tragic end of Jesus overshadowed the claim that he was acting in God's name. The temptation with which they were confronted was to conclude that God was not, after all, acting in and through him.

Thomas's encounter with the risen Lord in John's Gospel (20:24–29) would lift the veil of doubt for the next generations, who could rely on the foundational experience of the disciples. Indeed, when the occasion was given to Thomas to act on his precondition—"Unless I see in his hands the print of the nails, and place my finger in the mark of the nails, and place my hand in his side, I will not believe" (John 20:25)—he simply confessed, "My Lord and my God" (John 20:28). Thomas's doubt symbolically captured and somehow concluded the long road to faith in the resurrection.

Besides its appeal to trust in the testimony of the witnesses, the story of Thomas carries one fundamental insight: the risen Lord still carries with him the signs and marks of the crucifixion. He who has loved to the end by laying down his life has not simply left behind in the tomb the signs and marks expressing the pain and suffering characteristics of human existence. In his glory, Jesus Christ has carried those signs as reminder both of the task ahead for the disciples—"Do this in memory of me"—and as a testimony that he will be mindful of humankind up to the end of time. Thomas's confession can be understood as a true expression of his amazement of what indeed happened to the crucified and risen Lord: only God can love the world to the point of death in order to open up a new horizon to humanity. Thus, the signs of the passion on the glorified body, far from being an obstacle to faith, were the cornerstone of Thomas's confession, "my Lord and my God."

The joy of the resurrection will always be set in the background of the pain and suffering of the passion and crucifixion. This is part and parcel of Christian faith: "I delivered to you as of first importance what I also received, that Christ died for our sins in accordance with the Scriptures, that he was buried, that he was raised on the third day in accordance with the Scriptures, and that he appeared to Cephas, then to the twelve" (1 Cor. 15:3–5).

An Image of Christ When "Things Fall Apart"

When "things fall apart"—when a life is broken, suffering is unbearable, and death looms—the image of Christ that could illuminate a human journey is that of a God who is companion on the road. "The only Son, who is in the bosom of the Father, has made [such a God] known" (John 1:1, 14, 18). In Jesus Christ, "He came to his own home" (John 1:11), and "to all who received him, who believed in his name, he gave power to become children of God." (John 1:12).

When "things fall apart," we can turn to the Son who is "born of a woman, born under the law, to redeem those who were under the law, so that we might receive adoption as sons" (Gal. 4:4–5). His unique bond with God made Jesus's life in the flesh a true witness of how meaningful human existence can be, even with pain, suffering, and death: "Though he was in the form of God, [he] did not count equality with God a thing to be grasped, but emptied himself, taking the form of a servant . . . and became obedient unto death, even death on the cross. Therefore, God has highly exalted him" (Phil. 2:6–9). With Jesus Christ, there is no need to set in opposition he who is highly exalted and he who first humbled himself. It is indeed "in his flesh" that Jesus Christ "has broken down the dividing wall of hostility" (Eph. 2:14). He has definitively reconciled us with God, who is neither far nor exclusive to a particular people, and so has reconciled us with one another as brothers and sisters, sons and daughters of God (2 Cor. 5:17–20).

Founded and rooted in the experience of a "God with us," such as the early generation of Christian thinkers like Justin (c. 110–165) and Irenaeus (c. 120–202), each one can venture beyond the thought patterns of Scripture and tradition in presenting Jesus Christ. What really matters is not the particular name given; what counts is to hold fast and to experience oneself the fruit of the unique bond of Jesus Christ both with God and with humanity. So, by presenting Jesus Christ as the "seed of truth" (*logos spermatikos*) at the heart of any search for truth, Justin offered the insight that in every serious human quest for meaning, Jesus Christ is present. When "things fall apart" and the horizon of meaning is blurred by suffering and death, Jesus Christ in his passion and death on the cross is the seed of meaning. With Irenaeus we are reminded that, with Jesus Christ, there is no spiritual escapism because it is the "fleshy nature which was molded after the image of God" (*Adversus Haereses* V.6.1). The unique bond of Jesus Christ with God and with humanity appears to be the cornerstone for any answer to the new challenges.

The global context of the HIV and AIDS pandemic, where people of all ages, genders, races, nations, and cultures are affected, calls for a theological reflection sensitive to the basic experience at the origin of Christian faith. In Christianity, our understanding of God cannot be separated from our understanding of Christ. When things fall apart, as they often do in the case of HIV and AIDS, it matters to rediscover a God who, in Jesus Christ, loves unconditionally; a God whose presence, in Jesus Christ, is unfailing whatever the human tragedy; a God who, in Jesus Christ, cares without discrimination. Such bond with humanity is, in Christ, unending.

The basic Christian experience is the good news of the nearness of God: "The time is fulfilled, and the kingdom of God is at hand" (Mark 1:15). God's nearness opens the way to a new relation with humanity. God's nearness means that he is not afraid of the messiness and sinfulness of human life. His nearness is an open arm welcome to the sinner, the weak, the sick, the downtrodden, the prisoner, and so on. God, in Jesus Christ, is proclaiming a new beginning for all, without exception. John sums up what is at stake in God getting near in Christ: "To all who received him, who believe in his name, he gave the power to become children of God; who were born, not of blood nor of the will of the flesh nor of the will of man, but of God" (John 1:12–13).

When God makes himself at home on earth in Christ, humanity experiences something unexpected, utterly new: men and women partake in God's life. They become "children of God," "members of the household of God" (Eph. 2:19). This new parentage sets them into a brotherly relation that cuts across boundaries of age, gender, race, nation, culture, social status, or health situation. They are brothers and sisters, sons and daughters of the same Father: God. The fear, solitude, and distance stemming from the scary knowledge that the deadly disease has no cure can be overcome by looking at the unconditional expression of love and compassion that Christ has shown as a manifestation of God's nearness to all. "Do this in remembrance of me" (Luke 22:19) compels every Christian to act in the same manner toward his or her neighbor (Luke 10:25–37). In Christ, God's nearness is salvific. Indeed, it is "for us and for our salvation"[8] that Jesus Christ came down and became incarnate, that he was begotten from Mary, and that he suffered and rose up on the third day.

Because the totality of the existence of Christ is "for us and for our salvation," some early church fathers dared to envision that, prior to creation, the Son is foreseen as incarnate by the Father. This same fundamental intuition can be extended to his resurrection: in Christ, the Father has forever foreseen our glorification through the pain and suffering of the beloved Son. With the risen Lord we are called to "put off the old nature with its practices and put on the new nature, which is being renewed in knowledge after the image of its creator. Here there cannot be Greek and Jew, circumcised and uncircumcised, barbarian, Scythian, slave, free man, but Christ is all, and in all" (Col. 3:9–11).

One perspective on Christ in the context of HIV and AIDS is that which rediscovers and emphasizes the nearness of God. It stresses the unconditional love of God in Christ manifested in the very coming into the flesh of the eternal Son, the image of the fullness of humanity. "For us and for our salvation," he fully became one of us, sharing our joys and sufferings, including the anguish of misunderstanding and a sense of failure, as well as betrayal, solitude, and death. He experienced at critical moments of his passion the silence of the Father and overcame it in an uncompromising filial obedience. His resurrection sealed the Father's words of trust given at the beginning of his mission: "This is my beloved Son, with whom I am well pleased" (Matt. 3:7). The Father is ever faithful in keeping his words. In raising Jesus Christ from the dead, God expresses his total love and care for his only Son, and through him, of his care for our humanity. Indeed, "God so loved the world that he gave his only Son, that whoever believes in him should not perish but have eternal life" (John 3:16). The Son has carried this love to the end (John 13:1) by laying down his life, because "greater love has no man than this, that a man lay down his life for his friends" (John 15:13). The redemptive power of love carries only one imperative: the readiness to lay down one's life so that others may have life in full.

The love that goes to the end does not end in the tomb. By carrying the mark of his crucifixion into his new life, the resurrected Lord expresses once more that his bond with humanity is not just transitory. In this perspective, there is no need to pitch a "historical Jesus" against a "Christ of faith," or Jesus of Nazareth against the risen Lord at the right hand of the Father. The signs of the

---

[8] See Bernard Sesboüé, *Joseph Wolinski, Histoire des Dogmes*, t. 1., Le Dieu du Salut (Paris: Desclée, 1994), 342–45.

cross have indeed become the sign of salvation. The exalted Lord is the crucified Lord, and the crucified Lord is the eternal Son. Just as we have been created in his image and likeness, so our redemption will be in his image and likeness. As we journey in life, the Spirit within us that makes a turn to the Father and calls him "Abba" will help us alleviate the yoke of the pain and wounds of the world in Christ Jesus.

"No one has ascended into heaven but he who descended from heaven, the Son of man. As Moses lifted up the serpent in the wilderness, so must the Son of man be lifted up" (John 3:13–14). The resurrected Lord, elevated above all with the signs of the cross on his glorious body, is our hope and the source of healing and fullness of life to whoever turns to him—to God. In him everything is united, "things in heaven and things on earth" (Eph. 1:10).

CHAPTER 15

THE CHURCH AS FAMILY OF GOD AND THE STRUGGLE AGAINST AIDS IN THE ARCHDIOCESE OF KINSHASA (DRC)

Ignace Ndongala Maduku

The church is understood in different ways and exists in varied configurations in Africa today, which gives rise to a variety of perspectives on ecclesial fraternity. Because I do not wish to reduce this variety to a single portrait, nor ignore the specific character of particular regions and the distinctiveness of different local churches, in this chapter I offer some general observations about one situation only: the Archdiocese of Kinshasa in the Democratic Republic of Congo (DRC). But what is said of this place also applies to other Catholic churches in sub-Saharan Africa.

Starting from the fact that the AIDS pandemic challenges our understanding of the church's mission as well as our concrete ways of being church, my presentation continues in three steps. After outlining the main features of the Catholic Church's intervention in health care in Kinshasa, I raise the issue of pastoral care initiated by a church that formulates its identity as a family of God. Finally, looking ahead, I suggest some lines of action in health care for the construction of the church as a brotherhood of God's children: a community of service (*diakonia*), a healer, and a defender of life.

The Catholic Church's Health Activities in Sub-Saharan Africa

Since the colonial period, the Catholic Church in Africa has played a supplementary role in the area of health care, where its actions, making up for the shortcomings of the state, were appreciated both by the centers of power and by ordinary Africans. Care for the sick and alleviation of human suffering were central to the Church's missionary activities and entirely consistent with evangelization. These activities were theologically grounded in our shared humanity, which flows from the understanding of the human person as *imago*

Dei—a foundation that the Catholic Church needed to restore in view of its evangelizing mission with its ultimate goal to convert people to the Christian faith. Evangelization was therefore carried out as one of the ecclesial functions. Among the protagonists of this church mission were religious congregations whose medical work matched the requests and projects of the colonial powers.

The independence of African countries has not released the religious orders from their mission. States took control of the health-care sector and redefined the place of religious orders in it. African states prescribed that health-care organizations should be pluralistic and avoid all proselytism. Henceforth, state institutions were to be found alongside those in the networks of Catholic and Protestant health-care institutions. The state functioned both as a partner in and as regulator of the health sector. This led, on the one hand, to new relations between state and church, and on the other hand, to pastoral care becoming a rival to state-regulated health care. In many African countries, the organization of the state's health functions reflected public pressure on health issues, the dominant political ideology, and a logic of calculated equivalence.[1] This was not always consistent with the values of Christian denominations and how they legitimized this ministry.

With regards to the DRC, and specifically the city of Kinshasa, the way that the historical, cultural, and sociopolitical context evolved; urban growth; and the massive influx of those displaced by war from the east (1997–present) all have affected the church's health action and its social function. These conditions have influenced the ecclesial structure, resulting in a divergence from the meaning of Christian involvement and its mission. Let us remember that the preconciliar church was a hierarchical, centralized religious organization whose health action correlated with evangelizing missionary activity, aimed at conversion. Its doctrinal views emphasized salvation. The focus of health action for the Catholic Church was surely to relieve the misery of the population and contribute to its development. The church's engagement was geared to ensuring its visibility and thus demonstrating the vitality of its health institutions and their superiority over those of other denominations as well as the state's.

Despite the competition—sometimes hidden, sometimes open—with the state as well as with other religious groups, the health action of the Catholic Church of Kinshasa was also a matter of evangelization, and it was both a deliverable in itself and a way to convey meaning in life, death, salvation, and healing. The church organized its action according to a graceful logic. This activity and the associated meaning mirrored a particular view of the church. The latter served as a frame of reference for the sanitation practices, *diakonia,*

---

[1] On the distinction between calculated equivalence logic and gracious logic, see Étienne Grieu, *Un lien si fort. Quand l'amour de Dieu se fait diaconie* (Brussels: Lumen Vitae, 2009), 79.

and witnessing that have underpinned the pastoral praxis. What happened to this *diakonia* and this ecclesial witnessing when, confronted with the challenge of the AIDS pandemic, the local church of Kinshasa specified its identity as a family of God? In other words: What has been the impact on the pastoral health care of basing its ecclesial identity on the metaphor of the family of God? What changes followed at the level of the mission and practices of the local church of Kinshasa? These are the questions I wish to pursue.

Health-Care Ministry for a Family of God

Since the end of the first African synod, much has been written on the family as a legitimizing image of ecclesial structures. It derives its originality[2] and foundation both in Scripture[3] and in tradition,[4] and these provide impetus to pastoral proposals.[5] Reliance on the dimension of imagination to express the

---

[2] For more resources on this point see Friedrich Bechina, *Die Kirche als "Familie Gottes." Die Stellung dieses theologischen Konzeptes im Zweiten Vatikanischen Konzil und in den Bischofssynoden von 1974 bis 1994 im Hinblick auf eine "Familia-Dei-Ekklesiologie"* (Rome: Editrice Pontificia Università Gregoriana, 1998). For African works, see B. Roamba, "Pour une ecclésiologie de l'Église-famille de Dieu. Genèse théologique et pastorale de l'expression Église-famille de Dieu au Burkina-Faso," *Telema* 1, no. 1 (1997): 43–68.

[3] Jean Bosco Matand et al., *L'Eglise-famille et perspectives bibliques: Actes du huitième congrès de l'Association Panafricaines des Exégètes Catholiques* (Ouagadougou, Burkina Faso: 19–27 juillet 1997), t. 1 (Kinshasa: Association Panafricaine des Exégètes Catholiques, 1999); Jean Bosco Matand et al., *L'Eglise-famille et perspectives bibliques*, vol. 2, *Actes du neuvième congrès de l'Association Panafricaine des Exégètes Catholiques* (Abuja, Nigeria: 25–30 septembre 1999), t. 2 (Kinshasa: Association Panafricaine des Exégètes Catholiques, 2002); C. Mhagama, "The Church as a Family of God: A Biblical Foundation?" in P. Ryan, *The Model of "Church-as-Family": Meeting the African Challenge* (Nairobi: Catholic University of Eastern Africa, 1999), 36–45; Mhagama, "Pauline Churches as God's Family: A Search from the Roots," in *Inculturating the Church in Africa. Theological and Pratical Perspectives*, ed. C. Mcgarry and P. Ryan (Nairobi: Paulines Publications Africa, 2001), 183–91; Richard Mugaruka, "'Église famille de Dieu' dans le Nouveau Testament. Approche lexicographique," in *Église-famille; Eglise-fraternité. Perspectives post-synodales*. Actes de la XXe Semaine Théologique de Kinshasa du 26 novembre au 2 décembre 1995 (Kinshasa: Facultés Catholiques de Kinshasa, 1997), 161–68.

[4] Ntedika Konde, "L'Eglise-famille chez les Pères de l'Église," in *Église-famille; Église fraternité*," 223–37.

[5] For this, see Laurenti Magesa, "Christ's Spirit as Empowerment of the Church-as-Family," in Ryan, *Model of "Church-as-Family,"* 19–35; A. G. Msafiri, "The Church as Family Model: Its Strengths and Weaknesses," *Afer* 5–6 (1998): 304–17; M. C. Dohou, "L'image de la famille pour une ecclésiologie en Afrique," *La voix de Saint Gall* 76 (1998): 6–19; Modeste Malu Nyimi, "Église-famille/Église-fraternité. Proposition synodale d'une ecclési-

identity of God's church in Africa draws on evocative images of the church. It articulates precisely the church's epistemic and social place.

Understood as a new vital version of African traditions, this family image is found in various combinations, which, depending on the cultural referent or the specialization, vary from one theologian to another: descriptive, comparative, thematic, categorical, interpretative, exploratory, or prospective. The new interest in African traditions accommodates vivid metaphors related to the person of Christ. Ecclesiology is here developed based on various themes: family, community, ancestors, and the clan.

The extensive literature that favors ecclesiological images provides a bewildering variety of interpretations. Some theologians conceptualized the African understanding of the church through analysis and description of the traditional family.[6] Others see a concrete form of the church-as-family in the living ecclesial communities.[7] Some develop an idea of the church as God's fraternal family on the basis of a powerful new vision of the image of the church as brotherhood.[8]

---

ologie dynamique en Afrique," *Revue africaine des sciences de la mission* 5 (1996): 95–106; Pierre Lefebvre, *L'Église est notre famille* (Kinshasa: Épiphanie, 1990), 14–15.

[6] Jean-Marie Kusiele Dabiré, "L'Église famille de Dieu. Approche théologico-doctrinale et pastorale," *Revue de l'Institut catholique de l'Afrique de l'Ouest* 14–15 (1996): 81–119. Read also Bernard Désiré Yanoogo, *Église famille de Dieu au Burkina Faso. Contribution théologique et perspectives pastorales*, sl. (2004): 176s.

[7] Sylvain Kalamba Nsapo, "Une théologie de l'Église-famille en Afrique sub-saharienne," *Ephemerides Theologicae Lovanienses* 75 (1999): 57–174. In the same vein see D. Kyeyume, "The Small Christian Community in the Church-as-Family," in Mcgarry and Ryan, *Inculturating the Church in Africa*, 56–60. A. D.-S. Tidjani, "De la conception 'domaniale,' de la famille au concept d'Église-famille: cas du milieu yoruba," *La voix de Saint Gall* 7–8 (1998): 20–32.

[8] The thesis of Benjamin Ndiaye, *Jésus, "Premier-né d'une multitude de frères." Étude de Rm 8, 28–30.* Thèse de doctorat en théologie (Paris: Institut Catholique de Paris, octobre 1996). Francis Appiah Kubi, *L'Église famille de Dieu: un chemin pour l'Afrique* (Paris: Karthala, 2008); Augustin Ramazani Bishwende, *Eglise-famille-de-Dieu. Esquisse d'ecclésiologie africaine* (Paris: L'Harmattan, 2001). On the image of the church as brotherhood, see Atal Sa Angag, "La fraternité dans le Nouveau Testament," in *Église-famille; Église-fraternité*, 181–98; Paul Buetubela Balembo, "Église-fraternité selon le Nouveau Testament. Enquête exégétique dans les Synoptiques et les épîtres pauliniennes," in *Église-famille; Église-fraternité*, 199–209; Mgr. Robert Sarah, "La fraternité dans l'Ancien Testament," in *Église-famille; Église-fraternité*, 169–79; Michel Dujarier, *L'Ecclésiologie du Christ-Frère dans les premiers siècles. L'Église s'appelle "fraternité" Iᵉʳ-IIIe siècle* (Paris: Cerf, 2003); Dujarier, *L'Eglise-fraternité: I: Les origines de l'expression "adelphos-fraternitas" aux trois premiers siècles du christianisme* (Théologies) (Paris: Cerf, 1991); Ignace Ndongala Maduku, *L'Église de Dieu qui est à Kinshasa (1979–1989). Contribution à l'étude de l'image de l'Église-fraternité*, in Maurice Cheza and Gérard Van't Spijker (dir.), *Théologiens et théologiennes dans l'Afrique d'aujourd'hui* (Paris: Karthala, 2007), 83–230.

Still others address the problem of the church in the context of Christology and regard the church as an instrument of the ancestral mediation of Christ.[9] Much more interesting, in my opinion, is the study of A. E. Orobator. Very briefly, its intention is to make the term "family" a heuristic paradigm that illuminates the *diakonia* of society, where society is understood as a community of solidarity in service to life.[10]

Consistent with the first African synod, the church located in Kinshasa construes its identity as a church-as-family-of-God. It strives to embody the model of family. Scriptural and conciliar in essence (*Lumen Gentium* [*LG*] 6), this ecclesiological image fits with that of Church brotherhood.[11] Through this, the church shows itself as a brotherhood of the children of God. Such an ecclesial approach is rooted in traditional values as well as in the biblical data, the patristic tradition, and theological investigation. Its elaboration considers both the Trinity and Christology, which inspires new harmonies in the church; its nature is perceived both as visible and invisible, human and divine, institutional and spiritual, legal and mystical, temporal and eschatological. This approach suggests the question of whether the church manifests itself concretely as a family. This issue, of the empirical referent of the church, allows multiple responses. Distinctions must be made between what one desires and what already exists, between de jure statements and de facto assertions, between the church *in via* and the church *in fieri*. The collision of these two levels can lead to further analysis of an idealized church isolated from historical reality, whose structures exist only in an idealized sense without any real-life content.

The image of church as a family clearly provides a *telos*, a purpose that requires deconstruction, changes, and commitments so that the potential it contains—the desirable and the possible—transforms gradually into reality.

---

[9] Charles Nyamiti, *Christ as our Ancestor* (Gweru: Mambo Press, 1984); Nyamiti, "Some Items on African Family Ecclesiology," in Ryan, *Model of "Church-as-Family,"* 1–18. Completely different is the perspective of John Mary Waliggo, who seeks to enrich the notion and reality of the church by exploring the African experience of the clan and the extended family. In this perspective, the universal church is mother of all the clans, with Christ as the proto-ancestor. See John Mary Waliggo, "The African Clan as the True Model of the African Church," in *The Church in African Christianity: Innovative Essays in Ecclesiology*, ed. Jesse Mungambi and Laurenti Magesa (Nairobi: Initiatives, 1990), 111–27.

[10] Agbonkhianmeghe Orobator, "The Church in Dialogue as Family of God," in *What Happened at the African Synod?*, ed. C. McGarry (Nairobi: Pauline Publications Africa, 1995), 33–50; Orobator, *The Church as Family: African Ecclesiology in Its Social Context* (Nairobi: Paulines Publications Africa, 2000); see also Peter Lwaminda, "The Church as Family and the Quest for Justice and Peace in Africa," in McGarry and Ryan, *Inculturating the Church in Africa*, 249–71.

[11] In this sense, see Ndongala, "Église de Dieu qui est à Kinshasa (1979–1989)," 183–230.

It does not provide a conceptualization of the objective situation based on a trenchant analytical exercise. In this sense, to say that the church of Kinshasa is a family of God is to give it the mission to become a family of God. Saying this also helps to mobilize the church toward effectively realizing this family of God—hence the need to include the ecclesiological image in specific operational contexts, and the need for institutional mediations that give the image effective realization.

In this line, in search of fraternity,[12] the local church of Kinshasa has articulated its ecclesial structures around existing ecclesial base communities, which, in the image of the whole church, work as "a community of faith, hope, and charity" (*LG* 8), a "sign of the presence of God in the world" (*Ad Gentes* [*AG*] 15). Consistent with the teaching of Pope John Paul II, they are "living communities, where the faithful can mutually communicate the word of God and express themselves in the service of love; these communities are authentic expressions of ecclesial communion" (*Christifideles Laici* 26). They could be at the origin of the renewal of the terms of the mission, that is, the *leitourgia*, the *diakonia*, the *martyria*, the *oidokome*, and *koinonia*.[13]

Let us state, as others have, that one's ecclesiology shapes one's pastoral approach. This point being clear, what happens to the adoption of the ecclesiological image of the church as family of God to guide the evangelization of the local church in Kinshasa? This leads me to mention the request for ecclesiological images to be inscribed in reality. It is reasonable to suppose that, globally speaking, the ecclesiological image of the church as family of God introduces new values in the ecclesiastical field in Kinshasa, including the mobilizing value of brotherhood, supported by the image of brotherhood within the church.[14]

As Michel Dujarier shows, the church as brotherhood in Christ is rooted in the communion between the Father and his only Son, thanks to the power of the Holy Spirit.

God, the Father of all humanity, is thus the source of fraternity. The mystery of the love that reigns within the triune God is the model, origin, and goal of this brotherhood. As Joseph Ratzinger stresses, "Unlike the purely terrestrial brotherhood of Marxism, the Christian fraternity is first and foremost a fraternity founded on the universal fatherhood of God."[15] This brotherhood is rooted in communion "with the Father and with his Son Jesus Christ" (Eph. 1:10).

---

[12] Ibid.

[13] Grieu, *Un lien si fort*, 143–58.

[14] On this notion, see François Houtart, "Décisions critiques et tensions institutionnelles dans une institution religieuse," in François Houtart and Jean Remy, *Église et société en mutation* (Paris: Mame, 1969), 72–101.

[15] Joseph Ratzinger, *Frères dans le Christ. L'esprit de la fraternité chrétienne* (Paris: Cerf, 1962), 57.

There is a significant convergence of filiation and adoption. A new fraternity is created between men, who were promised the same heritage (*LG*; *AG* 32]; *Nostra Aetate* [*NA*] 5; *Gaudium et Spes* [*GS*] 24, 25, 32). It should follow, therefore, as outlined by Dietrich Bonhoeffer, that "if we can be brothers, it is only through Jesus Christ and in Jesus Christ."[16] As Dujarier explains, "All humans, present and future, are already inserted into a 'fraternity' that we may call 'Creation.' All are brothers, not only because they were created by one and the same God, but also, and above all, because they all have the same vocation: to enter into a communion of love with this God."[17] Their likeness to the first-born Son gives Christians a way to be brothers through the Son. Brothers in Christ, men become members of the same family (Eph. 2:15–19): the family of God (Eph. 2:19). Communion with God truly changes their relationships (Rom. 8:29; Heb. 2:10–12; Col. 3:10–12).

This innovative embrace of the idea of brotherhood is fundamental and decisive; it shapes the role and functions of actors in the ecclesial field. It affects the way that the relationship with disease is lived and how action against HIV and AIDS is planned. Henceforth, the mission of the church as "family of God, a fraternity that has but a single soul" (*Presbyterorum Ordinis* [*PO*] 6a) is to work to encourage humanity—according to the will of God (*GS* 24)—to become the family of the children of God (*LG* 51b; *GS* 42a; *AG* 1b; *Unitatis Redintegratio* [*UR*] 2d). The family comprises a universal brotherhood (*GS* 3b) gathered and united around Christ, the purpose of whose death was to unite the scattered children of God (*LG* 7, 13). This family is *ex Deo in Christo*, that of the children of God in Christ, of all families of peoples (*LG* 69). As such, this family supports people living with HIV, is active in the prevention of the pandemic, and takes care of AIDS orphans—the result shown by analysis of the ecclesial base communities' action in Kinshasa.

What Sort of Church for the Future?

In order to answer the above question from the viewpoint of ecclesiology, we need to take into consideration the sense and meaning given to the predication (God's family), which characterizes the church's nature and substance. The crucial perspective here is the church's health action for the future. Facing extreme situations, including the HIV and AIDS pandemic, God's family, which gathers at both the level of ecclesial base communities and at the level of the local church, lives as a body linked to the Lord—"Emmanuel, God with us, God for us," from

---

[16] Dietrich Bonhoeffer, *De la vie communautaire, Foi vivante* 83 (Paris: Delachaux & Niestlé, 1968), 16.

[17] Michel Dujarier, "Vers une mission de fraternité," in *Christianisme et humanisme en Afrique. Mélanges en hommage au cardinal Bernadin Gantin* (Paris: Karthala, 2003), 226.

which the church cannot be separated (Rom. 8:39). When she suffers in her members ravaged by the disease, she suffers with God, and it is in God that the church builds its confidence in a life of abundance (John 10:10), promised by the prophet whose *diakonia* and *pathos* remain a Scripture of "divine *Pathos*."[18]

Called to be the church and to manifest the signs of the kingdom announced by her Lord, this community is invited to become a herald and a sign of the good news to those who suffer disease. To do this, the church broadens its horizons and goes beyond ecclesial borders. Perceiving itself as sent to the whole of humanity, especially to suffering humanity, it strives to make God's considerate, merciful, and compassionate love present in current history. The God proclaimed by the church, and who gives the ecclesial family its identity, is a compassionate God. What follows is a way of "being church" for communities that are ecclesial witnesses to the fragility of a God who suffers through his creatures. For such communities, building the kingdom takes into account the social and political dimensions of its emergence. In so doing, communities imitate God's compassion and initiate a *diakonia* articulated around the *"pathos* of God." The God for whom the Christians of Kinshasa constitute a family is partial. He is not neutral, nor does he accept injustice. He is a God who is infinitely conscious of social justice and human dignity. His partiality lies in the fact that he defends the weak and those left behind. It is He whom the prophets called the God of widows, orphans, and strangers. His salvific will enjoins Christians to participate in the implicit battle that God leads in current history. This fight is for freedom against inhuman economic structures, oppressive political institutions and alienating religious organizations. It seeks the communion of Christians with "God's *pathos*" for the sick, in order to join the explicit daily struggle that combines disease prevention, care, and support to the ailing members of Christ's body and God's family. Therefore it can be asserted that to "be familiar with Christ," "to do Church," "to be with" Jesus, "to live with" him, is like "fighting with" him to restore human dignity. Belonging to the family of Jesus's God (*fides in Deum*) and confessing faith in his God is to engage in the fraternal relations of an active *diakonia*. This explicit call to combat gives birth to a church that is compassionate as well as rooted in and committed to solidarity.[19] Those who engage in this *diakonia* exemplify the archbishop of Kinshasa's call: "Kinshasa, rise, shine in the light of Christ" (John 5:1–9).

---

[18] This reflects Abraham Heschel, *The Prophets* (New York: Perennial Classics Edition, 2001).

[19] Lise Baroni and Yvonne Bergeron, "Les orientations, les idéologies et les spiritualités des groupes chrétiens impliqués dans la modernité au Québec," in Lise Baroni et al., *L'Utopie de la solidarité au Québec. Contribution de la mouvance sociale chrétienne* (Montréal: Pauline, 2011), 46.

In this regard, note that social learning has brought about a new style of interaction in Kinshasa. The term *ndeko* (brother/sister) is used as a designation and common identification for Christians. The new horizon of meaning that it opens, referring to universal brotherhood,[20] carries a pragmatic value that mirrors value at the purely linguistic level (phatic value)—namely, the identification and the integration suggested by the Christian greeting, "Boboto, bondeko, esengo" (peace, fraternity, joy). The inherent aim lying within these terms is that of assigning and specifying the task that belongs to the mission of the baptized: to make peace, to spread joy, and to build a fraternal society.

The Christian identity evidenced by such self-referencing and by the greeting suggests a particular mode of living together, with specific rules under the sign of fraternity. In this regard, care for patients is no longer a matter to be solely addressed by specialists (such as doctors and nurses), but the entire living ecclesial base community.

With regard to the challenge posed by HIV and AIDS, the expected result of the evolving mode of living together is an approach to the disease that is entirely at odds with any guilt and marginalization of the victims. It requires a new attitude toward the sick from Christians, one that does not stigmatize or exclude. In concrete terms, people living with HIV are members of living ecclesial base communities; they have a face and a name. They must be treated with humanity, with the same sympathy that people in good health receive, but also with the caring attention that helps them feel that they belong to the church. These expectations put the risk of HIV infection into relation with justice, as well as with socioeconomic and political problems. They denote underlying responsibilities of Christians and their communities, called now to become responsible communities of healers and defenders of life. In this regard, Christians refocus on the suffering of the most affected among the members of the community. Sharing in their suffering, they may see their action as reflective of the assistance offered by Simon of Cyrene to Jesus. They carry the cross of the sick on a journey that brings about an encounter with the fragility and precariousness of the human nature. The members of the living ecclesial base community discover themselves to be brothers and sisters in suffering that is shared and lived in communion with the suffering Christ. Backed by a Christology of the suffering Christ, such support of the sick and coping with the illness richly embody Christian hope. It does not separate the disease and suffering from the sacrifice of Christ and his victory over death.

---

[20] In a retreat for students of UNAZA in 1976, Cardinal J.-A. Malula expresses this universal fraternity when he says, "Tout homme devient et est mon frère." See Léon de Saint Moulin, *Oeuvres complètes du cardinal Malula*, vol. 6 (Kinshasa: Facultés Catholiques de Kinshasa, 1997), 127. The statement enlarges fraternity beyond the restrictions of identification based on baptismal grace. It is the human being as creature, baptized or not, who is identified as a brother or a sister.

In this respect, the involvement of the ecclesial base communities in prevention, care for patients, and support to orphans, widows, and widowers of AIDS takes on significant and inventive practices associated with the Eucharistic liturgy. It gives new life to "the bowl of the poor" (for needy travelers) and the "poor basket" (for the rural needy) of the Jewish tradition. Offerings include donations in kind collected in the ecclesial base communities; at the end of the celebration, these are gathered by such communities and redistributed to the poor.

Among the poor are many HIV carriers who are also supported by the spirituality of the parish. Onetime collections are also organized to fund urgent medical care or hospitalization. A home service to assist patients, which depends on Caritas International, mobilizes Christians and inspires them to be the human presence of a church that visits, relieves, soothes, and comforts. One must recognize that Christians constitute a family for many of the patients who find the varied help they need in them, and in the church, for their primary needs, their daily hygiene, and the long-term management of their illness. They are, to recall A. E. Orobator, a community of solidarity at the service of life.

To support their use of faith's theological and ethical resources for the purpose of defending life, I believe that Christian communities must engage in further learning, and I think it should have three axes: cultural, sociopolitical, and economic. Cultural learning will help ecclesial communities overcome discrimination between the sick and the healthy, to cross linguistic and cultural boundaries, and to transcend ethnic and religious barriers, social disparities, and political opposition (Acts 2:1–13; 11:18). Sociopolitical learning will promote engagement with social and political realities in ways that promote the political, social, and administrative justice referred to by Pope Benedict XVI (*Africae munus* 27). Economic learning will help recast how goods are exchanged and how the needs of individuals and the community are met, with an eye to critical and fair social practices (*Africae munus* 72).

Based on justice and governed by the ethics of the "divine *pathos*," these different learnings require the church not to critique the absence of the state but to call upon it to accept its responsibilities and become more involved in prevention and support for patients. Thus, we can say that based on the "divine *pathos*," living ecclesial base communities see their mission as rediscovering *diakonia* in support of a wounded humanity. It directs them to become a place of living together and "making together" oriented toward support of people living with HIV, tailored to the needs, hopes, and aspirations of individuals, their families, and their communities.[21]

---

[21] Ibid.

Conclusion

Starting from the position that the HIV and AIDS pandemic calls into question our concrete ways of being the church and our vision of its mission, I have provided a general overview of the fertile link between professed ecclesiology and pastoral implementation. I described the approaches of African theologians to ecclesiological images and supplemented them with a position that emphasizes the features and the importance of God to the ecclesial family's foundation. The most obvious observation is that the local church of Kinshasa is a brotherhood of the family of God's children. The fraternity that dwells in its living ecclesial base communities provides support to patients, which absolves the state of some of its responsibilities.

In my opinion, the current situation in the DRC should lead the social action of the Church toward a *diakonia* founded on the *pathos* of God. The expected results that follow from such a *diakonia* are a balancing between the risks for HIV infection on one side, and justice—and therefore socioeconomic and political problems—on the other. This engages Christians' responsibility and requires learning in their communities in order to infuse the codes of living together with the values proper to a responsible diaconal church that heals and defends life—in short, a community that, like its Lord, "lives in doing good" (Acts 10:38).

CHAPTER 16

THEOLOGICAL ANTHROPOLOGY AND THE POLITICAL ECONOMY OF HIV AND AIDS PANDEMIC FROM AN AFRICAN PERSPECTIVE

Odomaro Mubangizi

From the time the HIV and AIDS pandemic became a major public health concern in the 1980s, numerous conferences, programs, publications, and initiatives have been spawned. Some have focused on prevention, while others have focused on treatment and advocacy. HIV and AIDS, being an issue of life and death, has attracted heated debates on the best approach to address this deadly pandemic. The debate has also caught the attention of theological ethicists, who raise issues of what norms can guide interventions for public health in the prevention of the disease and care of the infected and affected. However, an area that has not been sufficiently interrogated is the theological anthropology and political economy of the HIV and AIDS pandemic from an African perspective. How do we theologically perceive the human person vis-à-vis forces of production and power in the context of the HIV and AIDS pandemic in Africa?

Since HIV and AIDS is a theological and anthropological issue as well as a public health and political economy issue, this chapter takes an interdisciplinary approach to address the deeper issues surrounding the HIV and AIDS crisis. The conceptual and theoretical framework employed covers creation, sin and grace (social and personal), freedom and responsibility, *Ubuntu*, and death and eternal life. Certain African cultural anthropological beliefs and practices that aggravate the spread of HIV and AIDS are also interrogated. African theological anthropology grounded in cosmology provides a critique of the global political economy that neglects the care of people affected and infected by HIV and AIDS. In conclusion, I propose a theology of global compassion (Matt. 25:31–46) as both a theoretical and practical solution to the HIV and AIDS pandemic.

The Perspective of Theological Anthropology and Political Economy

The extant research on HIV and AIDS necessarily covers a wide range of themes and issues. In *Rays of Hope: Managing HIV and AIDS in Africa*, Mombe provides useful scientific information that includes medical and nutritional information for the treatment of AIDS.[1] Accessible and affordable means are well presented, and implications for policy and governments' role are discussed.[2] The various approaches to HIV and AIDS by various Jesuit apostolates have been documented by the African Jesuits AIDS Network (AJAN); these approaches demonstrate a Christian anthropology, with principles of solidarity, a holistic view of the human person, the dignity of the human person, and ending stigma and discrimination.[3] The impact of HIV and AIDS on society and development, and how vulnerability to HIV is closely linked to structural injustice, prejudice, racism, and gender inequality, are well addressed by Robert J. Vitillo.[4] The other complex issue that has been researched is the relationship between armed conflict and the spread of HIV and AIDS. Women and girls have been sexually exploited in northern and eastern Uganda by rebel groups, thus exposing them to HIV and AIDS infection.[5] Many Congolese women have been abused by rebel forces in Eastern Congo, but this situation has also spread AIDS in Congo, Rwanda, and Uganda.[6]

The role of nongovernmental organizations (NGOs) or faith-based organizations in influencing global policies on HIV and AIDS has also been researched. Such a role has been best exemplified in the HIV and AIDS network's global campaign against pharmaceutical companies and the demand for cheaper drugs.[7] The church as a major segment of global civil society has a

---

[1] Paterne-Auxence Mombe, *Rays of Hope: Managing HIV and AIDS in Africa* (Nairobi: Paulines Publications Africa, 2006), 113–34.

[2] Ibid., 137–46.

[3] African Jesuit AIDS Network, *Linked for Life* (Nairobi: Paulines Publications Africa, 2007).

[4] Robert J. Vitillo, *Pastoral Training for Responding to HIV-AIDS* (Nairobi: Paulines Publications Africa, 2007), 99–138.

[5] Eric Awich Ochen, "A Feminist and Rights-Based Analysis of the Experiences of Formerly Abducted Child-Mothers in Northern Uganda," in *Conflict and Peacebuilding in the African Great Lakes Region*, ed. Kenneth Omeje and Tricia Redeker Hepner (Bloomington: Indiana University Press, 2013), 199.

[6] Mungbalemwe Koyame and John F. Clark, "The Economic Impact of the Congo War," in *The African Stakes of the Congo War*, ed. John F. Clark (New York: Palgrave Macmillan, 2002), 213.

[7] Mary Kaldor, *Global Civil Society: An Answer to War* (Malden, MA: Blackwell Publishing, 2003), 96.

right and a duty to play a prophetic role in challenging the dominant discourse that tends to promote certain economic agendas disguised as humanitarian motives to fight the HIV and AIDS pandemic. In the same way, the church needs to challenge certain fundamentalistic religious views that tend to overlook the wider socioeconomic factors that contribute to the spread of HIV and AIDS and instead reduce the AIDS crisis to a sexual morality issue.

If it is true that the HIV and AIDS pandemic is closely linked to other vulnerabilities such as poverty, inequality (both gender and economic), and conflict, then it is important to look at the pandemic as a symptom of a deeper crisis facing humanity—namely, the paradox of poverty amid plenty.

It is therefore important to examine briefly elements of theological anthropology offered by some leading scholars that can help us understand why HIV and AIDS is, at a deeper level, an anthropological problem. Any true theological anthropology must be Christocentric, since Jesus Christ is the perfect human being, to whose perfection all humans should aspire. To what kinds of people did Jesus dedicate his time and energy? On what section of the population did Jesus focus his attention? Albert Nolan, in his *Jesus before Christianity*, identifies the target group of Jesus's ministry and care:

> the poor, the blind, the lame, the crippled, the lepers, the hungry, the miserable (those who weep), sinners, prostitutes, tax collectors, demoniacs (those possessed by unclean spirits), the persecuted, the downtrodden, the rabble who know nothing of the law, the crowds, the little ones, the least, the last and the babes of the lost sheep of the house of Israel.[8]

Clearly, the marginalized of today would include the same people Jesus showed compassion to, plus those infected and affected by HIV and AIDS. True to his liberationist approach, Albert Nolan, thirty years after his celebrated *Jesus before Christianity*, wrote *Jesus Today: A Spirituality of Radical Freedom*, in which he outlines the spirituality of Jesus Christ and how it can help us address contemporary challenges of hunger for spirituality, individualism, globalization, and science.[9] For Nolan, a true theological anthropology must be grounded in Christology. What does the spirituality of radical freedom entail? Nolan posits the following:[10] reading the signs of the times; Jesus's spirituality, which is revo-

---

[8] Albert Nolan, *Jesus before Christianity* (Maryknoll, NY: Orbis Books, 1981), 21–29. The biblical passages that show Jesus's preferential option for the oppressed and marginalized include Luke 4:18; 5:27; 6:20–21; Matt. 5:10–12; 21:31–32 (New Jerusalem Bible).

[9] Albert Nolan, *Jesus Today: A Spirituality of Radical Freedom* (Maryknoll, NY: Orbis Books, 2008).

[10] Ibid.

lutionary, prophetic, mystical, and healing; personal transformation that can only happen in silence and solitude, knowing oneself, being generous, being like a little child, and letting go or detachment; experience of oneness—with God, oneself, fellow human beings, and universe; and finally, being radically free.

Wherever a section of society is marginalized, a privileged class also exists that benefits from the exploitative system. At the time of Jesus, the privileged class included Roman citizens, royal households of the Herods, the Pharisees, scribes, chief priests, and elders.[11]

Our main concern should not be whether we are doing theology, but rather what kind of theology we are doing. Faced with this issue of a relevant theology amid societal challenges, Joseph Donders is critical of a personalistic theology that engages in abstract thinking about structures of society from which the well-off profit, while the majority of humanity is oppressed by these very structures.[12] Similarly, some biblical texts justify oppression of certain groups, such as women, the poor, and several minority groups. In order to come up with a genuine Christian anthropology, there is need for the theological task that Donders describes: "Theology should be busy analyzing society; it should serve the liberation of all those who are oppressed; it should be an instrument to change society."[13] What emerges is a theology of liberation,[14] which in turn challenges other theologies to be authentic in addressing pressing human concerns.

Inspired by the theology of liberation, some leading African theologians have carried out profound theological reflections about HIV and AIDS. Ghislain Tshikendwa Matadi, S.J., reflected on the theme of suffering caused by AIDS from the perspective of the book of Job, debunked the view that AIDS is God's punishment, and showed that those suffering from HIV and AIDS can grow in deep relationship with God.[15] For much more developed theological reflections on AIDS in Africa covering a wide range of issues—holistic healing; solidarity; suffering and hope; compassion; community ethics; the church's collaboration with secular actors; use of antiretroviral medicines (ARVs); working, playing, and living together as an alternative to miraculous medicines; virtues of compassion; hospitality; and the role of women—*AIDS in Africa: Theological Reflections* offers helpful insights.[16]

---

[11] Ibid., 27.

[12] Joseph G. Donders, *The Global Believer: Toward a New Imitation of Christ* (Mystic, CT: Twenty-Third Publications, 1986), 30–33.

[13] Ibid., 31–32.

[14] Gustavo Gutiérrez, *A Theology of Liberation* (Maryknoll, NY: Orbis Books, 1973).

[15] Ghislain Tshikendwa Matadi, *Suffering, Belief, Hope: The Wisdom of Job for an AIDS-Stricken Africa* (Nairobi: Paulines Publications Africa, 2007).

[16] Bénézet Bujo and Michael Czerny, *AIDS in Africa: Theological Reflections* (Nairobi: Paulines Publications Africa, 2007).

The other major issue researchers have addressed in relation to HIV and AIDS is education in HIV and AIDS prevention. A leading study on education for the HIV and AIDS pandemic is one by Michael J. Kelly, who covers a whole range of issues, such as distressing challenges that children face in the school environment, children's right to education, the role of educational institutions and use of ARVs, developing new curriculum, the role of Catholic schools, and behavioral change.[17] Among the crucial policy options that governments can embrace are increasing opportunities for girls; mainstreaming of HIV and AIDS in the education sector; supporting a broad, holistic approach to HIV and AIDS education; promoting public-private partnership in preventing HIV; and providing care and support for the affected and infected.[18]

How does political economy fit into the HIV and AIDS discussion? It is important to briefly clarify what political economy is. The main concern of *political economy* is "the interaction of state and market, or, in different terms, politics and economics."[19] This conception of political economy raises the complex issue of who or what controls the economy. On this question, two approaches still compete: market-oriented and state-oriented. This is why political economy is further defined as "concerned with structures within which political and economic activities take place."[20] Market forces influence who has access to ARVs. The poor are mostly affected by HIV and AIDS. Politics determines what percentage of the national budget goes into HIV and AIDS programs. When pharmaceutical companies produce ARVs, they give priority to profit instead of patient health. Even at the international level, the choice of what social and economic programs to fund is a political economy issue.

Constance Bansikiza well articulates the strong connection between economic status and the prevalence of HIV in Africa as he highlights the factors that increase poor people's vulnerability to infection: lack of information on one's HIV status; exposure to other opportunistic diseases such as diarrhea, malaria, and tuberculosis; resorting to immoral behavior to earn income; poor nutrition; unemployment; lack of health insurance; and poor national health-care systems.[21]

---

[17] Michael J. Kelly, *Education: For an Africa without AIDS* (Nairobi: Paulines Publications Africa, 2008).

[18] Ibid., 171.

[19] Björn Hettne, "Introduction: The International Political Economy of Transformation," in Hettne, *International Political Economy* (London: Zed Books, 1995), 2.

[20] Ibid., 6.

[21] Constance Bansikiza, *Responding to Poverty in Africa* (Eldoret: AMECEA Gaba Publications, 2007), 94–97.

From Demographics of AIDS to
Theological Anthropology and Cosmology

Sub-Saharan Africa has the world's largest burden of people infected and affected by HIV and AIDS.[22] The 2006 UN Program on HIV and AIDS (UNAIDS) Report indicates that out of 38.6 million people living with HIV today, 24.5 million (70 percent) are in sub-Saharan Africa.[23] Africa is the most affected continent with regard to HIV and AIDS, with estimates that "one in every twenty adults (4.9 percent) [are] living with HIV."[24] The impact of HIV and AIDS on society has also been documented. Since its appearance, HIV and AIDS has robbed Africa of as many as 15 million people, leaving behind over 12 million orphans. Mombe summarizes effectively its social and economic impact: "[The HIV crisis's] impact on human development has led to a drastic decrease in life expectancy in many countries; reduced economic growth; resulted in a loss of agricultural and qualified manpower, including teachers and medical staff; and increased poverty. It seems that its impact will remain for years to come."[25] At this time, no one can claim not to know the grave impact that HIV and AIDS has on communities. Still, the need exists to push the boundaries of discourse on HIV and AIDS to theological anthropology and cosmology. The holistic African view of reality suggests that when one aspect of the cosmos is affected, so is the rest of the cosmos.

An African theological anthropology consists of an *Ubuntu* ethic and a Christian anthropology grounded in Scripture. Feminist theologians have brought to our awareness the oppressive cultural practices and beliefs that need to be addressed if women are to develop their full potential. Such practices and beliefs include widow inheritance, forced marriages, polygamy, and genital mutilation. These practices taken as cultural dogmas diminish the dignity of women, and their potential to expose women to HIV and AIDS infection has been well documented.[26] However, these cultural practices are not the major causes of the HIV and AIDS crisis.

---

[22] Unless otherwise noted, the term "Africa" is used in reference to the forty-eight sub-Saharan African nations.

[23] See UNAIDS, *Report on the Global HIV/AIDS Epidemic*, May 2006.

[24] Veronica Jamanyur Rop, "Giving a Voice to African Women through Education," in *Feminist Catholic Theological Ethics: Conversations in the World Church*, ed. Linda Hogan and A. E. Orobator (Maryknoll, NY: Orbis Books, 2014), 44.

[25] Paterne-Auxence Mombé, "Moving beyond the Condom Debate," in *Reconciliation, Justice, and Peace*, ed. Agbonkhianmeghe E. Orobator (Nairobi: Acton Publishers, 2011), 204.

[26] See Anne Arabome, "Woman You Are Set Free," in Orobator, *Reconciliation, Justice, and Peace*, 127–28; Jamanyur, "Giving a Voice to African Women through Education," 45.

Ironically the African worldview best conceptualized as *Ubuntu* can still, on the basis of gender, exclude others from positions of power and public participation. According to *Ubuntu* philosophy, "A person becomes a person through other people. In other words, your identity depends upon the family, the friends, and the community who relate to you and to whom you relate."[27] Unlike the African ethic of *Ubuntu*, Western individualism holds that a person becomes a person through independence and autonomy. While many generous individuals contribute to humanitarian causes, many others are not bothered about the plight of the suffering on the basis that people should take care of themselves. The basic teaching on Matthew 25:31–46 is "how those who appear before the judge have treated their fellow human beings. No questions are asked about their attitude to God, their faithfulness to their duties or to Sabbath laws or any other laws."[28] *Ubuntu* practices what traditional theology calls "corporal works of mercy": feeding the hungry, giving drink to the thirsty, welcoming the stranger, clothing the naked, caring for the sick, and visiting those who are in prison.

Contrary to those who want to claim that *Ubuntu* promotes ethnocentrism, the notion of *Ubuntu* in fact is premised on the view of the human person universally conceived, since the word *Ubuntu* means "human person" and not "Bantu ethnic group." Genesis 2:23–24 puts it well: male and female are created as "one flesh." To show how the concept of *Ubuntu* is pervasive among Bantu-speaking Africans, consider the many ethnic groups that use this concept: *Ubuntu* among the Zulu, Xhosa, and Ndebele of South Africa; *Botho* among the Sotho and Tswana of Botswana; *Umunthu* among the Chewa of Malawi; and *Obuntu* among the Ganda, Kiga, and Nyankore of Uganda.[29] Concretely, *Ubuntu* entails values of respect, care for others, generosity, kindness, patience, and cooperation.[30] Consider how these African values are similar to the criteria for accessing heaven at the last judgment in Matthew 25:31–46. The idea of solidarity in *Ubuntu* is well captured in some African proverbs: *Omwana omwe tarinda mishure* (Kiga/Nyankore) is translated as, "One child does not keep away birds (*emishure*) that feed on crops." *Indo nĩku'rĩmithinio* (Kikuyu) is translated as, "Riches are found in cultivating together."

Does *Ubuntu* extend to the cosmos? What is the cosmological basis for a holistic approach to HIV and AIDS intervention? As Nolan points out, "The whole universe is alive with divine action and creativity."[31] This charge is what Placide Tempels referred to as "vital force": "an inner invisible power in

---

[27] Nolan, *Jesus Today*, 15–16, 18.

[28] Ibid., 160.

[29] See Laurent Magesa, *What Is Not Sacred? African Spirituality* (Nairobi: Acton Publishers, 2014), 13.

[30] Ibid., 13–14.

[31] Nolan, *Jesus Today*, 168.

anything at any given moment . . . This is the harmony that must be sought in life; it must be cultivated and carefully respected if life is not to be harmed."[32] Health issues, in this worldview, are not just a medical condition that can be fixed by medication. If we consider vital power as "shorthand for the whole of life . . . the sum total of the individual or community's approach to the totality of life,"[33] then it is clear why any interventions to address the HIV and AIDS pandemic need a holistic approach that includes spirituality, theology, medicine, economics, politics, and policy.

It is interesting to see how various thinkers from different cultural backgrounds can converge on this notion of vital force rooted in deep cosmology. The claim that humanity and the rest of the universe are intimately interconnected, as are their common destiny and fate, has been asserted by Pierre Teilhard de Chardin, Brian Swimme, and Thomas Berry.[34] This mutual interdependence between human beings and the universe calls not for human beings having dominion over nature, but for humans to cooperate with nature in a symbiotic way. For instance, HIV and AIDS patients rely on foods that boost immunity, while human beings help in preserving those food crops through proper farming methods. We need to befriend nature, not fight it. While relationship "is a participation in the vital force of the Other," it "reaches its peak in God who created the founders of the clan and the tribe."[35]

The cosmos sustains us, and we sustain it in return; we have a symbiotic relationship with the universe. Creational theology is the solid foundation for a new cosmology that is attributed to mystical theologians like Matthew Fox, Meister Eckhart, and Hildegarde von Bingen.[36] This creational theology has some similarities with African vitalogy[37] or the belief that all reality is composed of forces. HIV and AIDS disrupt not only the human immune system but also the cosmic immune system, and clearly the political economic immune system of society. To use Pauline theology, HIV and AIDS disrupt the mystical body of Christ. That Christ is the unifying principle of all things and ultimate vital force is affirmed by Teilhard de Chardin: "Through the force of his magnetism, the light of his ethical teaching, the unitive power of his

---

[32] Magesa, *What Is Not Sacred?* 27.

[33] Ibid., 28.

[34] See Brian Swimme, *The Hidden Heart of the Cosmos* (Maryknoll, NY: Orbis Books, 1996); Pierre Teilhard de Chardin, *Hymn of the Universe* (New York: Harper & Row, 1965); Brian Swimme and Thomas Berry, *The Universe Story: From the Primordial Flaring Forth to the Ecozoic Era, A Celebration of the Unfolding of the Cosmos* (San Francisco: HarperSanFrancisco, 1992); and Martin Nkafu Nkemnkia, *African Vitalogy: A Step Forward in African Thinking* (Nairobi: Paulines Publications Africa, 1999).

[35] Nkafu Nkemnkia, *African Vitalogy*, 171.

[36] Donders, *Global Believer*, 35.

[37] See Nkafu Nkemnkia, *African Vitalogy*, 166–70.

very being, Jesus establishes again at the heart of the world the harmony of all endeavors and the convergence of all beings."[38] Christ, therefore, provides the paradigm of the emergent cosmology; after all, Christians believe that all things were created through him.

Toward a New Theological Anthropology of Sexuality

The subject of sex remains taboo in Africa amid the HIV and AIDS pandemic. It seems that the whole discourse about HIV and AIDS prevention and cure betrays a deeper problem of a wrong understanding of human sexuality, which in turn betrays a faulty theological anthropology. Consistent with the holistic approach suggested for addressing the HIV and AIDS pandemic, we need a new theological anthropology of human sexuality and love. Given the dangers related with HIV and AIDS as a primarily sexually transmitted infection, there is major concern that many people are likely to develop a negative attitude to sexuality.

A new theological anthropology has to start with the original creation intuition that all that God created is good. Practically, this approach entails loving one's body and owning one's gender and sexual orientation, as Nolan suggests.[39] Only after one has loved oneself can he or she love others. If a person genuinely loves himself or herself, then one can also avoid any harmful behavior.

This point leads us to the role of performance and aesthetics in the African worldview. As Laurenti Magesa rightly points out, to become "fully human is to participate in the dance of life, one's own dance within that of the community."[40] What does this individual and communal dance include? It comprises all the elements that nurture life: "social institutions, economics and politics, cookery, painting, sculpture, architecture, the art of speech, music, gestures, and sense of beauty"[41] This is why celebrations accompany major events in life, such as birth, initiation into puberty, marriage, death, entering a new house, harvest, and many others. According to Magesa, the ultimate celebration that integrates all essential elements of the African worldview is sexual performance:

> Sexual performance plays a central role in African aesthetic values because it constitutes the fundamental energy that makes the life-giving relationships in the universe possible. In the experience of the African community, nothing unites one person to another, to the ancestral and divine spirits, and to the universe as a whole as much

---

[38] Teilhard de Chardin, *Hymn of the Universe*, 153.

[39] Nolan, *Jesus Today*, 150–51.

[40] Magesa, *What Is Not Sacred?* 69.

[41] Ibid.

as the conjugal bond; this is where the energy that activates life in the form of conception and birth is most present.[42]

HIV and AIDS make this conjugal bond a threat to life, which is such a great tragedy for Africans; the pandemic disrupts the aesthetic harmony and vital dance. This aesthetic approach to reality brings about a holistic approach to the body that is celebrated in dances and initiation ceremonies whereby sexuality is embedded without being commercialized or reduced to genital expression.

Political Economy of HIV and AIDS: Toward a Holistic and Integrated Approach

The existing literature on HIV and AIDS eloquently demonstrates that the various heated debates on what interventions are more effective are premised on an either/or approach and not on both/and. Consider the whole range of approaches: one school claims the quick fix is abstention; another suggests antiretroviral therapy; another advocates condom use or "zero grazing," a term for sticking to one sexual partner; some advocate accompaniment and care; another mentions proper nutrition; the politically inclined argue that the whole problem is governance and political will—and the list goes on.

The prevalence of HIV and AIDS in the poorest parts of the world, especially in sub-Saharan Africa, suggests a positive correlation between extreme poverty and illiteracy, and high HIV and AIDS infection. Among the other factors identified for the rapid spread of HIV and AIDS are lack of control of women's sexuality due to unequal power relations on the basis of gender, prostitution due to poverty, polygamy due to cultural beliefs that large families are a source of security and cheap labor, rural-urban migration in search of jobs and better facilities while wives are left at home, and early marriages for securing a dowry.[43] Young girls are not able to negotiate safe sex. People who are illiterate are not able to read advertisements or booklets on safe sex and prevention measures.

Focusing too much on HIV and AIDS can distract us from recognizing that other health issues like malaria, tuberculosis, and general infant mortality due to poor nutrition are in fact killing more people in Africa than the AIDS pandemic. Why have these killers not attracted as much attention as AIDS? Some Africanist activist scholars, such as Patrick Bond, hold that Africa is deliberately marginalized by global capitalism through strategies such as structural adjustment programs, brain drain, capital flight, unequal exchanges, neoliber-

---

[42] Ibid., 72.

[43] Goran Hyden, *African Politics in Comparative Perspective* (New York: Cambridge University Press, 2006), 90–91.

alism, repression, militarism, and subimperialism.[44]

The need for an integrated and holistic approach is well articulated by Michael Czerny, who demonstrates the connection between provision of ARVs, injustice, poverty, conflict, and vulnerability: "Many people live more positively with HIV, and fewer are dying of AIDS-related illnesses. However, widespread ignorance, prejudice, poverty, injustice, and conflict mean that access to treatment remains a distant dream for many. Those who have obtained access to ARVs represent less than half of those who need them, especially among the poorest and those outside major urban centers."[45]

"I Am Because We Are": HIV and AIDS as a Theological Anthropological Issue

John Mbiti's often quoted phrase, "I am because we are, and since we are, therefore I am," can be taken as a point of departure for an African theological anthropology of HIV and AIDS. The phrase is clearly an assertion of an African communitarian and relational ethic. When applied to the HIV and AIDS pandemic, this adage can be interpreted to mean that when one member of the community is suffering from or affected by HIV and AIDS, the other community members are also affected.

This African communitarian understanding is consistent with the social dimension of sin and grace that calls for solidarity and compassion. Since sin has a social dimension, grace also has a social dimension. While disrupting society's social fabric, the HIV and AIDS pandemic also provides an occasion for solidarity and mutual support.

The *Ubuntu* philosophy, which holds that a person is a person because of other persons, reinstates the view that one's survival is premised on the support of others. The *Ubuntu* ethic does not permit the suffering of others while people are watching. With a tragedy such as HIV and AIDS, the community steps in to offer support and compassion. A grave sin would be for neighbors to just stand by when people are suffering from HIV and AIDS. Christian theology refers to this as a *sin of omission*—sinning by what one has failed to do.

Matthew 25:31–46 suggests that the final judgment will be based on how people took care of the concrete needs of those who were sick, hungry, homeless, naked, and in prison—a guide on how people should live in anticipation of eternal life. This passage demonstrates that to do good for the needy other, one does not have to be a follower of Jesus Christ, since those who did the right

---

[44] Patrick Bond, *Looting Africa: Economics of Exploitation* (London: Zed Books, 2006), 5, 59, 55–60, 98–127.

[45] Michael Czerny, "The Second African Synod and AIDS in Africa," in Orabator, *Reconciliation, Justice, and Peace*, 193.

thing did not even know they were doing it for Christ, just as those who failed to do good for the needy did not know that they were not doing it for Christ. The appeal implied in Matthew 25:31–46 is universal.

Conclusion: A Call to Global Compassion

The famous rhetorical question that God put to Cain, "Where is your brother?" is relevant for all people in the world amid the scourge of HIV and AIDS. Cain responded thus: "Am I my brother's keeper?" Cain's answer in the form of a question to God demonstrates a lack of concern for his brother. But Cain was also responsible for the death of his brother—he had killed him. God is posing the same question to all those now living: "Where are your brothers and sisters who died of HIV and AIDS?" By not sharing information about HIV and AIDS prevention and cure, by promoting stigma and discrimination, by not sharing food, by sticking to moral dogmas that stifle the use of one's conscience and critical reasoning, regardless of our country of origin, we all have contributed to the death of AIDS victims.

Do we have duties beyond our borders? Several arguments can be made for the claim that we do. First, helping those beyond one's border is the result of altruism or humanitarian concern. The motive could be based on one's religious conviction or just on the basis of humanism. Even though many people tend to put interests of their fellow citizens first, most other people "unquestioningly support declarations proclaiming that all humans have certain rights, and that all human life is of equal worth."[46] A deeper ethical argument for helping those in need comes from St. Thomas Aquinas: "Whatever a man has in superabundance is owed, of natural right, to the poor for their sustenance."[47]

The landmark UN Millennium Summit that came up with the list of Millennium Development Goals clearly shows how global compassion based on a secular humanism is possible. Those goals are "to halve the proportion of people who suffer from hunger or who live on less than $1 per day; to see that all children have primary education; to reduce by two-thirds the under-five child mortality rate; to halve the proportion of people without access to safe drinking water; and to combat HIV and AIDS, malaria, and other diseases."[48] ARVs cost about $10,000 per person per year, yet if they were produced locally they would cost about $350 per person per year.

For Christians, the neighbor is not the person who lives close by, but rather the one who is in need. In answer to the lawyer who asks Jesus, "Who is my

---

[46] Peter Singer, *One World: The Ethics of Globalization* (New Haven, CT: Yale University Press, 2004), 152.

[47] Quoted in ibid., 185.

[48] Ibid., 184.

neighbor" (Luke 10:29), Jesus tells the story of the Good Samaritan. "Jesus tells the lawyer in effect that he is a neighbor to any and every man, that his group or community is mankind, and even includes his enemy, people of the other group which his own group hates and/or despises."[49] Christian anthropology asserts the two main principles on which any acts of compassion and care are based: the inviolability of every human being and the equal worth of all human beings.[50]

The belief of a people in the supernatural matters, just as a people's conception of the human person also matters. Some African cultural practices and beliefs—such as widow inheritance, marrying of underage girls, denying of reproductive rights to women, crude methods of circumcision, female circumcision, and polygamy—are some of the major factors that have contributed to the spread of HIV and AIDS. Such practices and beliefs need policy interventions and appropriate legislation to be eradicated, but religious beliefs are also a great motivation in fighting HIV and AIDS. Hope in eternal life, compassion, charity and love, solidarity, and trust in a provident God are some of the deeply ingrained beliefs that most HIV and AIDS health-care providers hold.

There is also the need to take medical anthropology seriously, since it helps to bridge the gap between medicine and the deeper issues of the human person, sexuality, love, and cultural beliefs, and to link issues of social justice, corruption, and poverty with the HIV and AIDS pandemic. Medical schools should integrate ethical and economic issues in their curriculum. Health budgets need to be analyzed from the perspective of how they address medical issues from an integrated approach. Finally, the church, as a major provider of health care in Africa, needs to be supported by governments and donor agencies, but also to be given space to contribute to policy debates that affect public health, especially on the prevention and treatment of HIV and AIDS. It is necessary to link faith-based interventions with governmental interventions, and to establish public and private partnerships, in combating the HIV and AIDS pandemic in order to share and learn from best practice.

---

[49] Edmund Hill, *Being Human* (London: Geoffrey Chapman, 1984), 125.

[50] Ibid., 125–26.

CHAPTER 17

ECUMENICAL HIV THEOLOGY
FROM WOMB TO TOMB

Nyambura J. Njoroge

How do we talk about sex, sexuality, the womb, semen, the breasts, and blood in doing ecumenical HIV theology in the context of multilayered social evils of gender inequalities, sexual and gender-based violence, conflicts, harmful cultural practices, global economic injustices, and failed leadership and governance in sub-Saharan Africa? Put differently, how can we do ecumenical HIV theology when the carriers and givers of life, pleasure, and the ability to cocreate humanity with God become the epicenters of destruction, pain, suffering, and death—despite the gift of medicine and scientific knowledge that help to arrest viruses, infections and diseases?

With these questions in mind, this chapter attempts to capture the kind of theologies and methodologies Christians in Africa have created in response to the HIV and AIDS pandemic as a public health crisis. These theologies are shaping the daily lives of many children, youth, women, men (including clergypersons), theologians, and scholars. The chapter in particular traces the contributions of the World Council of Churches' ecumenical HIV response since the 1980s, the Circle of Concerned African Women Theologians, and the African founding members of the International Network of Religious Leaders Living with or Personally Affected by HIV and AIDS (INERELA+).[1] Therefore, in this chapter, I am particularly interested in some of the marginalized groups or what UNAIDS has named as key populations[2] in the HIV pandemic context.

---

[1] Originally in 2003, the International Network of Religious Leaders Living with or Personally Affected by HIV and AIDS (INERELA+) was known as the African Network of Religious Leaders Living with and Personally Affected by HIV and AIDS (ANERELA+), the name it held until 2008. Religious leaders outside Africa had shown interest on ANERELA+'s vision and mission, and it eventually became an international and interfaith network. For more information, see inerela.org/.

[2] Namely people living with HIV, adolescent girls and young women, prisoners, migrants, people who inject drugs, sex workers, gay men and other men who have sex with men, transgender people, children and pregnant women living with HIV, displaced persons,

The World Health Organization describes the transmission and progression of HIV as follows:

> The human immunodeficiency virus (HIV) is a retrovirus that infects cells of the immune system, destroying or impairing their function. As the infection progresses, the immune system becomes weaker, and the person becomes more susceptible to infections. The most advanced stage of HIV infection is acquired immunodeficiency syndrome (AIDS). It can take 10–15 years for an HIV-infected person to develop AIDS; antiretroviral drugs can slow down the process even further. HIV is transmitted through unprotected sexual intercourse (anal or vaginal), transfusion of contaminated blood, sharing of contaminated needles, and between a mother and her infant during pregnancy, childbirth and breastfeeding.[3]

Over the years, these modes of HIV transmission have provoked societal, cultural, political, legal, ethical, and theological issues that the churches and global institutions like the World Council of Churches (WCC) have been forced to address by engaging pastors, theologians, religious scholars and other academic professionals, people living with HIV, and many marginalized groups—for instance, people with disabilities, men who have sex with men (MSM), sex workers, and prisoners. But sometimes we seem to forget that before the scientific medical community gave us the language of AIDS and then HIV, the disease was known as GRID (gay-related immune deficiency),[4] and many religious communities and hospitals wanted nothing to do with patients who were dying from this mysterious disease. In this context, the late Jonathan Mann, head of the Global Program on AIDS at the World Health Organization (WHO), predecessor to today's Joint United Nations Program on HIV/AIDS (UNAIDS), approached the general secretary of the WCC to mobilize its member churches to examine sermons and theologies that associated sin (in particular, sexual immorality) and punishment from God with people dying from AIDS.[5] In this chapter I take a chronological approach because this

---

people with disabilities, and people ages fifty year and older (UNAIDS, *The Gap Report* [2014], 120–270). See the full document at www.unAIDS.org.

   [3] See http://www.who.int/topics/hiv_aids/en/.

   [4] See Calle Almadel, "A Thirty-Year Personal Journey with HIV," *Ecumenical Review— HIV: Ecumenical and Interfaith Responses* 63, no. 4 (December 2011): 370.

   [5] This meeting took place in early 1986. Soon after, the WCC held its first consultation on "AIDS and the Church as a Healing Community" in June 1986, which led the WCC Executive Committee to issue its first groundbreaking policy statement on the AIDS crisis. See www.oikoumene.org.

initial contact between WHO and the WCC was crucial, and one thing led to another. Most importantly it was no longer business as usual in dealing with health and healing from a Christian approach in the HIV pandemic context.

Facing AIDS—Be Compassionate

From the beginning, the World Council of Churches benefitted significantly from any new scientific medical knowledge about HIV and AIDS from the World Health Organization[6] and medical professionals working in church-sponsored health facilities in various countries, particularly the German Institute for Medical Missions in Tübingen, Germany, and the Christian Medical College in Vellore, India. However, given the many social evils fueling the pandemic, the WCC intentionally took an educational, pastoral, and liturgical and missiological approach. Soon the WCC became a learning community, even as it continued its role of encouraging churches to be competent healing and compassionate communities and "safe spaces" for people living with HIV and AIDS. Musa W. Dube, a leading New Testament scholar from the University of Botswana, makes a strong case for how churches can carry out the Gospel mandate of being compassionate, just as our Father-Mother is compassionate (Luke 6:36).[7]

However, two seminal documents demonstrate how the WCC took seriously pastoral, ethical, and theological perspectives on the HIV pandemic.[8] This was the beginning of an ecumenical HIV theology as the WCC continued to play its critical role of attracting churches, theological institutions, and other actors. As the medical scientific community continued to explore and share more knowledge about HIV and AIDS, the focus moved from the gay community to heterosexual infections among Africans, women in particular.

---

[6] Fortunately WHO had signed a memorandum of understanding (MOU) with WCC in 1974 (becoming the first faith-based organization to have a nonstate membership at the WHO annual assembly) and knew the great potential that churches and the WCC could offer for arresting stigma and negative stereotypes toward people diagnosed with HIV.

[7] Musa W. Dube, *The HIV and AIDS Bible: Selected Essays* (Scranton, PA: University of Scranton Press, 2008), 145–67. Musa Dube has written widely on HIV postcolonial feminist biblical theology. At the time of writing these essays (2001–2004) she was theology consultant with the World Council of Churches Ecumenical HIV and AIDS Initiative in Africa (WCC/EHAIA).

[8] *A Guide to HIV/AIDS Pastoral Counseling* (Geneva: WCC Publications, 1990) and *Facing AIDS: The Challenge, the Churches' Response*, A WCC Study Document (Geneva: WCC Publications, 1997), which was accompanied by a study guide for use in local congregations that was translated into French and Spanish. The pastoral counseling guide was later augmented with Fr. Robert Igo's *Listening with Love: Pastoral Counseling—A Christian Response to People Living with HIV/AIDS* (Geneva: WCC Publications, 2005).

Coincidentally, in the 1980s, African women theologians and religious scholars under the leadership of Mercy Amba Oduyoye,[9] a Ghanaian ecumenical theologian, started to address the dearth of theological writings by African women. The women started scrutinizing African religiosity, cultures, socialization, Christianity, and Islam through women's realities, experiences, and perspectives. Inevitably, African women theologians named social injustices of gender discrimination and marginalization, patriarchy, stigma, sexual and gender-based violence, among others, creating a powerful theological ecumenical and interfaith platform that also addressed HIV and AIDS. African women's theological voices and perspectives on the HIV pandemic, sex, sexuality, and sexual and gender-based violence transformed the ecumenical theological discourse, especially the more that women of faith living with HIV gathered the courage to disclose their status. Tragically, women living with HIV also discovered that without medical interventions, it is possible to transmit HIV to their infants, which remains a major challenge for millions of women the world over, but mostly in sub-Saharan Africa.

Christian women theologians and religious scholars in abundance turned to biblical narratives on women and Jesus as they articulated their God-given dignity to overcome negative stereotypes and long-held lies about women.[10] This small but significant community of women has worked with male theologians in the World Council of Churches (Ecumenical HIV and AIDS Initiative in Africa) to create a biblically sound ecumenical theology on HIV and gender justice, and an HIV theological curriculum for theological institutions in Africa.[11] In addition, this community of theologians and scholars has taken

---

[9] Mercy Amba Oduyoye was the youth education secretary for the World Council of Churches from 1967 to 1979 and later the deputy general secretary from 1987 to 1994 and now is the director of the Institute of Women in Religion and Culture at Trinity Theological Seminary in Legon, Ghana. In 1989 she was the lead founding member of the launch of the Circle of Concerned African Women Theologians, an ecumenical and interfaith network committed to research, writing, and publications. Some of the earlier writings of the circle are Mercy Amba Oduyoye and Musimbi R. A. Kanyoro, eds., *The Will to Arise: Women, Tradition, and the Church in Africa* (Maryknoll, NY: Orbis Books, 1992), and Mercy Amba Oduyoye, ed., *Transforming Power: Women in the Household of God* (Accra: Sam-Woode Ltd., 1997).

[10] I have addressed "age-old sin: the big lie about women" in "Women as Compassionate Champions: The Doers and the Leaders," in *Women, HIV, and the Church: In Search of Refuge*, ed. Arthur J. Ammann with Julie Ponsford Holland (Eugene, OR: Cascade Books, 2012), 97–109.

[11] See Musa W. Dube, ed., *HIV/AIDS and the Curriculum: Methods of Integrating HIV/AIDS in Theological Programmes* (Geneva: WCC Publications, 2003); Isabel Apawo Phiri, Beverley Haddad, and Madipoane Masenya, eds., *African Women, HIV/AIDS, and Faith Communities* (Pietermaritzburg: Cluster Publications, 2003); Musa W. Dube and Musimbi Kanyoro, eds., *Grant Me Justice! HIV/AIDS and Gender Readings of the Bible*

seriously the liturgical and pastoral nature of the church and has produced practical guides, handbooks, toolkits, and manuals on methodologies for use in local congregations and various church groups. This literature focusing on local congregations and communities has helped to demystify theological reflection and biblical interpretation as a preserve of the academy.[12] Equally important, it gives some of the key populations—for example, prisoners, people with disabilities, men who have sex with men, and sex workers—the opportunity to participate in workshops organized to meet their particular needs.

Providentially, the entry of people living with HIV—as well as Christian faith leaders and African women theologians—has provided much-needed compassionate leadership, thus calling faith communities to be prophetic and to preach truth to power in the HIV pandemic era. Compassionate leadership speaks out against all manner of injustices and structural factors that fuel HIV transmission, especially stigma, discrimination, and exclusion of particular groups in faith communities and society. For people living with HIV and those most affected by it, ecumenical compassionate encounters promote a nonjudgmental, nonstigmatizing, and welcoming environment in the spirit of Jesus Christ, the compassionate Healer and Teacher (Matt. 7). Musa W. Dube writes,

> The identity of the Christian church and of its member believers revolves around the person of Christ. Accordingly church leadership should reflect the vision and perspective of Christ. Although believers are influenced by their church and its constitutions, theologies, and policies, as well as by their various secular cultures, ultimately the Gospels, and the deeds, words, and identity of Christ, remain the central and authoritative canon of believers' faith and practice. As long as believers regard themselves as the church of Jesus Christ, then they should constantly go back to assess if they are still faithful to his vision

(Pietermaritzburg: Cluster Publications, 2004); Musa W. Dube, series ed., *HIV and AIDS Curriculum for Theological Education by Extension in Africa*, 10 modules in CD-ROM (Geneva: WCC Publications, 2007); T. M. Hinga, A. N. Kubai, P. Mwaura, and H. Ayanga, eds., *Women, Religion, and HIV/AIDS in Africa: Responding to Ethical and Theological Challenges* (Pietermaritzburg: Cluster Publications, 2008); Ezra Chitando, ed., *Mainstreaming HIV and AIDS in Theological Education: Experiences and Explorations* (Geneva: WCC Publications, 2008); and Eunice Karanja Kamaara, *Gender, Youth Sexuality, and HIV/AIDS: A Kenyan Experience* (Eldoret: AMECEA Gaba Publications, 2005).

12 For instance, Musa W. Dube, ed., *Africa Praying: A Handbook on HIV/AIDS-Sensitive Sermon Guidelines and Liturgy* (Geneva: WCC Publications, 2003); Sue Parry, *Beacons of Hope: HIV-Competent Churches—A Framework for Action* (Geneva: WCC Publications, 2008), and its sequel, Parry, *Practicing Hope: A Handbook for Building HIV and AIDS Competence in the Churches* (Geneva: WCC Publications, 2013).

for life and relationships. To help with that assessment we will examine the Gospels on the question of "Was Christ compassionate? Is God compassionate?"[13]

Undoubtedly, facing HIV and AIDS with compassion has motivated many Christians to think outside the box and not to be complacent as we encounter, with very limited financial resources, new challenges of taking care of millions of orphans and people dying from AIDS. In sub-Saharan Africa, the HIV pandemic is one among many challenges, as we contend with rampant violence, internally displaced persons, refugees, and people living in extreme poverty, people with disabilities, and prisoners who are more often than not neglected and excluded in the national HIV strategic plans. Committed and compassionate faith leaders, especially women, had to discover holistic ways of creating an environment for dignified life and for justice-seeking strategies.

Contextual Feminist Biblical and Cultural Hermeneutics

It is important to emphasize that the cornerstone of ecumenical HIV theological discourse in Africa has been contextual feminist biblical and cultural hermeneutics.[14] Individually and communally, women and men have innovatively and creatively taken time to offer their God-given talents and skills in identifying lasting solutions to the multilayered pandemics confronting the continent. The World Council of Churches through its Ecumenical HIV and AIDS Initiative in Africa (2002–2013; now renamed Ecumenical HIV and AIDS Initiatives and Advocacy [EHAIA]) has also worked with biblical scholars, clergy, activists, and advocates who have embraced the contextual Bible study (CBS) methodology, which has helped to change the way we conduct workshops on HIV and AIDS with "ordinary" members of the community and churches.[15]

---

[13] Dube, *HIV and AIDS Bible*, 152–53.

[14] For more information, see Musimbi Kanyoro, *Introducing Feminist Cultural Hermeneutics: An African Perspective* (Cleveland: Pilgrim Press, 2002), and Musa W. Dube, *Postcolonial Feminist Interpretation of the Bible* (St. Louis: Chalice Press, 2000).

[15] In addition to Musa W. Dube and Musimbi Kanyoro, already mentioned in this chapter in earlier notes, Gerald West, Old Testament scholar at University of KwaZulu Natal in South Africa, has written extensively on the processes of doing contextual Bible studies (CBS). See Gerald West, *Biblical Hermeneutics of Liberation* (Pietermaritzburg: Cluster Publications, 1991; 2nd ed., 1995); *The Academy of the Poor* (Pietermaritzburg Cluster Publications, 2003); and "Contextual Bible Study," in *Contextual Bible Study Manual on Gender-Based Violence*, ed. Fred Nyabera and Taryn Montgomery (Nairobi: FECCLAHA, 2007), 6–25. Among Christian faith leaders living with HIV who have made great contribution in

Briefly, a CBS methodology allows intensive participatory and interactive engagement with sacred texts and always begins with people's reality (including cultural practices and beliefs) in the local community. A well-facilitated CBS helps participants identify issues or themes that a particular community is dealing with. Even though facing HIV and AIDS has been the entry point, the WCC has been able to develop an ecumenical theology that addresses gender disparities and discrimination even within ecclesiastical leadership, sexual and gender-based violence, and most recently masculinities, femininities, and comprehensive sexuality education.[16]

In the process of doing contextual Bible studies and theological reflections in workshops with women, HIV prevention methodologies such as the ABC approach—Abstinence, Be faithful, use Condoms—have been found wanting by women because of the local reality in their families, faith communities, and society. For instance, married women living with HIV have asserted, "HIV found me in my bedroom and in the church. Besides I have no power to negotiate for safe sex with my husband or even say no because the culture dictates that I must submit to him." Other women have shared their painful encounters with rapists who left them HIV-positive and pregnant.[17] These experiences have rendered many women and girls traumatized, stigmatized, and with little hope. Worst of all, many churches and theological institutions remain ill-prepared to address rape as a criminal act. Some church leaders silence those who speak out and are ashamed to accept that marital rape happens, or they literally deny it exists in the name of "male headship" in the marriage. Few have learned to listen with compassion to girls who have simultaneously been sexually violated, become pregnant, and become HIV-positive.[18]

---

this genre of biblical scholarship is Phumzile Mabizela, a South African Presbyterian clergywoman and the executive director of INERELA+. Together with Gerald West, Sarojini Nadar (another South African Old Testament scholar at University of KwaZulu Natal) has trained a cohort of CBS facilitators in Africa and beyond, a contribution whose research and documentation is long overdue. Among those they have trained are WCC/EHAIA staff who use the methodology extensively in workshops and lectures in Africa and elsewhere.

[16] On some of these themes see Ezra Chitando and Sophie Chirongoma, eds., *Redemptive Masculinities: Men, HIV, and Religion* (Geneva: WCC Publications, 2012); Ezra Chitando and Sophie Chirongoma, eds., *Justice NOT Silence: Churches Facing Sexual and Gender Violence* (Stellenbosch: Sun Press, 2013).

[17] See *I Am Now Free: Diaries of a Survivor of Child Rape and Sexual Abuse* (Kingston, Jamaica: Eve for Life, 2014). Together, For Girls: Ending Violence against Children in collaboration with UNICEF is collecting data and narratives of survivors that are proving to be very useful as we reach out to children on HIV prevention.

[18] Because scientific evidence shows a strong link between sexual and gender-based violence and the HIV pandemic, the World Council of Churches has joined other Christian institutions in promoting the We Will Speak Out Coalition on Sexual Violence (www.

Voices and Actions from INERELA+

Nonetheless, all is not lost. African women theologians and people living with HIV are unrelenting in their call for gender justice and an end to stigma, shame, denial, discrimination, inaction, and misinformation (SSDDIM). At this juncture we must acknowledge the contributions of Gideon Baguma Byamugisha, a Ugandan Anglican priest who was the first to disclose his HIV-positive status in 1991 and a founding member of INERELA+ (originally ANERELA+). A prolific writer, public speaker, and theological educator on HIV, Byamugisha has enlightened and educated faith communities that stigma kills. In his own words,

> It is now common knowledge that in HIV/AIDS, it is not the condition itself that hurts most (because many other diseases and conditions lead to serious suffering and death), but the stigma and the possibility of rejection and discrimination, misunderstanding and loss of trust that HIV-positive people have to deal with.[19]

Over the years, Byamugisha's courage to disclose his HIV status helped other faith leaders living with HIV to disclose their status, and has helped many churches to accept people living with HIV in local congregations and to end SSDDIM.[20] For instance, Phumzile Zondi (neé Mabizela) has powerfully and eloquently used contextual Bible studies to empower people living with HIV, especially rural women.

> Women are affected most directly by HIV/AIDS because they look after the sick and the dying. Whenever I ask women's groups about their main problems, AIDS is always in the top five. They say they don't know what to do about the disease that's killing their children. Even discussing AIDS is difficult because of its connections with sex and sin. . . . Whenever I have

---

wewillspeakout.org), which is spearheaded by Tearfund, UK. WCC has also revived and rejuvenated its own campaign from the 1980s on "Thursdays in Black: Toward a World without Rape and Violence" (www.thursdaysinblack.co.za). WCC/EHAIA is on the forefront of promoting both movements.

[19] Rev. Canon Gideon Byamugisha in *Plan of Action: The Ecumenical Response to HIV/ AIDS in Africa* (WCC, Global Consultation on the Ecumenical Response to the Challenge of HIV/AIDS in Africa, Nairobi, Kenya, November 25–28, 2001), 3. Byamugisha has received many awards, among them an honorary doctorate from the University of Botswana in 2010.

[20] Read Gideon Byamugisha and Glen Williams, eds., *Positive Voices: Religious Leaders Living with or Personally Affected by HIV and AIDS* (Oxford: Strategies for Hope Trust, 2005).

an opportunity to preach I mention these things. I am very clear about where God stands in their relation to HIV/AIDS. God stands with those who are living with the virus. When you help people to read the Bible in this liberating way, they will go out and help others to read it with their own eyes, and from their own experience. If you aren't infected or affected by HIV, you don't even think about AIDS when you read the Bible—you think of the issues that affect you more directly.[21]

These painful experiences of faith leaders led them to create ANERELA+, a network that took their own experiences very seriously. Here is the experience of Johannes Petrus Mokgethi-Heath, a South African Anglican priest and former director of INERELA+ who is currently working with the Church of Sweden:

> The journey of forming, belonging to and working for INERELA+ over the past eight years has been a journey of joy, pain, discovery, reinforcement, longing and celebration. We started as a small group of religious leaders, lonely and isolated, separated from colleagues and society by the effect a virus had on our lives. Solidarity joined us; our unique calling inspired us and determination to make a difference for all people living with HIV directed us. This journey took many of us down a road of self-discovery, self-acceptance as creations of God, and self-actualization within the love of God. God's self-giving sacrificial love challenged us to reach out not only to those whom we were comfortable with but rather reach out to those whom God is comfortable with; God's people, God's creation, the ones who God had given God's self for in sacrificial love.[22]

With this deep commitment, this small group took women's testimonies seriously that ABC was very often inadequate in HIV prevention and in relation to SSDDIM. On his part, Byamugisha started to look for other ways of communicating HIV prevention effectively, based on the latest scientific medical information on how HIV is transmitted, by asking, "What can I do"?[23] He also initiated SAVE:

---

[21] Gideon Byamugisha, Lucy Y. Steinitz, Glen Williams, and Phumzile Mabizela Zondi, eds., *Journey of Faith: Church-Based Responses to HIV and AIDS in Three Southern African Countries* (Oxford: Strategies for Hope Trust, 2002), 34–35.

[22] Ezra Chitando and Peter Nickles, eds., *What's Faith Got to Do with It? A Global Multifaith Discussion on HIV Responses* (INERELA+, 2010): 72.

[23] Byamugisha recorded an almost fifty-minute video (Strategies of Hope Trust and the Friends of Canon Gideon Foundation, 2004) sharing lessons from his journey with HIV and encouraging churches to spread hope and offer love and support in nonjudgmental approaches.

Safer practices
Access to treatment and nutrition
Voluntary, routine, and stigma-free HIV counseling and testing
Empowerment of children, youth, women, men, families, communities and nations living with, or vulnerable to HIV or AIDS and other preventable and controllable infections, disasters and epidemics.[24]

With Mokgethi-Heath's leadership at INERELA+, SAVE was tested in various countries and eventually put into a toolkit.[25] Together with contextual feminist biblical and cultural hermeneutics, the toolkit is helping motivate women and men to expose patriarchy and its deadly and dangerous contributions to HIV's spread in Africa. This means digging deep into biblical, cultural beliefs and practices that dictate how women and men relate to each other sexually, in the marriage setting as well as in faith communities. Many women and key populations are being empowered to speak out on their own behalf and saying no to intimidation and isolation. For instance, Mmapula Diana Kebaneilwe, a Hebrew Bible lecturer at the University of Botswana, has brilliantly demonstrated that women do not have to conform to societal expectations in the HIV context. By reading and contextually interpreting the first chapter of the biblical book of Esther through HIV transmission dynamics, women can take a cue from Queen Vashti, who said no to her husband's demands, even though he happened to be king!

Vashti is one of the unsung heroines of the Hebrew Bible. She acted on her own initiative against what she clearly saw as violence to her integrity as a woman. Her decisive actions against male dominance and control resulted in her husband the king commanding that she suffer the ultimate punishment of forfeiting her status as queen. The ramifications of her refusal are much larger than a domestic squabble. In challenging her status of being subject to her husband, she is seen as a threatening social order. . . . I suggest that Vashti has left behind a true legacy of female power, courage, and resilience, which is particularly relevant in the era of HIV and AIDS. She is an example for women who find themselves oppressed, with their autonomy suppressed.[26]

---

[24] Gideon B. Byamugisha, *Church Communities Confronting HIV and AIDS* (London: SPCK, 2010), 63. Since 2009 Byamugisha has spent most of his time and creativity multiplying anti-SSDDIM– and pro-SAVE–focused leadership in faith communities around the world.

[25] INERELA+ has developed the idea of SAVE into a toolkit, which is accessible on its website. WCC and Christian AID are among some of the faith institutions that have promoted and used SAVE widely to reduce SSDDIM.

[26] Mmapula Diana Kebaneilwe, "The Vashti Paradigm: Resistance as a Strategy for

Women, Girls Say No to Violence

Women are demanding safer sex practices and saying no to violent relations, and are at the forefront of promoting the SAVE toolkit, Thursdays in Black, and the We Will Speak Out Coalition to End Sexual Violence. But two biblical narratives have won the hearts and minds of women and girls in Africa: the rape of Tamar, daughter of King David, by her half-brother Ammon in 2 Samuel 13, and the nameless hemorrhaging woman and the raising from death of the name-less daughter of Jairus (Matt. 9:18–26; Mark 5:21–43; Luke 8:40–56).

First we look at the Tamar narrative and its endearing impact. For over twenty years, Tamar has been a heroine in sub-Saharan Africa, especially among girls and women survivors of incest, rape, and other acts of death-dealing violence in the home. The fact that Tamar said no to Ammon twice (vv. 12, 16)—and publicly demonstrated that she had been raped by putting ashes on her head, tearing the long robe that she was wearing, putting her hand on her head, and going away, crying aloud as she went (v. 19)—has encouraged and taught many survivors that they also can speak out. In contextual Bible study workshops, this text has empowered many participants, which has motivated hundreds if not thousands of Africans to address sexual and gender-based violence in the family, faith communities, and society at large. Furthermore, in South Africa, a community of biblical scholars, advocates, and activists—some of whom are living with HIV—started the Tamar Campaign on sexual and gender-based violence (SGBV). Consequently, a group of faith leaders and biblical scholars produced Bible studies in the name of the Tamar Campaign.[27]

The most significant development is that the Tamar rape narrative has raised critical questions about the socialization of women, men, and power: "Why do men rape? Why this violent behavior even toward their siblings and intimate partners?"[28] The endearing impact of this narrative is yet to be researched or documented, especially in the context of constructing an ecumenical theology on HIV and SGBV and life-affirming theologies that lift up the God-given dignity of each and every human being created in God's image.

Combating HIV," in *The Ecumenical Review—HIV: Ecumenical and Interfaith Responses* 63, no. 4 (December 2011): 378–79.

[27] Fred Nyabera and Taryn Montgomery, eds., *Tamar Campaign: Contextual Bible Study Manual on Gender-Based Violence* (Nairobi: FEECLAHA, 2007). Because of the growing demand for Bible studies on masculinities, WCC/EHAIA has responded by publishing Ezra Chitando and Nyambura J. Njoroge, eds., *Contextual Bible Study Manual on Transformative Masculinities* (WCC/EHAIA series, 2013).

[28] See Gerald West, "The Contribution of Tamar's Story to the Construction of Alternative African Masculinities," in Chitando and Chirongoma, *Redemptive Masculinities*, 173–91.

Next are the nameless woman and girl and their encounters with Jesus in his healing miracles. At the launching of the Circle of Concerned African Women Theologians in Accra, Ghana, in 1989, the lead text was the healing of the nameless hemorrhaging woman and the raising from death of Jairus's nameless daughter. *Talitha qumi*[29]—Little girl, arise! Child, get up! These are words that speak volumes to many women and girls in Africa, especially because the words come after the healing of a woman who touched the cloak of Jesus in a huge crowd pressing from all sides. Amazingly, without a word, without asking for permission or begging to be healed, Jesus allowed his healing power to restore her health and peace. This text means a lot to women and girls, and has even gained more mileage as men look for positive male role models and find one in Jairus. No doubt, in this narrative, patriarchy is on its knees, which has given women and girls the opportunity to speak out about their experiences, not just on HIV but many other illnesses, as well as a life without sex due to maladies that affect their reproductive organs, such as the womb and the cervix. The narrative breaks the silence on taboo topics, such as an irregular menstrual cycle, fibroids, cervical cancer, fistulae, cancer of the uterus and breasts, and the pain of losing children to stillbirth.

Given the way that HIV is transmitted, especially from mother to child, I contend that an ecumenical womb-to-tomb HIV theology is long overdue. Such a theology would help us amplify the critical themes of life and death in this narrative, which puts the well-being of women's and girls' lives at the center of Jesus's healing, and restoration of life in a continent where thousands of women and girls die at childbirth while others are subjected to rape, unwanted pregnancies, and illegal abortions. Indeed, this biblical text empowers us to theologize about women's reproductive organs, health, and even blood (including the menstrual cycle), and above all, the burden that women living with HIV carry to bear and rear children who are HIV-negative. Men should also be encouraged to talk about semen and issues related to infertility (impotence) or even what it means to have a spouse who cannot have vaginal sex because of continuous bleeding. Children and young people born with HIV should also be given opportunities to enrich an ecumenical womb-to-tomb HIV theology, because theirs are journeys unlike any other. Certainly, even though such a theology is initiated and motivated by

---

[29] *Talitha Qumi!* is the title of two Circle publications and the name of the Centre of the Institute of Women in Religion and Culture at the Trinity Theological Seminary in Legon, Ghana. See Mercy Amba Oduyoye and Musimbi R. A. Kanyoro, *Talitha Qumi! Proceedings of the Convocation of the African Women Theologians 1989* (Ibadan, Nigeria: Day Star Press, 1990), and Nyambura J. Njoroge and Musa W. Dube, eds., *Talitha Cum! Theologies of African Women* (Pietermaritzburg: Cluster Publications, 2001). See also Thandeki Umlilo, *Little Girl, Arise ! New Life after INCEST and ABUSE* (Pietermaritzburg: Cluster Publications, 2002).

women, women and men should undertake it. After all, we all come into this world through a woman's womb.

Most importantly, because there is no HIV cure despite all the gains from antiretroviral treatment, the theme of healing, compassionate relationships (including sexual relationships), and life-affirming theologies should take center stage. Musa W. Dube, who has invested much of her HIV writings on the theological meaning of Jesus's healing narratives, writes,

> HIV & AIDS raises fundamental questions for those infected and affected. Why me? Why does God allow this suffering? Does God care? Does God love me or reject and condemn me? When I die, where will I go? The spiritual nature of these questions makes spiritual issues central to HIV & AIDS healing. A compassionate church offers spiritual healing to the affected and infected by assuring them that God has not sent HIV & AIDS to plague any of us nor is God punishing anyone with HIV & AIDS. God created life and God loves all of us regardless of our HIV & AIDS status or our past lifestyle. Spiritual healing helps eliminate HIV & AIDS stigmatization and discrimination, which kill people before the virus kills them. . . .
>
> Psychological healing is essential because HIV & AIDS breed fear and hopelessness among the infected and the affected. The fears are numerous, and include fear of suffering from a biologically incurable disease, fear of infection, fear of death, and fear of an uncertain future. It is hopelessness. Affected communities are psychologically ill. This manifests itself in many different ways. It manifests itself in the discrimination, isolation, and rejection inflicted on those who are infected and their relatives. It manifests itself in increased violence, mainly in the rape of children, young girls, and women.[30]

The Body of Christ Is HIV-Positive

Dube articulates issues that have forced African theologians to dig deeper into Scripture to come to terms with some of the negative treatment of people living with HIV and their families in the churches. In this regard, theologians (beyond Africa) have reflected on 1 Corinthians 12—Paul's discourse on the body of Christ. In the early days of the HIV pandemic, there was much talk about "them and us," those who are blamed for bringing the virus into the society: gay men, and in the family the culprits are the women, including female

---

[30] Dube, *HIV and AIDS Bible*, 159–60. For further exploration on healing, see Ezra Chitando and Charles Klagba, eds., *In The Name of Jesus: Healing in the Age of HIV* (Geneva: WCC Publications, 2013).

sex workers, and truck drivers, among others. Many in the church could not acknowledge they knew Christians in the pews, let alone clergypersons, who were HIV-positive or who had died from AIDS-related illnesses. Many Christians who were rumored to be HIV-positive were denied Holy Communion, while others were refused Christian burial. The denial, shame, and silence were deeply entrenched in the hierarchy of the churches until clergy living with HIV started to disclose their status, as we have observed with the founding members of ANERELA+.

Eventually, a new ecclesiological Christology emerged that asserted that the body of Christ is HIV-positive. Others stated that the church has AIDS. In other words, Christians living with HIV contend that they are authentically part of the body of Christ. As Dube has eloquently argued, people living with HIV need both spiritual and psychological healing as well as a compassionate church to facilitate the healing processes. Others communicated through painting, as did the late Maxwell Lawton, an American Baptist gay man living with HIV, in his *Man of Sorrows: Christ with AIDS*. This painting depicted Jesus covered with AIDS lesions. In 1993 Archbishop Desmond Tutu invited Lawton to reproduce this painting in St. George's Cathedral in Cape Town. Later Lawton enriched the WCC's ecumenical HIV theology by displaying the painting at its headquarters in Geneva, Switzerland.[31]

Many churches still close doors to members of the key populations or have no clue how to practice compassion and an inclusive theology. Despite frequent preaching on the body of Christ, the Beatitudes (Matt. 5–7), and Matthew 25, many churches continue to judge and exclude people living with HIV.

Life-Affirming Theologies and the Vision of Jesus

Creation of an ecumenical HIV theology in Africa is an ongoing project that is mostly motivated by the faith and hope of people living with HIV and women who yearn for fullness of life, as promised by Jesus Christ (John 10:10). This community of people believes that HIV does not have the last word, and that it is possible to change the trajectory of AIDS-related deaths by following Jesus's vision. This community of theologians, scholars, and committed people of faith know too well that even if the international medical community was to announce the production of an HIV vaccine and an AIDS cure today, work will

---

[31] On the ongoing theological discourse on this theme and the painting, see Gideon Byamugisha, John Joshva Raja, and Ezra Chitando, eds., *Is the Body of Christ HIV-Positive? New Ecclesiological Christologies in the Context of HIV-Positive Communities* (Delhi, India: ISPCK/SOCMS, 2012); and Rachel Mash, Johan Cilliers, Keith Griffins, Edith Chemorion, and Archwells Katani, eds., *Our Church Has AIDS: Preaching about HIV and AIDS in Africa Today* (Stellenbosch, South Africa: NetACT 2009).

continue because one of the fundamental truths that the HIV pandemic has revealed are the multilayered social evils we have tried to name in this chapter. The church and all other people of goodwill have no business being complacent, especially when the latest UNAIDS statistics show that AIDS is the number-one killer of people eleven to nineteen years of age, and the same age group has the highest rate of new HIV infections, with girls being the most affected.[32]

Through other ways of reading and interpreting the Bible,[33] African women and people living with HIV have demonstrated the possibility of deconstructing patriarchy, for instance, and constructing life-affirming theologies that inspire people to pull out of despair and hopelessness. Revisiting the encounters of Jesus with women, the sick, and the dead offers a powerful reminder that women and any other marginalized groups do not need "permission" to touch the cloak of Jesus, let alone wash his feet (Matt. 26:6–13; Mark 14:3–9; John 12:1–8). Indeed, the HIV pandemic has had a devastating impact, but the most affected populations have nevertheless shown enormous resilience, endurance, and tenacity.[34] Recently, nonheterosexual people in Africa (including people living with HIV) have been slowly but steadily demonstrating this resilience and their emerging theological voices.[35]

Many more people who yearn for fullness of life in the HIV era have voices, cries, joy, and laughter that are yet to be amplified. Their theological contributions need to find their rightful place in the ongoing ecumenical HIV theological discourse. Life-affirming theologies are not the preserve of a few. Jesus came so that we may have life in abundance from womb to tomb.

---

[32] In February 2015 in Nairobi, Kenya, the Kenya government, UNAIDS, and other partners launched the global initiative "All In" to End Adolescent AIDS. See allintoendado-lescentAIDS.org/.

[33] This evokes the title of a book by Musa W. Dube, ed., *Other Ways of Reading: African Women and the Bible* (Geneva: WCC Publications, 2001).

[34] This reality has motivated Ezra Chitando to write *Troubled but not Destroyed: African Theology in Dialogue with HIV and AIDS* (Geneva: WCC Publications, 2009). In this book Chitando takes time to showcase African women theologians' contributions to HIV theology. See also Ezra Chitando and Nontando Hadede, eds., *Compassionate Circles: African Women Theologians Facing HIV* (Geneva: WCC Publications, 2009).

[35] See Ezra Chitando and Peter Nickles, eds., *What's Faith Got to Do with It? A Global Multifaith Discussion on HIV Responses* (INERELA+, 2010): essays 4–7.

Part Five

AIDS, Theological Ethics, and Social Changes

CHAPTER 18

ETHICAL AND PASTORAL APPROACHES TO DEALING WITH AIDS IN AFRICA

Peter Kanyandago

AIDS is not just a single disease confronting humanity: it is a complex syndrome resulting from many factors. In 2013 it was estimated that 78 million people had become infected with HIV, and 39 million had died of "AIDS-related illnesses."[1] Africa had about 70 percent of the people living with HIV, although some indicators show a decline in the case of new infections. Whatever one's opinion about the figures, there is no doubt that Africa is the continent most infected and affected by AIDS. Seen in the context of the church's mission to promote life in its fullness, this disease is not only a medical problem. It has generated orphans, widows, widowers, and broken families and social structures. It has also caused strains on livelihoods. The church in Africa, and more specifically Christian communities and families, have tried to combat the disease and its effects, but over the past two decades AIDS has continued to kill and create problems. Moreover, the response and the means taken have not been commensurate with the epidemic's gravity. Still, clear ecclesial and theological invitations exist for the church in Africa to assume its responsibilities.

Looking at how the world reacted with urgency to the recent outbreak of Ebola in West Africa—although even here some unexplainable delays took place—it would appear that AIDS-related issues have been relegated to the background. Furthermore, science has tended to focus on preventing the spread of the disease, and little attention is given to continue searching for AIDS' origin. Despite all indications that AIDS poses a very serious threat to Africa, raising many ethical issues, the urgency needed to deal with the disease seems to have declined with time.

In this chapter I suggest that AIDS can only be adequately addressed if situated in a wider general and ethical context that takes into account what is necessary to promote and defend every person's dignity and identity. All that dehumanizes humans will be considered here as unethical. I am suggesting that

---

[1] UNAIDS, Global Statistics, www.unAIDS.org.

while the terrible effects of AIDS on Africa are largely due to the lack of means
to deal with the problem, the main issue is Africans not receiving the attention
they deserve. In this wider ethical context I would like to add a more specific
ethical and theological consideration grounded in the principle and practice
of promoting life in all its dimensions, echoing Jesus's words that he has come
that we "may have life and have it to the full" (John 10:10, Jerusalem Bible).
AIDS has doubtlessly disturbed the life of Africans in most of its dimensions.
In light of these ethical considerations, I argue here that the African church has
a moral and ecclesial mandate to come up with ways of dealing with AIDS that
are original and specific to its context.

Some Unanswered Questions and Controversies

Outside of scientific and academic circles, conventional knowledge has it
that all is clear about the origin, testing, diagnosing, causes, transmission, and
management of AIDS, but this is not the case. Actually, this misconception can
lead to serious medical and ethical issues. I outline a few of these controversial
issues below and link them to Africa's increased vulnerability.

Thabo Mbeki's Presidential Advisory Panel on AIDS

One of the ways of approaching these issues has been to use a report
from eminent scientists that President Thabo Mbeki of South Africa commissioned.[2] The report presents controversial issues and debates without
pretending to offer solutions or answers where none exist. The panel consisted
of thirty-two scientists, some of whom held orthodox views and others who
held dissident views on AIDS.[3] Some of the unresolved issues, according to
the report, are as follows:

- Questions about the causes of AIDS are not yet completely resolved,
  since some other conditions exhibit similar medical symptoms as
  AIDS.
- There are differences between the African epidemic compared with
  HIV and AIDS in Europe and the United States. For the latter areas,
  the epidemic is originally more linked to the gay milieu, while in Africa
  it has a heterosexual characteristic.

---

[2] See *Presidential AIDS Advisory Panel Report: A Synthesis Report of the Deliberations
by the Panel of Experts Invited by the President of the Republic of South Africa, the Honourable
Mr. Thabo Mbeki* (unpublished), 2001.

[3] The "dissident" group has a website on which one can find their views. See *Virusmyth,
A Rethinking AIDS Website*, www.virusmyth.com.

- Some people question results from AIDS tests, since in some cases other conditions can give positive results.
- Socioeconomic factors in addition to medical ones should be considered in the HIV and AIDS context.

In addition to the above points, I add a few others related to this discussion.

Alternative Views on the Origin of AIDS

Despite the fact that AIDS first became publicly known in the US gay community, it has been more or less accepted in other sectors that the disease's origin is in Africa.[4] However, some credible research indicates that the AIDS and Ebola viruses were made in the laboratory. Leonard G. Horowitz's book *Emerging Viruses*[5] offers an example. He contends that development of the two mentioned viruses is linked to research in the development of vaccinations, viruses that cause cancer, and US efforts to develop and defend against biological weapons. Regarding the latter, a document declassified by the US government contains information from a House of Representatives subcommittee in 1969, noting, "Within the next 5 to 10 years, it would probably be possible to make a new infective microorganism which . . . might be refractory to the immunological and therapeutic processes upon which we depend to maintain our relative freedom from infective disease."[6] Another source, a video called the *Strecker Memorandum*, presents similar arguments affirming that AIDS is a synthetic biological invention.[7]

These alternative explanations about the origin of AIDS are not well known, but they are closely linked to factual projects and documents (mainly from the United States) stating that overpopulation is to be taken as a security threat and measures to control overpopulation therefore should be put in place. I cite two US studies that see overpopulation as a security problem. The first is *The National Security Study Memorandum 200*.[8] The study, also known as NSSM 200, was conducted and classified by the National Security

---

[4] See, for example, James Gallagher, "AIDS: Origin of Pandemic 'Was 1920s Kinshasa,'" BBC, October 2, 2014, www.bbc.com.

[5] Leonard G. Horowitz, *Emerging Viruses: AIDS and Ebola—Nature, Accident, or Intentional?* (Las Vegas: Tetrahedron, 1996).

[6] Department of Defense Appropriations for 1970, H.B. 15090, 91st Cong., 1st Sess., pt. 5 (1969).

[7] The Strecker Memorandum can be found at www.youtube.com.

[8] National Security Council, *The National Security Study Memorandum 200: Implications of Worldwide Population Growth for U.S. Security and Overseas Interests* (Washington, DC, 1974).

Council under Henry Kissinger, adopted as an official program by President Gerald Ford in 1974, and declassified in 1990. NSSM 200 recommends that measures to limit population growth be put in place, including birth control and legalization of abortion, indoctrination of children, and withholding of aid, accompanied by a cover-up of US population control activities. The second study, called *The Global Report to the President*, was ordered by President Jimmy Carter in 1977 and made public in 1980.[9] In the letter of transmittal to the president, the study's authors say that their findings about population growth are very disturbing.[10]

The issues I have briefly presented here have not been conclusively shown to be linked to the origin and spread of AIDS. However, rather than brushing them aside as conspiracy theories, they should be properly investigated by natural and social scientists, especially keeping in mind that science is usually driven by and sometimes (ab)used for political and economic interests, as the last three studies cited indicate. This is the wider socioethical scope within which African churches must situate the challenges of dealing with AIDS. These studies are all the more imperative, especially when we consider the significant historical precedent for similar incidents of experimenting on people. It is important that qualified scholars, especially in Catholic institutions, in collaboration with their counterparts outside Africa, take up and follow these issues, trying to find the origin, and hopefully the cure, of AIDS.

The Ethics of Research on AIDS in Developing Countries

Another important area worth mentioning relates to the ethics of research. In research carried out in Rakai, Uganda, a study was designed to determine whether treating sexually transmitted diseases (STDs) could be reduced by treating other STDs in the population. A second study asked whether the viral load affected the heterosexual transmission of HIV. In the latter case, the couples were discordant (that is, one of them was HIV-negative). Marcia Angell raised serious ethical questions about these studies.[11] They include, in general, whether ethical standards in research depend on where it is done. More specifically, Angell asks whether it was ethical to involve subjects in such a study without treating HIV with antiretroviral drugs (ARVs). Second, with the discordant couples, the seropositive participant was not obliged to reveal

---

[9] Council on Environmental Quality and Department of State, *The Global Report to the President*, 3 vols. (Washington, DC: US Government Printing Office, 1980).

[10] Ibid., iii.

[11] Marcia Angell, "Investigators' Responsibilities for Human Subjects in Developing Countries," *New England Journal of Medicine* 342 (2003): 967–69.

his or her status to the other. Third, some of the people with STDs were left to look for their own treatment. The authors of the study try to defend themselves, among others, by saying that the research was cleared by government and university authorities, and that Uganda did not have the capacity to manage antiretroviral treatment.[12] As Angell herself notes, and I agree with her, such an approach subscribes to the idea that ethical standards in research should depend on the places where the research is being done. This concept is unacceptable. If Uganda did not have the capacity to manage antiretroviral treatment and it was needed, the study should not have been carried out in Uganda. Moreover, the fact that institutions cleared the studies does not make them ethical. Without going into details in this discussion, what emerges is that some people still believe that ethical standards should be lowered when it comes to doing research in so-called developing countries.

Affordable ARVs

Another point that deserves our attention is the controversial issue of access to antiretroviral therapy (ARVs) for most people. There are enough drugs to assist people who have AIDS, but most are very expensive, and patent holders often do not allow use of their equivalent generic counterparts, even when the patents have expired. Generic drugs are far cheaper, and making them available would help to prolong the lives of many people with AIDS. The current economic stance of some pharmaceutical companies, which want to maximize profits, can be said to be insensitive, and one could even call it inhuman, given the ravages of AIDS in the lives of many poor people. The callousness of this position is compounded by the fact that patents are selectively applied in different countries, which usually disadvantages Africa.[13] The ethical consequences of an economic policy like this one are not too difficult to imagine. The clear tendency has been to deal with Africans as if they do not enjoy full human dignity, as is evidenced in the short discussion about research on AIDS and availing people of generic ARVs. Statements made in this regard must be qualified since, in some cases—like the research on AIDS patients in Rakai, Uganda—African scholars also participated in the unethical study.

---

[12] Ronald H. Gray et al., "The Ethics of Research in Developing Countries," *New England Journal of Medicine* 343 (2003): 361–63.

[13] Hannah Keppler describes how this happens. See "The Untold AIDS Story: How Access to Antiretroviral Drugs Was Obstructed in Africa," October 1, 2013, theejbm.wordpress.com.

The Church and AIDS in Africa

Let me turn now to a theological and pastoral reflection on our topic. AIDS is dehumanizing in all its aspects because it militates against having life in its fullness. Pastoral and theological undertakings must aim at contributing toward this primary aim, for which Jesus came into the world. The promotion of fullness of life can only be done if each person and society is respected in their identity and dignity. Before focusing on the African churches' role in promoting life in the context of the AIDS pandemic, we need to address people's dignity and identity.

The Importance of Dignity and Identity

Dignity refers to what is considered worthy of or deserving of respect, admiration, and promotion in a human being. *Identity* refers to what distinguishes us from others. Dignity and identity are differentiated at the cultural, personal, age, professional, and gender levels. Erosion of dignity and identity has disastrous effects for Africans,[14] which could explain generally why Africans have lost self-confidence and harbor an inferiority complex that sometimes prevents them from looking for original solutions to their problems. For example, Africans have been—and still are—despised and humiliated because of their collective identity as blacks. Racism in international football (soccer) can serve as an example here.[15] Problems affecting Africans are often not treated with the urgency they deserve, since in some cases Africans are not seen as fully human.

More specifically, John C. Caldwell, Pat Caldwell, and Pat Quiggin, while trying to explain why AIDS is more prevalent in Africa, say that in Africa, sexuality has hardly any moral value.[16] The demeaning of Africans in their dignity and identity was and is still a reality. Even Christian evangelization in some of its aspects contributed to the negation of Africans.[17] John Paul II recognized

---

[14] In the following writings, I have touched on the effects of the dehumanization of the African: "Violence in Africa: A Search for Causes and Remedies," in *From Violence to Peace: A Challenge for African Christianity*, ed. Mary Getui and Peter Kanyandago (Nairobi: Acton, 2003), 7–40; "Rejection of the African Humanity: Search for Cultural Reappropriation," *SORAC Journal of African Studies* 1 (2000): 57–72.

[15] See, for example, Neil MacLeman, "Suspended: Roma vs. Milan Series Halted after Fans Racially Abuse Mario Balotelli," *Daily Mirror*, May 13, 2013. www.mirror.co.uk/. In this match, Kevin Prince Boateng, an African, was also an object of racist insults.

[16] John C. Caldwell, Pat Caldwell, and Pat Quiggin, "The Social Context of AIDS in Sub-Saharan Africa," *Population and Development Review* 15 (1989): 194.

[17] On this, see, for example, Peter Kanyandago, "Violence in Africa: A Pastoral Response from a Historical Perspective," in *Pastoral Care in African Christianity: Challenging Essays in Pastoral Theology*, ed. Douglas W. Waruta and Hannah W. Kinoti (Nairobi: Acton Publishers, 1994), esp. 38–43.

this clearly in his *Encyclical on the Third Millennium* and in no. 33 asked that the church "should become more fully conscious of the sinfulness of her children, recalling all those times in history when they departed from the spirit of Christ and his Gospel."[18]

The way AIDS is handled therefore depends a lot on the value we attach to Africans in relation to other people. Some anthropological, ethical, economic, and political elements are still in play. Experts must find equivalent solutions that seek to rehabilitate Africans' dignity and identity.

Ecclesial and Pastoral Grounds as a Springboard for Action

Let me now specifically turn to what we can find in church documents with regard to Africa's responsibility in dealing with its issues in light of the teaching of the universal church, in matters of human dignity, and in dealing with AIDS.

Christians in Africa and their leaders repeatedly argue that they cannot do much to find adequate answers to their problems because they are often hampered by the rigid doctrines of the Catholic Church. While perhaps true in some cases, there are also enough documents for the African church to look for solutions that are theirs, including for AIDS. The Decree on the Church's Missionary Activity (*Ad Gentes*) of the Second Vatican Council posits a key theological principle for appreciating and using traditions and cultures of people in evangelization.[19] Other documents have been issued calling upon Africans to inculturate the gospel in their cultures. John Paul II's Post-Synodal Apostolic Exhortation *Ecclesia in Africa* calls for inculturating the gospel in Africa.[20] In Benedict XVI's *Africae Munus* (no. 62), the pope speaks about the importance of African traditional religions and calls for "a theological study of those elements of the traditional African cultures in conformity with Christ's teaching."[21] All this is to emphasize the fact that the struggle against AIDS in Africa must be situated within the framework of promoting and defending human dignity. I do not see concrete and original cases of theologizing and inculturating in the context of HIV and AIDS.

---

[18] John Paul II, Apostolic Letter *Tertio Millennio Adveniente* (Nairobi: Paulines Publications Africa, 1995). See also International Theological Commission, *Memory and Reconciliation: The Church and the Faults of the Past* (Nairobi: Paulines Publications Africa, 2000).

[19] Second Vatican Council, "Decree on the Church's Missionary Activity (*Ad Gentes Divinitus*)," in *Vatican Council II: The Conciliar and Post-Conciliar Documents*, ed. Austin P. Flannery (Dublin: Dominican Publication, 1977).

[20] John Paul II, Postsynodal Apostolic Exhortation, *Ecclesia in Africa* (Nairobi: Paulines Publications Africa, 1995).

[21] Benedict XVI, Postsynodal Apostolic Exhortation, *Africae Munus* (Africa's Commitment) (Nairobi: Paulines Publications Africa, 2011).

Statements and Proposals for Dealing with AIDS

In documents dealing with AIDS, one finds general expressions of solidarity with suffering, the need to educate people to change behavior and accompany patients, an appeal to organizations to provide resources so that the people affected can be treated, and encouragement to abstain and be faithful. The Symposium of Episcopal Conferences of Africa and Madagascar in 2003 repeated these ideas and interestingly referred to use of traditional medicines and other natural remedies in looking for the means to combat AIDS.[22] In the Propositions of the Second African Synod (no. 51), the bishops exceptionally make a strong recommendation that there be "a pastoral support which helps couples living with an infected spouse to inform and form their consciences, so that they might choose what is right, with full responsibility for the greater good of each other, their union and their family."[23] This recommendation draws our attention to the importance of human dignity and promoting the fullness of life, which I have emphasized. The bishops' document also—exceptionally again—refers to the couple's responsibility in choosing what is right after they have been informed and formed. Rather than insisting only on doctrinal issues, the recommendation takes on a pastoral perspective that engages the consciences of those concerned. What has been said here in the case of a discordant couple can be applied to other difficult pastoral situations.

In his homily during the opening Mass for the Third Extraordinary General Assembly of the Synod of Bishops,[24] Pope Francis said, "We . . . are not meant to discuss beautiful and clever ideas . . . [but] to help realize [God's] dream. . . ."[25] Francis is concerned with a pastoral approach and spirit to address problems that are affecting Christian families. This same spirit should provide inspiration when we are looking for pastoral means to help a continent ravaged by the AIDS pandemic. In his final address to the assembly on October 18, 2014, Francis warned against the temptation of hostile inflexibility, "that is, wanting to close oneself within the written word . . . and not allowing oneself to be surprised by God. . . ." The pope speaks about the church that has its "doors

---

[22] The Symposium of Episcopal Conferences of Africa and Madagascar, "The Church in Africa in the Face of the HIV/AIDS Pandemic, Message Issued by Symposium of Episcopal Conferences of Africa and Madagascar (SECAM)," October 7, 2003, www.oikoumene.org/.

[23] Synodus Episcoporum, II Coetus Specialis Pro Africa, "The Church in Africa in Service to Reconciliation, Justice, and Peace," *Elenchus Finalis Propositionum* (Vatican City: General Secretariat of the Synod of Bishops, 2014).

[24] It was held in Rome from October 5 to 19, 2014, under the theme, "The Pastoral Challenges of the Family in the Context of Evangelisation."

[25] "Pope Francis's Homily at Opening Mass of Extraordinary Synod on the Family," www.zenit.org.

wide open to receive the needy, the penitent, and not only the just of those who believe they are perfect." These words must guide us in the search for means to help Africa in need of healing from AIDS.

The important takeaway here is that Christians in Africa have sufficient ecclesial, ethical, and theological grounds for finding appropriate and adequate solutions to AIDS-related problems. For this, we have to undertake the task of informing and forming consciences, avoid closing ourselves within the word, and accept the possibility of being surprised by the Spirit of God. Let us see what this approach can tell us about actualizing *Humanae Vitae*.

Contextualizing and Actualizing *Humanae Vitae*

Talking about Paul VI's encyclical *Humanae Vitae*[26] is difficult without polarizing the discussion between those who say that the church is right in prohibiting all means of artificial means of contraception and those who say that the church is rigid and not realistic. I would like to share some reflections, especially taking into account the African churches' mandate to find more adequate and holistic solutions to the multiple problems that AIDS poses and the deliberate pastoral openness that some documents present as a necessary companion of doctrine. These two elements can help us not to oppose doctrinal and pastoral concerns, but to consider the two. To do this, we must look, as Pope Francis recommended, for what is not yet achieved. Let me briefly recall the context of the promulgation of the encyclical and summarize its salient points.

Humanae Vitae was published in a context in which problems of rapid population growth were being discussed in relation to employment and lodging, with the fear that some authorities might take some radical measures to counter the problems. Changes in the way of considering the personhood of women, the value attributed to conjugal love in marriage, and the value of conjugal acts in relation to that love are also considered. A commission with different experts was put in place to study these matters, and their results, on which there was no consensus, were submitted to Paul VI for his final decision. The magisterium replied by laying down doctrinal principles about marriage that emphasized a total vision of the human person, situated conjugal love in the divine plan, and presented it as human, total, faithful, exclusive, and fecund. Abortion, direct sterilization, and all actions "which, either in anticipation of the conjugal act, or in its accomplishment, or in the development of its natural consequences" aim at rendering procreation impossible, are illicit (no. 14). In view of this teaching, hormonal contraception is excluded, as was later the use of condoms.

Actualization of *Humanae Vitae*, therefore, must be done in the wider perspective of the Christian vision of marriage in particular, and generally of

---

[26] Paul VI, *On the Regulation of Birth* (Kampala: Saint Paul Publications, 1968).

promoting human dignity and life in its fullness. The AIDS pandemic has raised new questions in this area, where it is no longer only a question of preventing conception but, in the case of a discordant couple, preventing infection of the other partner. The discussion in this area should not lose sight of the fact that at stake is a moral issue that engages the consciences of the faithful in light of the church's teaching. For this reason, the bishops' recommendation in their already cited proposition about informing and forming consciences is quite significant.

The difficulties found in this area were detailed in the *Instrumentum Laboris* of the Third Extraordinary General Assembly of the Synod of Bishops, which notes, in the context of HIV and AIDS,

> The responses and observations reveal a deep understanding of the difference between "abortive" and "non-abortive" contraceptive methods, which is often used as a criterion in judging the moral integrity of the different methods. Moreover, some responses and above all different observations point out the difficulties associated with the prevention of HIV/AIDS, which is a grave problem in some parts of the world, where the disease is widespread.[27]

Note the distinction made here between abortive and nonabortive contraceptive methods. They were not taken up in the *Lineamenta* for the synod in October 2015. Before the celebration of the synod on the family in October 2015, the churches in Africa had the chance to discuss these questions and proposals, and to be particular about this problem of preventing transmission of AIDS in Africa. In this regard, Pope Francis's encouragement in his final communication during the Third Extraordinary General Assembly was important: "Dear brothers and sisters, now we still have one year to mature, with true spiritual discernment, the proposed ideas and to find concrete solutions to so many difficulties and innumerable challenges that families must confront; to give answers to the many discouragements that surround and suffocate families."[28]

Conclusion

AIDS poses serious personal and societal problems for the population on the continent that is most affected and infected. The following points need attention to confront seriously the challenges that AIDS presents in Africa:

---

[27] Synod of Bishops, *III Extraordinary General Assembly, The Pastoral Challenges of the Family in the Context of Evangelisation*, Instrumentum Laboris (Vatican City: General Secretariat of the Synod of Bishops, 2014).

[28] Address of His Holiness Pope Francis at the conclusion of the Extraordinary Synod on the Family (October 18, 2014), http://en.radiovaticana.va/.

- The African churches must use their ecclesial mandate to look for an appropriate solution in collaboration with other churches. This will necessitate collaboration between leaders, Catholic universities, other institutes of higher learning, and scientists.
- AIDS poses serious moral and ethical issues that can be sufficiently addressed only if the pastoral agents can inform and form consciences so that people facing challenges can take decisions with full responsibility, especially in the area of preventing the disease's spread.
- Some areas still need further clarification and research, especially with regard to the origin of AIDS. The Catholic Church in Africa and its partners outside Africa must study the existing literature carefully in order to throw some light on this matter.
- Dealing with AIDS is not just a medical problem: it involves anthropologico-ethical, economic, and political issues relating to how Africans have been treated as regards their dignity. A holistic pastoral approach is needed to undertake rehabilitative actions for Africans.
- With regard to preventing the spread of AIDS, the known means must be used, and available resources should be equitably shared so as to reinforce the Africans' ability to ward off AIDS.

CHAPTER 19

AFRICA'S TRANSFORMATIVE RESPONSES TO THE GENDERED GLOBAL HIV AND AIDS SYNDEMIC

Teresia Hinga

One of the most enduring crises that the world has faced in the last three decades and more is the HIV and AIDS crisis. The crisis has been exacerbated by a variety of issues, including stigma against the African continent itself as well as against people living with HIV (PLWH). Feminized extreme poverty, gender-based injustices, and violence have taken a terrible toll on vulnerable groups, particularly women and children. These exacerbating factors make it possible to describe the HIV and AIDS crisis both as a pandemic and a syndemic. While AIDS is a pandemic insofar as it reaches far and wide geographically, it is also a syndemic because it thrives in a symbiotic relationship with other diseases and comorbidities such as tuberculosis. I also consider the HIV and AIDS crisis as a syndemic since it also thrives in the context of "metaphorical viruses" such as stigma, denial, sexism, racism, and other situations affected by what Paul Farmer calls "pathologies of power."[1]

Against this background, this chapter explores the implications of HIV and AIDS as a syndemic and suggests that part of the reason why this has been such an enduring crisis is failure to adequately address exacerbating factors that help AIDS thrive. Beyond epidemiological factors and biological comorbidities such as cancer and TB that accompany AIDS, and which should also be addressed in efforts to eradicate it,[2] I argue that metaphorical viruses such as the ones listed above also need to be addressed, which calls for transformation at multiple levels. At the very least is the need for transformation of consciousness as well as transformation of unjust social structures or systems of domination, which

---

[1] Paul Farmer, *Pathologies of Power: Health, Human Rights, and the New War on the Poor* (Berkeley: University of California Press, 2005). In this book Farmer discusses the deadly impact of pathological power dynamics, including sexism, racism, and colonialism.

[2] See ibid., 115–33, for an analysis of inequalities that make people living with HIV and AIDS (PLWHA) vulnerable to multiple-drug-resistant tuberculosis.

Elizabeth Schüssler Fiorenza calls *kyriarchies*.[3] Such structures, as Paul Farmer insists, are "pathogenic" and are most conducive to diseases such as AIDS.[4] The transformation of consciousness as well as structural transformation is needed at the individual and collective levels, in the church and in the wider society.

In this chapter, I explore sites where this transformational work is afoot and examine strategies and best practices worthy of recognition and even of scaling up to ensure more sustainable solutions to the enduring AIDS crisis. The sites and strategies include the church and its transformation to be a beacon of hope by cultivating HIV and AIDS competency, academic scholars and their trans-formation into activists and advocates for those infected and affected by HIV, and even people living with HIV transformed from being victims of despair to doctors of hope. The strategies to transform consciousness explored here include mainstreaming HIV and AIDS in the theological curriculum, as well as constructing and reclaiming redemptive masculinities to replace hegemonic and troubling ones that have been named as major factors exacerbating HIV and AIDS in Africa and beyond. Transforming power dynamics to enhance mutuality instead of domination is also a fundamental strategy. This global and gendered syndemic thus becomes a locus of transformation. We now turn to a discussion of the selected sites and strategies of transformation.

From Stigma and Condemnation to a Beacon of Hope

During the earlier days of HIV and AIDS, the church and faith-based responses to the crisis tended to exacerbate the impact of the disease, because many viewed it as punishment for "sin," particularly sexual sin. The impact of this interpretation betrayed a distorted theodicy or theology of suffering,[5] a distortion that proved most costly. Not only did it contribute to the condem-nation and stigmatization of many infected and affected by the disease, this distortion also distracted from a more timely development of responses more conducive to interrupting and containing of the rampage.

Fortunately, due to the determined intervention of many resilient AIDS activists, the syndemic nature of the disease is now better understood and the exacerbating impact of the metaphoric viruses better recognized. Today, due to this recognition, churches and faith communities address the disease's medical

[3] See Elisabeth Schüssler Fiorenza, *The Power of Naming* (Eugene, OR: Wipf and Stock, 2006), xiv, for a detailed definition of the notion of kyriarchy.

[4] Farmer, *Pathologies of Power*, 20.

[5] See Teresia M. Hinga, "AIDS, Religion, and Women in Africa: Theo-Ethical Chal-lenges and Imperatives," in *Women, Religion, and HIV-AIDS in Africa: Responding to Ethical and Theological Challenges*, ed. Teresia M. Hinga, A. N. Kubai, and Philomena Mwaura (Pietermaritzburg: Cluster, 2008), 77–103.

and epidemiological dimensions as well as its root causes, particularly where the latter are embedded in structures and pathologies of power.

One such church context in which intentional and specific efforts have been made to address the deadly root causes of AIDS is the World Council of Churches through its Ecumenical HIV and AIDS Initiative in Africa (hereafter EHAIA).[6] Launched in 2002, EHAIA was initially meant to enable churches in Africa simply to access information, training, and resources, and to make contact with other church bodies[7] working in the same field in order to help them deal with the problem of HIV and AIDS.[8] To date, EHAIA has become a strategic and successful platform through which the churches in Africa have striven to become what Susan Parry calls "HIV/AIDS Competent."[9] Here I explore how EHAIA has facilitated the much-needed transformation of consciousness as well as a transformation of social structures—changes that are vital in the struggle against HIV and AIDS.

With regard to the imperative that the church be transformed into a beacon of hope, EHAIA calls the church to become HIV- and AIDS-competent. Susan Parry explains that an HIV- and AIDS-competent church "has first developed an inner competence through internalization (i.e., acknowledgment) of the risks, impacts, and consequences of HIV/AIDS and has accepted the responsibility and imperative to respond appropriately and compassionately."[10] A prior step in the direction of becoming a beacon of hope, therefore, is transforming the church's mission to embrace the imperative to respond to AIDS with compassion, accountability, and intentionality in dealing with factors that increase vulnerability, such as stigma, denial, and discrimination. Such attitudinal change allows the church to move to the outer competence more confidently, effectively, and credibly. This latter competence, Parry further explains, is multidimensional and involves "building theological and institutional capacity in socially relevant, inclusive, suitable collaborative ways that reduce the spread of HIV virus, mitigate the impact, and ultimately restore hope and dignity."[11] Outer competency thus defined calls, at the very least, for transformed and transformative leadership with appropriate resources and knowledge.[12]

---

[6] EHAIA is one of the several projects under the WCC Health and Healing Desk. Other initiatives involve mental health and healing from violence and trauma. For details see www.oikoumene.org.

[7] For example, member churches of the World Council of Churches, an ecumenical body comprising mainly Protestant churches.

[8] World Council of Churches, *EHAIA Impact Assessment, 2002–2009*, www.oikoumene.org.

[9] See Susan Parry, *Beacons of Hope* (Geneva: WCC Publications, 2008), 14–19.

[10] Ibid., 20.

[11] Ibid., 21.

[12] See examples of transformative leadership in the stories of Asunta and Canon Gideon Byamugisha below.

Enhancing HIV and AIDS Competency
through Curriculum Transformation

To generate such transformed and transformative leaders, and to equip them with appropriate knowledge, the WCC through EHAIA has launched several strategies, including two that I find most pertinent for this chapter. The first strategy is called Mainstreaming HIV and AIDS in Theological Curriculum; the intent is to change the theological curriculum so that it better equips theologians, service providers, pastors, and ministers to deal with the crisis. Under the leadership of specially commissioned scholars and theologians including Nyambura Njoroge, Musa Dube, and Ezra Chitando, the WCC has spearheaded this curricular transformation and implemented a template for HIV and AIDS curriculum that Dube developed.[13] Judging by the tenth-year self-study and impact assessment, EHAIA has seemingly been successful in this regard, at least among the member churches and allied institutions. The impact assessment, for example, reports St. Paul's United Theological School in Limuru as a successful trailblazer in mainstreaming HIV and AIDS in the curriculum. At Limuru,

> Faculty integrated HIV/AIDS in their curriculum and introduced a Post-Graduate Diploma program . . . [in which] . . . students worked with grassroots peoples infected or affected with HIV/AIDS . . . [and] as a result, graduates became more open to discussing HIV/AIDS and gender-based violence.[14]

While EHAIA is primarily a WCC initiative, and while WCC is primarily an ecumenical platform for Protestant member churches, the initiative is also intentionally multifaith-oriented in its implementation and encourages transformative leadership among Protestant faith communities as well as among Muslim and even Catholic communities.[15] I submit, then, that this effort to mainstream HIV and AIDS in the curriculum needs to be evaluated, expanded, and scaled up for an enhanced inner competency of the church and other faith communities. Such an inner competence is a prelude to outer competence, as defined by EHAIA.

---

[13] See World Council of Churches, *HIV and AIDS Curriculum for Theological Education by Extension (TEE) Institutions in Africa* (Geneva: WCC Publications, 2002), for details of this template curriculum.

[14] See World Council of Churches, *EHAIA Impact Assessment, 2002–2009,* 25–26. The World Council of Churches has commendably and strategically made all the publications emerging through this initiative freely accessible both online and in print.

[15] See Robert Igo, *Listening with Love: A Christian Response to People with HIV/AIDS* (Geneva: WCC Publications, 2005). This is an example of a Roman Catholic priest participating in the (predominantly Protestant) EHAIA program.

Transforming Consciousness and Enhancing
HIV and AIDS Competence:
EHAIA's Strategic Quest for "Redemptive Masculinities"

The inner competency of the church described above demands that the church address risk factors that increase vulnerability. Recognizing the problem of distorted notions of sin and punishment, sexuality, and specifically masculinity as a driver of vulnerability to HIV, EHAIA developed yet another strategy—namely, seeking and nurturing what has been called "redemptive masculinities." This strategy involved facilitating a pan-African theological conversation on the question of masculinities in a bid to unmask how hegemonic and one-sided accounts of gender—that is, dominant ideals of masculinities—have contributed to the pandemic's escalation.

This strategy is based on several prior recognitions. First is the recognition that the feminization of HIV and AIDS is a palpably gendered condition. The disease affects not only the impoverished but also women disproportionately. Digging deeper for root causes, scholars and ethicists have located gender (the way society constructs, transmits, and enforces roles and gender norms pertaining to men and women) as a factor that makes some in society particularly vulnerable.[16] EHAIA recognized the gendered dimensions of HIV and AIDS and thus pushed for a pan-African discussion of how masculinity and notions of manhood are constructed, disseminated, and reinforced in society and their implications for HIV vulnerability. One outcome of this conversation was the publication of *Redemptive Masculinities: Men, HIV, and Religion.* Contextualizing this title, Chitando, a key player in EHAIA, observes that

> the title *Redemptive Masculinities* can be problematic in a world dominated by men . . . [but in] this book . . . , we employ the concept of redemptive masculinities to characterize and identify masculinities that are life-giving in a world reeling from the effects of violence and the AIDS pandemic. . . . We underline the importance of liberating, more peaceful and harmonious masculinities.[17]

Interestingly, EHAIA speaks of *masculinities* rather than simply *masculinity*, offering evidence of the second recognition to the effect that even though hegemonic masculinity often dominates individual and collective conscious-

---

[16] See Ezra Chitando and Nontando Hadebe, eds., *Compassionate Circles: African Women Theologians Facing HIV* (Geneva: WCC Publications, 2009). The book documents and analyzes the substantive and quite comprehensive input and critique by the Circle of Concerned African Women Theologians, who have written several volumes detailing how gender-based injustices have exacerbated women's and girls' vulnerability to HIV/AIDS.

[17] Ezra Chitando, *Redemptive Masculinities* (Geneva: WCC Publications, 2012), 1.

ness, alternative masculinities, even liberative and redemptive ones, also exist. There is also recognition that masculinities, even troubling and dangerous ones, are socially constructed and transmitted, so they can be deconstructed and changed as well. Conversely, if the troubling masculinities are natural, and if all men are essentially the same, then efforts to bring change in gender relations of unequal power would be futile. This twin recognition—that genders and masculinities are constructed, and that the possibility exists of multiple masculinities—has the immediate and healing effect of avoiding essentializing, stigmatizing, and demonizing men en masse in the contexts of the AIDS pandemic and other crises. It signals the possibility that men, even those caught up in troubled and dangerous masculinities, can change. The notion of redemptive masculinities also recognizes the possibility of men as allies (rather than enemies) and partners with women in the common struggle to eradicate AIDS.

Thus, in its journey toward HIV and AIDS competency, EHAIA deliberately and strategically embraces the idea of multiplicity, fluidity, and transformability of masculinity, taking this idea into account in the deliberate quest for redemptive masculinity as a major key in search of an AIDS-free world. EHAIA's strategic goal here is to encourage such redemptive masculinity and hence nurture and support "gender-equitable men."[18] Such men

- Believe that men and women have equal rights.
- Are opposed to violence against women.
- Are respectful to women and seek relationships with them based on equality.
- Are involved domestic partners and as fathers are responsible for at least some of the household chores and their children's caregiving.
- Are not homophobic.[19]

Significantly, the church as exemplified by EHAIA has made great strides in the journey toward the transformation of consciousness through mainstreaming HIV and AIDS into the curriculum and by nurturing redemptive masculinities. Yet, much work remains to be done if such redemptive masculinities are to be mainstreamed not only in the curricula but in church and society. Such mainstreaming would allow redemptive masculinities to hold more sway in a world much in need of redemption and liberation from AIDS and other contexts of woundedness and brokenness.

---

[18] Ibid., 26.

[19] Homophobia has been a major cause of vulnerability to AIDS and violence against members of the LGBT community. Some people have been raped, ostensibly to cure them of their homosexuality. For details of this troubling, morally reprehensible phenomenon, see Andrew Martin et al., eds., *The Rise of Corrective Rape in South Africa*, Action AID Report, www.actionaid.org.uk.

HIV and AIDS Transforming Scholars and
Their Scholarship: From Mere Academics to Scholar Activists

Remarkably, at the helm of these EHAIA strategic interventions in search of an AIDS-free world has been the work of several socially engaged African theologians who have worked with EHAIA in various projects responding to the HIV crisis in Africa. These include Musa Dube's instrumental role in curricular reform and the work of Ezra Chitando, who has been articulate in naming the issue of masculinities as a major theoethical concern, particularly in the context of AIDS. These scholars' capacity to propose and implement new strategies to address the AIDS crisis springs from their own prior transformation as scholars in the face of the crisis. Many of the scholars involved in AIDS work consider themselves or are considered scholar activists, which means that beyond an academic interest in the crisis, they are personally invested in the quest for lasting solutions.

Such a transformation from a "mere academic" to a fervent HIV and AIDS scholar activist is here palpably exemplified in the case of Musa Dube. Like many in Africa who have witnessed firsthand the harrowing impact of HIV and AIDS on families and communities, Dube saw the urgency of working to transform theological education so that it serves rather than subverts Africans' quest for health and wholeness. Dube herself intentionally reoriented her whole scholarly and research agenda toward this goal and invites other scholars to follow suit.[20]

She considers this transformation of scholars and their scholarship as analogous to becoming "firefighters," determined to put out seemingly ubiquitous crises or fires ranging on the continent. Comparing responses to the HIV and AIDS crisis to various responses that people might have to a burning hut, she identifies a "typology" of responses to AIDS in Africa. Some may be indifferent to the burning hut and continue with a business-as-usual attitude, while others may be in so much shock that they become overwhelmed and helpless. Dube calls on scholars to move out of a business-as-usual mindset and also to avoid giving up too soon in the face of the seemingly herculean task of putting out the HIV and AIDS fire.

Reflecting on her own journey as an academic responding to HIV and AIDS,[21] Dube speaks of how she moved from seeming "indifference" and inaction, possibly born out of a sense of helplessness in the face of the complex HIV and AIDS crisis, to becoming an active firefighter. Initially she fought the fire at the personal level through her own research and writing. Later, she became a

---

[20] See Ezra Chitando, *Troubled but Not Destroyed* (Geneva: WCC Publications, 2009), 61–65, 81–94, for an analysis of Musa Dube as a scholar activist.

[21] See Musa Dube, "On Being Fire Fighters: Insights on Curriculum Transformation in HIV and AIDS Contexts," Institute for Theology and Religion, UNISA, 2008.

"lead firefighter" as EHAIA appointed her to help mainstreaming AIDS in the theological curriculum. There and elsewhere, she collaborated with and benefited from being in the company of other firefighters, particularly colleagues and fellow sisters in the Circle of Concerned African Women Theologians.[22]

In her case and that of other scholars,[23] or collectivities of scholars such as the Circle of Concerned African Women Theologians (more about them below), we witness how the AIDS pandemic and other crises have transformed academics into socially engaged scholar activists. Many would agree that a business-as-usual attitude by scholars when Africa is burning in so many ways would be morally unconscionable.

Dube's and other African academics' transformation into scholar activists in the face of AIDS is reminiscent of the transformation of Paul Farmer, who testifies to how working among radically impoverished Haitians transformed him from a mere academic (a medical and cultural anthropologist) to an activist determined to make health care accessible to all as a human right. His scientific background and training notwithstanding, and inspired by Latin American liberation theology, Farmer became a prophet of justice, seeking to address structural root causes of ill health among the impoverished. He also embraced the liberation theology notion of the preferential option for the poor and called upon scholars to do the same. In Farmer's view,

> Such an option for the poor offers a new way of analyzing health systems. It demands that the analysis (of the Haitian context, for example) be historically deep enough to remember that modern-day Haitians are descendants of a people enslaved in order to provide our ancestors with cheap sugar, coffee, and cotton.[24]

While acknowledging that the transformation from being mere academics to activists on the side of the poor is not easy, Farmer considers such a transformation morally obligatory and a necessary ingredient for reaching viable solutions to disease and its roots in structures of violence. In his words,

---

[22] See Musa Dube, "HIV and AIDS Research and Writing in the Circle of Concerned African Women Theologians, 2002–2006," and "In the Circle of Life: African Women Theologians' Engagement with HIV and AIDS," in *Compassionate Circles*, ed. Ezra Chitando and Nontando Hadebe (Geneva: WCC Publications, 2009), 174–96, 197–227. These two chapters constitute Musa Dube's appreciative yet analytical assessment of the Circle of Concerned African Women Theologians as "fellow fire fighters" against HIV/AIDS.

[23] The list of such scholars includes Dr. A. Orobator (Hekima College) and Professor Mary Getui of Catholic University of East Africa, who is a long-standing member of the Circle of Concerned African Women Theologians and, until recently, chairperson of the Kenyan National AIDS Control Program.

[24] Farmer, *Pathologies of Power*, 158.

If we (i.e., doctors, physicians, nurses) fail in this task, we may never be able to contend with the structures that create and maintain poverty, structures that make people sick. . . . We can expect more and more of our services to be declared cost ineffective and more of our patients erased. . . . In declaring health care a human right [we] join forces with those who have long labored to protect the rights and dignity for the poor.[25]

Many African scholar activists would agree that a preferential bias for the poor helps them more credibly and effectively come to analytical grips with the scourge of AIDS, among other crises that the impoverished face.

AIDS and Its Wounded Healers:
PLWH Transformed from Victims of
Despair into Doctors of Hope

One of the most remarkable sites of transformation is among people living with HIV (PLWH). During the early years of the pandemic, many diagnosed with HIV were given up for dead and were encouraged to think about dying from the disease rather than thinking about how to live with it. While the news of impending physical death was the biggest blow, stigma around those diagnosed with the disease also occasioned a sense of social death among PLWH. This stigma triggered in them a deadly cocktail of fear, isolation, guilt, desperation, and a sense of worthlessness.

Asunta Wagura, one of the most articulate AIDS activists in Kenya, recalls the sense of despair that nearly drowned her when she was first diagnosed with AIDS over twenty-five years ago.[26] Expelled from the medical school where she was studying and warned that she had a short time to live, her dreams for a career and family were shattered. She reports that, for her, facing physical death was not as scary as the prospect of dying of AIDS "in the glare of society." Dying in that manner was even more shameful because AIDS was a sexually transmitted disease; it was assumed that if a woman contracted AIDS, then she was a promiscuous prostitute. As Asunta recalls, "I was judged harshly. . . . No one listened to my side of the story. . . . With time I decided to tell the world that I didn't get infected because I was careless or promiscuous."[27]

In response to this rather desperate situation, Asunta gathered four other similarly rejected PLWH to create a surrogate family for themselves. This surrogate family and support group has since grown to be an internationally known

[25] Ibid., 159.
[26] See KENWA (Kenya Network of Women With AIDS), "Asunta's Diary," www.kenwakenya.org.
[27] Ibid.

and award-winning organization: KENWA (Kenya Network of Women with AIDS). Transformed from desperation, Asunta has grown over the years from a mere survivor of AIDS to a healer of those infected and affected. Not only does her organization help PLWH get resources to help manage the biological aspects of the debilitating disease, Asunta also addresses the pain of desperation, social death, and loss of hope that accompanies those diagnosed or living with HIV. She celebrates her own resilience and asks fellow PLWH to remember that they are more than victims. In her words,

> I am in charge of my life and my destiny as long as I live. . . . That is the message we have been driving in KENWA—that we are in charge of our lives and we don't need to be reduced to dependence on handouts and reliefs. I am in charge of my life. I can work for the sustainability of my life.[28]

Asunta has reinvented herself as a healer, a "doctor" who dispenses more than ARVs. As she celebrates in a recent blog post, she has become "a doctor who dispenses hope."[29] Through creative partnerships with the government and with people of goodwill, KENWA has brought hope where there was none and made it clear that those infected with HIV can live healthy, robust, and positive lives.

Similarly transformed is Canon Gideon Byamugisha, who has been living with AIDS since 1992 and who is one of the many courageous religious leaders to publicly announce his HIV-positive status. In going public, Byamugisha helped religious leaders living with HIV come to terms with the stigma, which, for such leaders, is compounded by shame since they are religious leaders and yet have HIV, a sexually transmitted infection.

Having to some extent overcome shame and stigma to announce his status, Byamugisha went on to challenge the prevailing wisdom regarding solutions to AIDS. The mantra, particularly for Uganda where he lives, was that the solution to AIDS was ABC: Abstinence, Be faithful, and use Condoms. Byamugisha challenged this ABC solution on several grounds. First, he challenged its exclusive focus on sexual transmission and, conversely, its failure to address other modes of transmission, including mother-to-child or through contaminated needles. Second, he challenged the exclusive focus on HIV prevention and thus ABC's failure to address the needs of those already living with HIV. Third, the ABC approach focused on the voluntarily sexually active, thus leaving out children and others who, though not active sexually, are vulnerable to HIV through rape, including marital rape.

---

[28] Asunta Wagura, cited in David McKenzie, *CNN*, "AIDS Activist Proves There Is Life after HIV," July 5, 2011.

[29] See Asunta Wagura, "I Am an Expert at Dispensing Hope," *Daily Nation* (Kenya), May 26, 2015.

Going beyond a critique of the ABC model of HIV intervention, Byamugisha proposed an alternative model: SAVE (**S**afer practices, **A**ccess to treatment, **V**oluntary counseling and testing, and **E**mpowerment). This now globally accepted model seeks to overcome the inaccurate connection that the ABC model was making between AIDS and (sexual) immorality, a situation that increases stigma against PLWH by assuming that those who are HIV-positive have failed to abstain and to be faithful. ABC also suggests that condom use is only a measure of last resort for those who won't or can't abstain or be faithful, rather than a legitimate prophylactic measure integral to HIV prevention and AIDS management.[30]

Like Asunta, who founded a supportive network to address problems of isolation born out of social rejection, Byamugisha founded a supportive network known as ANARELA (African Network of Religious Living with AIDS). In time, this group has morphed into an international platform (INERELA) through which religious leaders who are PLWH find a voice to speak for themselves and for others who are also voiceless and vulnerable. Such religious leaders stepping up to fight HIV and AIDS are an example of wounded healers. They exemplify and model resilience, courage, and hope in the face of HIV and AIDS.

Moreover, in his journey as a wounded healer, Byamugisha has specifically named and amplified the syndemic nature of HIV and AIDS, pointing at the cumulative impact of the metaphorical viruses mentioned earlier. He specifically identifies and works to subvert these viruses, for which he coined an acronym, SSDDIM (**S**tigma, **S**hame, **D**enial, **D**iscrimination, **I**naction, and **M**isaction).[31] Understanding the impact of these viruses became key in his fight against HIV and AIDS.

By going public and organizing a network of similarly publicly engaged religious leaders who are PLWH, Byamugisha and his colleagues struck major blows against stigma and shame, the first two ingredients of the deadly virus cocktail. Overcoming shame and despair and proposing alternative causes of action such as SAVE, Byamugisha, Asunta, and other activist PLWH also model transformative leadership, which is much needed in the context of HIV and AIDS as well as other crises that Africa faces.

Wrestling with Kyriarchies and Building Circles of Compassion and Solidarity

A fundamental strategy in the struggle for an AIDS-free world is the transformation of power dynamics in interpersonal relationships. Ever since AIDS

---

[30] See INERELA, SAVE Toolkit, inerela.org/.
[31] See Global Working Group on Faith, *SSDDIM and HIV Strategic Plan, 2012–2016*, globalworkinggroup.wordpress.com.

made global headlines in the 1980s, analysts of the pandemic have considered the analytical relevance of power and its dynamics in history in the quest for lasting solutions. Paul Farmer, as noted earlier, has identified "the pathogenic" impact of what he calls "pathologies of power," which, according to him, revolve around several "axes": gender, race, class, and colonialism. Working toward the dismantling of such structures of violence so that the impoverished can access health care as their right became morally obligatory for Farmer.

Farmer's diagnosis and response echo that of feminist theologians of liberation, here exemplified by the Circle of Concerned African Women Theologians. They also have identified systemic and pathological power dynamics (which they call *kyriarchies*) as root causes of many of the issues that African women face, including HIV and AIDS. So, when in 2002 they deliberately took on the AIDS pandemic as an urgent target for their scholarship and advocacy, this circle of women theologians committed to address the cumulative impact of stigma, denial, violence against women, and the feminization of HIV and AIDS. The theologians considered these issues to be symptomatic of sexist, racist, and patriarchal mindsets and worked toward transforming consciousness, raising the awareness of the deadly impact of these mindsets in the context of HIV and AIDS.

At the same time, the scholars recognized that sexism, racism, and classism are not just a matter of individuals' faulty thought and practice. Rather, these mindsets inform the way society is organized and lead to systemic or structural injustices. Thus, African women undertook the task of bearing prophetic witness against these systemic injustices that disproportionately affect women and children, and that make women and children extra vulnerable to HIV and allied states of ill health. The Circle women diagnosed distorted notions of power as the root causes of these injustices and vulnerabilities. Given this diagnosis, it is not surprising then, that—determined to articulate and make public their insights into the question of power—the circle women dedicated their 1996 pan-African Congress to the theme of "Transforming Power Women in the Household of God."[32] The very title of the conference was a sign that African women are aware of the need to transform power and to use it so that it would be more conducive to better human flourishing for women, many of whom have been victims of the abuse of power.[33]

The Circle women go beyond bearing prophetic witness against kyriarchies. They have proposed, and indeed practice, alternative ways of wielding power

---

[32] See Mercy Oduyoye, ed., *Transforming Power: Women in the Household of God* (Accra: Samwoode, 1997). The volume is an anthology of the papers presented at the 1996 Circle Conference in Nairobi, Kenya.

[33] Teresia Hinga, "The Dialogical Imperative: Listening to Concerned and Engaged African Women," in Colleen Griffith, *Prophetic Witness: Catholic Women's Strategies for the Church* (New York: Crossroad, 2009), 83.

and authority. De jure, if not entirely de facto, the ideal for them is to nurture and implement the ideas of "power with" and "power for" others rather than "power over" others. To express this ideal, the African women theologians deliberately adopted the idea of the circle as a metaphor describing their vision of church and society. Naming themselves the "circle" signified their intention to overcome hierarchical thinking, which facilitates the use and abuse of power as domination. Determined to implement the ideal of "power for" and "power with" instead of "power over" others, the circle members intentionally avoided hierarchical terms like *president* and *chairman* and deliberately chose a nonhierarchical leadership model. To date, Circle affairs are managed by a rotating steering committee and a pan-African Circle coordinator.

Through these intentional efforts to replace hierarchical and pyramidal thinking with Circle thinking and practices, African women made a significant step in the direction of transforming power. Instead of pyramids of power, the women have forged what has been called "compassionate circles."[34] Such efforts to forge compassionate circles of solidarity and care become a major breakthrough in the search for lasting solutions to the AIDS pandemic. Circle thinking and practice would indeed subvert kyriarchies that sicken those at the bottom of intersecting power pyramids.

Conclusion:
Toward an AIDS-Free World

Although many important steps in the quest for lasting solutions to the AIDS crisis have been made over the years, major and enduring roadblocks persist on the way to an AIDS-free world. The viruses of stigma and denial continue to haunt many, while sexism and patriarchal thought and practices continue. Globalization has exacerbated poverty and its feminization, which in turn exacerbates women's vulnerability to HIV. Greed and abuse of power seem to be the norm today, while many continue to benefit from the AIDS crisis as they partake in what has been dubbed the "AIDS industry."[35] Instead of demanding justice for those affected and infected by AIDS, the tendency is still for many to settle for charity as the preferred intervention.[36] Clearly there is work to be done in search for an AIDS-free world.

---

[34] See Chitando and Hadebe, *Compassionate Circles*.

[35] See Helen Epstein, *The Invisible Cure: Africa, the West, and the Fight against AIDS* (New York: Farrar, Straus, and Giroux, 2007), for a detailed analysis of this problem.

[36] For a critique of charity as a preferred intervention against poverty, see Teresia Hinga, *Becoming Better Samaritans: Quest for New Ways of Doing Social Justice in Africa*, in *Applied Ethics in a World Church*, ed. Linda Hogan (Maryknoll, NY: Orbis Books, 2008), 85–95.

At the same time, however, encouraging developments have taken place along the way as more nuanced diagnoses of root causes yield more effective responses. The emergence of strategies such as SAVE and the deliberate nurturing of alternative structures of interpersonal relations, such as the Circle of Concerned African Women Theologians is doing, are indeed signs of hope. In the context of HIV and AIDS, a most gendered crisis, the vigorous efforts to replace dangerous, hegemonic masculinities with redemptive masculinities is a major cause for celebration. Considering the insight that patriarchy and sexism are driving forces for the AIDS syndemic, it is particularly encouraging to witness the emergence of male feminism and to hear men calling on others to become feminists and deliberately work to dismantle patriarchy. I conclude with the hope-inspiring words of ethicist Jim Keenan, who invites fellow men to become male feminists as a matter of moral duty. This duty involves men's

> awareness of their privilege in order to vigilantly dis-assemble male dominance . . . and incorporate principles of equality in one's daily life. [It] means taking steps to shift societal dynamics that benefit men as a group . . . being accountable for the deconstruction of male privilege, [and finding] creative ways to undermine and disassemble patriarchy.[37]

Such innovative proposals for structural transformation as well as transformation of consciousness suggest that, although AIDS continues to be a most daunting and deadly crisis, recognizing the complexities that make it a syndemic and working toward dismantling its allied viruses give cause for hope, a hope that is itself vital for a world en route to being AIDS-free.

---

[37] James Keenan, "The Gallant: A Feminist Proposal," in *Feminist Catholic Theological Ethics: Conversations in the World Church*, ed. A. Orobator and Linda Hogan (Maryknoll, NY: Orbis Books, 2014), 229.

CHAPTER 20

GLOBAL HEALTH, AIDS,
AND THE CATHOLIC CHURCH IN AFRICA

Anthony Egan

Although points of convergence outweigh divergence, tensions exist between global health organizations and the Catholic Church's theological understanding and pastoral practice (notably condom usage and gender justice) with regard to HIV and AIDS in Africa.[1] Yet, cooperation is essential to serve the common good and fundamental to this is a *ressourcement* by the church of a number of classical themes in moral theology.

Global Health and the Challenge of AIDS in Africa

Global health is the study, research, and practice of health-care professionals aimed at promoting health for everyone on the planet. Global health also emphasizes the elimination of disparities in access to health, and protection from health threats not on an individual or local basis but as part of a global human development policy. The field is holistic in that it rejects a narrow biomedical understanding in favor of health policies and programs that integrate with political, economic, and social issues in developed and developing countries.[2] A survey of key themes in global health[3] reveals that the field recognizes the importance of economic and social inequality, war, and conflict, as well as ecological-environmental issues as crucial to human well-being, and in some ways more important than the treatment of specific symptoms. This approach makes perfect logical sense. Malnutrition is both a disease and a major contributory factor to disease; poorly fed people are simply more vulnerable to

---

[1] Hereafter "AIDS" is used as a form of shorthand for the condition of HIV and AIDS.

[2] J. P. Koplan et al., "Toward a Common Definition of Global Health," *The Lancet* 373, no. 9679 (2009): 1993–95; Global Health Initiative, *Why Global Health Matters* (Washington, DC: FamiliesUSA, 2008); Peter Muennig and Celina Su, *Introducing Global Health: Practice, Policy, and Solutions* (San Francisco: Jossey-Bass, 2013).

[3] See, for example, Solomon Benatar and Gillian Brock, eds., *Global Health and Global Health Ethics* (Cambridge: Cambridge University Press, 2011).

opportunistic illnesses than those who enjoy a proper diet. Food security is thus essential.[4] So, too, is greater social equality: unequal societies are by definition societies where the gap between haves and have-nots is greater, not only in terms of access to adequate nutrition, but also access to adequate and affordable health care. Often in the face of opposition from governments and multinational pharmaceutical companies, global health advocates lobby for easier and cheaper access to essential drugs and treatments for people who cannot afford them, even challenging international economic policies protecting the intellectual property rights of corporations.[5] Conflict situations are also quite obviously situations where health is adversely affected, not simply by the direct effects of warfare, but indirectly through damage to the social infrastructure. The expenses of building a war machine and replenishing weapons of war further exacerbate the situation by drawing public funds away from health, welfare, and education into feeding the military industry.[6]

Global health, in short, sees social justice as integral to physical and mental well-being. It also integrates international organizations, governments on every level, nongovernmental organizations, the academy, and civil society in the pursuit of the common good of human flourishing.

The global challenge of AIDS is simply one aspect of the global public health agenda, albeit a crucial one. Yet AIDS has been seen as transforming and renewing the idea of global health in an era where the neoliberal capitalist agenda was dominant in three key ways: (1) by being a disease of both rich and poor, developed and developing peoples, it transformed public health into a "global endeavor"; (2) because many politicians and civil society groups were initially unwilling to face the disease, it highlighted the centrality of politics in public health; and (3) it brought the voices of people living with AIDS into

---

[4] Lynn McIntyre and Krista Rondeau, "Food Security and Global Health," in Benatar and Brock, *Global Health and Global Health Ethics*, 261–73; O. Müller and M. Krawinkel, "Malnutrition and Health in Developing Countries," *Canadian Medical Association Journal* 173 (2005): 279–86.

[5] Thomas Pogge, "The Health Impact Fund: How to Make New Medicines Accessible to All," in Benatar and Brock, *Global Health and Global Health Ethics*, 241–50; Peter Singer, "Famine, Affluence, and Morality," *Philosophy and Public Affairs* 1 (1972): 229–43; Wolfgang Hein, "Global Health Governance and WTO/TRIPS: Conflicts between 'Global Market-Creation' and 'Global Social Rights,'" in *Global Health Governance and the Fight Against HIV/AIDS*, ed. Wolfgang Hein, Sonja Bartsch, and Lars Kohlmorgen (New York: Palgrave Macmillan, 2007), 38–66.

[6] Salahaddin Mahmudi-Azer, "The International Arms Trade and Global Health," in Benatar and Brock, *Global Health and Global Health Ethics*, 166–72; R. M. Garfield and A. I. Neugut, "Epidemiological Analysis of Warfare: A Historical Analysis," *Journal of the American Medical Association* 226 (1991): 688–92; V. W. Sidel, "The International Arms Trade and Its Impact on Health," *British Medical Journal* 311 (1995): 1677–80.

the public arena.[7] This has led quite a few scholars to suggest that the pandemic more or less "invented" our current understanding of global health.[8]

Central to the United Nations' Millennium Development Goals[9] (notably Reduction of Child Mortality [no. 4], Improve Maternal Health [no. 5], and Combat HIV and AIDS, Malaria and Other Diseases [no. 6]), global health is pursued directly and indirectly by a range of international organizations, including specifically the World Health Organization (WHO), the United Nations Children's Fund (UNICEF), the World Food Program, and even the World Bank. Global health is also the focus of a range of national and international governmental and nongovernmental bodies.

The Catholic Church's Response to AIDS in Africa

I do not deal directly with the specifics of the Catholic Church's response to AIDS in Africa, since other chapters in this book deal with it more fully. On a continent with the highest levels of HIV infection and people living with AIDS (PLWA), the Catholic Church, together with many other Christian churches and other faiths, has played an admirable role in both pastoral and medical care. UNAIDS itself has recognized this fact, pointing out that the Catholic Church, with its extensive network of hospitals and clinics in Africa and elsewhere, is the world's largest private provider of medical care to PLWH.[10] All major global health organizations and researchers broadly acknowledge this fact, as do theologians engaged in ethical-pastoral reflection, who stress the importance of what they call "faith-based organizations" (FBOs) in the fight against AIDS. The church's pastoral care for PLWAs is outstanding, as is its campaign against stigmatization, which it rightly sees as a major social justice issue. Kenyan-born church historian Stephen Joshua has documented some of this activity in his study of the Catholic Church's combination of medical care, creation of AIDS orphanages, and advocacy for antiretroviral treatment in South Africa.[11] In fact, if one were to revisit my description of global health's

---

[7] Wolfgang Hein, Sonja Bartsch, and Lars Kohlmorgen, "Foreword: Governing Interdependence," in Hein, Bartsch, and Kohlmorgen, *Global Health Governance and the Fight against HIV/AIDS*, xi.

[8] Allan M. Brandt, "How AIDS Invented Global Health," *New England Journal of Medicine* 368, no. 23 (2013): 2149–52.

[9] www.un.org/millenniumgoals/.

[10] UNAIDS Press Statement, "UNAIDS Congratulates Newly Elected Pope Francis," March 14, 2013, www.unAIDS.org/en/resources/presscentre/pressreleaseandstatementarchive/2013/march/20130314pspopefrancis/.

[11] Stephen Muoki Joshua, "A Critical Historical Analysis of the South African Catholic Church's HIV/AIDS Response between 2000 and 2005," *African Journal of AIDS Research* 9, no. 4 (2010): 437–47.

agenda, it becomes obvious that the church echoes all its primary concerns. Yet global health also acknowledges that FBO engagement is not without tensions and complexities.[12]

So why are there tensions between the Catholic Church (and other religious communities) and the global health initiatives?

The Church and Global Health: Common Ground and a Few Points of Tension

On the face of it, the Catholic Church and global health should be inseparable allies.[13] Catholic social thought (CST) stands firmly against unjust war, economic and social injustice, and all factors that adversely affect health, and for greater socioeconomic equality and access to the necessities of life, including health care. The holistic discourse of global health could be lifted from the great tradition of the social encyclicals' proclamation of the common good, dignity of persons, and (insofar as global health insists on local agency in promotion of well-being, over aid from "outside," wherever possible) the principle of subsidiarity. Indeed, I would argue that at least 90 percent of the global health agenda accords perfectly with CST.

Also, as we have noted, the churches and other faiths in Africa and elsewhere have played a vital role in treatment and pastoral care of AIDS patients.[14]

---

[12] Elizabeth Ferris, "Faith-Based and Secular Humanitarian Organisations," *International Review of the Red Cross* 87, no. 858 (June 2005): 311–25; R. Morgan, A. Morgan, and J. Boesten, "Aligning Faith-Based and National HIV/AIDS Prevention Responses? Factors Influencing the HIV Prevention Policy Process and the Response of Faith-Based NGOs in Tanzania," *Health Policy and Planning* (2010): 1–10; R. J. Vitillo, "Faith-Based Responses to the Global HIV Pandemic: Exceptional Engagement in a Major Public Health Emergency," *Journal of Medicine and the Person* 7 (2009): 77–84; Fiona Samuels, Reina Geibel, and Fiona Perry, *Collaboration between Faith-Based Communities and Humanitarian Actors When Responding to HIV in Emergencies*, Project Briefing no. 41, May 2010 (London: Overseas Development Institute / Tear Fund / Worldvision, 2010); Vhumani Magezi, "From Periphery to the Centre: Toward Repositioning Churches for a Meaningful Contribution to Public Health Care," *HTS Teologiese Studies / Theological Studies* 68, no. 2 (2012).

[13] In this section I must acknowledge the important work done by, in particular, Lisa Sowle Cahill. See "Bioethics, Theology, and Social Change," *Journal of Religious Ethics* 31, no. 3 (2003): 363–98; "Global Health and Catholic Social Commitment," *Health Progress* (May–June 2007): 55–57; "Catholics and Health Care: Justice, Faith and Hope," *Journal of Catholic Social Thought* 7, no. 1 (2010): 29–49.

[14] Some useful localized examples can be found in Michael Mbona, "The Response of the Roman Catholic, Anglican and United Methodist Churches to HIV and AIDS in Manicaland, Zimbabwe (1985–2007)" (PhD dissertation, University of KwaZulu Natal, 2012); Mark Krakauer, "Churches' Responses to AIDS in Two Communities in KwaZulu Natal, South Africa" (MPhil thesis, Oxford University, 2004); African Religious Health

Similarly there has been a deliberate attempt to orient the theological education of pastors toward dealing with the crisis.[15] Where the divergence emerges, heightened by the AIDS pandemic, is in two areas: gender justice and the use of condoms in preventing HIV infection. Based on overwhelming evidence that all the key factors affecting global health—poverty, poor education, violence, social discrimination, lack of access to resources (including medical care), and so on—are heavily weighted against women, particularly in Africa where young women are still the most at risk, the global health community emphasizes the importance of gender justice. This emphasis includes specifics—like promotion of reproductive health rights, including access to contraception and, if needed, abortion—and more general issues like full equal rights for women in a world where patriarchal attitudes and practices persist in almost all countries, and where access to education, jobs, and resources (including health care and nutrition) are skewed toward men.

The other point of divergence is the important but not exclusive emphasis on the use of condoms in the prevention of HIV infection. Global health simply finds the anticondom attitude of the Catholic Church and other churches incomprehensible and at times dishonest, particularly given the clear disparity between church teaching on sexuality and practice, especially among youth.[16] The condom, properly used, *is* a scientifically effective way of preventing HIV transmission, although they admit that sexual abstinence is even better: Abstain if you can, Be faithful to one partner, or Condomize if you can't (the ABC rule) is for secular global health organizations a reasonable scientific (and hence ethical) proposition. That its side effect is contraceptive as well is seen by some

---

Assets Programme, "Appreciating Assets: The Contribution of Religion to Universal Access in Africa," Report for the World Health Organization, Cape Town, October 2006; Stuart Bate and Alison Munro, eds., *Catholic Responses to AIDS in Southern Africa* (Pretoria: Southern African Catholic Bishops Conference / Grace and Truth, 2014); Constance M. Mamba, "Prevention within a Pastoral Strategy: Assessing the ABC Model, with Reference to the HIV/AIDS Pandemic in Swaziland" (MTh thesis, University of Stellenbosch, 2012).

[15] See, for example, Hannu Happonen et al., eds., *Toward an HIV- and AIDS-Competent Church* (Iringa, Tanzania: CUAHA / Tumaini University, n.d.); Gillian Paterson, ed., *HIV Prevention: A Global Theological Conversation* (Geneva: Ecumenical Advocacy Alliance, 2009); Paula Clifford, *Theology and the HIV/AIDS Epidemic* (London: Christian Aid, 2004); Ezra Chitando, ed., *Mainstreaming HIV and AIDS in Theological Education* (Geneva: EHAIA, 2008).

[16] See, for example, Elisabet Eriksson et al., "Faith, Premarital Sex, and Relationships: Are Church Messages in Accordance with the Perceived Realities of the Youth? A Qualitative Study in KwaZulu–Natal, South Africa," *Journal of Religion and Health* 52 (2013): 454–66; Joanne E. Mantell et al., "Conflicts between Conservative Christian Institutions and Secular Groups in Sub-Saharan Africa: Ideological Discourses on Sexualities, Reproduction, and HIV/AIDS," *Global Public Health* 6, no. S2 (October 2011): S192–S209.

in global health as a socioeconomic and ecological bonus, reducing the pressure on bearing and raising children for women in particular (giving them greater opportunity for advancement in work, and hence more equality) and reducing rapid population growth's negative ecological impact.

Engaging the Tensions: Gender Justice

Gender justice has become a red-flag term in parts of the Catholic Church, often because it's seen as explicitly advocating abortion rights and implicitly challenging the church's rejection of women's ordination. On the former, abortion is indeed seen by many in global health as integral to broader reproductive health. This view is based on medical science's understanding that the fetus is a potential person, not a person, and that potentiality simply does not have the same rights as the actuality. In fairness, abortion is not seen as standard practice for pregnant HIV-positive women: cutting-edge research has developed ways of preventing mother-to-child-transmission by administering antiretrovirals to newborn infants.

The latter issue is ours. Many in the Catholic Church see a contradiction between our social ethic that promotes equality of the sexes "outside" and a kind of "different but equal" discourse within. While a source of dispute within the church, global health has no authority or comment here.

Fundamentally, the problem between the Catholic Church and global health policy is the current official Catholic understanding of women, particularly as found in John Paul II's *Mulieris Dignitatem*, understood by many to be rooted in an anthropology of biological essentialism and difference. Here a woman's primary role is interpreted as mother and nurturer, and women are seen as fundamentally different from men. A number of Catholic feminist scholars would share this understanding, though arguing against any notion of inequality and for a broader anthropology.[17] Many scientists, anthropologists, and philosophers—and most in the global health field—reject the theory outright but comment on it only insofar as it may be used to maintain patriarchal cultures that disadvantage women's abilities to protect themselves from HIV.

Clearly this is a topic too broad to address adequately in this chapter. What we need here is a major global dialogue between all sides of the debate. Rather, what I'd suggest for the moment is to see that much of the area that gender justice covers needs to be read through Catholic social thought. Also, on our continent, an African theology should at the very least recognize the degree to which justice for African women in general, and their health in particular, is negatively affected by cultural practices that all too often (but not always)

---

[17] For example, Tina Beattie, *New Catholic Feminism: Theology and Theory* (London: Routledge, 2005).

reflect an oppressive patriarchal worldview, backed up (knowingly or unknowingly) by Christian and often Catholic thinking. The point is not to portray African culture as hopelessly patriarchal and irredeemable; if moral theology, and theology in general, is to have an impact, it must engage with African cultures in all their complexity. Theology must continue to draw on the riches of African religion,[18] proverbs, songs, folktales, and above all, the dialogical emphasis on palaver[19] rooted in what may be summed up in the southern African concept of *Ubuntu*. But such engagement, though already critical, must be increasingly aware of the gendered emphases and biases within culture so that a potentially liberating source (to adapt Aquinas, perhaps a "third source of revelation") does not become a source of sexism and irrationalism. Groups like the ecumenical Circle of Concerned African Women Theologians—and increasingly some male theologians—are already raising this issue. What we need here is a constructive dialogue with global health rather than enmity.

Engaging the Tensions: Condoms

On the question of condom use, I would suggest that we start with the insights of Pope Emeritus Benedict XVI in the book of interviews *Light of the World*,[20] where he argued that in certain cases, condom use in a time of AIDS might be a lesser evil. While Benedict XVI did not change his mind about artificial contraception or even the usefulness of condoms in HIV prevention, the new view is a substantial step forward for a number of reasons.

While not abrogating the controversial 1968 encyclical of Paul VI banning the use of artificial contraception, Benedict XVI intimated, cautiously, that with AIDS we are dealing with two different things altogether: contraception and prevention of disease. If we look at the example the pope uses, we see that he is using a case—a homosexual male prostitute—where there is in fact no chance of the sexual act resulting in pregnancy! Nor, it should be added, has the pope declared condoms to be the panacea for the AIDS crisis. He clearly affirms in the interview that condoms should not be seen as *the* solution, or even a major solution, to the problem—a point that global health now concedes: abstinence and marital fidelity are the 100 percent certain solutions to the problem.

---

[18] For example, Laurenti Magesa, *African Religion: The Moral Traditions of Abundant Life* (Maryknoll, NY: Orbis Books, 1997); Bénézet Bujo, *Foundations of an African Ethic* (New York: Crossroad, 2001); Peter Knox, *AIDS, Ancestors, and Salvation: Local Beliefs in Christian Ministry to the Sick* (Nairobi: Paulines Publications Africa, 2008).

[19] For example, Agbonkhianmeghe E. Orobator, *Theology Brewed in an African Pot* (Maryknoll, NY: Orbis Books, 2008).

[20] Benedict XVI (with Peter Seewald), *Light of the World: The Pope, the Church, and the Signs of the Times* (San Francisco: Ignatius Press, 2010), 113.

What we see, rather, is that a slightly different application of Paul VI's *Humanae Vitae* might be in operation here. Before and after Benedict's interview, the Vatican officially rejected the suggestion that the use of condoms to prevent the spread of HIV was permissible under the exception that *Humanae Vitae* allowed with regard to the medical use of the Pill (for purposes of regulating menstrual cycles). Yet this is precisely what the text allowed for: medical exceptions. This little-known exception says,

> The Church, on the contrary, does not at all consider illicit the use of those therapeutic means truly necessary to cure diseases of the organism, even if an impediment to procreation, which may be foreseen, should result therefrom, provided such impediment is not, for whatever motive, directly willed. (*Humanae Vitae*, 15)

In the context of preventing HIV infection, the condom is a clear example of artificial contraception serving a therapeutic purpose. Careful research shows that the proper use of condoms substantially reduces the risk of HIV transmission.

What we see here is perhaps an acknowledgment of the classic doctrine of double effect, which might be simply stated as follows:

> An action must be good or at least indifferent; the agent must intend the good effect but not the bad effect, even though he or she may foresee the bad effect; the bad effect cannot be a means to the good effect; and the good effect must outweigh the bad effect or there must be a proportionate reason for allowing the bad effect to occur.[21]

Applied to the question of condoms in prevention of HIV transmission, we can see how this might work: the "bad effect" (contraception) is not the means to the "good effect" (prevention of HIV transmission), but a side effect of the intended good. My sense is that, whether Benedict intended it, this clause of *Humanae Vitae* objectively applies to the present situation, albeit perhaps in very limited circumstances.

This proposed innovation echoes what many moral theologians, conservative as well as liberal, have been arguing for a number of years. Martin Rhonheimer, a theologian in Rome, articulated many of the points the pope made in an article in the *Tablet* in 2004[22] (and in other academic

---

[21] James Childress, "Christian Ethics, Medicine, and Genetics," in *The Cambridge Companion to Christian Ethics*, ed. Robin Gill (Cambridge: Cambridge University Press, 2001), 264.

[22] Martin Rhonheimer, "The Truth about Condoms," *The Tablet*, July 10, 2004.

writings[23]), where he argued that intended HIV prevention rather than contraceptive intention did not violate *Humanae Vitae*. This might also be seen as an application of the principle of totality, where one looks at the overall picture of a problem in order to situate the morality of a controversial act. Even when one accepts the overall principles behind *Humanae Vitae*, and acknowledges the risk that the use of condoms might encourage sexual activity outside marriage (which, given the acceptance of intentional and when properly applied highly effective Natural Family Planning methods of fertility regulation, seems to be the only coherent reason for the teaching), we are still faced with a dilemma. Given that scientific studies of sexual activity deemed immoral by the church persist—in Africa and elsewhere—*despite* the teaching, should one then *increase* the amount of real or potential harm or evil, or seek to reduce it? The analogy traditional ethics has used of medical amputations—removing a diseased limb to save a person's life—seems to apply here. (Note, too, that medical scientists and global health proponents would say that amputation is in certain contexts a positive good, at least the lesser evil. But, given the result, we can live with our different opinions.)

Many of these classical traditions of applying a contextual or historical consciousness to moral problems have been lost in much official moral theology, particularly as it applies to matters of sex. Since HIV transmission in Africa (and elsewhere) is primarily *sexual transmission*, the ethical prevention of HIV transmission has up until now been subsumed in, and often confused with, the ethics of sex. The official ethics of sex[24] has determined (and arguably limited) what the church deemed morally acceptable means to prevent the spread of HIV. The problem is that we tend to focus on sex from the perspective of personal sin, which some argue "pales in comparison to the structures of poverty and gender discrimination that [place] most HIV-infected persons at risk."[25] AIDS places poor people and especially women at risk, as numerous theologians have noted.[26] In Pope Benedict's statement, we perhaps saw the

---

[23] See Martin Rhonheimer, *Ethics of Procreation and the Defense of Human Life* (Washington, DC: Catholic University of America Press, 2010); Rhonheimer, *The Perspective of Morality: Philosophical Foundations of Thomistic Virtue Ethics* (Washington, DC: Catholic University of America Press, 2011).

[24] I use "official" specifically because evidence suggests that it is at best acknowledged rather than widely practiced within the church. Likewise, *Humanae Vitae*, however firmly its promulgation, has largely not been "received" by the majority of Catholics.

[25] Lisa Sowle Cahill, "AIDS, Justice, and the Common Good," in *Catholic Ethicists on HIV/AIDS Prevention*, ed. James F. Keenan et al. (New York: Continuum, 2000), 291.

[26] Gillian Paterson, *Women in a Time of AIDS* (Maryknoll, NY: Orbis Books, 1996); Kevin T. Kelly, *New Directions in Sexual Ethics: Moral Theology and the Challenge of AIDS* (London: Geoffrey Chapman, 1998); Kenneth R. Overberg, *Ethics and AIDS: Compas-*

beginning of an attempt to address the HIV crisis in its wider context. It needs to be taken further.

Historically, pastors like Bishop Kevin Dowling of Rustenburg, South Africa, and numerous moral theologians[27] whose interpretation of the problem is based on a wider, more justice-focused reading of Catholic moral tradition have been seen as "dissident." What Benedict's statement suggested is not a theological vindication of their views, but a possible narrowing of the gap between the Vatican and such pastors and theologians. The new style of Pope Francis seems to echo this: we talk to each other; we examine each other's ideas in a respectful and collegial fashion. We even presume that each truly seeks both the True and the Good.

Underlying the new approach has been a combination of traditional Catholic methods of doing moral theology, rooted in a renewed casuistry,[28] often tied into a pragmatic concern for pastoral care, justice for women (and, in the case of Margaret Farley,[29] justice as a basis for the underlying sexual ethics that need to be part of HIV prevention), virtue ethics, and a renewed theology of conscience. A very helpful example of this new integration is provided by Maria Cimperman,[30] who outlines a virtue ethic for a time of AIDS. Hope gives us a social vision that is communal, inclusive, paschal, and eschatological; fidelity is rooted in mutual love and faithfulness; self-care strikes a balance between selfish autonomy and inappropriate self-sacrifice; justice demands a responsibility to seek and do the good for individuals and the community. Last, like Aquinas, she argues that Prudence mediates the other virtues by calling us to conscientiously and wisely discern what needs to be done; in doing so, this sets a new moral agenda, one that I would argue echoes the best African dialogical and culture-mediated theological tradition—and the new openness of Francis.

---

sion and Justice in Global Crisis (2006; Mumbai: St. Paul's, 2009); John Mary Waliggo, "A Woman Confronts Social Stigma in Uganda," in Keenan, *Catholic Ethicists on HIV/AIDS Prevention,* 48–57.

[27] See, for example, Kelly, *New Directions*; Keenan, *Catholic Ethicists.* On Bishop Dowling, see Stephen Muoki Joshua, "The Dowling Controversy, the 'Message of Hope,' and the Principle of Oikonomia: A Historical-Critical Reflection on the South African Catholic Church's Stance on the Use of Condoms in HIV Prevention between 2000 and 2005," *Journal of Theology for Southern Africa* 137 (July 2010): 4–27.

[28] See Keenan, *Catholic Ethicists on HIV/AIDS Prevention.*

[29] Margaret Farley, "Partnership in Hope: Gender, Faith, and Responses to HIV/ AIDS in Africa," *Journal of Feminist Studies in Religion* 20, no. 1 (2004): 133–48, and *Just Love: A Framework for Christian Sexual Ethics* (New York: Continuum, 2006).

[30] Maria Cimperman, *When God's People Have HIV/AIDS: An Approach to Ethics* (2005; Mumbai: St. Paul's, 2006).

Conclusion

We are, at least partly, what we do. Part of my work is within the church, part at a secular bioethics department attached to the health sciences faculty of a South African university. In the latter, the necessarily secular ethical discourse includes global health. I have come personally to see much value in it, more common ground than disagreement with Catholic theology. My chapter affirms this. Similarly I see the tension between official Catholic teachings on AIDS prevention that seem to emphasize personal sexual behavior at the cost of broader justice, health, and flourishing, and a more pastoral, pragmatic, and social ethic that I would argue (no doubt contentiously to some) reflects a broader and deeper approach to Catholic moral theology. Paradoxically, though not without problems, the ethics of global health seems closer to the latter, what I might call the long tradition of Catholic theological ethics.

Clearly there are differences and difficulties between both forms of Catholic thinking and global health philosophy, and by extension between their respective agencies at work in Africa and elsewhere. But mutual excommunication is unhelpful and has potentially lethal human consequences. Dialogue is essential, not denunciation.

On another level I am struck by how much more African theologians need to engage both with the long tradition and with African culture in this regard. Though theology and the church have grown from greater numbers of women theologians simply being given an ear, we maintain a strongly masculinist way of thinking in faith and culture. Male theologians, particularly clergy and bishops, need to listen to the *critical* voices—not just those who echo traditional religious and cultural views. Failure to listen and engage may not only render us irrelevant; it may make us part of the problem global health addresses rather than a partner in its solution.

CHAPTER 21

PUBLIC POLICY AND AIDS IN AFRICA

A Theological Approach Using the *Ukama* Concept

Ezra Chitando

The HIV epidemic has left an indelible mark on the continent of Africa. While bringing out serious challenges, the epidemic has also demonstrated many strengths that the continent possesses. Faced with a devastating epidemic, the continent has shown incredible resilience, coordination, compassion, and leadership. Whereas stigma, discrimination, poor theology, and ineffective leadership allowed HIV to spin out of control in the late 1990s, solidarity and embracing new theological paradigms enabled the continent to get HIV under control. Despite the notable achievements, major challenges remain. The international community has also contributed in stemming the tide of HIV, although much more needs to be done in order to ensure that Africans can experience life in abundance.

This chapter applies a theological approach to examine and critique the role of public policy in responding to HIV in Africa. Operating with the concept of *ukama* (relatedness of all citizens), which is equivalent to the biblical notion that we are each other's keeper (Gen. 4:9–16), the chapter challenges public policy in the time of HIV to take seriously the need to protect the poor, the marginalized, and the stigmatized in society. The concept emerges from the Shona people of Zimbabwe but is found across most African cultures. *Ukama* maintains that by acknowledging the relatedness among all the people of God, public policy can become more attuned to the struggles and needs of the most vulnerable citizens. Whereas a few African governments have demonstrated impressive levels of sensitivity to the struggles of people living with and affected by HIV and AIDS, there is a need to increase awareness around the concept of relatedness.

The chapter argues that by appreciating the concept of the relatedness of all citizens, public policy in Africa will prioritize the welfare of the oppressed in the context of HIV and AIDS. It identifies the gaps that public policy needs to fill in Africa in order for responses to HIV and AIDS to become more effective. Relatedness implies that those tasked with crafting public policy do not conceptualize the process as involving "others" out there, but the policy makers recognize the extent to which their very own interests are inextricably intertwined with those of the poor. By realizing that HIV is a serious matter, they will be compelled to acknowledge the importance of "names, not just numbers."[1] In the chapter's first section, I examine public policy in Africa in the context of HIV and AIDS. The second section takes up the concept of *ukama* and analyzes its theological value. In the third section, I discuss the benefits of applying the concept of relatedness to public policy in the time of HIV and AIDS in Africa. I conclude by reiterating the importance of theologians contributing to reflections on public policy in Africa. Given the bewildering diversity that characterizes Africa and its theological traditions, I must state my social location upfront: I write as a Zimbabwean scholar of religion and theologian who operates in ecumenical contexts. I am familiar with, and influenced by, African Catholic, Protestant, Pentecostal, and Independent Church theological traditions.

Public Policy in African Contexts of HIV and AIDS:
An Overview

In a real sense, Africa's response to HIV and AIDS has laid bare the major weaknesses of the continent's systems, as well as providing some insights into its notable strengths. For example, while President Thabo Mbeki's initial denialism and the actions of his Minister of Health, Manto Tshabalala-Msimang, caused untold suffering and death in South Africa,[2] there are also alternative narratives of policies that enabled people living with HIV to enjoy very early access to treatment. Despite the challenges that Mbeki's policies had, they drew attention to the need to address the issue of poverty in the response to HIV and AIDS. Musa W. Dube observes, "From the outbreak of the HIV epidemic in 1985, Botswana has demonstrated a strong and committed response characterized by a series of strategic plans."[3] In these often contradictory narratives of poor leader-

---

[1] Donald E. Messer, *Names, Not Just Numbers: Facing Global AIDS and World Hunger* (Golden, CO: Speaker's Corner Books, 2010).

[2] Warren Parker, "The Politics of AIDS in South Africa: The Foundations of a Hyperendemic Epidemic," in *African Responses to HIV/AIDS: Between Speech and Action*, ed. Segun Ige and Tin Quinlan (Pietermaritzburg: University of KwaZulu-Natal Press, 2012), 228–29.

[3] Musa W. Dube, "'We Pray, We Give Hope': The Faith-Sector Response to HIV and AIDS in Botswana," in *The Faith Sector and HIV/AIDS in Botswana: Responses and Challenges*, ed. Lovemore Togarasei, Sana K. Mmolai, and Fidelis Nkomazana (Newcastle upon Tyne: Cambridge Scholars Publishing, 2011), 23.

ship and outstanding interventions, Africa's story of responding to HIV and AIDS must be told.

Public policy essentially refers to "deciding who gets what and who pays."[4] It can also mean, "Who says what." In many African countries, public policy has sought to ensure that formerly disenfranchised citizens are well catered for in the postcolonial period. However, the effects of colonialism and the challenges facing the post-colonial state have compromised public policy in Africa. The uncritical acceptance of development blueprints supplied by global financial organizations has also contributed toward challenges associated with public policy in Africa. The posturing of politicians compounds the problem. The net result has been a general failure to uplift the quality of life for the majority of citizens. Without subscribing to the doctrine that "nothing good comes out of Africa," one can accept that "most of these policies are beclouded with politics and implementation bottlenecks."[5]

One of the biggest challenges that public policy in Africa has faced in the wake of HIV is that many governments have been slow to act. Although all bureaucracies move slowly, failure to recognize that HIV and AIDS represented a new and urgent threat constituted a major hindrance. As many governments adopted a business-as-usual approach, many lives were lost. Fear, stigma, discrimination, and apathy allowed the epidemic to spin out of control. The need to rethink public policy in the wake of the epidemic was urgent. According to Elias K. Bongmba,

> The social world created by HIV/AIDS challenges status quo public policy and calls for new priorities in Africa today. HIV/AIDS is the greatest threat to the political, economic, and social stability of African countries because it is causing the polis to disintegrate at an unprecedented rate. This could have been avoided if African governments had acted on time.[6]

Public policy in Africa has, therefore, been slow in responding to the challenge of HIV and AIDS. Prominent politicians, however, can play a major role in mobilizing communities to respond to HIV and AIDS. For example, President

---

[4] David Bromell, "Doing the Right Thing: Ethical Dilemmas in Public Policy Making," Centre for Theology and Public Issues Working Paper 2012, 1.

[5] Brahima Awaisu Imana, Rufai Kilu Haruna, and Annin-Bonsu Nana Kofi, "The Politics of Public Policy and Problems of Implementation in Africa: An Appraisal of Ghana's National Health Insurance Scheme in Ga East District," *International Journal of Humanities and Social Sciences* 4, no. 4 (2014): 196.

[6] Elias K. Bongmba, *Facing a Pandemic: The African Church and the Crisis of AIDS* (Waco, TX: Baylor University Press, 2007), 28.

Yoweri Museveni of Uganda was instrumental in providing leadership to his country's response to the epidemic. He went public about the impact of the epidemic at a time when acknowledging the reality of HIV and AIDS was taboo. Unfortunately, not many other leaders have followed his example.

Among the numerous public policy issues that need to be tackled in Africa, in this chapter I concentrate on stigma, funding, treatment for children, and the urgency of services for key populations. I have selected these issues to highlight the need to address abiding challenges such as stigma and to be attuned to emerging realities. By tackling these challenges, public policy in Africa will become a valuable resource for enhancing the quality of life of people living with HIV, as well as their communities. The chapter does not discuss these themes in an exhaustive way, but teases out the key issues before analyzing how the theological concept of *ukama* can be applied in order to contribute toward a greater sensitivity in the overall response to HIV and AIDS.

Regrettably, the early phase of the HIV epidemic was characterized by denial, inaction, and misaction. Stigma and discrimination tended to dominate, with religious communities playing a leading role. Stigma prevented communities of faith from contributing to HIV prevention. Gideon Byamugisha, one of the most outspoken and committed Christian leaders in the response to HIV and AIDS, contends that stigma remains a challenge.[7] While African public policy has sought to address stigma and discrimination by adopting a human rights framework, more still needs to be done to enable people living with HIV (PLWH) to feel fully accepted. Even with the availability of lifesaving medication, stigma remains a reality.

Across many African countries, the integration and normalization of services for PLWH remains a forlorn ideal, which has sustained stigma as PLWH are "marked out" by accessing services at points designated for them. Although no signs are posted that indicate a service point for PLWH, most people in health-care settings and those who use health services regularly do figure it out. The net effect has been to entrench stigma, with some PLWH hesitating to take up services. As a result,

> Stigma and discrimination in the health care setting and elsewhere contribute to keeping people, including health providers, from adopting HIV preventive behaviors and accessing needed care and treatment. Fear of being identified as someone infected with HIV increases the likelihood that people will avoid testing for

---

[7] Gideon Byamugisha, "Reconstruction of '*Missio Dei*' in the Context of HIV," in *Is the Body of Christ HIV-Positive? New Ecclesiological Christologies in the Context of HIV-Positive Communities*, ed. Gideon Byamugisha, John Joshva Raja, and Ezra Chitando (Delhi: ISPCK, 2012), 130.

HIV, disclosing their HIV status to health care providers and family members, or seeking treatment and care, thus compromising their health and well-being.

With its potentially devastating consequences on care-seeking behavior, stigma represents a major "cost" for both individuals and public health. Both experienced and perceived stigma and discrimination are associated with reduced utilization of prevention services, including programs to combat mother-to-child transmission, HIV testing and counseling, and accessing care and treatment.[8]

Alongside the ongoing challenge of stigma in health-care settings, public policy on HIV and AIDS in Africa continues to grapple with the issue of funding. While international initiatives such as the Global Fund to Fight AIDS, the President's Emergency Plan for AIDS Relief (PEPFAR), the Bill and Melinda Gates Foundation, the Stephen Lewis Foundation, and others have played an important role in stemming the tide of HIV and AIDS in Africa, it remains critical for African countries to fund their own programs. The funding must include research, securing medication, and support for orphans, as well as meeting other needs. Domestic funding for HIV and AIDS interventions is an absolute priority, as external partners have set a clear trend of reducing funding. It is, therefore, crucial to find ways of indigenizing the production of medicines and the financing of HIV and AIDS projects in the region.[9]

Public policy in Africa must emphasize mobilization of local resources for an effective response to HIV and AIDS. It must ensure that all protocols that have been signed are implemented and that governments do not prioritize luxury items ahead of the needs of people living with and affected by HIV and AIDS. Governments must be held accountable in honoring their commitments to financing health on the continent. While Zimbabwe has done well by instituting an AIDS levy and Botswana has sought to meet its health costs, much more remains to be accomplished. As one author observes,

The importance of government funding for health services has been emphasized for a number of reasons. Government health funding is typically more predictable and flexible than donor funding. It is also a demonstration of government's commitment to invest in its citizens' health. The underinvestment in health against a backdrop of slow

---

[8] Laura Nyblade, Anne Stangl, Ellen Weiss, and Kim Ashburn, "Combating HIV Stigma in Health-Care Settings: What Works?" *Journal of the International AIDS Society* 12, no. 15 (2009); www.jiasociety.org/.

[9] C. Gwandure and T. Mayekiso, "The Impact of Dwindling Donor Funding on HIV and AIDS Projects in Sub-Saharan Africa," *Africa Insight* 42, no. 4 (2013): 44–58.

progress toward the MDGs has been a concern for African governments since the beginning of this century. Commitments were made
in Abuja in 2001 and in several health financing panels for Ministers
of Health and Ministers of Finance in Kampala (July 2010), Addis
Ababa (March 2011) and Yamoussoukro (September 2011), all in an
effort to explore ways of increasing government investment in health.[10]

By ensuring that African governments invest in health, public policy will
be laying a solid foundation for the health and well-being of present and future
citizens. As I argue below, governments that invest in the health of citizens are
making sound decisions and will win the future by preparing for the development
of their nations. The Abuja Declaration expresses the April 2001 commitment
by heads of African governments to commit at least 15 percent of their annual
budgets to improve the health sector. In its evaluation after a decade, the World
Health Organization poignantly observes, "Only Rwanda and South Africa have
achieved the Abuja Declaration target of 'at least 15 percent.'"[11]

The third challenge that public policy in the contexts of HIV and AIDS
must address more seriously is the availability of lifesaving medication for children living with HIV. That many children living with HIV in Africa have not
been put on treatment is scandalous. What kind of a world are we living in,
when we leave children facing death when scientific progress has been achieved?
Whereas Africa has led the way in expanding access to treatment, UNAIDS
notes that "pediatric coverage is exceptionally low." Furthermore, "Treatment-
eligible children living with HIV in sub-Saharan Africa are only about half as
likely to receive antiretroviral therapy as HIV-positive adults."[12]

Apart from the ethical challenges that emerge from a world where we as
adults prioritize our own survival, some practical challenges are associated
with meeting the unique medical needs of children living with HIV. Getting
the right dosage has been a challenge, along with ensuring that the formula-
tions are palatable or not too difficult for children to swallow. In addition, in
some instances, refrigeration for some children's medications is required. Public
policy must prioritize children's access to antiretroviral therapy, which will
restore children's confidence and demonstrate the seriousness of policy makers
and implementers.

The final challenge has proved quite problematic in Africa. After the earlier
debates surrounding the use of condoms, key populations have emerged as a

---

[10] Tatah Mentan, *Africa: Facing Human Security Challenges in the 21st Century*
(Bamenda, Cameroon: Langaa RCPIG, 2014), 240.

[11] WHO, "The Abuja Declaration: Ten Years On" (Geneva: WHO, 2011), 2.

[12] UNAIDS, "Access to Antiretroviral Therapy in Africa: Status Report on Progress
toward the 2015 Targets" (Geneva: UNAIDS, 2013), 5.

contested group in Africa. Due to the undeclared influence of religion, policy makers have often minimized the importance of ensuring that key populations in Africa are covered in programming if the overall response to HIV and AIDS is to be more effective. UNAIDS says the following regarding this particular category of persons:

> Reliable estimates of antiretroviral therapy coverage are not available for men who have sex with men, people who inject drugs, sex workers, or transgender individuals. However, there are strong indications that key populations face substantial barriers to access essential health services and have extremely low access to antiretroviral therapy.[13]

Whereas documents by some national AIDS councils make references to key populations, most public policy documents and official discourses do not address the reality. In particular, the issue of men who have sex with men has been moved from the public health platform to the realm of public morality. Church leaders and politicians have joined forces to demonize, ostracize, and further stigmatize men who have sex with men. Regarding the phenomenon of men who have sex with men as an attack on "pure African culture," many African church leaders and politicians have sought to challenge public policy when addressing the needs of men who have sex with men. Overlooking the incompetence of most of the ruling elites, they bring up homosexuality as one of the most significant "signs of the end times." Writing from the context of Nigeria, Ebenezer Obadare clarifies this development:

> The upshot has been a situation in which homosexuality (and the moral degeneracy that it presumably epitomizes) is held responsible for problems as diverse as the destruction of African families, the HIV/AIDS pandemic, cultism and violence in the universities, female prostitution, increased divorce rates, the erosion of discipline in the military, moral decay in society and natural disasters. Because religious leaders are central to the construction of this discourse, it meshes with an eschatological imaginary which interprets global structural transformations as a sign of the imminence of "the second coming." According to this thinking, homosexuality and associated sexual and moral "perversions" are not just poignant evidence that we are in the "last days," they vindicate a divine program whose inexorable climax is the termination of human culture.[14]

---

[13] Ibid., 6.

[14] Ebenezer Obadare, "Sex, Citizenship, and the State in Nigeria: Islam, Christianity, and Emergent Struggles over Intimacy," *Review of African Political Economy* (2015): 3.

Although most African states claim to be guided by secular constitutions, the influence of African Indigenous Religions and cultures, Christianity, and Islam on the formation of public policy is noticeable. Versions of conservative and "biblical" Christian ethics, as well as Islamic tenets, have found their way into public policy with a negative impact on the health and well-being of key populations, who have been marginalized as a result. While it would be strategic for positive ethical values to permeate Africa's public policy, the situation becomes untenable when retrogressive values and fundamentalist ideologies gain ground. In the following section I propose the concept of *ukama* as a possible resource for theological contributions to public policy in Africa.

Ukama (Relatedness):
A Theological Resource for Public Policy in Africa

As noted above, conservative religious ideologies have found their way into public policy in Africa, frustrating efforts to ensure that nobody is left behind in the response to HIV and AIDS. While the turn after 2000 toward acknowledging the role of faith-based organizations in addressing HIV and AIDS is welcome, policy makers must ensure that only progressive values from the religions are distilled and appropriated. When religion compromises access to health, as is the case generally in its approach toward key populations, there is a need to recover religion's liberative dimension. African theologians need to become prophetic. According to Tukunboh Adeyemo, prophets are "bold, courageous, daring, and decisive. They fear no man: presidents, priests, or philosophers. Prophets command an incredible authority and power."[15] Such a prophetic outlook can be inspired by the ethical concept of *ukama*, a concept that needs reinvigoration, as negative attitudes toward people living with HIV have persisted in most communities in Africa.

The concept of *ukama*, deeply rooted among the Shona people of Zimbabwe but finding expression in various other African communities as well, suggests that each human being is related to the other. Although closely related to the more popular concept of *unhu/Ubuntu*, *ukama* is more directly connected to the notion of relatedness among all members of the community. (*Unhu* refers more to the qualities of good citizenship.) As its proponent, Zimbabwean philosopher Munyaradzi F. Murove, has argued, *ukama* expresses the idea that life is an interconnected whole. It suggests that a person must recognize that she or he is intrinsically related to the other humans around her

---

[15] Tukunboh Adeyemo, "The Church's Strategic Role," in *The Hope Factor: Engaging the Church in the HIV/AIDS Crisis*, ed. Tetsunao Yamamori, David Dageforde, and Tina Bruner (Waynesboro, GA: Authentic Media, 2003), 287.

or him.[16] *Ukama* is a reminder that the fate of others is bound up with one's actions. Although the individual does have freedom, that freedom is exercised within a communal context. Murove elaborates on the etymology and expansiveness of *ukama*:

> *Ukama* is a Shona word implying relationship and an understanding of reality in terms of interdependence. Grammatically *Ukama* is an adjective constructed *U-kama*. *U-* is an adjectival prefix and *-kama* an adjectival stem. *Kama* becomes a verb meaning to milk a cow or a goat. In Shona thought the idea of milking suggests closeness and affection. Those related by blood are *hama*, which is a noun. . . . In its adjectival form, *Ukama* means being related or belonging to the same family. However, in Shona, as in many other African languages, the meaning of *Ukama* is not restricted to marital and blood ties. This culture tends to see all people as *hama* (relatives).[17]

When a culture tends to regard all people as related, there is hope for the poor and the marginalized because relatives have some responsibilities and expectations. There are no strangers or outcasts, as all belong to the community of relatives.

I believe that a dynamic equivalence exists between *ukama* and the Catholic social teaching on solidarity. Solidarity means that one recognizes that we are one human family, whatever differences we might have. *Ukama* expresses the theological notion that we are our brother's and sister's keeper, communicating the responsibility that each member of the human family has toward other family members. The concept challenges the human family to cultivate the feeling of belonging, which is captured by its sister concept, *unhu* (also expressed as *Ubuntu* or *Botho* in other Bantu languages).

> *Unhu* is a social philosophy which embodies virtues that celebrate mutual social responsibility, mutual assistance, trust, sharing, unselfishness, self-reliance, caring and respect for others among other ethical values. It means behavior patterns acceptable to Shona people. This means ethos and attitudes which influence the way people participate in various departments of their lives.[18]

---

[16] Munyaradzi Felix Murove, "The Shona Ethic of *Ukama* with Reference to the Immortality of Values," *Mankind Quarterly* 48, no. 2 (2007): 179–89.

[17] Munyaradzi Felix Murove, "An African Environmental Ethic Based on the Concepts of *Ukama* and *Ubuntu*," in *African Ethics: An Anthology of Comparative and Applied Ethics*, ed. Munyaradzi Felix Murove (Pietermaritzburg: University of KwaZulu-Natal Press, 2009), 316.

[18] Evans Mandova and Agrippa Chimombe, "The Shona Proverb as an Expression of

Ukama expresses the value of solidarity. Where some ideologies seek to emphasize variables such as ethnicity, class, race, gender, sexual orientation, HIV status, and other factors that deepen divisive pluralism, solidarity emphasizes the point that we all belong together. Like *ukama*, solidarity recognizes that we are all members of one human family. In the quest for justice and human dignity, solidarity implies acknowledging the fundamental right to quality of life for all of God's people. Solidarity empowers individuals and the church to challenge the many situations of inequality, poverty, and injustice because they distort the sense of *ukama*.

Applying *Ukama*:
Enhancing Public Policy in the Context
of HIV and AIDS in Africa

The interface between religion and policy on HIV and AIDS in Africa has not been as effective as many would have wished.[19] One of the major challenges, as I indicated in the previous section, is the impact on public policy of conservative religious ideologies. However, there has also been a general absence of progressive and activist theological voices to influence African public policy. Despite this, the efforts of the International Network of Religious Leaders Living with or Personally Affected by HIV and AIDS (INERELA+) needs to be acknowledged. In addition, other bodies, such as the World Council of Churches and the Ecumenical Advocacy Alliance, have promoted advocacy to challenge stigma and discrimination and to urge governments to be more accountable. With particular reference to Christianity, the quest has been to promote the emergence of "HIV-competent churches."[20] *Ukama*'s entry point would be primarily from the perspective of indigenous knowledge, although it touches on religion, ethics, and culture. A full elaboration of these points lies beyond the scope of this chapter.

Applying the ethic of *ukama* will go a long way toward eliminating stigma and discrimination. When all human beings are regarded as belonging to the family of God, the basis for stigma and discrimination is removed. Integrating *ukama* in public policy in Africa contributes toward acknowledging the role of indigenous knowledge systems in policy formulation. Combining it with

---

Unhu/Ubuntu," *International Journal of Academic Research in Progressive Education and Development* 2, no. 1 (2013): 100.

[19] Jill Olivier, "Religion and Policy on HIV and AIDS: A Rapidly Shifting Landscape," in *Religion and HIV and AIDS: Charting the Terrain*, ed. Beverley Haddad (Pietermaritzburg: University of KwaZulu-Natal Press, 2011), 81–104.

[20] Sue Parry, *Practicing Hope: A Handbook for Building HIV and AIDS Competence in the Churches* (Geneva: World Council of Churches, 2013).

Catholic social teachings on solidarity would appeal to millions of Christians. Furthermore, the concept is consistent with the teachings of various other religions of the world, thereby contributing toward an interfaith theology of liberation in the time of HIV and AIDS.[21] While the contours of such a theology are yet to be teased out, one can already anticipate an emphasis on the relatedness of all human beings.

Building on the concept of solidarity, public policy in Africa needs to acknowledge that all citizens deserve to be treated with respect and that stigma is an affront to the intrinsic dignity of every human being. While the wording may differ (in keeping with the secular character of public policy), the underlying notion of relatedness should be communicated when addressing stigma and discrimination. This concept can also be linked to citizenship: all citizens have the right to high-quality lives.

Ukama is a powerful resource for mobilizing greater state investment in health in the time of HIV and AIDS in Africa. In outlining the challenges, I mentioned the Abuja Declaration, in which states undertook to devote at least 15 percent of their budgets to health. Unfortunately, most African governments have chosen to politic over this very serious matter. *Ukama* challenges policy makers to recognize their intrinsic connection to PLWH and all those affected by the epidemic. Solidarity demands that the policy makers and implementers prioritize the needs of PLWH over the grandiose projects that many African states pursue. Where resources are misallocated or even looted, prophetic Christians must speak truth to power. They must ensure that public policy protects the poorest and most vulnerable members of the community. Christians must insist on the rights of "the wretched of the earth" to receive protection from the state. According to Musa W. Dube, an African theologian who has led the way in reflecting theologically on HIV and AIDS,

> The concept of community, the *Botho/Ubuntu/Buthu* paradigm, should become the cornerstone for propounding the African philosophy of justice and liberation by constantly revisiting what it means to be community and live in community, what violates community, and how to live in community in the new and hybrid twenty-first-century contexts. Being a community is not something set. It is a process that must be continually cultivated by its members. Relationships should be constantly assessed. Anything that is oppressive must be reviewed. Only when society is healthy can it be claimed that "I am because we are and we are because I am."[22]

---

[21] Gerald West, "Sacred Texts, Particularly the Bible and the Qur'an, and HIV and AIDS: Charting the Textual Terrain," in Haddad, *Religion and HIV and AIDS*, 139.

[22] Musa W. Dube, "'I Am Because We Are': Giving Primacy to African Indigenous

The ethic of *ukama* or solidarity can contribute toward urgency in investing in children's access to medication. As I indicated, public policy in Africa must take seriously children's rights in the time of HIV and AIDS. Unfortunately, the low position of children in most African communities makes their situation quite desperate. Although this assertion is open to debate, one can argue that adults tend to take precedence over children in most African communities—a concept that also applies to children in other contexts, beyond Africa. Through the concept of *ukama*, public policy in Africa can promote the full participation and citizenship of children. By recognizing that children constitute full, productive, and intrinsic members of the community, theologians can influence public policy, which would go a long way toward ensuring that children are taken more seriously in African communities. For Kenneth Mtata, a Zimbabwean theologian who seeks to promote African child theology, we must learn to appreciate the need for advocacy and solidarity in this particular model of theology. He writes,

> Advocacy approach to child theology emerges from the understanding that in other liberation theologies the affected persons speak for themselves. Women theologians speak for themselves and other fellow women. Black theologians spoke for themselves even though there are some sympathizers among white people. . . . Since children cannot do child theology by themselves, all those who accompany them see themselves as involved in some task of advocacy. In this case advocacy approach emphasizes the aspect of solidarity and empowerment. As such solidarity is the foundation of child theology. Since it is a theological reflection of adults in solidarity with children, it is a representative theology or one that seeks to mediate between childhood and God.[23]

Finally, *ukama* offers radical insights into the status of key populations. The description "key populations" has been used in HIV and AIDS discourses to express the particular vulnerability of members of these groups to HIV infection. Although there are differences among members of these groups, they have been grouped together in order to increase understanding of their vulnerability to HIV infection. Solidarity obliterates distinctions based on sexual orientation, drug use, or sex work. It critiques holier-than-thou approaches and readily recognizes the full dignity of every human being created in the image of God.

Values in HIV and AIDS Prevention," in *African Ethics: An Anthology of Comparative and Applied Ethics* (Pietermaritzburg: University of KwaZulu-Natal Press, 2009), 202.

[23] Kenneth Mtata, "African Personhood and Child Theology," in *Befreiung vom Mammon/ Liberation from Mammon*, ed. Ulrich Duchrow and Hans G. Ulrich (Berlin: LIT Verlag, 2015), 248.

It challenges all members of the community to share in each other's struggles and to embrace difference on the understanding that God accepts all human beings as we are. *Ukama* equips African theologians who seek to contribute to public policy to refuse to allow prejudice and false superiority to hinder the formulation of sound policies. Although some critics will declare doom and destruction, theologians who are guided by the ethic of solidarity will be courageous enough to recognize that key populations are essential to understanding God's love and mercy. No class, gender, sexual orientation, professional occupation, or any other distinguishing characteristic has the right to monopolize God and exclude part of God's creation from enjoying God's warmth and acceptance.

Conclusion

Many Africans are tired of HIV and AIDS. Unfortunately, HIV and AIDS are not yet tired of Africa. To put it in Southern African parlance, "Aluta continua!" (the struggle continues). In this continuing struggle, public policy has a major role to play in directing Africa's ongoing engagement with HIV and AIDS. In this chapter I have explored some of the key themes that public policy in Africa needs to address in order to improve the effectiveness of the overall response to HIV and AIDS. I drew attention to stigma, funding, lack of medication for many children, and the exclusion of key populations. I proceeded to suggest that the concept of *ukama* could be appropriated and deployed to provide theological insights to public policy in Africa. *Ukama* enjoins African theologians to regard public policy as an integral part of their sphere of influence as it reminds them that, in the face of HIV and AIDS in Africa, God stood up.[24]

---

[24] James Cantelon, *When God Stood Up: A Christian Response to AIDS in Africa* (Ontario: John Wiley and Sons Canada, 2007).

CHAPTER 22

HIV AND AIDS AND STIGMA

Elias Kifon Bongmba

The most powerful contribution we can make to combating HIV transmission is the eradication of stigma and discrimination; a key that will, we
believe, open the door for all those who dream of a viable and achievable
way of living with HIV/AIDS and preventing the spread of the virus.
—*World Council of Churches Consultation in Nairobi, 2001*

During the last thirty-three years, the global community and the African
community in particular has lived with the tragedy of the HIV and AIDS
pandemic that has coexisted with the stigma against people living with HIV,
children orphaned by AIDS, and family members affected by HIV and AIDS.
In this chapter I discuss stigma at a time of AIDS, its impact, and responses to it
from faith communities. This interpretive essay draws materials from previous
studies and my research for the book *Facing a Pandemic*.[1] In writing this chapter,
I am mindful of the claim by Harriet Deacon that stigma has "suffered from
'conceptual inflation' and a consequent lack of analytical clarity."[2]

---

[1] Elias K. Bongmba, *Facing a Pandemic: The African Church and Crisis of AIDS*
(Waco, TX: Baylor University Press, 2001); see Gillian Paterson, *AIDS-Related Stigma:
Thinking outside the Box: The Theological Challenge* (Geneva: World Council of Churches,
2005); Paterson, "HIV, AIDS, and Stigma: Discerning the Silences," in *Religion and HIV
and AIDS: Charting the Terrain*, ed. Beverley Haddad (Pietermaritzburg: University of
KwaZulu-Natal Press, 2011), 350–65; Philomena Njeri Mwaura, "Violations of Human
Rights of Kenyan Women with HIV/AIDS through Stigma and Discrimination," in *Women,
Religion, and HIV/AIDS in Africa: Responding to Ethical and Theological Challenges*, ed.
T. M. Hinga, A. N. Kubai, P. Mwaura, and H. Ayanga (Pietermaritzburg: Cluster Publica-
tions, 2008), 126–43; Harriet Deacon, "Toward a Sustainable Theory of Health-Related
Stigma: Lessons from the HIV/AIDS Literature," *Journal of Community and Applied Social
Psychology* 16 (2006): 418–25; Harriet Deacon and L. Simbayi, *The Nature and Extent of
HIV- and AIDS-Related Stigma in the Anglican Church of the Province of Southern Africa: A
Quantitative Study* (Cape Town: HSRC, 2006).

[2] Deacon, "Toward a Sustainable Theory of Health-Related Stigma," 419.

Defining Stigma

I consider *stigma* to be attitudes and actions that characterize a person or group of people as different in a disapproving manner. People stigmatize others because they think that those people have acted in a manner that is not normal, done or neglected to do something that sets them apart, or they caused a condition that others perceive as a threat. Erving Goffman, in his famous work *Stigma*, argued that it encompasses beliefs and actions that discredit a person deeply and demote that person "from a whole and usual person to a tainted, discounted one."[3] People suffer stigma for different reasons, which range from belonging to a certain race or nationality, class or immigrant community, or they have a sexual orientation of which others disapprove. People also express stigma because they fear illness, such as a sexually transmitted disease or the Ebola virus disease. In case of illness, those who stigmatize others think that the person who has the illness has done something to become ill and could have acted differently to avoid the illness. Acts of stigma set apart those considered disapprovingly, and the consequences of stigma could be as mild as facing an embarrassment, or as severe as a sense of loss of identity or belonging, unequal treatment, and acts of violence.[4]

The root of the term *stigma* comes from slaveholding in ancient Greece. To ensure that, if a slave ran away, the slave would be apprehended and returned to the owner, slaves were tattooed with their owner's mark. The process of making a mark was called "stig in Greek."[5] Emile Durkheim argued that stigmatization takes place when other people are described as deviant and society then unites itself around core moral values to exclude those who have been deemed deviant. Durkheim argued, "Imagine a society of saints, a perfect cloister of exemplary individuals. Crimes or deviance, properly so called, will there be unknown; but faults, which appear venial to the layperson will there create the same scandal that the ordinary offenses do in ordinary consciousness. If, then, this society has the power to judge and punish, it will define these acts as criminal (or deviant)

---

[3] Erving Goffman, *Stigma: Notes on the Management of Spoiled Identity* (New York: Touchstone, 2010); Betsy L. Fife and Eric R. Wright, "The Dimensionality of Stigma: A Comparison of Its Impact on the Self of Persons with HIV/AIDS and Cancer," *Journal of Health and Social Behavior* 41, no. 1 (March 2000): 50–67.

[4] My definition has borrowed several elements from the conceptualization of stigma by Bruce G. Link and Jo C. Phelan. See their essay, "On Stigma and Its Public Health Implications," www.stigmaconference.nih.gov/FinalLinkPaper.html. See, for instance, William Shakespeare, *The Merchant of Venice*; Charles Dickens, *Oliver Twist*; John Steinbeck, *The Grapes of Wrath*; Emile Durkheim, *Suicide: A Study in Sociology* (New York: Free Press, 1951).

[5] Gerhard Falk, *Stigma: How We Treat Outsiders* (Amherst, NY: Prometheus Books, 2001), 17. I am indebted to Gerhard Falk for this historical perspective to the term.

and will treat them as such."[6] Gerald Falk argues that stigma thrives when people assign essences to things and create distinct categories.[7] Some consider stigma as a temporal phenomenon because people's views always change. While stigma is a global phenomenon, we know more about stigma from contextual studies.

Paterson has argued that stigma is grounded on fear and demonstrates a lack of knowledge. Fear is based on the risks associated with certain conditions and causes *instrumental stigma. Symbolic stigma* depends on symbolic meanings, which can promote moral judgments. Clergy focus on sin reinforces symbolic stigma. Paterson points out that stigma could be an instrument of promoting moral values and cultural norms. Overall, it promotes inequalities.[8]

The literature from medicine, sociology, anthropology, psychology, and institutional theory has contributed significantly to our understanding of stigma. Paterson argues that Mary Douglas's analyses of pollution, gender, sexuality, sin, and body taboo might have given ideas for some people to stigmatize others in religious communities. For example, people treat a person with HIV as a tainted individual who has violated sexual norms, lived a promiscuous life, and defiled the body, the temple of the Holy Spirit.[9] Research on HIV and AIDS indicates that people have discriminated against individuals who were infected with the virus because of preexisting prejudices and social segmentation. For example, some people discriminated against women, blacks, and homosexuals. Some perceived that homosexuals were immoral or lived lives that placed them at risk of contracting the virus. With time, many of these perceptions changed, as churches and faith-based organizations fought to reduce the rate of infection and provide care for people living with HIV.

Stigma and Health

Health epidemics and pandemics produce stigma because they pose a threat to other people. People who think that the situation could have been

---

[6] Emile Durkheim, *The Rules of Sociological Method* (New York: Free Press, 1964), 68–69. I am indebted to Falk for the quote and for pointing me to reread this classic discussion. See also Bruce G. Link and Jo C. Phelan, "Conceptualizing Stigma," *Annual Review of Sociology* 27 (2001): 363–85; G. Petros, C. O. Airhihenbuwa, L. Simbayi, S. Ramlagan, and B. Brown, "HIV/AIDS and 'Othering' in South Africa: The Blame Goes On," *Culture, Health, and Sexuality* 8 (2006): 67–77; S. B. Adebajo, A. O. Bamgbala, and M. A. Oyediran, "Attitudes of Health-Care Providers to Persons Living with HIV/AIDS in Lagos State, Nigeria," *African Journal of Reproductive Health* 7 (2003): 103–12.

[7] Gerhard Falk, *Stigma*, 23. The quotation is from Karl Popper, *The Open Society and Its Enemies* (New York: Harper Touchbooks, 1963), 31.

[8] Paterson, *AIDS-Related Stigma*, 3–5.

[9] 1 Cor. 6:19–20.

avoided tend to stigmatize the victims for wrongdoing; they are seen as "other" and blamed for their infection.[10] The AIDS pandemic has given the global community a perfect storm of stigma. At the beginning of the HIV and AIDS crisis, certain communities were singled out and stigmatized. Fear and panic caused some people to disown family members, employers discriminated against infected workers, and people killed HIV-positive relatives because they had brought shame to the family. The communities that experienced stigma included homosexuals, hemophiliacs, intravenous drug users, and sex workers.

Although AIDS was a public health issue, the logic of stigma worked out with this pandemic in profound ways. Many people thought it was preventable and thus urged people to do everything to protect themselves. They gave the message that people were infected with the virus because they engaged in deviant behavior. Some religious leaders described AIDS as a disease that God sent to punish people for the "sin" of homosexuality.[11] The virus spread and took roots in different places, and Haiti was stigmatized became it was considered the epicenter of HIV infections.[12] Later, Africa, where the rate of prevalence remains disproportionately higher than any other place, became the epicenter. In addition to maintaining that HIV and AIDS was a gay disease imported from the deviant West, many Africans blamed the infections on truck drivers, prostitutes, and witchcraft. This perception widened the scope of the stigma, and many communities were plunged into fear.

In my research of the church and HIV in Cameroon in 2005, I met James Ngeh, who told me that he suffered in silence when he received the diagnosis that he was HIV-positive. I asked him if he received any support from the Christian community, but he told me that he did not tell anyone. Informing the pastor of his church was not an option. He feared that the pastor and the rest of the church leadership team would be very disappointed with him and "excommunicate" him since he was also on the leadership team. I reminded him that as a member of a Protestant church, he could not be excommunicated, but he argued, "If they know my situation, they will immediately blame me for committing adultery . . . , and I do not think I can take that." I asked him if his wife knew about his status, and he said she did and was supportive and would not tell anyone. He knew people avoided him because he was ill frequently and had lost weight. He suspected that people despised him and said many bad things about him behind his back.[13]

---

[10] Deacon, "Towards a Sustainable Theory of Health-Related Stigma," 421.

[11] Adebajo, Bamgbala, and Oyediran, "Attitudes of Health-Care Providers."

[12] Paul Farmer, *AIDS and Accusation: Haiti and the Geography of Blame* (Berkeley: University of California Press, 1992); see also Paul Farmer, *Infections and Inequalities* (Berkeley: University of California Press, 1999).

[13] Musa Dube, personal comment.

Scholars have pointed out that HIV-related stigma became an exercise of us-versus-them discrimination in South Africa, where people blamed blacks *and* whites; gays and lesbians were all held up for ridicule. Some South Africans blamed people from other Southern African countries for exporting the virus to South Africa.[14] Women were accused of being the vectors of the HIV virus. In some African countries, the deaths of parents created an orphan crisis never before seen. The orphans faced stigma in different forms. They were now the children whose parents committed sinful acts, contracted the virus, and then died. People feared that these orphans could also be infected with HIV. Some orphans were abandoned to survive on their own, making them vulnerable to sexual exploitation.[15] Even when they received support from overseas nongovernmental organizations, they were further set aside and called "American children"—a dubious distinction that isolated them.

Stigma has had a chilling effect on people living with HIV. On broad public issues, even developed countries like the United States in the 1980s heard calls for the quarantine of people who tested positive for the HIV virus. Some people recommended compulsory testing, and international travel was severely restricted for people infected with the virus, even by the United States. Ryan White faced challenges attending public school in the United States because many in his community feared that their children could be infected with HIV, despite that fact that the doctors said that Ryan White did not pose a risk to the public.

Even health-care workers expressed attitudes of stigmatization against HIV-positive persons. In a discussion about the M. D. Anderson Cancer Center in Houston, some physicians who were very bold in starting treatment for HIV patients recall how some of the center's staff feared contagion. In an interview in 2003 Dr. Peter Mansell recalls some of the innovative approaches they took at the time, but many people still feared having direct contact with the patients.[16] Some people even avoided contacts with health-care workers treating patients at M. D. Anderson Cancer Center because of the fear that the workers might have been infected with the virus.[17]

Health-care stigma is not benign; it can and has been deadly. Gideon Byamugisha laments the reality of stigma: "Many community members, political leaders, policy framers, and legislators do not hide their feelings that preferably HIV-positive people should be withdrawn from society by resort to tough laws that criminalize both HIV infection and

---

[14] Petros, Airhihenbuwa, Simbayi, Ramlagan, and Brown, "HIV/AIDS and 'Othering' in South Africa."

[15] Adebajo, Bamgbala, and Oyediran, "Attitudes of Health-Care Providers," 396.

[16] See interview at library.mdanderson.org/hrc/interviews/mansellp1/mansell.html.

[17] Richard L. Sowell and Kenneth D. Phillips, "Understanding and Responding to HIV/AIDS Stigma and Disclosure: An International Challenge for Mental Health Nurses," *Issues in Mental Health Nursing* 31 (2010): 394–402, 396.

transmission."[18] In South Africa, neighbors killed Gugu Dlamnini, an HIV-positive volunteer for the National Association of People Living with HIV, at her home in KwaMashu, near Durban.[19] In parts of Africa, people have been verbally assaulted and denied food.[20] Stigma and discrimination have intensified fears, feelings of abandonment, neglect, despair, and isolation, and compromised global attempts to control the spread of the pandemic.

Responding to and Fighting Stigma

Beginning in November 2001, in the midst of the fight against HIV and AIDS, some African church leaders confessed that they have not been able to address human sexuality in an honest and realistic manner, opening the door for the churches of Africa to address stigma and end their silence.[21] People living with HIV have been denied the opportunity to strive, and they continue to live on the margins with little bargaining power. Some could not respond to stigma because of the threat of summary execution. For example, in 2006 a Kenyan paper, *Daily Nation*, reported that a Kenyan man killed his HIV-positive nephew and orphan because the HIV status brought shame on the family.[22] Elsewhere, a South African woman who disclosed her HIV status was stoned to death.[23] Studies by members of the Circle of Concerned African Women Theologians document these lack of opportunities to strive. Elesinah Chauke discusses the case of Janet and Susan, cousins who married two brothers. Janet's husband died of AIDS complications, and her husband's relatives urged her to marry her brother-in-law, who was married to Susan. Janet became ill two years after the death of her husband and died. However, she had consummated the union with Susan's husband, and both Susan and her husband would also become ill and die of AIDS complications. There was a wall of silence around the cultural practice of wife inheritance that did not give Susan a fighting chance.[24]

---

[18] Gideon Byamugisha, *Practicioner Response in Religion and HIV and AIDS: Charting the Terrain*, ed. Beverly Haddad (Pietermanizburg: University of KwaZulu Natal Press, 2011), 366.

[19] Donald G. McNeil, Jr., "Neighbors Kill an H.I.V.-Positive AIDS Activist in South Africa," *New York Times*, December 28, 1998.

[20] I am indebted to Sowell and Phillips, "Understanding and Responding to HIV/AIDS Stigma and Disclosure," 396, for these references.

[21] Michael Kelly, "The Significance of HIV/AIDS for Universities in Africa," *Journal of Higher Education in Africa*, 1, no. 1 (2003): 1–36.

[22] M. Ndirangu, "An Act Most Cruel," *Daily Nation* (Kenya), April 26, 2006.

[23] C. Campbell, *Letting Them Die: Why HIV/AIDS Prevention Programmes Fail* (Cape Town: International African Institute, 2003), 110.

[24] Elesinah Chauke, "Theological Challenges and Ecclesiological Responses to Women

In Africa, *ecclesial communities worked through their health-care systems, hospitals, health centers, and ecumenical organizations* like the African Christian Health Association and the Ecumenical Pharmaceutical Network *to address stigma.*[25] These faith-based organizations have provided medical treatment as acts of love that also help reduce stigma.[26] These groups joined with other ecumenical organizations like the World Council of Churches, nongovernmental organizations, the Joint United Nations Program to Combat HIV and AIDS (UNAIDS) to offer a variety of programs that would encourage dialogue and discourage stigma. The African Network for Religious Leaders Living with or Affected by HIV and AIDS (ANERELA+) has worked tirelessly to end stigma through its message of love and safe sex practices.[27] Paterson points out that the Anglican Primates boldly declared, "We raise our voices to call for an end to silence about this disease— the silence of stigma, the silence of denial, the silence of fear. We confess that the church herself has been complicit in this silence. When we have raised our voices in the past, it has been too often a voice of condemnation. We now wish to make it clear that AIDS is not a punishment from God. Our Christian faith compels us to accept that all persons, including those who are living with HIV, are made in the image of God and are children of God."[28]

One of the organizations that worked with churches around the globe to provide assistance and education and established programs that would change people's perspectives on HIV and AIDS is the World Council of Churches (WCC). Its Ecumenical HIV and AIDS Initiatives and Advocacy (EHAIA) was launched in 2002 to implement the concept that "the AIDS crisis challenges us profoundly to be the church in deed and in truth: to be the church as a healing community."[29] EHAIA has worked tirelessly to develop a theological perspective that builds AIDS-competent churches and poured resources into education and training to make churches welcoming and healing communities. EHAIA developed programs, electronic communication, and videos and sponsored several publications addressing HIV and AIDS.

Experiencing HIV/AIDS: A South Eastern Zimbabwe Context," in *African Women, HIV/AIDS, and Faith Communities*, ed. Isabel Apawo Phiri, Beverley Haddad, and Madipoane Masenya (ngwana' Mphahlele) (Pietermaritzburg: Cluster Publications, 2003), 131.

[25] Bongmba, *Facing a Pandemic*, 23.

[26] Ibid.

[27] M. W. Dube, "We Pray, We Give Hope: The Faith Sector's Response to HIV and AIDS in Botswana," in *The Faith Sector and HIV and AIDS in Botswana: Responses and Challenges*, ed. L. Togarasei (Newcastle upon Tyne: Cambridge Scholars Press, 2011), 22–43; Paterson, *AIDS-Related Stigma*, 2–3.

[28] *Statement of Anglican Primates on AIDS*, Canterbury, April 2002, quoted in Paterson, *AIDS-Related Stigma*, 3.

[29] World Council of Churches, "Ecumenical HIV and AIDS Initiatives and Advocacy," www.oikoumene.org/en/what-we-do/ehaia.

EHAIA's work on Africa has now been extended to include other parts of the world. EHAIA appointed Dr. Musa Dube of the University of Botswana to serve as consultant on HIV and AIDS, and during her tenure Dube published pioneering texts addressing theology, biblical analysis, and liturgical approaches for an AIDS-competent church.[30] In addition to teaching at the University of Botswana, Dube carried on research; met with people living with HIV, religious leaders, and political leaders across Africa; published several works addressing the church and its response to HIV and AIDS; and prepared individuals as well as congregations to accept the situation, but fight it with all the resources available to them in and outside their faith communities. Dr. Ezra Chitando from the University of Zimbabwe and Dr. Sue Parry, a physician, followed Dube in the position of HIV-AIDS consultant. They published research work for the church and worked with congregations and denominations across Africa to provide support for churches to address HIV and AIDS. The work of EHAIA and these publications have strengthened African communities to deal with stigma. Chitando and Parry both published works centered on hope for individuals and the community.[31]

Stigma has been reduced because of the availability of antiretroviral drugs. Getting drugs to those infected with the virus took a long time. In South Africa, activists such as Zachi Achmat campaigned for treatment through the organization Treatment Action Campaign (TAC) to get the South African government to provide AZT to people living with HIV. This was a rough struggle because the government complained that the drugs were expensive and toxic. In 1998 the government abandoned the trial program that gave AZT to pregnant mothers to prevent transmission of the virus to their unborn child. TAC, under Achmat's leadership, continued the fight, and their stand expedited the availability of antiretroviral drugs for many people.[32] New combination medications such as highly active antiretroviral therapy (HAART) were introduced, and zidovudine was found to be effective in preventing transmission from mother to child.

[30] Musa W. Dube: *HIV/AIDS and the Curriculum: Methods of Integrating HIV/AIDS in Theological Programmes* (Geneva: World Council of Churches, 2003); *Africa Praying: A Handbook on HIV/AIDS-Sensitive Sermon Guidelines and Liturgy* (Geneva: World Council of Churches, 2003); Dube, *Grant Me Justice: HIV/AIDS and Gender Readings of the Bible* (Maryknoll, NY: Orbis Books, 2005); Dube, *The HIV and AIDS Bible: Selected Essays* (Scranton, PA: University of Scranton Press, 2008).

[31] Ezra Chitando, *Living with Hope: African Churches and HIV/AIDS* 1 (Geneva: World Council of Churches, 2007); Chitando, *Acting in Hope: African Churches and HIV/AIDS* 2 (Geneva: World Council of Churches, 2007); Sue Parry, *Beacons of Hope: HIV-Competent Churches: A Framework for Action* (Geneva: World Council of Churches, 2008).

[32] See www.africansuccess.org/visuFiche.php?id=424&lang=en. See also www.avert.org/history-hiv-AIDS-africa.htm.

Important developments on the political front changed the picture as the United States introduced a flexible implementation of patent laws, making it possible for developing countries to get drugs. This move cleared some of the hurdles that bogged down advances in treatment due to the debate on patents at the World Trade Organization, especially on compulsory licensing. When Brazil and India started producing generic drugs, more medication was available to people in developing countries.

UN secretary-general Kofi Annan called on richer nations to work together to make treatment available to all. UNAIDS set the initial target of 3 by 5, meaning that by 2005, 3 million people living with HIV would be taking medication. By 2001, about eight thousand people were receiving treatment in Africa—a small fraction of the millions infected with the virus, but it was a great improvement. That number has since grown with treatments now available in many countries. There was a global effort to provide treatment, and some of the organizations involved in this effort include UNAIDS; the Global Fund to Fight AIDS, Tuberculosis, and Malaria; the US President's Emergency Plan for AIDS Relief (PEPFAR); the Bill and Melinda Gates Foundation; the William Jefferson Clinton Foundation; and African governments that expanded treatment for their people.[33]

While these medicines have not cured people of HIV, their effectiveness in reducing the viral load in the infected person has made it possible for people to live normal lives, working and taking care of their families. These medications have contributed significantly to the creation of a new environment where people have accepted and supported people living with HIV because they no longer look emaciated and frighten others. HIV-positive people who have started a regime of ARVs have shown that a person can live with the virus; it is no longer a death sentence as people once thought.

I have followed two women in the Northwest Province of Cameroon; let's call them Miriam Takem and Magdalene Ndi. They were infected with HIV in the early 1990s. When treatment became available through a church hospital, they started taking their medication and have continued to live healthy, productive lives. The rejection that they experienced early on is not there anymore, although people occasionally tell them that they are worried about getting the HIV virus from them.

Christian organizations in Africa have intensified their fight against HIV and AIDS in ways that help reduce stigma. Here I highlight just two effective programs, both of which embraced counseling and testing. The Cameroon Baptist Convention Health Board, through its AIDS Control and Prevention (ACP) program, increased its hospital chaplaincy programs by recruiting and training new counselors to talk with people and encourage them to take the HIV test, with testing followed by counseling. The ACP developed nine training modules as part of their program to control the spread of HIV and AIDS, and encouraged people

---

[33] www.avert.org/history-hiv-AIDS-africa.htm.

to get treatment. Module 5 addresses stigma and trains people on how to handle stigma and discrimination.[34] These counseling programs gave people living with HIV and AIDS a new perspective on the infection and the disease, and about all the different ways of reaffirming themselves and fighting it.

Christian organizations also started home-based care. This was certainly something new for many of the African Christian organizations that decided to start these programs. They worked with a core group of caregivers who were trained and understood the HIV infection, the progress of the disease, its impact on a person, the impact on relatives, and the fear that the disease generates. These workers were also trained to communicate in ways that would convince a person to do the HIV test, then to talk about the disease if the test was positive and go on antiretroviral drugs. Studies of community home-based care in Swaziland demonstrate that this initiative established a client-based support group that facilitated education, and encouraged people to begin taking antiretroviral medicines.[35] These community home-based centers changed people's lives, but more importantly encouraged them to start drug therapy that significantly improved the quality of their lives and reduced the fear and stigma that surrounded them before the availability of these services. These developments also proved an important expression of the Christian faith from the churches involved—a clear indication that churches had turned a corner on negative attitudes to HIV and AIDS that had fueled stigma and discrimination. For these churches, this new service was an expression of their Christian love.[36]

Moving Forward

The fight against stigma is not over, although the church in Africa has made tremendous progress. As the ecclesial community moves forward in its combat against HIV and AIDS—and, one should add, the Ebola virus disease—faith communities can do several things to eliminate stigma and discrimination. In addressing stigma and moving forward, ecclesial communities must remember that they have gone through a rough history of responding to HIV and AIDS and the stigma that has accompanied it.[37]

---

[34] Cameroon Baptist Convention, *Module 5 Stigma and Discrimination Related to MTCT*, n.d.

[35] Robin Root and Alan Whiteside, "A Qualitative Study of Community Home-Based Care and Antiretroviral Adherence in Swaziland," *Journal of the International AIDS Society* 16 (2014): 17978.

[36] Robin Root and Arnau van Wyngaard, "Free Love: A Case Study of Church-Run Home-Based Caregivers in a High-Vulnerability Setting," *Global Public Health: An International Journal for Research, Policy and Practice* 6, no. S2 (October 2011): S174–S191.

[37] Gillian Paterson, *AIDS-Related Stigma: Thinking outside the Box—The Theological Challenge* (Geneva: World Council of Churches, 2005).

1. Ecclesial communities should build on the success story of counseling, testing, and collaboration with larger faith-based organizations and other nongovernmental organizations to provide a context for dialogue and treatment. Antiretroviral drugs have gone a long way in reducing fear and stigma and encouraged a positive and embracing attitude from relatives and friends of those who are HIV-positive.

2. Ecclesial communities should continue to read the Bible in progressive ways that would offer new theological tools for dealing with HIV and AIDS. Gerald West has argued that there are texts that "stigmatize, discriminate, and bring death," and we must read them critically.[38]

3. To address stigma effectively, ecclesial groups must rethink the human body. Recent literature invites new perspectives on the body, including rejection of the view that the flesh is always sinful or points to sin.[39] Although the body is open to pollution and infections, it is still the image of God and remains sacred, even if a disease robs it of its vitality. The pathologization of the body in HIV and AIDS makes the body simply a receptacle of sinful impulses, a position that has failed to live up to Christian claims that God created the human body and sexuality. People of faith need to appreciate the body and see sexuality as a thoughtful and spiritual expression. To remove sexual stigma, it is important to see the body and human sexuality from the perspective of desire, the right context, and responsibility, and as an affirmation of both divine and civic virtues. Religious leaders should pay attention to new research and ideas about the human body rather than focus on the sins of the flesh. These leaders should also pay attention to the perspectives coming from feminist theologians such as Denise Ackermann on issues of embodiment as a way of eliminating the stigma that is present in Christian analysis of sexually transmitted diseases.[40]

4. Ecclesial communities should return to their roots in the African community and culture to rekindle a culture of care and sustenance. The structure of care in the African community can be conceptualized in different ways, but so far, the notion of *Ubuntu* has received wide discussion in the literature. *Ubuntu* offers a relational ethic that embraces community, and in those communities one can see practices of love and compassion.

---

[38] Gerald West, "Sacred Texts, Particularly the Bible and the Qur'an, and HIV and AIDS: Charting the Textual Territory," in *Religion and HIV and AIDS: Charting the Terrain*, ed. Beverley Haddad (Pietermaritzburg: University of KwaZulu Natal Press, 2011), 135–65, 159.

[39] Susan Sontag, *AIDS and Its Metaphors* (London: Penguin, 1991), 179.

[40] Denise M. Ackermann, "'Engaging Stigma': An Embodied Theological Response to HIV and AIDS—The Challenge of HIV/AIDS to Christian Theology," *Scriptura* 89 (2005): 385–95.

Part Six

Worship, Education, and Conflicts
in Times of AIDS

CHAPTER 23

APPROACHES TO LITURGICAL SPIRITUALITY IN TIMES OF DISEASES, EPIDEMICS, AND DISTRESS

Elochukwu Uzukwu

The rage of HIV and AIDS in Africa is being silenced by the ravages of Ebola. Children and young people, elders and caregivers are victims. Father Augustine Barewa captures the socio-pastoral-ritual constraints imposed by Ebola virus disease (EVD) in Sierra Leone: "We omit the 'sign of peace' at Mass. We have suspended administering the sacraments of Baptism, Confirmation and the Anointing of the Sick because they require that the celebrant anoints the persons receiving these sacraments. Holy Communion must be gently dropped into the hand of the communicant so as to avoid touching the saliva of the communicant. . . . The presentation of a death certificate is a prerequisite for a funeral Mass."[1]

Struck by EVD, West Africa writhes like a snake! "I am like one struck by God," laments the psalmist, "a hidden illness from the spirit-world overpowers me; the snake is weighed down by the big game it swallowed."[2] The lament is not smothered by chants of realized eschatological optimism like the song Musa Dube improvised. Reacting to the devastations of the AIDS pandemic (that carried away a dear friend) in her native Botswana, she went lyrical:

Jubila ni Afrika inkosiikhona (Rejoice, Africa, your Lord God liveth)
Jubila ni lonke, Jubila ni Sizwe (Rejoice all, rejoice nation)
Jubila mama loba baba (Rejoice, mothers and fathers).[3]

---

[1] *Spiritan Newsflash* no. 306, Congregazione dello Spirito Santo, October 2, 2014.

[2] I paraphrase Ps. 41:9 translated into Igbo by Raymond C. Arazu, *Abu-Oma Nke Bible*, vols. 1–3 (Enugu: SNAAP Press, 1993). See below for my use of this psalm.

[3] Musa W. Dube, "Mainstreaming HIV/AIDS in African Religious and Theological Studies," in *African Traditions in the Study of Religion in Africa: Emerging Trends, Indigenous Spirituality, and the Interface with Other World Religions (Vitality of Indigenous Religions)*, ed. Afeosemime U. Adogame, Ezra Chitando, and Bolaji Bateye (Farnham, Surrey: Ashgate, 2012), 79.

The terms of the rejoicing are not clear, except, perhaps, the weak's radical faith in a God whom the African American religious imagination confesses as "making a way where there is no way."

What does this disease, the Deity that sent this monster, want us to do? Where have we gone wrong—in interrelationships between community and neighbors, humans and ecology—to provoke such reprisal? What rituals should we perform?

The stigma of Ebola equals that of HIV and AIDS. Frustrated and terrified communities, denied healthy social interaction, pose one question after another (medical-spiritual) without receiving a satisfactory answer: Where is the deity of healing (Agwu of the Igbo, Ifa Orunmila of the Yoruba, even Sakpata of the Fon) and those initiated devotees, *dibia-nganga-babalawo-bokono*, that (West) Africa relied on?[4] Where are the diviner-doctors and healers, ancient and modern? Jesus, Holy Spirit, where are you? Heal—save us!

In this chapter I address the monstrosity of HIV and AIDS from the indigenous African perception of ominous diseases (the result of unheeded warnings from the deities?). (I assume that the indigenous ritual/spirituality throws light on and clarifies the modern/Christian.)[5] I indicate some ritual gestures of community and individual toward the disease (a demanding spirit-force), toward the patient, and toward the deities, Jesus-God. Narratives and poetic liturgical texts are evoked from the indigenous West African ritual repertoire and interfaced with the Judeo-Christian. Then, I note the symbolic power of narratives of misfortune suffered by the innocent, the lament in African and Judaic-Christian traditions, and the *aporia* (theodical) raised by the suffering of innocent communities and individuals. Finally, I indicate liberational clues from liturgical spiritualities that appear to claim that suffering empowers community and individuals. Schooled by suffering, the besieged Christian community and suffering individuals search for better reasons for life through the mimesis (anamnesis) of the God that, in Jesus Christ, is revealed as powerfully weak; the community gains new insight into the fragile condition of human existence, appreciating the fragility of creation that is "groaning in labor pains" (Rom. 8:22) to be freed from bondage to become children of God.

---

4 The Igbo say "Chukwuwelu, oludibia" (after God, it is the doctor, *dibia*). See John Anenechukwu Umeh, *After God Is Dibia*, 2 vols., vol. 1: *Igbo Cosmology, Divination, and Sacred Science in Nigeria* (London: Karnak House, 1997); vol. 2: *Igbo Cosmology, Healing, Divination, and Sacred Science in Nigeria* (London: Karnak House, 1999).

5 Magesa agrees; see Laurenti Magesa, *What Is Not Sacred? African Spirituality* (Maryknoll, NY: Orbis Books, 2013), 20–22.

Wrathful Visitation:
The Why and Wherefore of Monstrous Diseases

Not so long ago, among the Igbo of Nigeria, it sufficed to learn that Kitikpa (the smallpox deity) struck a homestead for the whole clan or village to take a ritual distance from the unfortunate ("unclean") family. Ritual, a symbolic pattern of action, demarcates a social group (ethnic or religious). Through ritual performance, under the gaze of the group's spiritual originators, the group recognizes and affirms who they are in the world and how the world is.[6] The stigmatization of victims is part and parcel of contextual ritual behavior.

Chinua Achebe, in *Girls at War*, mused on smallpox (scourge of Kitikpa, a ritually grounded spirit-force[7]). Kitikpa struck the fictional Umuru village and its sprawling market. The epidemic was punishment for communal moral failure, a sequel to unfettered modernization—the failure to uphold the ancestral ecological balance by keeping the market clean and offering sacrifices as and when due.[8] Achebe captures the savagery of Kitikpa in "The Sacrificial Egg": "Who would have believed that the great boisterous market could ever be quenched like this? But such was the strength of Kitikpa, the incarnate power of smallpox. Only he could drive away all those people and leave the market to the flies."[9] AIDS and Ebola cause similar ravages today in West Africa.

What marks this "spirit-terror," the "silent killer," is the imposed solemn silence that a community breaks at its own risk, because "Kitikpa is in that village."

> Such was the state of the town when Kitikpa came to see it and to demand the sacrifice the inhabitants owed the gods of the soil. He came in confident knowledge of the terror he held over the people. He was an evil deity, and boasted it. Lest he be offended those he killed were not killed but decorated, and no one dared weep for them. He put an end to the coming and going between neighbours and between Villages.[10]

Achebe is on target. In the 1950s, in Nnewi, Nigeria, death from smallpox was described as *ode nkeoma degbu luya* (the beautiful decorator, decorated him/her to death/perfection.)

---

[6] See Elochukwu E. Uzukwu, *Worship as Body Language: Introduction to Christian Worship* (Collegeville, MN: Liturgical Press, 1997).

[7] On the grounding of deities in West African *vodun* religion and spirituality in shrines and figurines, see Nadia Lovell, *Cord of Blood: Possession and the Making of Voodoo* (London: Pluto Press, 2002).

[8] See the interesting comments on Kitikpa by Magesa, *What Is Not Sacred?*, 15.

[9] Chinua Achebe, *Girls at War, and Other Stories*, African Writers Series 100 (London: Heinemann, 1972), 45.

[10] Ibid., 46.

In West Africa, epidemics and abominable diseases challenge the community's theological and ritual imagination. Groups take measured steps for their security, though at the expense of victims. Such diseases are omens, signaling oncoming disaster.[11] The "failure to heed warning signs is catastrophic. . . . This failure to read and, in so doing, to develop a viable response turns signs into . . . *sign continua* of the disaster of which they warned. They become part of the destructive tide, allowing initial events to cast larger shadows and to create disastrous people and projects."[12] In *Things Fall Apart*,[13] Achebe narrates the ominous disease suffered by Unoka, father of Okonkwo, the novel's hero: Unoka had "the swelling which was an abomination to the earth goddess." The abomination is ritually removed from the community: The afflicted was isolated—left to die in the Evil Forest, an eschatological bad story! The person "died and rotted away above the earth, and was not given the first or the second burial. Such was Unoka's fate. When they carried him away, he took with him his flute."[14] (I argue below that Unoka's attachment to the flute is a contestation of traditional piety.)

Stigmatization or taboo did not start with Ebola and AIDS. Nevertheless, stigma undermines the "effectiveness of care." A 2001 WCC resolution, in its Nairobi assembly, offered a corrective to the taboo attached to Kitikpa, Ebola, and AIDS: "For the churches, the most powerful contribution we can make to combating HIV transmission is the eradication of stigma and discrimination."[15]

Smallpox, "swelling" disease, EVD, and HIV cause fear. Their visitation could lead to the extinction of the group. The community takes ritual-medical steps to remedy the situation. Rituals were abundant. There were apotropaic rituals or disaster rituals similar to medieval rituals to contain plagues.[16] The rituals compare with rituals of the postmodern world where master narratives no longer capture the imagination (e.g., the Dutch rituals following the plane crash in Amsterdam on October 4, 1992, with forty-one dead; and the café fire in Volendam on January 1, 2001, with fourteen fatalities. The Dutch rituals were marked by mass participation in a silent procession and memorial service).[17]

---

[11] See Jane Anna Gordon and Lewis R. Gordon, *Of Divine Warning: Reading Disaster in the Modern Age*, The Radical Imagination Series (Boulder, CO: Paradigm Publishers, 2009).

[12] Ibid., 2–3.

[13] See Chinua Achebe, *Things Fall Apart* (Oxford: Heinemann,1958), 5.

[14] Ibid., 18.

[15] Cited by Gillian Paterson, "HIV, AIDS, and Stigma—Discerning the Silences," in Bev Haddad, *Religion and HIV and AIDS: Charting the Terrain* (Scottsville: University of KwaZulu-Natal Press, 2011), 351.

[16] See René Girard, *The Scapegoat*, trans. Y. Freccero (Baltimore: Johns Hopkins University Press, 1986).

[17] See P. Post et al., *Disaster Ritual: Explorations of an Emerging Ritual Repertoire,*

What do we learn about indigenous liturgical spirituality from the above cases? What light do these throw on the effectiveness of ritual symbolic action vis-à-vis diseases like Ebola and AIDS? I begin with reflection on the smallpox epidemic to illustrate how isolation and prayer and a community's imaginative creativity ritually, spiritually, and medically empower initiates/devotees to heal diseases/epidemics. Next, I use the rejection of the community's wisdom-piety by Unoka (dumped in the Evil Forest) to introduce the contestation of the received indigenous and Judaic-Christian ritual repertoire and spirituality in West Africa.

Reflection: Isolation, Prayer, Ritual, and Healing

Communal experience and indigenous wisdom dictate the isolation of patients. In extremis, indigenous religious piety ordered the abandonment (in the Evil Forest) of those struck by the "swelling" disease—an omen of worse things to come. Similarly, the victims of Ebola and AIDS are isolated (just as the Hebrew tradition ritually separated "unclean" lepers from the community [see Lev. 13–14]). They are a risk to the group that isolates them for security. One understands the protestations over the location of EVD isolation centers in Sierra Leone, Guinea, and Liberia. However, isolation and restrictions of social contact, including restrictions on sacramental administration, are necessary to stem the tide of contagious diseases. However, the stigma appears ineradicable.

Rituals and prayers were credited with securing the social group from smallpox, and today they are thought to secure communities from Ebola and AIDS. Apotropaic or preventative rituals are believed to be effective. Early in the twentieth century, C. K. Meek recorded a ritual performance that secured an Igbo clan (Nigeria) from smallpox. The clan consulted the powerful Oracle, Igwe-ka-ala of Umuneoha. A priest of Igwe-ka-ala supervised the ritual. On the appointed day, "the minister of Igwe," in the midst of the market assembly, "holding a rattle in his right hand and a chicken and ram, would walk through the confines of the market saying, 'May Igwe protect the people of this community; may he help their crops to grow well; and their women to bear children abundantly.'" Then he sprinkled the people with medicine saying, "I wipe away the evil of this community, and if this community prospers in consequence of these rites then I direct that a share of the prosperity be paid to Igwe."[18] All

---

Liturgia Condenda 15 (Leuven: Peeters, 2003). The mass processions in France and elsewhere in Europe following the attack on the magazine *Charlie Hebdo* (January 7–11, 2015) qualify as disaster ritual, including the massive assembly of close to 2 million people in Paris with over forty heads of government in Europe and other parts of the world participating.

[18] C. K. Meek, *Law and Authority in a Nigerian Tribe: A Study in Indirect Rule* (1937; New York: Barnes and Noble, 1970), 46.

salute Igwe by raising their hands, and the elders concur by placing the sacred symbol of authority and honesty (*ofo*) in a dish. This will be sent back to Umuneoha with the sacrificial offerings.

Prayers, on the other hand, assure the afflicted communities of the Presence of God, the deities and ancestors. In Malawi (the 1920s), ancestors were solicited to halt an influenza epidemic:

> Let the great ones gather!
> What have we done to suffer so?
> We do not say, Let so-and-so come, we say, all!
> Here your children are in distress.
> There is not one able to give a drink of water to another.
> Wherein have we erred?
> Here is food, we give to you;
> Aid us, your children.[19]

The current Catholic Rite for Anointing of the Sick rhetorically destroys or exorcises "by the laying on of our hands" on "any power the devil has over" the sick, and prays,

> Holy Lord, almighty Father, everlasting God, in pouring out the grace of your blessing on the bodies of the sick, you show your loving care for your creatures. And so now as we call on your holy name, come and free your servant from his (her) illness and restore him (her) to health; reach out your hand and raise him (her) up; strengthen him (her) by your might; protect him (her) by your power; and give him (her) back in all desired well-being to your holy Church; through Christ our Lord.

Indigenous communities anchor the power of controlling-healing diseases in deities. For example, in Dahomey (Benin Republic), initiates into the cult of Sakpata, the deity of smallpox, are empowered to provide holistic health care (spiritual, medical, and ritual) for the community. Today, initiates take care of the victims of HIV and AIDS. Through initiation, they move in and out of spirit-land, capture vital medical knowledge, and bring cure and security to the community through healing the patients.

Ethnographic data collected by Serpos Tidjani in the late 1940s gives insight into the pattern of ritual-medical empowerment of devotees, integrating science into the community's ritual repertoire. Initiation was preceded by the slaying of the candidate by Sakpata:[20] one dies and is resuscitated by the deity

---

[19] John S. Mbiti, *The Prayers of African Religion* (London: SPCK, 1975), 47.

[20] See A. Serpos Tidjani, "Rituels," *Présence Africaine* 8–9, no. spécial—Le Monde

to mediate cure of the deadly disease. Initiates become mystically empowered. They are born again, into "the life of initiation and the penetration of the world of spirits."[21]

Serpos Tidjani witnessed the initiation of seven slain young women, "struck dead" by Sakpata. Deposited (isolated) in the "convent" of Sakpata, their bodies were in the process of putrefaction. The worms emerging from them were carefully deposited in a medicine pot that, mixed with medicinal herbs, would be crucial in their ritual resuscitation. On the day of ritual reintegration, the slain candidates are dissociated from families, consorts, debtors, and so on. They belong totally to Sakpata to assume the task of mediating health and wholeness to the community. Early that morning (8:45 a.m.), all assembled in the public square. The drums vibrated. The bodies were brought out one after another. As each slain candidate lay in view of all, the high priest addressed the assembly:

> Chiefs and armies, [free] people and slaves, men and women, listen. It has pleased our great fetish [spirit],[22] the "KING," to choose from among our children, his handmaids, his wives, in whose body he will enter to dance. Since seven days, he killed the person that you behold. Already her body is decaying. Through the power of this "fetish" [spirit] we are going to call her back to life. With this in view if she is indebted to anyone let the person come forward and make claims. If the person does not come forward . . . the person would have no grounds to claim that the gods retain this woman definitively in their palace.[23] Regarding this particular case I say "chekounouhélou" for that! I exclude that possibility.[24]

Furthermore, the high priest addressed "creditors, lovers, friends of the victim, and all those to whom she may have made promises": such commitments were no longer binding. To ensure the freedom of the elect to belong and minister to Sakpata, "all possible cases" of wrongdoing that may provoke reprisals were ritually excluded. As the diviner-doctors (all female) were anointing and massaging the body of the slain candidate with concoctions from the medicine pot, the

---

Noir—dirigé par Théodore Monod (1950). The ritual is analyzed in a lecture delivered in Leuven (2001): "African Inculturation Theology: Path of Liberation [Explorations in Ritual]," *Liberation Theologies Forum*, Faculty of Theology, Katholieke Universiteit Leuven, June 2001. This section draws freely from that lecture.

[21] Tidjani, "Rituels," 305.

[22] Note that Tidjani uses the term *fétiche*, which is a derogatory appellation of *vodun* or deity.

[23] If one fails to come back to life (and the account claims that there have been such cases), one is retained by the *vodun* in his palace.

[24] Tidjani, "Rituels," 301–2.

slain was called seven times: "In the name of our great god Souviningui, O you here present, when I call you seven times, come back to us alive."

At the seventh call, a shrill cry was heard from the convent of Sakpata. And, instantaneously, within the assembly, the deity took possession of three devotees who danced their *vodun* (deity's) dance. The drumming was fast and furious; the community was elated; participation was intense. The person summoned came back to life, very weak. She was carried on the back of one of the older women initiates into the convent, where the rest of the initiation concluded with a ritual bath.

Possession, as heightened mystical experience, is the peak of African spirituality: container (initiate) and contained (deity) become one. Initiates see with the eyes of deity and penetrate "the world of spirits," the world of the night. As "traditional medical practitioners,"[25] they protect the community from the attack of smallpox. In the power of the *vodun*, initiates parade Sakpata's healing might and bring solace to the community. Initiates belong to Sakpata; they are holy and horrible! Today, in the name of Sakpata, diseases like AIDS are treated.[26]

The smallpox epidemic, widespread in West Africa, perhaps influenced conversions to Christianity; the indigenous ritual-pharmacopeia caved in before the Christian medical/ritual vaccine.[27] Today, African-Initiated Churches (AICs) deplore the worship of Sakpata. AICs claim that Sakpata is an agent of Satan (Christians generally make such claims about African deities).[28] *Vodun* are exorcised in the power of the Holy Spirit. In the Holy Spirit, diseases are eradicated by trained and consecrated Christian ministers. However, the liturgical language of consecration of *woli*—visionaries and prophets-seers of the Celestial Church of Christ—fuses indigenous and Christian ritual vocabulary:

---

[25] This is WHO's technical definition of *nganga* and all such African practitioners; see Eric de Rosny, *Les yeux de ma chèvre: Sur les pas des maîtres de la nuit en pays douala* (Paris: Plon, 1981), 48–49.

[26] See the highly suggestive study of Eric de Rosny, *Healers in the Night*, trans. Robert R. Barr (Maryknoll, NY: Orbis Books, 1985). Note that priestly ministry in the shrines of the *vodun* is exclusively male, while initiation into the cult is more often than not exclusively female. This scenario is reproduced in the ministries of some African-Initiated Churches in the Benin Republic (e.g., the Celestial Church of Christ): pastors are male while ministers of healing, possessed by the Holy Spirit, are female (pastors are never possessed, while ministers are possessed as in the *vodun*). See Nadia Lovell, *Cord of Blood: Possession and the Making of Voodoo* (London: Pluto Press, 2003); Albert de Surgy, *L'Église du Christianisme Céleste. Un exemple d'Église prophétique au Bénin* (Paris: Karthala, 2001).

[27] See Felix K. Ekechi, "The Medical Factor in Christian Conversion in Africa: Observations from Southeastern Nigeria," *Missiology* 21, no. 3 (July 1993).

[28] See Brigit Meyer, *Translating the Devil: Religion and Modernity among the Ewe in Ghana* (Edinburgh: Edinburgh University Press for the International African Institute, London, 1999).

God, save us for we are your children. Save us from evil spirits. Save us from evil people. And help us to worship you, as we should unto our death. . . . You that spoil the works of Satan, come and show your laborers (those who through suitable intercessions contribute to the extension of the kingdom of God) the plan to be followed. Come and stay with your laborers. Your servants (the visionaries) are prostrate on the floor in your name. Descend and enter into them.[29]

Western Christian ritual, supported by the smallpox vaccine, superseded the indigenous ritual and pharmacopeia. The indigenous medical practitioners, however, still play an irreplaceable role. They certify the therapeutic economy of indigenous religious spirituality. They "display the capacity to recapitulate and reintegrate . . . [the] cosmic, social, psychological, religious, and pharmaceutical—into one great struggle against violence, against the enemies of life."[30]

The AIDS epidemic remains a challenge to all rituals and pharmacopeia, indigenous or Christian. How do victims of AIDS and other epidemics lend voice to the struggle and inspire piety-spirituality that reimagines the world and transforms social relations?

The Ritual Voice of the Voiceless: Liturgical Lament Challenging Taboo/Stigma

Unoka, in *Things Fall Apart*, was judged for his shortcomings by his clan: "Unoka, the grown-up, was a failure."[31] When clan piety led him to the Evil Forest to die, he clung to the symbol of his passion, the flute: "When they carried him away, he took with him his flute."[32] Achebe made no further comments about what Unoka did with the flute. However, earlier in *Things Fall Apart*, Unoka's flute is indexed as symbol of innovation and liberation.

He was very good on his flute, and his happiest moments were the two or three moons after the harvest when the village musicians brought down their instruments, hung above the fireplace. Unoka would play with them, his face beaming with blessedness and peace.[33]

---

[29] See Elochukwu E. Uzukwu, *God, Spirit, and Human Wholeness: Appropriating Faith and Culture in West African Style* (Eugene, OR: Pickwick Publications, 2012), 181. Text from Surgy, *L'Église du Christianisme Céleste*, 205 (my translation).

[30] I summarize de Rosny; see Uzukwu, *God, Spirit, and Human Wholeness*, 89; Rosny, *Les yeux de ma chèvre*, 48–49.

[31] Achebe, *Things Fall Apart*, 5.

[32] Ibid., 18.

[33] Ibid., 4.

This appreciation of Unoka gives voice to the stigmatized to interrogate their community's moral and ritual imagination. The afflicted artist, carried in silent procession (communal piety) and ritually dumped in the Evil Forest—bloated stomach, playing his flute—challenges the society that called him a monster.

Another thought: *Was the afflicted Unoka at prayer?* Was he appealing to the Powers beyond the community and its limited perception of reality, to behold and come to the rescue, or lamenting and bewailing the intolerable dehumanization like Jeremiah: "Look and see if there is any sorrow like my sorrow, which was brought upon me" (Lam. 1:12).

Unoka symbolizes the theodical voice of the stigmatized Ebola and AIDS patients. Lament built on hope shores up the community's and individual's will to live. In lament, the Powers are invited to show up.[34] Judaic tradition provides insight into suffering through the Psalms of Lament or Complaint that bewail the woeful plight of the suffering people or person with copious tears. Where is Yahweh of the covenant? (Where is Jesus, the savior?)[35]

Psalm 41 presents an individual lament, applicable to those abandoned in the Evil Forest, and to the victims of EVD and HIV. The Igbo folk rendition of the psalm by Arazu reinterprets suffering with local cosmological idioms that shed light on the received Judaic spirituality.[36] The following chart lists four verses in Igbo, in the literal translation, and in the New Revised Standard Version.

The symbolic expressions—"illness from spirit-land," "stirring the hornet's nest," and the snake swallowing big game—are interpretations of diseases such as AIDS as retribution. How should the hope that underlies liturgical lament infuse new Spirit into the dry bones to reinvent society? The Judaic-Christian-Igbo– patterned lament (before evil, AIDS, and Ebola) is not a palliative, not mere resignation before incurable diseases (cf. Jer. 15:18)![37] The new piety proclaims that the Lord is not a "deceitful brook, like waters that fail" (Jer. 15:18).

New Conversion, a New Spirituality

Achebe does not walk away from the communal interpretation of evil as depicted by the dominant piety—ritual dumping in the Evil Forest. Other unfortunates dumped in that forest of horror included twins whose intru-

---

[34] See Esther E. Acolatse, "God, Where Are You? Theological Reflections on HIV/ AIDS in Africa," *Bulletin of Ecumenical Theology* 26 (2014).

[35] See H. Gunkel, *The Psalms: A Form-Critical Introduction* (Philadelphia: Fortress, 1967).

[36] Arazu, Abu-Oma Nke Bible, 100–102. See Elochukwu E. Uzukwu, "Bible and Christian Worship in Africa: African Christianity and the Labour of Contextualization," *Chakana* 1, no. 2 (2003).

[37] Like in the Igbo adage: The hen that lost its chick to the predatory kite is crying, not for its chick to be returned, but that all may hear its voice/lament.

Abu Oma	Literal translation	NRSV
v. 6: Ndiilo mu naajun'obi ha joronjo, keduoge mu g'anwu, kaafa mu rienammiri?	My enemies are asking in their evil heart, when shall I die, so that my name be drowned in the water [river]?	v. 5: My enemies wonder in malice when I will die, and my name perish.
v. 7: Nee ha n'abia i neta mu oh // Okwu e kwuru ha n'onubuasi, obi ha n'akpunjo, asirik'ebuh'agaghari.	Look, they are coming to visit me-o-o // the word they spoke from their mouth is lie, their heart molds evil, they are carrying around rumors.	v. 6: And when they come to see me, they utter empty words, while their hearts gather mischief; when they go out, they tell it abroad.
v. 8: Ndikporo mu asinaagbaizumaka mu oh // siisikot'ebunyagbagbueya	Those who hate me take counsel about me-o-o // they say, "the head that stirs the hornet let it be killed by its sting"	v. 7: All who hate me whisper together about me; they imagine the worst for me.
v. 9: Ana h'asin'oriammuo / e jidenay'aka, kaagwon'ih'- ogburugbasara / o m'ekunizi.	They are saying that a spirit-illness / has laid hands on him, let the snake and what it killed [swallowed] lie down together / it won't get up again.	v. 8: They think that a deadly thing has fastened on me, that I will not rise again from where I lie.

sion into the community was ominous: left in earthenware vessels to die or be devoured by wild beasts. Achebe introduced the whiteman's religion and penciled in the son of the uncompromising Okonkwo as a symbol of the challenging and liberating alternative. Christian missionary rhetoric focused on the Trinity, a laughable discourse to Okonkwo. However, Achebe insists,

> There was a young lad who had been captivated. His name was Nwoye, Okonkwo's first son. It was not the mad logic of the Trinity that captivated him. . . . It was the poetry of the new religion, something felt in the marrow. The hymn about brothers who sat in darkness and in fear seemed to answer a vague and persistent question that haunted his young soul—the question of the twins crying in the bush and the

question of Ikemefuna who was killed. He felt a relief within as the hymn poured into his parched soul. The words of the hymn were like the drops of frozen rain melting on the dry palate of the panting earth. Nwoye's callow mind was greatly puzzled.[38]

Igbo conversion to Christianity confronts the theodical puzzle raised by the flute-playing Unoka, the crying twins, and today, Ebola and HIV and AIDS victims. The Christian removal of stigma on twin births and the siting of churches in the Evil Forest presented alternative piety, ritually rescuing and giving voice to the voiceless. The continued impact of stigma today calls for new conversion and new piety.

Jesus, who welcomed the unclean and excluded lepers, continues to empower Christians in the struggle against exclusion and stigma:

A leper came to him begging him. . . . "If you choose, you can make me clean." Moved with pity, Jesus stretched out his hand and touched him, and said to him, "I do choose. Be made clean!" Immediately the leprosy left him, and he was made clean. (Mark 1:40–42)

Welcoming, touching, and affirming the humanity of lepers (healing them integrally as God, the ultimate healer) Jesus rejected the Levitical code's ritual expulsion of "unclean" lepers from the community (Lev. 13–14). This affected his disciples, affected the group of Christians in Igboland, and must continue to affect African Christians today to reinvent a society without stigma.

The medical factor (Western pharmacopoeia, the vaccine supported by Christian ritual) and the removal of the stigma on twin births and dreaded diseases in the name of Jesus strengthened the liberational tone of the liturgical hymn about "brothers who sat in darkness and in fear": an alternative piety. "Surely he has borne our infirmities and carried our diseases" (Isa. 53:4). Victims of incurable diseases feel the "dry bones" come to life (Ezek. 37) because God listens, sees, and touches. The Kenya Eucharistic Prayer (inspired by Galla tradition) evokes God's caring Presence: "Listen to us, aged God. Listen to us, ancient God, who has ears. Look at us, aged God. Look at us, ancient God, who has eyes. Receive us, aged God. Receive us, ancient God, who has hands!"[39]

The African experience of HIV and AIDS, according to Acolatse, "makes 'a mockery' of the suffering undergone by Job who is held up in the Christian faith as the epitome of suffering"; the devastation inflicted by the disease on childbearing

---

[38] Achebe, *Things Fall Apart*, 147.
[39] See Aylward Shorter, "Three More African Eucharistic Prayers," *African Ecclesial Review* 15, no. 2 (1973): 155.

young women has been catastrophic.[40] But the lament in African indigenous religions interfaced with the Judaic-Christian tradition positions sufferers to live in hope or reinvent piety. Smallpox and Ebola survivors develop immunity. As initiated caregivers, they expand medical-spiritual practices to eradicate diseases.

God's response to Job's lament was a wakeup call: "'Who is this that darkens counsel by words without knowledge? . . . Where were you when I laid the foundation of the earth?'" (Job 38:2, 4). God shows up as an ally, a friend! The impossibility of probing the length and breadth of the universe is a call to mobilize all forces, "cosmic, social, psychological, religious, and pharmaceutical," in the struggle "against the enemies of life."[41] The indigenous interfaces with and sheds light on the modern and Christian. "God's own friendship with the world" shores up hope[42] and clarifies the alternative piety: "I had heard of you by the hearing of the ear, but now my eye sees you" (Job 42:5). Sick, weak, and fragile humans cooperate with God in healing God's world! As the Igbo say, *onyekwe chi yaekwe* (when a person says yes strongly to one's *chi*, the *chi* responds strongly and positively): humans and God collaborate in the health ministry.[43] Christian liturgical spirituality locates this cooperation within the anamnesis or ritual representation of God's choice to suffer with humans in Jesus Christ so as to transform the world.

Christian Mimesis (Anamnesis)
of the Lord's Founding Ritual

The ritual performance of Jesus brings God's healing to the "unclean" leper and instigates new rituals, a foundational healing rite: "Moved with pity, Jesus stretched out his hand and touched him, and said to him, 'I do choose. Be made clean!'" (Mark 1:41). By touching the "unclean," he declared "all" clean (cf. Mark 7:19). In order to entrench and memorialize health and cleanness in the community, Jesus relocated to the "unclean" margin (leper colonies, the Place of the Skull, EVD centers, the Evil Forest). There Jesus challenged suffering and held it hostage; *Christus Victor* led captivity captive (cf. Eph. 4:8).

The theo-drama (Balthasar) at the Place of the Skull is the highpoint of the Trinitarian script that removes the stigma of HIV and returns voice (humanity) to the voiceless. There, God reveals Godself as powerfully weak.[44] There God

---

[40] Acolatse, "God, Where Are You?" 73.

[41] Uzukwu, *God, Spirit, and Human Wholeness*, 89.

[42] Acolatse, "God, Where Are You?" 74. Acolatse draws from John Swinton, *Raging with Compassion: Pastoral Responses to the Problem of Evil* (Grand Rapids: William B. Eerdmans, 2007).

[43] See Acolatse, "God, Where Are You?" 75.

[44] This expression is taken from Etienne Babut, *Le dieu puissamment faible de la Bible*, Coll. Lire La Bible 118 (Paris: Cerf, 1999).

hung; the outcast of and for the outcasts: "And I, when I am lifted up from the earth, will draw all people to myself" (John 12:32).

At the Place of the Skull, the final ritual-drama threw the hanging bridge between the wisdom of the ancients and the novelty of the present. The suffering Jesus, supported perhaps only by his mother and the women, had his final struggle with his *Chi* (God): "'Eloi, Eloi, lama sabachthani?'" (My God, my God, why have you forsaken me? Mark 15:34; cf. Matt. 27:46). This Lament of Psalm 22:1 raises the theodical question because "hanging on a tree" is a curse, a pollutant (cf. Deut. 21:22–23). The outcast of and for the outcasts raises this question at the sacrificial point and complexifies the question because it was also the cry of the Just: *Elî 'atta,* "You are my God" ("You are my God, and I will give thanks to you; you are my God, I will extol you" [Ps. 118:28]).[45] Jesus—in this liturgical drama, the victim and the sacrificer—says yes strongly to his *Chi*, and his *Chi* responds positively and strongly: "He was heard because of his reverent submission . . . [and] designated by God a high priest according to the order of Melchizedek" (Heb. 5:7–10). God responded, speaking in a sound of "sheer silence"!

Why does the *theo-drama* prefer the response in deafening silence: "'Eloi, Eloi'" or "*Elî 'atta,*" Silence! (Recall the silent procession bearing Unoka to the Evil Forest; recall the silent processions in Holland following the plane crash and the fire!) Silence: the foundational ritual-solidarity of the Triune God! Elijah at Horeb reinterpreted Yahweh's Presence as "a sound of sheer silence"— "The LORD was not in the wind. . . . The LORD was not in the earthquake. . . . The LORD was not in the fire; and after the fire a sound of sheer silence" (1 Kgs. 19:11–12).[46] God is present and speaks in the cry of the sufferer and the cry of the just, in the cry of the AIDS victims and the abandoned Ebola patients, not in a violent wind and earthquake, not in the fire and brimstone of condemnations, but as participant and motivator in quiet and silent solidarity, in the services and research, to bring the succor that alleviates Ebola and AIDS, to enable the excluded to reclaim their humanity, and to renew the community.

---

[45] Brown and Dufour favor this interpretation. See Raymond E. Brown, *The Death of the Messiah: From Gethsemane to the Grave—A Commentary on the Passion Narratives in the Four Gospels*, ed. David Noel Freedman, vol. 2, Anchor Bible Reference Library (New York: Doubleday, 1994). 1087–88; Xavier Léon-Dufour, *Lecture de l'Évangile Selon Jean*, 4 vols., vol. 4: *L'Heure de la glorification* (chapitres 18–21), *Parole de Dieu* (Paris: Éditions du Seuil, 1996), 152–53.

[46] See my analysis of this in Uzukwu, *God, Spirit, and Human Wholeness*, 122–23.

CHAPTER 24

HIV AND AIDS AND SPIRITUAL DIRECTION

Compassionate Accompaniment

Susan Rakoczy

When HIV and AIDS enters a relationship, everything changes. Although antiretroviral medications are now available, fear and stigma continue to permeate in powerful ways the lives of those who are HIV-positive. In South Africa we say, "Everyone is either infected or affected by HIV and AIDS."

This also applies to the experience of spiritual direction. Perhaps the director is HIV-positive. What effects will this experience have on the way he or she listens to seekers?[1] How will the director respond when a seeker discloses an HIV-positive status? How will the depth and quality of the direction experience be affected? How will the director respond if the seeker shares that a family member or friend is HIV-positive?

HIV and AIDS presents major challenges to all facets of life: to the public health system of a country, to gender issues since women have a higher infection rate than men, and to pastoral care because it affects a person's self-identity, self-worth, and all her or his relationships, including the one with God.

In this chapter I focus on some of the inner dynamics of spiritual direction when HIV and AIDS becomes part of the conversation because of the personal experience of the director, the seeker, or both. The extent of the pandemic in Africa, especially South Africa, is evident through UNAIDS statistics. In a brief literature survey I assess the state of the question. After locating spiritual direction within discernment, the experience of interpathy is applied to direction experiences that include HIV and AIDS. Discernment is essential in spiritual direction, and the presence of HIV and AIDS significantly impacts the experiences of consolation and desolation. Excerpts from interviews and a focus group conversation with spiritual directors in South Africa are woven throughout the chapter to illustrate aspects of the spiritual direction experience.

---

[1] I prefer the word "seeker" to that of the traditional term "directee," which to me connotes passivity.

HIV and AIDS in Africa: Some Better News

Current statistics about HIV and AIDS in Africa present an essential context for discussion of the theme of HIV and AIDS and spiritual direction. The good news is that the HIV and AIDS pandemic in Africa has begun to abate. The 2014 statistics from UNAIDS report that in 2013 there were 2.1 million new infections around the world, a decline of 38 percent since 2001. In sub-Saharan Africa, AIDS-related deaths dropped by 39 percent between 2005 and 2013.[2] A major factor in the better news is that antiretroviral medications are now affordable. The cost of a year's supply of medication now costs $140, compared to $10,000 in the 1990s.

The news is also encouraging in South Africa. In January 2014 there were 6.1 million people in South Africa living with HIV and AIDS. The new infection rate has dropped by about one-third from 2004 (540,000 new infections) to 2012 (370,000 new infections). Since 2009 the South African government has made antiretrovirals widely available in government hospitals and clinics, and thus in 2014 about 2.2 million persons were on treatment.[3]

HIV and AIDS and Spiritual Direction: A Brief Literature Survey

While the literature on HIV and AIDS is huge and studies of spiritual direction are many, few publications bring the two together.

A small number of sources directly address the interface of spiritual direction and HIV and AIDS.[4] Walter J. Smith discusses the spiritual care of persons living with HIV and AIDS, which he describes as a "path not travelled before."[5] The director is "a fellow sojourner, an advocate, an intercessor."[6] This type of direction relationship is very emotionally demanding: "They [seekers] become like a sponge: if a relationship is nurturing, they absorb the energy and feel more whole; if the encounter is detached and impersonal, they may feel they are losing energy and becoming less whole."[7]

---

[2] "UNAIDS Gap Report 2014," www.unAIDS.org.

[3] "New HIV Report Finds Big Drop in New HIV Infections in South Africa," www.unAIDS.org/.

[4] Different versions of this research have been published in Susan Rakoczy, "Spiritual Direction and HIV and AIDS: An Exploration of Experience," *Grace and Truth* 30, no. 2 (2013): 73–91; and Rakoczy, "Spiritual Direction and HIV and AIDS: South African Experience," *Presence* 21, no. 1 (2015): 41–49.

[5] Walter J. Smith, "Spiritual Care of Persons Living with HIV/AIDS," in *Handbook of Spirituality for Ministers*, vol. 1, ed. Robert J. Wicks (New York: Paulist Press, 1995), 448.

[6] Ibid., 455.

[7] Ibid.

Juan Reed uses the images of margin and center in his discussion of spiritual direction and HIV and AIDS.[8] Persons on the margin include the poor; the physically disabled; women; gay, lesbian, and transgendered persons; people of color; prisoners; persons who are chemically addicted; homeless people; and those infected or affected by HIV and AIDS. Reed calls attention to two temptations to directors who accompany marginalized persons. Once the difference is acknowledged, they "are seen as so foreign that they come to be seen as less than full human beings," or they are "idealized and romanticized and seen, not as unique human beings, but only as representative of groups."[9] In both cases, the director is not in conversation with a real person who is HIV-positive or is affected by AIDS, but with an abstract type. He emphasizes that the director must be aware of his or her own location and experience with the pandemic. One person may have lingering fears about HIV and AIDS, while another may come to be aware of his own judgmental attitudes. Directing at the margin involves pain and suffering, but Reed also stresses that "it is also home, a place of joy and love. Marginal space, however, is always a site of struggle."[10]

Writing from an African perspective, Benjamin Kiriswa of Kenya discusses HIV and AIDS within the broader area of pastoral counseling, which is a cousin to spiritual direction. He states, "HIV/AIDS counseling can be described as an interpersonal relationship to help persons living with AIDS to experience God's presence in their suffering and to find spiritual healing."[11] Dimensions of this relationship include dealing with self-acceptance, self-rejection, the purpose of life and trust in God, relating pain and suffering to the redemptive work of Christ, fostering a sense of prayer and inner peace, and integrating death and dying into life.[12]

James E. Korzun analyzes the experience of shame in spiritual direction.[13] He describes two types of shame: *toxic shame*, which is often the experience of persons who are HIV-positive, and *discretionary shame*, a healthy type in which we see ourselves as God sees us. Since the experience of HIV and AIDS may lead to experiences of shame, this perspective is helpful.

---

[8] Juan Reed, "Can I Get a Witness? Spiritual Direction with the Marginalized," in *Still Listening: New Horizons in Spiritual Direction*, ed. Norvene Vest (Harrisburg, PA: Morehouse Publishing, 2000), 93–104.

[9] Ibid., 94.

[10] Ibid., 101.

[11] Benjamin Kiriswa, "Pastoral Care and Counselling of Persons Living with HIV/AIDS," *African Ecclesial Review* 46, no. 1 (2004): 88.

[12] Ibid., 89.

[13] James E. Korzun, "The Dynamics of Shame in Spiritual Direction," *Sewanee Theological Review* 46, no. 1 (1969): 69–76.

Spiritual Direction as Codiscernment

The term *spiritual direction* is a classical term in the literature of the Christian spiritual tradition.[14] But it can be misleading because in contemporary usage, the practice is neither wholly "spiritual" nor about following the "directions" of the director. *Spirit* refers to the Spirit of God; *direction* is about seeking the presence of the Spirit of God. Anything and everything that is important to the seeker can be brought to the spiritual direction conversation.

Spiritual direction is an experience of codiscernment: seeking the presence and action of the Spirit together. It is triadic: God, the seeker, and the director are intimately connected. Both the seeker's and the director's prayer and experience of God are crucial. A director cannot listen for the signs of the Spirit in another's life if the director has no experience of this presence. A seeker who is not praying regularly and deeply has only superficial life experiences to share.

The spiritual direction relationship is one of communion and the creation of community. *Africae Munus*, the document of the Second Special Assembly for Africa of the Synod of Bishops (2009), describes different forms of community and emphasizes, "Each member of the community must become a 'guardian and host' to the other" (no. 133). This form of community includes spiritual direction in which the director receives the seeker with compassion and the desire to help the seeker grow in the Spirit of God. We are to "'make room' for our brothers and sisters, bearing 'each other's burdens' (*Gal* 6:2)" (no. 35). When HIV and AIDS is part of the direction experience, this compassion becomes even more imperative.

People Living with HIV (PLWH)

Because of the continuing stigma associated with HIV and AIDS, knowledge of a person's HIV status is not easily learned by the director. In my research conducted in September–October 2012 with a variety of spiritual directors in South Africa, very few of them had had actual disclosure experiences.

A director commented, "I haven't had any of my formal directees coming to me speaking about HIV and the ways that they have been affected. But mostly I give spiritual direction to religious sisters, one priest, one businessman. Not at

---

[14] Among many sources, see William A. Barry and William J. Connolly, *The Practice of Spiritual Direction*, 2nd rev. ed. (San Francisco: HarperOne, 2009); Kathleen Fischer, *Women at the Well: Feminist Perspectives on Spiritual Direction* (New York: Paulist Press, 1988); Margaret Guenther, *Holy Listening: The Art of Spiritual Direction* (Cambridge, MA: Cowley Publications, 1992); Janet Ruffing, *Spiritual Direction: Beyond the Beginnings* (New York: Paulist Press, 2000); Nick Wagner, ed., *Spiritual Direction in Context* (Harrisburg, PA: Morehouse Publishing, 2006).

the coalface of HIV" (Luke).[15] Another said, "In spiritual direction, awareness is low; the questionnaire was the first, perhaps with married couples, pastoral counseling as a psychologist, haven't dealt with this much either; certain contexts would be more aware but not much awareness" (Matthew).

Nontando, who accompanied a young woman in spiritual direction who was HIV-positive until her death from AIDS-related illnesses, described the disclosure process:

> Firstly I can say that you need to be strong because most of the time when a person reveals his status, it comes with emotions. And you need to be able to hold the person, hold all his emotions, to try to stabilize the person, that is the important thing, and bring the person to an understanding that the step you made to reveal it's a step to life. That will bring the hope, the desire to see that the future is still there. And the person will feel comfort, will feel supported.[16]

What does affect a director's openness is previous experience with HIV and AIDS in his or her family or community. Two spiritual directors who participated in the research shared their experience of HIV and AIDS in their family. One man's sister died of AIDS-related illnesses, and denial by her and the family persisted to her death. Thandi's brother-in law also died of AIDS-related illnesses. She described the trauma for the whole family and her courage to share it with a member of her community:

> My brother-in-law died of AIDS-related illness in March 1991. In 1986 he was diagnosed, and at that time not only HIV and AIDS was hushed about a lot, people just didn't know a lot; people did not speak about and did not know about it. . . . Two years prior to his death this time the doctor gave him two years. Five years seemed a long time. Two years seemed a very little time. I remember saying to my sister, "If you want the family to support you have to tell the others." . . . My father and brother were angry, wanted to kill him on the spot. My other sister went into a shell. Whole family under a cloud. Each one had to make a journey and it was not easy. . . . By the time we got to his last days, he actually died on Good Friday, and his Requiem was on Easter Tuesday. The thing is, dying on Good Friday—Lord, what are you saying?

---

[15] All names are pseudonyms. The research was conducted in September and October 2012 in various cities in South Africa through one-on-one interviews and a focus group.

[16] Quotes from the interviews are presented verbatim (they were tape recorded with permission) with minor edits for clarity.

She finally had enough courage to share it with her community. One day while she was cooking supper, she said to one of the sisters, "'I want to share something but it is very difficult to get it out of me.' . . . Eventually I said, 'My brother-in-law is dying of AIDS. Has AIDS and is dying.' Once out, such a load off my shoulders."

These experiences appear to give the director a "sixth sense" of openness to the possibility of HIV and AIDS entering the spiritual direction conversation. There must be a high level of trust before people share their status. Of course, the director may herself or himself be HIV-positive, but that is knowledge that the director will not share freely with a seeker unless the dynamics of the direction relationship include HIV and AIDS. Since in South Africa, HIV and AIDS pervades every facet of life, most directors probably know persons who are HIV-positive.

The director must have accurate knowledge about HIV: facts, not myths. Directors need to know about antiretroviral medication protocols and their possible side effects. Directors also face the challenge of confronting their own fears about HIV and AIDS, to reflect on how they may internally stigmatize people. All of this is part of the increasing self-knowledge that is demanded of all spiritual directors, but especially in the context of HIV and AIDS.

Cross-Cultural Spiritual Direction: The Experience of Interpathy

Accompanying a person who is HIV-positive is a huge challenge for the director. It is one of the many experiences of directing someone who is "different" in a significant way from the director.[17] These differences can include age, class, educational background, gender, race, and sexual orientation.

The work of David Augsburger provides a triad of experiences that can assist directors in growing in the ability to enter even more deeply into a seeker's experience. Augsburger describes three types of interaction between counselor and client—here applied to director and seeker—which lead to ever greater engagement with the experience of the other.

Sympathy is the experience of "feeling with" the other. Augsburger describes it as "a kind of projection of one's own inner feelings upon another as inner feel-

---

[17] See Leonard Blahut, "The Spiritual Director as Guest: Spiritual Direction in a Cross-Cultural Situation," *Presence* 3, no. 2 (1997): 57–61; Sophia Park, "Cross-Cultural Spiritual Direction: Dancing with a Stranger," *Presence* 18, no. 3 (2012): 46–52; Susan Rakoczy, "Unity, Diversity, and Uniqueness: Foundations of Cross-Cultural Spiritual Direction," in *Common Journey, Different Paths: Spiritual Direction in Cross-Cultural Perspective*, ed. Susan Rakoczy (Maryknoll, NY: Orbis Books, 1992), 9–23; Theresa Utschig, "Bridging the Gap: Cross-Cultural Spiritual Direction," *The Way* 42, no. 2 (2003): 16–28.

ings are judged to be similar to experiences in the other."[18] The director is both "frame and picture," and the seeker remains outside of the director's experience. If the seeker raises the issue of HIV and AIDS, the director stands outside that experience, listening to it but not feeling with the seeker. *Empathy* goes one step further since it is an experience of "feeling with": "In choosing to feel your pain with you, I do not own it; I share it. My experience is the frame, your pain the picture."[19] When the seeker speaks of anguish on learning that a family member is HIV-positive, the director draws her experience into his frame along with the kinds of suffering he has experienced. But still there is a gap.

Augsburger adds a third type of experience, that of *interpathy*. Here the director moves out of her or his experiences and crosses over into that of the seeker who is speaking of HIV and AIDS. Interpathy challenges the director to allow the seeker's experience to become the director's frame and picture. This experience is temporary since the director later "passes back" into her or his own frame and picture. Augsburger states, "Interpathic 'thinking and feeling with' another across cultural boundaries requires a willingness to bracket one's own way of knowing and enter another."[20] For example, the feelings associated with the stigma of being HIV-positive become the director's feelings, albeit briefly. The director feels the isolation, the fear, and the loneliness that many HIV-positive persons experience. Interpathy is a type of kenosis, a self-emptying (Phil. 2:1–11) that allows the director to hear the seeker's experience and make it the director's own.

Interpathy has two important theological foundations. The first is the dignity of the person, specifically the seeker, who images God (Gen. 1:26). HIV and AIDS represent one—very significant—aspect of a person's experience, and while it certainly affects a person in myriad ways, it does not comprise the totality of who that person is before God and others.

Second is the faith conviction that the Spirit of God is ever present in the spiritual direction relationship. A deepening sense of this theological truth can assist the director to "pass over," however briefly, into the seeker's experience with true interpathy. The director "returns" to his or her own experience enriched. In the personal reflection time that follows a direction session, the director takes time to note experiences of interpathy: *What did I feel in crossing over and into the seeker's experience? What was challenging? What do I feel now?*

Interpathy in a spiritual direction relationship in which HIV is present (explicitly or implicitly) can be limited because of the director's fear and hesitancy to speak of HIV and AIDS and her or his conscious or unconscious

---

[18] David Augsburger, *Pastoral Counseling across Cultures* (Philadelphia: Westminster Press, 1986), 31.

[19] Ibid.

[20] Ibid., 32.

feelings that the HIV person "deserves" this because of some types of behavior or projections of stigma.

One director in the focus group was very honest about his feelings:

> Obviously we are taught that we had to accept people where they are at, not judgmental, accompany them. I suppose in the early years of the pandemic I really tried not to do that. . . . But I find these days young people, urbanized young people, discover they are HIV-positive in a way I feel less compassionate because there it is. No one in urban areas can say that they aren't aware, see the campaigns, they haven't been made be aware of the risk. (John)

Another director stressed the strength that is needed when the seeker is HIV-positive. She emphasized the need for gentleness and support, to reassure the seeker that there is hope and that life still continues.

The Kaleidoscope of HIV and AIDS

A spiritual direction conversation can focus on one theme or many. HIV and AIDS may be the dominant aspect of today's session or it may not reenter for several months. Just as a kaleidoscope constantly changes its colorful patterns as it is turned to the right or left, so also a spiritual direction relationship in which HIV and AIDS is one of the colors will not always focus on the HIV color.

As a spiritual direction relationship develops and deepens, various themes emerge at different times and in different ways: images of God, images of the self, self-knowledge (which is key in discernment), prayer, relationships, work, problems of various kinds. When the seeker shares the theme of HIV, the director is challenged to listen deeply and help the seeker relate it to his or her relationship with God. HIV and AIDS should never be seen outside of that relationship.

In the interview, Gertrude described how the experience of learning he was HIV-positive changed this man's image of himself:

> He came to me and he said, "I am so grateful for this virus. I had lost my moorings. And I'm back in that space of really longing for God and realizing my mortality." . . . He was aware of living a fairly promiscuous life and he was acknowledging that he was coming back to God's way.

Another man told her, "Every morning I wake up and I am so grateful for life and just living a completely different life from those years of that profligate living." Elizabeth commented, "The one thing I found out for sure that people need is self-esteem. Work with people so that they know they are precious, they are with God." She described an exercise with nature that is part of a retreat for caregivers who are HIV-positive. One man found a stone in the road and at first saw it as useless. But then he realized it could be part of a foundation. "He was so convinced when he came back that he had a purpose in life, value, a gift the stone gave him."

The feeling of trust in the spiritual direction relationship unfolds gradually. Thandi, who had experience of HIV and AIDS in her family, stressed, "I had to go through that whole conversion experience before I could help anyone else." She shared the importance of the director's presence with the seeker and emphasized the need "just to be present, to be, to give them the time they need, to affirm them in whatever space they are in, to be present in that. But to help them to recognize their own space, their own goodness, whatever needed affirming in their life. To gently help them see no blame but just being in the situation."

Nontando spoke of using the story of the Prodigal Child (Luke 15:11–32) with a person she was accompanying who was HIV-positive and whose faith was increasing:

So when you are working with the person that reaches at this level, strengthen their relationship with God, bring God into this acceptance, refer to the Prodigal Child, who went and wasted everything, but when he came back and accepted I have sinned, this is who I am, broken as I am, the parents accepted him.

Discernment

Discernment is a very significant dimension of the spiritual direction experience. The key discernment questions are always, "Where is the Spirit present? What are the signs? Where is the Spirit leading?" As in all discernment processes, when HIV and AIDS enter the spiritual direction conversation, this involves interpreting the affective responses the seeker is experiencing in order to judge where the Spirit is present and active. Ignatius of Loyola named these experiences as "consolation" and "desolation."

In the *Spiritual Exercises* (*SpEx*) Ignatius describes consolation as a deep affective experience in which the person is "inflamed with love for its Creator and Lord," and sheds tears in sorrow. The key discernment sign of consolation is "every increase of faith, hope and love, and all interior joy which calls and attracts the soul to that which is of God and to salvation by filling it with tranquility and peace in its Creator and Lord" (*SpEx* 316).[21] Desolation is the

---

[21] Quotations from the *Spiritual Exercises* are from *The Spiritual Exercises of St. Igna-*

opposite and painful experience. Ignatius describes it also in powerful language. It is "darkness of soul, confusion of spirit, attraction to what is base and worldly, restlessness caused by many disturbances and temptations which lead to lack of faith, hope, or love" (*SpEx* 317).

Two key questions emerge in discerning consolation and desolation: Are faith, hope, and love increasing or decreasing? Where is the forward movement of grace?

The directors who were interviewed described consolation in various ways:

> I will talk about her last moments. Even though I could see that she was in her last time, she would smile to you. I would feel very happy that at least the work I did with her at least is the reason she is feeling comforted; she's feeling that when time comes she will sleep peacefully. For me it made me strong, it gave me the strength to continue in the work with people in need like her if they are presented to me. (Nontando)

Charlotte said, "I feel great compassion and deep care for the person who is struggling with a so-called terminal illness. My task is to offer them hope in a loving and merciful God." Thembi described consolation as "seeing people accepting the situation as it is and praying about it." For Gertrude, a doctor, it is, "Seeing people get onto meds and deal with the illness and get better!"

Desolation is also present in the direction experience as affected by HIV and AIDS. Luke said,

> I think consolation is truth, veritas, coming to know reality. Desolation, turning back on God, has to do with denial, stigma, veil of secrecy and not wanting to talk about it. For me that's the work of the bad spirit, however we want to talk about it. Stigma.

Charlotte's feelings were very clear: "I have felt desolated when a directee feels depressed and together we are struggling to find meaning and purpose in life." While this sadness is not necessarily Ignatian desolation, it can affect one's life of faith.

Nontando had some very difficult experiences of desolation while she accompanied a seeker who was HIV-positive:

> I think there's a time when I was supposed to meet with her and I found out that she started smoking; there's this powder that South

---

tius Loyola, trans. Elisabeth Meier Tetlow (Lanham, MD: University Press of America, 1987).

Africans use through the nose, all those kinds. I knew how fragile this person was, struggling with the cough, all the time. I saw her doing that. When I went and reflected I was very angry. I said maybe I wasted my time. I was like fighting with myself. I couldn't handle that.

When they next met she expressed her anger and the seeker told her, "I know what I am doing.... I listen to you but I can't stop." It took her time to acknowledge that this is the way she is handing her pain, and she had to respect it even though she "had a hard time to accept and to cope."

Interpreting Consolation and Desolation: The Forward Movement of Grace

These statements from seasoned directors about their experiences of consolation and desolation in the spiritual direction relationship in which HIV and AIDS is present demonstrate that directors must be aware of their own feelings as they listen to the seeker. The forward movement of grace has two dimensions: listening to the seeker and listening to one's own heart, mind, and feelings.

Discernment includes the ability to sense either the forward movement of grace as the increase of faith, hope, or love—or its weakening in experiences of desolation. A director without this self-awareness is a danger to the seekers they accompany. They will be unable to sense the direction that the Spirit is leading the seeker and may lead the person down dangerous pathways of the lessening of faith, hope, and love.

Supervision sessions, either one on one with a more experienced director or group supervision, can help the director work with their negative feelings that HIV and AIDS may generate and also learn how to be more aware of the presence of the Spirit of God in the seeker's often painful experience.

What Are Spiritual Directors Learning about HIV and AIDS in the Direction Relationship?

"AIDS is not a sin," said Charlotte. "Every person needs to be understood, listened to with love and understanding. No one is unaffected by the HI Virus." Diane insisted that directors "need to offer nonjudgmental support, to guide in decision making, to offer forgiveness to those who are hurt, to suggest reconciliation and the sacraments to some, to express that HIV is only a virus! You are alive and have a purpose in life." Busisiwe emphasized the African gift of hospitality in spiritual direction: "Simply to receive people as they come, help them to hear themselves speak, and gradually accept their reality. My learning is simply to be present to them and listen."

Conclusion

The HIV and AIDS pandemic in Africa challenges spiritual directors in many ways. Because everyone is either affected or infected, directors must be alert to any signs of this experience in the seeker's sharing. Directors must be aware of their own feelings and perceptions toward people who are HIV-positive. If conscious or semiconscious feelings of judgment and stigma surface, the director needs to bring these feelings to a more experienced director as a supervisor in order to process them more deeply.

A person who is HIV-positive is a person; that person's HIV status is not the sum total of his or her identity. A director must be careful not to focus on a seeker's HIV status to the detriment of addressing the depths of that person's relationship with God.

The presence of HIV and AIDS in the spiritual direction relationship through the experience of seeker and director offers the opportunity for growth in both persons' relationship with God. Reflection by directors on these experiences offers the entire spiritual direction community an opportunity to learn something more of the gracious gift of the Spirit of God among us.

CHAPTER 25

ANOINTING THE SICK, MINISTERING TO THE DYING, AND SPIRITUAL HEALING IN TIMES OF AIDS

Stuart C. Bate

The fundamental pastoral exercise of prayer care for the sick and dying is the bringing of life to the sick, their families, and the communities they inhabit.[1] It is a journey that leads to being raised up to new life whether in recovery from the sickness or in passing on to new life in the reign of God. The life, sickness, and death of a Christian is a journey along a road constructed in the vision and promise of Christ and his church as manifest in the paschal mystery. It is in some ways prefigured in Jesus's response to the sickness, death, and raising up of Lazarus. This juxtaposition between life, sickness, death, and being raised from the dead presents the central truth of the Christian faith: Jesus gives life by giving up his own life on the cross. The final journey of Jesus begins by giving life to Lazarus as he is raised from the tomb and from that begins the journey to his own death.

The text of the raising of Lazarus thus provides a powerful backdrop for understanding the issues around prayer care for the sick and dying in terms of the wider journey of human salvation of which they are part. They also point to various aspects of the ministry of pastoral prayer care for the sick and dying. These may be liturgical, as in the anointing of the sick, communion to the sick, and the reception of viaticum as "in their passage from this life Christians are strengthened by the body and blood of Christ."[2] They may also be nonliturgical in prayers for the sick and dying in various contexts.

---

[1] The notion of life in African cultures is wider than the life-death paradigm of Western cultures. Life is tied to health as well as personal and communal well-being. "In African thinking, life is a whole and a person becomes an embodiment of the community. This implies being in harmony with the whole environment which comprises the family, the clan, the ancestors, and the community as a whole" (Stuart C. Bate, *Evangelisation in the South African Context* [Rome: Centre "Cultures and Religions"—Pontifical Gregorian University, 1991], 59).

[2] *Pastoral Care of the Sick, General Introduction*, no. 26, catholicsensibility.word-press.com/.

The Lazarus Story of Sickness, Death, and Raising to New Life

The Lazarus story is a foundational metaphor of sickness, healing, death, and life in the Christian community. It is based on the relationship between God and his people in creation and salvation. Note Jesus's relationship of friendship, love, and care with the family of Martha, Mary, and Lazarus (John 11:5). Relationship in pastoral care is essential. In relationship we walk together in journey as a Christian community. It reminds us that pastoral care of the sick and dying is ministry to fellow members of God's family.[3]

The text also describes some of the important aspects of prayer care for the sick and dying in a world of HIV and AIDS. First, Jesus receives information about the situation (John 11:6a). This information is sent as a result of the care and concern of the family for Lazarus and the recognition of their need for Jesus's help. The church refers to this in its pastoral practice:

> If the sickness grows worse, the family and friends of the sick and those who take care of them have the responsibility of informing the pastor and by their kind words of prudently disposing the sick for the reception of the sacraments at the proper time.[4]

Once he has been informed about the situation, Jesus begins preparation to journey to visit the family (v. 6b); he then undertakes the journey to encounter the sick and dying Lazarus (vv. 7–10), reminding us that journey is an important dimension of prayer care for the sick and dying. The journey is undertaken in terms of a statement of pastoral purpose expressed here by Jesus as "to awake him out of sleep" (v. 15).

Jesus arrives and finds the people consoling Martha and Mary (vv. 17–19), which reminds us of the powerful healing effect of consolation. He specifies his statement of pastoral purpose: to raise Lazarus up and bring him to life (vv. 20–23). This is Jesus's message regarding sickness and death and it is a message in word and deed as he calls Lazarus out from the tomb (v. 43). His mission to heal the sick and raise up the dead is one he has mandated to his disciples: "And as you go, preach that the Kingdom of heaven is close at hand; heal the sick, raise the dead, cleanse the lepers, cast out demons" (Matt. 10:7–8).

---

[3] John Paul II, *Ecclesia in Africa*, no. 63; See also Benedict XVI, *Africae Munus*, no. 7.
[4] *Pastoral Care of the Sick, General Introduction*, no. 34.

Pastoral Care of the Sick:
Raising Up, Saving, and Healing People

Pastoral care of sick in the rite of anointing makes an important connection between anointing of the sick, raising up the sick and saving the sick: "The Letter of James states that the sick are to be anointed in order to raise them up and save them."[5] The importance of the journey to visit the sick is also emphasized: "Priests, particularly pastors and the others mentioned in no. 16, should remember that it is their duty to care for the sick by personal visits and other acts of kindness."[6] In addition the hope that Jesus gives to Martha and Mary and those present is also seen as a necessary component of the ministry:

> Especially when they give the sacraments, priests should stir up the hope of those present and strengthen their faith in Christ who suffered and is glorified. By bringing the Church's love and the consolation of faith, they comfort believers and raise the minds of others to God.[7]

From the story of Jesus and Lazarus and the teaching around the rite of anointing the sick, we learn that the fundamental pastoral exercise of prayer care for the sick and dying is the bringing of life to the sick, their families, and the communities they inhabit. Jesus explains this to Martha in John 11:24–25: "Martha said to him, 'I know that he will rise again in the resurrection on the last day.' Jesus said to her, 'I am the resurrection and the life. Those who believe in me, even though they die, will live'" (RSV). This reveals the real goal of primary pastoral care of the dying as part of the journey to being raised up to new life, whether in recovery from the sickness or in passing on to new life in the reign of God.

The Lazarus story tells us three important truths: Jesus visits the sick and dying and comforts their family and those close to them; Jesus heals the sick; and Jesus raises the dead and brings life. Another important teaching of this text is found in the very name of Lazarus, which means "God is my help." This name describes the real situation of all who find themselves in a context of sickness to death—a situation that for many years has informed the lives of those infected and affected by HIV and AIDS: God is their help. The minister and those who accompany to visit the sick and dying are the ones who must evangelize the sick and dying, their friends, and community about the truth that God is their help and then through their actions mediate his helping presence to them.

---

[5] Ibid., no. 8.
[6] Ibid., no. 35.
[7] Ibid.

All ministry to the sick and dying needs to be constructed around four principal activities where God is acting in the Spirit through his ministers: healing the sick, bringing life to what is dying, promoting the journey from death to life in raising up the dead, and preparing the dying for new life. These activities can be unpacked as four pastoral strategies:

1. The principal response to the sick and dying is that of mediating healing, life, and resurrection.
2. The response to the family is one of concern, comfort, and hope.
3. Healing and life are family and communal events, not just those of a sick or dying person.
4. The principal prayer mode is to God who is our help.

Mediating Healing, Life, and Resurrection

Pastoral prayer care of the sick needs some important clarifications. First, healing the sick person means that even if the disease may not disappear, the person lives in the fullness of life through faith in Jesus and the promise of eternal life. Second, pastoral care of the dying has as its goal that even though the person may die of the disease, that person dies healed. This is the fundamental truth of this ministry. Prayer care needs to mediate this truth into the life of the person under care. Third, the healing ministry needs to raise up the sick person in the fullness of awareness that they are saved. This implies the effective transmission of the real meaning of the words "the sick are to be anointed in order to raise them up and save them."[8]

Such raising up, healing, and saving take many forms, including strengthening, support, and consciousness of God's presence, because people are crushed down and broken by the experience of serious illness, troubles, and difficulties that life brings.

> Those who are seriously ill need the special help of God's grace in this time of anxiety, lest they be broken in spirit and, under the pressure of temptation, perhaps weakened in their faith. This is why, through the sacrament of anointing, Christ strengthens the faithful who are afflicted by illness, providing them with the strongest means of support.[9]

However, and in some ways most importantly, the faith of the minister, the community, and the sick person should not discount the possibility, if it be

---

[8] Ibid., no. 8.
[9] Ibid., no. 5.

God's will, that the sick or dying person is restored to the fullness of life in this world. "The sick person will be saved by personal faith and the faith of the Church, which looks back to the death and resurrection of Christ, the source of the sacrament's power (see James 5:15)."[10]

Accepting this in the fullness of its evangelical meaning calls us to widen our notions of healing, saving, raising up, and bringing life in order to understand the deeper meaning of the gospel and prayer care of the sick, particularly as it refers both to the human body and human relationships.

Deepening Our Understanding of the Recurring Cycle of Life and Death in the Human Body

The question of life, health, sickness, and death in the human person is more complex than first meets the eye. On the physical level, life, health, sickness, and death are part of a continual process within the body. The same is also true within interpersonal relations between people and in the life of communities and societies.

Our bodies are made up of cells that all descend from the original cell at fertilization. However, less well known is that most if not all of the cells that make up our body die after a period of some years and are replaced by new cells.

> Jonas Frisen believes the average age of all the cells in an adult's body may turn out to be as young as 7 to 10 years. But Dr. Frisen, a stem cell biologist at the Karolinska Institute in Stockholm, has also discovered a fact that explains why people behave their birth age, not the physical age of their cells: a few of the body's cell types endure from birth to death without renewal, and this special minority includes some or all of the cells of the cerebral cortex. . . . About the only pieces of the body that last a lifetime, on present evidence, seem to be the neurons of the cerebral cortex, the inner lens cells of the eye, and perhaps the muscle cells of the heart. The inner lens cells form in the embryo and then lapse into such inertness for the rest of their owner's lifetime that they dispense altogether with their nucleus and other cellular organelles.[11]

However, and perhaps more surprising, is the fact that Frisen's view regarding the long life of some cells is a disputed question in science, with recent articles

---

[10] Ibid., no. 7.

[11] Nicholas Wade, "Your Body Is Younger Than You Think," *New York Times*, August 2, 2005, www.nytimes.com. See also Ratan D. Bhardwaj, Maurice A. Curtis, et al., "Neocortical Neurogenesis in Humans Is Restricted to Development," *Proceedings of the National Academy of Sciences of the United States of America* 103, no. 33 (August 15, 2006): 12564–68.

providing convincing evidence for adult neurogenesis, meaning that all body cells die and are regenerated.[12] My intention is not to pursue this avenue except to note that the question of life and death and raising up in a living human body is already a reality, even in the verifiable and repeatable world of scientific "certainty." We should not discount it elsewhere in human life.

*Deepening Our Understanding of the Recurring Cycle
of Life and Death in Human Relationships*

Perhaps it is more easily understandable that human relationships also go through experiences of life, health, sickness, death, and even raising up. From the most intimate relationships in marriage to the more casual relationships between friends and acquaintances, daily life is also caught up in events of life and death within relationships that may both flourish and fade and then sometimes revive. Even in the personal project of the individual, initial life choices are often modified, revised, and even abandoned, and new ones may emerge and take over. Similarly, relationships with other people are born, fade, renewed, and sometimes die. The same is clearly true of the life of the community.

Understanding the ubiquity of diversity of the human condition in the many strata of life as people journey through life, death, sickness, health, and revival allows us to understand the complexity of human needs that call for a response in faith. This is pastoral care. The more difficult needs and concerns of people often transcend our ability to respond on a merely human level, and at this point we raise up our hearts and commitment in faith to the transcendent. This is when we present needs in prayer, and this is what we celebrate in prayer ministry for life, healing, sickness, death, and raising up. This should help us recognize the importance of the ministry of prayer care and reinforce our commitment to it.

The Response to the Family
Is Concern, Comfort, and Hope

So far we have considered illness from the perspective of the sick person, but illness is rarely just a personal matter, because a person's illness also generates a series of feelings within the family and local community. These feelings enter the family and community by means of perceptions regarding the illness, local knowledge about the illness, and values and disvalues associated with it.

The story of Lazarus reminds us that personal sickness makes the family sick, too, and family members also become a site for healing, saving, being

---

[12] Simon M. G. Braun and Sebastian Jessberger, "Adult Neurogenesis: Mechanisms and Functional Significance," *Development* 141, no. 10 (2014): 1983–86.

raised up, and resurrection. The family will be concerned and discomforted for a variety of reasons. The sick person may be someone of power in the family and thus necessary for its functioning—for example, a principal breadwinner. Alternatively the sick person may be dependent on a family in great need itself. The family is, thus, often the starting point as the minister and those who accompany them reach the family home. The goal here is twofold: first to console and pray for the family, and second to construct out of the suffering and despair of the family a caring, supportive group that is empowered to minister to the sick member.

Family and communal feelings can make things much better or much worse, particularly with illnesses considered serious in the cultural system of the family and the community. Then, far from being a personal matter, the illness becomes a family and community issue. Indeed, communities and cultures themselves construct illnesses that are unfelt, unknown, and of no value to other people, communities, or cultures. These are known as *culture-bound syndromes*.

> Simons and Hughes (1985) have collected studies of these sicknesses which they call "folk illnesses" from around the world. The collection includes such exotic illnesses as "The Cannibal Compulsion Taxon," "The Fright Illness Taxon," and the "Sudden Mass Assault Taxon" ("Amok"). At the end of their book they list almost 200 different "culture bound" syndromes from around the world, which are by no means an exhaustive list.
>
> Coming to the South African context, Edwards *et al* (1982) describe fifteen Zulu culture bound psychiatric syndromes which fit into the category, referred to by Ngubane (1977) as *"ukufa kwabantu."* For Edwards (1982:86) the culture bound syndromes "reflect culturally flavoured versions of problems in living that are common to all people in all cultures."[13]

AIDS is indeed constructed differently in cultures as an illness, especially on the moral level. AIDS stigma is part of this. In some cultures, AIDS patients within the family are often hidden away. The diagnosis of a person with HIV and particularly its manifestation in AIDS and AIDS-related sicknesses has consequences that create negative feelings in the family and local community. This aspect of AIDS can reduce the personal dignity and worth of the sick person as the community sees a sinner, a morally weak person, and a bringer of

---

[13] Stuart C. Bate, *Inculturation of the Christian Mission to Heal in the South African Context* (New York: Edwin Mellen, 1999), 106. Note that *Ukufa kwabantu* (or its synonym *isifosabantu*) are terms in *isiZulu* that refer to sicknesses that cannot be healed just by medicines but that require cultural healing rituals.

shame on all, which can create feelings of anger about the sick person. People construct all kinds of coping mechanisms to deal with this, such as silence and not naming the illness, even at the funeral. Such feelings are also a manifestation of illness, an aspect that needs to be dealt with in the process of ministering concern, comfort, and hope to the family and community.

In addition, concern, comfort, and consolation also need to be supported by rituals that help people name their fears and cast out the negative feelings, scapegoating, and other worries that possess and oppress them. The experience of casting out demons in order to raise people up out of their oppression and fear is an important part of pastoral care and healing of the sickened community. Here the ministry of raising up is particularly significant. Culture-based sickness on this level must also be healed as a communal therapy and as family therapy. This may often involve African cultural rituals of reconciliation that involve the family and the ancestors as well as the greater community. The Second African Synod called for greater inculturation of the Sacrament of Reconciliation with concerns like this in mind.[14]

Healing Is a Family and Communal Event

The healing ministry must also be a ministry of the family and community. Healing has to mediate the experience of an enhanced quality of life to the sick person but also to the immediate family context and that of the local community. The healing of the person's life is also linked with the healing of the person's interpersonal and communal lives. The outcome is that all should participate in feeling well.

> If one member suffers in the Body of Christ, which is the Church, all the members suffer with that member (1 Corinthians 12:26) (*Lumen Gentium* 7). For this reason, kindness shown toward the sick and works of charity and mutual help for the relief of every kind of human want are held in special honor.[15]

Many things can go wrong. A medical doctor may report to a patient suffering from HIV and feeling sick that all the tests are negative, and "there is nothing

---

[14] The Second African Synod has called for the creation of inculturated forms of the Sacrament of Reconciliation, "based upon an in-depth study of traditional African ceremonies of reconciliation" (Proposition 7) and "further scientific research on African cultures and religion" (Proposition 13). See Stgan Chu Ilo, "Toward an African Theology of Reconciliation: A Missiological Reflection on the Instrumentum Laboris of the Second African Synod," *Heythrop Journal* 53, no. 6 (2012): 1005–25.

[15] *Pastoral Care of the Sick, General Introduction*, no. 32.

wrong with you." A preacher may castigate those who are HIV-positive, accusing them of being sinners. A community may blame the family for their child's sickness because the family didn't raise the child properly.

Healing of sickness and ministry to the dying should include therapies to deal with perceptions like these. Healing and ministry also have to respond to the sick person's level of cognition, providing an understanding of how the disease is caused and how the therapy heals. Similarly healing and ministry must respond to the healing of the morals and values of the sick person and the community so that immoral behavior on both sides is identified appropriately and forgiveness and reconciliation are effected in the life of the sick person, the community, and the spiritual world.

Christians in the family and the local community are the best to take these matters into account as they live there. They, too, must participate in finding ways for a person, a family, and a community to become healed as the full experience of life is manifested and mediated to all. Then they are raised up!

> It is thus especially fitting that all baptized Christians share in this ministry of mutual charity within the Body of Christ by doing all that they can to help the sick return to health, by showing love for the sick, and by celebrating the sacraments with them. Like the other sacraments, these too have a community aspect, which should be brought out as much as possible when they are celebrated.[16]

Deepening Our Understanding of the Human Experience of Sickness and Health

Sickness and health are human experiences articulated first by feelings. The first experience of illness is when a person feels unwell, and the first experience of healing is when a person begins to feel better.

The feeling of unwellness is a perception of how the illness enters the world of the sick person, but perception clearly has a strong cultural dimension to it. Some people perceive a natural cause as the source of the unwellness and look for a natural remedy in rest or herbs or medication. Mediating healing here usually occurs in the world of medical practitioners, and their counterparts in traditional healing who focus on herbs and natural medicines.

However, if the sickness does not easily respond to these remedies, people may look to other causes in the interpersonal world. Perception may lead to another living person who may be suspected of bringing harm through witchcraft or sorcery, or it may lead to the identification of an ancestor who is harboring

---

[16] Ibid., no. 33.

anger.[17] Alternatively, sickness may be perceived as spiritual in nature caused by an evil spirit or demon or as a punishment from God for sinful behavior.[18]

All of these feelings and perceptions lead to the need to identify the sickness and give it a name. This is a move from the level of perception to the level of cognition, where we try to answer questions about what this illness is and where it comes from: its etiology. But cognition also has a cultural dimension to it, because the labels that a person gives to the experience of illness are always given within their cultural framework, whether within a scientific Western culture (a germ or infection), within a religious culture (an evil spirit or demon or sin), or within a traditional culture (witchcraft or angry ancestors).

In addition, feelings about illness also raise issues on the level of values and morality. Some sicknesses, like a headache or a cold, are morally quite neutral, whereas others are morally problematic, such as when a family taboo is broken or when ancestors are offended by some behavior. Then the illness becomes an issue of the whole family or clan. Known immoral behavior in the Christian community similarly becomes an offense against God and the church, which can lead to sanctions and a bad reputation for the person and indeed the person's community. The church's teaching here is very clear: "Although closely linked with the human condition, sickness cannot as a general rule be regarded as a punishment inflicted on each individual for personal sins (see John 9:3)."[19]

Finally the understanding generated by both cultural cognition and cultural values or disvalues linked to illness will generate their own level of emotion and stress, which may exacerbate to a lesser or greater extent the experience of the illness in the sick person's life. All of these matters have been experienced when it comes to HIV infection and disease and AIDS deterioration into death.

When we speak about a person's healing, such healing has to respond to the sickness as it manifests itself on all these levels. Outcomes are seen preeminently on the level of feelings. We have seen this at the center of the experience of sickness, and so it has to be at the center of the healing process.

The Principal Prayer Mode
Is to God Who Is Our Help

Spiritual therapies recognize the importance of supernatural factors in both illness etiology and healing remedies. Illness etiologies may be ascribed to the activity of spirits, demons, or other malevolent spiritual beings as well

---

[17] Stuart C. Bate, "Constructing a Theological Model of Salvation and Life to Inform the Ministry of HIV and AIDS Prevention," *Journal of Theology for Southern Africa* 150 (November 2014): 20–45, 36.

[18] Ibid.

[19] *Pastoral Care of the Sick, General Introduction*, no. 2.

as to immoral human behavior usually understood as sin. Healing therapies include the casting out of demons or evil spirits, the confession and forgiveness of sin, anointing with oil, laying on of hands, and prayer for the sick person. The Catholic tradition has two sacraments of healing: Penance and Anointing of the Sick. Receiving communion also has a healing effect.

As Christians we believe in the power of God to heal the sick. Indeed the church was given a specific mandate to heal the sick and to cast out demons (see Jas. 5; Matt. 10). Often forgotten is that the ministry to heal the sick and raise the dead in a local community is actually a participation in the common healing ministry of the whole of the people of God throughout the world. Local ministry is always tied to the global pastoral activity of the church, which is one and holy. This is true whether in the sacrament of Anointing of the Sick or in viaticum or in family and community prayers for healing that may call on the charism of healing given to people for building up the body of the community.[20]

This ministry is carried out in communion with the whole church and in solidarity with its faith and teaching, which recognize both liturgical and nonliturgical forms of this ministry.

Liturgical and Charismatic Forms of Healing

The *Instruction on Prayers for Healing* is a very important document that all involved in this ministry should know. In its doctrine the Catholic Church makes a clear distinction between healing rites in the liturgy and "prayer meetings for obtaining healing."[21] "Prayers for healing are considered to be liturgical if they are part of the liturgical books approved by the Church's competent authority; otherwise, they are nonliturgical.[22] In addition, prayer meetings for healing are further distinguished "between meetings connected to a 'charism of healing,' whether real or apparent, and those without such a connection."[23]

However, while nonliturgical prayers for healing allow more freedom of expression and format, the rules regarding formal worship services in the church and its liturgy are much more strictly controlled. It is important for the sake of the solidarity mentioned earlier that these rules be followed.

The teaching about charisms of healing is also nuanced. Romans 12 and 1 Corinthians 12 both teach that the Holy Spirit "grants to some a special charism of healing in order to show the power of the grace of the Risen Christ."[24]

---

[20] Cf. 1 Cor. 12; Rom. 12.

[21] Congregation for the Doctrine of the Faith, *Instruction on Prayers for Healing*, September 14, 2000.

[22] Ibid., part 2, *Disciplinary Norms*, art. 2

[23] Ibid., part 1, *Doctrinal Aspects*, art. 5.

[24] Ibid.

However, this charism is not necessarily given to a particular class of people, such as priests or other church leaders. Nor is the healing dependent on the intensity and emotion of the prayer and the meeting.[25] Indeed, every Catholic has the right to pray for healing, and prayer meetings for healing may be led by nonordained Catholics even in a church. However, while nonliturgical prayers for healing allow more freedom of expression and format, the rules regarding formal worship services in the church and its liturgy are much more strictly controlled.

An Essential Mission

God's plan is that we should struggle against sickness and try to ensure good health and well-being in all people. This is part of the church's mission today. The sick, the dying, the poor, and the oppressed are at the center of God's compassion, and God seeks to use those called from all walks of life to be apostles ministering life, salvation, raising up, and healing to all. The sacraments are the principle sign of God's saving grace within the intimate reality of our created and saved reality where divinity is most fundamentally present. But sacred presence is also found in the most conflicted, evil, sick, and unjust situations of human suffering to oppression and death. This is the paschal mystery.

> The sick person will be saved by personal faith and the faith of the Church, which looks back to the death and resurrection of Christ, the source of the sacrament's power (see James 5:15). When in their passage from this life Christians are strengthened by the body and blood of Christ in viaticum, they have the pledge of the resurrection that the Lord promised: "Those who eat my flesh and drink my blood have eternal life, and I will raise them up on the last day" (John 6:54).[26]

---

[25] "Not even the most intense prayer obtains the healing of all sicknesses. St. Paul had to learn from the Lord that 'my grace is enough for you; my power is made perfect in weakness' (2 Cor 12:9)" (ibid.).

[26] *Pastoral Care of the Sick, General Introduction*, no. 7.

CHAPTER 26

THEOLOGICAL EDUCATION, LEADERSHIP FORMATION, AND HIV PREVENTION IN THE COMMUNITY

Edwina Ward

The majority of churches in South Africa require some form of theological education that includes HIV and AIDS in the curriculum, for the training of their leaders who are the priests, pastors, ministers, and caregivers. In this chapter I argue that the curriculum in theological education must include leadership training for seminarians and students of theology if they are to become active and informed leaders in their respective communities. The church is being challenged to once again find its prophetic voice. HIV and AIDS is a preventable disease, which must be properly communicated to those infected and affected, and people must be taught ways to prevent further spread of the disease. The leaders in the church are challenged with this task of communication and education, as theologians, educators, and others need to find new ways to educate the people of God. But they in turn need to be educated, trained, and equipped to address this ministry in a meaningful manner.

The Function of Theological Institutions in Leadership Education

Most priests, pastors, ministers, and caregivers are ready to accept the calling to be a disciple of Jesus, by which they understand that they are called to be missionaries and to evangelize others. Many feel they are only called to preach and manage a parish. Inevitably they forget the missionary nature of their calling as Christians. As evangelizers they are called to educate, to go out and into the community, to be close to those who need to hear the gospel, and to be involved in the hands-on education of men, women, and children. As stated in the Second Special Assembly for Africa of the Synod of Bishops, "The new evangelization needs to integrate the intellectual dimension of the faith into the living experience of the encounter with Jesus Christ present and at work in the ecclesial community" (*AM* 165).[1] One concern is that students of theology and seminarians preparing for active ministry lack training and formation in leadership skills for the communities they are to serve. Many communities in South Africa have issues related to the HIV epidemic. Leadership in the community means being one with the people's needs, guiding the people, educating them, supporting them in times of crisis, and offering them healing spiritually and emotionally where possible.

Theological training and seminary formation do not realistically prepare men and women who are to be ministers for their role in the local church. The difficulties arise from conflicting expectations of the role of the ministers in the community as they lack practical preparation in specific ministerial skills. The possible stress comes from a presupposed measurement between the performance of ministerial skills and the expectations of the congregation members. Five skills would seem to stand out: congregational leadership; development of worship, which includes the ability to give a good sermon; caring for people who need counseling; ministry to the community (especially those with HIV); and social justice.

Theological institutions and seminaries are challenged to work out some means to educate their students in leadership for the church of today and tomorrow. Many theology students have not worked within a community that is ravaged by HIV and AIDS. They will leave their places of education not being trained or equipped to address this issue in a meaningful way. Theological institutions should realize that the church looks for theological interpretation of any new issue that confronts humanity. Needed are leaders who are equipped to cope with the HIV and AIDS crisis and address this problem biblically, spiritually, relevantly, and meaningfully. The crisis of HIV and AIDS must be incorporated in the curriculum to prepare students to be informed and equipped to address this crisis when they enter into full-time ministry. The time for theories has passed; community leaders now need to take action. Many relevant textbooks are available that could be used in such curriculum.[2]

---

[1] Second Special Assembly for Africa of the Synod of Bishops, *Africae Munus* (2011) (*AM* 165).

[2] Phillip V. Lewis, *Transformational Leadership: A New Model for Total Church Involvement* (Nashville: Broadman and Holman, 1996); Alta van Dyk, *HIV/AIDS Care and Counseling: A Multidisciplinary Approach* (South Africa: Maskew Miller Longman, 2008); Gillian Paterson, ed., *HIV Prevention: A Global Theological Conversation* (Geneva: Ecumenical Advocacy Alliance, 2009); Beverley Haddad, ed., *Religion and HIV and AIDS: Charting the Terrain* (Scottsville: University of KwaZulu-Natal Press, 2011); Edwina Ward and Gary Leonard, eds., *A Theology of HIV and AIDS on Africa's East Coast* (Uppsala, Sweden: Missio Series, Swedish Institute of Mission Research, 2008); E. Chitando, *Troubled but Not Destroyed* (Geneva: WCC Publications, 2009); M. W. Dube, *The HIV and AIDS Bible: Selected Essays* (Scranton, PA: Scranton University Press, 2008).

A New Course in Community-Based Education

I was part of a hands-on experience in learning leadership skills when overseas, where the students in the classroom learned alongside homeless people (these could also be people living with HIV and AIDS) to solve social problems and advance the well-being of both groups, especially the homeless. The seminarians and theological students were challenged to learn how to interact with their congregations as well as how to interpret that interaction. The theological goals were to investigate questions such as, Where is God in homelessness? What should a theology of homelessness look like? A further goal was to open a dialogue between the students of theology and the homeless—a dialogue that builds community and offers support for and between the two groups as they learn about each other. Encouraging a nonhierarchical relationship helps to create a sustainable community on a journey toward social transformation.

The homeless persons were selected from the neighboring area and invited to attend the classes each day for two weeks. They were encouraged to reflect on the course topics and join in the discussions. The main presentation each day was on relevant topics. There were video presentations; guest speakers, one of whom was Gustavo Gutiérrez, who spoke about Basic Ecclesial Communities (BECs); chapel and worship services daily; and a final reflection by the students and the homeless as they reflected on their immersion events. The reflection led the homeless students to get in touch with their anger at the realization that society was not working for them and that they had lost so much, including basic elements such as a place to sleep and companionship. The homeless students had a difficult time accepting the theological language used, as this seemed to be out of touch with their lived reality. The students in turn were exposed to the need to organize community ministries—such as the need for soup kitchens, group entertainment, and a safe place to sleep—and volunteer services for the homeless community. Many of the students suggested that the theory and practice of the course should be separated and further courses offered as community-based education.

A bridge was built between the students and the homeless where the students were now prepared and willing to converse with homeless people on the street, to engage in eye contact and conversation with them, and to keep in contact with those who had shared the module after it was over.

Such a new course could be developed in theological institutions, with local communities who are living alongside people affected and infected with HIV and AIDS. I have some pointers on the main objectives of a course, which could be named, "Awareness of the Crisis of HIV and AIDS, and Preventing Its Spread for the Wholeness of Life in the Church and Society: A Community Leader's Role." Course objectives would be

- To learn the basics and have an excellent understanding of the HIV and AIDS crisis to humanity. HIV and AIDS is a preventable disease.
- To equip students with appropriate knowledge, skills, values, and techniques in AIDS management.
- To have knowledge of legal elements relating to AIDS, and an understanding of the medical elements.
- To provide biblical and theological perspectives on health, healing, and wholeness of life in South Africa.
- To learn and experience the skills necessary to become a valued leader in the community.
- To learn about different cultures and their rites and traditions.

The goal of this course would be to offer students adequate opportunities to incorporate into practice the skills they have learned in the classroom and translate them into the community, where they would be accepted as ministers who are leaders as well as compassionate caregivers to church and society.

What Can the Church Do?

Obviously churches cannot cope with AIDS alone, but with the relationships the church has in society every day and every Sunday, coping with AIDS will not happen without the church. The church needs leaders who are able to educate the community openly about the fundamental point that HIV and AIDS can be prevented. Leaders must come face-to-face with the people and understand their needs, problems, and fears, along with their hopes and desires. Church leaders can only lead if they have followers, meaning that the leader is trusted, respected, and capable of talking in a convincing and truthful manner. In turn, as the people of God are empowered, are able to accept more responsibility, and can lead one another, a new sense of vision will be born that will manifest as a sense of support and genuine caring for the other in all areas of life. We cannot just pray for one another, but we must discover that a person is alive and deserves all the healing available—in the form of medication, ARVs, nutritious food, and human love.[3]

As many of the church community attend a church service on Sunday, here we can reach people through sermons, Bible study, Sunday school, and group sessions with adequate teaching material in sex education for men and women, and incorporate the youth in being taught responsible sexual behavior. Pastoral counselors with appropriate training must be available to minister to and care for church members, just as Jesus reached out to the lepers who were duty-

---

[3] Edwina Ward, "Different Ways of Increasing Community Spirit," in *Becoming a Creative Local Church* (Pietermaritzburg: Cluster Publications, 1991), 78.

bound to shout, "Unclean, unclean" (Lev. 13:45–46). He touched them, healed them, and showed compassion for them. They were doomed to live the rest of their lives isolated and in tears, shame, pain, and loneliness, as are many people living with HIV and AIDS. In his exhortation to the church, Pope Francis implores the people of God, "No one can say that the demands of their own lifestyle prevent them from being attentive to the needs of the poor" (*EG* 201).[4]

How serious is the church about differentiating the roles of leadership, management, and administration? Has the church listened and dialogued with the community about the present-day needs? How can this information be given and filtered to the institutions of learning?

When first assigned to a parish and a community, a young minister would feel responsible for managing the congregation through administration. This is a far cry from the purported reason for their formation and training as leaders in the ecclesial community. What are young clergy called to anyway? We know of the definition of leaders as being persons who are charismatic—people who are born natural leaders, having vision, being democratic, having a sense of justice and fairness, being able to cope with conflict, empowering others, and calling for change. They are required to be managers, administrators, and leaders simultaneously and synonymously, yet not many people are good at everything. The present leadership crisis in many parishes is partly due to the confusion resulting from the perception that management, administration, and leadership are interchangeable.

Management and Administration

Management is described as more results-oriented than people-oriented, even though the people are the final recipients of those results. This situation is evident when a project is put to the parishioners, and those in charge come up with the best plan after full consultation. Once the plan is finalized, the managers convince the people to support and pay for the project. Thus, *management* keeps the parish functioning well and running smoothly. All aspects of the parish are coherent: liturgies are well planned, readers prepared, music is rehearsed, and the ministers of the Eucharist, sacristans, and altar servers all know their places. The outreach groups in the parish, such as caring groups, catechism classes, and teen outreach, are up to date. These are all management issues through which the parish is maintained.

Administration is defined as "the carrying out of tasks necessary for the management of a group or an institution."[5] Management and administra-

---

4 Pope Francis, *Evangelii Gaudium* (Rome: Vatican Press, 2014).

5 B. M. Bass and R. E. Riggio, *Transformational Leadership* (Mahwah, NJ: Lawrence Erlbaum, 2008), 3.

tion are both necessary to parish life. Initiative and expertise are important in managing a parish or group. Yet in differentiating leadership from administration and management, we can say that leaders have the vision to know what's best to do, and use their power as energy in life-giving ways while administrators and managers have the skills to accomplish it. The parish is changed and experiences growth through leadership. "Transformational leaders motivate people to do more than they envision, by raising awareness of different values and transcending self-interests."[6] Margaret Wheatley says that leadership is shown in the quality of relationships and goes on to state, "I have never in all my years as a consultant seen anyone change an organization in any fundamental way through rational planning . . . but by intuition, guided by strongly held intentions."[7]

*Influence of Leadership in the Parish
and Community It Serves*

In a community ravaged by the HIV crisis, where the people of God are suffering, confused, afraid, and stigmatized, the leader is responsible for influencing the behavior of others toward some positive goal or objective. In order to have an effect, leaders must have a strong and empowering relational base. They "cannot hope to influence any situation without respect for the complex network of people who contribute to the community."[8] People only support something in which they have a stake. Ultimately what unifies a group toward a common vision is a sense of being valued, respected, and esteemed.

Within parish life and in the community, we see that leaders are not born but rather evolve, become transformed, and mature in a participative, interrelational way within their context. What young ministers learn when they are studying and are in formation is the foundation of who they will become when in active ministry. They come to realize that collaboration is not an end in itself, but a way of ministering together for the sake of accomplishing a mission, a goal. This collaboration does not mean that everyone does everything together, and there still can be one designated leader with the authority to make unilateral decisions. As Sofield and Juliano express, "The end is always the mission. Collaboration is merely a way of accomplishing that mission and can take many different approaches."[9] In sum, leadership and followership are about how

---

[6] Lewis, *Transformational Leadership*, 8.

[7] Margaret J. Wheatley, *Leadership and the New Science* (San Francisco: Berrett-Koehler, 1992), 86.

[8] Ibid., 91.

[9] Loughlan Sofield and Carroll Juliano, *Collaboration: Uniting Our Gifts in Ministry* (Notre Dame, IN: Ave Maria Press, 2000), 156–59.

people are influenced each in different ways. In management, administration, and leadership, the one constant is the issue of power.

Power and Relationships

Power in itself is not bad, but it can have bad effects. Power is apparent in all organizations and can be exercised vertically, horizontally, or circularly. *Vertical power* is represented by hierarchy—up and down the organization, top management to the lowest employee or vice versa. *Horizontal power* refers to relationships across the organization with the focus on joint problem solving and coordination of work flow. *Circular power* revolves around the leader as a resource member or team enabler.

In the circular organizational structure, the leader does not operate above others but is seen as the enabling center of a team. Formal and informal relationships between people are recognized and appreciated, and differences are valued and respected. There is a continuous striving for balance between achievement or organizational goals and the care and development of the organization. The leader is not expected to be the sole originator of the organization's vision but to listen to ideas emerging from the organization's members to discern and articulate the vision.[10] The circular organization focuses on people, purpose, renewal, and growth, and the leadership style is one of collaboration. The church's greatest temptation is to survive, but its aim is to increase in service.

Power is an energy that is actualized within relationships. What gives power its strength, positive or negative, is the quality of the relationships involved. The most potent source of power in the church and the community is love. This power within leadership is the ability to call forth the people's vision and gifts. This power invites and nurtures new energy within the community. Leadership, which brings forth new skills and learning, demonstrates that the teacher is the learner; the learner, in learning, teaches the teacher. Information is mutually shared, and as applies to this chapter, the community receives information about the background, prevention, and treatment of and attitudes toward HIV and AIDS. Being a learner requires the leader to be humble and to demonstrate the essence of servant leadership.

Servant Leadership

The leadership style of Jesus was that of servant leadership. When he responded to a power conflict among his disciples as to who was the greatest, he said, "Let the greatest among you be as the youngest and the leader as the

---

[10] Lewis, *Transformational Leadership*, 23.

servant. . . . I am among you as the one who serves" (Luke 22:24–27). Yet the very notion of being a servant is challenging and has negative connotations. We in South Africa have a past that understands the meaning of servanthood, where one race of people were "servants" to a more superior race. A servant is the one hired to do the work or the dirty jobs. The idea of a servant suggests one who is less than or not as good as the master or mistress. The model that Jesus demonstrated is based on reciprocal servant leadership-followership and is based on equality, respect, and mutuality. A new model of leadership would include common goals of vision (Luke 9:57–62), communication (Rom. 10:13–18), and motivation (Acts 2:14–47). How do we live this way of being a servant leader in a hierarchical and oppressive church? How do we develop ecclesial structures that offer empowerment for both leader and follower? The temptation of the church leader is at times to use Christian preaching and teaching to maintain the power structures. "Power with" is servant power, where the leader of the church community encourages the energy within the community to overcome the crisis of the stigma and discrimination of HIV. The community and the leader work together in a reciprocal relationship as they listen to one another, learn from each other, and create a new vision for a brighter future. Thus they create a space for the vision that allows for deep questioning of the core questions that require kenosis, metanoia, and transformation. As Bass notes, "Religious leaders require unusual wisdom not to become intoxicated with power and lord it over their followers."[11] So it is in faith, hope, and love that leaders work in mutuality alongside the community.

Within the church and the local community we can see the lack of differentiation between the roles of management, administration, and leadership. The choosing of new seminarians and theology students seems to lack careful discernment, psychological testing, teaching, and formation. Within the Roman Catholic Church, those wanting to serve as priests are dropping in numbers, and the mainline Protestant churches are experiencing much the same. Only within the Pentecostal Evangelical churches today do we see young men and women wanting to become pastors and ministers. Answering the question "Why" is a topic for much further exploration. Transformational leadership and its responsibilities would seem to scare off many prospective ministers and leaders today.

HIV Prevention and the Role of the Church

Educating and training seminarians and theology students with HIV and AIDS knowledge and skills before their placements with the local community should be mandatory. In this way, people are instructed about HIV and AIDS

---

[11] Bass and Riggio, *Transformational Leadership*, 44.

at the grass roots in order to prevent stigma, discrimination, and marginaliza-tion—and bring about a change of attitude and behavior. This new thinking around developing a curriculum for theological institutions could include a choice of modules as developed by MAP International.[12]

The church has the role of shaping behavior and attitudes by example and by promoting an understanding of the values and the context of HIV in the local community. The church is influential, as those attending church are a captive congregation. In Africa the church is a significant part of people's lives that can offer support, guidance, and healing and become a powerful place of prayer, all offering signs of hope. Leaders in the church need to educate people to change their attitudes and become an influence to the powerful. The church engages in ministries that are often prophetic, because the leaders can journey alongside those in distress and suffering. In his exhortation *The Joy of the Gospel*, Pope Francis writes, "Our faith in Christ, who became poor and was always close to the poor and outcasts, is the basis of our concern for the integral devel-opment of society's most neglected members" (*EG* 186). The leaders of the church are encouraged to go and search for the one lost sheep, leaving the other ninety-nine behind (John 10:7–16). Pope Francis calls for greater solidarity with the poor and the marginalized so that we may be "attentive to the cry of the poor and come to their aid" (*EG* 187).

Education about and Prevention of HIV

The leaders and ministers are tasked with unveiling the mysteries, fear, and ignorance that surround HIV and AIDS. The correct information given in a clear and factual manner is the most empowering of ministries. This awareness comes through preaching, educational sermons, and testimonies. The church needs to encourage people to talk about responsible sex, because without this frank and open conversation, HIV education is impossible. People must also be encouraged to make use of Bible study group materials to involve people who themselves are living with and affected by HIV or AIDS.

Prevalence of HIV among Women

One cannot write about HIV and AIDS prevention without mentioning the disease's prevalence among women and girls. In some areas of KwaZulu-Natal where AIDS has affected almost every rural house-hold, we are given to understand that over 60 percent of those infected are

---

[12] Peter Okaalet, *Choosing Hope: Eight HIV and AIDS Curriculum Models* (Nairobi: MAP International, 2003).

women and girls.[13] We also know that women are mostly the caregivers for people living with HIV or dying from AIDS. The women are responsible for keeping the family together, and orphaned teenage girls often become the sole caregivers for the family once both parents have died of AIDS.

Education for women and girls is essential if they are to understand their bodies. They need to know how to protect themselves biologically and culturally. Many women are under cultural pressure to keep their marriages together at all costs. They may be expected to undergo female genital mutilation (FGM), or widow cleansing after the death of their husband. Many are raped by their own husbands or other senior members of the family, and some are expected to endure "dry" sex for the pleasure of the male partner. Women and girls are vulnerable because of poverty and being treated as second-class citizens.[14]

The church could be open to uphold positive cultural values and propose alternative rites and rituals in this time of HIV. New rituals could be developed in pastoral-care practices around *ukubuyisa*, the recalling of a dead person's spirit to the ancestral home. Pope Francis himself calls for a cultural change in the vast institution that is the Roman Catholic Church. He sees the need to work on the system and create a "critical mass" of people in the church, especially among the leadership, in order to create the total effect he wants. He states, "It is up to each Christian community to analyze the situation which is proper to their own country" (*EG* 184).

A Vision for the Future

There are so many ways to collaborate with people living with HIV. The church can forcefully address gender inequalities, violence, and stigmatization by allowing women to have equal representation in the church, allowing women to be represented in nonordained positions of decision making, and working with women's groups and marginalized communities to implement prevention programs.

An example of interdenominational collaboration is evident in northern Swaziland. The Methodist and the Roman Catholic clergy were well aware of the numbers of infected and affected families in their congregations. The concern was that people on ARVs were not well nourished and so were not responding well to treatment. The clergy realized that between the two churches was a parking lot, only used on Sundays. After deliberation, the parking area was turned into two hundred "door gardens" producing healthy vegetables. Soon

---

[13] Stephen Lewis, interview, 2006, www.un.org.

[14] Isabel Apawo Phiri, "A Theological Analysis of the Voices of Teenage Girls on 'Men's Role in the Fight against HIV/AIDS in KwaZulu-Natal, South Africa," *Journal of Theology for Southern Africa* 120 (2004): 34–54.

these gardens were able to feed many more of the local community and became financially viable—an excellent example of local community and church collaboration. This was one way for the churches to work together and for the community to learn about prevention and self-empowerment.

Church leaders need to acknowledge the reality of the problem of AIDS in their local communities. They in turn must educate the local community, listen to their needs, and not be afraid to speak the truth about this disease. Leadership is necessary at all levels: local, regional, national, and international. The process of doing theology results in action that moves leaders beyond mere talk and into deeper commitment.

Conclusion

The purpose of this chapter is to outline the need for church leaders to be trained and formed as community leaders and educators, to become prophetic in an era of HIV and AIDS. Unless we have men and women in the local community who are prepared to guide, teach, and offer caring and compassion to people living with HIV or AIDS, the church will find it has no relevance in the everyday lives of the people of God. The pain, fear, suffering, stigmatization, and marginalization of those affected and infected with HIV is showing in the ultimate lack of trust that many have in church leadership.

We are looking toward a theology of hope—hope that the church produces leaders who care, who will educate and lead the community through the pandemic that threatens our lives and show ways of prevention. We know now that HIV is not a death sentence. People live with AIDS, thanks to the availability of ARVs. But the hope they need is to be inspired by the leaders, whose mission is to bring about healing and a change of attitudes in the church.

The paradigm shift required of the church is to change people's knowledge, emotions, attitudes, and skills. One approach is redesigning some of the church's characteristic behaviors, which can improve the perceptions of church members toward their leaders and vice versa. Good leaders choose the style that best suits the situation they face. Leaders of the local church are called to be managers—administrators in most cases—but even more so they are challenged to grow as leaders in a community serving humanity.

Chapter 27

Conflict and Vulnerability to HIV in Africa

A Theological Approach

Bernard Tondé

The AIDS pandemic doubtlessly represents a serious threat to human life in general and to the socially disadvantaged in particular, given that many victims around the world and especially in Africa fall within this category. While Africa accounts for a tenth of the world's population, it is also where nine out of ten new cases of HIV infection occur and where 83 percent of all AIDS deaths take place. We therefore understand the United Nations' call for intervention in an effort to contain the pandemic.[1] While the number of people living worldwide with HIV has increased from 34.6 to 35 million between 2012 and 2013, the latest data on the pandemic and the announcement of a possible end to AIDS within fifteen years are a cause for cautious optimism.[2]

I intend to demonstrate that, in Africa, attempts to address the HIV and AIDS pandemic should take conflicts into account, since it has been proven that they increase vulnerability to the HIV virus. My specific goal is to outline the contribution of a culturally conscious and ethically sound theological reflection on the link between conflicts and vulnerability to HIV. Such a reflection cannot help but call for the promotion of peace and a greater political will to prevent conflicts, while more direct HIV prevention efforts will still go on until the complete eradication of the virus.

Wars and Vulnerability to HIV in Africa

Independence and the end of the Cold War led to high expectations for development in Africa, but this progress is clearly slow to come. Reasons for this

---

[1] Marcela Villarreal, *SIDA: Menace pour l'Afrique rurale*, www.fao.org.

[2] See "Afrique/Santé publique / VIH.SIDA et hépatites: bilan et perspectives" (July 2014), www.paixetdeveloppement.net.

inactivity include the many poorly healed wounds of slavery, the slave trade and colonization, neoliberal imperialism, and a growing urban criminality where religious and ethnic intolerance prevail. Migration due to wars and conflicts has become "a multi-dimensional drama, which seriously affects the human capital of Africa, causing the destabilization and destruction of families."[3] "The number of African countries in conflict has doubled from 11 in 1989 to 22 in 2000,"[4] before experiencing a decline in 2012 (thirteen armed conflicts) and a new rise in 2014 (eighteen conflicts);[5] there were 144 armed groups in the same year.[6]

Causes and Consequences of Conflict on HIV Vulnerability

Armed conflicts and wars in Africa have both internal and external origins,[7]: socio-political and economic crises compounded by ethnic rivalries and fratricidal conflicts such as the Rwandan and Darfur genocides, massacres in Algeria, the expansion of corruption,[8] and chronic recurrence of embezzlement.[9] We should also mention the incompetence of some tribalist heads of state who neglect and torment their people and whose access to power is almost always contested by the opposition parties. We also note conflicts between radical Islam and other faiths, including Christianity, as well as substantive insecurity and chronic poverty, due mainly to embezzlement of public funds, desertification, drought, and famine.[10] This list is not complete without "the deplorable ravages of drug and alcohol abuse, which destroy the human potential of the continent and especially afflict young people. Malaria and tuberculosis and AIDS are decimating African populations."[11] Ebola has already killed many in a few months: 9,604 people, including 490 health workers.[12]

---

[3] Benedict XVI, *L'engagement de l'Afrique* Africae Munus, *Exhortation apostolique sur l'Afrique* (Paris: Bayard / Fleurus-Mame / Cerf, 2011), no. 84.

[4] UNICEF, "Le VIH/SIDA et les conflits armés" (February 2015), 3.

[5] See "Gouvernance politique et économique en Afrique," www.africaeconomicout-look.org, 120, 122.

[6] See Symposium des Conférences épiscopales d'Afrique et de Madagascar/Johannes-burg/Seminar SG 2014.

[7] Francis, Exhortation apostolique *Evangelii Gaudium*, sur l'Annonce de l'Évangile dans le monde d'aujourd'hui (Rome: LEV, 2013), nos. 99, 98, 100.

[8] Raymond B. Goudjo, "Justice et paix en Afrique—Expérience de l'Afrique de l'Ouest (CERAO)," in *Bible et problèmes de sociétés en Afrique "Où est ton frère?" Gn 4,9.* Actes du 6è Séminaire Continental des Coordinateurs de l'Apostolat Biblique en Afrique Dar es Salaam, 30 July–3 August 2007 (Accra: CEBAM, 2008), 75–77.

[9] See *Africae Munus*, no. 76.

[10] Ibid., no. 80.

[11] Ibid., no. 72.

[12] See World Health Organization, "Ebola Situation Report" (February 2015), apps.

External causes, on the other hand, are due to the greed for and pillaging of the continent's teeming natural and human resources[13] by the French, British, German, Spanish, Portuguese, and Italian former colonial powers,[14] who are also joined by the Chinese, American, and Indian presence on the continent. The French presence in Francophone Africa is one of the major sources of conflicts:

> The Franco-African policy, otherwise known as Françafrique, is extremely harmful. After the proclamation of independence of the former French colonies in Africa, politicians' networks have ensured the continuity of the looting of the continent, particularly in favor of men of power in France, by placing corrupt dictators at the head of the newly independent States.[15]

It is worth underscoring the fact that AIDS is also a rural problem; not because it ruins sustainable development efforts but also because it threatens food security, hitting agriculture by decimating the workforce.[16] Moreover, not only has the revelation of the high prevalence of HIV in the armies hit the headlines (over 50 percent in several countries),[17] but the use of HIV as a formidable

---

who.int. If, since the first case in 1976 in DRC, there were 2,000 dead, there are 23,729 dead today in West Africa.

[13] The African continent abounds in many natural, mining, agricultural, and human resources that sharpen appetites and lusts: Africa has nearly one-third of global mineral reserves: 81 percent of the world's manganese, 68 percent of the chromium, 55 percent of the platinum, 44 percent of the vanadium, 40 percent of the gold, not to mention the rare earth deposits so indispensable to modern industries; Africa also has 13 percent of proven oil reserves in extraction costs and competitive production. Alongside the three African oil giants—Nigeria, Angola, and Libya—there are other countries, such as Algeria, Equatorial Guinea, etc. Besides the natural resources, demography is an important lever of the continent: the working-age population is expected to increase from 430 million to 960 million between 2000 and 2030, exceeding subsequently that of India. A Deloitte study reveals that Africa is on track to be, by 2017, the second largest market in the world. See Jean-François Fiorina, "L'Afrique convoitée. Entre coopération et prédation, un continent 'sous influence,'" *CLES* (*Comprendre Les Enjeux Stratégiques*), Note hebdomadaire d'analyse géopolitique de l'ESC Grenoble 102 (2013): 1.

[14] Thirty-two percent of the oil and 30 percent of the uranium needed for the French economy comes from Africa.

[15] François-Xavier Verschave, *De la Françafrique à la Mafiafrique* (Bruxelles: Tribord, 2004).

[16] See "Afrique: pas de lien prouvé entre conflit et propagation du VIH- Étude (IRIN Plus News)," www.unhcr.fr. See also United Nations, *Population, développement et VIH/sida et leur rapport avec la pauvreté*, July 2005.

[17] See Jean-Marie Milleliri, "Le sida transforme le paysage des conflits armés en

weapon of war has transformed civilians into strategic targets, making rape an integral part of the military arsenal. HIV is used as a biological weapon by the deliberate transmission of the virus, carried by soldiers aware of their infection. HIV is also a psychological weapon, arousing fear at the prospect of contamination in communities where stigma regarding infection is marked. This contamination of civilians is part of a deliberate strategy.

Links between Conflict and Vulnerability to HIV and AIDS

The impact of conflicts and violence on the spread of HIV is complex and can vary from one location to the next. In some cases, the conflicts appear to have slowed the spread of the epidemic, for example, by limiting the movement of people. P. Spiegle shares this view (although his analysis has been challenged due to insufficient data).[18] Many other reports postulate the opposite: conflicts increase the vulnerability to HIV. Indeed, thirteen of the seventeen countries with over one hundred thousand children orphaned by AIDS are either in conflict or on the brink of armed crisis. It is no coincidence that the populations of countries in conflict are so vulnerable to HIV.[19] Armed conflict creates difficult conditions and encourages human rights violations, making people particularly vulnerable to infection. Over two-thirds of war victims are afflicted by malnutrition and disease, with AIDS as a major cause of death.

In the countries in conflict, needs for available services can vary greatly, due to the destruction and deterioration of the health infrastructure and efforts to raise awareness of HIV and AIDS. On top of that, law enforcement systems crumble, fostering the growth of inexpensive drug trafficking: 10 percent of the HIV infections in the world are due to drug use by injection.[20] Moreover, armed conflicts usually trigger a lack of medical equipment, including blood testing equipment as well as gloves and sterile needles, considerably increasing the risk of infection.[21]

The deterioration of public order, the proliferation of physical and sexual violence, forced displacement, and prolonged separation from family members are factors that expose the entire population, especially the young, to an

---

Afrique," *Revue critique de l'actualité scientifique internationale sur le VIH et les virus des hépatites* 110 (2003); Stefan Elbe, "HIV/AIDS and the Changing Landscape of War in Africa," *International Security* 27, no. 2 (2002): 159–77, www.pistes.fr/.

[18] See note 15.

[19] See UNICEF, "Le VIH/SIDA et les conflits armés" (February 2015), 1–4, itinerairesdecitoyennete.org/.

[20] Ibid.

[21] Ibid.

increased risk of HIV infection. Individuals carrying the virus are neglected or are the last people to receive assistance. During the last conflict in Sierra Leone, for example, nearly 62 percent of health services were not operating.[22] Refugees are six times more likely to be infected than people living in more stable communities; fleeing the fighting, they bring the virus with them to their host countries.[23] The poverty and misery that accompany conflicts accentuate the sex trade, making it a viable survival option for women and girls. One-third of the twenty-five countries with the highest proportion of AIDS orphans have suffered a conflict in recent years.[24]

Gifty Baka, executive director of the Society of Women against AIDS in Africa (SWAA), which is established in forty countries on the continent, argues that civil wars and political struggles determine women's vulnerability to HIV infection.[25] She denounces the disproportionate vulnerability of women to HIV during and after conflicts, due to the disappearance of law and order, and the subsequent increase of sexual abuse perpetrated by the military. Women and girls are often used as weapons of war and systematically abused; examples include conflicts in Sierra Leone, Liberia, Côte d'Ivoire, Rwanda, Democratic Republic of Congo, Burundi, and Sudan. Unwanted pregnancies and fatherless children are often the by-product of war and sexual violence, resulting in mother-to-child transmission of the virus. In 2005, 75 percent of women and girls over eighteen years of age who went through the Disarmament, Demobilization, Rehabilitation, and Reintegration (DDRR) process in Liberia said they were victims of some form of sexual violence.[26]

While war can lead to higher risks of HIV infection, consider also that the AIDS epidemic can extend conflicts—for example, "when fighters find, in looting or anarchic use of local resources (diamonds, gold . . .), a way to finance access to antiretroviral treatment for themselves or their families."[27] If the complex link between HIV and conflicts cannot easily be understood in terms of cause and effect, "In Africa the AIDS pandemic leads to more instability and conflicts on the continent; and how, in turn, a violent conflict generates favorable conditions for spreading the virus."[28] With the AIDS and develop-

---

[22] In Rwanda, out of the two thousand women (many of whom had survived rape) who submitted to the AIDS test for five years following the genocide of 1994, 80 percent were HIV-positive. Many were not sexually active before the genocide.

[23] Coalition interagence sida et développement, *Le VIH/SIDA et les personnes déplacées* (Ottawa, 2001).

[24] See UNICEF, "Le VIH/SIDA et les conflits armés."

[25] IRIN, "Afrique: Protéger les femmes contre le VIH/SIDA lors des conflits armés," June 2005, www.irinnews.org/fr/.

[26] See ibid.

[27] Milleliri, "Le sida transforme le paysage des conflits armés en Afrique," 4.

[28] "Le VIH/SIDA comme problème de sécurité en Afrique: Les leçons de l'Ouganda," www.crisisgroup.org/.

ment coalition, one must also consider a link between displacement, violence, psychosocial tensions, and HIV spread.[29]

Identification of Groups Vulnerable to HIV and AIDS

The 2014 UNAIDS information sheet shows that optimism is warranted, but there is no reason to lower our guard.[30] Indeed, in 2013 in sub-Saharan Africa, there were 1.5 million new HIV infections, including 210,000 children, and 1.1 million AIDS-related deaths. UNESCO and UNAIDS have globally identified three categories of vulnerable groups called more specifically target groups.

Disadvantaged populations	Culturally destabilized groups	Specific hazardous groups
• The poor • Young people • Uneducated and illiterate populations • Elderly people, women, widows, street children, children abandoned or orphaned by AIDS, minorities.	• Broken families • The unemployed • Refugees and displaced persons • National and international migrants • Mobile workers	• Excluded groups and communities • Prostitutes • Members of the military

This table has the advantage of clearly pointing to vulnerable groups and grouping them in relation to the causes and reasons for their vulnerability. Thus, the common denominator of the first group is to be among the poor; the second, to be among the culturally destabilized groups; and the third, to be in specific risk groups. Poverty, insecurity, conflict, violence, destabilization, cultural uprooting, and exclusion are the breeding ground for HIV vulnerability. To understand HIV vulnerability would require scrutinizing the socioeconomic and political context in which infection occurs.

The Church as Family and Reconciliation

The HIV and AIDS epidemic, thanks to its complexity and link to sustainable human development, requires a multidimensional control strategy that relies on mentality, traditions, beliefs, and value components specific to each society, that could strengthen the necessary changes required. On the other

---

[29] See note 22.
[30] See "Information Sheet 2014," www.unAIDS.org.

hand, this strategy must mobilize cultural resources to benefit from the population's support both in the way of thinking and acting to reach the desired human development level. There is no doubt that the politics and methods of HIV prevention and AIDS treatment will be better and more effective if they are culturally appropriate, understood, appreciated, and integrated. The approach to HIV and AIDS must draw upon all the assets available to the continent, beginning with the family institution.

African Vision of the World

> In the African view of the world, life is seen as a reality that encompasses and includes the ancestors, the living and the unborn, all creation and all beings. . . . The seen and unseen are considered a living space of men, but also a space of communion where past generations coexist invisibly alongside the present generations, themselves mothers of generations to come.[31]

Traditional African religions inform the entire life of the African long before one's birth until long after death, thus determining its *modus vivendi*. This is the central element of its culture—so much that African religions are considered cultural religions the same way African culture is considered a religious culture. Religious diversity does not, however, distract from the unity of black Africa, which offers a rather unitary vision of man.[32] The African lives in constant contact with his family, his tribe, his age group, and especially his ancestors and deities. Thereby, "A man's worth is through his relationship with his family and the effective solidarity that leads from that relationship toward his community, then toward the place of his son or his daughter."[33]

African Root of Evil:
Anthropo-Ethical and Religious Causes

The ecclesiological figure of the church-family of God is welcome because it is an appropriate expression of the church's identity in Africa: a unique Trinitarian image with cultural and anthropological repercussions for the African.[34]

---

[31] *Africae Munus*, no. 69.

[32] See Kipoy Pombo, *Qui è l'uomo? Introduzione all'antropologia filosofica in dialogo con le culture* (Roma: Armando, 2009), 104–19.

[33] Bernard-Désiré Yanoogo, "Église-Famille de Dieu en Afrique: originalité du concept," *RICAO* 14–15 (1996): 140.

[34] See *Ecclesia in Africa*, no. 63. The history of the expression is all African; the fundamental option of the Burkinabe Episcopal Conference for all dioceses in the country dating

The disciples of Christ in Africa are aware of a common destiny and real kinship in baptism. To achieve this, they will need to further testify in their African adherence of faith in Christ in a real emotional solidarity and effective fraternity.[35]

For St. Paul, no doubt, "The root of all evil is the love of money" (1 Tim. 6:10). The masters of suspicion, meanwhile, denounce "the accumulation of material assets, a desire that has the power to inhabit any human. They also denounce empathy when it comes to dealing with otherness and their relationship with it."[36] Welcoming and deepening the plan of God for people to live it in the church-as-family of God may actually really help Africa solve its problems at their root.

The question asked by God about Abel, "Where is your brother?" (Gen. 4:9), and the one that Jesus asks, "Who is my mother and who are my brothers?" (Matt. 12:14), are, according to Moses Adekambi, questions at the center and source of the evils in Africa. The answers to these questions would be the only safe remedies for Africa because they refer to the origins, to God, and to humanity created by God in his image and likeness. These responses would offer a redefinition of humanity and fraternity as well as an increased awareness of one's own responsibility as brother or sister, with the daily mission to be a guardian so that blood is no longer spilled (Gen 4:10–11). Jesus will provide the key to holiness and social justice, to trigger for all, but especially for every African, the duty of the support of the other (Luke 10:29, 36). Redefining the notion of family and parenthood, starting from the necessity to obey God, Father of all, or Mary, Mother of all, becomes a strong invitation to fraternity,[37] and from this common fraternity we can think afresh of the new requirements of forgiveness and reconciliation that the African continent needs so much.

Responsibility, Forgiveness, and Reconciliation in Africa

The Word of God reveals a person to himself or herself and shows that person his or her dignity as a being created in the image and likeness of God. However, the Word of God also shows this person his or her sin against other people. It purifies his or her heart so that this person becomes in turn an artisan of justice, peace, forgiveness, reconciliation, and fraternal communion beyond

---

back to 1977 has become an issue for all the churches of Africa and Madagascar: Barthélemy Adoukonou, "Théologie de l'Église-Famille de Dieu 10 ans après dans l'espace CERAO," *RUCAO* 20 (2004): 176.

[35] See *Evangelii Gaudium*, nos. 69, 70.

[36] Moïse Adeniran Adekambi (dir. CEBAM), "Conférence inaugurale," in *Bible et problèmes de sociétés en Afrique*, 21.

[37] Ibid.

bloodline: a new, broader relationship based on listening to the Word of God and the accomplishment of his will (Luke 8:21; Matt. 12:50; Heb. 4:12).

The personally experienced mercy of God should transform Africans, to the point that it makes them, if they agree to cooperate with the grace from God, the agent of divine mercy toward those who do him harm (Matt. 6:12; Mark 11:25). The example of Christ on the cross and of St. Stephen forgiving his executioners shows the way of being church-as-family of God, where the availability and exercise of forgiveness has no limits (Matt. 18:21–22).

The fight against evil is meant to ensure that Christ, Light of the World and Salt of the Earth, Force and Food, Word and Bread of life, is welcomed by each and all, in all the Basic Ecclesial Communities (BECs). It is important that the Word of God is at the center of the awareness-raising efforts of Africans toward reflection and debate on social issues, also making use of Catholic social doctrine and papal messages.[38]

The church-as-family of God in Africa will work with all authorities—the political and governmental, public bodies, private authorities, traditional leaders, NGOs, and community-based associations—in maintaining social justice and promoting the common good. The church-as-family of God in Africa will have to study and suggest "restorative justice as a means and a process to promote reconciliation, justice and peace, and reintegration in the communities of victims and offenders."[39] In the name of the same belonging to the bloodline of Christ, the baptized living in oppressive African countries should show concrete gestures of solidarity worthy of those who live in Christ toward victims of neoliberal capitalism and political corruption.

Conscious of his Christian dignity, the baptized African should approach, head on, the fate of the despised and marginalized, whoever they are and wherever they come from, without limiting himself to his own family, his ethnic group, or even less, to his country. For the baptized African, it will be about setting in motion the fundamental option of the *Sequela Christi* by making his own life a path for others to participate in the construction of his nation and in the strengthening of the church-family of God in Africa.

Theological Approach to Suffering as Related to HIV

The dual challenge in the pursuit of victory over HIV and AIDS lies in overcoming the errors and lies of the past, to be able to consider the ministry and role of people living with HIV, as well as the duty of families and the entire

---

[38] See Synodes des évêques, *IIème Assemblée spéciale pour l'Afrique. L'Église en Afrique au service de la réconciliation, de la justice et de la paix "Vous êtes le sel de la terre . . . Vous êtes la lumière du monde" (Matt. 5,13.14). Lineamenta* (Cité du Vatican: 2006), no. 56.

[39] *Africae Munus*, nos. 81, 83.

community. The church-as-family of God will always be a place of welcome and support, compassion and education, fight and victory over the painful experience of physical, moral, and mental harm. With the active presence of its members, it will convey the compassion of Christ to people in need. In all this, the church-as-family of God will be a supportive educator, a companion to those who carry the burden of HIV by being an example of the active and compassionate presence of Christ.

African Theology of HIV and AIDS: A Theology of the Cross

Wilfrid Okambawa has already shown how the theology of HIV and AIDS, which is a theology of the cross, continues, in its African version, on its path in the theological disciplines, including ethics; a biblical, pastoral ecclesiology; and spirituality.[40] On a moral level, the identification of Jesus with human suffering and the biblical teaching of the *imago Dei* can help overcome stigma, because AIDS cannot undermine human dignity. Indeed, human dignity is an inherent quality for each human being; a quality whose value is not a factor of any sociohistorical contingency. A pastoral ministry that takes into account traditional religions and values becomes closer to man—to comfort and to help manage anger, despair, anguish, fear, and refusal of patients. If spirituality overcomes suffering, even without taking it away, it also cultivates hope of liberating from the fear of death.

A good interpretation of the Bible can avoid a view of AIDS as a divine punishment. The church, rich in the dialogue between the Holy Scriptures and Christian tradition, becomes the place of a strong and inventive solidarity toward the sick and the rejected of society. Ecclesial solidarity toward the sick and the poor would allow for the realization of how much the passion, the cross, and the death of Jesus lead to the resurrection, crown of Christian faith and hope.

Ministry of People Living with HIV

Supported by the entire Christian local community and their families, people living with HIV should be helped to see HIV and AIDS as a test, a "difficult time when the body is diminished, and where one finds it difficult to hope. The real being is revealed, like gold in the furnace, but the test will end."[41]

---

[40] See Wilfrid Okambawa, "African HIV/AIDS Theology toward a Holistic Approach to the HIV/AIDS Issue," in *AIDS, 30 Years Down the Line: Faith-Based Reflections about the Epidemic in Africa* (Nairobi: Paulines Publications Africa, 2012), 335–48.

[41] John Paul II, "La compassion aide les malades à vaincre le désespoir et à garder courage," in *Insegnamenti di Giovanni Paolo II*, vol. 13/2 (LEV, 1990), 492.

Jesus Christ is always with them, to support them with his grace and give them courage and strength (Matt. 28:20; Acts 18:10; John 14:18–23) to participate, in their own way, in the life of the city.

Because grace and mercy are offered to us by Christ's suffering, each of the persons living with AIDS is also called "to participate in the suffering, through which the redemption was accomplished."[42] To pray and intercede for one's self, one's family, those who may fall into the trap of HIV because of the lightness of morals and wrong sexual behavior, one also has to participate in awareness raising by testifying. John Paul II indicated that people living with HIV have an important role to play in the vital struggle for the good of their own country and invited them at the same time to offer their suffering in union with Christ for their siblings who are at risk.[43]

Action Plan of the African Church against HIV and AIDS

> Through Christ and in Christ, the riddles of sorrow and death ... On the cross stands the "Redeemer of man," the Man of Sorrows who has taken upon himself the physical and moral sufferings of men of all time, so they can find in love the salvific meaning of their sorrow and valid answers to all their questions.[44]

The text adopted in Dakar by the bishops of Africa in 2003 marks a turning point in the effective participation of the church-as-family of God in the fight against HIV.[45] Not only does this document emphasize solidarity with the victims, it is also accompanied by an action plan with fifteen concrete, achievable commitments to overcome discrimination, facilitate access to health care, and educate the Christian people. Most African bishops have courageously chosen a comprehensive, full, and concrete approach toward HIV and AIDS by opting for a ministry of closeness and competence, materially and spiritually supporting people infected and affected by the pandemic in hospitals, clinics, and Catholic care centers and chaplaincies—offering visits and specific support attendance, schooling of orphans, and advocating for effective and accessible treatment for all.

---

[42] John Paul II, Lettre apostolique *Salvifici Doloris*, sur le sens chrétien de la souffrance humaine (Vatican: LEV, 1984), nos. 19, 29, 30, 31.

[43] John Paul II, "Le fléau du SIDA, un défi pour tous," in *Insegnamenti di Giovanni Paolo II*, vol. 16/1 (LEV, 1993), 336.

[44] *Salvifici Doloris*, no. 31.

[45] See *Les Évêques Catholiques d'Afrique et de Madagascar brisent le tabou et parlent du VIH/SIDA* (Kinshasa: Médias Paul, 2005).

Family, school, and other training institutions should work, in synergy and with perseverance, toward the awakening and refinement of sensitivity toward one's neighbor and his suffering. To educate the human heart for compassion, true love, self-giving, and sacrifice is, ultimately, to reach out to the suffering of others.[46]

The prevention of wars by an effective system of conflict management is another challenge that African countries and the local churches in Africa have for showing their pastoral creativity. Human sciences, psychology and sociology in particular, have already demonstrated the utility of conflict in social and human development and their unavoidable presence in the heart of any free society. The church-as-family-of-God ought to find methods to manage normal conflicts without them being transformed into violent and armed conflicts. "Only a cooperative relationship that seeks neither to find responsible nor guilty nor a victim in the conflict is a method to manage conflicts without getting into the field of war."[47] This is the lateral approach, which focuses more on the needs and fears of each party, and grants them the right to have these needs and fears, rather than seeking the wrongs and reasons of both parties.

Beyond the courage to denounce the evils that plague the continent, local churches ought to propose concrete solutions and get involved with other social constituencies to prompt the transformation of social structures and promote the common good of all. The church through its community should do so by emphasizing evangelical values of solidarity, dialogue, service, promotion of life and love, protection of property and individuals, and the responsibility of each person in the integral development of all, starting with the less fortunate.[48]

Conclusion

This chapter has demonstrated how violent conflicts and wars contribute to an increased vulnerability to HIV and thus its spread. A credible fight against such a complex pandemic must succeed in combating those who seek to exploit Africa, whether they are outside or inside the continent. The cessation of hostilities must allow a truce, even a symbolic one, to allow mutual forgiveness and reconciliation.

The theological, spiritual, and pastoral vision of the church-as-family of God—rooted in the Trinity, illuminated by the Word of God, and strength-

---

[46] *Salvifici Doloris*, no. 29.

[47] Jacques Poujol, "Le conflit: définition, nature, importance," November 8, 2004, www. relation-aide.com. Cf. Ac 6 sur la gestion du premier conflit dans l'Église par l'apôtre Pierre.

[48] Francis Appiah-Kubi, *L'Église famille de Dieu. Un chemin pour les Églises d'Afrique* (Paris: Karthala, 2008), 231.

ened and led toward the existential peripheries[49] by the Holy Spirit—must bring about the good news of peace, true joy, and new life received from Christ. Through the BECs the fight against the pandemic will be possible through an empowering awareness-raising approach that calls for real change in behavior and shared caring for the sick and those orphaned by AIDS. In addition to the inculturation of the good news of Christ, the African Church will substantially contribute to an effective fight against cultural practices that favor the spread of the virus. These practices include female genital mutilation, early and forced marriages, and levirate marriage that ignores serology. No effort will be spared in therapeutic and pharmaceutical research, both modern and traditional (pharmacopoeia), and in accessibility to effective care for all, to be able to defeat the virus.

In dialogue with social institutions, the church can contribute to conflict prevention efforts through peace education, constructive dialogue, and training and information that move individuals and social actors out of ignorance. The goal should be to train church institutions and movements in conflict prevention and peace promotion, in such a way that they become agents of God's love, placing human needs at the center of any ecclesial endeavor. The Justice and Peace Commission in dioceses and parishes could contribute greatly both to nonviolent conflict management and to restoring peace through forgiveness and reconciliation.[50]

In this sense, the church-as-family of God in Africa will truthfully inspire and support the political players, NGOs, and all persons of goodwill who are seriously committed to the victory against the pandemic.

---

[49] See *Evangelii Gaudium*, nos. 20–24.
[50] See *Ecclesia in Africa*, no. 46.

CHAPTER 28

AIDS, NATIONAL SECURITY, AND POLITICAL LEADERSHIP IN SUB-SAHARAN AFRICA

Evelyn Namakula Mayanja

Sub-Saharan Africa has the world's largest number of people infected with and affected by HIV.[1] It is also the region most affected by armed conflicts, poverty, and social injustices, all of which contribute to HIV transmission. Religious organizations play significant roles in prevention and caring for, treating, and supporting the infected and affected. The Ecumenical HIV and AIDS Initiative in Africa plays a leading role in transforming theological thinking and mainstreaming AIDS in theological education. An important element overlooked by theologians and the entire church in the colossal battle against the impasse is the need to strengthen stewardship, political leadership, and security. In Africa, the quality of the person at the helm of society is more important than in nations with developed political systems and economies.

I argue in this chapter that unless this leadership deficit and insecurity are viewed as contributing factors to the pandemic and strategies are formed to strengthen stewardship leadership and national security, the AIDS pandemic will continue to escalate. Countries with positive interventions toward AIDS are those with stewardship leadership and the political will for national security. The chapter uses an interdisciplinary approach to address the issues of HIV and AIDS, political leadership, and national security. The conceptual framework includes governance, security, and social ethics, with principles from Catholic social doctrine: the common good, solidarity, and subsidiarity.

Africa has borne the burden of AIDS for decades. The UNAIDS July 2014 Report on HIV and AIDS noted that 24.7 million out of 35 million people infected worldwide are in sub-Saharan Africa.[2] The impasse has devastating socioeconomic, political, and security effects. HIV is aggravated by armed conflict, poverty, and policy makers' lack of respect for human rights and

---

[1] Unless otherwise noted, "Africa" is used in reference to sub-Saharan Africa.

[2] A UNAIDS report shows that 19 million of the 35 million people living with HIV today do not know that they have the virus (www.unAIDS.org).

dignity. The Second African Synod of Bishops noted that "Africa is the most hit" by "tragic situations of refugees, abject poverty, disease and hunger."[3] These conditions "are largely due to human decisions and activities by people who have no regard for the common good and this often through a tragic complicity and criminal conspiracy of local leaders and foreign interests."[4]

Faith-based organizations' (FBOs) interventions for prevention and the care, education, and treatment of the infected and affected are making remarkable strides. FBOs care for Christ's metaphorical body, the church, and the eschatological body of the whole of humanity—the entire creation that is groaning for physical, spiritual, and social healing and liberation (Rom. 8:22–23). From the perspective of the Church's preferential option for the poor, health care is fundamental as a civil and political right, and as a continuation of Christ's mission for all to have fullness of life. During the Second African Synod, the bishops noted, "The Church is second to none in the fight against HIV/AIDS."[5] An element overlooked by theologians and priestly and religious leaders who minister to those impacted by AIDS is the irreplaceable importance of strengthening ethical, principled, steward-based leadership and national security.

Progress in the war against AIDS requires breaking the silence against the intersectionality of AIDS with the approach to leadership and security that characterize church preaching and education. What holds Africa back and contributes to intensifying AIDS is "lack of principled, ethical leadership"[6] that cares for the common good, people's well-being, and security. This element of Africa's liberation theology must not remain a monopoly of the theologians, but must become popular theology to ensure that Africans from all walks of life recognize and seriously embrace the challenge of leadership to fight AIDS and other ills that beset the continent. Katongole Emmanuel wonders what "liberation in Africa would look like in the face of HIV/AIDS" and suggests the usage of "interruption" rather than "liberation."[7]

National security and peace must not be limited to the "absence of war," a currency that politicians use to solicit votes: "If you do not vote for me, the country will return to war," and the civilian response is, "The devil you know is better. . . . At least we can sleep." How do we sleep peacefully when our neighbors, loved ones, and those who serve our nations are perishing with AIDS?

---

[3] *Second Special Assembly for Africa of the Synod of Bishops*, art. 4.
[4] Ibid., art. 5.
[5] Ibid., art. 30.
[6] Maathai Wangari, *The Challenge for Africa* (New York: Pantheon Books, 2009), 25.
[7] Emmanuel Katongole, "AIDS in Africa, the Church, and the Politics of Interruption," in *Heil und Befreiung in Afrika. Missionswissenschaft und Dialog der Religionen*, ed. F. D'Sa and Jurgen Lohmayer (Würzburg: Echter Verlag, 2007), 168.

True peace and security are devoid of structural[8] and cultural violence,[9] which perpetuate the abuse of women and contribute to the scourge of HIV and AIDS. The traditional concept of national security was based on how states use force to curb threats to territorial integrity and domestic political order.[10] However, the militaristic approach to security predominant in the Cold War epoch is too narrow to understand contemporary security challenges[11] that emanate from within the state, including social, political, economic, and environmental issues. Africa is grappling with both the old and new security challenges.

In this chapter I argue that unless AIDS is viewed as a security threat—and the deficit of leadership and national security viewed as contributing factors to the pandemic, with strategies created to strengthen leadership and national security—the AIDS crisis will continue to escalate with further devastating repercussions. The deficit of principled, ethical, steward-based, and responsible leadership that cares for citizens' well-being is one of the obstacles hampering Africa's progress and the implementation of preventive and curative interventions. Equally, African nations need to create comprehensive, robust, and effective security policies and frameworks that guarantee citizens' safety. Such strategic frameworks need to address structural and geopolitical elements beyond military prowess.

Although African nations share many similarities, they are different in terms of governance, national leadership, culture, history, and education, elements that affect the spread and prevention of HIV. Subsequently, there are variations in how the HIV epidemic affects the continent, ranging from high- to least-concentration nations. Also, the responses to the impasse vary, ranging from intense interventions to denial of HIV's existence or denial of medical treatment, to consulting witch doctors in the belief that one who gets the disease is bewitched or has sinned in relation to some biblical passages (Mark 2:1–10).

The chapter is divided into three parts. The first part discusses the securitization of AIDS. The second explores AIDS, leadership, and governance. The third section attempts to embrace the whole predicament of AIDS, national security, and leadership and to suggest possible interventions.

---

[8] Johan Galtung, "Violence, Peace, and Peace Research," *Journal of Peace Research* 6, no. 3 (1969): 167–91.

[9] Johan Galtung, "Cultural Violence," *Journal of Peace Research* 27, no. 3 (1990): 291–305.

[10] Kanti Bajpai, "Human Security: Concept and Measurement," Kroc Institute Occasional Paper #19:OP:1, August 2000, www.hegoa.ehu.es/.

[11] Barry Buzan, *People, States, and Fear: An Agenda for International Security Studies in the Post–Cold War Era* (Boulder, CO: Lynne Rienner, 1991).

Securitizing HIV and AIDS

There is a dilemma as to whether HIV and AIDS should be considered a matter of national security,[12] because including every threat to human security under national security risks losing the meaning and the need for strict categorization.[13] MacFarlane and Khong do not consider "natural disasters, accidents, diseases such as HIV/AIDS or SARS, and economic privation"[14] as national security threats.

What constitutes national security and threats to it? What is not a security issue? By the middle of the twenty-first century, the HIV and AIDS pandemic was securitized with the UN Security Council's January 2000 meeting on HIV and AIDS in Africa and the subsequent passing of Resolution 1308. The securitization process occurs when an issue is taken beyond the realm of merely political discourses because it presents an existential threat to nations suffering from it.[15] In Africa's security landscape, AIDS is a grave national security threat in reference to legitimate security claims: uniformed militaries, including peacekeepers, are vulnerable to AIDS and may act as agents in spreading it; state stability is at risk where AIDS is prevalent; and conflict and postconflict phases create significant risks for spreading the virus.[16]

While Africa is embroiled in armed conflicts with implications for AIDS, not all Christian formation and higher education curriculums have embraced Musa W. Dube's insights for engaging education with the paradigm of shattered dreams.[17] The intersectionality of AIDS and Africa's shattered dreams for health, security, and peace is not yet conjectured. How contextualized are those curriculums? AIDS cannot be eradicated without leadership and "growth-enhancing governance"[18] that will not only restrain institutions but also transform them to guarantee human security, eradicate poverty, and reconstruct sustainable peace. What must Africa do to move forward? How effective are the current interventions?

---

[12] Stefan Elbe, "Should HIV/AIDS Be Securitized? The Ethical Dilemmas of Linking HIV/AIDS and Security," *International Studies Quarterly* 50, no. 1 (2006): 119–44.

[13] S. Neil MacFarlane and Khong Yuen Foong, *Human Security and the UN: A Critical History* (Bloomington: Indiana University Press, 2006).

[14] Ibid., 257.

[15] Barry Buzan, Ole Wäver, and Jaap De Wilde, *Security: A New Framework for Analysis* (Boulder, CO: Lynne Rienner, 1998).

[16] Colin McInnes and Simon Rushton, "HIV/AIDS and Securitization Theory," *European Journal of International Relations* 19 (2012): 122.

[17] Musa W. Dube, *The HIV and AIDS Bible: Selected Essays* (Scranton, PA: University of Scranton Press, 2006).

[18] Noman Akbar and Joseph E. Stiglitz, "Strategies for African Development," in *Good Growth and Governance in Africa: Rethinking Development Strategies*, ed. N. Akbar, B. Kwesi, H. Stein, and E. J. Stiglitz (Oxford: Oxford University Press, 2012), 3–50.

For more than three decades, AIDS has interrupted our lives, and we continue to live "under the paradigms of shattered dreams."[19] Life in Africa is short—threatened by disease, armed conflicts, injustices, poverty, violence, and gender and ethnic discrimination. National and international annual figures of the infected and the dead are given. We risk getting used to them. Yet behind every number is a human person who was created in God's image and likeness. AIDS-associated problems are more complex than just numbers. While we may have the moral imagination—"the capacity to imagine something rooted in the challenges of the real world yet capable of giving birth to that which does not yet exist"[20]—we are not yet at the end of the tunnel to see the light clearly. More strategic, creative thinking and implementation are still needed. Governments must complement FBOs' efforts and church endeavors. While some political leaders are engaged in fighting AIDS, "The linkage between public health and national security has so far been missing."[21]

Resources to prevent and address AIDS infections are wanting in national budgets, compared with resources for other government priority areas. For example, the Stockholm International Peace Research Institute (SIPRI) data on military expenditure for the 1988–2011 period indicate huge expenditures by African nations,[22] while only six nations achieved the 2001 Africa Union (AU) commitment to the Abuja Declaration of allocating 15 percent of the annual budget to the health sector.[23] Governments that allocate high proportions of their national gross domestic product (GDP) to military expenditure do so at the expense of the poor, who are denied health care, education, and food.

AIDS is inextricably linked to other factors that affect families and communities. Africa has millions of AIDS and war orphans, with households headed by children as young as twelve years of age. Dogs and cats in developed nations live in better conditions and are more adequately fed than many African children, who struggle for daily nourishment and receive no medical care. Even with universal education, these children lack the required scholastic materials, are left to scavenge in garbage, and become targets for sexual abuse, trafficking, and recruitment into rebel groups.

---

[19] Emmanuel Katongole, "Embodied and Embodying Hermeneutics of Life in the Academy: Musa W. Dube's HIV/AIDS Work," SBL Forum, sbl-site.org/.

[20] John Paul Lederach, *The Moral Imagination: The Art and Soul of Building Peace* (Oxford: Oxford University Press, 2005), ix.

[21] Harley Feldbaum, Lee Kelley, and Patel Preeti, "The National Security Implications of HIV/AIDS," *PLOS Medicine* 3, no. 6 (2006): 0774.

[22] Stockholm International Peace Research Institute (SIPRI) military expenditure data, 1988–2011.

[23] "Delivering Results toward Ending AIDS, Tuberculosis, and Malaria in Africa: African Union Accountability Report on Africa–G8 Partnership Commitments" (2013), 25, www.unAIDS.org/.

What does it mean for a nation to have hundreds or thousands of disenfranchised children and youth with no care, education, and economic security? How will the orphans on the streets be educated and trained to become responsible citizens and future parents? What security challenges does this predicament pose? The 2000 U.S. National Intelligence Council Report concluded that a third of children under fifteen in the hardest-hit countries constitute a "lost orphaned generation" with little or no hope of educational or employment opportunities. These nations risk "further economic decay, increased crime, and political instability as such young people become radicalized or are exploited by various political groups for their own ends."[24] Due to poverty, unemployment, lack of opportunity, and an unpromising future, Africa's youth are running away, often to perish in the waters of the Mediterranean Sea. The UNHCR estimates that between July 1 and September 30, 2014, 165,000 people "ran away" from the miseries in Africa, and 2,200 never made it safely. Sadly, this trend is increasing, as in 2013, only 60,000 people "ran away" from Africa. The Mediterranean waters are becoming an African cemetery. Can a country or continent develop when its youth are not empowered? The same youth are further exposed to HIV.

Parents who would have lived longer to raise their children have no access to antiretroviral medicines and other supplies necessary for their conditions. The same conundrum applies to pregnant mothers' lack of access to medicines that would prevent transmission of the virus from mother to child. Some cannot even access hospitals due to poor roads, insecurity, or their simple absence. In conflict zones and refugee and internally displaced camps, mass rape of girls and women (and boys and men) is a major contributor to AIDS transmission. Violence against women is a structural cultural violence that increases their susceptibility to HIV.[25] Women are also more exposed to HIV infection due to cultural practices that propagate gender inequality, such as widow inheritance, early marriages, and polygamy. One can also add feminization of poverty as a key factor in HIV's spread. Poorer and marginalized women have less power to negotiate their reproductive rights, let alone the ability to insist on safe sex. Threats to women risk crippling societies for generations. Thus, "'Security' must be redefined to mean the satisfaction of human needs, including comprehensive safety for women."[26]

Of the 21.2 million people in Africa eligible for antiretroviral therapy in 2013 under the 2013 WHO guidelines, only 7.6 million people were receiving

---

[24] Environmental Change and Security, "National Intelligence Estimate: The Global Infectious Disease Threat and Its Implications for the United States" (project report), issue 6 (2000): 61.

[25] World Health Organization, "Gender Inequalities and HIV 2008," www.who.int.

[26] Cynthia Cockburn, "War and Security, Women and Gender: An Overview of the Issue," *Gender and Development* 21, no. 3 (2013): 433.

HIV treatment as of December 2012.[27] UNAIDS' Treatment 2015 Initiative targeted 15 million people living with HIV to have access to ARVs by 2015.[28] It cannot be overstated that the African Union, the United Nations, and the global community must redirect attention to making ARVs free and readily accessible. While treatment is crucial, the wounds and trauma of AIDS are very deep in Africa. It is a tragedy that we can hardly "understand in biomedical terms, but a wound that reveals an underlying sense of disorder and decay."[29] In the words of Ivan Illich, "It is time to state clearly that specific situations and circumstances are 'sickening' rather than people themselves are sick," thus pointing to disorders and systems that are entrenched in society, beyond the "symptoms which modern medicine attempts to treat."[30]

Addressing systemic injustices and structural violence is vital to the fight against AIDS. What political, security, economic, and psychological challenges do African nations face when parents, professionals, medical and security personnel, politicians, economists, and researchers inter alia are lost to the pandemic? AIDS prevalence among leaders, military elites, and middle-class groups intensify the political power struggle and control for resources, which in turn stifles effective governance and economic and political progress.[31] For such reasons I argue for engaging and challenging the Realpolitik of leadership and national security. While the church acts as a "'spiritual solvent' of social crises," with bishops' national conferences passing communiques and pastoral letters "in which they vociferously express their opinions on a wide range of socioeconomic and political issues,"[32] more than thirty years of grappling with the impasse call for further strategizing and expedient responses. The Second African Synod proposition 51 acknowledges that AIDS "is an issue of integral development and justice, which requires a holistic approach and response by the Church." The approach requires a political response that involves advocacy and a struggle with those who wield political power.

Historians understood long ago the deleterious implications of epidemic disease on the security of nations and communities. William McNeill argues,

---

[27] UNAIDS, "Access to Antiretroviral Therapy in Africa: Status Report on Progress toward the 2015 Target," www.unAIDS.org/.

[28] UNAIDS, "Treatment 2015" (2014), 1–44, www.unAIDS.org/.

[29] Katongole, "AIDS in Africa," 172.

[30] Ivan Illich, "Brave New Biocracy: Health Care from Womb to Tomb," *New Perspectives Quarterly* 11, no. 1 (Winter 1994): 10.

[31] David E. Bloom and Ajay S. Mahal, "Does the AIDS Epidemic Threaten Economic Growth?" *Journal of Econometrics* 77, no. 1 (1995): 105–24.

[32] Agbonkhianmeghe Orobator, *From Crisis to Kairos: The Mission of the Church in the Time of HIV/AIDS, Refugees, and Poverty* (Nairobi: Paulines Publications Africa, 2005), 14.

The disruptive effect of such an epidemic is likely to be greater than the mere loss of life, severe as that may be. Often survivors are demoralized and lose all faith in inherited custom and belief which had not prepared them for such a disaster. Population losses within the twenty-to-forty age bracket are obviously far more damaging to the society at large than comparably numerous destruction of the very young or the very old. Indeed, any community that loses a significant percentage of its young adults in a single epidemic finds it hard to maintain itself materially and spiritually. . . . The structural cohesion of the community is almost certain to collapse.[33]

AIDS, Leadership, and Governance

There is a strong empirical association between AIDS, leadership, and governance.[34] The leadership and governance crisis in Africa contributes to the pandemic, and in return, AIDS worsens leadership and governance. Unethical, ineffective leadership and governance are critical challenges given that, in Africa, the men or women at the helm of society control the running of the state. Yet there is a disconnect between citizens, the leaders, and state institutions. The state-citizen gap runs deep, and the sense of belonging to a nation and being protected from threats, including threats to health, is inconceivable. Inequality, government ineffectiveness, corruption, dysfunctional institutions, and shoddy or nonexistent public services are the reality for the majority, different from that of the governing elites, who seek medical treatment abroad. With stewardship and effective and ethical leadership, the corruption that swindles both from the drugs and foreign aid for ARVs would be curtailed.[35] The resources spent on medical care abroad would be invested in bolstering domestic health-care systems.

Corruption illustrates a lack of empathy toward the needs and sufferings of others. Self-centered seeking of one's interest transgresses the principle of the common good. Political philosophy's history, as old as Plato's *Republic*, alludes to leaders ruling not for personal interests but in the interest of those whom they rule.[36] The same ideas pervade in Aristotle's *The Politics*,[37] Aquinas's *On*

---

[33] William McNeill, *Plagues and Peoples* (New York: Doubleday, 1976), 61.

[34] Alex de Waal, "Reframing Governance, Security, and Conflict in the Light of HIV/AIDS: A Synthesis of Findings from the AIDS, Security, and Conflict Initiative," *Social Science and Medicine* 70, no. 1 (2010): 114–20.

[35] Roger Bate, "Africa's Epidemic of Disappearing Medicine," *Foreign Policy* 11 (January 2011), www.foreignpolicy.com.

[36] Plato, *Republic*, trans. G. M. A. Grube (Indianapolis: Hackett, 1992).

[37] Aristotle, *The Politics*, rev. ed., trans. T. A. Sinclair (New York: Penguin, 1981).

Kingship,[38] and even Machiavelli's *Discourses*.[39] All distinguish good from bad leadership by whether it advances the interests of the ruler or the ruled. In *The Prince*, Machiavelli justifies "acting meanly towards the few" as necessary for acting generously towards the vast majority."[40] Contemporary leadership scholars differentiate between leaders and power wielders by defining leadership in terms of meeting the common good.[41] Nation-states are responsible for delivering essential political goods to the citizens, including "safety and security; rule of law and transparency; participation and respect for human rights, sustainable economic opportunity and human development."[42]

A popular adage holds that "Africa is cursed by her resources." As the Angolan journalist Rafael Marques stated, however, "It's fashionable to say that we are cursed by our mineral riches. That's not true. We are cursed by our leaders . . . because they are killing us for money. They are our CEOs of war"[43] and disease. The fight against AIDS necessitates war against corruption and unethical leadership. Having grown accustomed to corruption, ineffective leadership, and structural violence, the African Church risks considering these practices as normal. How far is the African Church disassociated from corruption and structural injustice? That is why the challenge of AIDS cannot be overcome only by the acts of mercy and compassion, without engaging politics and economic policies but also "cleaning house." To provide real hope, the church must not only condemn corruption but also dissociate from corrupt officials' gifts. Soliciting and accepting corrupted funds risks condoning the vice. Thus, the AIDS pandemic is a *kairos* moment that invites the church not only to serve Christ in the poor (Matt. 25:31–46) or to be good Samaritans (Luke 10:25–37), but also a revelation to the church of her weakness, "an interruption in a social history marked by illusions of power and self-sufficiency."[44]

The African Union recognizes the importance of a political commitment to AIDS and the need for good leadership to "take personal responsibility and provide leadership for the activities of the National AIDS Commissions/

[38] Thomas Aquinas, "On Kingship, to the King of Cyprus," in *Classics of Moral and Political Theory*, ed. M. L. Morgan (Indianapolis: Hackett, 1981), 397–99.

[39] Niccolo Machiavelli, "Discourses on the Ten Books of Titus Livius," in Morgan, *Classics of Moral and Political Theory*, 397–99.

[40] Niccolo Machiavelli, *The Prince*, ed. Q. Skinner and R. Price (Cambridge: Cambridge University Press, 1988).

[41] MacGregor J. Burns, *Leadership* (New York: Harper and Row, 1978), 56.

[42] Robert I. Rotberg, *Africa Emerges: Consummate Challenges, Abundant Opportunities* (Malden, MA: Polity Press, 2013), 174.

[43] Paul Salopek, "CEOs of War Bleed Angola," *Chicago Tribune*, April 2, 2000, www.pulitzer.org.

[44] Katongole, "AIDS in Africa," 174–75.

Councils"[45] by inspiring, motivating, and creating supportive environments for action. The MDGs Progress Reports—Africa[46] identifies some improvement on health, with concerns that progress could be stifled by political instability, natural or man-made disasters and armed conflict. Ineffective leadership contributes to man-made disasters, such as the embezzlement of funds for ARVs and exposing civilians to death. Do government leaders trust the local health systems? If so, why do the leaders seek treatment abroad when they are sick? Africa is still engaged in primitive, selfish accumulation that hampers the development of public services. While the majority poor fail to obtain the basic right of medical care, education, and housing, those in public service will never rest until they own mansions in different nations and have huge offshore bank accounts. Such public servants do not qualify to be leaders.

Embracing the Predicament:
AIDS, National Security, and Leadership

The fabric of Africa's society has changed with HIV and AIDS, necessitating a broadening of the discussion about the pandemic to include people from all levels of society. The liberation and interruption that the tragedy poses calls for concreteness, forging a strategy with the marginalized, the oppressed, the infected, and the affected. AIDS dehumanizes humanity on the African continent, including for those who make policies without considering AIDS as a tragedy. How do we develop authentic, effective, ethical, and stewardship leadership? How do nations ensure national security amid devastating diseases, deadly war, and underdevelopment? A blueprint? An ideology? The discourse that the church has nothing to do with politics and secular matters still lingers among politicians, journalists, and even scholars. Forgotten is the fact that church members are citizens with equal rights and responsibilities to participate in the decisions pertaining to their nation's well-being. According to *Gaudium et Spes*, the church "has the right to pass moral judgments even on matters touching the political order, whenever basic personal rights, or the salvation of souls make such judgment necessary,[47] in accordance with the signs of the time. More than ever, the church needs to play the advocacy role as "an expert in humanity"[48] and apply the gospel and Catholic social teaching in real-life experiences. Mother Teresa, a hero to millions, used to say to her admirers, "Find your own Calcutta," which could be interpreted to mean that wherever

---

[45] "Delivering Results toward Ending AIDS," 23.
[46] *The MDG Report 2014: Assessing Progress in Africa toward the Millennium Development Goals* (Addis Ababa: Economic Commission for Africa, October 2014), www.undp.org/.
[47] Second Vatican Council, *Gaudium et Spes*, no. 76.
[48] John Paul II, *Sollicitudo rei Socialis*, no. 41.

you find yourself, seize the opportunity for social involvement and work for justice. To this effect, I suggest the following as basic interventions for dealing with the challenges of AIDS, national security, and leadership.

The starting point is the *promotion of the common good*—"the sum total of those conditions of social living, whereby men (and women) are enabled more and more to achieve their perfection."[49] It is empowering people to have life to the full (John 10:10), to thrive and not just to "survive."[50] Education is one of those means that contribute to thriving. During the slave-trade era in the United States, it was illegal to teach a slave how to read and write. Why? Quality education liberates people. The question arises whether Africa's education systems as to whether they liberate learners from oppression or enhance enslavement to AIDS and other structural injustices. Education is key to motivate the oppressed: "to be able to wage the struggle for their liberation, they must perceive the reality of oppression not as a closed world from which there is no exit, but as a limiting situation which they can transform."[51] It is crucial that AIDS and peace become key components in the education curricula, the seminary, and religious formation.

Second is *advocacy for human security as a prerequisite for national security*. According to the United Nations Development Programme,

> Human security is a child who did not die, a disease that did not spread, a job that was not cut, an ethnic tension that did not explode in violence, a dissident who was not silenced. Human security is not a concern with weapons—it is a concern with human life and dignity.[52]

Third is *transforming leadership from being a source of personal aggrandizement to serving people's social, political, economic, and moral development interest*. Presumably, leaders should be at the self-actualization level of Maslow's hierarchy of needs and, through life examples, invite and inspire others to higher levels of motivation and morality. AIDS will persist as long as we have leaders who consider the national treasury as their private property and the nation as a personal business. To this effect, the church's mission in response to the signs of the time must include training leaders. Addressing the enormity of Africa's problems requires a continent-wide think-tank of well-motivated, enlightened individuals with different expertise, inclusive of gender, ethnic group, and polit-

---

[49] John XXIII, *Mater et Magistra*, no. 65.

[50] "Called to Be a Good Samaritan," Message of the 15th AMECEA Plenary Assembly (Mukono, Lugazi, June 10, 2005), 143–44.

[51] Paulo Freire, *Pedagogy of the Oppressed* (New York: Continuum, 2010), 49.

[52] UNDP, *Human Development Report: New Dimensions of Human Security* (New York: United Nations, 1994), 226.

ical and religious affiliation. Many young professionals and talented people on the African continent need guidance and opportunities for making a difference in leadership. Traditional institutions—formal schools, political parties, and religious organizations—do not have the flexibility and innovative spirit that these young people require.

Fourth is the *urgent need for civic education.* Africa's population must learn their civil, political, and economic rights and responsibilities enshrined in every African state bill of rights and demand service and accountability from the leaders. Catholic social teaching places these rights at the heart of political and economic life,[53] and it is inherent that they be implemented by the church. Respect for every person's rights and dignity is the surest way to peace on earth. Without a people-centered approach and ensuring that those affected and infected by the epidemic are involved in devising solutions, even in the post-2015 era we risk not going far.

Fifth is *solidarity as a central virtue of social life that enhances interdependence.*[54] We are still faced with the challenge of faith doing justice. The experience of Rwanda in 1994 rings in our ears with unimaginable suffering in our hearts on how believers hacked each other with machetes. Those who empty the national coffers and go as far as stealing the ARVs are not alien to the church.

Sixth is *subsidiarity, empowering and educating people to do what they can for themselves.* Also involved is allowing subsidiary organizations to carry out certain programs and not rely only on the top institutions. This is where FBOs' and NGOs' roles are crucial to render humanizing services and not to control people.

Seventh is *women's empowerment,* which deserves a critical consideration beyond feminist advocacy. Women are not given sufficient space to exercise their leadership roles. Even in countries like Rwanda and Uganda, where female representation in politics is significant, the predicament of grassroots women is pathetic. Without women's active involvement in leadership and policy formulation, the struggle against HIV and AIDS will not succeed. Women form more than half of Africa's population and are most affected by HIV. If women are more than half of every community, are they not also more than half of every solution?

Conclusion

The link between AIDS, national security, and political leadership in Africa suggests real and potentially significant threats to national, regional, continental, and global security, necessitating strategizing and engagement with

---

[53] John XXIII, *Pacem in Terris* (Washington, DC: US Conference of Catholic Bishops, 2003), 225.

[54] John Paul II, *Laborem Exercens, Sollicitudo rei Socialis,* and *Centesimus Annus.*

Realpolitik. Africa is affected by armed conflicts, poverty, and social injustices that contribute to HIV transmission. Religious organizations play significant roles in the fight against the pandemic. Theologians and all those involved in church efforts need to consider strengthening steward-based political leadership and national security as serious factors in eradicating the pandemic.

Part Seven

Pastoral Initiatives

CHAPTER 29

METHODOLOGICAL CHALLENGES
IN TIMES OF AIDS AND PASTORAL
REFLECTION IN CÔTE D'IVOIRE

Fabien Yedo

Côte d'Ivoire, a sub-Saharan country, continues to bear a disproportionate share of the burden of HIV and AIDS on both the African and the global scale. Indeed, since 2001, 40 percent of hospital beds in the main port city of Abidjan were occupied by patients with HIV and AIDS, with the cumulative number of people who died of AIDS put at 420,000.[1] The epidemiological situation of Côte d'Ivoire highlights the dire individual and social implications of the epidemic. The major question that comes up here is, What do we do with our lives? Our lives depend on our health, which in an African paradigm is subject to a kind of fluctuation, like a natural barometer that oscillates between disease and vigor, in order to establish a balance that is physical, moral, mental, and spiritual. The holistic well-being of the person includes harmony of body and soul. At the sociological level, even today, millions of people still seek traditional medicine in the treatment of HIV-related health problems and AIDS. The complexity of the phenomenon places the church right at the nexus of pastoral care for health. The church must ask herself what her theological reflection and its methodology can contribute toward preventing and managing HIV and AIDS.

Pastoral care is a social action, in as far as it represents an effort of a group, or of an individual, to inscribe something of its own identity in society. That is, if there is action, there must also be organization in view of acting, its operationalization with regard to taking into account the other. As one can see, prevention and management of HIV and AIDS and the promotion of health are the objective of this struggle. It implies struggling to protect the lives of the

---

[1] P. Msellati, L. Vidal, and J.-P. Moatti (under the direction of), *L'accès aux traitements du VIH/sida en Côte d'Ivoire. Evaluation de l'Initiative Onusida / ministère ivoirien de la santé publique. Aspects économiques, sociaux et comportementaux*, Collection sciences sociales et sida (Paris: Edition ANRS, 2001), 2.

people and the well-being of communities. Health in the case of the method-ological study we present here includes a

- descriptive method of evaluation that is progressive;
- prospective method of dissemination and information;
- structural praxis; and
- pastoral strategy in times of HIV and AIDS.

Description and Progressive Evaluation of HIV and AIDS

Côte d'Ivoire is one of the first African countries to have directly engaged itself in the fight against HIV and AIDS. As early as 1995, the country created a national program against HIV and AIDS, other sexually transmitted diseases (STDs), and tuberculosis. At the time of publication of the first results of anti-retroviral triple therapies, after the World Conference on HIV and AIDS in Vancouver in 1996, the Ivorian authorities actively demanded that people living in the countries of the Southern Hemisphere have access to treatments against the HIV infection. Today, Côte d'Ivoire remains the country of Francophone West Africa most affected by the epidemic in the countries of the South.[2]

Indeed, from 1996, major advances in basic and clinical research have changed the medical management of AIDS.[3] Introducing the multiple anti-retroviral therapies has translated into a dramatic decrease in the incidence of opportunistic infections and mortality. Côte d'Ivoire, because of its difficult epidemiological situation,[4] had a cumulative death toll from AIDS of 420,000 by late December 1997. The Ivorian Ministry of Public Health estimated that at least 1 million people were living with the virus in 1998, a significant propor-tion of its 15.4 million inhabitants.

During 2011–2012, in a Demographic and Health Survey with Multiple Indicators (EDS-MICS),[5] 5,671 women ages fifteen to forty-nine years and 5,677 men ages fifteen to fifty-nine were tested for HIV. The results show that 3.7 percent of people ages fifteen to forty-nine were infected with HIV. HIV prevalence was higher among women (4.6 percent) than men (2.7 percent).

---

[2] Ibid., vii (Foreword).

[3] J.-P. Moatti, P. Msellati, L. Vidal, and Y. Souteyrand (collective), "Raisons et enjeux de l'évaluation," in Msellati et al., *L'accès aux traitements du VIH*, 1.

[4] According to UNAIDS, 24.5 million men, women, and children were living with HIV/AIDS in sub-Saharan Africa at the end of 1999; almost 4 million of these infections were contracted during the same year.

[5] The Demographic and Health Survey and Multiple Indicator (EDS-MICS) was conducted in Côte d'Ivoire from December 2011 to May 2012 by the Ministry of Health and the Fight Against AIDS (MSLS) and the National Institute of Statistics (INS).

HIV prevalence is lowest among women and men living in rural areas. Generally, the rate of infection of women and men increases rapidly with age, reaching a maximum at forty-five to forty-nine years old. HIV prevalence has, however, declined since 2005. The decrease in prevalence among women and all adults is statistically significant, but not among men. In the regions of the country, the prevalence is distributed as follows: South, 3.5 percent; city of Abidjan, 5.1 percent; South West, 4.3 percent; West, 3.6 percent; Central West, 2.2 percent; Central, 3.0 percent; East Central, 4.0 percent; North Central, 4.4 percent; Northwest, 2.3 percent; Northeast, 2.3 percent; and North, 2.5 percent. Abidjan has the highest prevalence, and the Central West region has the lowest. Study by marital status shows that HIV prevalence is highest among widows (17.3 percent), the widowed (11.5 percent), and divorced (8.0 percent), and lowest among single women and single men (2.9 percent and 0.7 percent, respectively). In general, HIV prevalence increases with the number of sexual partners through life. HIV prevalence among young people ages fifteen to twenty-four is 1.3 percent. The infection rate is highest among young women in urban areas (2.5 percent). For young men, it is higher in rural areas (0.6 percent).[6]

In sub-Saharan Africa, a 2004–2005[7] assessment revealed that nearly 1.7 million Africans died each year as a result of AIDS or complications stemming from the disease. "Since 2001, HIV incidence [number of new cases] has declined by over 25 percent in 22 countries of sub-Saharan Africa. Among the young people of many countries, the tendency to adopt sexual behavior that helps to protect oneself and others against HIV infection is increasing. The coverage of programs to prevent mother-to-child HIV transmission has increased considerably. The number of people receiving antiretroviral therapy has increased by 16 since 2004."[8]

In 2010, approximately 1.9 million people were newly infected with HIV in sub-Saharan Africa, a decrease of 16 percent compared to 2001. This brought the number of people living with HIV in the region to approximately 22.9 million. As the treatment is extended, fewer people die of HIV-related causes and the number of people living with HIV increases,[9] an increase of 12 percent from 2001 to 2010.[10]

---

[6] Response rate and methodology: Data on HIV prevalence were obtained from a sample of dried blood spots, collected on a voluntary basis by a prick to the fingertip to women ages 15–49 and men ages 15–59. Almost 82 percent of women and 77 percent of men in this sample were tested. Overall, 79 percent of 11,348 surveyed were tested. Source: National Institute of Statistics, BP V 55, Abidjan, Ivory Coast.

[7] Le VIH/sida en Afrique Subsaharienne: le point sur l'épidémie et les progrès du secteur de la santé vers l'accès universel—Satus report 2011—OMS—ONUSIDA—UNICEF (Geneva: OMS, 2012), 1.

[8] Ibid.

[9] Ibid., 3.

[10] Ibid.

The high-level meeting of the General Assembly of the United Nations Program on HIV and AIDS in 2011 gave new momentum to the political commitment to fight the disease, and the final political declaration on HIV and AIDS reaffirmed the central role of universal access to prevention, treatment, care, and support in order to achieve all the targets of the Millennium Development Goals. Clear objectives were set for 2015, including a 50 percent reduction of sexual transmission, halving the number of people living with HIV who die of tuberculosis, and provision of antiretroviral therapy to at least 15 million people. The international community also approved a detailed global plan to support the elimination of mother-to-child transmission of HIV and to improve maternal health by 2015.[11]

The changing nature of the phenomenon of HIV and AIDS highlights the need to reflect on articulating how information about the pandemic is disseminated. One must know how to transmit information well, as pastoral efficacy demands the art of communication in all circumstances. The ability to communicate is important for carrying out pastoral and ecclesial activities, and for knowing how to choose one's collaborators in the mission.[12] Proper communication also helps in ordering in a unified manner parish and ecclesial life. All this, however, does not go without its challenges, alongside positive signs in the parish community and in the evangelizing mission of the church.[13]

In all, one must know what to say and what not to say about HIV and AIDS, and to "say well"[14] what has to be said about the pandemic. The use of the correct language in communication is important, in order to avoid empty rhetoric and misinformation. In all cases in pastoral work, asking these important questions is a good step: What should I do, and how do I do it? What should I say, and how do I say it?

Health professionals and pastoral actors' evaluation of the HIV and AIDS pandemic should lead to specific goals, including

- Analyzing the functioning of our parish communities, and families in particular.
- Identifying strengths and weaknesses of national health pastoral care (NHPC).
- Identifying strengths and weaknesses of diocesan health pastoral care (DHPC).

[11] Ibid., 16.

[12] F. Yedo Akpa, *La paroisse, une vie de foi, de charité et de gestion* (Abidjan: Paulines, 2010), 82.

[13] Ibid., 83.

[14] D. Koné, *Dire bien. 1997–2007. Dix ans de mots qui témoignent* (Abidjan: Vallesse Editions, 2009), cited in Akpa, *La paroisse*, 83.

- Making recommendations to church, political, and ecclesiastical decision makers as well as to managers of the health systems.

All this activity should be managed by competent people on the political, state,
and ecclesiastical levels.

Structural Praxis

For the reasons stated above, a commission and several pastoral ministries
should be created:

- A National Commission for Health Pastoral Care (NCHPC), which
  constitutes the central office for church action.
- A Diocesan Pastoral Health Board (DPHB), responsible for imple-
  menting the NCHPC at the diocesan level.
- A Parish Board for Health Pastoral Care (PBHPC).
- An Episcopal and Priests Board for Health (EPBH).

These three listed boards will constitute the sectorial ministry. The commission
and the three boards should be assisted by health professionals, appointed or
designated by the competent authorities or communities. Methodologically,
these structures will contribute at church level to maintain a national directory
for research and data on health information on the policy, planning, institutions, human resources, and funding of the National Commission for the
Health Pastoral Care. The prospective role of the pastoral care office will be to
arrange meetings at all levels of the pastoral pyramid to analyze information and
make decisions.

Faced with the HIV and AIDS pandemic, health pastoral care must obviously change its method and praxis. The public health crisis created by the HIV
and AIDS pandemic in the past decades has given rise to a major social crisis. It
is urgent to design a pastoral care program that helps men and women, young
people, and indeed the entire population to access information and to break old
habits. It is an opportune time for the church to change its vision and its analysis
on society and ecclesial communities and to improve its way of evangelizing.

The AIDS pandemic is clearly not just a simple public health crisis. It is
a global phenomenon that, unfortunately in Africa, brings us to this question: What can we do without life in our families, villages, cities, and ecclesial
communities? To respond to this challenge we must avoid creating anguish
within ourselves and around us. The aim is to give a new trajectory to life
through individual and collective consciousness. Only under these conditions
can a qualitative approach to pastoral health care be implemented, to promote a

quantitative transformation in the lives of people with HIV and AIDS. To this end, pastoral care in times of HIV and AIDS may also develop in its "spiritual quality."[15]

The Pastoral Strategy in Times of AIDS— A Question of Method

Taking into account what has been described as a pandemic where no country is spared, some hot spots require more in-depth pastoral reflection. If through the progressive method we identify some clear warning signs, there are also some indicators of hope and a way forward for strategy. We now turn to these indicators in order to mark out a reflection at the level of education, Christian responsibility, and its relation with the NGOs, Joint United Nations Program on HIV and AIDS (UNAIDS), President's Emergency Plan for AIDS Relief (PEPFAR), UNICEF, Global Fund, ecclesial communities, and the family. In fact, the management of the pandemic can be done through education at all levels. In education, freedom is the indispensable presupposition for human growth. It is not simply a starting point but a continuous process.[16] Therefore, awareness of the seriousness and urgency of the problems related to the pandemic and to the area of health care should be valued and encouraged.

In the current African world, which exhibits a tendency toward sexual perversion, sexual degradation, and uncontrolled morals, the situation is sometimes alarming.[17] That is why parishes and ecclesial communities must be challenged by the plight of the sick, the actual risk of infection, and the spread of the pandemic. Pastors and laypeople obviously have a great duty and an urgent responsibility to see and help all these people who, in distress, and sometimes without any support, challenge us.[18] They will, moreover, be committed to provide an educational dimension to their evangelization, because mission cannot be achieved without education.

In the momentum of the strategy, communities as well as pastors need adequate training in terms of knowledge of the modes of action of the virus, HIV prevention, and management of the AIDS disease in order to establish a

---

[15] P. Viveret, "L'émergence d'une nouvelle société," *Développement et civilisation*, no. 418 (2014): 4.

[16] F. Yedo Akpa, *Vivre sa foi et son baptême dans l'Eglise d'Afrique aujourd'hui* (Abidjan: Editions UCAO, Paulines, 2012), 34.

[17] F. Yedo Akpa, Foreword to Gilbert E. Sambou, *Le droit ecclésial. Pastorale familiale en Afrique et dispositions canoniques connexes* (Dakar: Imprimerie Saint Paul, 2013), 4.

[18] D. Ntigulirwa, "Jean-Paul II et l'accompagnement pastoral des malades," in *Revue de l'Institut Supérieur de Pastorale (Devins, sorciers et féticheurs, que faire? Santé, occultisme et foi, que comprendre? Comment réagir?)*, no. 2, Abidjan (1997): 75.

consistent pastoral strategy. Moreover, the Christian community cannot shun its responsibility. It has a mission to accompany the sick and support them physically, materially, morally, and spiritually, especially if they are members of their local church, because "visiting the sick is a duty for all Christians, as well as comforting them in their sufferings, praying with them and for them."[19]

The Christian communities and parish pastors are invited to pursue an active ministry among the sick. The ordinaries (bishops) and the hospital chaplains are also included. Each ordinary, being primarily responsible for the pastoral care in diocese, cannot neglect the pastoral care of the sick. Pastoral care for AIDS will always have to be in harmony with diocesan planning, which follows well the diocesan directives and rules. This requires, in conscience, establishment of a regular and comprehensive contact between all the actors involved in managing this pandemic in order to take into account the realities and emergencies in this area, including the necessary or indispensable means for proper administration of this ministry. It also requires acquiring appropriate logistical structures to be secured over time. This action is necessary, especially for the continuity and maintenance of structures of pastoral evaluation and actions.

Managing the pandemic at the level of ecclesiastical and civil authorities in its related structures—state, NGOs, UNAIDS, PEPFAR, UNICEF, Global Fund—has the same objective, namely to eradicate the pandemic and save people and their integrity. There should be no separation or overlap between the two authorities, but interconnection and collaboration, even an effective complementarity between the two. Pursuing the same ideal of human service, the two forms—NGOs and international health institutions—will collaborate in order to care for patients.

This is why the church should adapt its pastoral praxis to the contemporary situation, taking into account the demands and challenges of this pandemic. In today's world, stagnant pastoral work achieves little. The church needs a structured ministry, renewed and renovated by the signs of the times in relation with the state and NGO structures, as well as international organizations specialized in the fight against AIDS and in the investment of funds for prevention and care of patients. The church could benefit from the support of the state and its partners to fight HIV and AIDS. The value of such collaboration lies in the sharing of experiences and the communication of pastoral ideas and strategies, with mutual assistance between churches on the one hand, and meetings between state structures, NGOs, international organizations that fight against AIDS, and the pastoral health professionals at the international level for the case of AIDS on the other.

---

[19] John Paul II, *Dolentium hominum*, Lettre apostolique par laquelle est constituée la commission pontificale pour la pastorale des services de la santé, Ed. Cité du Vatican, 1985, no. 19.

Action requires revisiting the ecclesial communities in rural and urban areas and renewing from within their management structures, promoting a spiritual and pastoral dimension for the patients' development and self-reliance.[20] This legitimate concern can be seen as a challenge but also in terms of sustainability, because rural and urban church structures need to adapt to current articulations of modern society. Our Christian communities in general face organizational and structural difficulties that undermine their stability. Indeed, "Without the ability to develop its own internal resources and possibilities, a community cannot hope for a better future."[21]

Faced with existential tensions, one will have to pertinently address obstacles and inefficiencies that hamper the emergence of our communities as centers for development of humankind. One should not accuse the structures themselves, but the people and their behavior, often due to ill will, indifference, and lack of discipline about which everyone complains. One can add to this a lack of effort, creativity, and initiative. The struggle for life requires an acute awareness of the pandemic. Thus, pastors, laypeople, and efficient pastoral assistants[22] in HIV prevention will organize themselves as a relay team[23] for the pastoral ministry. Additionally, management of the pandemic requires a spirituality of communion as a fundamental and integral element. Faced with this pastoral reality, communities and health professionals will have to serve in humility and not in rivalry.

In all cases, the establishment of new consultative structures and of action as set out above can, in the case of the fight against HIV and AIDS, encourage the gradual emergence of a shared pastoral responsibility and a dynamism that is increasingly real in the church, and therefore in the parishes.[24] It will be a question of searching for appropriate methodology for pastoral changes, such as that of listening,[25] as well as of the double role of education and inclusion[26] of the sick. Praxis in this area shall be done through a network of intelligent and thorough understandings of the needs of the community and area for an effective ministry,[27] through an orthopraxis—that is, the right action in the service of the construction of a HIV-free society. The complexity of the methods used in this evangelizing strategy must be the responsibility of priests and laypeople trained for this service

[20] I. Bessi Dogbo and F. Yedo Akpa, *L'autonomie des églises locales d'Afrique et la charité pastorale* (Abidjan: Editions UCAO, 2014), 9.

[21] J.-M. Ela, "Ministère ecclésial et jeunes Eglises," *Concilium* 126 (1977): 66.

[22] F. Yedo Akpa, *Stratégie d'évangélisation. Notes sur le dialogue* (Abidjan: Paulines, 2008), 39.

[23] Ibid.

[24] Ibid., 40.

[25] J.-C. Larchet, *Le chrétien devant la maladie, la souffrance et la mort* (Paris: Les Editions du Cerf, 2002), 92.

[26] Akpa, *Stratégie d'évangélisation*, 40.

[27] Ibid., 41.

of the church. Those who have received the proper training need to be the first facilitators of prevention and management of HIV and AIDS programs.

Indeed, for those battling the HIV and AIDS pandemic, the challenge is real: to ensure that the method of struggle for life really means something to the people, meeting their demands for meaning, and acknowledging their individual lived experiences, because in the church everyone has a position and an irreplaceable role, however small it may be:[28] "From him the whole body, joined and held together by every supporting ligament, grows and builds itself up in love, as each part does its work" (Eph. 4:16).

In the search for a unified method in the fight against HIV and AIDS, for the preservation of life, the relationship between actors and communities in an ecclesial structured action will be developed. In this dynamic of method the sense of *otherness* will need to be cultivated. Very often the other can be an *aliud*, that is to say, the otherness of a thing, or an *alius*, and therefore the otherness of a subject. Often the attitude toward the *alius* is similar to the one reserved for the *aliud*; the other can be denied with indifference, contempt, and denigration, or manipulated with a possessive attitude; or the other can be sought and welcomed for his or her value and in his or her diversity.[29] From this we can say that, faithful to the gospel, the Christian makes himself or herself available for the service, in various ways, in the struggle for life in the church and in society. In view of contributing toward a positive cultural change,[30] the church and the laypeople cannot remain silent today, nor let events decide for them.[31]

The church will need to focus on the family because it requires special attention in Africa, and especially in Côte d'Ivoire, in the fight for life, against HIV and AIDS. It is often a place of tension, between the complexity of therapeutic uses that draw from both the "modern" and "traditional" methods of care,[32] in short, a medical syncretism.[33]

Conclusion

The AIDS pandemic is a challenge to our scientific convictions. Its changing nature calls for constant questioning of everything that may have been

---

[28] Ibid., 78.

[29] P. Sequeri, "Il sapere orientato al senso," in G. Colombo, ed., *L'evidenza della fede* (Milan: Glossa, 1998), 149–85.

[30] F. Sedgo, *Prévention et éducation chrétienne de la sexualité humaine* (Lomé: La créativité perpétuelle, 1998), 8.

[31] Akpa, *Stratégie d'évangélisation*, 83.

[32] H. Mêmel-Fotê, *La santé, la maladie et les médecines en Afrique. Une approche anthropologique*, Oeuvres complètes III (Abidjan: CERAP, 2008), 34.

[33] Ibid., 37.

seen as a scientifically or otherwise known fact.[34] Programs cannot be implemented without taking into account the circumstances in which people live, and it is necessary to adopt a very broad approach, involving all sectors of the community.[35] In the context of the struggle against HIV and AIDS, the fight for life and the aggression of the disease are inseparable. Therefore, we must provide a method that strikes a balance between behavior change, societal intervention, and ecclesial solidarity.

It is up to the collective bodies—individual, ecclesial, and state—to implement methods of cooperation, symbiosis, and solidarity to overcome the AIDS pandemic, by regularly taking stock of the pastoral actions that all the actors have recommended, and by implementing the strategy—that is, the monitoring and evaluating of the achieved progress.

---

[34] J.-S. Hendje Toya, *Le sida. Perspectives africaines* (Yaoundé: Publication CLE/CIPCRE, 2003), 11.

[35] Institut Panos, *Le vrai coût du sida. Un nouveau défi au développement* (Paris: l'Harmattan, 1993), 195.

CHAPTER 30

EARLY AFRICAN CATHOLIC CHURCH INVOLVEMENT IN THE AIDS PANDEMIC

A Fire That Kindled Other Fires

Ted Rogers

The advent of AIDS was first recognized in Zimbabwe in 1983, and there was a general panic in the world about this new disease. At that time I was principal of the School of Social Work, and with the staff I learned about AIDS and discussed this problem and the possibility of helping in some way people who were HIV-positive. However, shortly after my involvement I was transferred to a new post in 1985 and left the School of Social Work after twenty-one years. I then had a year's sabbatical overseas at Oxford University but still kept up an interest in the development of HIV and AIDS. When I returned to Zimbabwe I was appointed secretary to the Archbishop of Harare and managed to carry on some interest in this new AIDS problem.[1]

Zimbabwe Catholic Bishops Conference (ZCBC)

The first task was to set up an ad hoc committee with E. Ndoro, a local medical practitioner, and other interested persons. Our first meeting was held on September 16, 1987, where it was decided to make a draft statement for consideration by the ZCBC at their next meeting on October 5. The final draft was presented to the bishops at their meeting by Dr. Ndoro and I, and

---

[1] Much of the material in this chapter derives from my memoirs of the early years of the HIV and AIDS situation in Zimbabwe. See Ted Rogers, *Jesuit Social Pioneer and AIDS Activist* (Dorpspruit, South Africa: Cluster Publications, 2012). I wish to pay tribute to all those who worked with me in a dedicated way to combat the threat and the results of this disease, especially Christine Mtize; Noreen Nolan; LCM; Elizabeth Matenga and her husband, Jonathan Matenga; as well as ongoing help for decades from Alison Brydone and Gordon Chavunduka, who with Sister Noreen Nolan have now gone to the Lord. May they rest in peace.

the bishops said that after their small amendments, it could be published as a pastoral letter in English, Shona, and Ndebele. The bishops also agreed that seminars should be held on the topic for clergy, religious, and lay leaders and that the people should be informed as soon as possible. They commended the work of the ad hoc committee and said it should examine the possibility of setting up counseling offices in each diocese and decided that the Jesuit bishop Helmut Reckter would be their liaison person. A meeting was therefore called for October 21 to discuss these matters and also to arrange for the first national Catholic seminar on HIV and AIDS.

The School of Social Work made its facilities available for this national seminar on December 12, 1987. Doctors Felicity Zawaira, Jonathan Matenga, and E. Ndoro, who were well known to the church and interested in AIDS problems, and I all gave inputs, as did Clara Mutiti from the Medical Department of the city of Harare. Ambrose Vinyu, a Catholic diocesan priest, took part in the panel discussion. Each of the six dioceses participated, and other churches were also invited to send three representatives each. In all, forty-five delegates participated. We had invited Dr. Geoff Foster of the Salvation Army to attend, but he declined due to other commitments. In the "Short Report" on the seminar, the recommendations requested establishing an office in each diocese with a full-time coordinator, training in counseling for those working with people with AIDS as well as a stress on Christian and African traditional values, which cherished virginity and sexual morality. We realized that there needed to be much publicity about the disease and how to avoid it, all of which should be done in liaison with other agencies. A list of resource persons in each diocese would be compiled to assist when needed. Brigid Willmore, social worker and facilitator, prepared the notes on the meeting. Unfortunately, some years later she was killed in a car accident with a truck in South Africa. She had lived a full life.

The pastoral letter on AIDS was published by the bishops' conference in October 1987. It was the second letter on the problem from an African bishops' conference. The first was from Kenya in June 1987. At that time the problem of AIDS was not well recognized in Zimbabwe, and most people were in denial. However, tests for HIV and AIDS had been done in Zimbabwe in about 1983, which was one of the first countries in Africa to take this step. We managed to get some experts involved in a prognosis of the disease, from which it emerged that the disease would soon develop exponentially to create a major problem in Zimbabwe, as in other countries of Africa. We contacted Misereor, the Catholic funding agency of Germany, to see whether they could fund a program, and they responded so positively that they even asked if we would need expert medical help from overseas. To this we replied that we had enough medical people to cope. Misereor agreed to fund a structure to combat HIV and AIDS with a national office and an office in each of the six dioceses.

In the meantime we began work with concerned people such as Fr. Chad Gandiya of the Anglican Church, now Anglican bishop of Harare. We held a number of meetings, some at the Anglican Cathedral hall. The coordinating church body, the Heads of Christian Denominations (HOD), now became interested, and with assistance of the Anglican bishop of Harare, Peter Hatendi, I wrote a booklet on HIV and AIDS for the HOD that was published by the Christian Council. However, six months after we started on the national program for the Zimbabwe Catholic Bishops Conference (ZCBC), the Bishops of Southern Africa asked me if I would be prepared director of their organization, which comprised all the bishops of Southern Africa and was named IMBISA, which covered South Africa, Botswana, Lesotho, Swaziland, Namibia, Angola, Mozambique, and Zimbabwe. With my superior this was agreed, so I started work with the IMBISA in 1988 and moved into their headquarters in Highlands' suburb Harare, but I kept up my interest in AIDS. In my place Mrs. Christine Mtize, who had been working with me on a voluntary basis, was appointed national coordinator of the AIDS program for the ZCBC.

Community Involvement
in AIDS Counseling Trust (ACT)

There was no lay organization working in the field of HIV and AIDS in Harare or the whole of Zimbabwe except the one started in Mutare by Dr. Foster, as mentioned above, of the local government hospital, of which he was the doctor in charge. Thus there were two church-related bodies—ZCBC and the Salvation Army, to which Dr. Foster belonged—but there was nothing for the general population in Harare except government hospitals, which dealt with medical but not social and cultural problems. Obviously there was a dire need for other approaches.

With Sister Noreen Nolan, LCM (Little Company of Mary), of St. Anne's Hospital and Dr. Alison Brydone also concerned, we decided to hold a public meeting on March 24, 1988, to discuss the problem and see the way forward. This meeting was held at St. Anne's Hospital and, though well attended, with forty-two persons present, there were only thirteen local Africans attending— and these were clergy, religious, or social workers. The problem was not well recognized in the African community, but the meeting was well attended by the Anglican clergy: seven priests and three religious brothers. There were three Catholic priests, three sisters, and three lay representatives of the ZCBC organizations, including the Justice and Peace Commission and the Catholic Development Commission (CADEC). Four social workers and three social work lecturers from the School of Social Work, as well as three university academic staff, and a number of teachers and housewives were also present.

From this meeting a steering committee was formed to investigate the problem and see what could be done. The main issues appeared to be how to make information widely available and how to provide counseling. Medical personnel were busy and did not have sufficient time or skills to counsel people who were HIV-positive and their relatives. One of the major problems was that the medical understanding of counseling was to give practical information and access to medication. However, we were aware that AIDS was a social problem that affected whole families and their livelihoods. The counseling, therefore, was to be more of social workers' approach rather than that of medical personnel. We agreed to start a trust to deal with the problem, called it AIDS Counseling Trust (ACT), and applied for funds to various organizations. CAFOD of the UK was the first donor to help. On February 16, 1989, the trust was registered. The following persons who were already involved were cited as donors: Sr. Patricia Walsh, OP, Helen Jackson, Brigid Willmore, Clara Mutiti, Jan Majuri Shamu, Susan M. L. Laver, Chad N. Gandiya, and I, who also represented CAFOD. The board of trustees were mostly high flyers: Fay King Chung, minister of primary and secondary education; Lovemore Mbengeranwa, the city medical officer; Professor Gordon Lloyd Chavunduka, president of ZINATHA (Traditional Healers); Tendai Bare, the Secretary to Ministry of Community Development and Women's Affairs; and I as convenor.

I would like to pay a special tribute here to Gordon Chavunduka, who was professor at the time in the University of Zimbabwe's Department of Sociology. He went on to become vice chancellor of the university and worked with me, on a voluntary basis, in many areas of need. Another person to whom I wish to pay tribute here is Helen Jackson, who was a lecturer at the School of Social Work. In addition to being a professional social worker she had a degree in biology, which gave her a good understanding of the background of the HIV and AIDS virus. She was assiduous in helping to establish ACT and wrote a book on AIDS—also one of the first in Africa—which was updated and sold well.

Once the trust had been established, we needed an executive body as well as a director and full-time workers, premises, and transport. This required considerable effort, but we found that donors were forthcoming as there was no real competition for donor funding at this time. The board appointed Elizabeth Matenga, a senior nurse with considerable medical and administrative background, whose husband, Jonathan, was a medical doctor and had already been working with us in a voluntary capacity. There was considerable discussion about the location of the center. I felt it should be in one of the township areas where the majority of the population lived, especially the poor. However, the majority felt it should be near the major hospital in Harare, and this view prevailed. We managed to obtain premises by sharing some medical rooms at 22 North Avenue, Harare. As work and staff expanded, ACT acquired its own premises at 15 Rowland Square, Milton Park, Harare.

Dangers of Overinvolvement

In my opinion, ACT tried to take on too many activities and to meet too wide a variety of needs. This involvement was, however, accepted by the executive committee and led to staff and other logistical problems. As chair of the trustees, I felt obliged to point this out, but my reflections were in vain. More and more organizations were entering this field of HIV and AIDS activities, and ACT should then have withdrawn from some of them, especially the outreach program in rural areas, which involved also a mobile cinema projector, to focus on the unique local contribution it could make. Eventually it overextended itself, and some donors lost faith. It had then to go into recession and restart in a more modest way. Fortunately in this way it is still active today.

Incidence of HIV and AIDS in Zimbabwe

An article published in the Zimbabwe *Sunday* Mail, on February 23, 1997, reported on a projection of infection for HIV and AIDS in the country. The research was carried out by the local Blair Research Institute and Oxford University. It predicted that in the following twenty years, the population would be the same, at 11.5 million, or even decline. They also projected that life expectancy would reduce from the then current fifty-seven years to thirty years. These projections were made on the basis of the population not changing its behavior and no cure for AIDS being found.

By 2011 it was difficult to verify whether these projections had proved correct, but the life expectancy then was estimated at thirty-two years for women and thirty-four years for men, so their projected thirty years was not far out. In 2011 it was difficult to estimate accurately the population size as it was widely held that over 3 million Zimbabweans had left the country and were in the diaspora. There were no updated figures for the population, but an estimate was about 12 million. However, if access to antiretroviral drugs (ARVs) was widespread, the population figure now would be much higher. It was estimated for 2011 that 3,000 people per week were dying from HIV and AIDS as reported by the National AIDS Council, and of the 1.7 million living with HIV, only 150,000 were obtaining ARVs. On the other hand, the rate of infection in Zimbabwe had dropped from over 30 percent in 2000 to 17 percent, and the incidence among youth was lower than among older persons.

With increased funding from the Global Fund and other international donors, there is an increase in Zimbabwe of the number of HIV-positive persons obtaining ARVs, which in 2014 was reported to be 77 percent for adults but only 46 percent for children. In research conducted by the London School of Hygiene and Tropical Medicine in 2013 of children ages six to fifteen who might have contracted the disease at birth from the mother, it was found that 90 percent had not even been tested for HIV. One of the main difficulties is stigma as the child needs the consent of an adult for the testing and many family adults are scared of this in case it reflects badly on the family itself.

IMBISA and HIV and AIDS

In 1988 I was appointed director of IMBISA. As the regional body of the Catholic bishops IMBISA had a number of programs on its agenda: a refugee service, social communications and an interest in justice and peace activities, as well as the more normal pastoral and theological issues. During my period with IMBISA a major item was preparation for, and follow-up activities for the First African Synod which was held in Rome in 1994. However, I was able to follow up my interest in HIV and AIDS and some other relevant activities during the time I spent with IMBISA. As the headquarters were in Harare it was possible to carry on with some of the local work in which I was involved and also to bring items referring to HIV and AIDS to the attention of the bishops. With other interested persons I managed to have input on seminars, lectures, and contacts in South Africa, Mozambique, and other IMBISA countries.

As director I attended certain meetings of constituent bishops' conferences, and I remember being present at a meeting of the Southern African Catholic Bishops' Conference (SACBC), at Marianhill, Natal, in 1988 and being asked by those present to discuss the issue of condom use as they were rather confused about it. They knew I had been involved for some years with this problem. I said that my position was that I did not approve of condoms in general and certainly did not distribute them. However, in cases where people were going to engage in illegitimate sex in any case, they should use a condom in order to protect themselves and their partner. But they should also know that condoms did not give a very high degree of protection in Africa owing to exposure to heat, misuse, and the type of condoms supplied, some of which were dumped into Africa by some donors who could buy them cheaply from Asia.

The bishops appear to have accepted this policy, but later, when the new bishop of Rustenburg, Bishop Kevin Dowling, put forward similar ideas, they appeared to reject them. Near the end of his papacy Pope Benedict XVI more or less endorsed my point of view when he said that prostitutes could use condoms to protect themselves.

During the time of my contract with IMBISA I still kept up with local contacts and organizations in Zimbabwe, and in 1995, near the end of my contract with IMBISA, I was investigating the possibility of AIDS programs in schools. Saint George's College was the first one I contacted and worked with, and then later, the secondary school at St. Paul's Mission, Musami. This was also because I had good contacts at Musami as I had been acting superior there for three months at the beginning of 1996. In that same year I went overseas to study peer education. Christine Mtize's post at the ZCBC had finished, and I was asked if I could find a job for her. She agreed to come to work with me on a schools' program, and I was able to find some funds to assist her on a temporary basis. These were the early days of the schools' programs of Jesuit AIDS Project.

Jesuits of Africa and Madagascar's AIDS Network

In 1995 I completed my contract with IMBISA and was able to go on a sabbatical leave. On returning to Zimbabwe during the middle of 1996 I was met by Father Konnie Landsberg, the Jesuit Provincial, who said he had given me away to the Jesuit Superiors of Africa and Madagascar (JESAM). They wanted me to research the situation and work on HIV and AIDS in the various Jesuit provinces in Africa in which Jesuits were working in HIV and AIDS programs. This was to be a part-time job and certain minimal expenses would be provided. This work could be done at the same time as I was working on the schools' program on HIV and AIDS in Zimbabwe.

On October 8, 1996, I sent out a questionnaire, in English and French, to the twenty-four countries in Africa in which Jesuits were working, requesting information on the size of the problem of HIV and AIDS, effectiveness of control, agencies and Jesuits involved, technical and financial assistance, esti-mated growth of the problem and plans for the future. There were twelve responses, varying in length from one to twenty pages from Côte d'Ivoire, Kenya, Madagascar, Malawi, Mozambique, Senegal, South Africa, Sudan, Tanzania, Uganda, Zambia, and Zimbabwe.

It was obvious that most of the Jesuits involved in HIV and AIDS work were isolated, and so a newsletter, *JESAM AIDS Newsletter*, was started to help them share ideas and problems. The first edition went out in July 1997 in English and French and was transmitted by fax or by email, which was becoming beneficial to Africa as postage by surface/airmail was slow and erratic. In the newsletter I gave a report on the survey, asking that "perhaps each region or province could have a contact person."

Contact persons were slow in being appointed and local submissions to the newsletter sparse, so I had to dig around myself for information and news. My French was rather rusty, so the newsletter was translated by one of the French-speaking Jesuits at nearby Arrupe College. I informed French-speaking countries that they could write to me in French, and I would reply normally in English. In this way letter writing was acceptable.

Having submitted a new budget to JESAM for visits to other African countries I was able to see the problems and work at firsthand through visits to Malawi, Kenya, Zambia, Uganda, and South Africa. The newsletter of June

1999 gave a short report on my visits to Malawi, South Africa, and Kenya and also a description of the work in Zimbabwe. I visited Malawi at the invitation of Fr. Willie Reynolds, S.J., from April 17 to 25, 1999, held talks and discussions at the two seminaries, and participated in the Inter-Diocesan Coordination Program meeting on home-based care. The problems were similar to Zimbabwe's, except that people were poorer, had less education, and more cultural practices that could lead to transmission of HIV and AIDS. The church had taken a lead, but needed to pay more attention to work with youth.

West Africa was much less infected than central and Southern Africa, but our report from Côte d'Ivoire showed that it had a high incidence. The survey showed that Jesuits were reasonably involved in Kenya, Tanzania, Uganda, Zambia, and Zimbabwe and that, on the whole, the Catholic Church seemed to be more involved than any other church, but, given the size of the problem, even that involvement was still too limited. I offer here an abbreviation of two reports—one on South Africa and the other on Malawi. All the other reports are detailed in my Memoirs.

South Africa had a rapidly increasing infection rate, up from 14 percent in 1997 to 22 percent in 1999, but KwaZulu-Natal was much higher, being in the range of 25 percent to 30 percent and the infection rates were higher among youth. In 1998, one hundred thousand children were orphaned as a result of AIDS deaths. Fr. Alan Peter, a medical doctor as well as a Jesuit, had a program for youth and believed that an educational outreach was of enormous importance because the average age for first sexual intercourse in South Africa was thirteen to fourteen years. Fr. Peter later left the Jesuits so that he could concentrate more on his hospital work with HIV patients.

Foundation of the African Jesuit Network in Nairobi

Perhaps the most important meeting we held was in Durban after the International Conference on AIDS, which was held there in 2000 and attended by a number of Jesuits involved in AIDS programs, especially veterans Fr. D'Agostino, with his work with infected children at Nyumbani in Nairobi and Fr. Michael Kelly, who had a long history of combating AIDS through education. After the international conference we held a Jesuit meeting to decide on our priorities. This was held for two days in a conference center, Coolock House, outside Durban. It was hosted generously by the South African Jesuits.

The main item for discussion was the future of Jesuit involvement in HIV and AIDS programs. It was felt that there were not sufficient resources to enable broad Jesuit involvement, and it was decided that a letter should be written to the father general in Rome. This letter, drafted by Kelly, explained that what was needed was a full-time secretariat located in Africa and sponsored by Rome. It should be rather similar to the well-established Jesuit Refugee Service. The letter was signed by all present and sent off to the Jesuit father general, where it was graciously received and later implemented in cooperation with JESAM, when this was made known at the subsequent meeting of JESAM in Kinshasa, and I handed in my resignation as the part-time coordinator of the JESAM AIDS project in order to carry on my expanding work with the Jesuit AIDS Project in Zimbabwe. The implementation was the setup of a secretariat in Nairobi under the leadership of Father Michael Czerny, who had just finished his contract with the Jesuit Social Apostolate in Rome. He had the advantage of knowledge of social affairs and also was bilingual in French and English. The project was called the Jesuit African AIDS Network (AJAN) and has since done sterling work in coordination and publications.

Holistic Programs

The Catholic Church is involved in many social and health services, along with other churches. It started many of these services, but some have now been overtaken by NGOs with more resources. What is the difference of approach, and should the church be still engaged in such activities? As in the educational field, the church social services seek to serve the interest of the whole person in development, not just a specific activity or need. Some NGOs are also concerned about such development, but the majority seek to serve a specific material need, be it food, clothing, housing, or aspects of education. They mostly do a good job, but some tend to spend too much money on administration and the care of their own staff. This often is given witness by the beautiful 4x4 vehicles that many of them drive, whereas a double cab pickup truck would usually meet their transport needs.

Some church social services are tempted to emulate secular NGOs, but they should be aware of this temptation and always struggle to maintain their own identity. I know of a vibrant youth organization that had a change of director who appeared to have been influenced by the NGO syndrome. Previously most of the training was done at youth camps where the participants themselves helped in cleaning and other activities, making for some ownership of the project. But the new director held training in conference centers instead, which were expensive and did not raise the funds. The director also employed more salaried staff. The result was that the project ran out of funds and had to close down, a great loss to the youth and the church.

Many Catholic Church social organizations are run by religious sisters who become dedicated to the problems of those in their care. In Zimbabwe a good number of these sisters are professional social workers who have been trained at the School of Social Work, which was started by the Jesuits in 1964. Unlike many lay social workers the sisters stay helping the local people and communities instead of going overseas to greener pastures. In order to have maximum impact it is necessary to involve the local community in an AIDS project and encourage them to run it themselves and not look upon it as a church project, although the church may also be involved in providing skilled personnel and some finances raised from donors.

Mission hospitals in Zimbabwe were the pioneers of health care for the rural areas and are still providing essential care to such an extent that even many people in towns go there for treatment instead of the poor and expensive government hospitals that are in town.

AIDS and Social Justice

The social services of the Catholic Church should also contain an element of social justice. The concern should not only be to help those in need but also to try to change unjust structures that cause poverty or other personal or community needs. Communities and nations need to be aware of the concept of *structural sin*, about which Saint Pope John Paul II spoke strongly. Archbishop Tutu in South Africa expressed this also in a recent speech that outlined the benefits that the white community had from apartheid and still enjoy the fruits of it in terms of education, jobs, and businesses. He said they all benefitted and should make some reparation to the black community now, even though many of them may say that they themselves were not responsible for the introduction of apartheid. This also applies to some postcolonial African states in which policies favor the black elites who enjoy many riches and privileges to the disadvantage of the poor who may as a result die early. Sometimes such persons give large donations to the church for their own personal support and enhancement, such as Mobutu used to do in the Congo. Church organizations must beware of such entrapment as the money usually comes from ill-gotten gains, and such policies keep the people in poverty and do not help: for instance, many of those who are HIV-positive do not have access to antiretroviral drugs that are necessary for their survival. Others may die because of lack of food, shelter, or other necessities.

Another problem that needs to be addressed is that of stigma, which exposes other persons unknowingly to the disease and lessens community response. This comes within the parameters of justice as well as health. In some areas there appears to be a conspiracy to shield the clergy and religious who are HIV-positive while preaching the need for openness in the community. It is difficult for bishops and superiors to publish the status of their subjects who may be infected, but at least they could encourage the infected themselves to be open about it. This will help communities also, as most of the contacts of the infected persons in the parish or communities recognize the symptoms in any case. I remember in the early days when Mrs. Mtize was speaking about HIV and AIDS. There was opposition from some clergy at the time, one of whom chastised Mrs. Mtize, saying, "We don't talk about sexuality in church, so you are out of order." The struggle continues.

CHAPTER 31

FIGHTING AIDS FROM THE GRASS ROOTS

History, Theology, Values,
and Challenges of Home-Based Care in Zambia

Leonard Chiti

This chapter reflects on the emergence of the home-based-care (HBC) system in Zambia in the late 1980s as a complement to the mainstream health-care delivery system for people living with HIV. It draws upon personal and pastoral experiences of working for a brief moment with home-based-care providers. It is rooted in experience and supported by sectional research, and pays particular attention to the faith dimension of HBC. I also attempt a brief theological reflection in order to read the signs of the times and discern what God could be saying to us through the intervention of the HBC system.

Caring Women

In 1995 I had the rare privilege of accompanying a retired nurse who was a coordinator of a local parish's home-based-care program. The group was called Caring Women. This group of women was going around their neighborhood bringing medicine and praying for those who were terminally ill, many of whom had AIDS. They brought words of comfort and encouragement, and in many cases provided some counseling. Many of them were members of a Catholic sodality group that encouraged its members to carry out works of charity in their neighborhoods. These women also offered some psychological, emotional, and social support.

Following my experience in Libala and surrounding areas, I wrote an article with a colleague sharing my experience, titled "Caring Men."[1] The article highlighted the challenge of facing some illnesses that have no known cure. Approaching patients who were afflicted by such illnesses from the perspective of faith proved a daunting experience. The patient knew that he or she was

---

[1] Leonard Chiti, "Caring Women," JCTR Bulletin 26 (1995).

dying, so had lost hope. The Christian message was meant to revive hope but in the face of the absence of a known cure, many people initially resisted such people's visits. At the time, to be diagnosed with HIV was like a death sentence. Many formal health institutions were not interested in caring for people who had HIV. Health-care professionals instead encouraged relatives and friends to look after a person who at the time would be considered terminally ill, waiting to die. Today, it is no longer a death sentence to be diagnosed with HIV. With the availability of anti-retroviral drugs, many people now live longer and healthy lives.

HIV and AIDS in Zambia

The first official report of an HIV infection in Zambia was recorded in 1984.[2] The immediate response by government was to put in place institutional and administrative processes and systems as a way of dealing with what was to become a pandemic. A national framework was developed that contained policies and programs to combat the onset of the virus.[3] However, this approach was not very successful, partly due to the increasing numbers of people who were infected by the virus. Also no vaccine was available to treat patients. Moreover, life-prolonging drugs were not developed at the time.

The HIV and AIDS crisis has had a tremendous impact in Zambia. While not everyone is infected, all Zambians are affected in one way or another. Nearly every family has had at least one member contract the virus. Thousands of Zambians have died from AIDS, and many children were left orphaned.

In terms of numbers, the latest data from the UNAIDS Gap report for 2014 indicated that the country has an HIV prevalence of 12.5 percent of the population ages fifteen and above. By the end of 2013 there were 1.1 million infected people, of whom 500,000 were adult women and 460,000 were adult men. The rest were children.[4] The above figures have not changed much compared, say, to 2008, when the total number of infected Zambians stood at 1.1 million, with the number of children infected standing at 95,000 while the number of adult women stood at 560,000 and the rest being men.[5] It can be noted that the infection rate among women has declined since 2008. Of the figures given for 2014, up to 750,000 people over fifteen years of age

---

[2] Leonard Chiti and Chidzulo Aaron, *The Response of the Catholic Church to the HIV/AIDS Pandemic, Lessons to be Learnt* (Aachen: German Episcopal Conference, forthcoming).

[3] Ibid.

[4] UNAIDS, Gap Report, Beginning of the End of AIDS Epidemic, 2014, www.unAIDS.org.

[5] UNAIDS, Report on the Global HIV/AIDS Epidemic, 2008, un-ugls.org.

needed antiretroviral therapy.[6] However, figures showing how many were actually receiving ARV are not available. In terms of fatalities the number of people dying due to AIDS drew back from 68,000 in 2005 to 27,000 in 2013.[7] The decline in both infection rates and the number of deaths has been attributed to the availability of life-prolonging antiretroviral therapy.

Public Disclosure

In terms of public disclosure, not many Zambians are brave enough to publicly state that they are infected. HIV/AIDS disclosure still attracts stigmatization. However, a Zambian priest, Fr. Lewis Watuka, has openly talked about the personal struggles he went through when told he had the HIV virus. He hailed the support that he received from his fellow brothers at a time when it was customary to dismiss candidates to the priesthood and religious life if they tested positive for HIV. His superiors decided that they would practice the virtue of solidarity with those afflicted by accepting Lewis into their religious congregation.

The Home-Based-Care (HBC) System

The Medical Concept

The home-based-care system for treating people living with HIV emerged in the late 1980s. Initially, HBC provided nursing care to patients referred to it by the local health institution. Caregivers monitored the patient's history and provided medication to deal with some of the patient's immediate medical needs. Thus, initially the home-based-care system emerged as a community/grassroots–based initiative to deal with a very serious matter of inadequate capacity of the state health delivery system to cope with the challenge of increasing numbers of patients testing positive for HIV.

At the time when no life-prolonging drugs were available, the health delivery system failed to cope with increasing numbers of people who had developed full-blown AIDS. Many patients were allowed to leave hospitals and other health centers to be cared for by relatives. It would appear that at this point in time a complement to the mainstream health-care system had emerged out of necessity, filling the gap left by a system inundated with patients for whom it could not adequately care.

---

[6] UNGASS, Country Progress Report, 2014, unAIDS.org.

[7] UNAIDS, Gap Report.

What Is Involved in HBC?

As indicated above when describing the Caring Women project, care-givers provide medication, attend to the physical needs of the patients such as washing their bodies, and help with household chores. This is clearly in response to the immediate problem patients face when ejected out of the mainstream health-care system. Many caregivers were also trained to monitor people on antiretroviral drugs.

HBC also helped address some aspects of stigmatization in the sense that those who had the virus were "marginalized and excluded" from regular social interactions.[8] Caregivers stepped in and provided some companionship. In the early years, caregivers also helped the family of the patient deal with the possi-bility of the patient dying.

Relationship to the Catholic Church

A report by the Jesuit Centre for Theological Reflection (JCTR) in early 2011 shows three interesting elements regarding the relationship between HBC, the Catholic Church, and the state health-care system in Zambia. HBC provided a holistic approach to patients through curative services, attending to moral and social challenges as well as providing spiritual support. This holistic approach reflects the ministry of our Lord when he refers to his mission as one that brings life and life to the full (John 10:10). The report by JCTR also indicates that the success scored in dealing with the HIV and AIDS pandemic in the Eastern province of Zambia can be attributed to the Catholic Church's intervention through the establishment of home-based care (HBC).[9] It points out that the church has had enormous success in the treatment and curative approach to the pandemic in addition to its pastoral interventions.[10]

Relationship to the Health-Care System

In the same report there is evidence that, in some parts of the province, the HBC was evidently the only health-care delivery system. Data from the research established that the Catholic Church was the only institution providing primary health services in some remote parts of the eastern province of Zambia. Consequently, the HBC expanded its services to include many primary health-care services.

---

[8] Robin Root, "Being Positive: A Phenomenology of HIV Disclosure in Swaziland," in *Disclosure in Health and Illness*, ed. Mark Davis and Lenore Manderson (London: Rout-ledge, 2014).

[9] Chiti and Chidzulo, Response of the Catholic Church to the HIV/AIDS Pandemic.

[10] Ibid.

Theological Reflection

Twenty years on from my time with Caring Women, what have I learned about tackling critical challenges affecting our society from a grassroots perspective? What made home-based care such a success? There are many lessons we can learn from the intervention of HBC in the lives of patients. The following theological reflection highlights just a few. It takes the form of employing the Christian faith to reflect on the phenomenon of HBC and applying faith to the negative ramifications of people discovering that they were living with HIV.

At the heart of HBC is the experience of suffering, marginalization, and exclusion. HBC helped address the problems of pain and the seeming absence of God in the patients' lives. HBC transformed people's lives,[11] and mediated the presence of God to the patients. This strengthened their faith in spite of the pain and social marginalization they were experiencing. In dealing with issues of suffering, marginalization, and exclusion, I show in this chapter that the manner in which the church has responded to the HIV and AIDS crisis represents not only a prophetic ministry but also an example of reading the signs of the times and taking concrete steps to face the challenge. The chapter also argues that the HBC was an instrument "created" by God to respond in a concrete way to the suffering of his people. HBC mediates God's presence to the afflicted. It brings God's compassion to the patients who have to struggle with the depression of a noncaring society. The commitment of the men and women to serving those who were pronounced with HIV through home-based care is an illustration of the response to the Gospel teaching in Matthew 25. These devout Christians saw the sick in the neighborhoods and attended to their needs. In so doing, they met the Lord through encounters with the sick.

A Faith-Driven Intervention

This chapter recalls the origins of the home-based-care system in the late 1980s with a view toward discerning lessons for our faith and hearing the voice of God anew. Not long after the emergence of HBC, it became apparent that many of the caregivers called themselves Christian. This identification of the carers with Christianity brought a faith dimension HBC.

In Zambia, in the Catholic Church, which accounts for a third of all people calling themselves Christian, the home-based-care system followed closely the pattern of Small Christian Communities. Many of the carers volunteered to attend to the patients out of a Christian virtue of showing compassion to those in need. It seems as though the faith of individuals or a group of people inspired many to respond to the challenges of delivering a modicum of health

---

[11] Root, "Being Positive."

care to people living with HIV. In addition, a third of the mainstream health-care system is run by faith-based institutions. Therefore, it is not surprising that faith-based communities embraced the challenge of caring for terminally ill patients. Many people saw the plight of HIV-positive people as an invitation from God to put the virtue of compassion into practice. In this case, members of the caring women group were inspired and motivated by the Gospel teaching of attending to the needs of those who were suffering.

The witness of these women and other men and women around the country is in line with recent church teaching from the Second Vatican Council. In one of its important declarations, the church states, "The joys and hopes, sorrows and anxieties of the people of our time, are the joys and hopes and the sorrows and anxieties of the followers of Christ."[12] The women described above took this teaching to heart and acted according to its dictates. The women assumed the concerns of their patients and made them theirs. This is a wonderful example to all of us to assume the concerns of those around us, even when we are not obliged to do so.

In those days those who were diagnosed with the virus were ostracized and carried with them a stigma. In many cases they were abandoned by their communities and sometimes even by close relatives. In many cases death was hastened by the depression and isolation that people living with HIV developed because of stigmatization. In addition to this, full-blown AIDS was accompanied by excessive weight loss which meant that people with AIDS stood out because of the deterioration of their physical condition. Another important factor to remember is that many people acquired HIV from unprotected sexual intercourse with multiple partners. This contributed to stigmatization in the sense that people were also seen to have lived a careless and reckless life. However, this chapter argues that the emergence of HBC also reminds us of the truth of our faith that God is continuously calling us to encounter him in difficult and stressful times. Traditional piety sometimes gives the impression that God is encountered in pleasant and peaceful times. This is true, but sometimes this piety underplays the truth that God is present in all circumstances of our life. Failure to appreciate that God is present in a crisis situation leads to despair and can sometimes hasten the death of a person who could otherwise have lived longer to fully experience God's compassion.

HBC brings hope where there is despair. The solidarity that HBC members show and the companionship they share with the patients bear testimony to a God of love. One of the important lessons we can discern from the success of the HBC is that out of the depths of despair comes hope. In a brief life story that focuses on the discovery of his HIV-positive status, a Zambian Marrian-hill priest, Fr. Lewis Watuka, reveals that facing the reality of living with HIV

---

[12] Second Vatican Council, *The Church in the Modern World* (Rome: The Vatican, 1965).

brought him closer to a God of consolation. This encounter with a compassionate God engendered in him hope in the face of despair.[13] Further, HBC challenges our notion of sin because not everyone who is infected with HIV has acquired it through a careless sexual lifestyle. Many people acquired the virus from accidental contact with contaminated medical equipment, such as needles. Others acquired it through mother-to-child transmission. And still others acquired it through contaminated blood via medical procedures such as blood transfusions. Surely people such as these could not be seen as sinners who perhaps deserved their suffering as punishment for their misdeeds.

From Crisis to Hope, a Kairos

Looking back into history invariably brings about new lessons. The genesis of home-based care had everything to do with meeting an emergency. In fact, its beginnings had something to do with despair. In the absence of a cure, and in the face of increasing numbers of infected people, our health system failed to deal adequately with the challenge of HIV and AIDS. In desperation, many people who had HIV were rejected by the system that should have embraced them. They were also rejected by their own society, which, confronted with the severity of the problem and a lack of immediate solutions, led to a collective paralysis.

One of the questions frequently asked by those afflicted is about the presence of God. God seemingly abandons those who are suffering, a theme we come across repeatedly in the Scriptures. There is no better illustration of that theme than the cry of Jesus on the cross:

"My God, my God, why have you forsaken me?'" (Mark 15:34)

It is a cry that we first come across in the Psalms.

"My God, my God, why have you forsaken me?" (Ps. 22:1)

HBC addressed issues of stigmatization, sin, despair, and pain from a faith-inspired perspective. HBC brought God into the homes of patients. Into a situation of severe suffering and a feeling of rejection steeped in traditional way of dealing with those afflicted. Family and friends took over the responsibility of looking after those whom society had rejected or abandoned to die. HBC provided the care that patients needed. It also helped patients feel they belong and could find meaning for life even in their miserable situation. Patients found acceptance through the ministry of HBC.

---

[13] Lewis Watuka, *From Positive to Negative* (unpublished).

Perceptions of God in Times of Suffering

In many ways, HBC addressed the experience of feeling neglected and abandoned. Many people in this situation project their rejection by society to represent a rejection from God. However, Christian revelation affirms that God is ever present to his children. To those in special circumstances, God is present in a special way. HBC restored patients' faith in an abiding and faithful God. Those men and women diagnosed with HIV in the late 1980s and early 1990s turned to God in despair and uttered words perhaps different from those of the psalmist and our Lord but words to the same effect. God is silent when I am suffering. What have I done to deserve this? Why has God abandoned me?

Fr. Lewis Watuka in his story also points to the support that he received from his fellow brothers at the time it was customary to dismiss candidates to the priesthood and religious life if they tested positive. His superiors decided that they would practice the virtue of solidarity with those afflicted by accepting Lewis into their congregation. "Can't we see Lewis's problem not only as a problem, something to get rid of, but as a sign of the times for us, a chance to be grasped . . . Can't we keep Lewis? Can't we knowingly stand by his side and support him as a loving and understanding family would?"[14]

Many in our society, including within the church, saw the HIV and AIDS crisis as a problem to be solved. And those who were afflicted were rejected. They had to be hidden from society, confined to their homes until they died. Society had given up on them. Members of HBC refused to follow this well-trodden path. They not only confronted the pandemic head-on but also exhibited great courage and faith in a compassionate God. They became witness to the unfailing and unchanging love of God.

The Pastoral Dimension of Home-Based Care in Zambia

The reflections in this chapter are a reminder to many pastoral agents in countries like Zambia facing serious difficulties in finding God in those challenges and recovering the hope that comes from acknowledging that nothing can come between us and the love of God. The work of Caring Women that I referred to earlier is a classic illustration of a pastoral approach to critical challenges. We can truly surmise that the work of the Caring Women was a wonderful example of the efficacy of a Pastoral Cycle.

---

[14] Ibid., 5.

The Pastoral Cycle

At the time of writing this chapter, I was assigned to work at the Jesuit Centre for Theological Reflection (JCTR). At the time of its formation the center was designed to provide support to Jesuits in various ministries to appreciate their ministry from a theological perspective. Over time the center has expanded to include other works. However, what has remained a key element of the work of the center is its pastoral cycle approach. The work of the center begins with insertion in time and place. In other words, the JCTR keeping to the principles of the pastoral cycle begins with lived experience and then moves to analysis, theological reflection, and action. The work of the center is rooted in the lived experiences of the people. It is a grassroots-led ministry.

HBC strengthened the faith of patients in the presence of God amid pain and exclusion. A Christian does not give up on those who are too sick to be helped. The story of Mother Teresa of Calcutta and many other heroes and heroines is emblematic of this commitment to those in need. It seems to me that the early members of HBC were following in the footsteps of the likes of Mother Teresa.

The encounter between the home-based caregivers and the sick reveals a double dimension as far as our faith is concerned. On the one hand, this encounter brings much-needed solace and consolation to the afflicted. This is similar to the man who was left for dead and a supposed enemy came and bandaged his wounds and took care of him (Luke 10). Clearly, the sick were strengthened by these encounters. They also received the compassion of the Lord. On the other hand, this encounter between the afflicted and the carers also brings the carers into contact with God. "Insofar as you did this to the least of my brothers, you did it to me." Whether these words of the Lord were foremost in the minds of the carers or not is immaterial. What matters is the truth of our Christian faith that an encounter with a person in need is an encounter with God.

The above reflections remind us of a fundamental truth of the Christian faith. God lives among us. God is present in the people in special need. Affliction, suffering, and difficulties of every kind can become opportunities and occasions to encounter the divine.

The Christian Scriptures are replete with references to the fact that God lives with his people at all times and in all circumstances. The traumatic experiences of the Hebrew people in Egypt and Babylon and the emergence of prophetic utterances is testament to the fact that God lives among his people. "Yahweh then said, 'I have seen the misery of my people in Egypt. I have heard them crying for help on account of the taskmasters. And I have come down to rescue them from the clutches of the Egyptians and lead them out of that country, to a country rich and broad, to a country flowing with milk and honey."

Through the emergence of HBC, God responded to the cry of his people. Just as he sent Moses to liberate them, so did God send the HBC to bring consolation and solace to those suffering from the pandemic. The fact that God is present in our lives is a truth that we should not tire of repeating. And the fact that God is especially present in the afflicted is a critical and cardinal article of our faith.

The prophets of the exile are another example of the assurance from God that God lives among his people.

"And now, thus says Yahweh,
He who created you, Jacob, who formed you, Israel:
'Do not be afraid, for I have redeemed you; I have called you by name.
Should you pass through the waters I shall be with you, or through rivers, they will not swallow you up.'" (Isa 43:1–3)

God is present even in the messes of life. He always takes the side of the afflicted and redeems them. The work of the Catholic Church in general and the Caring Women in particular is a good reminder that God lives with us. The testimony of Fr. Lewis Watuka is another reminder that God hears the cry of the poor. The three testimonies together suggest that God from time to time raises up weak and limited human beings to be his instruments to bring about good in the face of evil. These instruments rely on the power of God through his grace to bring about positive change in individual and communal lives.

What the two fundamental truths of our faith remind us is that at various times in history, God chooses to manifest God's self in a crisis. The group of women I refer to above not only ministered to the afflicted but also met every week to share, reflect, and pray over their experiences. They were opening themselves up to discern the voice of the Lord in their work. Therefore, a crisis may turn out to be an opportune time to encounter God afresh. It can be a kairos. The Chinese proverb reminds us that the term crisis connotes two truths: danger and opportunity. Throughout history a time of crisis has turned out to be a time of grace as well. God is present in the crisis and calling us to return to him in a radical way.

Inculturation Revisited

One of the elements underpinning home-based care is the traditional value of care found in many African traditional societies. Many African families attend to weak and vulnerable members of the community even when there is no catastrophe. It is part and parcel of what it means to be community. This traditional value is well captured in the often repeated phrase of "I am because you are," frequently referred to as Ubuntu. The philosophy of Ubuntu that is a common feature of many African societies frequently finds its expression in acts of mercy and compassion. The experience narrated above shows how this philosophy can be put into action. The women who attended to the needs of those who were suffering were not necessarily related to the patients. They acted out of a recognition that a community is made whole by the contribution of every member. This value is also found in our Christian faith.

Challenges

The emergence of a home-based-care support system is emblematic of how God works in surprising ways in our societies. Those who had HIV in the late 1980s and early 1990s felt rejected and abandoned by society. Many of the people who encountered terminally ill patients shrunk from the horror and sight of people experiencing extreme and intense pain. Many felt inadequate. My first reaction when I encountered terminally ill patients was one of paralysis. I just did not know how I could help someone who was in so much pain at a time when there was no known remedy.

However, the emergency of home-based care was a true reflection that God does not abandon his people. The success of home-based care challenges us to continually be searching for God, who is present to us in unexpected ways. However, when all is said and done, AIDS remains a killer in our communities. Notwithstanding the availability of life-prolonging antiretroviral drugs, many people remain without such important medication. Clearly, we need to increase the coverage of such treatment to as many as need it. We also must remember that a cure has yet to be found. Consequently, some of the points presented below are still relevant.

Lessons for Today and Tomorrow

Recommitment to Prevention of Infection

In the absence of a cure for the virus, the church cannot forget its education efforts in order to help people avoid being infected. It is assumed in our time that a lot of people know the dangers of practicing illicit and unprotected sexual activities. This position is dangerous to hold. There is growing evidence that new infections are springing up again.

Pastoral Approaches

The story of HBC reveals the efficacy of pastoral approaches to many critical challenges. HBC is a community-based intervention. It is essentially carried out by volunteers who expect very little recompense for their efforts and time. This fact is important because sometimes there is inertia in responding to emergencies due to limitations in human, material, and financial resources. What HBC demonstrates is that with a few committed individuals and limited resources, a lot of good can be done.

Rooted in Reality

HBC is also an important example of an initiative that is rooted and founded in reality. It is an intervention born of necessity but very much directed at resolving concrete life challenges, which is probably why it enjoys such high rates of participation from the local members of the community. Much can be learned from this ability to generate interest from local people in attending to local problems.

Cooperation with State Institutions and Agents

HBC is a reminder of the need for state institutions and agents to cooperate with other agents—in this case, pastoral agents. Given that the church operates a third of health delivery institutions, the HBC that draws its support and leadership from local health institutions has become an important partner of the state health delivery system. The HBC has emerged as a complementary infrastructure to the mainstream health delivery system. It is a decentralized system that has enabled health services to reach people otherwise left out by the state system that cannot reach every corner of the country.

Prophets and Kings

HBC is a good reminder of the role of ordinary members of the church in the church's evangelizing mission. Every baptized member of the church carries a threefold ministry of prophet, priest, and king. HBC is an occasion for ordinary members of the church to participate in the prophetic and kingly ministries of the church.

Primary Health Care

The expansion of HBC to include services beyond AIDS care has brought primary health-care services to people in remote parts of the country. Evidence from the research mentioned above is testimony to this emerging complex health delivery system.

Conclusion

This reflection on home-based care shows us a compassionate God at work, and reminds us, his followers, never to give up. The experience of suffering perhaps reminds us once again that God is sometimes found much more readily and easily when we are in pain. It is in some ways difficult to search for God when we are healthy and successful. We attribute our good fortune to our efforts and wisdom. However, when we have nowhere to turn, when our powers and wisdom fail us, we turn to God, who indeed hears the cry of the poor (Psalm 34).

CONCLUDING REMARKS

AIDS, EVIL, AND SALVATION:
AFRICAN LIGHT ON FAITH IN JESUS CHRIST

Lisa S. Cahill

Theological Reflections

The authors gathered here bring the reader into stark confrontation with the most profound mysteries of human life and Christian faith: the intransigence of evil and the possibility of salvation in Jesus Christ. Where does evil come from? What explains its hold on human hearts and its pervasive corruption of human societies? Why are there "natural" evils such as illness and death? How are such realities compatible with trust in a good Creator? If death is the destiny of every living thing, and domination the inner blight of every social system, then what hope can there be for human happiness, social harmony, and respect for the dignity of all? How does Jesus Christ embody God's word of liberation from sin, violence, and sorrow? Does the salvation Jesus brings mean transformation as well as forgiveness, community as well as cross, justice as well as eternal life? How can this question be given a positive answer, given the fact that evil so deeply marks human history and our world today?

The contributors to this volume take up these questions in response to the scourge of HIV and AIDS on the African continent, but the questions themselves are of universal Christian importance. Indeed, they are vital to the very possibility of faith. They also define the enterprise of Christian theology and lead on to the essential questions of Christian ethics: What kind of human relationships and transformational politics flow from an authentic experience of salvation from God in Jesus Christ? If God's defeat of evil is already effective in our lives, what kind of personal and structural change can and does that entail?

Stated briefly, the authors here show that evil involves but is not limited to personal sin; it has a social-structural dimension, and can even seem to be a cosmic force that is outside human control. Salvation from God in Jesus Christ culminates in resurrection life beyond all suffering, but it also has this-worldly effects and demands. One of these is the transformation of personal attitudes and behavior; just as importantly, salvation involves the transformation of social exclusions and structural violence in a new family of brothers and sisters in Jesus Christ. But we also see from this collection, and the decades-long struggle with AIDS that it represents, that Christian claims about God, Christ, and salvation must be credible in the midst of ongoing human suffering, not just as assurances of a better world after death. Salvation, faith community, and love of neighbor are genuine only if and when their power in human lives now is stronger than the inevitability of pain and the certainty of death.

All Theology Is Contextual

In this book, theology engages with and develops from a particular human context: contemporary African societies as they are affected by the disease of AIDS. One of the book's aims is to provide a model of theological reflection that can speak not only to the AIDS epidemic but to future public health crises. Specific theological insights and claims that are part of this model are highlighted below. An important preliminary point is that theology is not merely an intellectual exercise that takes as its point of departure biblical texts or doctrines about Christ and the Trinity as defined at various councils for the universal church. Theology first originates in the life of the local church, because it is always a reflection on faith as it is lived concretely. Theology is necessarily defined by the circumstances of communities, by the lives of Christians who claim to be practicing faith in the gospel of Jesus Christ, to be embodying its meaning in what they say and do. Theology can only be as true and authentic as the relation to Jesus Christ out of which it emerges, in the particular and daily existence of Christian communities.

Therefore, one of the main tasks of this book has been to challenge theologies (and pastoral practices) that inauthentically convey the relation of God to AIDS sufferers and to the families and communities to which they belong. One of its main goals has been to advance alternative theologies that are deeply entwined with alternative Christian practices—practices which, it is claimed, are more consistent with the truth of our salvation from evil by the power of God manifest and shared in the life, death, and resurrection of Jesus Christ, and the sending of his Spirit.

It is evident from the chapters collected here that the purpose of theology goes beyond refining and rearranging intellectual concepts and ideas. Theology and all language about God are very practical, both in their origins and in their effects. The U.S. theologian Elizabeth Johnson has protested all-male images of God on the basis that "the symbol of God functions." "Hence the way in which a faith community shapes language about God implicitly represents what it takes to be the highest good, the profoundest truth, the most appealing beauty.

Such speaking, in turn, powerfully molds the corporate identity of the community and directs its praxis."[1] The same is true of language about God's stance toward sin and suffering. Does God liberate and heal, or condemn and punish? Does God embrace and lift up, or does God turn away and cast down? And *whom* does God liberate, heal, embrace, and lift up—or punish?

Of the many examples in this volume, a striking instance of religious ideas and theologies that are implicated in questionable praxis appears in the essay by Philippe Denis. He asserts that although few priests and bishops would today still say outright that AIDS is a punishment from God, that message has not disappeared. One member of a South African parish AIDS support group was told by her pastor that the church "is a place to talk about the Word of God," *not* HIV and AIDS. The theology that such a statement assumes is a theology of exclusion, not healing—a theology, and therefore a practice, in which Jesus Christ as Word has no connection to real human suffering, and does not overcome the boundaries that separate the sick from the healthy, the "guilty" from the "righteous."

Because AIDS is a sexually transmitted disease (and can also be transmitted through the use of addictive drugs), the suffering and death that it brings are easy to legitimize as just recompense for immoral behavior. This kind of repudiation of the patient as well as the disease helps protect the accuser or the accusing church against the fear of similarly becoming a pariah or a scapegoat, or of falling prey to premature death. It protects society and the church from having to reexamine accepted norms of sexual behavior and gender conformity to see whether their inadequacies have been in part to blame for the spread of the disease. This book requires us to question traditional norms, especially about the roles and rights of women; it also inspires us to see whether the gospel demands different values and priorities than those that have contributed to the ravages of the disease.

Offering hope in this regard, several chapters recount instances of local church groups and ministries that embody the inclusive reign of God, and express symbolically and theologically that salvation includes reconciliation and communion with suffering brothers and sisters. Ignace Ndongala Maduku provides a theology of "the church-family of God" that creates an ecclesiology of the Church as "servant, healer, and defender of life," and that has produced concrete pastoral action of service and support to AIDS victims in the Basic Ecclesial Communities of Kinshasa. Philippe Denis observes specifically that the challenges of AIDS have changed the way people relate to their faith communities, and have thus changed theology as well. The epidemic requires that matters of health, sexuality, and gender be matters of explicit Christian

---

[1]   Elizabeth A. Johnson, *She Who Is: The Mystery of God in Feminist Theological Discourse* (New York: Crossroad, 1994), 4.

concern; church members living with AIDS are insisting that the church as a whole become more attentive to values such as love, compassion, reconciliation, and forgiveness, and more invested in ministries of health care and of pastoral support. From an ecumenical perspective, Nyambura Njoroge outlines the creative theologies of the World Council of Churches and the Circle of Concerned African Women Theologians to show similarly, not only that theology has adapted, but also that new theologies are already "shaping the daily lives of many children, youth, and adults, including clergypersons, theologians, and scholars."

The Contextual Reality of HIV and AIDS in Africa

It is obvious from these examples that to articulate or understand a theology of AIDS, it is important to understand the practical conditions with which it is interdependent. Virtually every essay in this book offers some description of the reality of AIDS in the particular location of the author, or in terms of the continent considered overall. From these chapters certain general features emerge. At a factual level, they tell us how AIDS spreads and persists, and how it devastates lives and communities. At a theological-ethical level, the chapters illustrate the complex nature of sin and evil, particularly how personal and social causes magnify and reinforce each other.

Some key points are the role of personal sexual behavior: the influence of social and cultural attitudes and practices (including "stigma"); the role of larger economic and political institutions, affected by colonialism and global capitalism; and most especially the practices and institutions of patriarchy, with its personal, local, and global manifestations. It is not necessary to repeat here the various contextual assessments, which converge in many ways. I lift out two especially pernicious aspects of the epidemic in Africa, factors that not only reinforce each other, but also illustrate the interdependence of personal and social forms of sin and evil that takes varying forms beyond Africa. These are stigma and gender discrimination.

First of all, on a culturally distinctive yet more positive note, several authors explain that notions of sin and stigma, as well as those of care and mutual support, have to be understood in light of the communal view of the person shared among African cultures. Laurenti Magesa explains that individual fulfillment, authenticity, and rights derive from membership in a community, and in serving the needs of community, particularly the generation of new life. This is the meaning of the traditional concept of *Ubuntu*, which Odomaro Mubangizi shows converges with Christian biblical ideals of reconciling community and works of mercy.

In this light, Caroline Mbonu discusses the African notions of moral responsibility as having both an individual and a communal character; sin does not reside only in the individual, but also has a familial or communal dimension. The sin of an individual affects everyone, and the community as a whole is called to make amends. Although this should lead to an aggressive communal determination to heal the sick and root out the causes of the disease, where it often leads to is stigma (Bongmba). Stigmatizing those living with HIV is simultaneously a way of putting the emphasis back on individual culpability, deflecting attention from communal complicity, and "purifying" the community by disassociating from it those viewed to have brought misfortune, disgrace, or punishment.

Jacquineau Azetsop calls stigma "the major enemy of HIV prevention" because people fear the consequences of admitting their HIV status. Stigma causes immense suffering of persons with AIDS who are ostracized from families and communities. Stigma also obstructs the discovery of the more systemic and far-reaching changes in attitudes, practices, and institutions that are essential to fight the disease successfully. Stigmatization moralizes the disease, takes the emphasis off vulnerability and routes of exposure, and avoids the reality that AIDS is a public health issue that can be addressed only by addressing gender, poverty, social exclusion, and the government dysfunction and corruption that undermine any hope of an effective systemic response (Mayanja). Not to be minimized as a contributing factor is the additional fact of war and civil conflict, now rampant in many parts of Africa—causing social disruption, forced migration, poverty, and violence against women, including rape (Tonde).

Women across Africa are both more vulnerable to HIV and more likely to be stigmatized and excluded from social, economic, and health-care resources, even as women are the major caregivers for ill family members (Mkenda). Structural factors that affect women's resources and choices are often neglected in public health strategies, as well as in Christian condemnation of behavior that leads to AIDS. "ABC strategies, for example, failed to take into account the context of vulnerability created by structural actors that shape women's lives in most African countries" (Azetsop). Women not only have less power in sexual decision making than men, and are more vulnerable to AIDS than men, they are also more likely to be stigmatized, not only when they contract HIV but also when their spouse or partner dies of AIDS, no matter how he contracted it. Several authors point out that "women" are not the problem, and that changing gender means changing models of masculinity as well as femininity (e.g., Njoroge, Hinga), calling for models of what Teresia Hinga follows the World Council of Churches in calling "redemptive masculinities."

The interdependence of personal and social responsibility in producing AIDS exposure shows the complexity of the AIDS epidemic, and even of assessing the dynamics of stigma. If it is culturally acceptable for men to have more sexual partners than women, thus making women more vulnerable to

AIDS, then more socially condemnatory attitudes toward having multiple sexual partners might work in favor of reducing women's exposure and reducing the transmission of HIV in general. At the same time, viewing AIDS as primarily a matter of personal sexual responsibility or sinfulness harmfully minimizes cultural and economic factors that undermine female self-determination and male faithfulness, and can result in refusal to seek testing and treatment rather than in the actual reduction of unprotected or multipartner sex. In Africa, the battle against AIDS must be fought on three fronts: taking individual responsibility; changing cultural attitudes and established practices; and reducing local, continental, and global structures that cause poverty and other forms of injustice (Lado). Considering the lessons of this book more broadly, the same is true for virtually every form of social injustice, no matter on which continent it is felt most acutely, or who is most responsible for its causes.

Theological Interpretations

The theological content of this volume is rich and varied. Biblical narratives are more salient than Trinitarian theologies, Christologies, models of Christian ethics, or even Catholic social teaching. Although the chapters here obviously do not cover every aspect of theology in an integrated way, some important themes and commonalities can be identified. First of all, specific biblical narratives are used to illumine the situations of persons and communities afflicted by HIV and AIDS and to offer hope. Second, biblical and theological interpretation refers concretely to African societies and cultures, and its normative content is developed in dialogue with them. Third, the nearness of God even in devastating and desperate situations is proclaimed as a source of hope. Finally, local churches and lay ministries are devising creative ways to bring to reality this hope for salvation as including human liberation from the natural evil of disease, the consequences of personal sin, and the exclusions and oppressions perpetrated by institutional violence.

Turning first to biblical sources, we find examples both from the New Testament and the Christian Old Testament (Hebrew Bible). Not surprisingly, Psalms of Lament (Folifack) and the sufferings of Job (Ngengi) find great resonance with the plight of many Africans. Yet even these narratives of deep grief and protest reveal a relation to God that extreme suffering cannot interrupt. Wilfrid Okambawa invokes the Suffering Servant of Isaiah 52 to envision even the excluded and rejected community member as a potential vehicle of love and salvation. To be a "suffering servant" does not require that one be totally blameless like Job, however. This is an essential point, given the realistic circumstances of human life, especially in the context of AIDS. The connection between AIDS and wrongdoing is admittedly complex. African traditional ideas of witchcraft and Christian symbolism of Satan even point toward the existence of larger forces at work that cannot be reduced to individual sinfulness, yet somehow implicate human agency, a reality also suggested by the idea of structural sin (Davy).

What is important is to seek repentance, reconciliation, and a way forward, a responsibility shared by the whole community (Mbonu, Davy, Chitando, Bate). To this end, uses of the Bible that have furthered the "blaming of victims" (often women) and the alienation of those who remind us of our own vulnerability must be interrogated and rejected. This is especially true of biblical texts that are read to subordinate women to men, and to target women with blame for unexplained misfortune (Djomhoué).

As a powerful resource for hope and transformation, New Testament narratives model a "preferential option for the poor" that is the essential Christian response to any public health crisis, or indeed to any social crisis whatsoever (Azetsop, Hinga). Social upheavals and emergencies are exacerbated by unequal power relations, unequal access to remedies, and unequal and unfair apportionment of blame. Crises from economic collapse, to failed states, to ecological disaster and war, all involve systemic factors that illustrate what Paul Farmer has called "the pathology of power." Theologically and universally, we are called to recognize the reality of social sin, and "the need for social transformation through the option for the poor, which transformation requires structural changes, for the redemptive work of Christ is achieved by grace-filled individuals and institutions that seek to alter the social causes that created opportunities for poor behavior" (Azetsop).

This does not apply only to Africa, even in the case of HIV and AIDS, much less in the multitude of other cases in which immense human suffering is propelled by the self-interested actions of a relative few. We are reminded that in any such situation, women are the poorest of the poor, yet are rarely the recipients of any meaningful social "option" for dignity, respect, and agency (Hinga). Women foremost among those who suffer from AIDS, and all persons everywhere who suffer various forms of silencing and exclusion, must not only be the recipients of "our" concern and assistance, they must be *empowered* to become full agents whose gifts enrich and transform their own lives and their communities (Njoroge).

The option for the poor visible in Jesus's ministry of the reign of God, and his formation of community with the poor, sinners, and outcasts, is reaffirmed in Christian theological claims that go far beyond Africa or AIDS: the incarnation as divine nearness and care, the cross as God's full solidarity with human reality and the radical character of divine compassion, and the resurrection as Spirit-empowered hope for healing and a different future (Goussikindey).

A striking ecclesial insight emerges from the theologies represented here that has universal Christian value: the vitality and creativity of the local church, where the love of neighbor is brought to fruition in very practical ways, often by laypeople, especially women. "For most people infected or affected by HIV what counts is the local congregation" (Philippe Denis). It is in the local communities that wider Christian or Catholic ideals and theologies take hold and become "African solutions" (Kanyandago). Perhaps most obviously families must be encouraged and empowered to become part of the caring process, to embrace their affected loved ones with a healing with love and compassion, even though physical death may be inevitable (Bate).

Christian churches, the Catholic Church, and smaller units within the local church can support this process both by assisting families and by undertaking ministries of caregiving under the auspices of the church or churches. In Africa, efforts by local bishops' conferences and dioceses go back to the 1980s (Rogers) and have been renewed in recent decades, in concert with activism, services, and funding from nonecclesial sources, some of them outside Africa (Yedo). Of course, however promising and a mark of good intentions, a policy document or program does not always mean that a diocese and all its member parishes have made AIDS ministry a priority. This is why it is especially vital and a sign of hope to see that Small Christian Communities and grassroots initiatives, frequently under the leadership of women, are "owning" this ministry as an inherent correlate of Christian identity and participation in the life of the gospel (Chiti, Healey). As Joseph Healey shows, such efforts have already created a network that is changing social attitudes and the prospects of persons with AIDS across Eastern Africa.

One of the most cutting-edge and enduring lessons for the global church to be learned from African Christians' efforts to combat AIDS is that vast social problems require an equally vast social response, and a very energetic one. This is a challenge that cannot be met by Christians or Christian churches working in isolation, give the increasingly pluralistic nature of most societies and the global stretch of most problems and their causes, including vulnerability to disease and premature mortality (Egan, Mayanja, Tonde). Something that comes through clearly in this AJAN book on AIDS is that change in public policy requires broad-based social cooperation across different ethnicities, regions, subcultures, and religions. This is exemplified in references to African traditional religions and concepts, such as *Ubuntu* (many authors) and *Ukama* (Chitando). Elochukwu Uzukwu details correspondences between Christian and Igbo traditional spiritualities and liturgies, showing that Africans have cultural reservoirs that should not be neglected if the excluded are to reclaim their humanity and communities are to be renewed. Similarly, Susan Rakoczy draws together the diverse yet powerful spiritualities that will be available if the worldviews of affected persons are given a receptive hearing.

The African experience illustrates for North Atlantic theologians that "secular" society and "secular" public discourse is a limited phenomenon prevalent mostly in Western Europe, and among certain North American academics and elites. Chitando of the World Council of Churches goes so far as to call for an "interfaith theology of liberation." It is certainly true that some traditional religious ideas and practices need to be corrected and rejected in light of the gospel. Indeed, this is true of Christianity itself, as multiple voices in this volume have shown. While Odomaro Mubangizi shows promising connections among creation theology, New Testament compassion, and the African traditional view of the person, for example, Jean Paul Ondoua offers that important contrasts exist between the biblical view of healing by Jesus and the Word of God and African traditional healers' attribution of illness and healing to witchcraft and sorcery. On the whole, however, a dialogue among faiths of symbols, narratives, liturgies, and practices of daily life will have constructive results for the transformative energy and creative thinking needed to rid human existence of scourges like AIDS, whose resilience is due more to selfishness and structural injustice than to sex and a virus.

Conclusion

This volume gifts the reader and the broader universe of Christian theology with six important "take-away" messages:

1. Sin has deep personal and social roots and can only be defeated by compassion, sacrifice, and committed action.
2. The gospel must be received and embodied anew in every context, and is not truly heard until it comes to expression in the cultural symbols of its hearers.
3. There is an inherent connection of "theology" and "politics," for salvation necessarily entails changed human relationships.
4. The option for the poor must become an empowering option with and by the poor.
5. The primary meaning of "church" is not the Vatican, ecclesial structures, or a body of teaching and doctrine, but the community in which the risen Christ lives by the power of the Spirit.
6. Despite the historical tenacity of evil, communities that become genuine families of brothers and sisters in Christ can change historical conditions and give birth to hope.

POST SCRIPTUM

EXPANDING THE DISCOURSE TOWARD
VIRTUE, SOCIAL SPIRITUALITY,
AND UNIVERSAL COVERAGE

James F. Keenan

As we come to the end of this splendid volume, I am left thinking of three concepts: virtue ethics, social spirituality, and universal health care. Let me share with you how these concepts flow into one another as I finish this significant investigation into the plentitude of African theological resources in the time of HIV and AIDS.

First, although a few of the writers in this book refer on occasion to virtue, I want to suggest here that virtue ethics has a *growing* role in any ethical investigations that seek to promote communities. Why? Because the language of virtue conveys the anthropological vision of any social context. No one can understand a virtue out of its context, but when we understand a virtue as it is lived in one social context, we understand a bit about the people of that place. If we talk about patience in Nairobi it is very different from patience in Kinshasa and in both instances as we see patience taught and expressed in one culture, we are better able to understand the people from that place. If we talk about hospitality as practiced by one tribe, it is never the same as it is for another tribe. The practices and habits of the Yorubas are very different than the forms of welcome by the Turkana. But the way we are greeted by the Yorubas tells us about the people there: the way they greet us tell us the way they envision themselves.

Of course, Laurenti Magesa taught us that these virtues could be more than regional or tribal; they could be pan-African. In 1997 he looked to hermeneutics and found in pan-African religious claims an unmistakable language of abundant life that animated the religious ethics throughout Africa.[1] He used this abundant life ethics to address questions of right, virtuous conduct in a time of HIV. There are virtues then that are found across Africa—virtues like hospitality, justice, friendship, and hope, to name a few, a few indeed that actu-

---

[1] Laurenti Magesa, *African Religion: The Moral Traditions of Abundant Life* (Maryknoll, NY: Orbis Books, 1997).

398

ally are appropriate for Africans as they face and respond to the moment of *kairos* that the AIDS pandemic provides.

Virtues across Africa find their own incarnation in the particular contexts where they are sustained, cultivated, taught, and lived. Virtues are important because they are the way we hand on our tradition. In our homes, we teach our children how to treat a guest, how to respect an elder, how to love one's siblings, how to make friends with one another. In his work, John Kobina Ghansah explored first the question of character formation[2] and then ten years later the peculiar way that friendship in Africa bridges the world of the individual with the social.[3]

Virtue is precisely what allows Benedict Chidi Nwachukwu-Udaku to frame his theological reflections on the context of HIV and AIDS among the Igbos of Nigeria.[4] He looks at what the AIDS crisis brings to bear on his homeland, but argues that the way the Igbos respond to the crisis will shape the character identity of the Igbos in the future: they will become what they do. The practices of virtue lead us to answer urgent challenges but also to become a people transformed. For Chidi Nwachukwu-Udaku, the virtues he recommends helps make the Igbo church a community of commitment and solidarity.

Chidi Nwachukwu-Udaku's interest in developing a community of commitment echoes in many ways earlier African turns to solidarity and compassion. For instance, Michel Kamanzi sees solidarity, the quintessential twenty-first-century virtue, as a new categorical imperative, and Paterne Auxence Mombe invokes the virtue of compassion to promote a responsive, hope-filled community.[5] Together solidarity and compassion are instructive virtues that teach community members to take risks with one another, enter into trust, and walk with one another as they struggle to find pathways of accompaniment together.

A very important work that brings the ethics of compassion and solidarity together is Annah Nyadombo's work, *A Holistic Pastoral Approach to HIV/AIDS Sufferers: Reduction of Stigmatisation in Zimbabwe.*[6] In this study she

---

[2] John Kobina Ghansah, *Narrative Ethics and Christian Character Formation in Post-traditional Africa* (Licentiate thesis, Weston Jesuit School of Theology, 1996).

[3] John Kobina Ghansah, *"Drink with pleasure when it is aged": A Model of Friendship for Contextual Christian Ethical and Liturgical Life* (STD dissertation, Weston Jesuit School of Theology, 2006).

[4] Benedict Chidi Nwachukwu-Udaku, *From What We Should Do to Who We Should Be: Negotiating Theological Reflections and Praxis in the Context of HIV/AIDS among the Igbos of Nigeria* (Bloomington, IN: Author's House, 2011). An earlier work on HIV/AIDS in Nigeria provides enormous theological and ethical resources: James Olaitan Ajayti, *The HIV/AIDS Epidemic in Nigeria: Some Ethical Considerations* (Rome: Gregorian University Press, 2003).

[5] Michel S. Kamanzi, "Solidarity, A New Categorical Imperative," in *AIDS in Africa: Theological Reflections,* ed. Bénézet Bujo and Michael Czerny (Nairobi: Paulines, 2007), 17–30; Paterne Auxence Mombe, "Compassion of Christ," in Bujo and Czerny, *AIDS in Africa,* 43–48.

[6] Annah Nyadombo, *A Holistic Pastoral Approach to HIV/AIDS Sufferers: Reduc-*

shows how the virtue of justice animated by a church filled with the compassion of God and the solidarity of the Spirit can lead us to eradicate the awful stigma that blind bias brings to HIV and AIDS. Her work shows how concretely virtue directs us to ethical solutions that affect our communities.

Some writings on virtue and ethics emerged from elsewhere, though prompted by experiences, voices, and lessons from Africa. In a work of great vision, the English theologian Kevin Kelly, deeply affected by the HIV crisis in Africa, wrote a landmark work on sexual ethics in light of the HIV crisis using the virtue of justice.[7] Later Margaret Farley would find the language of justice as having resonance with the language of love and provide a sexual ethics for the twenty-first century.[8]

The turn to justice in a time of AIDS, however, is an African turn. In *Catholic Ethicists on HIV/AIDS Prevention*, Paulinus Odozor invoked the language of justice in response to the challenges of the HIV and AIDS pandemic.[9] In 2010 Michael Kelly provided arguably the most comprehensive work on sexual ethics out of Africa, all in the key of social justice.[10] HIV has helped us theologians understand the relational connection between sex and justice. More recently, the Nigerian theologian Daniel Ude Asue provides an incredibly powerful example of the effectiveness of the virtue of justice in sexual ethics as he explores Africa's Tivland women living within patriarchy and threatened by husbands living with HIV.[11]

These virtues lead us to see that they help us form communities of commitment, active spiritualities that are fed by the faith, expressed in the liturgy and worshipped and practiced in the ethical and moral life of our communities. In Africa these spiritualities are fundamentally communal and social, embodied like virtues in the felt lives of the members. Inclusion as opposed to autonomous individuality moved the Congolese theologian Benezet Bujo to look to the deep social, communal spiritual claims that ethics makes on Africa today.[12] Through

---

tion of Stigmatisation in Zimbabwe (Saarbrücken: Lambert Academic Publishing, 2014).

[7] Kevin Kelly, *New Directions in Sexual Ethics: Moral Theology and the Challenge of AIDS* (Washington, DC: Geoffrey Chapman, 1998).

[8] Margaret Farley, *Just Love: A Framework for Christian Sexual Ethics* (New York: Continuum, 2006).

[9] Paulinus Ikechukwu Odozor, "Casuistry and AIDS: A Reflection on the Catholic Tradition," in *Catholic Ethicists on HIV/AIDS Prevention*, ed. James F. Keenan, assisted by Lisa Sowle Cahill, Jon Fuller, and Kevin Kelly (New York: Continuum, 2000), 294–302.

[10] Michael Kelly, *HIV and AIDS: A Social Justice Perspective* (Nairobi: Paulines, 2010).

[11] Daniel Ude Asue, *"Bottom Elephants": Catholic Sexual Ethics and Pastoral Practice in Africa: The Challenge of Women Living within Patriarchy and Threatened by HIV-Positive Husbands* (Washington, DC: Pacem in Terris Press, 2014).

[12] Bujo, "Community Ethics," in Bujo and Czerny, *AIDS in Africa*, 63–78.

his discourse or *palaver ethics* he offered a three-dimensional (the ancestors of the past, the present generation, and the not-yet arrived future) look at who needs to be included in our deliberations.[13] In a manner of speaking, Peter Knox took Bujo's multidimensional communal summons and located it in salvation in his deeply resonant work *AIDS, Ancestors, and Salvation*.[14] Knox's extraordinarily reconciling work is really one of the most integral expressions of both African ethics and spirituality.

Agbonkhianmeghe E. Orobator reminds us that social spiritualities are hardly ethereal but are significantly practical and helpful when he offers us a triptych of practical "spirituality" in a time of HIV: a tradition of pastoral engagement in the context of HIV and AIDS, a systematic body of theological resources (like this splendid volume!) on HIV and AIDS, and a contentious ethical education regarding neuralgic issues spawned by the pandemic.[15] Orobator more than many understands how central the church's life needs to be to these spiritualities. He reminds us that, early on, "The AIDS crisis . . . spawned an intriguing variety of expressions depicting its impact on the church." Phrases like "The Body of Christ has AIDS" or "Our Church has AIDS" arose early and quickly. Orobator writes, "Far from being simply opportunistic jargon or clichés, such expressions indicate(d) the need to engage the crisis."[16] His triptych embodies that social spirituality that is needed today.

A variety of questions were raised about how inclusive the discourse in Africa actually is. Like Asue above, Anne Nasimiyu-Wasike, Teresa Okure, and Teresia Hinga advocated that women's voices needed to be better incorporated into the African discourse.[17] David Kaulem asked: In the African Catholic Church, where are lay voices in church deliberations?[18] Reading these critiques I find myself hearing the demanding voice of the late Jean Marc Ela, who brought more assertive claims of justice into the discourse, asking, Does anyone hear the African cry?[19] Indeed, all

---

[13] Bénézet Bujo, *Foundations of an African Ethic* (Nairobi: Paulines, 2003).

[14] Peter Knox, *AIDS, Ancestors, and Salvation* (Nairobi: Paulines ed., 2008).

[15] Agbonkhianmeghe E. Orobator, "Catholic Responses to HIV/AIDS in Africa: The Long Road to Conversion," in *Catholic Responses to AIDS in Southern Africa*, ed. Stuart C. Bate and Alison Munro (Hilton, South Africa: Grace and Truth, 2014), 170–85.

[16] Agbonkhianmeghe E. Orobator, *From Crisis to Kairos: The Mission of the Church in the Time of HIV/AIDS, Refugees, and Poverty* (Nairobi: Paulines, 2005), 121.

[17] Anne Nasimiyu-Wasike, "The Missing Voices of Women," in *Catholic Theological Ethics, Past, Present, and Future: The Trento Conference*, ed. James F. Keenan (Maryknoll, NY: Orbis Books, 2011), 107–15; Teresia Hinga, "Becoming Better Samaritans: The Quest for New Models of Doing Social-Economic Justice in Africa," in *Applied Ethics in a World Church*, ed. Linda Hogan (Maryknoll, NY: Orbis Books, 2008), 85–97.

[18] David Kaulem, "Catholic Social Teaching at a Crossroad," in Keenan, *Catholic Theological Ethics*, 176–84.

[19] Jean Marc Ela, *African Cry* (Maryknoll, NY: Orbis Books, 1986).

these theologians are mindful of the need for a more robust but just engagement of different persons affected by ethical challenges in Africa. Their critical concern is common: Is there someone not heard?

African spirituality depends not only on solidarity and justice; it has the compelling need for a language of hope in the face of such uncanny vulnerability. Two new scholars, Ghislain Tshikendwa Matadi and Maria Cimperman, would turn one to the biblical tradition, the other to the tradition of virtue to use the language of hope.[20] In both instances, they found that the reality of Africa in a time of AIDS was a proper place for engaging a virtue that was born in Golgotha. There they each articulated a virtue that depends on realism in all its uncompromising expression. Hope is not a virtue born out of easy experiences. Rather, the experiences of these theologians prompted their brother bishops to reflect on the same virtue. The language of hope became the prayer of the African episcopate.[21]

Justice, solidarity, compassion, and hope animate not only our ethics but our spirituality. We have seen that, but another virtue that we should attend to is mercy that prompts us to enter willingly into the chaos of another.[22] Mercy is the virtue that helps us to shape our justice so that we bring justice to those who have been so abandoned by injustice. Mercy is that which moves us to the excluded, the stigmatized, the marginalized, the infected; a true virtue, it has no condescension but rather acts as the Samaritan did. That is, mercy teaches the entire church to be neighborly.[23]

Finally, these virtues and an anthropologically rich, other-centered spirituality lead us to go beyond the HIV and AIDS pandemic. This volume provides the theological resources to realize that responding to the HIV crisis means responding to the entire spectrum of health care. No one who has any contact with the human and public health crisis caused by the HIV virus thinks that a response is adequate if it does not engage the entire infrastructure of African health care. In an essay that I gave in Nairobi two years ago to mark the thirtieth anniversary of HIV and AIDS, I argued that the end of the pandemic had to include access to universal health care.[24]

[20] Ghislain Tshikendwa Matadi, *Suffering, Belief, Hope: The Wisdom of Job for an AIDS-Stricken Africa* (Nairobi: Paulines, 2005); Maria Cimperman, *When God's People Have HIV/AIDS* (Maryknoll, NY: Orbis Books, 2005).

[21] Catholic Bishops of Africa and Madagascar, *Speak Out on HIV and AIDS: Our Prayer Is Always Full of Hope* (Nairobi: Paulines, 2004).

[22] James F. Keenan, *The Works of Mercy: The Heart of Catholicism* (Lanham, MD: Rowman and Littlefield, 2007).

[23] Francis, *The Church of Mercy: A Vision for the Church* (Chicago: Loyola University Press, 2014).

[24] James F. Keenan, "Developing HIV/AIDS Discourse in Africa and Advancing the Argument for Universal Health Care," in *AIDS Thirty Years Down the Line: Faith-Based*

The more we respond to the HIV crisis, the more our health-care agenda inevitably expands. Moreover, the more we attend to the *language* we use in order to address the AIDS pandemic and related matters, the more we *expand* our agenda, our circle of interlocutors, and our ability to address even more issues. I conclude suggesting that now is the time to include universal health care in our HIV and AIDS conversations, if we have already not yet begun to do so. I believe that we have the conceptual and practical networks as well as the moral and economic urgency to do this and that as we strive for universal health coverage, we will better respond to HIV and AIDS.

In my essay I highlighted two authors whom I think help us move from the HIV crisis and related effects to universal access. The first was the legendary Jonathan Mann, who began looking for something that could analyze the social context in which people became ill. In 1997 Mann put before public health officials a long recognized but rarely addressed insight: "it is clear, throughout history and in all societies, that the rich live generally longer and healthier lives than the poor."[25] But immediately after this he added, "A major question arising from the socioeconomic status-health gradient is why there is a gradient."[26] This question was begging not only for a conceptual analysis but also for a practical resolution: we needed to remove the gradient.

If poverty is so much a cause of the spread of disease, why wasn't poverty incorporated into the analyses and strategies of public health officials? Mann, sounding almost like a theologian, answered, "Public health has lacked *a conceptual framework* for identifying and analyzing the essential societal factors that represent the conditions in which people can be healthy." He concluded by ruing the ineffectual babble that public health officials inevitably uttered without these critical tools: "Lacking a coherent framework, a consistent vocabulary, and a consensus about societal change, public health assembles and then tries valiantly to assimilate a wide variety of disciplinary perspectives, from economists, political scientists, societal and behavioral scientists, health systems analysts, and a range of medical practitioners. Yet while each of these perspectives provides some useful insight, public health becomes thereby a little bit of everything and thus not enough of anything."[27]

Mann turned to and appreciated in the language of human rights both its integral comprehensiveness and its moral urgency. Public health had a desperate need for the conceptual framework of human rights to effectively respond to

---

Reflections about the Epidemic in Africa, ed. Paterne Mombe, Agbonkhianmeghe Orobator, and Danielle Vela (Nairobi: Paulines, 2013), 63–82.

[25] Jonathan Mann, "Medicine and Public Health, Ethics and Human Rights," *Hastings Center Report* 27 (1997): 6–13, 7.

[26] Ibid.

[27] Ibid., 8.

the unprecedented nature and magnitude of the HIV and AIDS pandemic: "Modern human rights, precisely because they were initially developed entirely outside the health domain and seek to articulate the societal preconditions for human well-being, seem a far more useful framework, vocabulary, and form of guidance for public health efforts to analyze and respond directly to the societal determinants of health than any inherited from the past biomedical or public health tradition."[28]

Second, I relied on the advocacy work of the theologian and public health researcher, Jacquineau Azetsop, the editor of this volume, who advances the discussion of how advances in responding to the challenges of HIV prevention and AIDS management inevitably lead to advances in public health. In five of his important contributions from the last few years, he shows how the resources of theology and public health together advance the trajectory of the work of HIV prevention, AIDS management, and treatment to universal health care. First, he offered a final critique of the principle of autonomy and its explicit endorsement of medical individualism.[29] Later he showed that an autonomy-based ethics inhibits our understanding of patients' interconnectedness with others and their biological environments. Instead, it makes invisible the social causes of poor health. Its view of the mind and body are abstract, and in this model, disease is the result of choices made. In short, autonomy-based ethics is at least in global health a moral siphon. Instead he turned toward Africa, which teaches that illness is at the same time an individual, social, and cosmological event of significant importance.[30] Then he identified Magesa's life-centered ethics as a natural law claim and incorporated it into a vision of public health and healing in Africa.[31] Next he summoned us to move away from the crisis mentality of disease management into a much more ambitious and visionary strategy of health promotion and advocacy, a fundamental move.[32] Finally, his

---

[28] Ibid., 9. See also Mann, "Human Rights and AIDS: The Future of the Pandemic," in *Health and Human Rights*, ed. Jonathan Mann (New York: Routledge, 1999), 216–26.

[29] Jacquineau Azetsop and Stuart Rennie, "Principilism, Medical Individualism, and Health Promotion in Resource-Poor Countries: Can Autonomy-Based Ethics Promote Justice in Poor-Resource Settings?" *Philosophy, Ethics, and Humanities in Medicine* 5 (2010): 1.

[30] Jacquineau Azetsop, "Pluralisme Médical et Guérison en Afrique sub-Saharienne. Implications du pluralisme médical pour la santé publique et la bioéthique," *Le Pluralisme médical en Afrique. Hommage à Eric de Rosny*, ed. L. Lado (Pucac: Yaoundé, 2010): 449–60.

[31] Jacquineau Azetsop, "A Life-Centered Ethics, Public Health, and Healing in Africa," *Human Nature and Natural Law*, ed. Lisa Sowle Cahill, Hille Haker, and Eloi Messi Metogo (London: SCM Press, 2010), 99–109; *Concilium* 336 (2010): 129–42.

[32] Jacquineau Azetsop, "New Directions in African Bioethics: Ways of Including Public Health Concerns in the Bioethics Agenda," *Developing World Bioethics* 11, no. 1 (April 2011): 4–15.

most sustained contribution is his book promoting health equity. There he insists we should "create the policy environment that can favor the optimization of health potential for individuals and groups."[33] In many ways Azetsop leads us into the conversation on universal health care, HIV prevention, and AIDS management.

Any post-scriptum is really a statement about "what needs to be said after all has been written." Mine suggests that, for this volume, we ought to spend some time learning more from virtue, both for ethics and for a social spirituality. I also think, if we want to move beyond the HIV crisis toward a more inclusive vision of health care in African countries, we might want to embrace the need for a more stable, inclusive, and accessible health system, and I think, the first author on this topic is the editor of this volume—and that is what needs to be said, after all has been written.

---

[33] Jacquineau Azetsop, *Structural Violence, Population Health, and Health Equity: Preferential Option for the Poor and Health Equity in Sub-Saharan Africa* (Saarbrücken: VDM, 2010), 102.

CONTRIBUTORS

Jacquineau Azétsop, S.J. is Dean of the School of Social Sciences at the Pontifical Gregorian University in Rome. His research focuses on health justice, the role of Christian faith in society, the link between public health and social policy, and the social dimension of health.

Stuart C. Bate, OMI, is Director of Research and Development at St Joseph's Theological Institute, Cedara and Honorary Staff member of the School of Religion, Philosophy and Classics at the University of KwaZulu-Natal, South Africa.

Elias K. Bongmba holds the Harry and Hazel Chavanne Chair in Christian Theology at Rice University. He is the author of *Facing a Pandemic: The African Church and the Crisis of AIDS.*

Lisa Sowle Cahill, J. Donald Monan Professor at Boston College, researches Christian bioethics, gender ethics, and war and peace. Her most recent book is *Global Justice, Christology and Christian Ethics.*

Ezra Chitando is Theology Consultant on HIV and AIDS for the World Council of Churches' Ecumenical HIV and AIDS Initiatives and Advocacy.

Leonard Chiti, S.J., is the Director at the Jesuit Centre for Theological Reflection (JCTR). He is the author of numerous scholarly articles on HIV and AIDS, the environment, human rights, and constitutional and legal issues.

Davy Dossou, S.J. is a doctoral student in philosophy at the Gregorian University in Rome.

M. Shawn Copeland, a professor of systematic theology at Boston College, is the former president of the Catholic Theological Society of America and a former Convener of the Black Catholic Theological Symposium. She is the author or editor of several books and numerous articles.

Philippe Denis, OP, is Professor of the History of Christianity at the University of KwaZulu-Natal.

Priscille Djomhoue, pastor of the Protestant United Church of Belgium, teaches at the Faculté Universitaire de Théologie Protestante de Bruxelles.

Conrad A. Folifack Dongmo, S.J., is a PhD student in Old Testament at the University of Louvain in Belgium.

Anthony Egan, S.J., works at the Jesuit Institute South Africa in Johannesburg. A historian and moral theologian by training, he lectures part time in bioethics at the Faculty of Health Sciences, University of the Witwatersrand.

Eugene D. Goussikindey, S.J., is Director of Center of Research and Action for Peace in Abidjan, Côte d'Ivoire.

Joseph G. Healey, MM, is an American Maryknoll missionary priest who lives in Nairobi, Kenya. He teaches a full semester core course on "Small Christian Communities" (SCCs) as a New Model of Church in Africa Today" at various theological institutes.

Teresia Hinga, is Associate professor of religious studies at Santa Clara University. Her scholarly/research interests include women and religion, religion and the public square, ethics of globalization and gendered perspectives on religions.

James F. Keenan, S.J., is the founder of Catholic Theological Ethics in the World Church (CTEWC) as well as the Canisius Chair and Director of the Jesuit Institute at Boston College.

Peter Kanyandago, is Professor of Ethics and Development Studies at Ugandan Martyrs University in Uganda.

Ludovic T. Lado, S.J., holds a doctorate in social anthropology from the University of Oxford (UK) and is currently head of research office at the Center of Research and Action for Peace in Abidjan, Côte d'Ivoire.

Ignace N. Maduku holds doctorates in Religious Sciences (University of Montreal), the History of Religions and Religious Anthropology (Sorbonne University), and Theology (Catholic Institute of Paris). He is a visiting professor at the University of Montreal.

Laurenti Magesa, is professor of ethics at Hekima College, the Jesuit School of Theology in Nairobi, Kenya. His most recent books include *African Religion in the Dialogue Debate: From Intolerance to Coexistence* (2010) and *What is Not Sacred? African Spirituality* (2013).

Evelyn N. Mayanja is a PhD candidate in peace and justice studies at the University of Manitoba. Her research focuses on Africa's Great Lakes region.

Caroline Mbonu, a member of Congregation of the Handmaids of the Holy Child Jesus, holds a doctoral degree from the Graduate Theological Union. She is a senior lecturer in the Department of Religious and Cultural Studies at University of Port Harcourt in Nigeria. She is the author of *Handmaid: The Power of Names in Theology and Society*.

Albert N. Mundele is the Graduate Training Coordinator and Professor at the Catholic University of Eastern Africa in Nairobi/Kenya and professor of Old Testament and Society at the Catholic University of Congo, DRC.

Festo Mkenda, S.J., holds a DPhil in History and has an interest in contextualized theology and spirituality. He is the founding director of the Jesuit Historical Institute in Africa (JHIA) and he also lectures in church history at Hekima University College in Nairobi. He is the author of *Mission for Everyone: A Story of the Jesuits in Eastern Africa (1555-2012)*.

Odomaro Mubangizi, S.J. is the Dean of the Philosophy Department at the Institute of Philosophy and Theology in Addis Ababa, Ethiopia. He is editor of the *Justice, Peace, and Environment Bulletin*.

Nyambura Njoroge is a Kenyan theologian and ordained minister of the Presbyterian Church of East Africa. She has served as program executive for the World Council of Churches' Ecumenical HIV and AIDS Initiatives and Advocacy since 2007. She is a founding member of the Circle of Concerned African Women Theologians in 1989 in Accra, Ghana.

Wilfrid K. Okambawa, S.J. teaches at the Jesuit Theological Institute in Abidjan, Ivory Coast. His recent publications include *Pardon, une Folie Liberatrice* (2008) and *Les Béatitudes : le Médicament pour le Bonheur* (2014).

Jean Paul O. Ondoua, a priest of the Archdiocese of Yaounde, lectures in New Testament in the Faculty of Theology of the Catholic University of Yaounde in Cameroon.

Susan Rackoczy, IHM, is a professor of spirituality and systematic theology at St Joseph's Theological Institute and the School of Religion, Philosophy and Classics of the University of KwaZulu-Natal, South Africa. She has published in the areas of feminist theology, ecofeminism, cross-cultural spiritual direction and gender and religion.

Edward (Ted) Rogers, S.J., now retired, was a social worker and AIDS pioneer and activist in Zimbabwe and Southern Africa.

Eugene E. Uzukwu, C.S.Sp., an expert in liturgy, ecclesiology, and contextual theology, has published four books, including *God, Spirit, and Human Wholeness* (2012); *Worship as Body Language* (1997); and *A Listening Church* (1996).

Bernard Tonde, a priest of the diocese of Bondoukou, lectures in moral theology at the Pontificia Urbaniana Universita in Rome. His recent publications include *Famiglia e mutamenti in Africa* (2015) and *Coscienza e formazione* (2016).

Fabien A. Yedo, a priest of the archdiocese of Abidjan, teaches pastoral and catechetic theology at the Catholic University of West Africa. He is the director of publications for Revue RUCAO and editor of Revue CEREPTI. He has published *L'Autonomie des Eglises Locales d'Afrique et la Charité Pastorale* (2014).

Edwina Ward is a retired practical theologian at the University of KwaZulu-Natal. She is a clinical pastoral education supervisor and a counsellor. She has published numerous articles and edited two books in the area of Theology and HIV and Aids in Southern Africa.

INDEX

ABC approach (Abstinence, Be Faithful,
    Condom Use), 18, 22, 24–25, 28,
    31, 52, 245, 204, 235–36
abortion, 245
Abuja Declaration, 256, 261, 343
Achebe, Chinua, 279, 280, 286–87
Achmat, Zachi, 271
Ackermann, Denise, 145–46, 274
Acolatse, Esther E., 288–89
Adekambi, Moses, 333
Adeyemo, Tukunboh, 258
adult neurogenesis, 308
Africa
    abundant life ethics in, 398–99
    beliefs in, contributing to HIV/AIDS,
        18–21
    children in, 343–44
    church's task in, 100–102
    communalism in, 131, 135–38, 195,
        259
    communitarian spirit in, 47–48
    community structure of, sexuality and,
        20–21
    conflicts in, and HIV, 326–31
    conservative religious ideologies in,
        257–58, 260
    cosmology of, and HIV/AIDS, 19
    cultural challenges in, 257
    cultural diversity in, 31
    dysfunctional states in, 61
    economic weakness of, 9
    French presence in, 328
    gender and culture in, 144–45
    governance in, 34, 341, 346–48
    healing practices in, 30, 93
    health issues in, 194–95, 355
    historical woundedness of, 13–14
    HIV/AIDS' disproportional impact
        on, 190

independence in, 175, 326–27
inferiority complex in, 220
Jesuits in, HIV/AIDS work of,
    371–73
language in, transforming, 25–26
leadership in, 339, 340, 346–48
marginalization of, 57, 194–95
migration in, 327
national security in, 339, 340
patriarchal practices in, 73, 146
portrayal of, 61–62
public policy in, 251–63
reality in, holistic view of, 190
relationality in culture of, 55
religious diversity in, 332
resources in, 328, 347
restoring dignity to, 62
sexual practices in, 16, 28–29, 131,
    136–37, 193–94, 360
socioeconomic hardware of, 9
soul of, 137
theological anthropology and, 185,
    190, 193–95
traditional view in, on life, 47–48
virtue ethics in, 398–99
women theologians in, 201–2, 205
worldview in, 19–20, 22, 332
Africae Munus (Benedict XVI), 221, 294
African AIDS Epidemic, The: A History
    (Iliffe), 5
African Christian Health Association,
    270
African Indigenous Religions, 258, 281
African-Initiated Churches, 284
African Jesuits AIDS Network (AJAN),
    186
African Network for Religious Leaders
    Living with or Affected by HIV and
    AIDS (ANERELA+), 206, 236, 270

411